Crossing Lex

By

Debby Caruso

For Scott, Enzo, and Dagny
My very own
Holy Trinity

In the Beginning

I can remember it now as clearly as if I were still five years old; a memory that has distilled only slightly by the passing of time. The angst at being left out, shuffled away, as if I were some Saturday night obligation that she wanted none of–that feeling stayed behind. So I hated her. I hated her then as I lay beneath my powder-blue canopied bed with tears in my eyes, a lump in my throat, ears sharpened, waiting to hear the footfalls of my father on the stairs.

In what seemed like eternity, he would appear, napkin wadded tightly in his closed fist. His hands were humungous; almost totally concealing his treat, save for the sharp edge of the cheap paper napkin peeking out between his knuckles.

"I brought you some shrimps." I was too young to know that the way he said it was not proper, too small to realize that the plural of shrimp is *shrimp*.

"Thank you Daddy!" I would try not to squeal as I grabbed eagerly at the package between his fingers. My heart rate began to slow as I realized he remembered.

Every week, I would lay in bed scared that he forget, or worse, that he would one day simply be too bored with our ritual to continue. Every week, my mother would order Chinese food for the two of them after sending me upstairs to bed on my Saturday-night special: grilled cheese cut in four squares.

It had been the secret that we kept on every Saturday night since I could remember. Mom would send me to bed early. They would order Chinese food, the orders varying, but always with the constant of my Dad's favorite and mine: shrimp fried rice. Once Mom was preoccupied, Dad would sneak me up a few of the larger shrimp that he was able to pry loose from the rice, and deliver them to me in a napkin on my bed.

"Did you think Daddy would forget?" He asked with a twinkle in his eye, as was his habit.

"No Daddy, I didn't think you would forget," I would reassure him, never telling him the truth. The truth was that I was always afraid he would forget.

Four shrimps later, I would deposit the napkin back into his palm and snuggle deep into my covers.

"Sssssh, don't tell your mother." This was his customary exit line.

"I won't." With that, I would generally ease off into an easy sleep, dreams filled with my coveted seafood, and our little secret tucked deep into my heart.

1999

Chapter One

"Are you still angry with her?"
"Now?"
"Yes, now." Constance nodded and waited. Constance didn't know this, but I would always be her patient, and I was more than sure that if it ever came between paying my co pay and eating the last available plate of sushi on the face of this Earth… the love of sushi would never win out…because she waited.

She listened.

To understand how monumentally important this was in the big scheme of things: I come from a family of Interrupters. As the Irish revel in their storytelling abilities, the Italians are world-renowned Interrupters; their half-sentences ended abruptly by somebody else's more seemingly significant thought. And they yell. They interrupt at decibels intended only to shatter glass; a mere asking of a fork could make the family dog leap for cover, paws extended fully over his little doggy ears. The sad part was that I was so used to it–that until I started seeing Constance–I was barely aware of how much I desired somebody actually waiting on me to finish a thought.

"No, not really," I paused, sighed, as I tossed the idea around inside my head. Was I still angry with her? No, not for that, anyway. For countless other atrocities, but least of all that. "No, I'm older now. I can see that she wasn't shutting me out as much as she simply wanted some time alone with her husband. She was busy, too. She would work all day and then try and get me off to bed, in order to acquire some down time with him. I see now that she was trying to save her marriage."

"But you didn't know that then." It was a statement, not a question, and I took a moment to mull that over too.

"No, I was a child who rarely saw my father, and at that point...still considered him the 'Hero.'" My voice cracked as I said *Hero,* my heart still aching for my father and the man I wished he could have, would have, should have been.

"I'm sorry, Danielle, our time is up." Constance made the same face she always did; the crooked half-smile, half-frown, as if she really was sorry that her 45-minute 'hour' with me had come to an end.

"That's okay," In one deft motion, I handed her the twenty dollar co pay and shrugged on my jacket. "Thanks for listening."

"You're welcome."

As always, I contemplated our session on my walk back to work. Why did I always thank her when I left? I mean, I was paying her, wasn't I? Was I mired in such an act of pathetic longing for someone to listen to me that I felt the need to thank her profusely every time I walked out the door? Better yet, what the hell had possessed me to talk about my father today? Did I miss the fact that we were co-conspirators in something as trivial as shrimp-fried rice? Or did I just miss him? I knew I missed the vulnerability I saw, however infrequently, in his heart. In his eyes, which were exactly the same shade as my own. Back then, was he really only the age I am now? Time had skewed so many things for me.

I passed the Frozen Yogurt bar and almost made it by without indulging. I didn't need it. Except when I craned my neck as I strode purposefully past, I realized they had Cheesecake flavor, and I knew that Cheesecake was a rare occurrence.

Could I just walk by?

My girlfriend Lanie always accused me of needing comfort food post-therapy. In an effort to not let her down, I buzzed her on my cell.

"Yellie!" She screamed into my ear. "What are today's flavors?"

I grinned in spite of myself. "Cheesecake."

"I'll be down in a jiff!" With that, she slammed the receiver in my ear.

Seconds later, she was at my side and whooping it up due to our good fortune.

"I loooooove Cheesecake!" Lanie was grinning from ear to ear.

"So do I. It's a little sick how much," I admitted.

"So how was it?"

"Dad." One word seemed to say it all. Often we exchanged after-therapy notes, although sometimes the briefest description was enough.

We nodded.

"Yeah, I've been on 'Daddy Dearest' for three months now." She related this as flippantly as possible, as only Lanie could, as she snatched her FroYo from the girl behind the counter and darted outside to wait for me. The frozen yogurt shop was no more than a closet overflowing with over-eager Manhattanites from a five-block radius, claustrophobic at best, as well as the worst place to try and carry on even a semblance of personal conversation.

I grabbed my yogurt and change and headed out to join her.

"Ummmmmm," we groaned at the same instant, as the cheesecake frozen yogurt rolled its way around on our tongues, a perfect prize at the end of a difficult session.

"Do we have to go back?" Her eyes pleaded.

"Yes, we have to go back." I was the sensible one of us two.

"You first." She insisted as she pushed me towards our building.

"Follower," I hissed, eyes narrowed, head held high.

I was grateful to have to finish the workday with her. Lanie worked in the same manner of which I was accustomed to: *she actually worked.* Lanie was my partner and I could depend on her not to be late, to call if she was going to be late, to pick up the pieces if I forgot and to cover for me when things got totally out of control. Besides, Lanie could mimic any and almost every personal assistant that we dealt with in the course of the day. Her impersonations were dead-on, to the point where I sometimes could barely contain myself when the person called to make a reservation.

Oooh, and she was *evil* with the speakerphone.

"Travel." Lanie's curt, perfunctory greeting was standard to the poor unsuspecting patron on the other end of the speakerphone.

"Lanie? Lanie, it's Adrienne. Hiya, hons-a-buns."

As if on cue, Lanie is standing at her desk, headset freeing her from the constraint of the phone's receiver, arms flailing wildly, teasing imaginary hair circa 1988-Brooklyn-princess style.

"Hiya back. What can I do for Mr. Todd today?" Lanie had perfected Adrienne some time ago, so the hilarity was no longer in the accuracy, but rather in the fact that Adrienne failed to realize that Lanie did not normally sound just like her.

"Well, tootsie, ya know how it goes. Mr. Todd needs a nonstop flight to Miami tomorrow; let's say 8 am? His meeting is at twelve…will that be enough time?"

Adrienne had been booking Mr. Todd's travel for the past three years, yet she still felt the need to run everything by us.

"Is the meeting at the Delano?" Lanie sounded as if she was smacking a big wad of chewing gum, but I saw the FroYo still on her desk and I knew better. She was simply *in character.*

"Yes, and he doesn't want to stay…" Adrienne trailed off again and we heard papers rustling in the background.

Lanie muted her. "No overnight with the Bain de Soleil chick?"

"I guess not this time." I shook my head. Tsk, tsk. Maybe him being found out by the wife on the last Miami overnight had some affect on the scrounge.

"…So we'll put him on a five, five-thirty-ish return into LaGuardia?" Adrienne could make a New York City airport sound like a disease only a duck could contract.

La-gwuard-ghiah.

A three-syllable quack.

"Right." Lanie was abrupt, but never rude. She recapped his itinerary, dropped the call, swiped the headset off of her head, and turned to me.

"So what's up for tonight?" Lanie and I had standing dates for every Tuesday and Thursday night. Tuesday was her therapy day; Thursday mine. Over time, it had become an unspoken ritual. If we were being good, we went to the gym together. If we were being bad, it was out for drinks and junk food en masse.

"Well, I packed a gym bag, so methinks we should be good girls tonight." I lived right outside of the city, so the colossal effort of toting in the gym bag generally led me to make sure that that was not my only workout. Lanie, on the other hand, hated the gym with a passion and generally tried any conceivable trick to get me not to go.

Just then, the phone started ringing off the wall. Lanie mouthed *To Be Continued* to me and I nodded. I would duke it out with her as soon as I got Mr. Campbell a limo to shuffle him the seven blocks from his appointment to his apartment.

Did I mention that the temperature in New York City was a beautiful seventy-six degrees with a breeze?

Chapter Two

"So how did you win this one again?" Lanie glared at me as she adjusted the grade on her treadmill.

"I preyed on your insecurities," I shot her an evil grin as I adjusted the grade on my treadmill. Higher. "Besides, I promised I would stay out with you tomorrow night."

"I better not see that gym bag sneak its way into the office!" She threatened, huffing and puffing and glaring all the way.

"Never on Friday," I declared.

"Aren't you going Upstate this weekend?" Lanie asked.

"Yes, but on Saturday. Why? Wanna come?" I could always use an advocate on my forays into my former life.

"Surely you jest."

"I jest not."

"I love you, but not that much."

"Urban snob."

"I like it like that."

"Groceries are cheaper up there."

"*'Groceries are cheaper up there?'* That's all you've got to sell me? Dysfunction is free up there; does that mean I should join you?" Lanie looked at me as if I had finally lost my mind.

"There are very few selling points." I admitted this with chagrin.

"And I'm not buying! Groceries or otherwise! The only reason I gave in to this sheer torture was because I have sushi to look forward to tomorrow."

"Not to mention that the gym always presents the opportunity of running in to the Bradomeister." I reminded her.

"The Bradomeister is in D.C." She kicked it up a notch. "He said he would call when he returns."

"And you are…?"

"Waiting with baited breath."

"Bradomeister" was a decent enough guy that Lanie had been dating for several months now, if in fact we could use the term *dating* very loosely. Lanie was a therapist's wet dream: the woman who went after men who not only acted like her father, but actually resembled him in one way or another. Whether the eyes had it or the imposing stance, one could not deny that Lanie sought these men out for more than just a fabulous French dinner. The problem is that they always made her feel as nonexistent in their presence as her father did. In Brad's case, it was less obvious, and therefore enabled Lanie to declare him *different.* He was different. Brad could watch cable news twenty-four hours a day and actually ticked the days off on his calendar until the latest John Grisham release came out in hardcover. He was more bookish and less rakish than the men Lanie had aligned herself with in the past, and I know that Lanie sometimes felt at odds regarding just what to do with him. I for one had nothing against Brad. I always experienced him to be rather charming, albeit in another orbit at times.

"So will the Bradomeister be joining us tomorrow?" Tuesdays and Thursdays were strictly for us, but Fridays were always open to interpretation.

"If he can tear himself away from *The O'Reilly Factor.*" Lanie made a screwed-up face. I don't think that Lanie minded Bill O'Reilly and his outrageous news analysis as much as she minded that Brad could get so caught up in things that he seemingly forgot about her.

She thought I didn't notice. I noticed more than I let on. Because of my background, I had learned to be a keen observer of people. In order to protect myself, I had always had to read the signals, interpret the signs…and therefore had developed an uncanny sixth sense. I could tell a liar from a mile away, I could detect a fraud with merely a glance, and I could usually tell when the people I cared about were concerned about something, or anything, or everything.

"Tell him we're doing sushi and I'm sure he'll tear." I looked at my treadmill. Three miles, 197 calories. That's it? What was that, a muffin? A muffin with nothing on it? Disgusted, I decided to hop off the treadmill. "I quit! How 'bout you?"

"I was dying for you to call it a night," Lanie intoned as we made our way to the locker room.

"A night." I quipped.

"You going home?" Lanie ignored me.

"Yes, fair friend, you cannot coerce me into anything else tonight." I was looking forward to reading my new book on the train and then perhaps a hot cup of tea in bed.

"Okay, then I will see you tomorrow. Remember: NO GYM BAG!" Lanie warned me as if she would not let me enter the workplace tomorrow were I to show up with it slung over my shoulder.

"Gotcha." With that I hugged her hard and fast, one foot out the door. I needed to make the 8:23 or wait another hour for a train. As it was, I ended up running for that one and snagged a lowly center seat. It didn't matter. What mattered was that I was on my way home, to a place where I was safe. My own apartment with my own rules, where nobody had the key but me, and I didn't have to worry about being woken in the middle of the night by voices raised in anger or glass shattering.

Chapter Three

I confess: I people-watch on the train.

I people-watch until everybody settles in, book in one hand, beverage in another, and I make up stories about the people I see on the train. I am convinced they all lead better lives than me, how could they not? They disembark at stops such as *Chappaqua, Pleasantville, and Bedford Hills.* They live at the toniest of addresses, next-door neighbors to people of talent and fame such as Richard Gere and Mariah Carey. Westchester County, New York was the suburb to end all suburbs. Rich and famous people littered its landscape in a muted way, unlike Hollywood or Palm Beach, but they were here nonetheless.

And I lived among them.

Among them, but not one of them, I reminded myself. Sure, I had an Armonk address, and Armonk boasted the homes of the CEO of Chase Manhattan Bank and one of the many homes of billionaire Michael Bloomberg, but I was currently ensconced in an illegal studio on a residential road.

Once I decided I was bored with people-watching, I would usually delve into my latest read, but tonight I felt my mind begin to wander.

I still couldn't believe I was even here. Although the town where I had grown up was only a two-hour drive from Armonk, it felt like worlds away. For that I was grateful. It was a hard-won battle, the independence, and the peace. I was finally comfortable in my own home and in my own skin. At times it was lonely, but it was always better than what I had left.

I thought about Upstate as I trudged my way from the train platform to my car. Whenever I woke up late, I always paid for it by snagging the farthest spot from the platform and then having to not only run for the train in the morning, but also having to endure a forever trek back to the car at the end of the night. This was particularly trying after a hard workout, muscles aflame, my car but a dot on the asphalt landscape.

Funny, I never saw Richard Gere on the train.

Truth be told, I had never seen Richard Gere. I saw people in the city all the time, though…Joan Rivers on Park Avenue, John Cusack downtown, Paul Sorvino–also on Park, Jerry Seinfeld in Grand Central…it is truly amazing how many famous faces I've seen since I moved. Rather, *because* I had moved. Those little moments validated my choice to be in a living, breathing place with people who made things happen.

Upstate. I breathed deep, an audible sigh escaping my lips. Well, Saturday shouldn't be too bad. I was going up to see my best friend and her husband, and not either parent. The players always defined the game; no parents always made for a more enjoyable visit Upstate. Plus, I would make it a point to go food shopping while I was up there. I may have the Westchester digs and the Manhattan career, but I had yet to attain either bankroll.

I unlocked the driver's door to my trusty Cavalier, and within seconds, I had the moonroof open and the radio blasting. I found myself suddenly famished as I drove, realizing that there was perhaps a half of an eggplant parmigiana wedge left in my refrigerator from the night before, and hearing it call out to me as I made my way down the road.

Stomach rumbling, I made a beeline for the door the minute I parked the car in the drive. I unlocked the sliding glass door entrance, threw open the latch, and simultaneously hit the lights on as I shrugged off my jacket. I opened the refrigerator door to find the sandwich still there. I breathed a sigh of relief and looked down to find my fingers were shaking. Had I been speeding home? Was I still trapped in the events of the past, still believing that if I sped home I could catch him in the act and claim what was rightfully mine? I felt an immense shudder of relief as my heart returned to a normal pace and I realized that nobody had stolen my food.

Years after the food started disappearing, I still felt unexplainable paranoia about somebody rifling through my refrigerator in the hours that I was not there to keep an eye on it. My logical mind registered that I lived alone and that nobody would steal from me anymore; however my past sometimes dictated my future in ways both small and large. I knew it, I felt it, I lived it, and I was working on it. I reminded myself to say those four words that Constance had continually drilled through my skull: *I'm working on it.*

I inhaled the leftover wedge and then put up the kettle for some vanilla tea. Once the kettle started whistling, I poured and then let it steep while I rummaged through my mail and checked my answering machine. There were no messages and the mail was all junk. I checked to make sure that my sliding-glass so-called front door was locked and latched, slid into some leggings and a short-sleeved tee and put on a Jim Brickman CD. As the romantic and soothing piano strains filled my small studio, I took the bag out of my tea and settled in to bed with the new mystery I had been dying to read. Only long after the tea was finished did I get up again to double-check the lock on my door.

Some habits die hard.

When the dreams began, I forced myself to get up once again. With sleep-filled eyes, I trudged my way over to the door and tested the lock. One, two, three times.

Chapter Four

The train waits for no man…the train waits for no man…
Why don't they just say woman?
The train waits for no woman…the train waits for no woman…

I chanted this in my overtired little head the whole way as I ran for the train the next morning. I have no answer as to why I torture myself in such a way, but I do know that since I had moved, the song and my steps had formed a sort of rhythm that each morning transported me from car to track. Nine times out of ten, I make it.

Today I would make it. I had already climbed the stairs when I saw the train still approaching, my feet planted firmly on the platform as it came to a stop and the doors opened. I was the first stop in the morning, an express to Grand Central, therefore I had the pick of every seat type when boarding. Every commuter knows that the window seat in the morning is preferable, because you could prop your book against the window and lean in for a quick little nap before the day begins. Considering that I had probably gotten perhaps four hours of sleep the night before, I decided that a window seat was the way to go. Prior to my nap, though, I had to dab on a little makeup.

Makeup never takes more than eight minutes. If it does, it's too much. I pride myself in not wearing a lot of stuff: only a dab of concealer under each eye, powder across the entire face, a thin black line that we call eyeliner under the eyes, a swoosh of mascara and an alarming amount of Cherry Chapstick.

That's it. I check my look in the mirror, and I decide there's not much else that could or should be done here. My dark brown hair falls into my eyes and I brush it back off my forehead, reminding myself to schedule a trim. I wish for curly hair, or straight, anything but this Italianwavy-thick mop that looks like everyone else I grew up with. And whose fault is the nose? My mind flicks to my father, and I wonder if he holds any remorse for his hand in this gene pool concoction that stares back at me, making no apologies, the prominent Roman nose so much like his own. I give up, shut the mirror, and try to people-watch for a few minutes before the daily doze. The morning is not prime people-watching time, however, so I try to doze and then give up when the train ends up being too bumpy. Some mornings are like this, and on such occasions I read.

    I can't explain to you how much I love reading. It is my downtime favorite, my escape, my therapy, my friend, and my whole heart. I would kill or die to find a job where somebody would pay me to read all day. I once answered an ad where they had advertised just that: GET PAID TO READ! I answered that ad so fast that I practically tore the numbers off my push-button phone; only to find out that what they wanted me to read were technical journals. Then they wanted me to rate them, whatever that means.

    No wonder why they were paying people! I could barely get into non-fiction, much less a technical journal! I was of the camps that if books were not fun, why bother reading? There was no indulgence in reading something boring.

    The current whodunit that had captured my attention was still playing on my mind as the train pulled into Grand Central. It was never the most obvious character, I surmised, as I walked to the escalators that would take me up and out onto 45th Street. I generally walked down 45th, across Lexington Avenue, down to Third, and left two blocks to my office on East 47th Street.

    Crossing Lexington Avenue, mulling over the suspects, I bumped into someone walking in the opposite direction.

    "Ooooh, I'm so sorry, I wasn't paying attention." I would have laughed, but I felt incredibly dumb, and the man who was picking up his briefcase looked rather serious.

"That's OK," he replied hurriedly as he brushed off his case and made his way past me.

I found myself lagging among the pedestrians as the sign on the corner flashed from *Walk* to *Don't Walk*. I picked up my step and hurried to cross the street, still thinking about the person I had bumped into. He wasn't rude, as so many non-New-Yorkers perceived us Manhattanites to be: people actually did say they were sorry if they bumped into you on the street. He was cute though, and I allowed myself to think about him the rest of my walk to work, instead of the various suspects in the novel I was currently reading.

After all, he too was a mystery.

Chapter Five

"Gym bag?" Lanie accosted me the minute I strolled into our office. Thank God I loved her, or I swear we would have killed each other by now.

"Do you see a gym bag?" I gave it right back to her, flashing my biggest grin, knowing that my coworker was the biggest anti-morning person to ever set foot on the face of the earth. The smile alone would set her on edge.

"What are you smiling for?" She grumbled, like clockwork.

"Need some coffee?" I was a tea girl myself, but was able to concede the magical wonders of coffee for the rest of the working population.

"Need? I already had a double espresso and I am still Groucho Marx on crack. Don't try and pretend as if I don't know how I am." Lanie was tres grouchy today, which led me to wonder if anything had occurred with the Bradomeister since I left her last night.

"I say nothing." I sat down at my desk and began to log in to both my computer and phone. The phone currently had no calls holding, so I decided to try again with her. "Come on, take a walk with me. I haven't had my tea yet." In an effort to save on funds, I usually made my tea in the minute cubbyhole our company had the nerve to call a kitchen. "I'll treat you to a Chai tea, or another shot of espresso, or whatever we can get that will make you human."

"Okay," Lanie relented with a big sigh, and followed me to the elevator. "It's Friday, I suppose I can be human."

"What's going on?" It would be easier to pry national secrets out of the current CIA chief, I knew this, and yet I persisted because I also knew that this was not just the normal morning cranky routine.

"It's Bradomeister."

"I thought so."

"He hates me."

"He hates you? When did that happen?"

"From Day One." Lanie, although long on drama, seemed genuinely distressed.

"I guarantee that he doesn't hate you. What happened, Lane?" We were almost at the friendly neighborhood Starbucks.

As I went to swing the door open, I realized she was holding back tears. I checked my watch and instructed her to wait outside. There were benches along the sidewalk where we were, and I figured I could grab us drinks and talk for a minute before we went back to work.

"C'mon kid, you're in no shape to book a limo," I chided her after I picked up the coffees, and then led her over to the nearby bench. "Tell me what's going on, Lane."

"Nothing." She looked away from me, choking back tears while cradling the espresso I had just shoved into her left hand. "Nothing...that's the problem."

I held her right hand while balancing my Chai.

"And everything. Just...everything!" She waved her free hand in pronouncement. "Of course, it's Brad. He never called when he got in last night, he didn't email, and he just doesn't care about me. I don't know what it's going to take for me to figure that out. I mean, I follow him around like a friggin puppy dog, a pathetic little jerk, I..." her voice trailed off while she wiped the tears that were now flowing freely down her face. "This is so unlike me."

"I don't think you follow him. At least, I don't think you project that. I think you may want a little more definition in the relationship." I offered.

"Relationship? Who am I kidding? I go to the gym so that I can perhaps grab the treadmill next to him. I wait for his calls that don't come, and I get way too excited when he says that he does want to see me. All I want is his attention; all I want is for him to want me as much as I want him. Maybe I'm barking up the wrong tree." She waved her hand in the air again, summarily dismissing the napkin I had proffered.

I sighed. I knew that this was less about Brad and more about Lanie's feelings of being ignored and rejected. I was also smart enough to know that those feelings didn't just start when she met Brad.

"I think you shouldn't be so ready to declare Brad 'the wrong tree.' How long have you been seeing him?"

"Five months." She was facing me now, and took a deep sip of her espresso as I tried to make my advice not come out sounding like advice.

"Well, maybe you should talk to him then. I really think Brad is the type of guy that just doesn't have a clue. He usually has his head in a book, or maybe he sits home and ponders the latest economic theory. I don't know. I don't get the impression that he doesn't call or follow up with you intentionally. I actually think he may be good for you." I nodded as I sipped my tea and allowed this latest theory to roll around inside my head.

"How so?" Lanie asked me skeptically.

"Because maybe, on some level, he makes you deal with the feelings of being pushed aside, ignored, or abandoned in such a way that it will help you to better deal with them in every aspect of your life."

"Thanks, Clara."

"Did you ever think it odd that I have Constance and you have Clara? Perhaps they should join forces and become the C&C Therapy Team." I quipped, an image coming to life in my head that caused me to laugh out loud. "Our company could do their advertising."

"The C&C *Traveling* Therapy Team."

"Speaking of which…" I indicated the time on my watch. We had spent a half-hour commiserating with coffee. It was a sure bet that we had several voice mails by now.

"You, my dear friend, are right. Alas, we must return!" Lanie jumped up and strode gallantly to the nearby trash container. As we crossed the avenue to make our way back, she looked me directly in the eye and said, "Thank you."

"For what?" I gave her the same wave of hand that she had given me a few minutes earlier.

"For being you."

Being me was becoming a little easier every day. I felt so free down here, in New York City, leading my own life and having my own opinions. There was a freedom in having found a friend so like myself; struggling with issues similar to my own, thinking the same kinds of thoughts.

The rest of the day flew by in a haze of continuous phone calls, emails, reservations and cancellations. Lanie and I worked for a relatively large advertising firm that did enough travel to warrant the two of us being on-site full-time in their building. We worked in conjunction with a humungous travel conglomerate, but the ad agency really dictated our work schedule as well as paid our salaries. Besides the general chaos and countless personalities, the place was exactly what you might picture an ad agency to look like: a nice modern space full of black and white, print ads of past campaigns gracing every other wall, and television screens recessed into the halls, walls, even the floor in one spot. The TVs were functional, but their main purpose was to play our ads on a continual loop, almost like a form of electronic art. Aside from the fact that the agency resembled Melrose Place in more ways than one can count, it was sometimes a lot of fun working for a major creative outfit with so many young people.

Unfortunately, I had yet to meet any single men at work. Most of the men were either married or gay, the same way it was the world over. I had resigned myself to believing that my freedom was much more important than any thing that any man had to offer.

Especially since David, who was the one man that time and space had not enabled me to forget. David had been my one true love, at the very least, the only love I had known, and a part of my life Upstate that had yet to shuffle off into the sunset. David walked through my dreams sometimes, appearing in a way that he had never actually been, rather starring as the man that I envisioned him to be in my life. I would wake confused, feeling slighted, and although I only felt the ache now and again, it was more than a fleeting reminder of pain. It was that harrowing loss I decided I never wanted to encounter in the future. The future made me wince. Loving and then losing David had practically sworn me off of men forever. He was the man that still invaded my thoughts seven years after he both entered and exited my life with an intensity that I have not known–either before–or since. David was a thought best pushed aside. I got the next call, and as I did, I smiled for Lanie, placing David back up on the shelf, out of reach for now.

"Lanie, it's the Bradomeister." I saw excitement dance in her eyes though her mouth revealed nothing.

As she picked him up, I mulled over the Bradomeister. He really was a nice guy and I hoped that he realized how great Lanie was in turn. My gut told me that they were just having a connection problem. Once they talked it out, I'm sure they would be fine.

I really shouldn't talk. Ever since David, I had a major connection problem. I was afraid to connect with anyone, not wanting to cry the rivers of tears I had cried the summer after we split up. So I kept to myself, buried in my books, not even looking. Deep down, I wanted that connection more than anything else, but I was not willing to compromise to get it, or find it, or keep it.

Constance and Lanie both believed that one day I would meet 'Mr. Right.'

I wasn't so sure.

"Yellie, he will be joining us for sushi tonight." Lanie announced, as she disconnected her headset and gave me a silly little grin.

"So what did he say?" I was eager to hear whether his negligence was real or imagined.

"He *said,* he took the last shuttle home from D.C. last night and thought it was too late to call me. He also mentioned something about meetings this morning. Then he groveled enough that I decided to let him join us for sushi." She said this as if Brad was a charity case, and not as if she had been practically sitting atop the phone, waiting on his call.

"You seem devastated." I ribbed her.

"I am." Lanie threw a paper clip my way.

I ducked. "So what's the plan?"

"Outta here by six? He'll meet us there."

"You're on."

Chapter Six

"So what about you, Danielle?" Brad posed this question to me just as I was eyeing the last piece of avocado roll on the platter.

I had already eaten so much sushi that *rolling* back to Grand Central was looking more plausible than walking, but there I sat, greedily eyeing that lone unsuspecting piece of Japanese delight, until I was caught in the act by the Bradomeister's probing question.

"What about me?" The American obsession with not taking the last piece had caused me to go off the deep end and lose my place in the conversation.

"Just take the sushi!" Lanie, ever the mind-reader, exclaimed forcefully all while shoving the last roll onto my plate.

"Was it that obvious?" I speared it with my chopstick, and then turned back to Brad.

"Yes, it was obvious," he chuckled. "What I was asking was what about me setting you up with my friend Ryan?"

"Ryan?" How long had I been drifting? "Sorry, Brad, I think I missed something." I smoothed out the napkin on my lap and poured myself a second of the house tea.

"I was just telling you and Lanie, perhaps just Lanie," he said this in an under voice, which was more comedy than I had ever experienced from him. I couldn't help but grin. I liked Brad, and I liked Brad for Lanie. "That my buddy Ryan at work needs to meet a nice girl. He's a great guy, Danielle, why don't we all go out sometime?"

I looked to Lanie. How could I explain to Brad that I was deathly afraid of dating again? Would it make any sense to Brad, born in Connecticut, living in Chelsea, degrees seeping out of his nostrils, that ever since I was engaged and summarily left at the altar at the ripe young age of nineteen years old that I simply hyperventilated every time I had to go out on a date? Or would this confession come across like the trailer for a Lifetime movie? *Television for Women.* I never did get that.

It made no sense to me, how could I expect it to make sense to anybody else? The worst part of the whole thing was that what I wanted more than anything was to feel that kind of connection again, to feel someone's arms around me, to share a private joke with someone other than a friend. I wanted and I feared and the fear was still winning out, at least for now.

I'm working on it. I had to remind myself to say that rather often, but I found that it helped. Regardless of how stupid I felt reciting this silly little mantra, I did it anyway.

Lanie spoke up. "Brad, have I ever met Ryan?"

"No, I don't think so." He shook his head. "Would you like to screen him first?" Brad offered in such a way that he actually sounded as if he understood women. Just a practical question that needed a practical answer.

"I think that wouldn't be too bad of an idea," Lanie suggested. She looked across the table to me and proffered a tiny smile. "Not that I don't trust you, but I think I know what Yellie likes, and she happens to like cross-eyed guys. So if he's not cross-eyed…" and she shrugged as if there was nothing more she could do.

"Oh, he's definitely cross-eyed!" Brad acted outraged. "Do you really think I would recommend someone to Danielle that didn't meet her criteria?" The look on his face was pure, *Who me?*

"Good. Then let Lanie do the initial screening and I'll get back to you." I could acquiesce to at least that much. If I wanted to feel those arms again, how was I ever going to get there without the initial handshake?

From there, Lanie and I both had a sudden craving for some form of cheesecake. We found one of the many all-night gourmet places not far from Grand Central with the door open, beckoning us with New York style cheesecake with blueberry topping. Brad treated us, grabbed himself a slice of crumb cake, and enthralled us both with stories from *The O'Reilly Factor.*

They walked me over to my train and then proceeded to hop a subway home. I got on the train, found no people worth watching, and went back to read the thriller I was currently invested in.

Arriving home, I switched on all the lights and poured myself a tall glass of water. I couldn't take another cup of tea. I locked the door and checked it several times before getting ready for bed. I set my alarm for the next morning and settled in, waking to a sharp buzz only to find all my lights still on.

Great, the landlord would love that.

I showered and called Annemarie. Annemarie was my best-friend Upstate and the person I was going to visit today. She and her husband Steven were the people I made a point to keep in touch with, and ever since I moved, I made the drive up at least once a month. Sometimes I went up to see either Mom or Dad and even then I would try and pop over, even if it was barely a brief respite from the lunacy my parents fought to uphold. Annemarie knew me better than anyone, including Lanie, and she was there throughout the entire David fiasco. There was a bond that could never be diminished because of that, but the friendship had become harder to maintain as our lives kept shuffling us in different directions.

Still, Annemarie was like the sister I never had, and she knew all my secrets. I was lucky to have her in my life.

"I'm leaving in a few," I told her when she picked up the phone. "Need anything?"

"No, I'm okay. Just get here." Annemarie had some kind of seventies rock blaring in the background. "Steven made muffins."

"I'm speeding!" I declared as I grabbed cell phone, sunglasses, and bubble gum and threw them in my weekend bag. Steven made the best muffins on the face of the earth, regardless of flavor. He knew I loved them and always tried to accommodate my cravings, being the good husband that he was to Annemarie, and the good pal that he was to me. Steven was the type of guy you could always count on to make you feel comfortable, and I was grateful to him for that. I was smart enough to know that he could have dismissed or labeled me as Annemarie's friend, *The Third Wheel,* but he had yet to project that and therefore gained my favor.

I sifted through my CD's before I left, picking out the best entertainment for the long drive ahead. There was music and then there was driving music, and I was determined to have the appropriate music for every occasion. *Earth, Wind, and Fire* called out to me. What was better than driving sixty miles an hour in the merry, merry month of May, with the windows down and *Sing a Song* blaring from the speakers?

Sing a Song!

(It'll make your day.)

I grabbed that, Steve Windwood, an older Mariah Carey, and Journey's Greatest Hits. All drive-time tunes that could not be beat...think about it...*Bring me a Higher Love...*the song was a shell of itself when played indoors.

Now I was ready. I grabbed my keys, bag, and locked the door behind me. I got into the car and exhaled.

Upstate.

Forget David, who was believed to still be in the area, although I had no real reconnaissance on him any more. My parents still lived Upstate, separately, both remarried to people that simply made no sense. Their new partners were not only bad for them; one was a horrible individual, the other a helpless sort who would engender sympathy if she weren't entirely pathetic.

Both had destroyed whatever new beginnings they had been hoping for, either in complacency or subversion.

Not that I think it would have been better for them to stay together. I was old enough and wise enough to know now that had they stayed together, they surely would have killed each other.

As each mile slid by, my heart became more involved with the memories of things past, and I found myself thinking about my mother. She had called the other day, left a message, and I had yet to return her call. I could barely define my exasperation with her, but it was smoldering just beneath the surface and I refrained from calling her more often than not.

The sad truth is that we used to be the very best of friends.

Once she and my father had divorced, the Hero status had shifted from him to her and she had fulfilled her role with fervor: I smiled now as I remembered us dancing around in my bedroom, each shouting shamelessly into an air microphone, *The second time around...you got it! The second time around...not like the first time...talkin' 'bout the second time...*

I know you've come a long way, baby
But you don't need that heart of stone,
You proved that you could do it–do it, baby
You can make it on your own...
The second time around, the second time around...
Not like the first time,
Talkin' 'bout the Second Time...

She had convinced me that it was going to be our song. Who sang that song? I remember loving all things disco as a kid, and I remembered believing in her. A new beginning for both of us! I didn't know what that meant, I was only nine years old at the time, but I knew she was excited so I decided that I was excited too. I was her girlfriend then, and I wanted nothing more than to please her and be let in on everything.

Shalamar!

That was it. The name of the group was Shalamar! How could I have forgotten that? I had only heard the song seven hundred times the first year after they got divorced.

If my life had a soundtrack, that song would have definitely made it on. The Seventies Years. The Eighties. And now…at the close of The New Millennium…a Nineties Retrospective from Danielle D'Ambrusco.

What would that CD have on it, except a few suicidal love songs and teary odes to the way things used to be? My life felt so blank sometimes–afraid to reach out–and tired of looking over my shoulder.

The years between my father and her husband were the best years that I can recall with my mother. She was so lively and free. She was beautiful then, before years and scars had made their imprint on her and I longed for that woman, that mother, that friend back in my life. It was the late Seventies, and my mother was slowly beginning to figure out who she was and what she wanted out of her life. She was vibrant and social and all the other mothers were jealous. Hell, all the other kids were jealous because my Mom was by far the coolest one on the block. None of their mothers let them eat pancakes for dinner, or played Monopoly with them for hours on end, or listened to Donna Summer and Barry White and Shalamar and insisted that the Motown sound was *the sound.* My mother taught me how to match everything: from socks to underwear, shirts to jackets. She would sing her head off in the car and dance herself to exhaustion when a song she liked came on the radio. She wore Chanel No.5 as an everyday perfume and she never dabbed it on, I know this because the faintest whiff of that scent still arrests me to this day, as bold as she once was.

Now the years had passed and changed us both. She stands, barely, with knees wobbling, amidst a life filled with poor choices and pocketed with blame.

She has become the woman I never wanted to be.

From sheer worship, the turnaround so swift and harsh and outright cruel, I staggered from the weight of it, but still managed to feel guilt at the core.

I had to remind myself those years does not a lifetime make; but for almost three years she was the best mother anybody could ever ask for.

Enter The Monster. He has no name; he does not beg any introduction. The irony is that he could have had any name, for I fear that men like him abound in the good old U.S. of A. He will have no name here, as I have not uttered his name in so many years that I would hate to break that truce with myself now. Who he is is not nearly as important as what he is and what he is is the opposite of love, for he is hate and fear and oppression and evil.

Driving Upstate, I cannot help but think of him, as he ended up shaping some part of my life that would always be bent. The Monster is in jail now, serving many years and never enough for his various transgressions. I believe my mother goes to see him every so often, as she has found her Christianity again and feels compelled to love those that hate her.

I cannot be that much of a Christian. I was born a Catholic, because I believe if you are of Italian descent, you automatically get indoctrinated into that faith directly from the womb. I became an Atheist, because I grew up finding nothing to believe in. Eventually, I turned back to my original faith, zigzagged over to the Protestant church, and was happy to find out that they would take an Italian-American like me.

I prayed now as I drove, an almost silent uttering that I almost always fell into during these long drives Upstate. I loved driving Upstate because it gave me time to think. I also hated driving Upstate because it gave me time to think.

Almost there.

My stomach grumbled and I started waxing nostalgic about Steven's muffins. I had brought up a loaf of bread that I picked up yesterday on my lunch hour. It wasn't much of an accompaniment, but I figured I'd trade him. The muffins for the bread–I was only about a mile away now and I decided that was the best way to go about it.

It was perfectly fair.

So I decided to be funny when I got there and ran up to the door, bread under my arm, dancing away from them, shouting, "The muffins for the bread!"

"Danielle, you never change!" Annemarie laughed as Steven tried to wrestle the bread away from me, while we all fell into a three-way hug.

Oh, but I have, my friend. I have changed more than you are willing to admit. I am no longer the small-town girl I once was, because I identify more with Manhattan than I do up here, and because I am learning to leave the past behind. I have changed, because I walk at a faster pace, and I see the world in a broader scope, and I have this firm belief that because I left, I will have a better life now. I may seem the same to you, because I still keep my head up and find comedy wherever I can, and I still have that same buoyant personality that got me out of here to begin with, but we will have less and less in common as the days tick by. I can no longer believe that I wanted to be married by the age of twenty-five, and that if I wasn't, that somehow I believed I would never fit in and then be deemed a failure. I have changed in ways large and small, changes brought about by both time and space, and I know you want to see it even less than I do. At times, I sincerely wish that I had not felt so uncomfortable here and that I could have stayed and grown old with you.

I say none of this. I cannot. How can you explain to someone that you love that you loathe everything about their lifestyle? That you are conflicted by your ties to this place and a time that wasn't always good to you and the new life that beckons? Can you say it in such a way that it won't offend?

I think not.

So I pretend that I miss it more than I do, because I miss her and I miss the closeness that I sacrificed to answer the call my life has issued me.

Not to mention the muffins…I miss the muffins!

"This is good bread. I say we trade her," Steven suggests, and I have to bite my tongue from saying, *Of course it's good bread, it's from New York City!*

My duality sometimes represents a problem, even if it's only in my head.

I accuse Lanie of being an urban snob, but I am really almost as bad, however unspoken.

Plus, I have a theory about bad bread. If you're asking, 'how do you know if it's bad bread?' I can safely say that you have never had good bread.

Annemarie and Steven knew better. They knew that when I came up to visit, they had a monthly shot at the real deal.

When they came to visit me, they had even grander opportunities laid at their feet: The chance to inhale various delicacies from around the world, all within a walk, swipe of a Metro-card, or taxi ride.

Was it obnoxious of me to think this way? Did I somehow think that I was better than them now, or was it that the differences seemed more and more pronounced as time went on? Was different necessarily better?

I swallow these thoughts as we make our way to a beautifully laden brunch table. Annemarie has a knack for all things domestic, not in the Martha Stewart fluff sort of way, but in the way that charms you and comforts you as you settle in. Despite my reservations regarding small-town life, she makes it seem attractive for the short duration of my stay and I can't help but come under the spell that Annemarie and Steven cast whenever I visit their home.

"So what's new and exciting?" Annemarie asks as she fills my plate with fresh fruit and some other salad that although not recognizable, is sure to tempt the taste buds.

"Not much on my end." I relate to her the week's events, editing a little for Lanie's sake, but giving her the overall view of the situation between Lanie and Brad. Annemarie and Lanie had met a couple of times, and they always ask after each other. Before introducing them, I was concerned that there would be surreptitious jealousy between the two factions in my life, but they seemed to genuinely like and regard each other, perhaps knowing that each gave something the other could not.

Steven had never met Brad, (and Lanie only once, at that) but he felt the need to enthrall us with a man's point of view.

"Any new men on the horizon for you?" Annemarie asked this tentatively, already knowing that if the horizon had produced anyone worth mentioning, she would have heard about it already.

"Manhattan is a great big island, with many fishies in the sea." This was an old standby.

"So have you gone fishing lately?" This from Steven. Annemarie shot Steven another look, as if to tell him to shut up, but she did it so gently that I couldn't help but smile.

"That's OK, Annemarie." To Steven I quipped, "I'm afraid I'll have to throw them all back!"

"Ah, but unless you throw your rod out there, you will never know just what you can catch. I would venture a guess that a big city like New York has all kinds of fish."

"So far I've found a lot of carp." I shook my head. Who was I kidding? I hadn't fished in a long time; I found the water dangerous and polluted. Not to mention that I was terrified of drowning.

"Carp or crap?" Steven persisted.

"Both!" Annemarie and I said this at the same time and then shared a laugh that took over the whole room for more than a minute.

"Actually, Brad wants to set me up with his friend Ryan." I said this in a voice that relayed just how I felt about it: *No big deal.*

"So go!" Annemarie said this with a little too much flourish, as if I were the child and she the mother, wringing her hands at the thought of her only child never married.

"No, I mean...I'll see." I went on to explain how Lanie wanted to screen him first and how maybe I wasn't quite ready. Not ready? Who was I kidding? It had been seven, almost eight years since David and I had split up—what exactly was I waiting for?

I was waiting for someone to come by, knock me down, bowl me over, and still leave me standing in the midst of it all. I wanted someone who was attractive *to me*, I didn't need somebody who was gorgeous to the rest of the world; but I certainly didn't want the balding-at-age-27 paunchy boy that had a self-described 'great personality.' I wanted a man who was smart, but was similarly not offended by the fact that I never finished college. I wanted someone who understood that I loved my family in spite of all the hurt, someone who would never allow them to walk all over me, a man who would be my advocate and still let me be whoever I was when I was with them. I wanted somebody I could talk politics with, somebody that got my zany sense of humor, that loved plays-on-words, that was a Yankees fan, that loved New York City as much as I did, that was hard and soft and funny and likable and serious and harmless and loved me unconditionally.

That's all.

All in all, I was pretty sure that I wanted what everybody else did.

I guess that's the problem, isn't it? In a city of eight million plus people, how exactly do you find the one person that *gets it?* I moved so that I could find someone more like me, but what exactly had I done so far to get it?

I ran up here on the weekends!

Thank God that Annemarie understood all this and loved me just the same. The rest of my visit was as good-natured as she was, with Steven knowing enough to leave us alone for a while, getting in all the girl talk that we so desperately needed.

At the end of the day, I left with a smile in my heart; laugh lines more pronounced, an aura of relaxation around me.

I hit the supermarket on the way home.

Chapter Seven

When the alarm went off on Monday morning, I wanted to scream, but could only moan and toss my alarm clock up against the wall. I found violence worked better than the snooze button, although my mind did register that my current alarm clock was the fourth one this year thus far.

It was May; I probably needed to invest in an immobile alarm in the near future, otherwise at this pace…I would be broke by December.

Looked like one of us would be! The alarm or me!

It was six twenty. Another day in the rat race, operative word being race. Makeup on the train was a given, but if I skipped shaving, I could possibly forgo the jog to the train. My mind was moving a mile a minute as a typical Monday morning unfolded.

I jumped as the hand on my shoulder shook me to consciousness. Had I fallen into that deep a sleep? Apparently I had, as the train had already arrived into Grand Central. I said my thanks to the neighborly passenger then proceeded to trudge off to work. The trudging had less to do with the job and more to do with my lack of sleep. The nightmares had started again in earnest, and the train seemed to be one of the few places I was able to sleep soundly.

I was at the corner of 45th and Lex and starting to cross when I saw a familiar face in the crowd. Where did I know that guy? He was smiling as he walked past me, and I returned the smile as I shuffled through my mind to place the good-looking stranger. Did he work in my building? No! No, it was the guy I had bumped into last week. Was he that cute last week? Once safely on the opposite sidewalk, I looked over my shoulder to try and get a second glance at him, but he was long lost in the crowd heading up towards the MetLife building.

My curiosity was piqued. Who was this guy? Did he really smile at me, or had I imagined it? Did it matter? I would probably never see him again. But he was cute. Boy, was he cute. I felt my heart beating a little faster and found myself suddenly wide-awake.

Thoughts of the Mystery Man kept me occupied until I entered work and my reverie was interrupted by Lanie's ever so subtle, "Spill it."

"Spill what?" I asked her as I began to settle in.

"What's up? You've got this kooky grin on your face, like you have Man-on-the-Brain. Did you meet someone Upstate?" She persisted.

"Lanie, surely you jest. I moved down here so that I *could* meet someone. I wasn't able to meet anybody decent Upstate when I lived there. What's the likelihood of me picking up on a weekend visit to see Annemarie, who is married, and Steven, her husband?" I threw her an exasperated glance.

"You are so dodging! OK. So you didn't–and never will–hook up Upstate. Then why do you look like a Cheshire cat?" She was sitting on my desk now, legs swinging in front of her, not going anywhere.

Was I that transparent?

"It's stupid." I stammered a little bit. "I just saw a very hot guy on the way to work." I shrugged as I tried to dismiss the fact that I would have lunged into oncoming traffic just to get a second glance of said guy.

"We see very hot guys every day on every street in this city. No, this is something more." Lanie pronounced this as if she knew for sure, not just this fact, but everything. The legs were still swinging.

She was planted. I had to 'fess up. I suddenly felt so dumb and desperate.

"Alright! Alright! I will tell you *everything* and you will see how *nothing* this is. On Friday, when I was walking to work, I bumped into a guy while crossing Lex."

"Literally bumped into? Or figuratively…like, someone you know?" Lanie interrupted.

"Literally bumped into. Like, I knocked his briefcase out of his hand. I apologized, I just wasn't watching where I was walking, and he said, *'That's OK.'* He kept walking, so did I, but he registered as very cute and I basically forgot about him. Then I saw him again this morning, crossing at the same corner, and I think…I'm not sure, now…but I believe he smiled at me. And today…well, he was definitely very cute. Let's just put it that way." I was grinning again, this time even I could feel a silly little grin plastered across my face.

"Very cute! Don't tell me that's nothing! I mean, Yellie, I have never seen you this way. You look like you have a crush," she teased.

"On a total stranger that I know nothing about. That I may never see again." I think I was reminding myself all this as much as talking out loud to her.

"Wearing?" She asked, eyebrows up.

"Suit."

"Both times?"

"Yeah." Something told me that I liked the way he looked in a suit.

"Tall?"

"I think so, yes, he was definitely taller than me."

"Hair?"

"Brown, dark brown."

"Eyes?"

"Not sure." I tried bringing his face into focus, but having only seen him for a few seconds each time, it was tough.

"Smell?"

"Not close enough."

"Birthmarks?" She laughed at her own inquisition.

"You are a dork. I'm sorry I even told you." I swiveled my chair away from her and began to answer emails.

"Danielle, we all know I am not a dork." Lanie sighed. "He sounds good. I hope you run into him again."

"Yeah, maybe next time I'll maim him just so he will be immobilized long enough to talk to me." I had an obscene visual of me ripping his briefcase out of his hand, pounding him on the head with it, and then rescuing him from oncoming traffic, all the while casting an irreversible spell on him. If he didn't end up with a concussion, I might even be able to find out his name.

"Not a bad idea." Lanie interjected.

"Let's drop it. Mystery Man shall remain a mystery. I think it's a fluke that I even ran into him those two times." I wasn't into getting my hopes up.

"A mystery, perhaps...but I do not believe in coincidence. Everything happens for a reason."

"God is in control."

"Amen, sister."

"You're a dork, Lane."

"I am so not."

The phone ended this endless repartee and the day moved forward. I tried to forget the Mystery Man.

Except I liked liking him. A Mystery Man was as good as any man for me to have: he couldn't hurt me, and he could be anything I wanted him to be.

Chapter Eight

Crash!
I awoke with a start, my heart hammering in my chest, wondering what the noise was and where it had come from. In the next instant, I heard a resounding thud, followed by nothing but an eerie silence that seemed to be emanating from the general direction of our living room. What was going on now? I relied heavily on my hearing as I sat alone in my darkened bedroom, my other senses taking a backseat for the moment as my eyes adjusted slowly to the blackness. I waited silently, as I knew there would be more noise forthcoming. I strained to hear the muffled voices that were coming from downstairs, trying to make out whatever I could, actually hearing very little. I allowed fear to take hold of me and I felt a familiar panic settle deep into my bones, even as I tried hard to think. I couldn't think. I could only feel my heart pounding and my mouth running dry, even as there was a break in the static buzzing in my ears, the buzz below me now alternating with high-pitched screams, nasty words being thrown about at a rapid-fire pace. What should I do? I sat stock still in my bed and thought about the situation. Should I get up, or was I safer right where I was? I tried to listen, to hear what was being said, but all I felt and heard was blood rushing through my ears. The words being spit out in obvious anger seemed garbled to me, even though the volume was loud enough to shake the foundation of the house. A moment later, clarity pushed its way through a jumble of shouted expletives, but I realized then that it didn't matter, as my heart knew the extent of what was being said, regardless of the actual phrases.
It was the same old song.
"You bastard!" That voice was recognizable at least. My mother then said something else, and although I could not hear her words, her tone was ominous.

"I TOLD YOU NOT TO FUCKIN'..." The
*Monster's words were lost on me also, but I felt a fear
spreading over me like a rash, permeating every inch of my
psyche. What did he tell her not to do? Where were they
exactly?*

*I crawled out of my bed and made my way to my
door. I turned the knob carefully, so that they would not
hear me. I kept my back against the wall and slid down to
the edge of the landing, where I could see the downstairs
light flowing from my perch on the top of the stairs. I tried
to discern where they would be positioned in the living
room, but I couldn't get my bearings by the sounds alone.
The voices were much louder now, as I no longer had the
door to buffer me. Should I go downstairs and try to break
it up? A voice inside told me to stay put. What exactly
could I do anyway? I was trembling and didn't know just
what to do. I felt tears begin to edge out of my eyes and my
throat was tight.*

What should I do?

*Another crash, and the sound of people struggling.
Was he hitting her, hurting her? I couldn't see anything
and I couldn't hear save for my own voice screaming in my
ears. The voice said: Call the cops! My brain registered
the thought, but my body was unable to move as I craned
my neck towards the carnage going on downstairs.*

*I heard another powerful bang and then a door
slamming shut, with our screen door clanging directly
after. I was able to distinguish my mother sobbing in the
sudden quiet, and I contemplated running downstairs to
comfort her. Oh, how I hated The Monster! I felt an anger
building inside of me that I was not yet familiar with, a
helplessness that I would grow to resent. I don't know how
long I stayed riveted to that landing, but once I heard my
mother's tears subside, I can remember slinking back off to
the relative safety of my own bed and my own room. I tried
to convince myself that he was gone and that I could go
back to sleep. My heartbeat returned to its normal pace*

after a long while, but sleep was far in the distance, so I listened for signs of her retreating to her bedroom. I can still remember keeping one ear peeled for my mother's footsteps on the stairs. I don't know how much time had passed before I drifted off into a semi-conscious state of sleep, which I remained in until the morning hours. It is hard to sleep with one ear open. When I woke, I padded down the hall to find my mother's door still closed. I stood outside a minute, raised my hand to knock, but thought better of it. If The Monster was gone, it would be better off if I left her alone to get some sleep. I walked gingerly down the stairs, trying not to wake her, offering up silent prayers so that the floorboards would not squeak. I made my way downstairs and parted the curtains in the living room's picture window. Good, The Monster's car was gone.

  Good Riddance.
  I turned around to find the fireplace poker lying in the middle of the living room floor. What was it doing there? Our condominium boasted a beautiful stone fireplace, which was at the center of our living room. I can remember Mom being so excited about it; when we first moved in, we made fires all the time. She would buy logs from the supermarket, the pretty kind that burned different colors, and we would light a fire together every night that it was cold outside. I picked up the errant poker in order to return it to its place next to the fireplace and the poker snapped in half. I looked down in amazement to find the handle still fitted into my hand, while the bottom half laid at my feet. How on Earth did they break an iron poker?

  A fresh rage washed over me as I bent to pick up the broken piece. I had helped my mother pick out this poker. How dare he destroy it! What the hell had really gone on here last night? I was shamed by my inaction as I roamed the rest of the house looking for clues. I thought again about waking my mother, but was unsure of what to do as I came across a mess in the kitchen. There was a broken bottle of Jack Daniel's in the sink, its amber liquid having spilled out and spotted the top half of the counter.

I stared at the bottle and tried to figure out if I should pick it up and throw it out, or just leave it and pretend as if I had never come downstairs at all. Its jagged edges leered at me while my mind reeled with possibilities. I checked the clock above the counter. Nine thirty-five. It was a Sunday, and my mother knew rather well that any opportunity I had to sleep in late would be taken. I could hustle back upstairs, burrow into bed with a book, and pretend I knew nothing.

The more I mulled it over, the more this plan seemed the best course of action for me to take. I wouldn't want my mother to be embarrassed, would I? Better to let her come down and deal with the mess, and think that they had not woken me last night.

Besides, she still hadn't left out my Easter basket. Even though I had just turned twelve and knew full well that there was not a rabbit hopping by with chocolate treats in tow, I was also aware of how steeped in tradition my mother was, and that it would devastate her to know that I went downstairs before she put out the basket.

With leaden feet and a heavy heart, I made my way back upstairs and waited for her to come and wake me.

Chapter Nine

The next day at work a sudden meeting was called by one of our bigger accounts in Minneapolis, the executives panicking about trying to get in there as there was a convention in town, and it was our job to get them there, even in the midst of sold-out hotels and zero availability.

After driving us crazy for several hours, our only satisfaction was that every single car service and rental remained completely sold out. They ended up piling into the only thing we could find available: a minivan.

Victory came in the form of a soccer mom's mediocrity on wheels, for seven millionaires to share, in a city where they could still see snow in May.

Occasionally Lanie and I shared a smug satisfaction that only pee-ons could share: things that would not bother an everyday traveler that were sure to raise the dander of all concerned. This was one of those times, although the situation did not make the day conducive to any form of personal conversation.

It was the next day before we had a chance to catch up.

We made our way over to Starbucks and indulged. It was a beautiful spring day, so we opted to spend a minute outside before our oatmeal-colored cubicle walls became our only form of scenery.

"Okay, Lanie, as your friend and virtual twin, I must say: Spill it! What happened with the Bradomeister this weekend?" I was curious to see if she had taken the Nestea Plunge.

" I flaked."

"You flaked! Whaddaya mean? You didn't say anything?" I wasn't overly shocked, but she seemed so upset last week that I thought she might actually take some action.

"Not a word. Na-da. Nothing. I totally flaked, Yellie, I was having such a good time that I was afraid to approach it." She bemoaned her fate.

"That's okay if you're not ready, but Lane...the next time he gets too wrapped up to call, you are going to be upset all over again." I was pointing out the obvious, but I knew how she worked by now. Lanie would convince herself that it didn't matter, when it did, the same way it did with her father.

"I have Clara today, and I am hoping to explore all this with her. I'll give you the blow-by-blow when I return." Lanie grinned. "I have a theory. You turn a certain age, and you must report to therapy. It's almost inevitable."

"My theory is a little more geographical. You turn a certain age, you have divorced parents, you work in New York City...you should really be able to just get a Therapy Card, like when you go get your driver's license. You work in New York, they issue you a Therapy Card."

"Because you will go eventually."

"Absolutely."

We nodded assent and shuffled off to work. We got caught up again and the next time we had a moment to spare, Lanie asked, "By the way, did you see Mystery Man this morning?"

"I think he is *Gone With the Wind*. He was probably a figment of my imagination, anyway." I shrugged it off as if it didn't really matter.

"Okay, I'm off to get my head shrinked. Are we still on for tonight?" She pointed to my gym bag, guiltily lying in the corner.

"We are." I shook my head as she departed, because Lanie was nothing if not a bad influence in the gym department. Lanie was one of the few people I knew who could cancel her membership, eat nothing but Ho-Ho's all day, and still fit into a size six beautifully.

While Lanie was visiting Clara, the phone started ringing off the wall, as the phone is wont to do with only one person attending it. I generally check the display before picking up, ready to steel myself for particular invasions, but I was just busy enough to not screen.

"Travel." I greeted as I typed.

"Hi Danielle, how are you sweetie?"

I felt my body tense as the voice at the other end of the phone registered in my brain.

"Oh, hi Mom," I'm sure I sounded distracted. I was. She rarely called me at work, so what had happened now? I was conditioned for chaos.

"I was just wondering when I was going to see you again," my mother had a way of saying this that inflamed me almost instantly.

"I don't know." I answered as honestly and with as little emotion as possible. I had just gone Upstate last weekend, although she didn't know that, and I was not in the mood to take the ride again so soon. "Why, what's up?" *Had she used up all of her visiting hours at the jail already this month?*

"I just wanted to see you." She sounded pathetic. I felt the old animosity rise up again in my throat, and the closely checked rage pounding inside my heart. Interestingly enough, she did not want to see me when I had lived in her home.

"Well, I'm busy, Mom, you know, big city life and all." She wouldn't know the difference; we barely knew each other at all anymore.

"Okay, well…" she paused, as if I would relent. The most difficult part of this whole exchange was that I wanted to relent, more than I was willing to admit, that I longed for the way things once were.

"I'll let you know when I'm free. Mom, I've got three lines buzzing here, so I've got to go. I'll catch up with you soon." With that, I disconnected the call, leaned back in my chair and took a deep breath. One in, one out.

Enter Lanie.

"What happened while I was gone?" As she breezed in, I read her mood as one that did not want to discuss her recent session.

"They cancelled Minneapolis." I tried to keep as straight a face as I could.

"NO!" Lanie shouted. "I will *Kill Many People!*" She pronounced each word with such fervor that I was afraid of her.

"I hope you know I'm joking. My mother just called." I announced this and then made a face. Lanie knew a lot about my relationship with my mother, Annemarie knew more, and I was the only one who knew it all.

It made sense; I was the only one who had to live with it.

"So what did she have to say?" Lanie was curious, she knew all the players in the family game, but had yet to meet them face-to-face.

"Not much. I think she wants to spend time together. I just…" my voice trailed off as I swiveled my chair to face Lanie's desk.

"You just what? Are you afraid you might like spending time with her?" Lanie's leveled gaze made me shrink lower into my chair.

Oh, to have your thoughts hit the air in the form of a spoken word! For an instant, I hated Lanie. How dare she presume to understand how I felt about my mother? I shelved that irrational thought and relented.

"Yeah, and then The Monster gets out of jail and I cease to exist again." The phone was ringing but I ignored it completely, allowing it to go to voicemail. "I just don't know if I want to take that kind of chance again." What I didn't say was that the anger that enveloped me was used as an invisible barrier between her and I and that I was afraid to hold her any closer than arm's length. I had been burned too many times to jump right back in and play with fire.

"I understand it, because I do the same thing. It's this bizarre fear that I have, that if I spend too much time with him that I might get used to it and then when he blows me off, it will hurt more and then some. So I return his phone calls about three for five, and then I have the nerve to complain that he doesn't care." She sighed. "This is why we have our Therapy cards!"

I laughed along with her. What else could I do? Cry? I had already cried rivers of tears, for the loss of things I had never possessed anyway. I cried for the Brady-Bunch family prototype, lost in the belief that other people had partaken of this, and I had been slighted in the most unusual way.

The phone rang and I motioned for Lanie to get it. I wasn't in the mood all of the sudden as I sat, awash with an indefinable sense of guilt, thinking back to the events that had made that guilt possible. Why was I the one to feel guilty? My brain argued with my heart: shouldn't she be the one to feel guilty? My mother had decided long ago that she would sell me out the minute the opportunity presented itself. God forbid any man were to feel challenged by my presence; God help us all if The Monster ever felt second best to the person who had been in her life for a longer amount of time, who cared for her in the most genuine sense of the word, who wanted nothing more than her attention and something resembling love.

She should feel guilty, not me. Maybe she did, maybe that's why her phone calls had increased in their frequency, maybe that's why she was trying to reinsert herself in my life.

Or maybe she was just lonely now that The Monster was locked away.

My mind flitted briefly to the Harry Chapin song that had just come on the radio. *Cats in the Cradle.* Perfect.

Lost in the reverie, I didn't hear Lanie calling me at first, and although I felt the present tugging at my consciousness, my soul teetered somewhere between revenge and regret.

"Danielle!" Lanie was waving her hand in front of my face.

That caught my attention, because Lanie's favorite nickname for me was Yellie, and she had gotten to the point where she rarely called me anything but.

"Lane!" I varied with her, between Lanie, Lane, Penny Lane, even Crooked Lane, when she was being especially devious.

"Olive's on two. I think she wants you to do a site." Lanie raised her shoulders as she spoke.

Olive? Now what? Olive's name wasn't really Olive, either–it was Lucille. Lucille was the liaison between the travel company and the ad agency, and she usually checked in with us once a week or so, just to make sure that we actually showed up to work and that there were no problems to fix. Lucille worked downtown, in The World Trade Center, and only came to the Midtown neck of the woods about once each month. She would pop her head in, make sure we were keeping the savages at bay, and then go back to her view from the 59th floor of WTC Building One. I envied her the view and little else; the reason Lanie and I had renamed Lucille was because of her unmistakable resemblance to Popeye's girlfriend, the venerable Olive Oyl.

I picked up the phone with ill-concealed surprise, as we had just heard from Olive yesterday.

"Lucille?" When she acknowledged, I said, "What can I do you for today?"

"Danielle, I was wondering if you could do us a great, big, humongous favor? By the way, how are you, hon?" Olive was the Queen of the Colloquial.

"I'm alright. What type of favor?" I was not one to commit to much without a play-by-play prior, and Olive had been known to pull some crazy stunts in her time.

"Well! Mr. Todd's assistant, what's-her-name again? Anyway, she is about to toss her cookies because Mr. Todd wants to set up an impromptu meeting in…Boston! Boston, I have it right here. A meeting in Boston on Monday, next week, at a hotel called the Fairmont Copley Plaza. Have you seen it?" All this in less than one breath.

"The Fairmont?" I shuffled through the hotel encyclopedia that I had amassed in my brain. "I don't think I saw that on my last trip up there, but how bad could it be? It's a Fairmont." I stated the obvious. My point being this was not a No-tell Motel. If I remembered correctly, it was a four or five-star property.

"Exactly. My thoughts exactly. However…what Mr. Todd wants…well, I was wondering if you could possibly go up there this Saturday and check out their meeting and sleeping rooms for me? He wants to have this meeting this Monday upcoming, and he expressed to…what's-her-name…." I could hear papers shuffling in the background.

"Adrienne," I supplied for her.

"Adrienne! Yes, Adrienne, anyway, let's put it this way: Adrienne's shitting a brick."

"This must be a big client pitch," I offered as I held back laughter. Olive was funny without ever intending to be.

"It is, and the Ritz is booked, and she's paranoid, but she trusts you, so when I offered to send you, she took it down about twelve notches. Will you please, please go for me? I've got a Bar Mitzvah that I can't miss, and she will not let him stay there unless somebody actually goes up and sites the hotel. I know it's not a lot of advance notice, but I've already talked to HR at the agency, and they are willing to offer you a comp day in exchange for having to work on a Saturday, and…" she was still trying to sell it to me as I cut her off and answered.

"Lucille, I'll go."

"You'll go?" She took a deep breath and let out a low chuckle. "Danielle, I owe you one. You know how hard it is to get somebody to do this on a Saturday?"

Perhaps with most people it was a hardship, but I loved stuff like this and could barely call it work. I would take the earliest shuttle up and the last one back and make a day of it in Boston.

Suddenly, my demeanor changed and I allowed myself to get excited. I had loved Boston the last time I visited there, and I had no plans for the upcoming weekend anyway.

"Well, I have plans with Faneuil Hall." And lobster bisque, and Boston Baked Beans, and all things Beantown.

Things were looking up.

Chapter Ten

I love takeoff.
I can't even explain how much I love takeoff. It's the rush, the feeling of doing something extraordinary on an ordinary day that makes me grin like a little kid every time the plane takes off the ground. Then the clouds come into play, and I still feel amazed, every time. My mind argues against the tingle on my skin and says it is absurd to be as excited as I am right now. People do this every day. The LaGuardia to Boston shuttle makes this trip twelve or more times a day, and each shuttle does the same to the Nation's capitol. Big deal, right? A big deal for a girl who, until she was fifteen years old, had never gotten outside of the Tri-state area.

The day was a whirlwind, as I toured the hotel and took in the very good-looking guy who was my escort through the property.

Okay, he was hot like fire. And by the time I left the property, I had myself sending out wedding invitations.

Brian. Brian Wells.

I fingered the business card that he had given me, and carefully placed it inside my pack. I walked down to Quincy Market and blended in with all the rest of the tourists, filling in the cobblestone walkways from one end to the other. I walked through Faneuil Hall, checking out all the crafts and handmade goods. I bought Annemarie a set of oven mitts that looked like lobster claws and then I thought of Lanie. I should buy her something; she always bought me little tokens whenever it was her turn to do a site inspection.

There was nothing that screamed Lanie, so I kept walking. I happened upon a store called *The Christmas Dove,* and I wandered in knowing that I absolutely had to get Lanie something from this place. Lanie was an avid collector of Christmas ornaments, and her collection rivaled the likes of Kris Kringle himself. I thought that I had seen this store once before…perhaps at the Seaport? South Street Seaport, located at the tip of Manhattan, boasted a Christmas-all-year-round type of store also. I convinced myself that this one seemed different, and it did, so I proceeded to look for an ornament that was indicative of Boston. I found several, and although there was a little lobster that was tugging at my heart, I made an executive decision and got the one that said Boston College. Neither Lanie nor I had gone to Boston College, but Lanie had a thing for eagles, (not to mention all types of fowl, seals, dolphins, fish, you get the picture) and since Boston College's mascot was an eagle, I thought she would get the joke. Either way, I was quite sure that she wouldn't already own this one.

Back out into the sunshine. I thought about buying my mother a gift, but knew not what to do. She had once loved Christmas, and shared that love with me so that I could carry it forward and one day show my children the spirit of that special season. Had she experienced too many bad Christmases to ever feel the joy again? Had The Monster ruined that for her also, as he had ruined so many other of the joys life had to hold? Oh, I hated him with every fiber of my being. I hated what he had stolen from us, but I couldn't let go of the fact that I hated her too, for letting him. I shrugged off the same cyclical thoughts that plagued me at the most inconvenient times.

I was determined to have a good day. My thoughts had wandered and I resolved to enjoy the gift that I had been given: a day in another place, enjoying a little free time.

I felt free. Perhaps insane, I marched right back into *The Christmas Dove* and bought my mother an ornament. Chosen or no, her lot in life had not allowed her to be frivolous and I still believed in the Mom that loved to sing and started decorating for Christmas the day after Thanksgiving.

When did she start hating Christmas? I allowed my mind to wander as my legs took me from the market over to the Public Garden. People-watching being a favorite sport of mine, there was no better place than at Boston's Public Garden in Spring and there was no better venue than those who rode the famed swan boats. At least in Boston, there was no better venue.

I took a seat on an inviting patch of grass nearby the boats. The sun was warm enough to warrant an ice cream, so I grabbed my bag, treated myself to one, and then reclaimed my spot on the grass. My thoughts shifted back to my mother, even as I spied a mother and daughter team laughing, holding hands, alighting from their swan ride. The girl looked to be about eight, the mother in her late thirties, or more likely her early forties. Was that it? Perhaps this mother was a little older, a little more ready to be a mother when her time arose. My mother was thirty-three when I was eleven. I remember that so clearly because I could still hear her saying to anyone who would listen: *We're double digits! At the same time!*

11/33…that was a banner year for us. That year was a slice of life that would always stand out…a couple of years after she and my father divorced and the year before she married The Monster. I went back to my original question: when did she start hating Christmas? I can remember her and my father having raucous fights while decorating the tree. He would insist on tinsel, she on garland…and I would cry every time because I wanted to be able to hear the holiday music over their shouting.

Older and wiser, I knew now that I hadn't been crying about the music. Maybe she began hating Christmas then, and her abhorrent feelings simply gained momentum after she married The Monster and he began not showing up for holidays. It took me no time to realize that he could not face whatever the holidays represented to him: a normal life, a family connection, hurts buried so deeply that they only surfaced once or twice a year? He couldn't do it, and my heart believed that to this day he knew not the pain he had inflicted on all of us, his selfishness both prison and cancer.

What came first: the chicken or the egg?

Did I hate him more for stealing our happiness, or her for allowing him to do it?

Then there's my father: oblivious to everything but the new life he cultivated, with the new wife and the new child.

There was no Hero.

I had reached the end of my ice cream cup, and although I could sit in the park forever, I wanted to walk at least some of The Freedom Trail prior to the sun going down. I yawned, checked my watch, and got up to toss away my cup. I would enjoy the rest of the trip, knowing these thoughts would always be there for me to kick around at a later date.

I moseyed around on The Freedom Trail, dragging the day out as much as I could. The last shuttle back was around nine pm, but I had no desire to have dinner alone in a restaurant, so I opted for a quick bowl of New England clam chowder at a pub before I made my way to the airport.

I left wistfully, longing for another day, another minute, in another place. I knew I was lucky and I was quite sure that they would send me out on a project just like this one again, but I had picked up a weird sort of melancholy in Boston that I now found hard to shake. I boarded the plane, enjoyed takeoff, and then promptly fell asleep in my window seat. I dreamed about Brian and I on a swan boat and my mother putting a glittery star on top of a heavily laden tree, her eyes twinkling as much as the topper.

Chapter Eleven

I was sixteen by the time I knew everything.

I knew about the drugs, I knew about the beatings, I knew all about the funny smell coming from my mother's room. It hadn't taken too long to catch on. I knew The Monster was no good right away, but I also knew that for some strange reason, my mother couldn't see that. I knew we had no money, I knew my mother was trapped, and I knew that I was probably just as trapped as she: I had a father that I saw periodically, who wanted nothing of his old life, evident as he buried himself in the new.

I also knew that nobody knew all that I did.

And I probably didn't even know the half of it.

And perhaps nobody would believe me if I told them all I knew.

One day, when all I knew was that The Monster's car was not in the driveway, I breezed into the house with my senses lowered, not needing to be on the usual high alert status if he was not around. I called out for my mother and nobody answered. I breathed in and out, and made my initial inspection of the house. Maybe today was going to be a good day. They weren't home. There were no broken bottles lying around, no notes on the refrigerator to do this or that, just a semblance of peace in a house that usually revolved in chaos.

I walked throughout the downstairs and saw no signs of anything gone awry, and then preceded to finish the upstairs portion of my tour. I walked into my bedroom only to find my mother with her hands in my sock drawer.

"What are you doing?" I accused, temporarily shaken. I thought I had been alone; what signs did I miss? I was usually much more on top of things.

"I'm putting my checkbook in your drawer, under your socks." She said it as if hiding adult things in her child's room was completely natural. I noticed that she

was looking down, averting her eyes from my venomous gaze.

"Why?!" I was furious, tired of all the games, tired of being responsible for another one of her things.

"Because of The Monster." Except she didn't say 'The Monster,' but the same rules apply here. No name for him.

"Why?!" I demanded again, unable to articulate how angry I was by this action. Why couldn't she see that this was abnormal? Why couldn't she see that I could deal with not normal, with your Mom being the only divorced Mom on the block, with your Mom being a little off kilter…not normal was okay, but abnormal was out of control.

"Because he can't be trusted, and I just need you to do this for me!" She became indignant. "If you hadn't walked in just now, you wouldn't have even have known!"

"Of course I would have known! I want it out!" I yanked open my sock drawer and tried to shove the checkbook back into her hands.

"No!" She shoved it back in the drawer, even as I tried to stand in front of her. "Danielle, you just need to do this for me. You don't understand." Her eyes pleaded with me, genuine fear inching out of her eyes in the form of liquid tears.

"I understand. I understand that he bounces checks in order to support his habit, and that by doing this you're not taking care of the problem. I understand that you can't trust him with anything. That's what I understand!" I felt a flush in my face, and my hands were emanating heat. Why did she always have to put me in this position?

"It's only temporary." She was always trying to smooth things over with me, would promise me anything just so I wouldn't leave and go live with my father. What she didn't understand was that I could never leave her alone with The Monster, and that either way, my father had all but forgotten about me. Sure, he showed up every three *weeks for an obligatory visit, but did it really mean anything to him?*

"What do you mean by temporary?" I would like to hear her promise me, even though whatever promises she made would inevitably be broken.

"He's going into Rehab." Her eyes still downcast, as if she believed it even less than I did, knowing the various outcomes we had already lived through together. The Monster had already entered and exited Rehab three times that I knew of, all programs completed to no avail.

"And then you'll remove the checkbook?" I wanted a promise.

"Yes." She conceded.

I let her leave the checkbook, and when I was twenty-one years old and moved out of the house once and for all; I took it out of my sock drawer and handed it to her without a word.

Chapter Twelve

"So I don't like anybody touching my things," I wound up my story with this statement, knowing full well that it was the understatement of all time. Whether people ever knew it or not, I went absolutely bezerk when people helped themselves to my things. When I first moved out, I had a roommate named Kayla for a short time, only because I wanted the safety net of somebody else pitching in for half the rent. She didn't end up being my roommate for long, because I continually caught her going through my drawers and borrowing my clothes without asking. At first, I tried to explain to her how uncomfortable this made me, and that if she wanted to borrow something she should just ask me. She failed to understand this and stated that I wasn't always around to ask permission. I related to her that it made me very uncomfortable, and having grown up with three sisters who regularly traded attire, she was completely unable to see my point. This put me in a tough position: how could I explain to somebody the itch I felt all over when I found somebody with their fingers in my drawers? It finally sent me over the edge, and after one conversation too many, I insisted that she leave. I can still remember being scared about making the bills on my own, but knowing deep down that it was something I needed to do to preserve whatever sanity I had retained from my crazy home situation.

"That's understandable," Constance offered in return. She waited before she went on. "There were no boundaries in that house."

"No, none." I uttered this ominously, scenes flashing through my head at the speed of light. No boundaries. We touched, we took, we all expressed things that should never have been.

"Do you deal with this daily?" Constance asked me, forcing me to define the sweeping statement I had made.

"Yes. I mean, no. Well…" I trailed off and smiled as I thought hard about how I really felt. "I still don't like people touching my things." I related the story about my old roommate. "But I really don't have to deal with that now. I live alone and I am the only one that has a key to my house."

She waited.

"I don't even know why I brought this up today," I admitted, knowing full well that during our last session, I was stuck in a memory from a younger age, a different time. What had triggered this particular memory?

"It's okay. You can talk about whatever you wish." She offered me an encouraging smile.

"I think that, after this past weekend, I started thinking about living with someone again." I relayed to her my infatuation with Brian and the longing to one day be married. Believe it or not, after all the horrors of marriage that I had witnessed first-hand, I still held a hopeful attitude that one day I would meet the right person and live happily ever after. Except I wanted everything separate: separate drawers, separate closets, separate checkbooks.

"I think that's good, that you've begun to think about wanting another relationship in your life. I also think our time is up." Constance gave me the same parting face she always did. I handed her my co pay and thanked her for listening.

On my way back to the office, I buzzed Lanie, but she was unwilling to indulge in anything without caffeine. I decided on two Frappucinos and made my way back to the office. I loved the Frappucino's made fresh from the Starbuck's bar. It was liquid comfort food, spilling over with whipped cream, all gooey and ready to soothe. Whoever designed the imposters in the little glass containers should be shot. I had tried them once and all I could say was *Yech.* They reminded me of Yoo-hoo's on crack; they held no charm for me, and I refused to allow myself to be fooled by an imposter.

My mother…fooled by an imposter. Nice segue, huh? My heart beat out the same fervent question: how had she been so outrageously duped? She had divorced my father and started on the path to self-awareness, self-empowerment. She was a woman of the Seventies, when woman-power was all the rage. And then, just when her life began to reach a personal pinnacle…she met The Monster and she reverted all her stances, only to take on the life of a woman who was more out of control than any woman she had ever allowed herself to be before. When exactly did that loss of power occur? Had it built up over time, only to be revealed when the chips were down, that the woman who knew strength was only temporary? She occurred to me as someone who was so much more irascible than that, that even with my father, she had a will that rivaled his own, and therefore caused that marriage's demise.

I would rather that. She seemed all too willing to give up the fight with The Monster, defeated before she began, a shell of the ultimate self that she had pursued so vehemently throughout her singledom.

The stereotypical victim, in every sense of the word, victimized time and again.

Why?

I had arrived at work, so I determined to shrug off these thoughts along with my jacket. Lanie and I had pressing issues to deal with, such as slurping our drinks, and catching up on each other's lives. My questions would still be there, after the drinks, and they would stick around, only to resurface whenever I encountered a minute to myself.

Since my return from Boston, we had dubbed our workweek 'Hell Week,' inundated with phone calls and endless trips, emails plaguing us at every turn. We had not even spent a minute together after work this week thus far, and I was hoping to change that tonight.

"Caffeine in dessert form." I announced with a flourish, as I extended her the Frappucino.

"You are the best friend a girl could ever hope for," Lanie said in response, a thick slurp following. "Yummy."

"Am I a good enough friend for you to follow me to the gym tonight?" I gestured towards the gym bag hiding in the left corner by my desk.

"Ugh!" Lanie said through a slurp. "If you insist."

"C'mon, Lane, I haven't been there all week." I knew I didn't need her to go with me, but the week had gotten away from me and now I needed a push in the right direction.

"Neither have I. Okay, I have an idea. Workout tonight, Little Italy tomorrow night." The resolute look on her face warned me to brook no argument.

"Great. I can burn seventy calories tonight, with the goal of eating seventy thousand tomorrow night. What about Brad?"

She coughed up a tad bit of beverage. "I just thought, the way you said that, I just thought of that movie, *What About Bob?*"

"Loved it." I giggled a minute, picturing Bill Murray stalking an innocent family in a way that only Bill Murray could make look hilarious. "So what about Bob/Brad?"

"Bob/Brad is in D.C. again this Friday, so I am all yours, and…we have a tentative date for Saturday eve." She paused a minute and chewed on the end of the bright green straw. "That is, *if* he remembers to call."

"Well, what happened last weekend?" She had briefly mentioned her breakfast with her father, but so far I had gotten very little on the Bradomeister front.

"I had breakfast with the Dadster, interrupted by no less than a dozen phone calls on the cell. He seemed as if he was listening about twenty percent of the meal, and since that's progress for him, I decided to shrug it off and simply split town early. I did that, went to my fave Korean nail place, got a mani and a pedi, and then dried out waiting for the Bradomeister to ring me. He rang me, but when he finally ventured over, we went to dinner and I had to stop myself from having a full-blown panic attack over the Egg Foo Young."

"Why the panic attacks?" I was mulling.

"Because it was like deja-freakin-vu! I felt like I was having breakfast with my father all over again. He was there, but he wasn't there. His cell phone kept ringing, and even though he kept letting it go to voicemail, I felt like I was intruding on him, so I told him to please answer it. He answered it, it was obviously work…he was muttering to some guy named Ned, then he hung up, apologized, and proceeded to be distracted for the rest of the meal. By then, I was so disgusted, I turned down dessert, and allowed him to drop me off before midnight."

"You should have called me. I was still up, I fell asleep on the shuttle back, but then was wired when I finally got home, so I ended up reading until about two in the morning." I wished I could have done more.

"Yellie, he doesn't get it at all. He doesn't get me." Lanie bemoaned her fate. "I think it's time I pointed out the obvious, and maybe that time will be this Saturday night."

"I think he just doesn't get women." I thought about Lanie's background and I knew that this must be killing her, slowly, but killing her regardless.

"And I am Woman, hear me roar!" With that, Lanie held up both arms and showed me her great big muscles.

"Woman, we need to get back to work so that we can go to the gym, get out of there, and still get home before midnight." I leaned down to pick up the next incoming call.

"Amen, sister." Lanie saluted me.

Chapter Thirteen

Running for the train the next morning, I felt my legs begin to shake and when I climbed the steps up to the platform, the back of my legs throbbed something fierce. I should have never have done that extra set of lunges after that crazy Step class last night, I knew it even as I was pushing myself, but I had forced myself anyway, since it was probably the first and last time I would see the gym this week.

Now I was paying for it.

I told myself to stop complaining as I walked to work, knowing full well that I would be eating an inordinate amount of bread and pasta tonight. My mind fantasizing about the linguine curling onto my fork, I almost missed him.

Yes, him.

Him!

The Mystery Man.

Same time, same place, same smile. Like two ships passing in the night, I walked past him again, and when I reached the opposite side of Lex, I finally knew one thing for sure: he really did smile at me.

His smile was directed at me, pointed right at my face, deliberate and huge. I couldn't help but smile back, as my heart threatened to beat right out of my chest. Our eyes caught for that one millisecond, and I knew for sure that I had his attention. The pain in my legs was completely forgotten as I trotted to the other side of the street, afraid to look over my shoulder, but dying to sneak another peek at the man that made my heart beat way too fast. I told myself no, I warned myself against it, but then I couldn't help myself and ended up throwing a quick glance over my shoulder, only to find him lost in the crowd.

Ugh! Did I smile back in a way that was inviting, but didn't make me look like a total geek, or groupie, or stalker? Did he really smile first? Now that he was out of sight, I started playing the interaction over in my head. Maybe I smiled first, and he simply returned my smile to be polite, because he felt bad for me, because I was the dorky girl who had knocked his briefcase clean out of his hands, and he was a charitable type of guy.

Oh, he was so cute! Another suit today, with a yellow tie, that much I saw before he passed me…was he tall? I would have to pay more attention next time. Next time! What if there was never going to be a 'next time?' What if I never saw him again?

I convinced myself I was being silly as I entered the office that Lanie and I shared. I had seen him three times already. I would see him again.

Oh God, I hoped I would see him again!

"Lanie!" I interrupted her as she was already on the phone. Sometimes I couldn't tell whether she was on the phone or not, the headset being a constant accessory to her everyday work attire. She waved me away, so I proceeded to go and make myself some tea while I waited for her to get off the phone.

I grabbed a tea bag, a couple of Equals, and was about to add some milk to the mix when I heard her voice behind me.

"Yellie, what's up? You look about to burst!" Lanie helped herself to some coffee.

"I saw him again." I put my cup down temporarily; knowing that handling boiling water while swooning should be left only to the experts. I could feel myself grinning from ear to ear, and although I felt ultimately dopey, I couldn't hold back.

"The Mystery Guy?" She was grinning right back at me, obviously amused by this little obsession.

"The Mystery MAN," I corrected. "He smiled at me, Penny Lane, this time I'm sure!" I was positively giddy.

"Did you whack him over the head with his briefcase this time?" She was amused.

"No, I just gave him my killer smile." I was hopeful that it didn't look like a sinister grin.

"You better watch out, he may start thinking you are just that." Lanie pointed her finger at me as we made our way back to the little hole in the wall we called our office.

"Just what?" I lost her.

"A killer." She laughed.

"You are funny, Lanie. Can't you see that I'm in love here?" I threw her my most wounded look.

"Tonight we talk all this out over food, and we figure out once and for all why you can't possibly fall in love with someone you know." She was good at bringing me down to Earth.

"One word: David." I liked to blame David for everything I possibly could regarding men.

"Many words: David, The Monster, Daddy Dearest, Danielle…" Lanie corrected me.

This was part of the reason why we had become such good friends. Lanie was a straight shooter, even when I didn't want to hear it. I should say, *especially* when I didn't want to hear it.

"Lanie, let's not go there."

"Oh, but *there* is soooo much fun," she gave a threatening glance, as if to underscore her abilities as my personal psychologist.

"Okay, then I get to go there, too. You don't get to get off the hook, Lanie." I warned her with the most evil look I could conjure only minutes after seeing the Mystery Man.

"You can go there. I allow you full access to the craziness that takes up permanent residence inside my head." Lanie acquiesced.

"Agreed." I vowed to only give her as hard of a time as she gave me. We worked through the rest of the afternoon at our usual compatible speed, picking up the pieces for each other and often trading assignments so that we could utilize each other's strengths. Lanie did a few spot-on impersonations, and the next thing we knew it was six o'clock in the evening.

The phones sat silent and we decided to call it a week. We hopped a subway downtown and ended up at a little Italian place we both loved called Emilio's. Emilio's was off the beaten tourist path, and it boasted a classic menu as well as a cozy atmosphere.

"Now, I'm Constance and you, my dear pal, are Clara. Tell me what you would tell your crazy client, Lanie," Lanie suggested as soon as the hot antipasto hit the table and she had a glass of wine in her hand.

"I would tell her to let her dear friend Danielle eat in peace and then, and only *then* to grill her about her love life. Hungry women can be highly irrational." I was hungry, but I was also avoiding telling Lanie what she probably already knew.

"Hungry women tell the truth, if for no other reason than that they are nasty. I've seen you ravenous in the past, and you are one scary kid."

"Yeah, I'll give you that one. The blood sugar drops and out come the fangs." I bared my fangs.

"So shoot. And please, don't be nice." She glommed a piece of garlic bread and sat there, waiting for me to continue.

"Well, if you were my crazy client Lanie, and not my friend, I would tell you that you need to start manufacturing your own happiness. The reason you are so dejected and end up feeling totally pushed aside by the Bradomeister's actions is because you still haven't dealt with those feelings regarding your father. So you seek out a man that reminds you of him, and you convince yourself that it won't be the same, but then time passes, and inevitably the same problems crop up. You feel the same feelings, and instead of dealing with them, you push aside whatever or whoever prompted those feelings; for example, getting rid of the Bradomeister. Then you plunge right into another cycle of depression, only to break out of it, find someone to shower you with attention, and then the first time he forgets to call…you're right back where you were before. Except then you usually try to avoid your father for a little while too, to add to the turmoil, and whether you realize it or not, you add to your own heartache. I think that Lanie needs to be happy with Lanie, alone, with people, whether people give you half their attention or all of it. Once you're able to do that, you won't have the agony over Brad, you'll either decide you want Brad in your life or not, but either way, you'll be fine. You won't allow somebody's offhandedness to destroy you the way it does now." I picked two of the three remaining shrimp off of the hot antipasto platter and transferred them to my plate. They were dripping with mozzarella, and laden with sauce. I loved this place.

"What would you tell me if you were my friend?" Lanie asked over a sip of wine.

"The same." I gave Lanie a conspiratory grin.

"Some friend."

I threw her a look of mock pain, then groaned out loud as I tasted.

"I know," Lanie agreed as she took in her plate. "I love this place."

"Have some," I offered, knowing full well that Lanie would take me up on it. She loved tasting what everybody else was eating and there was no shyness in her.

"Well, Yell…" Lanie began as she stole off my plate, "The only thing I can say is that you're right. I just don't know what to do about it. I can't seem to stop these feelings, and because nobody likes pain, I'm willing to just walk away from it in order to get it to stop."

"What does Clara say?" I was her friend, but all I had to offer was a bunch of educated guesses, from what she had allowed me to see thus far. Clara had a little piece of paper on the wall that deemed her far more qualified than I.

"She says basically the same thing you do. She thinks I should talk to my father."

"About what?" How do you tell someone that you felt inconsequential in his or her life? Had I ever been able to do that with either one of my parents?

"Practical stuff. For example, like…when we're having brunch or spending time together. She seems to think that I should ask him to turn off his cell phone, so that I feel less threatened and our time spent together can actually be some quality time, instead of interrupted vignettes and a conversation that starts and stops and loses its place the whole time." Lanie shrugged her shoulders. " I don't know how practical that is, though."

"Is he that needed?" I would think that a man as important as Lanie's Dad would have enough underlings that he could shut his phone off during a one-hour breakfast with his daughter.

"I just don't know if I could ask him." Her voice wavered and she brushed away a lone tear that cascaded down her pretty face. "Isn't that stupid? I get nervous just thinking about him saying that he couldn't do it, and I feel the rejection even before I ask, and because of that, I freeze and I can't assert myself around him."

"And Brad?"

She made a garbled noise as she inhaled a forkful of linguine.

"Well; maybe you need to deal with *Lanie* before you deal with *Brad.*"

"Now I say we deal with you!" Lanie clapped her hands together, as if she were chairing an episode of Oprah.

"Go ahead, Constance." I was egging her on as I pushed my dish away. I figured that I owed her the chance to rip my life apart.

"Where should I begin? How long have we known each other?" She started counting on her fingers.

"Almost five years," I supplied for her.

"OK, so: for almost five years I have seen you date absolutely no one. You've had a crush on several men. One who ended up being married," she was about to go on, but I cut her off right there.

"I did NOT know he was married!" I had met a guy named Reilly at a hotel site inspection, traded business cards, and went out to lunch with him one time after that. Three weeks later, I saw him *and his wife* at a new hotel's Grand Opening Gala. I avoided him like the plague.

"I know that! I'm simply underscoring the fact that you routinely go after unavailable men. It's like you have a nose for it! Anyway…then there was the guy that you met at the Hotel Convention that conveniently lived in…Chicago?"

"Milwaukee."

"Okay, I knew it was somewhere in the middle."

"Lanie, if he lived here I would have dated him!" I insisted.

"That's the reason why you suddenly had to run Upstate the weekend he was back in New York." Her tone was accusatory.

"Well, by then I decided I didn't like him." It sounded lame, even to me.

"Then there was the Sales Rep from that trendy little boutique-y hotel in Los Angeles."

"You could not blame me for liking him; anybody with a pulse would like him, he was hot as fire." I shook my head. "I think I just have a thing for Hotel Reps."

"Sure, he was hot. My point is that if he repped a hotel in good ol' NYC, you wouldn't have looked twice, much less drooled. Then you ran into that guy you knew from childhood…at that fundraiser." She had a memory that rivaled my own.

"Joel. He went away to some entertainment school like *Fame* when we were kids, and then I saw him perform at the fundraiser Olive couldn't go to. It was great to run into him, but I had no genuine interest." I thought about Joel and smiled. He lived down the block from me growing up, and although we were only neighbors a short time, I had retained fond memories of him through the years.

"You had stars in your eyes for days."

"Fine, you win. Your point is…?"

"My point is that the last two men to catch your eye were Brian, may I please remind you that he is *yet another Hotel Sales Rep from yet another city?* And The Mystery Man…a player yet to be named." Lanie ended her diatribe with a self-satisfied grin.

"And your point is…?" I couldn't help myself. If she was playing Constance, she was not doing a very good job. Constance never badgered me; she just listened and waited.

"My point is that although I might be afraid to be ignored, to feel shut out or forgotten, at least I throw my hat in the ring. Sometimes I run, but at least I give it a whirl. When was the last real date that you had that was not a figment of your overactive imagination?" She was still badgering me, even as I mulled over the dessert menu, and consequently pondered a chocolate-filled pastry that could, in some states, be considered suicide.

"You know the answer to that. David." I shut the dessert menu and waived down our waiter.

"David. David was seven years ago!" Lanie grabbed the dessert menu from my clutches and did a quick scan of her choices as the waiter approached our table. I honestly don't know why she bothered. We had been here several times, and she always perused the menu eagerly, and then ultimately chose Tiramisu.

"I'll have the New York Style Cheesecake and a cappuccino with mocha." The chocolate-filled pastry was deemed runner-up to my all-time favorite.

"I'll have a cappuccino too, and the Tiramisu." Lanie handed the menu back to our waiter.

What did I tell you?

Soon she was back to the David Issue.

I can barely explain David to myself, much less to anyone else. To explain David would have to be to explain all the nuances of another time, another place, the whole Upstate mindset, and most of all, the Danielle that once was. The current Danielle would never give David a second glance. Well, maybe a glance, because his looks were by far his biggest selling point. David swept me off my feet when I was only nineteen years old, he with his disarming smile and dark brown eyes that lit up a chiseled face, square jaw and chin only making him stand out all the more. Once you could drop your gaze from the face to the rest, his six-foot tall muscular frame left you with no reason to be disappointed. David was a brushstroke of a man I had painted once, a dream come to life from the canvas of my soul.

I met David at the ripe young age of nineteen years old, having just disposed of my relationship with my high school sweetheart that had carried over two years too long, far too long after the graduation bell had tolled. The funny thing is that when I met David, I wasn't looking, and I could never have foretold the pronounced impact that he would have upon my life.

There are days that I am still stunned, standing stock still, a doe frozen in the headlights of her own life, wondering how I allowed him to affect me so deeply.

I also wonder how I allowed the memories to stay, to haunt, to keep me at bay, from my own opportunities, whenever they took the chance to present themselves. I would occasionally lie to myself, and tell myself that he didn't affect me in such a deep way, only to find my love life lying dormant after months that turned into years, and if I was real honest, I couldn't keep lying for too long.

I met David at a Christian concert at my old church. When I lived Upstate, I had once been part of an old, rambling church that regularly hosted area gospel concerts in its theatre in the round. People would come from all different types of churches, from all over the area, just to catch a glimpse of somebody they may have heard on the Christian radio station, which is a force to be reckoned with in the rural New York market. I went to a good portion of the concerts, partially because they were either free or cheap, but also because they were a part of my old life, a refuge in the midst of the chaos at home, a voice that would buoy me from the ongoing storm.

    I can still remember being very excited about that particular concert. It's funny the things that our mind recalls in retrospect; I can remember that I wore black pants and a red shirt that night, my hair sporting the 'high hair do,' a throwback from the 80's, but it was only 1991, and styles took a little longer to make it up the Hudson than it did to sweep across the five boroughs. Anyway, I can vividly recall getting there early, chatting up my friend Ramon, and being well ensconced in my seat prior to Helen Baylor stepping out on the stage. I was so involved in her performance that I didn't notice at first the man who had claimed the seat next to mine.

    Halfway through, my pastor broke for a brief intermission, and just as he gave a time check, I noticed the man sitting on the aisle to my right. It was David. My heart registered that I should not have lustful thoughts in church about thirty seconds after looking at him.

    "Hi. Did you want to get out?" His million-dollar smile captured me as his hand made a sweeping gesture towards the aisle.

    I stood there like an idiot for a full minute, my mind trying to process his words as my heart flip-flopped in my chest.

    "I probably should go to the Ladies' Room." I tried to smush my way past him and out into the aisle. I made my way to the bathroom, and as I stood on line, I made sure to hit my forehead several times with an open palm. Was that the only thing I could think to say to this

man that God, in his infinite wisdom, had brought to my church door?

As the night wore on, I found that I had a lot more to say and so did David. Although I was enjoying the Helen Baylor concert more than any other I had seen at my church's ongoing Concert Series, I found myself paying very little attention to Helen in the second half of the evening.

Now, I had met guys at church before, and they generally fell into two categories. One was the Usher-I-still-lived-at-home-with-Mommy-Praise-the-Lord type, the other was one whose testimony generally went a little something like this: 'Dude, I was so f***ed up on drugs, man, and then I met Jesus.' Neither of which had I ever been interested in, but the church was its own scene, and that was that. I had resolved myself to the fact that I would never meet a guy at church, and that was also that.

Then I met David, and I knew. I mean, I knew all the cliché type of garbage that people say they know, how *you just know*...and all of that, and to this day I know that was a large part of why I no longer trusted my own judgment.

I was so very wrong about David. So wrong, I shook my head even now as I thought about how utterly blind I had been. However could I trust myself, and my foolish heart again? So I stayed away from men, concocting stories about them in my head, making them as I liked or needed them to be, knowing full well that if I didn't reach out and touch that I could not get burned.

Hence, this theory was why Lanie was currently staring me down over the cappuccino, her eyes challenging me, and me knowing that although what I told her might make no sense whatsoever, that I knew one thing for sure. I never wanted to be that wrong again.

"Did I ever tell you the whole 'David Story?' " I took a deep breath in, knowing that I would have to relive it in order to tell it, but knowing that it was time.

"No. I've gotten dribs and drabs since I met you, sprinkled with cryptic little asides, but never the truth, the whole truth, and nothing but the truth, so help you God." Lanie answered.

"Well, maybe it's time." My words echoed my thoughts, and before I uttered another one, I felt my heartbeat begin to escalate.

"I just ordered my first cappuccino, and you know full well I can down about three of these and sleep perfectly fine. So I am all yours." Lanie pronounced, her eyes urging me on.

I recounted how I had met David at church that night, and it somehow sounded a little different explaining it to Lanie, far different than how I had explained it to Annemarie, because with Lanie I had to expound upon the church culture and how small-town life had dictated a lot of what I thought and felt, at the time as well as now.

"After church, David asked me out for coffee. We went to a little neighborhood diner and each had a coffee and a muffin. I can still remember that he had a blueberry muffin." I said this with a twist of sarcasm as well as a wistful undertone. Oh, how I wished I knew then what I knew now.

Lanie patiently waited for me to continue.

"He said he would call the next day, and he did. That alone was a big thing for me; I can't tell you how many guys I had met at that point who had never even bothered to call. I was only nineteen, and I was *the only one* out of every friend I had at the time, that was boyfriend-less. I actually had two friends planning weddings that year, which I know sounds bizarre, but up there it wasn't altogether too strange." I knew I sounded as if I was making excuses, and I decided to stop and just let the story unfold. "I found out he was from a smaller town than mine, across the Hudson River, about a half an hour away. I had never met him before, but he seemed less small-town than me somehow, or maybe it was my hormones talking. Anyway, I fell instantly and totally in love with him. I found out that he was home on his college break, so I willed myself not to get too close to him, but I fell hard anyway."

"Where did he go to school?"

"Tulane." I spat the word out, even now, so many years after the fact. "You have to understand one thing to understand how taken I was by this guy: maybe I lived in a bubble, but I had never even heard of Tulane before I met David. I went to the community college Upstate, and the few friends that I had at the time who actually went to college went to places like SUNY Oswego and SUNY Plattsburgh. Tulane? I didn't know Tulane from a hole in the wall, but I knew it was big, and I knew it was someplace else, and I knew that any adult I said it to was impressed."

"Hell, I'm impressed." Lanie chuckled as she scooped up some Tiramisu. "Go on."

"So. So, we met and all the pieces just seemed to fall right into place. I tried to steel myself from falling in love with him, but he was way too slick, and as the days turned into weeks and he had to go back to school, he convinced me to stay with him." I took another deep breath, remembering our conversation that night.

"Danielle, I love you, and I want to stay with you." *His hands kissed my own, one knuckle at a time.*

"You can't stay, silly, you need to go back to school." *My utmost hope was the same way God enabled us to find each other that we would find each other again when he graduated. I explained this to him, my plan woven into the dreamlike state that I had created for us.*

"I can't go back to school knowing that you're not mine." *His eyes bored into my own.* *"Promise me you'll wait for me."*

And I did. I promised him that I would wait obediently at home for him, as he went off and pursued all things college. He knew nothing of my home life, and I had simply to survive until he returned to rescue me.

"Like keeping in touch?" Lanie inquired.

"I wish now that he had only promised we would keep in touch, but he wanted me to wait for him, and not see anybody else until he came home from school, which would be late May. I agreed. I was convinced that God had sent him to my doorstep, and since he was a solace in my life of confusion, he fit in well with my dreams of a better life. All I had to do was wait." It had all appeared so simple.

"Did you wait?" Lanie was motioning the waiter for a second cup of cappuccino. I declined and stirred what was left of mine.

"Well, yes. But strange things started happening after he left. At first it was great; he wrote me often and called every couple of days. I was just as much in love with him two months after he left as I was on the day he first told me he loved me. But then things started to change, subtly at first, little stupid things that started speaking to me and telling me that maybe he wasn't the dream guy that he thought I was. I tried to ignore them, I kept trying to convince myself that he was somehow God's gift, after all I had endured, but over time, the pieces didn't seem to fit." I shook my head at the memories that came unbidden, riding through my mind like an overpowering wave.

"Like what? What didn't fit?" Lanie asked.

"Like...I don't know. Silly little things. Here I was, this faith-filled young woman, having lived through a lot of hard things...I was more aware than he probably expected me to be. For example, I remember him calling me drunk. If he were truly a Christian, would he be calling me up drunk in the middle of the night? Again, I could chalk that up somewhat to college life and the culture in New Orleans, but it just didn't match up to the David he had represented at home. David would call me up cursing, laughing, more than once trying to tell me a 'funny story' that I didn't find funny at all. After a few late-night heart-to-heart talks, he convinced me that all we needed was to see each other again, to reassure each other of the love we shared. I flew down that Easter." My mind was moving like a movie reel in reverse, picturing the way we embraced at the airport when I arrived. I could still smell his cologne, so many years later, wafting me back to a love that had pierced my very soul.

"What happened then?" I had Lanie's rapt attention.

"Well, I flew down, and everything seemed to be just as it had been before, only better. He was the quintessential host, showing me around New Orleans, and showing me off to all of his friends. He introduced me as 'The Love of His Life,' and I was extremely flattered. I had been nervous about going down to see him, but we had a wonderful time together, we reaffirmed the love we felt for each other, and by the time my plane landed back in New York, I had persuaded myself to trust him and to have some faith in our relationship. I firmly believed that if God had placed David in my life, that He would work it out for us, come what may."

"Were you afraid of finding out something when you went down there, like another girlfriend?" Lanie asked.

"I guess. I mean, it didn't really cross my mind, but…I guess I just had a feeling, a strange sense of foreboding that I wouldn't give voice to then. Maybe I was just afraid that I would find out that he wasn't who I thought he was, and being that I had built him up to Super-Human status, I wasn't interested in seeing the downfall. I don't know," I replied, shaking my head again.

"And then?"

"And then things returned to normal. I was surviving at home, and living for letters and phone calls from David. One night, he called me up real late, and as we got to talking, he broached the subject of marriage for the first time. I knew I wanted to marry him, I probably had known it less than a week after we met, and it seemed almost natural that we were talking about it only a few short months after we met. And he proposed."

"But you were so young!" Lanie protested, her eyes widening.

"I know that now," I blushed for a second. "Lanie, believe me, I know how ridiculous this whole thing sounds. But when I was nineteen, it seemed almost par for the course. I had come from a life of broken promises and destruction; this was better than anything else I had imagined thus far. Here was a gorgeous, smart, charming guy who was interested in marrying me. He knew where I came from and he didn't care. He was at Tulane as an undergrad, but he fully expected to continue on to Tulane Law. I had the prospect of a future with him; so what if he occasionally drank a little too much? He was better than anything I had ever known." I said this in a way that reminded me of how much I missed being loved. I didn't miss David anymore, I had come to terms with David himself, but I still waxed sympathetic over the way he had made me feel.

"I mean, after that phone call, I told Annemarie, and we went out and celebrated. I told my mother the next time she wasn't engulfed with The Monster…he told his mother, because she called me the very next day. David had a brother named Jason, and Jason started calling me Sis whenever I called the house. I mean, it was real, it was no less real just because I didn't have a ring on my finger…I was going to get my ring in June, when he came home, and then we had planned to get married over New Year's, while he was home on break, and then in January, I would fly down to New Orleans with him and we would start our life together." I felt so naïve now, knowing the outcome.

"What were you going to do in New Orleans?"

"Good question. Become a housewife? It didn't matter, as long as I was with David. I think back then I thought I would get a job at the mall, and take a painting class at Tulane or some other nearby college. I was working at a bank as a teller Upstate; I guess I supposed that I could always do that. I had no goals to speak of, I just wanted to escape my house and be with David. Those were my goals."

"Well, you were nineteen." Lanie gave me an encouraging smile.

"And lovestruck." I agreed.

"I think it's lovesick." She offered.

"Now, get back to your story. I need to know the end." Lanie insisted.

"You know the end." I insisted just the same.

"Our downfall was my brilliant idea," I began again. "Sometime at the end of May, I had a so-called brilliant idea to go down and see David one last time before he returned, and so I made up my mind to surprise him."

Lanie's sharp intake of breath indicated that she knew what was coming. "You flew down and surprised him?"

"No, flying would have at least been easy. I decided to go at the last minute," Lanie was nodding; we both knew how outrageous last-minute airfares could be. "So I drove…24 and a half hours down…smiling all the way, dreaming about how perfect it would be, visualizing David's face, and how excited he would surely be to see me. Back then; I was the *definition* of naïve." I was back there now, driving down south, watching the miles go by outside my window, feeling validated when our song came on the radio, singing out loud, enunciating each word as I sang, punctuating with false bravado, willing everything to be okay.

I broke the reverie and looked at Lanie. "This is hard."

"I know." Lanie replied, but she did not give me permission to stop.

"So!" I brushed some nonexistent crumbs from the table. "So I drove twelve hours or so the first day, then stopped to sleep. My goal was to leave the hotel by nine, and hopefully be there by about nine o'clock that night. When I asked if he had plans, he said just studying, maybe going out for a pizza with his roommates, so I figured I had a pretty good shot of surprising him in his dorm. I pushed myself to get down there that Tuesday, and I have to admit that it was exciting, and on some level fun and full of adventure. I was so caught up in the adventure that I kept ignoring that little voice inside that was nagging, and telling me to beware. As an aside: I will never stuff that voice or feeling again. If I allow myself to be really, brutally honest now, I will tell you that I stuffed that voice down or drowned it out with loud music the entire ride down. Anyway…I arrived closer to ten o'clock at night, totally exhausted, but riding high on adrenalin. I parked the car and ran off to see him."

"I ran up to his dorm," I continued, my heart getting heavier as I retraced the steps in my mind, "and walked into the suite. I remember thinking that they were probably out getting that pizza, and I decided I would just lay down on David's bed until he returned."

"And there he was in bed, with a coed, naked and writhing around, making so much noise that they didn't even hear me enter the room."

"Oh, God, Yellie…" Lanie's voice filled with: *That Bastard!*

"She said, *'I'll call you later,'* as she left the scene of the crime, and it was all I could do to not reach out and smack her square across the face. Once she left, David was nasty. I had never seen him act the way he did that day. He accused me of spying on him, he said I was paranoid, and he basically said that he didn't ask me to come down, so why didn't I just leave?"

"You're kidding me!" *That Bastard!*

"I wish I was. We ended up fighting, screaming at each other, but he knew he had no real excuse…I told him I couldn't just leave, that I was exhausted, that I needed sleep before I turned the car around and pointed it back North…he said I could sack out on the couch in the common room, and then he left the dorm. He probably ran to her. I cried until I couldn't cry any more, and then fell exhausted into a disturbing little piece of sleep on his couch; Thank God the roommates were nowhere to be found. I slept maybe three hours, and then awoke hoping it was all a dream, a nightmare, only to find out that it was not. I went back into David's room and found him dead asleep in his bed. I remember shaking him awake and telling him that I was going to go. He said, *'Just Go.'* His head was buried in a bunch of pillows and he didn't even look up at me. I stood in the doorway to his room and my last words to him were: *I really did love you, David.* Then I left. I left New Orleans and him, and any dreams I had of marriage, or love, or trusting men, or hope, or Divine Providence, or anything that mattered. I drove all the way home, only stopping to get some hot tea or go to the bathroom. I cried most of the ride, high on caffeine, I couldn't eat anything, my stomach was tearing up on the inside, and at one point, 'our' song came on the radio, and it took all that I had within me to not pitch my radio out the window. I still can't believe I got home alive. When I did arrive home, I can remember locking myself in my room for days on end, only coming out to go to the bathroom, or try and eat something. I recall that as the one time my mother was actually more concerned for me than for The Monster. She kept banging on the door and trying to get me to come out and eat something. Eventually, I called Annemarie and told her everything, and she came over to talk, and hand me tissues one by one, and thankfully, I had taken off of work, obviously thinking I was going to be in New Orleans during that time, so I didn't have to report in to anyone or anything…I have vivid memories of crying, just crying, and sleeping whenever I was too tired to cry any more. I had a physical ache in my heart, which I had heard of and had read about in no less than a thousand romance novels, but never really believed was real before, and then I was living with it, suddenly thrown into a realm of pain that I could not do anything but exist in. I survived, the same way I had survived all the family garbage through all those years, but somehow this hurt more, and I knew full well that if I didn't get through it, I didn't really care. It was that bad."

"So what did you do?"

"You mean, after the fact?"

"Yes. What happened next?"

"Nothing. I healed. I survived. My faith in God was shaken, my faith in men was destroyed, and I walked through a deep fog until one day I made my way through, and the sky was blue and I saw the sunshine again. I really can't tell you why or how I got through it, but I did…Annemarie helped, but I think that overused cliché about how time heals all wounds is true. It took a lot of time. I cried every day for months."

"Did you ever see him again?"

"Once. It was funny, because he came home just a few weeks after the whole thing occurred, but I never ran into him, because he lived across the river, and I tried hard to avoid any place I knew that he frequented. His mother had called me, weeks after the trip, and expressed how sorry she was that we had split up, but I didn't get the impression that he told her any details about what had happened. She was a sweetheart, but the wedding was quite obviously off, so she went her way and I went mine. Thankfully, any plans we had made for our so-called wedding were not permanent, and so even though she was probably as embarrassed as I was, there wasn't all that much to undo. I don't know why I ended up being embarrassed when he should have been, but I avoided all things David whenever humanly possible. I never ran into his brother, or any of his friends, but then one day I ran into him. Rather, he ran into me. I was working at a bank at the time, and he obviously knew that, I had been working there when we were together. Anyway, one night when we were locking up, I saw him outside, standing by the ATM machine. I remember doing a double-take at first; not sure if it was him or not, but then he approached me, and stumbled all over himself as he made some excuse about why he was there. I knew why he was there–let's be honest here–there's an ATM machine on every corner in the USA, there was no need for him to drive a half hour to go to my town to withdraw money from the ATM machine at my bank."

"So what did he say?" Lanie was sitting on the edge of her seat.

"It was really weird. He didn't say anything worth saying. He said he was in the area, and needed some cash, which we both knew was ridiculous. He told me I looked great, I said Thanks, and he left. That was it."

"That was IT?!" Lanie was incredulous. "The man you were engaged to, the one you were going to spend the rest of your life with, who cheated on you, who more or less threw you out after you went out of your way to see him, the man you gave your heart and body and soul to, he just pops by the bank one day to say hello? What the hell is the matter with him?"

"I don't know. I guess I'll never know. I never saw him again…not at a concert at my church, not in the street, or the mall…it was as if he wanted to act as if I or *we* never happened. One thing, though…I gave him my heart, and maybe even my soul, but never my body. Isn't that interesting?" I never talked about it, but I felt I needed to clarify, as I had chosen to trust Lanie tonight, more than I ever had before.

"What do you mean?" Lanie was obviously lost.

"I never slept with him." There. It was out.

"You never...?" Lanie looked more floored by that than anything else I had told her thus far.

"Nope. I can't even explain to you why; I think that during the course of events in our relationship, God's hand was over me, to protect me, knowing in advance how ultimately devastated I would be. At least, that's what I believe now. I didn't always believe in God, and I had slept with a couple of guys before I met David, so there was no logical reason as to why I abstained at that point. I just did, and now I'm glad I did. I can't imagine our breakup hurting any more than it did, but there is a large part of me that knows that I would have been completely destroyed by that betrayal." I was utterly convinced to this day that I had made the right decision in that department.

"Did you ever think that maybe that's why he was fooling around with that girl?" Lanie prodded lightly.

"Absolutely! I beat myself up the whole way home, wondering if I drove him to it...but once the clouds began to dissipate and my vision cleared, I realized that he would have done it no matter what. The betrayal would have only have been deeper, and the hurt prolonged."

"Danielle, I never knew, and I want to apologize for giving you such a hard time about not going out with anyone. Now I know why you fall in love from a distance, and stay there. It's understandable." If Lanie had the ability to look sheepish, this was it.

"It is understandable, but you're right...it's not just David. All things together, I don't trust men and I barely trust myself. The most incongruent thing though is this: I really, really want to feel that way again. More than anything, I want to meet the right guy and fall in love and get married–for real this time–and be victorious in love. I want to succeed in an area of my life that has always eluded me. I want to love and be loved completely, and that's why I fall in love with every other guy I meet, and that's probably why I also run away scared."

"I don't have a story like that, but I think after hearing your story, it makes me believe that we are more alike than I originally thought. You and I are both running scared." Lanie mused.

"Without a doubt, my friend. Although…" I looked at my watch. "I cannot drink fifteen caffeinated beverages a day, get three hours of sleep, and still be even remotely human in the morning like you can."

"Are you calling it a night?" Lanie checked her watch also. "Yes, I think we should!" She waved for the check. It was almost eleven. Had we really been sitting here all that time?

"We need to if I'm still going to catch a train home." We divvied up the check and were leaving the restaurant when I felt compelled to thank her.

"For what?" She asked as we walked towards the subway together.

"For being a good friend." I was so happy to have found a friend that understood the Danielle that I was trying to be. If a little bit of history helped Lanie to get the current Danielle situation under wraps, then I didn't mind sharing.

"You are an inspiration, and I never mind listening," Lanie gave me a kiss on each cheek as we parted ways, she downtown, and myself up.

An inspiration. Now that was a new thought for me to toss around inside my head. Was I an inspiration? Why? Because I had survived heartbreak? Was that enough of a reason to label me an inspiration? Because I still wasn't sure if it had not made me worse for the wear, I still hadn't determined if some scars were permanent.

I made it home and fell asleep with another cliché on the brain.

Time will tell.

Chapter Fourteen

"We've really got to stop meeting this way," The Mystery Man said, smiling as he passed me, leaving me just enough time to cross Lex, but not enough time to respond.

It really happened, and I knew for sure it was not a dream because I pinched myself so hard that I left a bruise.

OH MY GOD…he was flirting with me! Was he flirting with me? Maybe he was just super-friendly, a guy who hailed from some small town in Idaho, who didn't know the ways of the world or the rules for street-crossing in New York City traffic. But he didn't look like he was from some small town in Idaho, he looked like a guy I could fall in love with in a New York minute. Oh, there I go again! I am totally ga-ga over some guy I didn't even know.

He could be an axe murderer.

He could be an Idaho guy, here for just a few weeks on some auditing job, licking his chops because his boss, Mr. Misner, let him go to the big bad city for a couple of weeks of auditing and whatnot.

He could be a married attorney.

He could be gay, an adulterer, a man with a bad disposition, a man with no disposition, a politician with twelve dispositions…my mind had a hard time keeping up with my legs as I raced down the hall to Lanie's and my hole/office.

Or…he could be the guy who just said hello to me! Me!

"LANIE! LANIE, Lanie, Oh, Lanie!" She tried to shush me until I made maniacal cutting gestures across my throat, when she acquiesced and put the caller on hold.

"What?!" She pretended to be exasperated, but I could tell that she loved me.

"I saw him and he said hello! HELLO! Oh, hello…I love hello!" I did a little dance in front of my desk.

"The Mystery Man said Hello?" Lanie was catching on.

"He actually said, *'We've really got to stop meeting this way,'*" I squealed. "And then he smiled at me." He smiled.

"Omigod!" Lanie was almost as excited as I was…almost.

"And then he vanished!" I said with verve. "Well, he walked past me. But it sounds so much more dramatic to say *vanished*."

"Yes, it does. The important point is that you've made contact."

"He made contact." I was flying high.

"He made contact. Now, what are you going to do about it?" Lanie looked at me head on.

"Nothing!" I looked at her as if she was a crazy person. "What should I do about it? Knock his briefcase out of his hands again? He could in fact be a super-friendly guy from Idaho."

"I doubt it. What we need here is reconnaissance. What you need is me." Crooked Lane asserted.

"How are you going to help me? What do you suggest? Should I wear a 'Hello, my name is…' tag as I cross the street tomorrow?" I liked scheming with Lanie, but we needed something concrete to go on.

"How about I go with you?"

"You wanna sleep over?"

"No, I'll just meet you at the corner tomorrow morning."

"Before I cross?"

"Of course."

"What if he sees you?"

"I'm slick."

"How slick?"

"Very slick. Look, I can stand by the mailbox on the opposite side, and check him out as he passes." Lanie suggested.

"How will you know it's him?"

"I'll know by watching you."

"It's a crosswalk, Lanie, and there will be tons of Mystery Men. You'll just have to cross with me." I thought this was as good a plan as any.

"So I'll meet you in Grand Central."

"Sounds good, and I'll poke you when he walks by."

"No! You'll say HELLO, no pokes, no jokes; you need to meet this guy! That is the objective! I will not waste my spy expertise on a venture that will profit nothing. You must meet the Mystery Man."

"Just don't bat your eyelashes at him. I'll kill you dead." I warned her. I was claiming The Mystery Man for my own.

"Don't you worry, this entire stakeout and reconnaissance is being done on your behalf." She grinned. "We're both nuts, I hope you know."

"I know." I was reeling from the exposure. "I know I'm nuts, but this is more fun than I've had in some time. What if he says hello back to me?"

"You bat your eyelashes." Crooked Lane was in full force.

"Lanie! You are not helping." I couldn't help smiling, grinning from ear to ear, the entire incident playing its way out on my face. Was I that lonely, desperate, dying for an interesting man to pay attention to me? I didn't care. There was something about this incident that was fun, something about the man that was intriguing, and something about the situation that I couldn't turn away from.

"I am helping! Look, Yellie, think about what we were talking about the other night…this is an opportunity for you to make a move! You already think he's cute, and he seems friendly…he apparently lives in New York…all things for the plus column. You never know." Lanie was building a case for me to justify my stalking of The Mystery Man.

"Lanie, I agree with you on all of those points, but keep in mind that people just don't meet this way." I took myself down a few notches, knowing that fantasy so often was unable to transfer into reality.

"How do they meet? I mean, who's to say that this isn't meant to be?" Lanie could be just as much of a dreamer as I could.

"He could be another David." I warned, my head landing back on planet Earth.

"You just made my point…exactly!" Lanie exclaimed.

"What point?"

"My point that you cannot declare how things are done! God has His own agenda! I am a firm believer that if I locked myself in my house for the rest of my life, unwilling to go out and search for the man of my dreams, that God…the Universe, Fate…whatever you believe in…would send a UPS man to my door! Who's to say that you can't meet someone crossing the street? You met David in church, was that any kind of guarantee as to how the relationship would pan out? As Olive always says: 'Think Outside The Box!' Lanie orchestrated her hands in a Ta-da! Fashion, underscoring her theory.

"I can think outside the box, but I also want to think in the realm of reality. The reality of the situation is this: I have eyes for a handsome stranger, and I want to find out more about him. Period. He could be very taken." I resigned myself to that being a real possibility.

"He could be. Let's just wait until tomorrow, okay?" Lanie was on to another subject after that, and the day wore on.

In between calls, I thought about The Mystery Man, and I couldn't help but feel a tingle in my spine. Tomorrow was a big day.

Chapter Fifteen

Tuesday, 8:42 am.
"Lanie, Lanie, come in, Lanie!" I was wielding my cell phone as if it were a walkie-talkie, little rivulets of sweat pooling underneath my bra, my pulse pounding in my ears. I took a train a couple of minutes earlier than my usual so that I could meet Lanie in an inconspicuous sort of way prior to crossing Lex, working under the delusional thought process that he may see us setting up shop if I arrived at my regular time, and not wanting him to catch on to our mission.

"I'm in. I'm on the corner, sipping a cup of joe, waiting for you, all the while nonchalantly scanning the crowd. Get your butt down here," Lanie hissed into the phone.

"I'm walking out of the MetLife building right now," I informed her as I made my way down to Lex. Our plan was to act as if we had happened upon each other, shoot the breeze for a minute or two, and then cross as soon as I saw him coming in the opposite direction. I silently prayed that I would see him today; I didn't see him every morning, although since I originally noticed him, I had seen him more and more often. As I made my way down the street, it occurred to me that perhaps we had been passing each other for quite some time, but just hadn't noticed each other until I knocked his briefcase out of his hands. He was so adorable, how could I not have noticed him? I righted myself; perhaps it had something to do with the several million people that populated this city at any given moment.

The question then became: Why had I noticed him now?

I joined Lanie and smoothed down my skirt as I gave her a kiss on both cheeks. I was wearing a black skirt with a lime-sherbet colored shirt and a black jacket slung over my arm. It was a beautiful May day, sunshiny and breezy, warm enough for the black sandals on my feet, and pretty enough to engender hope and all things romance.

A great backdrop for a stalking!

Lanie took a sip of her coffee and we lingered a minute.

"Lanie, that's him! It's him, it's him, it's him!" I was screaming and whispering at the same time, and slapping her leg with my hand as I focused on the man across the street, waiting for the light to change.

"Get into position," Lanie commanded, as she and I made our way to the corner.

The sign flashed from *Don't Walk* to *Walk*. We proceeded, and about two steps out onto the runway, his eyes caught my own again and I made sure to flash him the most brilliant smile that I could muster.

"Hi," I said as we neared the point where we were about to pass each other.

"Hello again," He said back, and his eyes crinkled as he smiled.

We passed each other. In a second, he was gone, leaving me with a flushed face and a pounding heart.

I walked, back straight and eyes forward, and I did not even acknowledge Lanie until we had fully crossed the street.

"Is he gone?" I breathed, counting on Lanie's spy tactics.

"Elvis has left the building!" Lanie announced as she forced me to turn around and face her.

"Lanie, did you see him? I mean, you saw him, right? Isn't he cute? Do you think he's cute? Oh, God! He's so cute! Did you hear what he said? He said, *Hello again.* Hello again! Hello...again!" I was almost dancing in the street, skipping as we made our way to the office.

"I saw him." Lanie was laughing at me. "I have never seen you like this, however, and it's refreshing to say the least."

"Forget about me! What about him? What do you think of him?" We were at the entrance of our building, and I was practically jumping up and down, eager to get an answer out of her.

"He is cute, and he is tall." Lanie observed. "He doesn't look like an axe murderer, as if an axe murderer has a particular look...I approve. Good eye contact, nice smile...but Yellie, you've got to say more than just 'Hi.'"

"Lane, I've got about thirty seconds to work with here," I reminded her.

"Throw yourself in front of traffic, and let him rescue you." Lanie suggested.

"In New York? That would be tons of fun."

"You'll be able to see his character right away."

"You're a funny girl, Lanie, I need a plan!" I was on the border of whining, straddling the fence between hope and despair. Was it even remotely possible to imagine that one day I would meet this man, know his name, be his friend, go out on a date, fall in love?

Or was this the most comfortable place I could find myself in? A crush, an infatuation, a Mystery Man that I could make whatever I wanted to be...?

I was at war with myself, and I needed a plan of action so that I could focus on that and convince myself that I wasn't scared, or hiding in the guise of a ridiculous plan that resembled a hide-and-seek-make-sure-you're-at-your-locker-between-third-and-fourth-period-because-the-football-player-will-walk-by sort of thing.

"Ugh!" I wailed and pleaded at Lanie with my eyes.

"I'm coming up with a plan. Just give me a few minutes," Lanie patted me on the shoulder.

We settled in to work and the day flew by as the phones jumped and we threw maniacal plans back and forth. What could we do? Kidnap him? Hire a private investigator?

I proposed waiting.

"Wait for what? For him to get married and move to New Jersey?" Lanie excelled at sarcasm in addition to her stable of impersonations.

"More dialogue. You know, like, *'Hi, my name is Joe, would you like to go out sometime?'* Or something." I didn't know, but I also didn't have a better idea.

"You're the one that said you had thirty seconds! How can he introduce himself while passing you in the street? You need to cross the street earlier tomorrow, and meet him at the corner." Lanie seemed pleased with this idea.

"I can't."

"You can't? Why can't you?"

"Because I…" I trailed off. I wasn't shy, but I wasn't so sure that I was up for that. Plus, I wanted him to be the one to approach me. Had he already approached me? Was his flirtation pure friendliness, or had I caught his eye in the same manner of which he had caught mine? Could he be having this same conversation with a friend of his?

"Because you don't want a real, living, breathing man in your life again," Lanie asserted. "You want a Mystery Man; a dream guy, the kind you can look at but not touch."

"I want a breathing guy!" I insisted, at the same moment that Alex, our regular internal postman, decided to pop in.

"You don't ask for much," Alex observed, then winked at me, and nodded at Lanie. He dropped a FedEx package off on Lanie's desk, and was on his way.

"That was funny," Lanie giggled as she wrestled with the FedEx package. "I love Alex; he's the best guy in the mailroom."

"Not to mention the fastest." Alex always made sure airline tickets got where they needed to go fast.

"Omigod!" Lanie cried out as I raced to her side.

"What?" I was looking over her shoulder and saw what looked like a DVD on her desk.

"I can't believe him...I didn't even think he was listening to me...Omigod!" She was muttering and blushing, and I had never once seen Lanie look so flustered.

"Lanie! Talk to me! Who is it from? Is it good?" I was reading her signals, and she seemed happy, but at the same time overwhelmed.

"It's..." She laughed, a light little laugh laden with surprise. "It's from Brad. When we went out Saturday–" she began but I interrupted her.

"Lanie, I never asked about Saturday! I'm sorry! I've been so caught up!" I felt horrible, as she was always there for me.

"Don't worry, please! If I wanted to talk about it, I would have interrupted you. Just listen now. Okay, so: we went out Saturday night and then went back to his place to chill out. He was tired, so was I, so we ended up just sitting around, talking, and watching TV. At one point, he was flipping through the channels, and we came across the movie *Once Around* on cable. Have you ever seen it?"

"Was Richard Dreyfus a pilot?"

"No, that was another movie with Dreyfus and Holly Hunter. I think that one was called *Always*. *Once Around* is a family movie, it's very real, but it's also about true love and taking chances. Anyway," Lanie waved her hands to demonstrate that the plot was unimportant right now. "The point is that I told him how much I loved the film, and how every time I watched it I cried, and I made him change the channel because it was in the middle, and I wanted him to see it from beginning to end." She shook her head in amazement.

"So he sent it to you. Did he add a note?" I was touched, so I'm sure Lanie was touched.

"No. No note, but obviously, I know it's him." Lanie paused. "I remember feeling like he wasn't even listening. I can't believe he heard me, and even went so far as to act on it, to do a really sweet thing like this. Aaaaaahhhh! Yellie, what do I do?" She looked perplexed.

"You call him, and you thank him, and you ask if you can see him later." Easy.

"Exactly." She chewed the inside of her lip, her eyes off in space. "I guess this means that he is pretty genuinely interested."

"I'd say so." I smiled as I picked up a call. I mimed a call in process and pointed to Lanie, mouthing *call him*.

As I attended to a client, I overheard her on the phone with the Bradomeister. I heard the trill of her laugh and I hoped that this would enable them to both get on the same page.

"I am not going to the gym tonight!" Lanie announced a few minutes later with an air of triumph.

"I will forgive you as long as you have a movie date," I replied.

"I think we have a talking date."

"Even better. The movie will keep."

"Definitely."

"Should I get bagels tomorrow?" We treated each other to bagels whenever we especially needed to confer before the day began.

"I'll get caffeine, you get bagels, and we'll figure out both of our love lives." Lanie delegated.

"Sounds good." We had a plan. I went off to the gym, she went to meet Brad, and when I went home that night, I dreamed about the Mystery Man.

Chapter Sixteen

Jogging for the train, I considered the conversation with Lanie the day before. Could I ever really approach this guy? What if I approached him and he humiliated me on a street full of people: *'Oh, I'm sorry, did you think I was interested in you? Heehee. I'm just a super-friendly guy from a small town in Kansas...'* Idaho. Whatever. For all I knew, he was an Amway salesman, and he was looking at me as his next prospect. My mind sorted through the various options: Jehovah's Witness, Greenpeace recruiter, talent scout, serial killer, a man high on Ecstasy, the friendly-guy syndrome, new to the city...and none of them rang true.

My heart was telling me that this was something else, and that maybe I could take a peek through Door Number One and see what was inside. I was petrified. I had listened to my heart with David.

Once off the train, I walked my usual route to work. It was a beautiful day in the neighborhood, and I felt my heart drop as I waited to cross Lex. There was no sign of him today. I tried to look nonchalantly, out of the corner of each eye, to see if he was anywhere left or right of me, but he was nowhere to be seen. I debated waiting through another light change, but then decided I was bordering on the obsessive, plus I had promised to bring in bagels, so I shifted my butt into gear and crossed the street, only to make a left and continue down the opposite side of Lex, figuring I would cross over to Third closer to the bagel shoppe.

Good call.

As if my heart had summoned him, I saw him coming towards me in a walk/jog similar to what I did each morning as I hiked it to the train. Our eyes caught, and he slowed down. I had an insane moment of thought: Could he have been running to catch up with me?

I wished.

As each step brought us closer together, I focused on his face, and felt as if the entire street had evaporated around me. I concentrated my gaze on a point between his eyes and his mouth, and hoped he didn't think I had a weird thing about noses.

He literally took my breath away.

"Hi," He offered, and stopped in front of me. I might go so far as to say that he was blocking my way, but I didn't mind it.

"Hi," I began sweating and blushing simultaneously.

"I...ah, I seem to be bumping into you a lot lately," He flashed his incredible smile, as I stood there, rooted to my spot, smiling awkwardly.

"Looks like we're on the same schedule," I pointed out, shifting my feet and wondering how long I should stand there. I wished I had a coffee cup in my hand to play with.

"Not for long. I'm Paul," He offered me his hand and I shook it.

All the clichés exist for a reason. I felt electricity when we touched, and knew that the flush in my cheeks had deepened to dark rouge.

"Oh, Paul! I'm Danielle. Are you moving?" What did he mean by *'Not for long?'* Was he leaving me so soon?

"I just took at new job downtown, so I will have to get up earlier, and I'm sure I'll miss you in the morning." He smiled clumsily. "I, ah...Look, I know this sounds crazy, but...since I won't be seeing you...would you like to get together sometime? I can give you my card, and I can promise you that I'm not just some crazy lunatic, but I figure if you can meet people in bars, ya know...I don't know, I'm hoping this isn't much different." His eyes seemed to plead with me to give him a chance, as his words tumbled out, one after the other, in a race to convince me that he was not *just* some crazy lunatic.

I was stunned. Never, not in a million years, could I have predicted this. I stood there for what seemed like a full minute, speechless, my mind sending a signal to my head, to move, to nod, all the while hoping that I didn't seem like too much of an idiot.

"You have a card?" What? What did I just say? Oh, stupid, stupid, stupid!

"I have a card!" He produced it with flair. "The only thing is that you have to call me within the next two weeks. I'm going to work right now, and I'm putting in my notice today. So you have to call me, and let me prove to you that I have a real office, and a phone number, and that I am not a serial killer." He disarmed me completely, with his ease, and his eyes, and the smile that wouldn't stop.

"I'll call you," I said, my tone somewhat robotic, picking up all the words he said, registering only some of them right now.

"I look forward to it. Have a great day," he said, and then moved along, as if he had just brought a newspaper and a cup of coffee, while I commanded my feet to move, one in front of the other, all the way to the corner.

Once I rounded the corner, I snuck a peak back over my shoulder, and unable to see him in the steadily moving crowd, began jumping up and down and screaming.

"Yes! Omigod, omigod, omigod, oh, yes, yes, yes, YES, YES!" I was pumping my fist in the air, and dancing around in a circle on the sidewalk.

The great thing about New York City is that, even as you scream like a banshee and writhe yourself into the shape of a contortionist, nobody stops to look at you funny. Very few people even glance.

I dialed Lanie and willed her to pick up, all the while chanting, "Omigod, omigod. Omigod!" She picked up after the third ring.

"Travel."

"Lanie! I talked to him, I did, I…he…AAAHHH!" I couldn't even talk; I was so blown away by what had just happened.

"Great! Well, get your butt in here and we'll discuss it. Did you bring the bagels?" Lanie got ornery when she was hungry, and she was letting me know not to let her get that way fast.

"No, I have to go get them now. Lane, I was talking to him *all this time!*" I glanced at my watch. It was almost nine.

"Did you find out a name at least?" Lanie inquired.

"Paul!" I exclaimed. Paul, Paul, Paul. I loved it.

"Good! Now we have a name to go with the face. Now, go get me a cinnamon-raisin bagel before I expire!" Lanie threatened.

"I'll be right there." I clicked off with her and stared at his card for a moment. Paul Corsi. Paul Corsi. I liked it. The card had his name, title, phone, fax and cellular number on it, as well as the place where he worked. He worked on Park Avenue. He must walk to work, that's why I always saw him. Then where did he live? Somewhere not far from my work on the East Side, I presumed. Nearby.

I floated into the bagel shop and ordered Lanie and I both cinnamon-raisin bagels, toasted, with walnut-raisin cream cheese. I kept fingering the card, and allowing the name *Paul Corsi* to roll off my tongue.

What a morning! *Life can turn on a dime.* I remembered hearing that saying after David and I split up, and I thought: How true, how true.

I swiped all thoughts of David from my head and made my way to the elevator bank in my building. The elevator took forever, and by the time I made my way up to Lanie, I was about ready to burst.

"Lanie!" I screeched, ran to my desk, dumped the bagels, and danced a little jig. "Ah-hah!" I exclaimed, and pointed at her. "I kept my half of the bargain…I SAID

MORE THAN 'JUST HI!'" I yelled. He initiated it, but I did my part, and I wanted some acknowledgement.

"Ah-hah! Fork over the bagels! Your coffee is cold, and there are three calls holding!" She exclaimed, all with a twinkle in her eye. With one swift movement, she pushed all the calls to voice mail. "Tell me everything while we reheat the java."

I followed her into the cubbyhole kitchen. She threw her coffee in the microwave first and my words tumbled out faster than it took the coffee to reheat.

"Wait! What happened with you and Brad last night?" I was determined to be a better friend than I was yesterday.

"That will keep. Tell me everything!" She demanded, all while ripping apart her bagel and throwing my coffee in the microwave after hers. With a mouthful of breakfast, she turned all of her attention to me.

"I LOVE HIM!" I cried out, shaking all over. Okay, I admit I was being a little bit over the top, but I could not remember ever feeling this way, even when I first met David.

"You lust him." She corrected, as she removed my cup from the microwave and ushered me back into our hole/office.

"Fine. He is sooo…sooo cute, Lanie! His name is *Paul Corsi.* He works on Park, but he just got a new job, and he said that he wouldn't see me any more, because of the new job, so he gave me his card, and asked me to call him. And he promised me he wasn't a serial killer," I added, filling in the dots.

"Oh, I'm so glad he promised!" Lanie was dripping with sarcasm, and stuffed with bagel.

I shot her a wry grin.

"He intimated that it was no different than meeting someone at a bar," I offered, agreeing with his logic, no matter how strange it seemed. How would you tell people this story? Well, we met crossing the street. Yeah, we were just crossing the street, and in a city of eight million people, we caught each other's eye…

It was weird. But in a city where people met at work, or in Central Park, at rallies of every different flavor, bookstores, coffee shops, blind dates, seminars, night clubs, bars, museums…how weird was it really?

"He's right. So? Are you going to call him?" Lanie pressed.

"I guess so," I hadn't thought that far yet, and the mere thought of calling him made me nervous.

"You guess so? You are! Yellie, do you know how cool this could be?" Lanie was done eating now, and therefore back to being somewhat human.

"It could be cool." I agreed. I knew I needed to just go with it, so I decided to shake off the nervousness and just be.

"You look lovestruck," Lanie threw that in for good measure.

"Speaking of which…what happened with you last night?" I was curious to see if she had even spoken to him about their relationship.

"We hung out at my place. He grabbed sushi and some Snapples and then we ended up on the couch. He kissed me…and then, he stopped, looked me straight in the eyes…and told me he loved me." She almost whispered the last part of the sentence.

"Lanie!" For the second time that morning, I was whooping it up like crazy. "Omigod! He did? He told you he loved you? Woo-Hoo! Alllllll right! What did you say, what did you say?!" I was so very happy for her.

"Well, after my heart started beating again…I told him I loved him, too. I swear to God, Yellie, it's like my whole heart stopped. I only paused a beat, but I hope he knows it was because I was stunned, rather than repulsed." Lanie shook her head, and now the one facial expression that tuned out all the others was evident: disbelief.

"Are you shocked? Do you love him?" I pried. Lanie had never said anything before about loving him, or anyone else I had ever known her to date. She was outwardly the emotional opposite of me, I who was able to proclaim love at first sight several times annually; whereas she would never confess audibly the love she may have felt. The truth was that we were both scared, no matter how our tactical displays may have differed.

"I am floored. Positively floored. I never in a million years would have expected that. I had wanted to talk to him, but he came out with this new bit of information, and I couldn't go through with it. It was far better than I expected, and if I were to be brutally honest with you, far better than I had even hoped to expect. Do I love him? Yeah, I think I do." She was reveling in the surprise omission that was so much more than she had dared to ask.

"You know you do, you're just scared." I corrected.

"Very true. But, Yellie," She paused a moment and looked over at the incoming call display. "I've got to take this one." Headset on, she picked up for Mr. Todd's assistant, knowing full well that the Bigwigs did not wait.

I settled in to my desk, surprised to see that it was already ten o'clock, and not surprised to hear a stack of calls to be returned on my voicemail. Didn't they know that Lanie and I needed to compare notes in the morning?

I returned calls, Lanie picked up the new ones, and we reconvened sometime close to when normal people eat lunch.

"Mexican?" I suggested.

"You got it," Lanie agreed, as I hit speed dial and ordered up our busy-day specialties. Whatever socializing we did at work, we always paid for it in the end. We ended up working through lunch and got fully caught up somewhere about three.

Lanie left for therapy and I pulled Paul's card out from my bag, and played with it again, rolling it over and over again in my fingers.

Maybe things were looking up for both Lanie and I. Brad loved her, The Mystery Man had approached me…I tried to remember his face again, and the way he had looked at me this morning. Did he look like a serial killer? My heart said no. My heart actually banged against my insides, a slow drumbeat, and if it had lyrics it would say: *Give him a chance.*

I plunked the card back down next to my headset, and started sorting through my email. The phone rang again.

"Danielle? It's Dad." Said the unmistakable voice.

"Dad? What's the matter?" Instant panic gurgled in my chest. What was he calling me at work for? He never called me here. He rarely ever called.

"Nothing's wrong. I just had a break and figured I'd give you a call." He sounded sincere, but I had learned from him first to be wary of all things male.

"Oh." It was so awkward to speak to him now, too much time and space had passed between us, and yet he still saw fit to drop me a line every so often, as if he had one day a month marked on his calendar, with a little reminder sticker that admonished him to call his first child. "Not much is new here." I never let him in, never even tried to keep him up on the current events that detailed my life, knowing full well that he wasn't interested.

He left me when he left her. He still hadn't gotten a hold of that concept.

"Well, I got a new car in today." He proceeded to tell me all about the new car his dealership just received. My father was a car salesman, in fact a very good car salesman, and he enjoyed his work to no end. Often times, he would tell me stories about different cars, and I would sit and listen, wondering how anyone could love an inanimate object with such fervor.

"How's my brother?" I asked, interrupting his endless diatribe about all things automobile. My father went on to have another child, as if his new life dictated a new kid, and therefore he complied. I liked the kid, he was cute as could be, but there were so many years and differences between us that I considered him more like a nephew. His name was Michael Jr., and I tried to be the best absentee-sister that I could be to him, though our paths didn't cross very often.

"Your brother is getting big," he went on to brag about him, something I had never heard him do about me, and my mind drifted. Just what was the purpose of this phone call? About when I was going to fake an onslaught of incoming calls, my mind registered something to the effect of 'Grandmother coming up.'

"Did you say that my grandmother is coming up?" His mother lived in Florida, and only came up to visit a couple of times a year.

"Yes, and if you want to come up, by all means…no pressure." The purpose of the call presented itself.

I almost laughed in his face. No pressure? Damn right, no pressure. As far as I was concerned, neither one of my parents had the right to pressure me into any form of closeness or communication, or any act that would deem me to act as part of One Big Happy Family. They had walked out on me years before, both literally and figuratively, and now that their lives were more stable, now came the time for invites and interest? I wondered sometimes why I even tried to uphold relationships with them, but I alternately knew that there was no chance of my just letting go of them yet.

Cats in the Cradle.

My heart lurched every time I heard that old song by Harry Chapin, carefully detailing my life in a way that I still couldn't express.

I told him that I would see, but I knew as I hung up the phone that I would probably not make the trip Upstate to see them. I wasn't particularly close to my grandmother anyway; and the way I had been feeling as of late, well…I was still sorting out the feelings I had for both Mom and Dad.

I had been in therapy a little over a year, but I still found it remarkable how many things I had yet to discuss, and conversely, how many memories being in therapy had stirred up for me.

A new thought registered, and it left me feeling melancholy, and forced me to look at myself. Was I really that different from him? He had proceeded to do all the things that his 'new life' dictated, including having another child at the bequest of his new wife. Wasn't he trying to shut out the past, the same way I was, by running from Upstate to a town where I knew no one, to work in a city where I could be as anonymous as possible? Who was I to judge him, and his invitations to me, however contrived?

Perhaps he was just as lost as I.

I shrugged off the thought and proceeded to work through the rest of the day, my mind now focused on the past instead of the future. When Lanie came back from therapy, she seemed morose also, so we respected each other's energy and called it a day without further discussion.

That night, I had a dream about my father running after me, down Lexington Avenue, and as I tried to run away, I saw Paul, and when I jumped into his arms, my father was nowhere to be found.

Chapter Seventeen

"Did you call him yet?" Lanie badgered me over a hot cup of tea and a muffin.

"No," I answered her tentatively, preparing myself for her reaction. I kept my mouth as full as humanly possible, a tactic I hoped would dissuade her from forcing me to pick up the phone right away.

"You have to call him! Danielle, this kind of stuff just does not happen. Aren't you at least curious? What happened this morning?" Lanie grilled.

"I didn't see him!" I hung out long enough to begin to look like I had a profession that involved the street corner. "What if he already left his job?"

"That's exactly why you *must* call him today. Now. This minute!" Lanie barked.

"Can I finish my muffin?" I barked back, that old nervous feeling taking hold of my body. I wasn't ready. Who was I kidding? I hadn't had a date in forever…when was I going to be ready?

I was never going to be ready.

"Finish your muffin, collect your thoughts, and then call him, Yellie! Think of it this way: you have *less* than two weeks to contact him. And you have to do it! No excuses, NONE! Then think of it this way: this might be fate, banging down your proverbial door. You have to answer the door, Danielle, you can't be too scared now." She was softer now, and I knew she was right.

"Okay!" I stood up, wrapped my headset around my head, and flexed my muscles. "I'm dialing now." I announced with gusto.

"Go Yellie, Go Yellie, Go!" Lanie, once a cheerleader, always a cheerleader.

It rang twice, three, four, and just when I thought it was going to go to voice mail…he picked up!

"Paul Corsi, Corporate Development."

I couldn't breathe.

"Hello?" His voice was patient, with a deep, resonant quality that stuck out more over the phone than it did in person.

"Hi, Paul, it's Danielle, the girl you..." I was about to fill in the blanks for him, but he cut me off mid-sentence.

"Danielle! Hey, I'm really glad you called. Wait a sec, let me get your number down." There was a brief moment of silence, and then he came back on the line. "I'm really glad you called."

I was blushing profusely, I knew it like I knew my name, and I was grateful that he couldn't see me.

"Ummm," I felt a bit off center. "Can I give you my work number?" I asked him, and then chastised myself in my head. Why was I asking him?

"Of course! I'm sure it'll take time to prove I'm not a serial killer. I, ah...I missed you this morning. I had to meet a friend for breakfast."

He was so cute! He didn't have to tell me anything, but I loved the fact that he did anyway.

"I hope it was good. Anyway, my number here is..." and I gave him my number.

"Where are you located?" He asked.

"I'm on Third."

"Do you think we could meet for coffee?" He suggested.

"When?" The whole conversation felt terribly surreal.

"Tomorrow morning?"

"Ummm, sure. What time is good for you?" I could not believe this was happening.

"You tell me." His voice was friendly and even.

"I could meet you before work, I have a partner, so I can run a few minutes late and she won't kill me." I smiled at Lanie and she gave me the high sign.

"I'll meet you at the corner," I heard him chuckle.

"Sounds good. 'Bye." I hung up and made an unintelligible noise. "Did I keep saying, Ummm?!" I pounced on Lanie.

"Once or twice. But you're fine. You did well! What did he say? I want to know everything," she had a gleam in her eye for me.

I gave her the play-by-play, word-for-word recap of the call.

"Lanie, do you think this is weird?" I couldn't help but wonder if this was safe, or just too weird to pursue.

"Do you remember the part in *Sleepless in Seattle,* when Meg Ryan calls Rosie O'Donnell from her hotel room, and asks her if what she's doing is crazy?" Lanie asked.

"Yes," I could remember almost every scene from that movie, as it was one of my all-time favorites.

"What did she say? She said, *No,* that she was not crazy. And Meg Ryan was traversing the country over some guy that she hadn't even met!" Lanie insisted.

"Yes, but Lanie, that was the movies, and this is real life. Real life usually doesn't work out like that." I wasn't used to real life being anything like the pictures painted on the screen.

Well…maybe a horror flick, I mused.

"Who says? Who says it can't? Who says it isn't your turn, Danielle? I know you've gone through a lot, your family wasn't exactly what I would call nurturing, but who says that life can't change and suddenly be better than you ever thought it could be?" Lanie was being so optimistic that my heart hurt.

I was afraid to hope, and only someone who had lived continuous, bitter disappointments could understand the sentiment.

I'm working on it. Constance's words came to me, and I nodded my head at no one in particular. Maybe I could work on being more hopeful. Wasn't that what therapy was supposed to do? I didn't know. I know that I was currently going because I had too many secrets for my heart to hold.

I decided to be hopeful. It was just a coffee date, and last time I checked, coffee had never killed anyone.

"I know you're right, and I will make the decision to be happy about this, and not nervous, and less paranoid, and all things hopeful!" I announced this to Lanie.

"Good!" Lanie admonished.

"Now what do I wear?" If I was going to be anxious, I was going to waste my energy on something I had some control over.

"Black pants." Lanie offered, and we laughed simultaneously. Everybody who worked in Advertising had at least ten pair of black pants, all called to a different purpose, alternating between meetings with clients, days at the office, and after-hours events.

The day flew by, and the next thing we knew, we were at the gym, running on treadmills, lifting weights, and talking in the locker room. I watched the time tick by, knowing that each minute past was a minute closer to coffee with Paul.

When we left from the gym that night, Lanie wished me luck as she bid me farewell.

"Break a leg, and remember…be yourself. Yourself is the person that I love the most." Lanie kissed me on both cheeks, and I ran to Grand Central to catch my train.

Chapter Eighteen

It was so unbearably hot.

Here it was, only June 24th, and the heat was already permeating every square inch of the horrible contraption I currently called a house.

We had just moved into what my mother insisted on calling a 'modular home,' but was, for all intents and purposes, a trailer. The Monster had gotten her into so much financial trouble that we had finally lost the house with the fireplace, and we had been forced to move to the other side of town into a sorry excuse for a home. The new place of residence had no air conditioning and the sweat was steadily pouring down my face as I struggled to adjust the cap on my head.

For once, I was hoping they would fight, a true blowout, a brawl so huge that he would slam the door with a bang and disappear for days on end.

At the very least, he could vanish for this day.

I didn't want him attending my high school graduation, I didn't want him clapping for me, I didn't want him being introduced as any type of relation to me, and I certainly didn't want him thinking he had any part in getting me to where I stood tonight.

It was hopeless; the whole thing was hopeless and I knew it. The bobby pins would not hold my cap in place, and the sweat was counteracting whatever help the hairspray tried to lend to the effort, so I ripped the cap off my head and decided to try it all over again. Besides that, I knew that having The Monster around or not having The Monster around was as equally hopeless a battle; one I knew from experience that I would not win. Only the call of the demon, the lust for his drugs, would dictate where he would and would not be. Of all the times he went on a bender…couldn't God do me just one favor, and have it be now?

I checked my watch and my heart lurched. I had only fifteen minutes left to get to the school and assume my place in Homeroom. The school had instructed us all to wait in our respective Homerooms, and to shuffle out accordingly, the hope being that we would stay in alphabetical order. I had fifteen minutes left to get to the school, find a parking space, and get into my room. I snatched the cap off my dresser, threw the bobby pins and some hairspray in my purse, and made my way out the door.

"Danielle! We'll see you after, at the restaurant..." My mother's words were lost in the sound of my exhaust. She was waving at me, but I pretended not to see her face, glistening with tears, and her hand shaking as she waved.

I had had quite enough of her. If she deemed it necessary to orchestrate a façade for the family members that knew better anyway, then so be it, but I wasn't about to help her play this game. This was my day, my achievement, and I had asked her rather politely, no less than a dozen times to tell The Monster that he was not welcome. She couldn't do it.

She was more worried about how things would look than how I would feel. She dusted him off, and paraded him out, as if he was attached to her arm, and had every right to be there. My father was no better. He had informed me that I was expected at his house the next day, for a Graduation shindig with his side of the family.

Years after their bitter divorce, they still couldn't place their emotions on the shelf for me. I would always have two birthdays, two Christmases, and now, two graduation celebrations. Would I have to have two weddings, too?

I shook the thought from my head as I parked the car and sprinted from the lot into my Homeroom. Annemarie and I shared homeroom, as her last name was Ditullo, and I knew that she would come to the rescue regarding my stupid cap. I entered the room with three minutes to spare.

"Am, you've got to help me out here." I thrust the cap into her hands and straightened my gown.

"Turn around," She instructed. "I was starting to worry about you."

"You shouldn't have, you know I always make it." I flashed her a devil-may-care grin.

"By the hair on your chinny-chin-chin," she admonished me.

"Exactly." There was no time to argue, as the Homeroom teacher drove us from the room, down the hall, and out onto the football field.

I looked around before taking my seat, scanning the sea of faces both in front and in back of me. I was startled to find my hands shaking, and my lips begin to quiver. I willed away tears as I took my place, knowing that all good things must come to an end. High school had been a sort of haven for me. I knew what to expect when I went there. I had an established routine to follow, I had time to read without interruption, and there was no chaos, nobody screaming at me, no violence to speak of. I was the rare student that loved high school, and I wasn't so sure I was ready to leave just yet. Time shuffled on, despite my fears. I had no real plans to speak of; my only goal in the near future was to get out of my house once and for all. I intended to go to college part-time, but work was to be a central part of my future plans, because work produced money and money would enable me to leave.

The tears came unbidden, continuously throughout the various speeches from the platform, and then in a torrent that I could no longer hide the minute the caps flew up and into the air. It was over. I turned to find Am, and when I hugged her, I held on for dear life, until her parents came up and pried us apart, and I began to wander away, and look for my own camp.

My mother found me, bidding another friend goodbye, and as she came up to me, I could barely speak a solid word. I held on to her, and I allowed her to mother me in a way she had not in eons. I stepped away from her and The Monster offered his hand. I glared at him through tears, refused to shake, and turned my back, so that others might congratulate me. I looked around every so often, wondering where my father was, trying to make my scanning of the crowd as inconspicuous as possible.

I waited for him to find me, and when it seemed obvious that he just had not shown, I waved both friends and relatives away and told them I would meet them at the restaurant. They left me, and the tears began again, as I searched the thinning crowd for my father's profile. I waited, and I cried, and when I realized it was time to face the music, I made my way back to my car.

As I pulled away, I gave a last glance over my shoulder, and turned the radio up full blast. The song was most appropriate: 'I Wanna Go Back,' by Eddie Money.

Chapter Nineteen

I woke up to a damp pillow. One look in the mirror confirmed puffy eyes, and I moaned, because I wanted quite badly to look as good as humanly possible for my first date with The Mystery Man. The exact look I was hoping to achieve for my first date did not include puffy eyes and a tormented demeanor, rather a fetching look that would leave him with desirous thoughts of me throughout the day.

Paul, I reminded myself. He had a name now. Wow. I was fully awake at that thought, and I leaned over from mirror to alarm. I still had five minutes left. I never woke before the alarm, and I knew full well in this case that my dream had woken me.

Why had I been crying? I found out the next day that my father had been there, that we had missed each other in the crowd. I didn't believe him at first, but he showed me the video he had taken, and sure enough, there was a close-up shot of me receiving my diploma, and an artistic wave of 500-plus caps being hurled into the air.

It never took away the devastation I had felt that night, the feeling of being forgotten, the assurance nestled deep in my soul that I was not important enough for either parent to act selflessly. Had he not sought me out simply because he was overly concerned about running into her? Would it have been too much to ask for them to have stood side by side, silenced if need be, but near enough in proximity that I could have found and hugged them both? Were they completely unaware of my childish need, to see them bask in some sort of parental glory, shoulder-to-shoulder, distinctly apart, but still unified in spirit?

These questions had never been raised, except in my heart, and in my dreams; true-life queries that lived behind the eyes every time my head hit the pillow, challenging me to face the feelings behind the circumstances.

My next question was: Why today? Why that dream, why now? Was my subconscious somehow warning my conscious self that perhaps Paul wouldn't show? Was there any correlation between the dream, the remembrance, the perpetual haunting of all hurts past, and the event that was coming up today?

How much had I allowed my parents to shape me?

Too much, I decided, as I made my way out of the bed and into the shower. I was mulling over my fashion options as I allowed the scent of my favorite shampoo to wake me, and in my early morning grog, I decided that black pants would not be too bad of an idea.

Black pants. Great! Now, which ones? Lanie was only half-joking when she proposed the black pants solution. The ad culture in particular, and Manhattanites in general, swore allegiance to black pants, and was a staple that could always be counted on. I decided that black pants would do the trick, as they were casual enough to not scream desperation, and elegant enough to wow the victim.

I hoped.

I chose a red shirt, red being my fallback color for all things social. I checked the weather report on my television, and the man on the screen promised me a beautiful day, low humidity, and a breeze. Perfect. I arranged my hair, sprayed it into place, grabbed a light jacket, and I was off. No running for the train for me today, as I was ahead of time, and determined to look cool as a cucumber. Makeup would still be done on the train, but there was no napping, and the nervous energy coursing through my veins prohibited me from concentrating on the book I was reading. After reading the same paragraph several times, I shut the book, placed it on my lap, and watched the scenery as my mind wandered.

What was he going to be like? Would he be as good as he looked?

Sooner than I was ready for, the train rolled into Grand Central. I took a deep breath and made my way off the train, all the while smoothing out imagined wrinkles on the chosen pair of black pants. I wondered if he was nervous too. As I approached the designated corner, I flexed my hands and made circular motions with both wrists, in an effort to stave off the tremors that were causing my hands to look like The Monster's, happening in after a three-day disappearance.

"Danielle!" He was already there, and greeted me with an enormous grin, and a clumsy handshake, which I found myself far too glad to encounter.

"Hi, Paul," I smiled sheepishly, knowing full well that the color creeping its way into my cheeks was sure to stay there awhile.

"I'm so glad you made it. I was worried…" he trailed off a second, and then bounded forward, in a way I found admirable. "Hell, I'm just glad I got the new job, so that I was forced to ask you out. Shall we?" He pointed to the *Walk* sign, and we crossed Lexington Avenue together.

Forced? What did he mean by forced?

"Forced?" I felt the lilt in my voice, and even if he didn't realize, I *forced* what I hoped was an amused laugh from my throat.

"Yeah, well…I have a confession to make." He kept one eye on me and one eye on the pedestrian traffic coming our way. I was next to him, almost following on his right, because two of his steps equaled one of mine.

"You really are a serial killer?" I felt bold enough to ask this on a crowded street during rush hour.

"No," he grinned as he shook his head. "I made a bet with myself."

"Who won?" I liked bantering, and it was coming so naturally with him that I was almost caught off guard, taken aback by the ease with which I had slipped right into this repartee.

"Is this okay?" He motioned toward a neighborhood bakery Lanie and I had been known to frequent, a place with wrought iron tables dotting the entrance, perfect for a quick coffee and croissant.

"It's fine," I replied, noticing that he was temporarily ducking my question about the bet.

"Should I order for us? What do you like?" He was generously accommodating, almost chivalrous as he scraped a chair across the sidewalk in order to allow me to sit there.

"I like tea better than coffee, with milk and two Equals. Preferably skim milk. And any kind of pastry will be just fine, in fact, I think they have pretty good croissants here, so any type of croissant will be great." I was babbling.

"Sounds good, I'll be right back." With that, he disappeared into the shop and I sat outside, breathing in the beautiful day the weatherman had promised, while trying to sneak looks at him as he paid for our breakfast. He came back within minutes, and we busied ourselves with some high-level flirting while fixing our drinks, a silent current passing between us, my eyes on his hands. He had great hands. Not manicured, neither nails that had been bitten to the quick, just nice, strong hands that I fantasized holding my own.

"You still have to tell me about your bet," I reminded him, feeling a sexy tone enter my normal voice, and knowing that I was already in over my head.

"Oh! My bet! I…ah, well…I made a bet with myself that if I got this new job, that I would ask you out on a date." It was his turn to blush. "The only problem was, that I couldn't back out, because I had also told my friend."

"And your friend…?" I was curious. This conversation meant that he had been checking me out also, plotting as it were, how to ask a stranger out on a date. It thrilled me to my toes.

"My friend Rob is the best guy ever, and the biggest pain in the ass. He works where I am going to, he's basically the one who got me the job, and I had told him about you. He told me that if I got the job, I had to ask you out." He smiled that fantastic smile. "He said to consider it part of the contract."

"I'm glad you got the job." Overtly flirting, pouring it on. Good thing there wasn't a mirror around, as I wouldn't recognize myself.

"So am I." He paused a minute, and then looked directly at me. "Do you still think I'm a crazy lunatic?"

"A little." I admitted.

"That's okay, I hope to convince you differently." He had been pulling the middle of his croissant out, taking the long fluffy pieces and rearranging them on his napkin. The playing with his food made him all the more human, and besides the obvious lust that was clouding my view, I decided that I *liked* him. He took a sip of tea. He got extra points for being a tea drinker. What was that old saying? Real men don't eat quiche? A load of bull, because since that saying hit the airwaves, men had even taken to eating things called salads, and allowing sun-dried tomatoes to dot the landscape of their pasta. Most men drank coffee. It took a real man to order a hot cup of tea.

"It's okay, though–I understand. I once made a bet with myself, that if I got the job I have right now, that I would cut my hair short." I smiled at the memory.

"Did you?" He looked confused, and rightly so, as my hair was currently past my shoulders.

"I did. I've always had long hair, but I decided that if I got the job that I have right now, that I would need something sophisticated in order to fit in down here."

"Down here? Where are you from?" He asked me innocently, but I felt my heart sink just a touch, wondering if I had given away a little too much of myself.

"Upstate." I named the tiny town where I spent many of my growing up years. "Where are you from?" I was no longer betting on Kansas, as I detected a smidge of Lanie's accent in his speech, and I had a funny feeling that he would say somewhere out on Long Island.

"Commack, Long Island. Are you familiar with it?" He asked.

"I've only been out to the beach on Long Island, and I don't know the name of the town." I confessed. "Actually, I also went out there for a concert once."

"I have a great beach not far from me. I'll take you there sometime," he offered, and then stiffened almost imperceptibly. I say almost because I caught it. All those years of reading body language, trying to know when it would be safe to say or do certain things, all that living on the edge garbage had given me one thing I valued: an edge in the dating scene. Did he suddenly feel as if he was coming on too strong? Was he worried about being too friendly? Or was he just someone who threw out invitations, flippant in manner, as if the day might never come? I caught the slight change but decided not to comment on the beach. The mere idea of lying on the beach with this man was almost overwhelming…and the fact that he obviously liked the beach made me feel all warm and fuzzy.

"Anyway…" I decided to flip back to my haircut story. "I cut my hair terribly short, the operative word being terrible, and when I came in to start my first day of work, the woman who hired me didn't even recognize me." We both laughed. "After a month or so, I decided that short hair wasn't for me, so I grew it back, but my point was that I understand making a deal with yourself."

We sipped our tea simultaneously, and I found the silence not uncomfortable, but pleasant in a sort of way that I did not know silence could be.

"I felt like an elf." Oh, there I go again…filling up the blank spaces. What exactly was wrong with me?

"An elf?" He repeated.

"Yeah," I felt myself blushing and I wanted to kick my own leg under the table. "I got a very short 'do,' but because I'm so short, I felt like an elf. I never realized how much I valued my hair until I didn't have it."

"I bet you were a cute elf." He countered, and I found myself adrift, suddenly wondering how to switch topics.

He did it for me.

"So what do you do?" He asked this in a sing-songy kind of voice, as if this is the way people are supposed to talk to one another on a first date. We both chuckled.

"I work for Todd and Roth Advertising." I was encouraged to see him waiting for more. "I do their travel, meeting planning, fetch Mr. Todd limos, etc." I waved my hand as if to encompass all.

"Do you like it?" He seemed genuinely interested.

"I do. I love Lanie; she's my partner, and one of my best friends. It gets crazy sometimes, but I enjoy it for the most part."

"Do you get to travel a lot?" He asked.

"Sometimes. I just traveled up to Boston to see a hotel for Mr. Todd, and I usually get invited to see new hotels when they open. Once a year, I also travel down for the big Creative Conference in Miami, but that's a lot of running around and making sure everybody has a towel." I replied with a grin.

"I never get to see if anybody needs a towel!" He feigned outrage. "I…ah, tend to work on some pretty boring stuff. But I'm looking forward to the new job, the change…the great view. Did I tell you that I'd be working at The World Trade Center?"

"Really? We have an office down there, we work in concert with a major travel consortium." I explained Olive.

"Does she really look like Olive Oyl?" His laugh lit up his whole face, and I decided right then and there that I loved making him laugh.

"Trust me. If you ever met her, you might not be able to keep a straight face," I assured him.

"Which tower does she work in?" He inquired.

"I think Tower One. Yes, she's on the 59th floor. But I doubt you'll ever see her, it's a virtual city in just those two buildings."

"Have you ever been to the top?" He asked.

"No. Believe it or not, I haven't. I've been to the top of The Empire State Building, though."

"Oh, you've got to go sometime. It's fantastic. The Empire State is great, but there's something I just love about the World Trade. Anyway, Rob talked me into joining his team, and I have to admit, the location was a real pull for me. I think my new office is going to be on the 103rd floor, Tower One." He sounded excited.

"Wow. Won't you get a little…sick?" I wasn't afraid of heights, but that's also because I wasn't going to be up there all day. I had a weird thing about heights: I could go on the tallest roller-coaster, but I would barf my brains out after ten minutes on a chairlift ride, thirty feet from the ground. Lanie said I have a problem with suspended height.

"No, I love it. I love everything about this city, and the vista is just the icing on the cake. Say, Danielle, not that I want to call an end to this…but do you have to get going?" Paul pointed to his watch.

I looked at mine and almost had a heart attack. It was a quarter after ten! My, how time flies when you are sitting, and talking, and wondering if you had found a kindred spirit and a kind heart. I didn't want to stop talking to him any more than he wanted to call an end to our conversation, but if I kept lingering over tea, Lanie was going to eat me for lunch.

We got up, disposed of our trash, and he asked if he could please walk me over to my building. I answered in the affirmative, and the next thing I knew, we were there.

Too soon.

"Danielle, I hope you will give me yet another chance to prove to you that I am not a raging lunatic." His charm was palpable.

"You may as well have another chance, as I am not convinced." Although my heart had taken up its irregular beat, my hands were steady. I was praying a silent prayer that I would have more than one chance to see him again.

"Can I prove it to you this weekend?" He brushed a lock of hair from his forehead, and if that gesture was meant to endear me to him, he got his wish.

"Can you call me?" I knew I didn't have any plans Upstate, but I wanted to talk to him more.

"I can call you later." The smile.

"Sounds great." I had to get into the building before I began gurgling, and drooling all over myself.

"I'll call you later," he pledged, walking away, still looking over his shoulder as he moved.

"Bye!" I gave a tiny wave and then bounded through the revolving door with such force that I almost injured the person on the other side. "Sorry!" I directed this to him, and then practically ran over to the elevator bank. I pressed the up arrow no less than seven million times, willing it to get to me faster, faster, when finally the door opened. I jumped into the elevator cab and mimed a tap dance all the way up to our floor, cameras be damned.

"Lanie!" I announced myself rather loudly, and after Lanie threatened my life several times over, I spilled the beans.

"Yellie, you are *mooning*! Positively mooning! I love it!" She was as excited for me as any good friend could possibly be, and Lanie was a great friend.

"Do you think he'll call?" The old Upstate girl tried to sneak into my city skin, and a rapid flash of David's betrayal crept across my psyche, despite all the evidence thus far, that Paul was not David.

"Of course he'll call! Stop it!" Lanie insisted.

I had to stop, if for no other reason than that I had to get to work. Lanie had gone above and beyond this morning, and I intended to pay her in full.

Except I couldn't focus, and every time the phone rang I was a complete basket case for a fraction of a second, hoping that it was him and not a business call, and willing myself to calm down every second of the day. He said he'd call later, but how late was later for him? Did he know what time I worked until? I had yet to give him any other number except my business number. What if he got so caught up he forgot to call?

By two-thirty, I was enveloped in sheer panic, and almost forgot about my appointment with Constance. By three, I was in a closed-door meeting with the woman I chose to tell all my secrets to precisely because of her name. Constance. I remember when I picked her off the HMO website, that the name Constance reminded me of *Constant,* and so I chose her because of the feelings her name evoked. I was aware enough to realize that my life has been one perverse longing for something *constant.*

The session was an easy one, as I didn't teeter today between the past and the present, but concentrated on the new development called Paul. Constance seemed to think the introduction of Paul in my life was a positive thing, and she gave me some practical advice that I could apply to the enfolding situation.

As if I could be rational! I hauled major buttocks from her office back to my own hole/office, only to burst through the door, all rational thoughts gone to seed.

"Did he call yet?" I threw open the door and barraged Lanie.

"Not yet, Tootsie. Calm down," she instructed, and then smirked, "You sure are a hyper little elf!"

"I'll tear you limb from limb," I threatened. He was probably thinking about my elf comparison right now, that being why the phone remained silent.

"I'd offer you caffeine, but you certainly don't need any. Really Yellie, you know what they say…a watched phone never rings."

"I get it. I got it. You're right, I'm being a fool." I had always believed that what was meant to be would happen. If he was meant to call, he would. I forced myself to give up and I went to go make myself a hot cup of herbal tea.

Lanie entered the kitchenette and said not a word.

"Is it him?" I couldn't hide the excitement from my voice.

"Yes!" She rejoiced right along with me, and followed me back into the hole in order to eavesdrop.

I began breathing, hoo-hoo-hoo---like a Lamaze instructor on crack, five little breaths before picking up the handset.

"Hello?" Call me coy.

"Danielle, it's Paul. How's your day so far?" He was direct and his voice, sincere and strong, made me positively melt.

Call me melted ice cream.

"So far, so good. I just booked the Concorde, so that's always fun." I had booked Mr. Todd on a Concorde flight earlier in the day, and it was always fun, because I got to make the booking directly with my British Airways Sales Rep, and she was a dream. She often invited me for drinks at The Concorde Lounge, and although I had only taken her up on it one time several months back, the smell of money still encrusted my clothes.

"Book one for me, while you're at it." I could hear him smile. "Well, I'm just finishing up over here. I wanted to call you because I wanted to know if you're free on Saturday." He got right to the point.

"I'm free. What did you have in mind?" I gave Lanie a thumbs-up sign, and she high-fived me as silently as possible.

"Dinner. Do you eat, or are you one of those non-eating girls that nibbles?" He had a way about him that wasn't poking fun as much as it was pure fun.

"I nibble, then I chew, I devour if I'm really hungry, and sometimes I even tip the table, slant it right into my mouth, and inhale everything on top, tablecloth and all."

"My kind of girl! All righty then, can I surprise you?"

"With what?"

"A cuisine."

"Oh, yes…anything but Indian. I hate curry." An elf that hates curry.

"There's Indian food that doesn't have curry," he replied.

"Yeah, but I hate the smell, and for the most part, all Indian restaurants have the smell." I hated the smell of hot dogs, too, but I would wait awhile to drop that bomb. Most guys had a heart attack as soon as I let that little factoid out. Especially guys who liked sports events, or barbeques, or street vendors in NYC…you get the picture. This is not a popular quirk to have around men.

"The Smell. I love it. Anyway, I had Asian food in mind. Are you game?"

"I am game. Where should I meet you?" I was a little nervous about meeting him, but I wanted to more than I didn't, so I shelved the worry.

"How about I call you tomorrow, and we throw it around a bit?" He suggested.

"Sounds great." *Throw it around a bit…*I really did like this man. Very James Bondish: he was cool, but he didn't act as if he knew how cool he was. That was the perfect combination of cool, if I do say so myself, and I was falling for every little piece in his repertoire.

"Okay, 'bye." He hung up and I swooned.

Overtly.

"You are too much! When are you meeting him?" Lanie was on me like white on rice the minute I hung up.

"Saturday night." I replied, my heart full and a smile firmly in place. I don't care what Lanie said, I loved him, and I think I already had skipped right past lust.

"Prime Time!" Lanie yelled, for she had the 'rules' of dating practically tattooed on her forearm. She had taught me a long time ago that Saturday night *meant something,* whereas Thursday night, albeit better than a lunch date, was only so-so.

Lanie: the dispenser of valuable vocational advice.

"I know!" I gulped my tea and then made an unintelligible noise that signaled victory.

"Saturday Night Fever it is, my friend. *IF* Brad remembers to call and reconfirm, I also have a prime-time date, to watch the previously shipped film, imbibe some kickin' take-out, and cuddle The Bradomeister to death. Our lives are destined for greatness." Lanie pronounced.

"To Greatness!" I toasted her with my cup of tea.

Chapter Twenty

After a marathon conversation with Annemarie, I was emboldened enough to try to conquer my closet. It was Saturday afternoon, and we were heading towards Prime Time with each tick of the clock, and I had decided on nothing in terms of wardrobe.

I turned my back on the closet and adjusted the volume on my stereo. Mary J. Blige was on, an oldie but a goodie, the song of my heart.

Real Love,
I'm searchin' for a Real Love,
Someone to set my heart free…
Real Love…

I started dancing, moving the way you do when you know nobody's looking, and soon after found myself shouting the words I knew by heart, massacring the poor woman's song.

I wished I could sing. I had always wanted to be able to sing well, from those hairbrush-as-a-microphone moments in my bedroom mirror, to the silly moments that my mother and I had spent, just the two of us, singing and dancing in the living room, long after Dad left and far before The Monster took away all her moves. It was a secret desire I harbored, the ability to make people shed tears over the mere sound of my voice set to melody, the stage presence to tear down the house and leave 'em begging for more. I had delusions of grandeur as a child, how one day somebody would notice that I was the next Roberta Flack, and then the next Donna Summer, and eventually the next Mariah Carey. I envied these women, and wondered why God had blessed some and not others (namely me) but I resigned myself to my fate and simply belted out tunes, off-key and shamelessly, every chance I got. I lived alone so I figured I wasn't insulting anybody's eardrums but my own.

Real Love turned into *Always Be My Baby.* Another favorite by another favorite, Mariah Carey, belting it out with the background styling of Danielle D'Ambrusco. Once that song was finished, I bowed to no one in particular and headed back to my closet.

The radio was a fabulous distraction, but I really needed to pick out an outfit. When Paul called yesterday, he said he was taking me to an Asian restaurant in Midtown that, although I had never heard of it, was apparently a sort of institution for Chinese food with flair. Lanie said the only reason I had never heard of it was because it was not a regular destination for people in our tax bracket. Annemarie wouldn't know Shun Lee Palace from a Chinese curse word, so I had very little to go on, but I decided that I would pick a killer outfit that could adjust to any type of décor.

I just had to pick it. Oh, what did I want this outfit to say? Well, I quite obviously wanted it to say: *Love me, take me in your arms and take away all my fears, please love me in spite of everything else this world has thrown at me, and think I am sophisticated and pretty and the girl of your dreams.*

I didn't have an outfit that said all of those things, but I had a rather becoming dress in charcoal gray with a black overjacket, one that I had only worn to work once and no place else, because it wasn't work-y enough, it was more date-y, but until now I had no one to date and therefore no reason to don the dress.

I took it out and mulled it over, deciding it would definitely make the final cut, and pulled a pair of black strappy heels out of the shoe pond on the bottom of my closet. He was tall, so heels were perfectly acceptable, and I hoped not too dressy.

I couldn't wait to see him. I was nervous, sure, but I was more excited than nervous, and I had waited so long to have a date that excited me that I was almost beside myself, unable to corral the grin that exploded every so often across my face.

Annemarie had told me to 'Break a leg.' I promised her a call tomorrow with details, and Lanie and I had conspired to call one another late Sunday afternoon.

I turned the radio up a notch or twelve, thankful that my landlord wasn't home, and jumped into the shower in order to get ready to go, and of course, to give my legions of fans an encore.

Five songs later, I exited the shower and did all the girly things us girls need to do in order to knock a man off his feet. No makeup on the train tonight.

I was meeting him in Grand Central. I found out yesterday that he had an apartment not far from there, and he said he would pick me up. Pick me up being a figure of speech, as we were meeting at the clock in the center of the landmark at seven.

When the train pulled into Track 37, I breezed out, nervously fixing my hair, alternately flipping it and smoothing it out, praying that I would pass a mirror one last time, but looking straight ahead and trying to walk the walk of the ultra-cool, one straight line to the big clock. I allowed my eyes to flit around the clock and I willed my head not to move, as I didn't want to appear too eager, but I wanted to spot him before he saw me, and steady myself, and tell myself one last time that this was not a dream.

I got my wish. As I strode towards the clock, he had his back to me. Peering down towards Lexington Avenue, I caught a glimpse of him, and my heart skipped a beat, acknowledging that what I felt for him was the most exciting thing I had experienced in far too long. I pulled myself up straighter as I watched him move his head right to left, with a quick glance past the escalators, to settle on me not two seconds later.

My heart made up for the beat it had lost; double-beats permeating my every move once our eyes caught across the vestibule. I flashed him a tentative smile, put one foot in front of the other, and allowed his 1000-watt grin to soothe my nervous system.

"Hi."

"Hi."

We said Hi at the same moment and then chuckled together. I'm pretty sure we both glanced at our shoes before looking each other in the eye.

"You look different at night," he observed, and I sincerely hoped so. I had on a glittery eye shadow that I wouldn't be caught dead wearing on a weekday.

"So do you," I threw it right back at him. He did, he looked even better looking, and his terribly-GQ outfit led me to second-guess mine for a millisecond.

An old David feeling popped up: *Whatever was he doing with me?*

I shoved that thought aside and forced my mind to focus on the man of the moment.

"I hope different is better. In your case, you look great either way, but tonight you look I…ah, glamorous." He stumbled over it, and he blushed, and his heart was endeared to mine all over again.

Besides that, *glamorous* meant that I was going to buy a vat of the glittery eye shadow.

"Thanks." I blushed in spite of the fact that I willed myself not to.

"Shall we?" He extended his arms towards the escalators. I nodded and followed him up the same escalators I ran up every day, except tonight everything looked different, and I had to remind myself that it was just one date, a first date, and he may still show his fangs. I tried to remind myself, but he stood two stairs behind me, and suddenly we were the same height, and I was drowning in his eyes.

I tried not to stare, but his eyes were the perfect shade of brown, light enough to almost be called hazel, dark enough to be piercing. We smiled at each other as the escalator rode us to the top, each momentarily lost in a thought or two. When we reached the top, he suggested walking to the restaurant. It was a beautiful spring night, a slight breeze in the air, and we had the city lights as our backdrop.

"I love to walk," I agreed, and we proceeded to cross the street and exit out to Park from under The Helmsley Walk. I could still remember when I first moved, how I never wanted to take the subway, for fear that I would miss something. I found out after a while that the subway had its own stories to tell.

"I love to walk when the weather is nice," he agreed. He pointed across the street from where we were walking. "I would say that's my building, but I should say that's my old building." He let loose another grin.

"Will you miss it?" I asked it tentatively, not sure about how much he wanted to reveal.

"I will miss Park Avenue, but I know I will love The World Trade. I will miss my friend Pat, and the shorter commute, but I also know that it's time to move on." His ease permeated his walk as well as his conversation, and I found myself wondering if he was even the slightest bit nervous as we continued uptown.

"I knew that I had to move when I moved down here, so I know what you mean. Sometimes you just know." There I go, revealing myself again, talking about my old life, telling too much too soon. Had I learned nothing from the David fiasco?

"I told my mother that, and you know, she worried…like Moms tend to do, but I think she ultimately trusts me. She has a knack for worrying, but I assume all Moms have the corner on that franchise to a certain degree." He shook his head in mock frustration, but the smile in his eyes betrayed him.

"Are you close to your Mom?" I was always curious about people with normal families.

"Mom is the best. She lives out on the Island, has lived there her whole life, and she practically runs the town we live in," he continued, "My mother is the Charity Queen, involved in every imaginable thing the town can get her involved in. She pretends to hate it, she always acts overwhelmed and pestered by her responsibilities, but if you were to rip her away from a Bake Sale, she'd probably have your head on a platter and sell it to the next customer." I detected a genuine love for his mother in his voice, an admiration, and a closeness that made my heart lurch.

"So where is this place?" I was determined to change the subject, lest I be led into a conversation about my own inept mother. I knew that my heart was not ready to go there, especially after the June Cleaver picture he had just painted.

"Shun Lee Palace is between Lex and Third on 55th. Just a couple of more blocks," he answered. "Have you ever been there?"

As if.

"No, I haven't," I replied, "But I heard it's really good."

"I've only been there once, when my brother came into town, but I recall thinking that I wanted to take a date there." Apparently we had the same problem about sharing on the fast track.

Only I loved it when he did it.

"Well, thanks for taking me." I meant it.

"You can thank me after dinner, once we decide it's good." He suggested.

"It will be good," I decided for both of us. "You said you have a brother?"

"Yes, I have a brother named Peter, but no sister named Mary." He intoned. "My mother gets tired of people asking that question, *'As if there aren't two apostles named Paul and Peter!'*" He did what I assumed was an impersonation of Mom.

"Well, that just means that your Mom is a traditionalist." Not to mention the bake sales.

"That she is! Mom is nothing if not a traditionalist. She gets terribly pissed off when people suggest she named her kids after a rock band. Anyway, Peter is two years my senior, married, and currently living in D.C. We have very little in common, but we tend to get along really well in spite of that, and I love my brother to death. I only see him every couple of months, but I think that's what keeps us close. Ya know?" He was so open, saying stuff like love and brother in the same sentence, on a first date no less.

"Oh, I know." I thought about my family members, and how if I saw them any more often than I currently did, how I would probably have killed either them or myself by now, preferably them.

We were there. He opened the door for me, and then pulled out my seat. The restaurant was the nicest Chinese restaurant I had ever been to, and the décor was, if not a little bit intimidating, what you picture cool New York City restaurants to look like.

"I feel like I'm on a movie set," I admitted, as I took in my surroundings. There were times when I really felt like a hick, and the Upstate girl with all her Upstate insecurities came up to rear her ugly head, and this was one of those times.

I forced that girl back down in the annals of my stomach, and determined to pile Chinese food right on top of her. Hopefully she would suffocate.

"I know how you feel; did you ever have drinks or dinner at Windows on the World?" He shook his head. "I felt like they dropped me right onto the set of *Sleepless in Seattle.*"

"Did you get dumped there too?" Tactless; but also the first thing to pop out of my mouth. Smart.

"No, no, I...ah, went there to celebrate my brother's graduation from Law School." He thought a moment. "But what if I had?" His face revealed mock horror and the already famous grin escaped a second later.

"I would have felt like a total jerk." I admitted. "I was just thinking of the movie." I tried to make light of my faux pas, although the blush creeping up my cheeks chose to reveal me.

"Please don't worry, Danielle. I often say what I'm thinking, before I can even think to stop myself. It sometimes allows for some pretty funny moments, but most of the time, I get myself in trouble. I remember one time in college; I told this guy I knew that this girl was being a total jerk to me. I had met her at a bar a few weeks before, and she was all over me the first night, but then afterwards, every time I tried to call her, she blew me off. At first, I thought maybe she wasn't getting my messages, so I wasn't mad, but then I saw her at the same bar a week or two later, and she was hanging all over me again. This happened two or three times before I confronted her. I guess I was drunk, or maybe a little desperate, but I liked her, so when she gave me some silly excuse about why she had blown me off in between the couple of times I had seen her, I took it, and I ignored the little voice telling me that she was a twit. Ends up that she was using me to make her ex-boyfriend jealous, because he worked at the bar, so she would hang all over me in his presence, and then act as if she didn't know me any other time. Anyway...my point is, that I started telling this guy Joe that I was friendly with the whole story one day, just hanging outside, shooting the breeze, peppering my story with venom and obscenities, and I found out too late that I was telling the wrong guy." He shook his head at the memory.

"Was it her ex-boyfriend from the bar?" I guessed.

"No, worse. It was her brother." He chuckled now, as I sucked in a breath. "Plus, he was friendly with one of my roommates, so I always had to run into him after that, and if I would have known that, needless to say...I wouldn't have ever have told him anything, much less call his sister a few charming expletives."

"Did he get over it?"

"No. I think he knew she was a twit, but she was his little sister, so I think he also felt he had to protect her." Paul lifted his menu. "Should we decide?"

"Yes." I perused the menu and insisted, "That wasn't as bad as what I just said. At least you didn't know the guy was her brother. I just say stupid things sometimes."

"Trust me, I have a whole repertoire of foot-in-the-mouth stories that could enthrall you for hours." His self-deprecating humor was welcoming.

"What do you think of the Spring Rolls?" I asked, my attention back on the menu.

"I was actually thinking about the vegetable spring rolls, and 'Ants climb on tree,' because that sounds tasty." He flirted with his eyes.

"What's that?" I followed his finger as he pointed to the menu.

"Fine minced of filet stir fry with cellophane noodles in spicy garlic sauce garnish with greens." He repeated directly from the menu, with an accent that wasn't even close to Asian.

"That actually sounds good. Although, are you one of those people who gets upset if somebody else orders the same thing as you from a menu?" Lanie hated that; she always wanted the opportunity to try two meals.

"I am not one of *those people,* although I know some of those people." He teased.

"One of my best friends, Lanie, is one of those people. She is incensed when people try to copy her, and I know for a fact that she likes to sample off of everyone's plate."

"Ah, I get it. The same dish all around equals less sampling."

"Exactly."

"Well, although I am nothing if not an individual, I will tell you that imitation is the most sincere from of flattery."

"Are you imitating me or am I imitating you?"

"Does it matter?"

"Sure it does."

"Which way do you like better?" He was pandering to me, but I found myself flattered rather than bothered by it.

"You imitating me." I responded.

"You got it then," he replied, as the waiter approached. "I'll have what she's having," he began, and then ordered for both of us.

We ate and we talked and the night flew by, pretenses done away with quite early on, with ease our companion throughout the entire meal. Whatever nervousness I had originally experienced when we first met was long gone, and the night was sprinkled with a sense of comfort that clashed with the amount of time we had actually known one another.

By the time we moved on to tea, the conversation had drifted from college to work, family to friends, even quirky things like the fact that he loved potato chips with ketchup.

"Potato chips and ketchup?" I must have blanched, because his response was accusatory.

"Don't knock it 'til you try it!" He wagged a finger my way. "If you eat French fries and ketchup, what's the difference?"

"I guess there is no difference," I conceded, laughing at the way he defended his craving.

"And the best, the ABSOLUTE best: Sour cream and Onion Ruffles with ketchup!" He announced.

"Yech." This time I blanched openly.

"I've got to get you to try it sometime. You'll love it," he insisted.

"I'll take your word for it," and so it went.

As with all good things, the night came to an end. When we left Shun Lee Palace, he offered a cab, but I suggested we walk back to Grand Central, as the night was still beautiful, the weather perfect.

We walked slowly, both of us wanting to prolong the night. He didn't say it, but it was obvious to me that he was thinking along the same lines as me: we had definitely done more than just click. I not only wanted to see him again, I wanted to see him a hundred thousand times again, and I prayed that he felt the same. I walked close to him, on his right, and at one point, he moved behind me and positioned himself so that I was on the left.

I must have given him a curious look, because he answered my unasked question.

"I…ah, my father taught me that a man should always walk closer to the traffic." As we were on the East side of Park Avenue at that point, it made perfect sense, as well as told me something about the man.

Chivalry was not entirely dead.

Amen to that.

I shivered, and it wasn't about the temperature outside; I was terrified, because David had presented himself in all the same charming ways, coming on like a freight train, persuading me to fall madly in love with him before I even had a chance to catch my breath.

I knew one thing for sure: my heart would not survive another David.

Oh, God, please don't let him be like David.

"Are your Mom and Dad still married?" He hadn't mentioned his father until now, only his Mom, and I had wondered if they were still together, and now was the perfect opportunity to ask. I was pushing the family envelope again, wondering what it would have been like to still have your original parents in place, playing traditional roles in today's world.

"Yessiree, Mom and Dad are still very much together. They are embarrassing at times, dancing more than either one of their sons, having to be pulled off the dance floor at family weddings and the like." He shrugged his shoulders. "I could have worse problems."

Yes, yes, you could.

I must have nodded and not said anything, because he then asked the inevitable:

"What about your family? Are your parents still married?" He asked it innocently enough, but I bristled inside anyway, reminding myself that this was all part of getting to know each other.

"My parents are divorced, and both have remarried since." I skipped the part about the abandonment, the drugs, the abuse, the absence or presence, and of course, the jail. I resurrected a dead end conversation with, "I now have a brother too."

"From your Mom or your Dad?"

"My Dad. He remarried and had a son, Michael Jr. He's a fabulous kid, and we're close in our own way, I've just never lived with him." That's it. That's all I was willing to go into tonight. "So what did your friend Rob say when you told him we were going out for dinner tonight?"

Quick-change artist that was I.

"He said *it's about time!*" Paul chuckled. "It had only been a couple of weeks since I first saw you, but I think he was royally sick of hearing me." He looked me straight in the eye at that point. We were almost at Grand Central, and I was thankful that we were back underneath the Helmsley walk, so that I could look at him and not worry about getting mowed over by traffic.

There was a sizzle in the air, and the comfortable silence that passed between us was infused with a spark again, my heart beating fast, the nervous energy again coursing its way through my veins. I started worrying about how we would and should commence the evening, would he try to kiss me in the middle of Grand Central? Should I let him? How do you say goodbye before embarking on a train? These were not the days of old, the times when you could kiss a man as the train pulled from the station, he running alongside the train as it departed, smoke rising, a whistle blowing, hands waving and kisses being blown all the while.

We were making idle chitchat as we rode the escalator down to the center of the building, my eyes focused on the boards for information. Track 42 was where I was to depart from.

"What track are you pulling out of?" He asked solicitously.

"Looks like it's 42," I pointed at the boards.

"I'll walk you," he offered, and I nodded, my nervousness escalating with each step closer to the track.

"Thanks." We made our way over to my departure track, he still on my right, me focusing so much on the upcoming good-bye that I almost missed him asking me about the next day.

"I'm sorry?" I cursed myself for projecting so much that I was missing the moment.

"I just asked if I could call you tomorrow. Would there be a particularly good time?" He was waiting for my answer.

My heart screamed, OF COURSE YOU CAN! For another second, my mouth failed to work.

"Of course you can. Ummm, anytime after two would be great." Whether I chose to go to church or sleep in, either way I would be free and awake by then.

We were there.

Track 42.

"Well, I…ah, I had a great time." He stood there, leaning up against the departure board, looking awkward as could be, as the sign next to him stated all of the destinations that my train would go to.

"So did I." My shoes caught my interest again.

"I'll call you tomorrow." With that he offered his arms out to me. I leaned into him for a quick hug, but he held on an extra beat and gave me a quick squeeze. In the instant that it took for my mind to command my body to stop its shaking, he had exited the hug and was gone.

    I stood there, stunned, for all of one second, and then I turned on my strappy little heels and made my way to the train.

    I smiled to myself, he was human, albeit too good to be true, a real human being, a guy I could definitely fall in love with, if I wasn't already, and I knew beyond knowing that there would be more dates ahead, and time to perfect that hug.

    I didn't even people-watch on the train. I settled in without a book, and I stared out the window at no one in particular. When I arrived home, I had a tall glass of water and settled into a deep, dreamless sleep.

Chapter Twenty-One

"I love him," this being my greeting as Lanie picked up the phone.

"I know," she croaked, her voice still sleepy. "What time is it?"

"Eleven. C'mon, Lanie, wake up. I could've called you last night, but I didn't want to interrupt you and the Bradomeister. And I waited a whole hour to call you this morning!" I was impatient as I had ever been, dying to tell someone all the details, to relive every moment before he called and clouded the first memory. I had already tried Annemarie, forgetting she was still at church, and left her a funny message, regarding eloping last night.

"Didn't we say Sunday afternoon?"

"Did you really think I could wait that long?"

"No," She replied, with a yawn and a groan. "Go ahead."

I stifled a giggle, knowing full well Lanie was a good sport, but also knowing that she wanted to keep that information classified.

"Well, when I got into Grand Central–" I began, but she cut me off completely.

"Start with what you were wearing." Lanie directed. "You know I want the whole story."

Of course.

"Okay, I ended up wearing the gray dress, black overjacket, and black strappy heels." I waited for her critique.

"Strappy is good."

"Okay, anything else?"

"Purse."

"My little black one that I save for dates."

"I didn't know you had one."

"Witch!"

"Okay, go on. You arrive at Grand Central…" Lanie always wanted the blow-by-blow.

"And he was already there, standing by the clock, waiting for me. He looked gorgeous. We saw each other, and I almost died, Lanie, *he is so much better looking than I remembered!*" I could no longer keep the excitement out of my voice.

"Yellie, you saw him running past you on the street, then for a few minutes for coffee. He always had a suit on. You had yet to see his date face."

"Is that kind of like a game face?"

"Exactly. He had his game face on last night. So how was it?"

"It was fabulous. We walked over to Shun Lee Palace, because it was beautiful out, and the restaurant was gorgeous, Lanie, you've got to get Brad to take you there."

"More likely my father. Actually, I will file that for Daddy Dearest, as if I can get an hour with him." Lanie replied.

"Either. Okay, so, we sat down, flirted a little, and…Lanie, you're gonna barf: we ordered the same thing." I didn't have to wait for her reaction.

"Nooooooo! Ugh! Gross! Next week, are you going to get the same T-shirts with your name ironed on them, too?" Lanie's sarcasm was dripping through the phone.

"I think Iron-ons went out a little while ago, Lane." I scolded her.

"I think you're right. Did you have the Iron-on rainbow one?" She asked.

"Who didn't?" I countered.

"Anyway, go ahead. I smell marriage up ahead. Did you know that once you are married a certain number of years, that you begin to look like each other too?" Lanie acted disgusted, but the best part is that I knew she loved this almost as much as I did.

"God, I hope so. He is so hot, Lanie, he–no–you know what? He's actually a guy who fits the word handsome. He's handsome!" I was grinning like an idiot.

"So what did you and Handsome talk about?" I could hear her crunching something on the other end, which told me that by eating something she was working her way towards human being status.

"Everything. I mean, we talked about the city, our jobs, the beach, putting our feet in our mouths, restaurants, his family…you name it."

"I will name everything except your illustrious family. Am I right?" Lanie prodded as she chomped what sounded like chips.

"Affirmative. Lanie, he made his mother sound like freaking June Cleaver, what should I

have told him about first: the absentee father, or the Jailbird Monster?" I had never once

used the word stepfather in referring to him, not even now. He didn't deserve a name or

a title.

"No need to get defensive, not yet anyway. What did he say about his mother?" Lanie inquired.

I relayed to her the conversation about his mother, father, and brother. "I told him about Michael."

"Because Michael hasn't done anything to you yet. Well, I can't say as I blame you, I was just curious." Lanie kept chewing in my ear.

"What are you eating?" I asked, exasperated, because I could not eat chips the minute I woke up and still fit in my jeans later on in the day.

"Veggie chips. Stop getting testy. I realize that you want to pretend your family doesn't exist, but eventually you will have to pursue the topic." She warned.

"You're right. I just don't want to pursue the topic until I get to know him better. My father's side never met David, and my mother only met him once. The Monster was never around enough to meet–Thank God–and it really didn't matter anyway, did it?" I hated that every time I talked about my family, I got all riled up inside, no matter how minimal the conversation was, no matter what the topic ended up being.

"Alright. Enough about the family! Thoughts? Impressions?" Lanie was persistent.

"Thoughts? I love him. Impressions? I love him." I wailed.

"Real thoughts, deep impressions...let's try this again." Lanie was nothing if not persistent.

"Real thoughts: I think I can, if I have not already, fall deeply in love with this man. Impressions: He is undeniably charming, and real. Once I got over my initial nervousness, I felt extremely comfortable with him, and the conversation flowed naturally, and I found myself really enjoying the night with him. I have the impression that he is nice almost to a fault, but not the type of guy you can walk on...confident, but not overly confident. Smart, but not showy...an everyday guy that just happens to make a good living...a person who can be a good friend, a good boyfriend, a good son, etc." I didn't need time to think it out, as impressions are free-flowing if nothing else, but I had an innate sense that I had read him pretty well.

"All good stuff." Lanie paused a second and said, "Yellie, I am so very happy for you. I hope this works out. He seems like what you've been waiting for."

"God, I hope so. I'm just so scared, like when I allow myself to really think about it. We both know I'm being a tad bit facetious when I proclaim to love him, I can't love him yet, I barely know him...but I know that I darn well could, and it scares me, because I don't want to fall, not hard, not if it means getting hurt all over again." I was being very honest with both Lanie and myself.

"I know. But love doesn't always have to hurt, Yellie. I know you haven't seen that occur yet, not personally, but I bet it can, I have to believe it, and so should you. Belief is what keeps us all going, whether we *believe* it or not," Lanie pontificated.

"That should be on a bumper sticker."

"More like a billboard."

"So how's Brad?" I inquired.

"We watched the movie, ordered Chinese in- -nothing like yours, you see- and we had a very good time. He liked the movie, and I swear he got a little teary-eyed at the end." Lanie seemed rather proud of herself.

"Is the end a tear-jerker?" I hadn't seen it myself.

"Omigod, you have to see this movie!" Lanie insisted, appalled that I hadn't seen it yet.

"Lanie, I never even heard of it until you told me about it."

"That doesn't mean it's not good. It's so good, and I know you, you will cry, and you will then call me up and admit that I recommended a fabulous film." Lanie pronounced.

With that, having no further room to disagree, we discussed Brad and Paul some more, and eventually she ushered me off the phone. It was another great day outside, so I opted to go out for a walk instead of waiting around for Paul to call.

A watched phone never rings, I heard Lanie say in my head. So I suited up, put on a pair of cross-trainers, and made my way around the neighborhood. One of the nice things about living in a rich suburb was that my neighborhood was in great shape, the landscaping a beautiful accompaniment to houses that I could only dream about. I didn't need a Walkman to take a turn or two around the block; I only needed my imagination and the backdrop of house after mansion.

As I walked, I swooned a bit more over Paul, but eventually some flowers caught my attention, and I started thinking about painting. I had painted long ago, in what seemed like another life now, so long had it been since I committed brush to paper. Or, in my case…plastic. My favorite medium had been plaster craft, or anything three-dimensional. However, my eyes caught one flower arrangement in particular that was in full bloom, so I stopped a minute to size up the arrangement and try and figure out what kind of flowers they were; they looked like the type of flowers I might be able to paint.

I needed something that wasn't too complex. I hadn't painted in forever, and if I was even remotely serious about it, I knew I should start small and work my way back to where my skill level once was. I wasn't sure if I could still do it, but for some reason the desire to paint had come back recently, and I felt intrigued by it. I wondered if I had even kept any of my old brushes, or any of the plaster craft pieces that I had purchased, oh-so-long ago. I decided I would look around when I got back.

I kept walking, and the road I was walking on led me down a hill and around a lake. I didn't know if the lake had always been there, or was a man-made lake for the upper crust to peer out their windows and enjoy. By the time I got back to my place, there was a phone message from Annemarie, so I called her back and reiterated what I had told Lanie, receiving encouraging words from her as well as Steven, who was catching her half of the conversation in the background.

I made sure I was off the phone by two. I decided to try not to focus on it, however, so I started hunting for my paintbrush supply. A few minutes into my hunt, the phone rang.

I ran for it.

"Hello?" I tried not to sound overly excited, but I was grinning like an idiot the minute I heard his voice.

"Hello, Danielle, it's Paul."

As if I didn't know.

"Hi!" I said with perhaps a little too much eagerness.

"Hi!" He said back, and we laughed simultaneously.

"I just got in." I wanted him to know I wasn't waiting on top of the phone. Yeah, right. I was just talking about him on it all morning.

"Where did you go?" He asked, so I told him about the lake and the neighborhood I lived in.

"It's a great head-clearer…is that a word?" I asked.

"I think we can make it one. Did you ever make up words with your friends when you were a kid?" He asked.

"Yeah." I smiled at the memory, something I hadn't thought of in quite some time. "When I was in high school, the cool thing to do was to put a –ness on the end of every word. I don't know if they did that on Long Island, but it started out with Beat-ness, then Cool-ness, then we just started attaching –ness to every word we could think of: 'I'll have an ice-cream-ness,' or 'Jump into the pool-ness.' It was actually kind of dumb, but it became a way of speech for us for at least a year. It just didn't work if you had to go pee." I found myself screaming inside my head, SHUT UP! SHUT UP! NOBODY WANTS TO HEAR THIS!

I realized too late that I couldn't stop myself; it was like I was shooting from the hip every time I spoke to him, and whatever ridiculous thought crossed my mind, I just happened to blurt it all out, with no hesitation, embarrassment, or censure.

Thankfully, he was laughing. "Oh, I get it! Pee-ness?"

I nodded, and then realized he couldn't see me. "You get the picture."

"I suppose that one wouldn't work. Well, we never took it to that level, but I can remember saying Beatness! a time or two ourselves. No, our 'word' was redass." He admitted plainly.

"Redass?"

"Yeah, like 'More redass than you!' —As if to say, 'God, you're cranky.' Like when a baby gets a red butt, and cries all day long from diaper rash…" he trailed off a second. "I can't believe I'm telling you this."

"That makes two of us," I was an accomplice in the crime of made-up vocabulary, but a willing one, in spite of myself, enjoying this silly conversation more than I would like to admit.

"If I see my friend Jeff, and talk turns to high school, we will still revert to our old slang, using words and code that nobody but us understands. I guess there's a comfort level in it, or perhaps we're just trying to pretend that we're still teenagers."

"I know how you feel. Did you like high school?" I tried to picture him younger, convinced that he had been the most popular guy in school, dashing even then.

"I liked it, I didn't love it. I loved college. In high school, I was still trying so hard to find my way. I had Jeff and another friend, Vin, and we were like The Three Musketeers. We all played lacrosse together."

"Lacrosse?" My little high school in Upstate New York didn't even have a lacrosse team. I think that my impression was that lacrosse was a game that rich kids played, like polo.

"Yeah, believe it or not, lacrosse is a big thing out on the island. My cousin taught me to play when I was in junior high, and Jeff's older brother taught him, and I honestly don't know how Vin picked it up, but I know that by the time we were in high school, we were lacrosse nuts." He reminisced, a wistful tone wrapping itself around his words; his voice charged with an emotion I felt sure he couldn't hear.

I didn't have time for sports in high school, or drama club, or cheerleading, or anything else that I may have ventured into, simply because I was embroiled in trying to get home as fast as humanly possible, to protect my mother, to protect my things, to try and stay under the radar as far as The Monster was concerned. It was only once I met David that I realized that being out of the house was infinitely better than being in it, and over time, I came to realize that I couldn't protect my mother anyway.

"Did you play lacrosse in college?" I asked, curious to hear more about him.

"No, no, no. It pains me to say this, but I wasn't good enough. I went to a school where they recruited people, and you couldn't just try out and brown-nose the coach in order to make the team. Maybe I could have tried out, I don't really know, but the fact is that I never really tried." His voice still held a wisp of the wistful tone, although he didn't sound as if he regretted his decision.

"Where did you go to school?" I settled onto my beanbag chair then, relaxing into the soft sphere, my mind focused on nothing other than the conversation at hand.

"Boston College."

"No way!" I shot up off the beanbag, laughing at the coincidence. "I just went up to Boston on a business trip, and I bought my girlfriend Lanie a Boston College Christmas ornament because she loves eagles." I went on to explain Lanie's ornament collection and how she loved eagles, among other various forms of animal life.

"That's a funny coincidence. Well, that proves you have good taste." Paul suggested.

I thought about him and nodded, *so far so good.*

Then I thanked God quickly that there was no video screen attached to my phone.

"Speaking of which, dinner was great last night. I really enjoyed that place, thank you." I had already thanked him last night, but I couldn't help myself, so I thanked him again.

"You're so welcome. I really enjoyed the company." He replied in a voice that made my toes curl and a shiver run up my spine.

"I...so did I." There was the briefest moment of silence, and then I asked him: "Where are you?"

"Where am I? I'm home." His voice betrayed the fact that he thought my question strange.

Perhaps it was a strange holdover from the David era, but I like to picture the person I was talking to, where they were while they were talking to me, what they were wearing, eating, etc., so that I could have a visual to go along with the audio.

This from the girl that thanked God there was no video attached to the phone.

I know.

"I meant, like...are you outside? On the couch? Breakfast nook?" I used a playful tone with him, hoping that he wouldn't decide that I was just too kooky to pursue.

"Oh, I get it. I am lounging around on my terrace, my third cup of coffee in hand, a newspaper sprawled out all over my little breakfast-nooky-type table. I am wearing an old pair of jeans and a T-shirt that I got at the Gap about four seasons ago. No shoes, no socks, no hat, a cool breeze blowing through my hair." His voice said amused more than annoyed.

"I am laying on my beanbag chair, my running suit on, sneakers kicked off but lying nearby, socks also AWOL, an iced tea next to me, and no paper anywhere around." I gave him the scoop from my end.

"Does this constitute as phone sex?" He teased.

"I think if it did, and I charged money for the service, that I would be broke." I confessed.

"Let me guess: you're an artist." He said it so matter-of-factly that he nearly took my breath away.

"I...how did you know?" I asked incredulously.

"Because you need to see things. What is your medium, Madame Artiste?" He seemed genuinely interested, so I began to tell him what so few people knew about me.

"I love to paint." I couldn't remember the last time I had said those words out loud. "I used to paint a lot when I was younger, and although I haven't picked up a brush in quite some time, I was just thinking about painting this morning, for the first time in a long time." I told him about the flower I had found on my walk.

"Do you paint people?" Paul chuckled. "I mean, not actual paint on actual people, obviously I mean pictures of people."

"Nowadays there is a need to clarify, huh?" I joined him in easy laughter. "I am actually not that good at painting people, perhaps because I don't like it. I like painting landscapes, but I also enjoy plaster craft. I used to do a lot of that when I was young."

"What's plaster craft?"

"It's similar to ceramics, except the pieces are already fired in the kiln and made for you. You buy the pieces, and then you prime them, paint them, spray them, etc., -some people call it the lazy man's ceramics. I haven't done it in a while. It's a very 70's thing, I think, I haven't seen a shop or studio in quite some time." My heart was stirring, the prospect of painting again causing my soul to stand up and take notice.

"I think that's great. I have no talent like that." He sounded saddened by that.

"You play lacrosse." I reminded him.

"I used to play lacrosse, plus that's not a talent, it's a sport." He dismissed his ability the same way I would, as if it just wasn't significant enough.

"It's a sport that takes skill, a sport that someone like me knows nothing about." I pointed out to him. I knew none of the rules that governed that particular game, and when I gave it a minute's thought, I knew I had never watched an actual game.

"Alright, you win. I have a talent besides taking you out to dinner, although I would love to cultivate that particular talent." He shifted the conversation back to us, and my heart sang at the prospect.

"That could be fun," I agreed.

"So when can I see you again?" He was as persistent as Lanie.

I wanted to say, *Right now. Get on the train, come up here, and take me out to dinner tonight.* My fear held me in check, however, and I knew that whether I was fearful or not, it wouldn't be wise to push the envelope just yet. I shuffled quickly through my week, and knew that Tuesdays and Thursdays were reserved for Lanie and me to commiserate, and anything other than that may be too much, too soon.

"Friday night?" I suggested.

"Friday night the old work crew already has dibs on taking me out for a final round of drinks. You're welcome to come along, though I definitely want to spend some time alone, just the two of us." He thought a minute. "I'm free Saturday night, but I don't really want to wait until then to see you again."

I loved that about him.

"What about breakfast?" I thought maybe we could meet for breakfast again while he was still working nearby.

"What about tomorrow?" He was pushing the envelope.

"Tuesday?" I countered, knowing that although Lanie wouldn't mind, it still wouldn't be fair to leave her alone for any length of time on a Monday morning. Monday mornings could be crazy in our business, in any business.

"I will take what I can get!" He pronounced, with a jovial tone in his voice. "Tuesday morning and Saturday night, and perhaps Friday eve?"

"Perhaps." I felt all tingly again, agog with the reality of a man pursuing me, one that wasn't brandishing a meat cleaver, no less.

"I will take what I can get!" He repeated, and we both laughed.

"I'll see you Tuesday," I said by way of getting off the phone.

"I'll see you tomorrow, crossing Lex," he reminded me.

"Of course." And with that, I hung up the phone and hugged myself, allowing myself to drift into the happiness that had found me.

Chapter Twenty-Two

I can still remember being attracted to the clown's hand in the window. There was no clown attached to the hand, just a hand with layers of distinctive ruffles around the cuff of the absent man's sleeve, bursting forth in primary colors, almost detracting from what the hand held in its brightness, as it took several minutes for my eyes to trail upward from the singular hand, and follow the strings to the joyous colors that the balloons personified.

I wanted to be able to make something that pretty. As I peered through the window, I saw ladies at tables, painting their own clown hands, and balloons and all sorts of other pretty things. I wondered what they were doing. I had never seen such a place.

I ran across the street to where my mother worked at the beauty salon.

"Mom!" I can remember being so excited that I was gasping for air, trying to push the words out with each breath.

"What's the matter, Danielle?" She came out from behind the reception desk, surveying me for damage.

"I wanna show you something!" I tugged at her arm. "Can you come now?" I knew that if she had a customer she would have to wait, but I wanted to show her what had captured my heart.

"Yes, yes, I will come." She grabbed her purse and we skipped out the door, holding hands as we crossed the street.

"Look!" I pointed at the clown hand holding the balloons. I looked over at my mother and found a smirk taking over her face.

"I knew you would find this place eventually," she said, in the voice that all mothers tend to use.

I looked up at her, not understanding then that she already had something in mind for me, that moms sometimes know their children innately, and that she had spied this place long before me.

What did I know? I was only nine years old.

We entered the store, my eyes riveted upon the women that were stationed at the table, creating pretty things, aprons draped over them as they worked, paintbrushes in motion, bringing things to life. I heard my mother speaking, her voice sounding from a distance, enraptured as I was with the creativity going on around me.

I had taken art classes in school, but this was something else. So far in Art, I had only been allowed to make a paper mache animal and a dinosaur diorama, neither of which floated my boat. I had painted some, but never objects, and I was keen with interest, longing to be a part of all that was going on here.

"Danielle!" I turned towards my mother as she called my name. "Would you like to pick something out?"

"Can I?" I was awed by the shelves and stacks around me, fragile pieces laid gently atop another one by one, just waiting to be picked and given color and life.

I hesitated a minute and looked at my mother.

"I'll help you." She followed behind me as I made my way up and down the first two aisles. At first I would point, and she would lift, one object after the other, showing me all the angles and suggesting colors that I could use to paint it. After the first two aisles, I spotted the piece I knew I had to have.

"That one!" I said, as I pointed towards the rainbow with a cloud attached. The cloud was covering the entire bottom, almost as if to suggest that the rainbow sat on top of it. I looked at my mother and nodded. This would be my masterpiece.

The proprietor must have sauntered over at some point, and I, in my quest to find the perfect piece, had not noticed her standing right next to us.

"We can offer you a package where she can paint her first piece here, in the studio, and one of the girls will show her the steps to plaster crafting properly." She was speaking to my mother, but she was looking at me, and I smiled at her, because I wanted to learn and she was willing to teach me.

"Sounds good," my mother asked a few more questions as she wandered back over to the register, and I in my delight found that I would not have to use the two words mothers hear whined and wailed most often: Moooommm, puh-leeeese!

They talked shop, settled up, and we made my first studio appointment for the very next day. I handed my piece over to the shopkeeper, gingerly, not willing to let it go, and afraid they might break it. The woman assured me that they would tape my name on to it, and that it would be waiting for my arrival the next day.

I left the Plaster Craft Palace swinging arms with my mother, happy as a young girl could be, virtually unaware that I was on my way to becoming an artist.

Chapter Twenty-Three

"That seems like a very positive memory of your mother," Constance pointed out and then waited for my response.

"Yes, it is. It definitely is." I agreed, nodded, took a deep breath. "That was before The Monster."

"Did The Monster have anything to do with why you stopped painting?" Constance, perhaps without knowing it, hit the nail on the head.

I nodded again and began to cry, fat tears that dropped suddenly, my heart searching into the past, my eyes staring straight ahead.

"He broke it." I let the tears flow and Constance waited, for more explanation, for me to elaborate. "I can't even explain to you why it bothered me so much. I knew what he was all about by then, I knew he had no respect for life or property, but most of his anger had been directed towards my mother, and not me, and I guess it was stunning to me, and that's why I was so hurt at the time."

"Start at the beginning." Constance directed.

"The beginning. The beginning was what I just told you: I was attracted to the Plaster Craft Palace, and once I learned how to paint, I was off on a roll. I made my first piece–the rainbow–there, and then another. Eventually, my mother bought me a caddy to store my paints in, several brushes, primer, and even a sparkly spray that would protect the paint once the piece was completed. I learned how to dry-brush, so after I painted the cloud white, I dry-brushed on top of that with a pale sky blue, so it stood out even more. The rainbow started me off, but soon my hobby developed into a craft, and eventually I began making an artillery of plaster products, and I gave them out as gifts anytime I could. I made ornaments for Christmas, kitchen plaques, knick-knacks, whatever caught my eye…I would get lost in my painting, and I think my mother was thrilled, because I was an only child, and between that and my reading, I knew how to occupy myself for hours on end. It came to mean a lot to me, and once I got into high school, I moved up to painting landscapes and other things, but I always came back to the three-dimensional pieces that were my favorite. By the time I was in high school, we had pieces of my 'collection' dotting the landscape of our house." I threw out a laugh that felt sour, even though it sounded sweet. "At one point, I came across a cache of toilet seats and made one for every family member that I could think of, just because it had a silly saying on it."

"What did it say?" Constance asked.

"It said:
*If you sprinkle
When you tinkle,
Be a sweetie
And wipe the Seatie.*
It was incredibly droll, albeit tacky, but I whipped those toilet seats up one after the other, colors done according to the receiver's bathroom, a glitter rub on the letters in order to highlight the saying. My mother loved the sentiment, thought it so funny that she made me make one for each of our own bathrooms, and she hung each one on the wall behind the seat. I think it was the Christmas I was twelve that everyone got a toilet seat." I chuckled now, wondering how many family members were guilted into humoring me. "I'm sure they were thrilled."

Constance laughed.

"Then…" my voice trailed off again, my tears engulfing me. Oh, this was so incredibly dumb! Out of all the things The Monster did, after all he stole…why was I crying over something that was so…small?

Insignificant?

Or was it?

I looked at Constance, and she waited.

"…One day, I heard them arguing in their bedroom. He slammed into the adjacent bathroom, and I guess he slammed the door so hard that the toilet seat fell off the wall. I heard my mother say, *'Oh!'* and the next thing I knew, she was in my bedroom, asking me if I had another wall hanger, one that would hold it up better against the wall. I can remember thinking that if The Monster would just stop slamming doors and other things, that nothing would be falling off the wall. I kept that to myself and tried to help her anyway. I looked through my supplies, and when I couldn't find one, I went downstairs into the kitchen to try and find something to reaffix it with. I remember being downstairs in the kitchen, rifling through one drawer or another, when The Monster came in and asked what we were doing. I didn't answer him; not only was it evident, but also I had made it a rule to never answer him directly. I think in my mind I was willing him to not exist. Anyway, my mother offered up her explanation as to what we were doing, cowering as usual, and then he, rather gruffly, said something to the effect of, *'Gimme that.'* I wouldn't hand it to him, but my mother lifted it out of my hand, and handed it to him. I can still remember thinking that it was not a good idea..." I trailed off, because I had a knot in my chest that was so tight, I could barely breathe, I was reliving it, the whole debauchery, the same exact feeling, resurrecting itself, all over me again.

"Do you want a sip of water?" Constance pointed to the pitcher of water that was habitually on her desk.

I waved her away, determined to get past the knot, the moment, the pain.

"I'm alright." I breathed deeply, continuing and crying simultaneously, "So I knew it was not going to be good, and probably the minute I had that thought, he took it, rose it high over his head, and crashed it onto the floor right in front of us both. The toilet piece smashed, and broke into a billion little pieces, because we were still in the old house, and that kitchen had ceramic tile, and you know that ceramic tile isn't the easiest thing to clean. He looked me in the eye and said, *'I never liked that stupid thing anyway.'* And then he left. He left the kitchen and the house, and I can't recall seeing him for days after. He was probably as high as a kite, lost on a bender, but it didn't matter, because once he left I had peace for a day or two, and that's all that mattered."

I took another breath and continued on. "I cleaned up the remains, and I cried the whole time, but as heartbroken as I was, do you know what really bothered me?"

"What really bothered you?" She asked.

"That she just stood there." A fresh round of tears appeared and the hurt in my chest grew, expanded, and left me stunned again at the ineptitude of my mother to handle the situation. "I can still remember my mother mouthing, *'I'm sorry,'* and bending down to help me clean up the mess. I pushed her away and insisted on cleaning it up myself." I cried openly.

"What is it that's making you cry right now?" Constance asked in a level voice, but I could no longer articulate my position. I flailed my arms at her and grabbed a handful of tissues from the same end table that held the water pitcher, blowing my nose in a way that could be called anything but ladylike.

"I'm crying because of her…her…her lack of ability to protect me, or stand up for her…or me, what about me? It's like once he appeared on the scene, I ceased to exist…nothing mattered as much as him, or keeping him from getting upset, angry, playing the game so he wouldn't leave…making excuses for his bad behavior…she became so unlike the woman I had once known, the Mom that I had once worshipped, that it killed me inside and on some level it still kills me today."

Constance and I went on to discuss how inept she was, and I was just about to underscore that story with another, when she realized our time was up. I thanked her, paid her and left, sorting out my thoughts all the way back to the office. I never even stopped to get a frozen yogurt, never even thought about it.

"Paul called." Lanie greeted me with this as I walked back in to the office, and I acknowledged her with what I knew was a weak grin. I talked myself into shaking my mood as my blazer came off, and I determined that I would shake off the mood along with the blazer. What else could I do? Grieve more? I wasn't about to let another day be dictated by my past, another minute wasted over a hurt that had long been hiding underground.

She was on the phone another minute and then turned to look at me.

"Tough session." I informed her and then decided to make that valiant attempt at letting go. "What did he say?" Paul was much more intriguing than anything my past had to offer.

"He said to call him back." Lanie stated this matter-of-factly, and then flashed me a wicked grin. "I'll have you know I gave away some personal information."

"How personal?" I was wary of her, but not too, as I knew Lanie was harmless, no matter how fierce she pretended to be.

"Flower particulars." She threw this at me as she sashayed out of our hole/office, and I laughed out loud and buried the past right then and there.

Paul.

I had met him on Tuesday for a cappuccino muffin and tea. We went to a different place than we had the first time we shared breakfast, and we talked each other's ears off as if we were old friends. He was excited to be wrapping up things at the old job, and kept trying to convince me that I should join him for Happy Hour on Friday.

"I forgot, I already made plans with Lanie," I had said, and although I thought myself to be rather slick, he knew that I was fudging, and he called me on it. The truth was that I was just starting to feel comfortable with him, and I was amazed at how short of an amount of time that had taken. Not wanting to tempt fate, I decided that I didn't need to meet him out for Happy Hour just yet.

He seemed determined to convince me to come along, and had only accepted my No after securing the next three Saturday nights for dates with me.

I wasn't upset.

Now it was Thursday and he had called again, and my heart soared at the mere thought that I had a man who was interested in me, one that I found attractive, one that made me laugh, one that wasn't afraid to be himself around me.

Thus far, I liked himself very much.

I logged back into my computer as I returned his call. His voice mail picked up, so I left a quick message and then got back to work. Lanie and I wanted to hit a kickboxing class at the gym tonight, so I knew that I had to get done in order to get out.

I was immersed in a rooming list for an upcoming group going to Canada when the phone rang. The display read *Unavailable.* Thinking it might be Paul calling from a different line, I lunged for it.

"Hello, may I please speak to Danielle Damruco?" The voice was pleasant enough, but after massacring my name, I knew it wasn't anybody I knew.

"This is she." Could be someone from another company, adding their name on to the rooming list. The ad agency had sent out strict instructions to email and not call in individual reservations, but nobody ever read directions, so...I wouldn't be surprised.

"Hi. I don't know if you remember me, but my name is Violet. I used to work for Todd and Roth. You used to do my travel."

My mind was shuffling through names, Violet, Violet; did I remember anyone named Violet?

"Um, hi." I said this because I could think of nothing else to say. What did this person want? And who was she? For the life of me, I couldn't place a face with the name.

"You probably don't remember me," she reiterated, talking faster all the while. "I actually used to book travel for Mr. Endine, I was his First Assistant."

"Oh! Of course I remember you!" I interrupted her then, her face coming in to focus. Mr. Endine was the Ex-CFO or some such thing of Todd and Roth. Originally he, Todd, Roth, and one other guy started the agency as a little shop on Madison Avenue. They hooked a huge cola account and grew at leaps and bounds, bigger than they ever thought they would, faster than anyone in the Ad Game could have predicted. With great success came great stress, however, and rumor had it that Endine and the other guy left last year to paint their own face on a new ad agency. There had barely been a ripple in the travel department, so I hadn't given it much thought, except of course, until now.

"Yes, yes, I always remember you being so polite and helpful." Violet waited a beat and then asked, "Are you happy there?"

She could have asked me if my underwear were green and I wouldn't have been more shocked.

"I, umm…yes. May I ask why you're asking?" Was this call being monitored? I had heard of some companies doing that, posing fake offers out to their staff in order to test their loyalty. This call popping out of the blue sounded like it might fit into that category.

"Well, Mr. Endine has been extremely unhappy with the Travel Service we have been using as of late. I remembered that dealing with you had been so easy, so I thought I would call up and see if there was any way you might be interested in coming to work for us." She was so to the point that I really began to think that this call was a set-up.

"Well, Violet, I hate to admit this to you, but I'm *Very Happy.*" I put such emphasis on the words that it sounded like a song title. Just in case anyone was listening.

"Well, let me leave you our number, just in case you change your mind, or know someone who might be interested." She rattled off her number. With that and a quick good-bye, she was gone.

I must have had an interesting look on my face, because Lanie moved her chair closer to me and asked, "What was that all about?"

"Do you remember Violet?" I filled her in on the phone call. "Do you think it's internal?" I told her my suspicions.

"I don't think anybody here has the time or the patience to do that kind of stuff. The Ad Game is too cutthroat anyway–everybody knows that." Lanie shook her head. "Sounds like a legit offer. What are you going to do about it?"

"Nothing." What was she thinking? I could never leave her.

"You should at least go and see what they have to offer. You never know, it might be a lot more money." Lanie suggested.

"No, I'm not interested." I shook my head.

"You don't like change, and you're not high on taking chances either." Lanie shook her finger at me, suddenly Daddy's little girl. "My father says you should always, *always* have a resume circulating, no matter how happy you are."

"I resent that." I could barely look at her, as I spoke through clenched teeth. "I moved. Lanie, I left everything behind and moved far away with little to no money to work with, and nobody to rely on. So don't tell me that I can't change." I felt an overwhelming sense of anger towards her, and feelings were taking shape inside my heart that I couldn't even define.

"I didn't say that you can't change, I merely pointed out that you don't like change. Newsflash: NOBODY likes change! As for taking chances, what chances have you taken in your professional life?" She was standing over me now, as I pretended to ignore her and focus on my computer screen.

"Paul! Okay? I took a chance on going out with Paul!" My sudden outburst was shocking even to me. I had swiveled my chair back so that I was facing her now, and I glared at her with all my might. We had been friends now long enough for her to know how terrified I was.

"I said your *professional* life. And I am very proud of you for taking a chance with Paul, please keep that in mind and stop your glaring." She gave me her best bitchy look right back.

"I am happy here. Happy! Is that a crime? Should I be like your friend Jimmy, the King of hotjobs.com, prostituting himself for the highest salary?" I was outraged that Lanie was getting on my case.

The phone rang and neither one of us answered it. We stared at it and then at each other.

"C'mon, Yellie. Let's blow off the phone, get both our butts fired, and then sell ourselves on Hookers-For-Hire.com." She made a gesture towards the door, threw her purse over her shoulder, and pulled me out of my chair. "This hole/office is getting to me today. It's too small on a good day. I'm treating for FroYo."

I acquiesced, and by the time I latched myself onto some Berry Berry Delicious, I looked at Lanie and began to laugh.

"You're a pain, you know that?"

"Be all you can be."

"That's your comeback?"

"I think that's the Army's comeback, but I'm borrowing it." She gave me her evilest eye. "You're a tougher cookie than you pretend to be."

"I had to be." I whispered.

"I know." Lanie put her FroYo in one hand and slipped an arm around me. "You can't get scared now."

"Are you still harping on the job thing?" I needed a break.

"I am harping on the every thing." Lanie shrugged. "Sometimes I am my father's daughter. I don't imagine myself to be, but times like these I know that there's just no escaping it. My point is this: what would be the harm in finding out what they have to offer? Wouldn't it be a great big ego boost if nothing else? I mean, they are pursuing you. Doesn't that just ring your chimes?"

"Not really." I thought about what she said a minute. "I might be comfortable, Lanie, but I am also happy. *Happy* is not a dirty word. I have learned that I can't stay where I'm not happy–that's why I moved. I also know though, that Paul is more than enough change or chance for right now."

"So be it." She hesitated and then looked me directly in the eye. "I believe that you can do anything."

"I…thank you." I wasn't used to people believing in me.

"Get over it." She dumped her Fro Yo and we made our way back to the hole/office.

Chapter Twenty-Four

By the time I got on the train, I was exhausted, drained both mentally and physically. After work, Lanie and I had managed to hit the kickboxing class, and every last ounce of fight that was in me was now gone. As if that wasn't enough, I worked my arms further with resistance bands and now my whole upper half was tingling.

I sat on the train and mulled over the elements of my day: Paul. Therapy. Thinking about The Monster. My mother. Painting. Fighting with Lanie. Work. An unexpected offer to work elsewhere. More work. Paul. Kickboxing. Push. Pull. The train.

I was kicked, depleted beyond the physical. I tried to read, but I kept dozing off on the trip home, and eventually I gave up. I people-watched with fervor for the rest of the trip, willing my eyes to stay open, making up stories about people in my head.

On the drive home from the train station, I thought about a nice tall glass of pineapple juice. I had brought a half-gallon container of pineapple juice a few days earlier. I tried to tell myself that a hot cup of tea would be more sedating, but I could feel the ice cold juice sluicing down my throat, every pore in my body refreshed, the sweet and tangy taste compensating for the exertion I had put forth throughout my class.

I felt I owed myself some after that tough class, but as I made my way around each winding turn, a taunting little voice spoke up inside of my head.

It'll be gone by the time you get there.

That was ridiculous, and I knew better by now. I swiped a piece of hair straight off my brow and commanded the thought to move right along with it.

Another voice, this time sounding distinctly like The Monster's: *Oh, was that yours? I thought your mother brought it for me. Oh, were you saving that? Did you want the last one? Too Late. Sorry!*

Feigned innocence and evil intent abounded.

That was then; this was now.

I had to remember.

I could remember back to when I really believed that he didn't know that I loved cranberry juice, and I was able to convince myself that he had finished it unknowingly, not finish it *on me.* Survival was the theme, so I was sharpened like a knife, instincts honed in such a way that I lost a large part of childhood, and stepped right into having the wisdom of a woman who could discern truth from lies. It didn't take too long to realize that he was never sorry. I would catch him sneaking off with a bag of Twizzlers, cradling them under his arm like a football, straight from the shopping bag, directly into their bedroom, where he would squirrel them away in the nether reaches of his nightstand. My mother would ask me what happened to them, and I would point theatrically, knowing full well that she would never retrieve them from his grasp and place them in my own. Once I caught on to the game, I would make sure to unpack the groceries, and plaster certain items with Post-it Notes, stating: DANIELLE. Do Not Touch.

He always touched. I would see him slip silently into the kitchen, ignore my Post-it warnings and then stand in front of me and wipe crumbs from his wretched face. He ate my cookies, he drank my juices, and he played games with any aspect of my life that involved my mother.

I thought back to the times when I would see him eating things I knew he didn't even like in order to spite me. It was stupid, the games that we had played, using my mother as a pawn between us two. Did she remember my favorite shampoo, but forget to get him instant mashed potatoes? I would crow with victory, albeit silent, believing that I had taken up an instant of her thought life, a tiny edge of her heart that wasn't reserved specifically for him. Then he would retaliate by using my products or eating the food that she specifically brought for me.

At times, I would cry. The injustice of it all; the bare hatred that hung between us, my mother unable or unwilling to assert herself and insist that the brownies she brought were for me to enjoy. Full cereal boxes would disappear the day they were brought into the home. I found out later that they were undersold.

Street Value: one dollar.

Oh, how I would love the times when he left the house for days on end, seeming never to return. My house was my own, my mother, although crushed and consumed by the absence of his presence–safe–even if it was only temporary, and an illusion at best.

My food was mine to enjoy.

I turned the last curve into my road and determined that I would wave these ghosts away, once and for all. I would make a poster and hang it on the outside of my refrigerator door claiming my food for my own. I would remind myself that I no longer needed to be afraid, and if the taunting, nasty, reminiscent voice popped up again, I would shut it down completely.

I couldn't really do that, nor should I have to. I simply had to train my mind to know that those days were over. That way of life had made me suffer far more than I ever should have, and I commanded my soul not to perpetuate the horrors of my former life.

I entered my door and double-locked it immediately behind me. Noticed there were no messages to return and shrugged off my jacket as I swung open the door to my fridge.

It was there, reassuring me that all was well and that my place was still my own. I took a deep breath and then lifted the pineapple juice off the shelf. I poured myself a tall glass and enjoyed the feeling of sweet and cold as it made its way down my throat.

I'm working on it.

One step at a time, I felt my life coming back to me. Perhaps coming back to me wasn't even the most accurate way to put it. Coming at me? Coming towards me? I shook my head, as there were no words to define it.

They say you can't mourn what you have never had; I don't agree. I think I've mourned for quite some time now, the sense that everybody else had something a heck of a lot closer to what we all should have. I think I still long for The Brady Bunch existence, and although I've never experienced it first-hand, it's a picture that my heart still holds dear. I have a vision for my own life now, too…my own family. Could Paul be a part of that? I was afraid to hope, remembering with a lopsided grin my mother dancing in the living room to *The Second Time Around.*

It wasn't any better for her.

I was terrified over the thought that it may not be better for me.

Except I couldn't deny the changes I had made already and the call my life was issuing me now. Hope is an interesting commodity. It wouldn't let me go.

My heart full, my limbs tired, I climbed into bed and tried unsuccessfully to read once more. The murder mystery was good, the relationship between the detective and the witness contrived.

I laid my head on the pillow and drifted into a dreamless sleep.

Chapter Twenty-Five

"Alex!" I waved to him from the doorway of our hole/office, determined to flag him down. "I have rush tickets!"

"Danielle, I have something for you, too. I'll be right in, I have a rush for Media." He threw the brakes on his mail cart and made a quick dash backwards, towards the Media Department.

"Okay!" I called after him. I wasn't worried. I was still thinking about Paul, and how he tangoed across Lex this morning, his smile unstoppable.

Today was his last day and his excitement had been written all over his face. I chatted him up quickly and made my way to work, but my thoughts were still mulling over his final invite for this evening.

"Just go," Lanie interjected, reading my mind as I double-checked the package that Alex would be delivering to our client. Occasionally, someone from Mr. Todd or Mr. Roth's pool of assistants requested that we do travel arrangements for a client who would be traveling with the Head Honcho. Now, it would make sense to the average not-rich person that if Mr. Todd were traveling with Mr. X, that he simply hand said tickets over to Mr. X when they meet at the airport, since they are not only on the same flight, but we have already reserved the same conference room for them at the American Airlines Airport Lounge. However, in Corporate America, the goal for the Rich is to waste as much money as possible (such as needless Fed-Ex charges on a rush ticket) so the not-rich are not only stupefied by this behavior, but are also unable to obtain a raise because Mr. Rich/Todd would rather waste money than hand-deliver a ticket to Mr. X.

"Go where?" For a second, I thought she was talking about hand-delivering the ticket, but then I realized that Lanie's mind-reading abilities were as intact as ever, and she was telling me to go to Happy Hour.

"You know where. Happy Hour, Dork! He has only asked you, like fifty-seven times!" Lanie pointed out.

"I know. I know, Lanie, but I can't. I'm not ready."

"You went out with him alone. I would think a group of people would be an even easier venue for you to get to know him."

"It should be, right?" I was following her logic; I just couldn't bring myself to insert myself into his life in such a way. Not yet. I was about to offer her an explanation, when Alex came through the door to pick up the rush.

He had a bouquet of flowers in his arms.

"Danielle, looks like somebody likes you a lot," Alex teased and winked at both Lanie and myself.

"Nothing for me?" Lanie feigned outrage as our eyes caught, and then she let slip with her widest grin. *"I knew all about this!"* She sing-songed.

"I…" I was speechless, and my head was swimming. Too much, too fast. My heart ticked like a clock. Too much. Tick-tock. Too fast. Tick-tock.

"Sign please!" Alex indicated where and picked up the Rush with a flourish. "I'll get these over to them ASAP." And he was gone.

"I…" I started again and stared at Lanie. "I…" I couldn't enunciate all that I was feeling, so I promptly burst into tears.

"Yellie, No!" Lanie was by my side in an instant, gently taking the flowers from my hands as I bent and covered my face with them. I sat there and sobbed for a full minute, my heart a myriad of emotions, my hands getting soaked and my makeup streaking.

"I can't…it's too much. Too fast. I…what if…" My heart pounded out a familiar question. *What if he's like David? I can't take another David.*

"What can't you do?" Lanie asked plaintively. "You can't let a man buy you flowers?"

"I can't fall in love with him!" I threw this out with a yell that surprised even me in its force. "It's too much, too soon, too fast for me–can't you see that? What if he is just like David? Sure, he's wowing me now, but what about when he finds out that I'm not going to sleep with him right away? And that he'll never meet my highly dysfunctional family? I can't take another David!" I protested. I felt tremors reaching down deep into the depths of my being, my insides roiling, my heart fighting with my head. I was so scared.

Afraid to reach for what was right within my grasp. I knew it, Lanie knew it, and God knew it. Could this really be the answer to my prayers? If so, then why was I so scared? I wasn't ready to test the waters again. Was that it? What if you told God that you weren't ready yet? Did He give you another chance, or was it on His terms only, in His timetable or not at all?

What if God thought I was ready?

"Sssshh," Lanie tried to calm me, her hand softly rubbing my back as the tears flowed and the shaking continued. "This is what I was talking about, Yellie, taking chances."

"I want to," I whispered this, surprised to hear the words as they came out of my mouth. I sniffled and turned around to face her. "Do you believe me?"

"I do. I believe that you really do want to try it again with someone. And I don't blame you for being as scared as you are, considering your background and what I now know about David. But the same way that there are no guarantees that this guy won't screw you over the same way David did, there are also no guarantees that he will." Lanie's eyes were piercing. I paused a minute and thought about her analogy before I responded.

"There are no guarantees, period." I stated.

"You're right. There are only chances." Lanie responded.

"I don't know." I didn't know anything; I didn't even know why I was so scared of him. I wanted a future with a man I loved, why couldn't it be easy?

"I don't know either. I only know that I would hate to see you give up this chance. He seems like the right kind of guy, Yellie." Lanie lifted up the flowers so that I could see them. "I'll go get these guys a drink. You fix your face."

She left me alone and I was grateful for a moment to think and to try to collect my thoughts. She was right. I was getting myself totally crazy over something that wasn't anything yet. Only I sensed it could be something; was that why I was so scared? I shooed away every thought I had that bound me up in fear, and by the time she reentered the room, I felt almost silly.

"Thank you," I said to her, and we held each other's eyes for what seemed like a long time.

"You are so very welcome." She arranged the flowers on my desk. They were a beautiful arrangement of spring tulips, the colors vibrant, and the stems strong.

"They're beautiful." I muttered. "Lanie, did you tell him that I liked tulips?"

"Yesterday. I also told him that you don't wear underwear." With that, she put her headset on and answered the phone.

"Thanks." I pushed the vase around on my desk, looking for the perfect angle. I couldn't remember the last time I had received flowers.

David.

I pushed that thought far from my mind.

I noticed the tiny card that Lanie had laid carefully next to the vase. I reached for it and paused a moment, then ripped it open, curious to see the message inside.

There's something to be said for the road less traveled, but right now I'm sure glad I crossed Lexington Avenue. Can't wait to see you again. Paul.

Not too much. Not too fast.

Oh, God, why was this so difficult? Why is it that you wish for something, and then it happens, and then you don't know what to do with it?

Two breakfasts and one dinner does not a relationship make? What was I scared of? A few phone calls, a bouquet of flowers, a genuinely nice guy who was willing to ferret out a place within my life...I was being served what I wanted on a platter. This was not cause for alarm. I needed to try.

I picked up the phone and dialed Paul's work number.

"Hello, Danielle!" He answered the phone and his smile came through the wire.

"Do you have Caller-ID?" I asked, temporarily caught off guard. Either that or he was a mind reader.

"I do. It says, 'Beautiful Girl,' so I knew it was you." He sounded full of energy, and I knew that his last day was going to be a good one for him.

"You're funny." I waited a beat. "I just wanted to call and thank you for the flowers. They're beautiful." I gazed at them as we spoke.

"Ah-hah! You got them already? Well, well, well...I didn't expect you to receive them until after lunch." He seemed pleased.

"I just got them. I heard you had some help," I added, feeling my fears subside and taking comfort in his voice. It was truly uncanny the way I always felt at ease with him after even the briefest exchange.

"Yes, I am guilty of bribing your friend. Tell her the check is in the mail."

I laughed.

"Well, I'm sure you're busy packing up and all. I only wanted to thank you." I could hear the noise around his desk gaining volume.

"You are so welcome. No chance I can change your mind about meeting the crew later?" He tried again.

"No, I'm sorry." I shook my head, resolute in my anxiety. "But I'll see you on Saturday."

"Same place?"

"Same time." We had agreed to meet by the clock in Grand Central earlier in the week.

"I will be there. I'll call you later."

"Okay. Bye."

I hung up the phone and waited for Lanie to get off the phone.

"What did he say?" She asked.

"He said I was a beautiful girl," I felt girlish and silly, but better since I had cried, and the whole day felt lighter.

Chapter Twenty-Six

Once I got over the flowers, I decided to run with the flowers.

On the way home on the train I spied a woman with a Bible on her lap. She became the object of my people-watching activities, and slowly my mind began to think about an old teaching I had learned, way back in the "David Days," when scripture would readily roll off the tip of my tongue.

Faith and fear cannot exist in the same vessel.

I am sure that's a paraphrase of some sort, my old pastor famous for breaking down scriptures into memorable phrases, but the effect was positive, as I was able to recall now the teaching that my soul was in need of. I decided to set my mind on the path of faith and hope.

When I arrived home, I double-locked the door and did my regular check of the mail, the answering machine, and the refrigerator. I stood there for a minute with Paul's gift clutched firmly in my fist, my eyes set on the hope and the newness that the flowers represented. I determined anew to trust God, and to believe that I was right where I was supposed to be at this point in my life, fear or no fear. As I set the flowers into the only vase I owned, I set my mind firmly on faith and not fear.

Now if only that mind-set would last through to the morning.

I fell asleep with my book on my chest. I got up, stretched, and padded over to the fridge in order to pour myself the last of the pineapple juice. Give me pineapple, cranberry, mango/kiwi/exotic fruit, any juice other than orange, and I was the happiest girl in the free world.

It wasn't exclusively orange juice that I hated with a passion, it was orange everything. Orange Lifesavers got saved and pawned off on unsuspecting coworkers, and eventually tossed in the garbage, orange gummy bears got played with until they no longer resembled anything close to a bear, orange tea was not even allowed in the door to my humble abode.

This quirk, among others, has yet to have been explained by medical science.

I shook my head and as I busied myself making tea, my eyes flicked to the flowers. I wanted to make sure they were still there. I checked my watch and decided there was enough time to ransack my closet, throw a temper tantrum about every piece of clothing I owned, and still get to the mall and invest in a brand-new pair of Capris for tonight's date with Paul.

I wanted something…*kicky.*

Not dippy. Kicky.

Tea imbibed, I threw my hair back and slapped on a baseball hat. I would swoop down on the mall, incognito, and then transform myself into beauty rather than beast upon my return.

Aaaahhh…the mall on a Saturday. Filled with screaming babies, teenage rock-star wannabes, and women such as myself: on a mission to find the best outfit *ever.*

I swept in and out of several franchises; only to find myself wandering into a store I loved called *Lili's,* an independently owned bastion of quality clothing for women who actually had hips. Imagine that! I tried on a pair of coral-colored Capris, and they spoke *kicky* to me. I had several shirts at home that could go along with it, but once I exited the dressing room, I found a light beige boat neck sweater that I just had to have. It was a bit pricey, but I knew I would get some mileage out of beige, so I opted for the sweater. I grabbed a medium off the rack and the mission was over.

Screw the stores with their pants made for pencils!

I made my way home and decided to give myself a quick facial before I dove full speed ahead into the beautifying process. I allowed myself to fret for a millisecond, hoping that wherever he was taking me was truly casual, and wondering what type of shoes would complete the effect. I settled on a pair of brown sandals, figuring I could use my small brown purse and be done with it.

Fifteen minutes later, I was lounging on my futon with green goo lathered all about my face and the same trite novel in hand. The romance scenes were so…Ugh, is the only way I could put it, but I determined to finish the book regardless. No matter how awful, I had never not finished a book–not even once. I had plowed through plotlines that were so foreseeable they were scary, characters who I didn't give a flying leap about, scenes so unbelievable that I found myself yelling at the poor defenseless pages…but I kept on, no matter how hard it was to do so, all for the love of reading.

Soon it was time to wash off the goo and get going. I jumped in the shower, and an hour later I was converted into something resembling a woman going out on a date.

I found myself leaning more towards excited and farther away from nervous on my trip down to the city. Was that a good sign? I thought so. Perhaps I was letting my defenses down a little too fast, though, and perhaps I would pay for it later? I shook those thoughts from my convoluted mind, focusing instead on Paul's incredible smile.

It was the smile that accosted me the minute I got off the train. Instead of meeting me by the clock, he was standing right outside the track my train pulled into, his grin lighting up not only his face, but also several of the restored chandeliers in the middle of Grand Central.

"Hi!" I was surprised by him, but taken in by his disarming grin.

"Hi!" He opened his arms to me and I found myself leaning into him, and catching a whiff of some form of amazing cologne as he held me close.

Oh my.

We released each other and I gathered my thoughts. "I thought you said by the clock. How did you know that I would come into here?" Track assignments at Grand Central changed faster than Madonna let loose with a bottle of hair dye.

"There is an Arrival listing, as well as the Departure boards." He pointed over to a small television set recessed into a nearby wall. "The guy behind the desk said it's accurate about seventy percent of the time, so I figured I'd give it a whirl."

"Thanks," I said for a lack of anything better to say. Did that mean that he couldn't wait to see me?

"So!" He clasped his hands in front of him, as if he was giving a tour of Grand Central. "Are you in the mood for very good, very sloppy, Mexican diner food?" He suggested.

"Blockheads?" *Blockheads* was the name of a Mexican diner in our work neighborhood, one that Lanie and I frequented whenever one or the other of us had PMS. They made burritos the size of some people's legs, and the endless bowl of tortilla chips always served its salt-craving purpose.

"The one and only!" His excitement was infectious. "I take it you've heard of the place? That's why I recommended casual." He splayed his hands again, as if to demonstrate how he wore jeans and a button-down shirt, with carefully worn loafers ending the ensemble at his feet.

He looked great. Casual, suit and tie, naked…

I could only imagine.

"I think that's a great idea," I agreed. It was an entirely different speed than Shun Lee Palace, but I liked that about him. It made me wonder a little less if he was up to something.

We departed Grand Central then and wound our way over the short few blocks to Blockhead's. Essentially, Blockhead's was a dive. A neighborhood joint that most tourists knew nothing about, with tiny tables that packed in as many people as humanly possible, ambiance zero. The food was fabulous however, and on a clear May evening such as this, they would open up their tiny back patio and we could eat beans and lard under a starry night sky.

Once arrived, I deemed the place to have an altogether different feel in the evening, and shared that tidbit with the present company. Perhaps everything seemed different because of the present company?

Ah, food for thought.

"I really do love this place." I remarked.

"Good, I'm glad. I was afraid of outdoing myself after last time," he said as he settled into his chair.

I smirked. Throughout the week, I was more than charmed by his wit, and I found it positively refreshing that I had found someone who could keep up with me.

"So how was last night?" I was curious to see how his send-off had gone.

"It was fun. A lot more people showed up than I originally expected." He relayed where they had gone and then where they moved the party to once the general work population had left and he found himself surrounded by only his core group. "We ended up at this place with a cigar bar, and although I am not a cigar connoisseur myself, I decided that I liked secondhand smoke enough to stay, and I ended up bumping into an old buddy from college. We ended up shooting the breeze for quite some time, and we exchanged cards before we left. I told him to keep in touch. Apparently, he's going to be in the city for almost six months working on a project for his firm in Boston, so I told him that we have to get together for a drink or a steak or something."

"Do you like steak?" I asked.

"Yeah, I occasionally like a nice filet mignon with an old-fashioned baked potato and some creamed spinach. Do you eat steak or are you offended by people who do?" He threw this out at me as if to assume that everyone in the world belonged in either one of these two camps.

"I actually used to like steak very much. I have nothing against it, I just can't eat it because it doesn't like me." Great, now I sounded somewhat geriatric. Actually, the doctor said it was aggravating the bleeding ulcer that I had acquired at the ripe young age of sixteen. He recommended that I stay away from red meat, butter, and chocolate. He would have been better to recommend that I stay away from my own household. Since I left, no more ulcers. I just wasn't willing to take any chances with Mr. Moo.

"So you don't care about the cows?" He made another sweeping motion with his hands. Paul was a huge hands-talker.

"I could care less about the cows," I assured him. "I have a problem digesting red meat. I do eat fish though, and chicken, and turkey."

"And Mexican food? How does your stomach do with that?" He seemed genuinely concerned for a second, as if he had just created a major faux pas.

"It does just fine." I assured him once more, even though I was telegraphing for him to shut down this line of questioning. How the hell did we end up discussing my delicate stomach? "Besides, I usually order the spinach burrito here."

"Good." He looked pleased with himself again. "I guess I'm lucky; I don't have any stomach problems."

"You couldn't. You eat weird things like potato chips and ketchup, and still live to tell the story." I teased.

"Oh, like that's so different than this!" He made his point with a gesture towards the tortilla chips and salsa.

"Touché!" I cried and we shared a bold laugh. *I love this guy,* my heart announced, and my head paid attention.

Where did you come from? Oh, please, dear God…make him stay.

Our burritos arrived promptly, and the conversation continued throughout the collective ooohs and aaahs, good old comfort food in full force.

"So who was the old college buddy you ran into?" Inquiring minds want to know.

"Alex. Actually, Alexander Trent Walker III. My good buddy Alex was one of my suitemates my first year there, one of the richest kids in the world, and a very good guy to room with, especially to typically broke guys like me."

My eyes asked a question.

"For example, Alex's mom was always sending up baked goods, or toiletries, or money to buy those things. If you're suddenly broke and run out of razors, Alex was your go-to guy. He was also a genuinely great kid, and we became pretty good friends. Then, after college, we lost touch, as so many people do. I'm glad I ran into him." Paul elaborated. "Alex's dad owns all the Perfect Piper Pizza Pied restaurants on the west coast. His parents are positively rolling in it."

"Where on the west coast is he from?" I slathered some guacamole on the end of my burrito, calories be damned. "And if he's so rich, why did he go to Boston College?" I didn't mean it to demean Boston College, I meant the question in a manner that said, Why not Harvard?

"Why not Harvard, right?" Paul laughed as he dumped extra sour cream on his plate. Paul shrugged. "Alex isn't only rich. He's one of the most generous people I know. I'm pretty psyched that I ran into him last night, and I hope to see him as much as I can over the next few months."

"That sounds good. Where is he staying in New York?" I loved listening to Paul's stories. He seemed so much worldlier than me.

"He said his company got him some corporate housing on the East side. I forgot to ask exactly where."

"I suppose you gave him a business card?"

"Yes, I did."

"You're good at that." I smiled.

"I guess I am." Paul returned the gesture.

"I can imagine how the Dad/CEO thing can't be easy," I related a little about Lanie and her struggles with her father.

"Plus having money has its own struggles." Paul interjected.

"I wouldn't know," I said and then tried to kick myself under the table. Why, oh why couldn't I just keep my big mouth shut?

"Yeah, me neither," He waved that thought away. I wondered, though, if the watch he was wearing was a real Rolex. I got the impression that he came from a typical middle-class family, but he seemed like he did pretty well for himself since he had moved into the city.

It didn't matter to me one bit, but somehow it mattered to think that I still had that indefinable fear governing my life, the fear of being found out.

Trailer Trash!

I wiped that epithet from my mind, pushed down the fear, and tried to pay attention to the conversation at hand.

"So! You're going to the moon..." I began my standard date question, the one that I throw out to various unsuspecting individuals. Well, I hadn't tried it out on a date in quite some time, but it felt safe, so I gave it a whirl.

"I'm going to the moon?" Paul verified. "Okay. Cool."

"Yes, you're going to the moon, and you can only take 3 CD's with you.... for the rest of your life. You can never come back or switch those CD's. What are you taking?" I posed the question and took a big bite of my burrito.

"Wow, okay..." he seemed deep in thought for a minute. "The type of music is easy; you need something slow, something fast, and something classical. Right?"

"There is no right or wrong here. It's just a question." I tried to be flippant about my Spy girl capabilities.

"Well, one is so easy. It's Billy Joel's Greatest Hits."

"Isn't that a two CD-set?" I countered.

"Is that against the rules?" He looked appalled. "But he's from Long Island!"

As if that made all the difference.

"Being a local hero justifies a two CD-set?" I shook my head. He made a mournful face.

"Aw, c'mon, it's for the rest of my *life*." He put so much emphasis on the word *life* that I had to actually giggle. I liked the fact that he was taking my little game seriously.

"Alright! All right, between the forever thing and the Long Island thing, you get Billy Joel. What else?" I prodded.

"What else?" He was pensive. "I would take John Coltrane."

"Which John Coltrane?"

"Any one you would let me! I mean, I got away with the two-volume set of Mr. Joel, so I wouldn't want to push my luck!" He grinned and then took a big bite of food, still grinning as he chewed.

"And?" He still had one more.

"And," he hesitated as he swallowed. "Something by Bach."

"You're a better person than I am," I observed. I wanted to bring pop hits galore. Anything but the Rolling Stones. Oh, how I hated The Rolling Stones.

"So? Do you have a list?"

"Of course." I devised the game, dummy.

"And?" He gave it right back to me.

"Okay. Well, you can't laugh." I warned him with my eyes. "I would definitely take Amy Grant's *Lead Me On*." I waited for the obligatory reaction.

"Was she the one that sang, *Baby, Baby?*" He wasn't very good at concealing the fact that he thought my choice to be tres geek.

"Yes, but this album was way before that. It is fabulous, very moving–sort of folksy, but with a pop twist. It's uplifting, spiritual…I just love it." I couldn't imagine living without popping it on occasionally, therefore: right into the moon bag.

"Did you say album?"

"I think I did."

"Shows our age."

"Yeah, it does." I felt so lighthearted with this man, that chuckling became second nature.

"Back to your list." He pointed at me.

"The second one would have to be Jim Brickman's *By Heart*. I love soft piano music." I waited for a response.

"I've never heard of him," he admitted.

"He's great; probably a lot of people have never heard of him, at least not by name. Plus, I would consider it women's music more than men's."

"Chick music?" He acted appalled.

"Women's music!" I insisted.

"How is piano music considered genderized?" Paul picked up his drink and took a deep sip while waiting for my answer.

"You'd have to listen to it." How can you explain Jim Brickman to somebody who has never heard Jim Brickman before? His music evoked romance, his soft touch on the piano keys made my heart strain and pull with every chord. "It's soothing."

"I believe you. A third?"

"You can't laugh." I warned again. My choices were eclectic, but the astute listener would be able to piece together a little part of me. I guess that's what I was hoping for.

"I won't laugh." Earnestness all around the eyes, the smiling eyes.

"Grease." You would have to be dead or on another planet (the moon, perhaps?) if you weren't familiar with Grease, the movie, the soundtrack, ergo the phenomenon.

"The soundtrack? I love it! That's a great choice; I wish I had thought of it." He raised his glass to mine. "To Grease!"

"To Grease!" I allowed a great big grin to slide across my face.

"I have a secret." He was leaning over the table now with a conspiratory grin waving in my direction.

"Let me guess: you always wanted to be John Travolta?" I think every guy who was a boy in the seventies wanted to be John Travolta at one point or another. Hell, if *Grease* didn't do it, I'm sure *Saturday Night Fever* did.

"No. Kenickie." He actually blushed.

"Kenickie?" It was my turn to act appalled.

"Yeah, I thought he was cool."

"Because he almost got his girlfriend knocked up? Or because he chickened out the day of the big race?" Oh, Kenicke was not a good choice.

"I liked his hair." He flushed a deeper shade of red, and I burst out laughing. I couldn't help myself.

Only my boyfriend would like Kenicke better than John Travolta!

Wait a minute! Did I say the B-word? Did I even imply that this man was my boyfriend? Oh, slow down heart, please, do yourself a favor.

"You liked his hair." I shook my head as if to say, *Oh, what am I going to do with you?*

"Yeah, it was somehow more manly than Danny's."

"He was a pig."

"Kinda."

"Rizzo called him a pig."

"Tell me, are you one of those girls that knows the entire movie by heart, line by line?"

"Name one woman my age that doesn't."

"You got me."

We were smiling so much at this point that my face was beginning to hurt. Like a seriously depressed person that stumbles across an old George Carlin act on late-night television, one who realizes that laughter is lightening, and can't help but give in and stare, transfixed by someone paid to make them laugh, I felt that same kind of sudden realization and joy. I couldn't ignore that my face hurt in a way that it hadn't in quite some time.

I could only ease into it, like a toe into frigid water, and hope that my body would get adjusted to the temperature, and that I wouldn't need to extricate myself from the situation and run back to the shore.

The night wore on and we talked about anything and everything, often agreeing on things, and finding out more about each other with every uttered word, or in his case anyway, wave of the unfettered hand.

"If I tied your hands behind your back, could you finish this conversation?" I interjected at one point.

"Am I Italian?" He countered.

"I'll take that as a no," I answered, and the flirting went on. Soon it was time to vacate the premises. He paid the check and we exited the diner out onto Second Avenue.

"I have an idea, but it'll only work if you're not afraid of heights." He suggested that we continue our night elsewhere.

"I'm afraid of suspended height, not roller coasters." I tried unsuccessfully to explain this to him, and he got it enough to reveal where we were going.

"Well, I was going to take you to the *top-top-top-top-top of The Empire State Building!*" He was mimicking a NYC radio DJ now and I caught on fast.

"Omigod! Is that from Z100?" NYC's all-hits radio station that broadcast from...the top of the Empire State Building.

"Actually, I think they pawned it off from the old HOT 103, do you remember that?"

Did I ever! In my teenage years, Annemarie and I, and basically the entire high school class would tilt at windmills in order to get enough reception Upstate to listen to it. I remembered now that you could get it in clearly at my house, good unless it rained at Am's, and the car was sketchy. I could vividly recall how much we loved the music; we thought we were so cool listening to a New York City radio station, and we loved knowing all the hits way before they hit our tiny little Upstate Hits station. I would pray for The Monster to go away on a bender every time they played 'The Saturday Night Dance Party,' never wanting to invite my friends over unless I knew he was gone.

I shook the memory and chose instead to remember the music. I told Paul how we were addicted to it Upstate, and I felt linked to him in a weird sort of way, just to think that we had grown up listening to the same radio station.

"Wait!" He halted us both in the middle of Second Avenue. "Before we proceed, I need to know if you even want to go there."

"Yes, I'd love to." I thought it romantic, albeit another snapshot from *Sleepless in Seattle.*

"Okay. Second question: do you want to walk?"

"I would love to walk." It was a beautiful night and even though the famous skyscraper was probably twenty blocks away from where we were, I was vaguely aware of the fact that I had just inhaled about 70,000 calories in one sitting.

"Now, back to HOT 103...tell me you love Freestyle." His eyelashes fluttered and shadows fell across his face. He looked great in the streetlights, in any lights.

"I love Freestyle." For those of you who don't know, 'Freestyle' was a style of music that swept the Tri-state area in the late Eighties. It was a New York phenomenon, a Latin-infused style of dance/disco type music with a fabulous beat and strong vocals wailing about love lost and broken hearts.

I used to eat it up; all my high school friends loved it, but none like I. Had I found a partner in listening crime?

"YOU DO NOT!" He threw his hands up in the air as he screamed this, happy as I had ever seen him. The usual grin took over his whole face, and he actually hopped up and down on one foot in the middle of the sidewalk. "I never, *never, never,* in my entire life thought that I would meet someone who loves Freestyle, at least not like I do. I still love it. When I go home to visit my parents and my old friends, I still blast it in the car, and force all my buddies to listen to TKA before we go out."

"Yeah, TKA was one of my favorites." TKA was a group that stood for three guy's first names, the undisputed Kings of Freestyle. "I saw them in concert once."

"YOU DID NOT!" He was whooping it up now, genuinely pleased to find a confidante that knew all the words to all the same songs.

Music is such a personal thing, isn't it?

It draws forth so many emotions, it summons up memories that we may sometimes want to keep buried, and it enables us to see into another person's soul.

I can recollect one of The Monster's tattoos: The Famous/Infamous Rolling Stones logo, the red, raucous lips with the infernal tongue hanging out.

To this very day, I still could not listen to any single song by the group without flinching uncontrolled, and conjuring up images better left forgotten.

"I did." I nodded, recalling the night that Annemarie and I had driven out to Long Island to see them in a gargantuan night club that went the way of acid-washed jeans. "In fact, the place that I saw them at was on Long Island…you might have even have been there."

"No, I was probably up at BC by then, because if I had known they were out on Long Island, I definitely would have been there." He flashed me the look of a little boy who missed the ice cream truck.

"They were great, but the club was crowded, and being a little on the short side, I really couldn't see very well. But the music was thumping, and Cynthia showed up as a surprise guest." Cynthia was the Cher of the Freestyle set.

"I loved her, and Coro, and George Lamond, and Judy Torres." He was swept up in the nostalgia.

"So tell me why you didn't take one of those CD's to the moon."

"Because my choices are more long-term. I love Freestyle, but in a reminiscent, juvenile sort of way. It's not the type of stuff that would endure, on the moon, forever and ever. I mean, would it be easier to explain Lisa Lisa and The Cult Jam to aliens, or Billy Joel?" He asked pointedly.

"Do you believe in aliens?"

"Answer the question." He challenged.

"Answer mine." I challenged him right back.

"No." He stopped a minute.

"I think Billy Joel might be a little easier for them to digest, him being a local boy and all," I was trying to mock his fervor for Billy Joel, but he was stopped in the middle of the sidewalk again, the same place he had found me, and our eyes caught. Something happened in that moment, electricity in the air, and we stood there for a second or a million seconds, nobody knew, when he suddenly reached out and took my hand in his own.

"Is this okay?" His voice had shifted down a notch or twelve, but I couldn't verbalize anything at that moment, so I looked at him and nodded my response, my hand shaking in his own.

I forced my hand to still. It was as easy as stopping my heart from beating.

We continued down a few blocks more, his hand covering mine, the conversation resuming slowly, a different kind of air settling between us.

"Look!" I pointed up towards the lights, the city's emblem shining down on us, the lights lit tonight in red, white, and blue.

"It's great, isn't it." He grabbed my hand and led me towards the building. "C'mon!" Like a child, he dragged me into the building and towards the long line of people waiting to go up to The Observation Deck.

"It seems like everyone had the same great idea," I pointed out, smiling in spite of the line.

"This line is moving!" He exclaimed, determined to wow me with the city lights.

"I'm fine with it," I reassured him, not wanting him to think I had been complaining about the line. I shot him a full-fledged grin, drinking him in with my eyes.

Soon we were at the front of the line. He paid our way and we got on the next available elevator. Up, up, up we went, his hand still squeezing my own.

We walked outside and stood there in awe for several seconds, the city lights demanding a modicum of respect, and as we drank it all in silently, I felt a slight pull on my arm.

"Come over here," Paul urged me as he saw a spot open up near the edge. There were so many people standing up there, speaking in all sorts of different languages, oooohing and aaaahing and posing for pictures, each one dreaming a little piece of their American dream. We stood together by the railing, and a long moment passed before either one of us tried to utter even one syllable.

"It's so beautiful," I finally said, breaking the silence.

"So are you," his voice was lower now, and he titled my head towards him with a gentle finger under my chin. I knew before he moved in towards me, I knew it like I knew my name, I knew that he was going to kiss me.

When the kiss happened, it wasn't what I expected. He was so tentative that it made me more nervous, and I almost pulled away a little, not sure of what he was trying to do. I told myself to calm down and simply be present–enjoy the moment–and just a few seconds later; his kiss became something far more sweet and rewarding. We stood there for an indeterminable amount of time, the funny accents blocked out of my mind, the crowds all but forgotten.

"Danielle, you are fantastic." He paused a second, kissed my forehead, looked up at the stars, then back down to me and directly into my eyes. "I…ah, I've been wanting to do that for some time now," he hesitated, then asked again, "Is this okay?"

Was he picking up on some weird hesitancy vibe that was buried so deep that he could only pick up on it through physical contact? I was more than aware that he had asked me that when he took my hand also, and although I was charmed by his chivalry, I didn't want him to think that I was anything less than interested, and I wanted him to touch me more than words could even express.

"I'm fine." I looked deeper into his eyes and then I went for broke and started kissing him again. I told myself it was to reassure him, but I hadn't kissed anybody in so long that I was feeling a little heady with the power I found in hand.

He responded, our lips and tongues melding together, coming up for air only once it became absolutely necessary.

"No how do we top this?" He chuckled, his eyes crinkling, hands once again doing all the talking as they swept the skyscape.

"We don't." I shot him my best cat-ate-the-canary grin, realizing I was just as serious as I was joking. How do you top a fun-filled dinner, one heart calling out to another, a kiss filled with longing, and the New York City skyline practically at your feet?

"Look, there's where I'm going to be working on Monday," he pointed towards the Twin Towers.

"So that way must be the ocean," I pointed East.

"Not to mention Long Island." He pointed in the general direction of the island.

"West is…" I spun around to face our neighboring state.

"And North…" he gestured towards Upstate.

I turned my back on it.

"It's getting late," I announced, forever the killjoy, after about another half an hour had passed. I still needed to catch the train home before they shut down for the night.

"Yeah, I guess I should get you back." He looked wistfully at the skyline one last time before we descended. "Do you realize that there are people that will never see New York City? I can't imagine it; but there are people living in The United States today that have absolutely no interest in ever seeing my beautiful city."

Did I realize it? I felt like saying, *HA! I knew people that lived in Upstate New York–the same state, mind you–that would never see this building or any or all this city had to offer.*

I opted for, "Oh, I know." And then I added, "*Your city?*"

"Yeah," he replied with chagrin.

"It's my city too," I warned him. Hell, I had to fight to get here. He had just to move inland a few miles.

"I can share." We shared another little glance as we made our way out onto the sidewalk. He had resumed the hand-holding again, and unlike the first lightning bolt that had flashed its way through my body, it felt comfortable now, and I felt myself shelving the nervousness and enjoying walking by his side.

"Let's walk up Park back to Grand Central," I suggested. There was very little foot traffic on Park Avenue at this time of night, and the avenue always looked pretty with the trees all lit up in the middle.

"You're sure no cab?"

"No, it's still so nice out. We'll have all winter to cab it." And again I blanched inwardly, not wanting him to think that I was assuming we would be together come winter, just saying it as one New Yorker to another.

He seemed content, and we walked the length of Park together at a leisurely pace, hand in hand, as if we had known each other a very long time. When he dropped me off at my train track, he deposited another kiss on my forehead, and with a swift kiss on the lips, he disappeared into the depths of Grand Central.

I felt a curious smile playing on my lips the whole way home.

Chapter Twenty-Seven

I woke up to find the same smile plastered across my face, my mind wondering if it had lain there all night while I slept. The flowers were still winking at me from my kitchen counter and I snuggled deeper under the covers, trying to hold on to the feelings and burrow deeper into the memories we had made the night before.

I ran my tongue over my teeth and touched my lips with my finger. I hugged my pillow closer as I remembered the feeling of his lips on my own. Reveling in the moment, I almost didn't hear the phone ring.

Once I realized what the interruption was, I reached over from my bed and pulled the phone from its cradle on my end table to my ear.

"Hello?" I heard my answering machine click on, and I reached out from under the covers once more to shut it off. Ugh, I hate the way I sound on tape. I clicked it off about halfway between the message and the beep. "Hello?" I tried again.

"Good Morning." It was Paul. "I am sitting up in bed, I have the *Wall Street Journal and The New York Times* spread out all around me, a cup of amazingly good Kona coffee on the nightstand, and I can't even remotely concentrate enough to read, or sip, or enjoy anything."

"What's the problem?" I asked, hoping it was the same problem I was having, a giddy grin writing the problem across my face, no words needed, thank you very much.

"It's this girl I know." He paused a second. "I can't seem to get her out of my mind." His voice was suddenly deeper, and richer than in person.

Could it be the Kona?
"Me neither."
"Same girl?"

"Ah-hah," I giggled as I realized what I had inferred. "Yeah," I hesitated. "Ah, not the same girl. Just the same problem."

"So when can I see you again?"

Say right now, you dimwit.

I rebelled against my heart's advice.

"Um, I don't know when," I hedged. Why was I hedging? Lanie would kill me if she knew I was doing this again. I was reneging on the deal: faith, not fear.

"Are you busy right now? I can transport my coffee and myself and even my newspapers to your place."

"I wouldn't like your newspapers anyway," I informed him. I had a serious thing for the comics, and although I was endeared to the Arts and Leisure section of The Times, I usually got that in addition to a local paper that carried the Sunday Comics.

"I know the Journal can be a bit…let's say boring, for lack of a better word, but…everybody loves The Sunday Times. Even if they just use it to bench press." He sounded so cute, and I couldn't help but give into another chuckle as he referred to the fact that The Sunday New York Times was generally anywhere from five pounds to three tons.

"It's not that either paper is boring, it's just that I have a rare case of Comicsitis, and I have to fulfill that need every chance I get on a Sunday." I proceeded to 'fess up about my love for the Sunday Comics.

"So let me fill that need for you. I'll pick up yet another paper, jump on the Metro-North train, and we can read the Comics and drink coffee together." He was insistent, and although part of me wanted to scream, a larger slice of my heart responded and I found myself giving my place a quick once-over, trying to determine how much I would have to clean in order to have human beings over.

"Did you eat yet?" I was stalling, trying to figure out if I just wanted to revel in the last wisp of his scent, or to have another encounter with the man himself.

"No! In fact, I can stop at the bagel store and pick up bagels. Of course, I may have to bring my *Radio Flyer* wagon up in order to carry all this…the seven-pound New York Times, the Wall Street Journal, The Post or the News, or whoever carries the Comics, a dozen bagels, a block of cream cheese…" he was teetering into an endless diatribe when I decided to make an executive decision.

"Okay, okay, come up. I give in!" I didn't realize the words had escaped my mouth until they did, and I was glad he couldn't see the blush that was currently crawling up my face.

"I'll be up there in an hour." He sounded as if he were just waiting for the green light.

"Do you need a train schedule?" I ambled out of bed in order to get my own. What was I doing? Now I needed to dust and clean the bathroom, not to mention pick out an outfit, all in less than an hour.

"I scaffed one last night before your train got in. Should I call you as the train pulls in?" I could picture him then, rounding up his papers, packing them all in a bag.

"That sounds good." I was caught off guard for half a second, my heart sending my brain the message that he may have had this planned, grabbing the train schedule in advance and all. So what if he did? My brain and my heart were at war: wasn't every woman my age busy complaining that no man wanted a commitment, that men were unable to think ahead, that they all scared easily? Here I had a man who was planning to spend as much time as possible with me.

I willed my heart to tell my brain to shut up, got off the phone, and shifted my butt into fifth gear. I dusted and sprayed and spiffed up my tiny little place, measured out some coffee and jumped into the shower. Once I dried myself off, I stood in front my closet for far too long, wasting precious minutes trying to decide what to wear.

Danielle, what would you wear on a typical Sunday?

Sweats. Jeans.

Nothing seemed right. I wanted to wear something I would wear on any given Sunday, I didn't want to be fake, and yet I detested sloppy.

I settled on a clean pair of standard blue jeans, an ice blue short-sleeved sweater, and tan sandals. Not a minute after I was dressed, the phone rang again.

It was him.

"I have arrived!" He announced with fervor, and I felt my heart rate accelerate all over again, at the mere sound of his voice.

"I'm on my way," I assured him. I jumped into the Cavalier as if I was saddling up a horse in a hurry, threw her in reverse, and sang along to the radio the whole way to the train station. Whatever reservations I had felt disappeared the moment I saw him.

"Where's your wagon?" I teased as he opened up the passenger door, unloading a humungous bag into my backseat.

"Would you believe they wouldn't let me take it on the train?" His tone incredulous, his gleaming smile blinding me more than the midafternoon sunshine. He leaned over and gave me a quick kiss. "Hi."

"Hi," I responded, my heart thudding, and I suddenly felt as if I was standing outside myself, watching this impulsive girl have a good time and be ill at ease.

Who was she?

I'm working on it.

"Hi," he repeated, and then leaned in again to give me a deeper kiss. We stayed that way for what must have been maybe a full minute, but seemed like eons, his lips probing my own, and the warmth something I wished I could bottle.

"Hell of a greeting," I said as he pulled away, and I'm sure I blushed just for good measure. Besides the greeting, his appearance was yet another part I found so easy to warm up to: a pair of worn jeans that screamed comfortable, a loose button-down shirt, and a baseball cap with the Yankees logo. I was glad I wore the jeans.

"I feel better now." A smile played across the same lips I had just kissed.

"I'm so glad." I patted him on the knee.

"Really, you solved my problem." His eyelashes fluttered, and he shot me an innocent face.

"About the girl?" I was following.

"Yup." He said no more, so I started the car and found myself narrating as I wound my way home.

"You seem to really like it here," he observed as I told him a little history about Westchester County.

I stifled a laugh. "You could say that." Oh, if you only knew.

"Where did you used to live again?" His interest seemed genuine, but I cut him off at the pass.

"Upstate." I turned the wheel around a curve and pointed towards the stone wall coming up on our right.

Up ahead there is a magnificent stone wall that surrounds a house that I can never get more than a glimpse of, directly around the corner from my apartment, and it bears mentioning to any newcomer.

"Is that *one* house behind there?" He sounded as awed as I felt the first time I spied it.

"I believe it is." I made a left and in less than a mile arrived at my humble abode. "This is my mansion."

"I like it," He tossed me yet another beaming smile as he hefted his backpack from the backseat onto his shoulder.

"I'll give you the ten-cent tour." I made my way to the door, opened it with a flourish, and stepped back. I waved my hands across my studio apartment in one deft Abracadabra move. "That's the tour!"

He indulged me with a laugh. "It's cute."

Small=cute.

That's one thing I always hated about being short. I was never tall enough to be any of the good words, like *beautiful, gorgeous,* or even *hot.*

I was cute.

Anyway…

"The coffee's ready to roll." I indicated the small/cute machine on my counter.

"I also brought you up a pound of the good stuff," he stated as he unveiled a one-pound bag of what looked to be Kona coffee.

"Oh, would you rather me put that in?" I hadn't brewed the coffee yet and could quite simply transfer his grounds with my own.

"No, no, whatever you have is fine." He waved his hands again in an attempt to dismiss my hospitality. "I brought…" he struggled to get the brown paper bag out of his knapsack. "…two onion bagels in a separate bag, two sesames and one cinnamon raisin. I wasn't sure what you liked. I also brought," he dove in again, "a small tub of cream cheese with scallion, and another of plain cream cheese."

"Wow, you've really outdone yourself," I complimented him as he kept depositing things from the bag onto my table. The two papers he already had, plus a *Post* and *The Daily News.* Both were wrapped in an outer layer of comics.

"I tried." He scratched his head underneath his cap and then reaffixed it. "I figured it was the least I could do, after inviting myself over and all."

"It was." I couldn't hide the grin.

"Like I said…" he smiled back, then trailed off for a second. "Are those the flowers?" He pointed over to where the flowers stood on my counter.

"No, those are from the other guy." I turned my back to him and began taking mugs out of the cupboard. As if.

"Oh, I have competition? I like sports! Tell me about the other guy," He chided.

"His name is Herb." It was all I could do to not burst out laughing.

"Herb? Herb! A guy named Herb is *not* competition," he laughed a deep laugh that took up residence inside my heart.

"Herbie could very well be competition," I insisted, as I took two different jars of jam out of my refrigerator.

"No, he can't." He was standing behind me, close enough that I could feel his breath on the back of my neck. I felt his arms envelop me and I fell into his backwards hug for a moment. I turned into him, placed the jam on my tiny bistro kitchen table and hugged him again, forward this time, in a way that felt as if we were experts at hugging.

"Okay, you win," I whispered into the crook of his neck, and held myself there for a minute longer. I didn't want to let him go, and as I acknowledged that feeling, I shuddered just a little to think that I had come to feel this way so quickly.

The coffee machine rang, as it had a little built-in chime to let the maker know that their caffeine injection was currently ready. We broke apart at that point, but he kept his eyes on me as I made my way over to the machine, and I felt him the same way you feel a warm fire in the corner of the room.

"Should we toast these suckers?" He held up a bagel and motioned towards my toaster oven.

"Yes, we should. Which one are you having?"

"I say we both have onion bagels with scallion cream cheese, that way we both smell and we won't notice each other's bad breath when we kiss."

"I am overcome by your logic."

"Does that mean yes?" He was hopeful.

"Yes." I poured the coffee and set it up on the table. "Sugar, Sweet-n-Low, Equal, Milk, Vanilla creamer?"

"Ah, are you always this prepared?"

"I try to be."

"You are too much." He fixed his coffee with sugar and vanilla creamer, and then leaned closer to keep an eye on the toasting bagels. Once they were done, we enjoyed our impromptu brunch at the table, and then moved to the couch with the various papers.

I got up and fed a CD into my stereo before I settled in.

"This is Jim Brickman," I decided to share a moon CD with him.

"It's nice, very Sunday-ish," he commented as he sat back and listened for a minute. "So what's your favorite?" He indicated the papers.

"Well, I have Comic Categories." I had his rapt attention, so I continued. "All-time favorite would have to be Snoopy. Peanuts, actually, the whole crowd–but I have always and will always call that particular comic strip 'Snoopy.' Then, on an intellectual level, I love B.C. There's usually a pretty good message woven into the strip, but you have to be astute enough to see it. As a single girl, I love Cathy. Another all-time favorite is Calvin and Hobbes, although very few papers run that strip anymore. I have all the books though." I pointed over to a bookshelf across from the couch where we were sitting.

"You are a GEEK!" He was laughing at me. "You have Comic Categories?" His look was incredulous.

"So?" Great comeback, Danielle. I shot him my most wounded look because I was a trifle wounded. Here he was, wooing me with bagels and newspapers, so I open up my heart and what do I get?

I get called names!

"So, I have never met anyone like you in my entire life. A grown adult that admits to liking the comics more than most five-year-olds do?" He shook his head in disbelief.

"Comics are the last pure form of entertainment in the universe." I argued my position.

"You're right. But what about Prince Valiant? I mean, I didn't hear you mention Prince Valiant. Or is he too violent?" He countered.

"I have never, in my entire life, known anyone who read Prince Valiant." I said this with the assurance of someone who had studied this statistic.

"Neither have I." He paused a second, then leaned in a little closer. "I think it's cute."

"You're making fun of me." I slid away about an inch.

"I am. But I am doing it in a purely fun way, not an evil way, and the truth of the matter is that it warms my heart. I think it's cute, I think it's great, and there's something very original about it. Like I said, I have never met anyone like you before." His eyes were drawing beads on my own, and I found my heart pounding against the walls of my chest again, my lips anticipating him. He leaned forward as expected, and wrapped his arms around me once again, this time more than a hug, transferring from his body to my own a feeling of warmth and home.

I shook him loose after a few minutes. "Is that a good thing?" I asked with both my mouth and my eyes, as I tried as hard as possible to see into his soul.

"That is a great thing." He kissed me again, a quick one, and then turned his attention to the papers before us. "So show me your stuff."

I opened up the first paper with comics and continued to narrate my various opinions, likes, and dislikes. He seemed almost as animated as the comics themselves, agreeing and then arguing different points with me, all the while seeming to enjoy himself as much as I was.

"I have a theory about this one," I pointed to a one-frame strip entitled *Close to Home*. "Do you see the way the characters are drawn?"

He nodded.

"Do you remember Gary Larson's *The Far Side?*" He nodded again. "Well, I have a conspiracy theory about this one."

"A conspiracy theory?" He arched an eyebrow and pretended to stroke a mustache that didn't exist.

"I believe that Gary Larson still draws this strip. See, the guy's name is John McPherson. But do you see the way the character's noses are drawn?" I popped up and grabbed a Far Side Comics book from my shelf. I opened up to a random page and then placed the book next to the strip in the paper. "They're almost identical."

"You're right. Although Larson could be his mentor," Paul suggested.

"True. True, but do you remember when Stephen King started writing as Richard Bachman? He did it just to see if his talent was selling, or his name. This guy, McPherson, didn't come out until after Larson had 'retired.'" I gave him a knowing look.

"You really do know your comics." He returned my look with a look of reverence, and then a totally goofy grin.

"I warned you, I have Comicsitis!" I decided to laugh along with him.

"I always liked Beetle Bailey myself," He interjected.

I made a face.

"All boys like Beetle Bailey." A sweeping generalization steeped in truth.

"Is there any one you don't like?" Paul inquired.

"Yes. Besides Prince Valiant, I'm not really into Doonesbury."

"Too liberal?"

"Too political. I like comics for fun."

"Gotcha." Our eyes clicked, and he held my gaze for a long minute. The phone rang then, and I looked over at it, but decided to let whomever it was leave a message on the machine.

They deserved to get the machine for interrupting us.

"You wanna get that?" He asked in a conciliatory tone.

"No, it can go to the machine." I passed it off as no big deal. It wasn't. Now that he was here, everybody else could take a number.

"So tell me what else you like." His gaze was intent on mine again, the phone ringing ceased, the interrupter relegated to speaking into a virtual microphone.

"In terms of the Comics?" I racked my brain for a second, thinking I had went through them all.

"In terms of everything." He blushed a little then, and it endeared me to him all the more. He started again. "You know, I must confess that I'm rather crazy about you, and I find myself thinking about you all the time. I guess I just want to know everything there is to know about you."

His comment was innocent enough, his desire palpable, but it sent a chill up my spine nonetheless, because I was able to see shades of David in the words that he said. Plus, let's face it here: I was not cast in the starring role on a movie set, I was not some glamorous supermodel that men sought after with the tenacity of a defense attorney trying to get off a celebrity client, I was just me, Danielle. Danielle D'Ambrusco, an ordinary girl from Upstate New York, one who wasn't so sure that he or any man would stick around if they knew *the whole story.*

You so sure, Paul? You want to know *everything?* The whole enchilada? I have one question first: How much can you handle? Do you want to know about the father who doesn't know my favorite anything? Or would you rather hear about the mother who married the crack addict, who I could not defend, who ruined any chance I had at a so-called normal life? Be careful here: do you really want to know how I still sweep the house, the refrigerator, how I triple-lock the door behind me every night, even though I live alone and have done so for quite some time now?

I must have lost myself in these combative thoughts for more than a minute, my response time slow, because he suddenly reached out to tilt my chin, forcing me to look in those penetrating eyes.

"Am I going too fast?" His eyes were riveted on me, but his voice was soft, as if he realized that he had just crossed a line that he didn't anticipate.

More like trip wire. Suddenly, an indelible line was drawn: don't tell me that unless you mean it; you made me feel uncomfortable because I don't know you well enough yet to know if you mean it or not.

"You're not going too fast." I shook my head solemnly, trying to gather together words that were neither too harsh nor too soft. How could I make him understand what he had just triggered inside me? "Well, you are a little." I was scared. I could feel that same old heaving feeling in my chest. Stop it, I told myself. *Stop it!*

"I'm sorry," he took his hands in mine, and gently covered my top hand with his own. "Sometimes I think things, and they just pop right out of my head. There's no on/off switch, no censor, barely a filter. Especially when I really like something, or someone…I tend to go a little overboard, and I let my mouth run a little wild. I don't mean to scare you, I mean, I didn't mean to…" I saw he was struggling, so I cut him off at the pass.

"Paul, I understand. I do. Sometimes, it's a little hard for me to believe that people have a genuine interest in something without an ulterior motive. Can you understand that?" I was speaking in vagarities, but that's the best I could do at the moment in order to get my point across.

"I can appreciate it." I saw the gears turning inside his head. "I never even thought I would meet you. It's like a huge bonus that we have so many little things in common.

I guess I'm eager to see how much of the big stuff matches too."

He was honest and I loved that about him. There was no pretense, and my heart continued to mete out the same daring rhythm that said I should give him a shot, and trust him, even if it was just a little bit.

"Okay, one big question." I challenged him.

"Whaddaya mean, 'one big question?'" He looked confused.

"Ask me a question about something big. I'll answer one question, right now, on one big topic." I was a tad nervous, but I was presenting it in a way that was lackadaisical and fun, and I hoped he would just play along.

"Hmm. Wow, I wonder which one I should ask first. The big questions are: Sex, Family, God, Politics, and Future." He ticked them off on one hand. "I'll go with God."

"Alex, he'll take God for FIVE HUNDRED!" I made it sound as if it were a game show choice.

He indulged me with a laugh.

"Okay, the question is: Do you believe in God?" He straightened up in his seat, giving me his full attention.

"I do." I wasn't sure whether this was the 'right' or the 'wrong' answer to his question, but I didn't care. I wasn't about to deny my faith or get off on the wrong foot by trying to tell him whatever it was that he wanted to hear. I did that with David; enough said.

"That's it? You do? Care to elaborate?" He was fishing.

"Well, I believe in Jesus. I was brought up Catholic initially, but then…" and I went on to tell him my story.

"Do you attend church now?" He appeared to be truly interested.

"There is a church down the road that I sometimes visit, but I have yet to find one that really fits yet." I missed my old pastor, my old church, but it was all part of the old life that I wasn't ready to get into just yet. "What about you?"

Always safer to turn the tables.

"I attend church regularly when I'm home. I've been slacking a lot since I moved in to the city, but part of the reason for that is because I haven't really found my kind of church in the city yet. I know that sounds like a lame excuse, but it seems as if I am also looking for the perfect fit." He went on to describe what made his old church so comfortable and we compared notes about various Protestant churches we had each attended.

"Do people automatically assume that you're Catholic, just because you're Italian?" I asked him.

"Yeah, I get that a lot." He went on to tell me about how his mother had grown up Lutheran and his Dad was Catholic, but because Dad loved Mom they decided to get married in and then attend her church, and then they both decided to attend his home church together when Paul and his brother were preteens. "I think that Mom and Dad feared that if we didn't throw down roots in a serious church prior to our teenage years, that they'd have a handful with the two of us. So they started attending Christ Tabernacle when I was about nine or ten, and they've never looked back since. My mother is the chairwoman of almost every board!"

"So you've said." The June Cleaveresque this woman belied positively scared the crap right out of me.

We continued to chat from there, one topic leading right to another, none too painful, none too touchy, and even the God thing seemed easy after the fact.

Now we still had to get through Sex, Family, Politics, and Future.

The next time we looked at the clock, we were astonished to find out that it was four o'clock in the afternoon. After commiserating and checking the train schedule back to the city, he decided that he would head home in an hour.

"Which means we have time left for ice cream!" He rubbed his hands together like a little boy, eager to fill every last minute with fun and excitement.

"Ice cream?" I got up and checked the freezer. "Sorry, Paul, I'm fresh out."

"No, I didn't mean that you should make me some. Tell me that there's a Friendly's nearby."

"There are two different towns that have a Friendly's, either of which are about fifteen minutes from here." I explained to him that Armonk was a historic town, therefore preserved, read: no fast food, zero chains.

"Well, I must admit that Friendly's is the one thing I miss from suburbia. Let's recheck the schedule and go indulge in a *Reese's Pieces Sundae.*" He rechecked the train schedule and decided he could catch either a five or six o'clock train.

"You're sure?" I asked him. He started his new job tomorrow and I didn't want to horn in on whatever time he needed to unwind before the big day.

"I'm always sure about ice cream," he said with a wink.

"I'll drive," I joked and then bemoaned my fate inwardly. Between the bagels and the ice cream, I would have to spend at least twelve extra hours at the gym this week. Maybe thirteen.

He insisted on leaving the papers and all the brunch stuff with me, so he helped me clean up quickly and then we left, he with a decidedly smaller bag on his shoulder, myself with a childish excitement in my heart, a smile plastered across my face not for the first time that day.

I convinced him to share the sundae, our excitement spilling over the same as the chocolate sauce. One spoon in and I was glad he had recommended it. We flirted as the cool treats and candies shimmied their way down our throats, and ended the day talking about candies that we loved as children that they (whoever 'they' were) no longer made.

When I dropped him off at the train station, I knew that I was glad he had come up, and even happier that I wasn't as scared as I thought I would be. His kiss goodbye was comforting, and longing in a way that defies words. I left him off and I drove home with his scent in the car and his touch on my mind.

I let myself back in to the house and sighed, determined to finish the book I was currently reading and wind down before the workweek began again. I didn't even check my answering machine before I drifted off into an early evening nap, dreaming of Paul's lips moving tenderly all over my face.

When I woke, I read for a while. Paul called. Lanie called. I had a hot cup of tea. I checked the door before I fell into a fitful sleep, once again forgetting to check the message on the machine.

When I finally woke the next morning, I could have beat myself up for not checking it sooner.

Chapter Twenty-Eight

"What happened?" I demanded of her, my hair dripping into the mouthpiece of the phone as the makeshift towel turban fell from my head.

"He's threatening me." She was sobbing now, incoherent in her hysterical way, the way she got when she just couldn't take any more.

"Start at the beginning," I instructed her, trying to use a calm tone in the hopes that she might calm down also. Oh why, oh why had I not picked up the phone yesterday? It was an honest oversight, but so unlike me that I could do nothing less than loathe myself as my heart pounded fury and her tale unfolded.

"Well, the first time he called I accepted the charges." My mother gulped on the other end. I knew instinctively that she was afraid to admit even this much, knowing that I had a very low tolerance for anything Monster-related.

"What did he say to you?" I demanded, my blood pumping furiously, water sluicing down my back in accordance to the beat of my raging heart. I had just jumped out of the shower, was in the midst of rushing around to get ready for work, and I noticed the answering machine light blinking at me. I ended up having two messages from my mother, which is what prompted me to call her right away. The one she had left while Paul and I were chatting on the couch, but the other had apparently been left while we were out getting ice cream, and the by the time she left the second one, she sounded positively awful.

"He said…that he's up for parole soon. He said that he wants to come back." Her fear hung between us, across the many miles and the phone line, but I shut myself off as much as I could and tried to deal with her as rationally as possible.

"You don't want him back." I told her, I didn't ask her, because I knew damn well that if I asked her, she might cave. "I thought he was going away for a very long time." The truth is, I had never asked her, but I had inferred that from her roundabout conversations and had more likely than not talked myself into believing that over truth.

"He should be," Her voice was more coherent, but still trembling. "But they said since he's not violent…"

"Not violent! Who the hell are '*they*' kidding? I mean, what the hell are they thinking? What did he say to you?" I insisted, trying but failing miserably to keep my rage in check. I wasn't there; I couldn't help her, I could barely help her when I lived with her. I took a deep breath and forced myself to calm down a bit. Another deep breath and I said, "Is this what he told you?"

"Yes." She sniffed.

"Well, then he could be lying." I tapped my fingers on the small table that held the phone. The Monster was famous for being a Liar Extraordinaire: anything to get a fix. He had once stopped by Annemarie's parent's house when only her Mom was home, told her mother a sob story about my mother and I being stuck on the road in her car, and could he borrow fifty dollars for the tow? She gave him the money and The Monster took off for four days straight. What was his angle now? Or was he simply not through torturing her?

"He could be," she acquiesced and then cleared her throat. "The point is that he kept calling. The first call was collect, and I accepted the charges because he said he was Rich, then he started with me right away, taunting me, and saying how he was coming back whether I wanted him here or not. I told him it was over, I told him that he should start a new life once he gets out of jail. Then I told him to please leave me alone, but he called me all day, and once I started not picking up the phone, he left nasty messages on my answering machine. He was probably using a phone card."

First of all, Rich is my mother's cousin who lives in California. Why she thought that Rich, who is what his name implies, would call her collect is beyond me. Second, I can't exactly say that I don't understand why The Monster would believe her now; she has thrown him out and told him 'It's Over' more times than O.J. said he didn't do it.

Why would he believe her now? Back down? Never. Especially because the 'It's Over' scenes didn't begin until I left, years after she had perfected her backing down pattern, thousands of scenes after she established herself as someone who could not stick up for her child, much less herself.

I sighed audibly. I tried to collect my thoughts, but my mind was flying in twelve different directions. Did the jail or did *he* think that he was non-violent? Would they really release him early, only to set him out to be my mother's torturer, as well as a further menace to society? Was there anything I could do about it, a parole board I could go before, in a converted gymnasium with a bunch of sour-faced panelists like in the movies?

"I think you should change your phone number," I began thinking as logically as I could, starting with the easiest thing I knew to do.

"I can't do that." She brushed aside my suggestion the same way she had brushed me aside.

"Why not?" I ambushed her, those two words scaring even myself as they leapt from my mouth laced with venom.

"Because…" she trailed off a minute, no excuse forthcoming. "It's such a pain, and then I'd have to let everybody know."

"So? You let everybody know! You freaking call every friend and relative you have, you let them know your new, *unlisted* number, what would that take? Three minutes?" I was so angry at her incompetence that I was almost spitting.

"I just…" she was present, in all her pathetic splendor, silently waiting for me to take control. Or perhaps not? Perhaps she just wanted a shoulder to cry on? I was the wrong person, however, because after her countless episodes of inaction, I would insist on some action.

"You just what?" I sighed again, taking deep breaths, mentally trying to slow myself down. "You just can't tell him no? Are you afraid? Did you save any of the messages he left you on the tape? You could take them to the police…he's harassing you; maybe you can do something about that. What about an order of protection?"

"An order of protection is just a piece of paper. A piece of paper can't protect me. I watch *Law and Order*, you know. The dead girl always had an order of protection." She insisted.

If it weren't so sad, I would laugh.

"You have a point, but it helps. If you could put together some proof of him antagonizing you, then the wardens in the jail or the police, once he gets out, would be forced to pay a little attention to him." I ran a hand through my hair, trying to unknot it as it dried naturally.

"I just want to be left alone." My mother whispered. She sounded defeated, but then again she always did, whenever The Monster was the topic of conversation.

"I know that, Mom, and I want to believe you, but you've got to do something to get there." I urged her. "I'll find out about changing your number today."

"All right," She conceded. I heard a sharp intake of breath on the other end, followed by a sigh, and then she whispered again. "Thank you."

"For what?" I hadn't done anything yet. "Mom, I'll call you later." I hung up the phone then and speed-dialed Lanie's cell. As it rang, I calculated which train I could feasibly make next without cracking a rib or spraining an ankle in order to make it to work on time.

"Lane, it's me. Had a little Mom crisis, so I'm running late, but I should still be able to catch the 8:32, so I'll see you around 9:30ish." The train ride was only about forty minutes, but you have to allow for the X factor, so I left her that message and then ended up finishing getting dressed as soon as possible.

My mind was moving faster than my hands as I grabbed my gym bag, pocketbook, double-locked the door behind me and made my way out to my chariot. I would call Verizon later and see about a call-blocking system for her phone, and at the very least, I would get her Caller-ID. Would she still be tempted to pick up the phone? I shook my head, trying to abate my growing frustration, knowing deep down that there was little I could do about that. I would also have to call some Upstate services, find out about procuring an order of protection, and I reminded myself about contacting the jail also. The only problem is: whom do you ask for? *Hi, Mr. Correction Officer in Charge of Abusive Husbands and Drug Addicts, could you please tell me what The Monster's status is? Oh, what? You have a lot of Monsters there? Yes, I know…it must be confusing.*

Absurdity reigned supreme. As far as I was concerned, I shouldn't have to know any of this stuff; nobody should. What my mother needed more than anything was therapy. She would never be able to move on if she still felt compelled to pick up the phone every time he decided to call, if she still shivered at the mere thought of him being back in the real world.

As I situated myself on the train, I realized that she didn't feel as if she had a choice. He had controlled her for so long, even from a jail cell hundreds of miles away, she still felt as if he could control her. Therapy would give her strength. I knew her faith gave her strength, but I firmly believed that therapy would release her. I made a mental note to self to ask Constance about how best to suggest therapy to someone who may be opposed.

Once the train pulled in to Grand Central, I allowed my thoughts to shift temporarily to Paul. There would be no smiling face to greet me as I crossed Lexington Avenue today, but I hoped that he was happy and having a good first day.

I knew I loved him, I knew it like I knew The Monster was evil incarnate, the same way you know things you can't express, monumental truths that your soul speaks to your heart, even if there are no words attached to it.

Hmm.

I speed-dialed Lanie again, seeing if she needed a shot of caffeine before I got locked in the hole/office with her for hours on end.

"Yes!" She replied as I offered her coffee. "You okay? How's Mom?"

"She'll be alright, and so will I. Lemme just grab a cup o' java real quick, and I'll be right upstairs." I clicked off from her and made my way over to the caffeine altar: Starbucks.

Once the barista slammed our cups on the island, I grabbed all the essentials and high-tailed it over to work. I didn't like being late; even in lieu of a family crisis, being late made me anxious. Being late, being inconsiderate, being wrong…maybe I was too accommodating, maybe I was too interested in having things go a certain way…maybe I was going off on a tangent.

First things first: Work/coffee.

Then: Mom/phone stuff.

Then again: Lanie/catching up.

Next: Paul/a quick hello.

Should Mom take precedence, or should I allow myself to process this a little bit longer? I had advised her not to pick up the phone for the rest of the day; that if I needed to call her for any reason, I would ring once, hang up, and then call back. Our secret code. Then what? Then whatever else presented itself to me? I found I worked better with parameters, and that when I could compartmentalize things I could breathe easier, and think clearer. Mom would get done ASAP; I just needed to get myself in order first.

"So what happened?" Lanie greeted me with this and a concerned set of eyes as I walked in the door to our hole/office.

Lanie knew much, although nobody knew everything, but even so I felt comfortable enough telling her the events that had just transpired. I related to her my mental anguish over not picking up the phone earlier, the fear that I felt knowing that I could not protect my mother from this bastard, and the frustration that I experienced every time I dealt with this never-ending situation.

"So after I get myself situated, slug this coffee down my throat, and perhaps breathe deep several hundred times, I am going to call Verizon and see what phone services are available so that she can perhaps elude the monster." I wound up with this.

"You really don't think you can get her to change her number?" Lanie paused. "That would be optimum."

"I know, Lane, believe me, I know." I shook my head and rolled my neck around on my shoulders. I could feel the stress in my neck, shoulders, and upper back.

"Well, Paul called." Lanie, the bearer of glad tidings, and good news. Her smile sparkled. "I heard that you guys went out for ice cream." She looked like the cat that ate the canary.

"Did he tell you that at the locker, between first and second period?" I teased her, my countenance lightening as I thought of Paul and stretched my neck. All of my stress just seems to collect in one area: where my spine meets my neck. Ah. Oh. What I wouldn't give for a backrub.

"He left his new number." She flitted over to my desk and stuck a Post-it note right next to my phone.

"OK, let me just catch up with work first. You've already got me out of order. I was supposed to check my emails, then fill you in, then call him, and then deal with the phone stuff." I ticked off the things-to-do-list on my fingers.

"I know, I force you to talk to me." Lanie rolled her eyes. She knew enough to know that I only made lists like this when life was getting the best of me.

"You do." I shot her a quick grin and shuffled through a collection of emails, made a few callbacks, and generally got my workday in order. By the time I was caught up, she was in the middle of handling a group reservation, so I decided to call Paul before I finished catching up with her.

The phone rang twice before he picked it up. When he did, he sounded farther away and distracted.

"Hi, it's…" I trailed off a sec, unsure whether to say *'me'* or *'Danielle.'*

"I know who this is!" His voice came into focus and I grinned like a wild woman on the other end of the phone.

"So how's it going?" I wanted to kiss him again. And again.

"So far, so good. I've got Rob showing me the proverbial ropes, and I've got a view that would take your breath away." He took a deep breath before he continued. "I miss you."

As if I wasn't already bowled over by this man. Little did he know, I needed a little sweet talk right now.

"I miss you too." I said this so softly that I wasn't even sure if he heard me.

"So what happened to you this morning?" He asked then.

"I overslept." I offered no other explanation, sure that Lanie hadn't elaborated. If he stuck around, there would be time to clue him in on the drama.

"I hate that. Well, I had the exact opposite problem. I was up all night, pacing, and finally poured myself a glass of red wine about 3 AM, in a desperate attempt to get myself some sleep."

"Did it work?"

"Yup. Although I am sure I'm going to crash tonight. Unless…what are you doing tonight?"

"I have a gym bag that has already threatened me if I don't take it and my butt to the gym tonight."

"Just as well. Can I call you later?"

"Please do."

"Okay, I should run, I can't be slacking off for at least another week." He chuckled and then we said goodbye.

Lanie was still on the phone.

I logged online and went right to the Verizon site. Verizon was *the* phone service for the New York area; from Upstate to New York City, there were no choices to be had. I found a package that included Caller ID, call forwarding, and even call blocking for a minimal price. I decided that the hardest part would not be getting signed on (Have you ever heard of a phone company that wouldn't take your money?) but signing Mom on to the plan.

The next thing I did was get all the different phone numbers I might need to find out about assistance in her area. After about five different people told me I had the wrong department and I got transferred no less than twelve times, I finally landed with a woman from the family court system. She informed me that the complainant would have to make the appearance at the court in order to establish an order of protection.

Looks like I had some more convincing to do. I explained to her quite loosely about the situation at the jail and realized how very little I knew by the time I got off the phone with her. I didn't even know the exact name of the penitentiary The Monster was incarcerated in; I only knew the name of the town.

What I thought was the name of the town anyway.

I sighed. How would I ever convince this woman to get the albatross off of her neck? This is part of the reason that I couldn't easily decide on an order of events this morning; there was urgency only on one end of this seemingly endless conversation. She wasn't even amenable to switching her phone number. By now, I had reams of paper on my desk with information galore. Would it matter?

I must have sighed again, because Lanie looked over at me then and gave me a signal with her forefinger, as if to say one minute.

Less than a minute later she was off the phone.

"You wanna do lunch?"

"Yes. That's not why I was sighing, but I think I could use a break." I scraped my fingers through my hair. I probably needed to talk to Constance before pursuing all of this, but I felt time was of the essence as I didn't want to see her continually harassed.

Ugh.

"Let's switch topics." Lanie suggested on the way out in the elevator, even though neither of us were talking at the moment.

"Let's." I went along with her to a Tossed Salad bar, where you basically just point to what you want and the man behind the counter throws it all together and then tosses your salad for you with your choice of eighty-two different kinds of salad dressing.

"Tell me about the Paulomeister." Lanie tried to say this with a straight face, but she cracked, and I almost snorted some low-fat honey Dijon I was laughing so hard.

It wasn't her best material, but it was just what I needed.

"Only if you give it up about the Bradomeister," I pointed my fork at her and then speared a cuke. "The *Paulomeister*…I think I like it."

"The Bradomeister is…*attentive,* for lack of a better word. I almost don't know what to do with him," Lanie took a deep breath and elaborated as she shook her Snapple. "It seems like he really took to heart everything I said, and he has been a veritably changed man since we talked."

"But? I sense a 'But.'" I pushed.

"But, and there is a but, bigger than mine..." we both smiled. "The but is that it seems contrived."

"How so?" I was surprised. Brad may be a lot of things, but he doesn't come off as a fake.

"I don't know. I can't put my finger on it. But I know that Clara and I will have fun trying to put our fingers on it." She shrugged. "May be self-sabotage."

Ah, now there was a tactic I was familiar with. It seems like every guy I met between David and Paul was an instant case of self-sabotage, and even with Paul I've had to keep myself in check like crazy.

"May be." I quickly agreed, knowing that when she was ready to expound upon this, she would.

"So how was the ice cream?" She had a devilish look on her face.

"Great." I related to her the entire Sunday, and all of the emotions that went along with it. By the time I had segued into Mom and her drama, we needed to get back to work.

"Are we working out tonight?" Lanie asked on the way back up.

"We are kickboxing big-time." I announced with fervor. I couldn't just go along eating bagels and ice cream and falling in love with Paul, neglecting my program.

"You're on."

Chapter Twenty-Nine

"So tell me how your day was," Paul delved right into talking about my day, which endeared me to him even further because God knows his day was bigger than mine.

"It ended up okay," I still hadn't talked to my mother, as I wanted to come at her armed and ready, so I brought the phone information home in its entirety and decided to call her from home. I told him about my kickboxing class.

"I never worked out regularly at a gym. I always played lacrosse, or baseball, or I joined a gym every so often, but I have yet to make the gym a permanent fixture in my lifestyle." He returned.

"I find it to be a great stress reliever." I had started going when I met David, and had stuck with it through the years.

"It is. I actually belonged to a gym through my old company, but I can't say honestly that I went there any more than a dozen times total." Paul sounded almost wistful.

"Does your new company have a gym, or a discounted membership package at a gym downtown?" I suggested.

"They might. I'll have to check." He went on to say that things were quite different where he was right now, and that he hoped he had made the right decision.

"What makes you think you didn't?" He had seemed hesitant to talk about work thus far, but in the same token also seemed excited about the new job.

"It's not that I think I didn't make the right decision. It's just that I didn't hate where I was at; somehow I think it would have made it easier to leave. Up until now, I had only left a job because I was unhappy at one job, so I would look for another. I was always able to put my finger on when I got stagnant, or lazy, or simply uninterested. This time, I had Rob breathing down my neck, persuading me with the money and the prestige, the view…" his voice trailed off for a second. "I think I must have first-day jitters. I'm overtired and over thinking everything."

"I understand where you're at, though, and I can appreciate how that feels. When I was in high school, I worked at a Hallmark store. I loved it there; most of the customers were nice, they were looking for gifts or cards or something nice to do for someone, so it wasn't as taxing as another kind of retail store. I loved the work and the people, but when I came across an opportunity to do some filing at a local travel agency, I took the job because I knew that in the long run that I could develop some sort of career from that. But I still missed working at the Hallmark store for a long time after, because I hadn't been looking to leave for any other reason than to have a more career-oriented job." I paused a second and then continued the thought. "I think as humans, we always look for a more severe 'line of demarcation,' so to speak. We want definitions, we love lines drawn, and we expect God's direction to be clear. Sometimes we are our own worst enemy."

"You're right. I made this decision, and when I made it, I thought it was the right decision, but it was bittersweet in a way, because I keep looking over my shoulder. I'm sure it'll fade, but right now I find myself in unfamiliar territory." Paul replied.

"Keep in mind that it is just the first day," I reminded him. "You may feel totally different by the end of the week."

"I will feel totally better the next time I see you." Paul closed the topic.

"Nice segue." I felt my heart warm and I was aware of the smile that had just slid its way across my face. "Where are you now?"

"Ah-hah. No, you first." He insisted.

"I am laying on my couch, my feet are dangling over the arm, I am wearing comfy clothes and my hair is up in a ponytail." I was happy to have someone to play the game with.

"Fair enough. I am sprawled out on the couch, legs akimbo, also donned in comfy clothes, I have a cap on backwards and a tall glass of Dr. Pepper on the coffee table next to me. The television is on, but the volume is off, and I wish you were here." He said this so matter-of-factly, that I could have not put too much stock in it, but there was a catch in his voice that took my breath away.

"Legs akimbo?" I laughed.

"Read that in a book, and I've been dying to use it for…fifty-seven days now." Paul admitted.

"And I gave you the perfect opportunity." I chuckled softly and then nattily switched gears. "I wish I was there too," I replied, berating myself even as the words popped out of my mouth, still trying to press the brakes on a car that had already shot over the cliff.

"So come over." His voice was higher, and he presented it as if the suggestion was comical, but I had the distinct impression that if I had taken him up on it, he would not have been upset.

"Don't tempt me," I said, but left it at that. My car might have been soaring over the cliff, but I hadn't crashed and burned yet either.

I lost myself for a moment as my mind went elsewhere, wondering what it would be like to fall asleep in his arms.

Where were we? Ah yes, the weather.

"So when do I get to see you again?" Paul interrupted his own monologue about the impending rain.

"Well, what are you doing this weekend?" I bounced the ball right back to him.

"Spending time with you." Paul responded. "Seriously, when are you free?"

My mind shuffled through my week, knowing that I had planned to work out with Lanie both Tuesday and Thursday, but also highly aware of the fact that Wednesday was free, and that Lanie and I could hang out either before or after the gym.

"I'm free Wednesday and then again on Saturday." I would need a night to myself and Friday night seemed just as good as any.

"How about we do dinner in the city on Wednesday, and we do something up by you on Saturday night? Dinner up there should be different." Paul suggested. "Fair?"

"More than fair." I agreed. There were so many restaurants I had wanted to try in Westchester, and no man willing to take me until now. I had dragged Lanie up here to try two of them, and had coerced Annemarie into indulging in one with me, but a date was entirely different.

"I will see you in forty-eight hours." Paul finalized.

"And how many minutes?"

"Too many."

Chapter Thirty

One night my mother and I had thrown together some pork chops, rice and corn and called it dinner. It was just the two of us, and we were enjoying our meal in relative silence when we heard the screen door open and The Monster's footsteps hit the tile floor in the front hall. I looked up from my meat, and our eyes met briefly, both of us having thought that he would be out for the evening at the very least. The truth was that she never knew in advance whether he would be home for dinner or not, but that morning they had gotten into a fight, and he had left the house in a hurry, the screen door banging behind him.

All I could hear from their bedroom that morning were muffled voices and threatening whispers, but I felt sure that the fight had been about the night before and the man at the door.

The night before the doorbell had rung about nine o'clock. It startled me so much that I jumped off my bed and ran to answer it before I even thought to look out the window. When I opened the door, there was a man standing there that I had never seen before.

"Yeah, is _____ here? I gotta talk to'em." The man was looking for The Monster, except he said his name, and I knew by the way my spine straightened instantly that whoever this man was, that he was bad news. My body was on high alert as I took in his scraggly beard and worn leather jacket with chains hanging off of it.

I was about to tell him that I didn't know where The Monster was when my mother suddenly appeared behind me, shooing me away from the door. I moved behind her but I wouldn't leave.

She stood in front of the open door and I saw her slide the lock on the screen from left to right. It moved silently. I wished then that I had grabbed the phone, just in case I needed to call the police. This guy gave me the creeps. Whoever this guy was, he was up to no good, because of the way he was looking at my mother, and because I was smart enough to know that someone like The Monster had no real friends.

"The Monster isn't here." My mother stood with her feet planted firmly in front of the screen door. "Can I help you?"

"Sure. You can give me the money he owes me." The man's nonchalance was laced with malice, his voice edged with an evil undertone.

"I'm sorry, I don't have any money." My mother grabbed the door by the side as she said this, ready to bang the door closed on this menace to society.

"Don't be sorry. Just get me the money." He laughed a cruel laugh, but one that said that he actually found himself funny. " Tell ____ that I'll be back," With this, he left our front step and we saw him depart in an old, beat-up truck.

We stood together by the door, long after he departed, the only movement coming when she checked the screen lock again and then closed and locked the main door behind us. She then proceeded up the stairs and closed her bedroom door behind her.

The Monster was unaffected when she related this to him in the morning.

My mother, on the other hand, was genuinely scared. The Monster's little drug problem had finally come knocking on our door.

So here he comes, bounding in to the kitchen with a dog in tow, acting as if he is a normal man with a normal job who just took the family dog out for a walk.

"What is that?" My mother jumped up from her seat, her eyes betraying her fear as she set them upon the dog that would become a part of our dysfunctional so-called family for the next three years.

"It's a dog." He blew her off as he motioned towards the stove. "Is there any left for me?" As if he hadn't just made a major family decision on his own.

"There are left-overs," she responded by pointing to the plate she had left for him on the stove, her eyes not moving from the dog.

"Good." He maneuvered his way about the kitchen, as the dog looked us over one by one.

I wanted to choke him for his blasé attitude. I didn't want a dog. Mom didn't want a dog; I would bet all the money he owed that he didn't even know that Mom was allergic. Plus, this was not a friendly little puppy that he chose to complete the family circle, but a full-grown Doberman pincher that was currently eying my half-eaten pork chop.

"What's his name?" My mother asked him, and I almost retched right then and there. There was no mention of her allergies and she brooked no opposition, almost immediately acquiescing to the canine stranger sitting on his haunches, staring at us from the far edge of the kitchen.

"King." He chucked a piece of pork down his throat and proceeded to chew with his mouth half open. "But we'll just call him Protection."

His laugh was altogether too similar to the man who had darkened our doorway the night before. I pushed my plate away, strode past the dog, and went upstairs to call my father.

He wasn't home.

Chapter Thirty-One

The phone rang for the hundredth time that morning, and although I spied the number calling in, I picked it up anyway, knowing that I would have to deal with him eventually, conflicted as always, because I wanted to hear his voice.

"Hi Dad," I said as I picked up the phone, juggling three sets of airline tickets in my right hand. I was waiting for Alex to pop by from the mailroom, as these suckers had to go out fast.

"Hey, Danielle, what do you have, a spy phone there?" He was in a jovial mood and I felt happy that he called just then.

"I do. God knows I need one with this job," I chuckled softly into the phone. There were certain people that you needed to steel yourself for, and others that needed to be avoided at all costs.

Which category did he fall in? I swiped the thought from my mind and tried to join the conversation.

"...They have it in white and black and this new color they're calling denim, but it's basically blue...it's gorgeous, I tell ya, but a little too sporty for me. Plus, I'm too freakin' old for a car like that anymore." He was talking about a new car I was sure, although I had tuned in too late to find out which one.

"You're not old," I countered, for in my mind's eye, he would always be the young guy smuggling shrimp into my bedroom.

"I'm getting there," he threw out a laugh that could not hide the bitter edge. "Your brother's getting so big."

"How is Mikey?" They hated when I called him that. Apparently my father had been called Mikey as a child and when his wife insisted on a junior, he almost balked.

"Michael is fine," He got his point across as he responded. "Your grandmother was here last weekend."

Oh, yes. I had forgotten about the grandmother up from Florida. This was the infamous common ground that my father and I could trounce upon: we had dubbed her thrice-yearly visits The Aggravation Tour.

"So where is she currently at on her tour?" I asked as if inquiring after a rock

star, which for all intents and purposes, she was. Grandma Lacey was the rock star of

that side of my family, commanding attention and a particular type of pillow every place

she went. Whenever she came up to visit, she made the rounds to my father's, my

father's sister's house, and then still managed to impose upon various cousins prior to

jetting back south.

"Oh, please. She's at Michelle's; next is probably Cousin Velda or some other unsuspecting victim that she will be able to go to and then go home and decimate to her entire retirement community." He sighed.

"Yeah, did you ever notice that old people are bigger gossips than us young whippersnappers?" I saw my grandmother in my mind's eye and stifled a cough. She was a room as well as a throat-clearer.

"And everything's a scandal. She will go down to Florida and bitch for hours about how Velda made the most miserable cake or how I gained five pounds." He snorted this time.

"Good thing I didn't run up, huh?" I flagged Alex down as I spoke, motioning with the tickets in my hand. He called that he would be right with me. I saw him disappear around the corner.

"Well, you could have kept me company. We could have suffered her together," he offered and I suddenly felt bad for him. My father's father had died right after the divorce. I didn't see him much then, but I don't think he ever got over it.

"That sounds like great fun." I hesitated an instant, my heart rolling over with a need to reach out to him, to be in on something together, the way we once were. I must have hesitated too long, because I let the feeling wash over me and proceeded to get off of the phone. "I'll see you soon" was the last thing I said to him.

"Okay."

I gave Alex the tickets and took a time check.

Only a few more hours until I saw Paul.

It was Wednesday, and we had plans for dinner downtown. He wanted me to meet him and show me his new office. I told him I couldn't wait.

And I couldn't. Although I had just seen him on Sunday, I was getting royally excited at the mere thought of sitting under the glaring light of his smile for an hour or two.

"Do you want to go out for lunch or order in?" Lanie asked as she ripped her headset off her head and then in the same motion fixed her hair, which never seemed to get smushed from the headset anyway.

"Your call," I threw it back at her. We had a big group coming in, and although there were benefits to ordering lunch in and working nonstop, there was also a huge mental benefit to taking a breather that could not be discounted.

Just then, Alex zipped in and grabbed the tickets from my desk. He seemed in a hurry, so I called loud thanks after him, knowing that he knew what to do.

"I don't want it to be my call today!" Lanie was whining in a fashion that was rather unlike Lanie.

"PMS?" I asked.

"BS." She answered.

"Bull shit?" I wasn't following.

"Brad Syndrome." She bit the inside of her cheek.

"Okay, I call that we are going out to lunch." I grabbed my jacket and shuffled her out the door. "We're going to the diner." There was a small diner not far from where we worked, with two-person booths and comfort food galore.

Once we were settled into the plastic-y booth, Lanie proceeded to tell me why she was suddenly down in the dumps again over the Bradomeister.

"He's away again and I haven't heard from him. We have tentative plans for Saturday night, which are probably permanent in his little world, but I'll tell you right now that they are definitely holding at maybe status, slowly sliding towards *ixnay,* because I simply cannot contemplate how this man expects me to run on empty all week and then fill up my tank on the weekend." Her hands illustrated her frustration, moving a mile a minute in a tense concerto in perfect time with her words.

"I think he probably wants to fill up your tank more than once a week." I winked lewdly and shrugged, as if I couldn't help myself.

Her answer to this was a Sweet-n-Low packet thrown directly into my face.

"Are you going to help me out here?" Her eyes flashed annoyance.

Slapped by the pink packet, I tried again, "Lanie, I do want to help you. But you have to try and see the humor in this; you'll be much better off. Do you really think the Bradomeister is upset right now? He most likely thinks that all's well on the Lanie Front, and here you are molesting your best friend with artificial sweeteners."

This actually got a laugh out of her, but by the time our grilled cheese sandwiches arrived, she was right back on the topic of Brad ignoring her.

"What did Clara say?"

"Keep busy."

"Did she?"

"In a psychobabble sort of way. You know, explore why I am with this person…live my own life outside of him…a watched phone never rings, blah, blah, blah." Lanie checked her watch.

"Yeah, we should go." I nodded for the check by way of a wrap-up. Lanie already knew every word I just told her.

On the way back, she asked about Paul and the plans we had for the night. I almost felt bad telling her, but made a quick decision not to feel bad, as the tables had been turned many times in the past, and our friendship was not flimsy enough to let petty grievances push or pull it one way or the other.

"I don't really know. He told me that he wants me to meet him downtown, I guess he wants to show off the new digs, and then dinner?" I said this more like a question, because he had yet to give me definite plans.

"Sounds good. So when do I meet him?" Lanie was off the Brad topic now, and I knew better than to insinuate a double date. At least not right now.

"I don't know," I told her and then I caught myself blushing. I hadn't even thought about stuff like that yet.

"Soon, I hope? He still needs the Lanie stamp of approval." Lanie insisted.

"Is that sort of like Good Housekeeping?"

"Sort of."

By the time we got back, we both had a pile of emails and voicemails to return. Paul called about an hour later.

"Hi!" It was hard to hide the enthusiasm from my voice as I saw his phone number appear on my spy phone.

"Hi!" He returned my greeting with the same amount of enthusiasm, and for that I was grateful.

"So how's your day?" I asked. I felt a silly grin slide across my face. They were slowly becoming unstoppable; like a fast-speed train that was suddenly on the right track. My face had become *The Silly Grin Express.*

"It will be better once I see you." Paul cleared his throat. "Do you know how to get down here?"

"Which train do you recommend?" I waited for him to give me directions and then signed off. I had a lot to do in order to meet him by six.

The rest of the day was a whirlwind. I had a bunch of last-minute hotel cancellations and almost had to hang up on Adrienne in order to get myself ready to go by about 5:30. Lanie waved as she walked out the door, dejected, perhaps still a bit out of sorts, and I felt another slight twinge of guilt as I freshened up for my date with Paul. I couldn't seem to help myself. I wished and said a quick prayer on my way down to the train that Brad would call.

Once on the rumbling downtown train, I let my mind focus on Paul and the night ahead. He had given me no indication as to where we were going and although I technically liked the idea of surprises and romance, my heart was overly concerned with the clothes on my body and the fact that my trust was being stretched, the fast heartbeat within me belying the fact that I could begin to relate to the resistance bands at the gym.

Great analogy, Danielle.

But it's what just popped into my head.

As you push and pull you grow stronger.

Shut up, logic. Emotion suits me so much better.

Had any of those resistance bands ever broken? Or snapped? If they had, I hadn't seen it happen. I shook the strange comparison from my head as I got off the train and made my way over towards the towers.

In darkness, they were almost majestic. The World Trade Center, also known as The Twin Towers, glittered above me in the nighttime sky. I paused a moment and tried to figure out which one was the 103rd floor. They were too big and I too small. From the pavement, I had to crane my neck to try and see the tippy top.

Just as I was crossing the street, I heard a voice I recognized call out something familiar:

"We've really got to stop meeting this way," Paul called out as he approached me from farther down on the sidewalk.

"Sounds familiar," I crowed.

"I thought you'd like that. I also thought you might like this," he pointed as he indicated The Twin Towers standing above us. "That's why I asked you to meet me here."

"It's an amazing sight." I stood in awe for another moment. I felt his arm slide around my shoulders and I looked from the buildings to him.

"Now, if you want to see a truly amazing sight, you need to see my office," Paul made a funny face as he transferred his arms from my shoulders and then took a hold of my hand. "C'mon."

I followed him up and then into the bowels of the monolith that we called a building. One thing about New York, it really does have the biggest and the best of everything. From buildings to pretzels and bridges to shows, like it or not, the world turns on the axis of New York City.

Of course, I happened to love it.

Several elevator banks later, we had arrived at the new office of Paul Corsi, Corporate Development. It was manly in an unspoken sort of way; with wood on the walls and brass touches everywhere. His space looked used, but barely, as if he started work right away and barely had time to unpack anything personal.

"I haven't hung up one picture yet," Paul narrated the office as I stood agape beside one of his windows.

"It is breathtaking." However wonderful I thought the Towers were from street level, it was magnified up here, and the city that never slept shone brightly from my vantage point.

"Yeah, it is," He agreed as I felt him enclose me from behind. He wrapped his arms gently around me and I fell into him, all the while continuing to take in the view. His breath felt hot on my neck and as I turned around, his lips sought my own in a manner that suggested that we had not touched in years.

"Is the door closed?" I jumped just a tad as I turned around to check. It was closed and I was thankful. Even though there was only a smattering of people still left at their desks, it wouldn't look good to have the new guy making out with his girl for the entire world to see.

Paul stared at me and then wrapped me up in his arms again. I stayed there for a while, not willing to move until he did.

"So what do you think?" He moved away slightly and made a sweeping gesture with his hands.

"I think it's great." I nodded an affirmation.

"Yeah, I don't know what to do with this picture now," He dove into a box and pulled out a picture of The Twin Towers and we shared a quick laugh. "Do you want to put it up in your office? I just think it's a little, I...ah, pretentious, for lack of a better word."

"I would love it," I hesitated, "but I don't want to take it from you."

"Why not?" He looked at me as if I had just fallen from a tree. "I'm giving it to you. Hold on, I think I have a bag." And with that, he dove into another half-opened box by his desk. He rustled around and surfaced not a minute later with a shopping bag and what looked like the original bubble wrap that the picture came in. He wrapped it up and then handed it to me.

"Thank you," I said and felt a catch in my throat that I hoped he hadn't picked up on. What was the matter with me? It was such a small gesture, but I felt overwhelmed by the simplicity of it, which somehow made it beautiful.

"You are welcome." Paul cracked his knuckles and looked deeply into my eyes. "I want to kiss you again, but what do you say we grab some dinner first?"

I couldn't help but blush. He was far too much, more than David had ever been. It wasn't just the thrill, which was what David was all about, but there was a steadiness I detected and my heart responded to that in a way that defied fear.

"Where are we going?" I asked him on the elevator down.

"Well! We'll have to catch a cab, but *methinks it'll be worth the trouble, sweets.*" Paul proceeded to swagger as we alighted from the elevator, his accent and impersonation so terrible that I couldn't pick up on who or what he was trying to imitate.

"What was that?" I was incredulous.

"That was my gangster impersonation," he revealed, blushing himself as he successfully hailed us a cab.

"Oh, did you just watch *Goodfellas* or something?" I wasn't following, and I wanted to, otherwise I would deem him certifiable.

"No, I was trying to create a mood." He must have seen my expression because he laughed at himself then, a full and hearty laugh that shouted self-deprecation and whispered embarrassment. "You'll see."

Again, I felt a close kinship to the resistance bands at the gym.

Push, pull, and trust.

Ugh.

Soon we pulled up to the curb in front of a building that had no real demarcation, save a red neon "L" in the font style I could easily liken to Laverne and Shirley's initialed shirts. I looked at Paul and his eyes looked mischievous.

"I can see you're not familiar with this place. Good," he opened the door so that I could walk in first.

The hostess nodded at our entrance. I heard Paul say 'Corsi,' and then something that sounded like 'Old New York.' I shot him another inquisitive glance. His eyes were still dancing as we made our way over to our table, and only when we were settled in did he choose to explain.

"Danielle, I must apologize now for my very bad Meyer Lansky impersonation." He proceeded to chuckle. "Welcome to Lansky's Lounge. All the portraits you see on the wall are portraits of Al Capone, Bugsy Siegal, Meyer Lansky, who they named the place after, and the crowd they ran with. The entrance had only an "L" on the sign, the same way they used to disguise things in the Prohibition Era. This…" he waved his hands around, as if introducing me to a portrait in a museum, "is old New York."

"This is cool." I was interested now, not only in my surroundings, but also in a man who knew enough about the city to take me to such neat places. If I had to be honest with myself, I could tell you that I knew Midtown Manhattan rather well, but little places like this weren't on my compass, and until now, I hadn't had anyone to put these places on the map for me.

"I thought it would be fun." Paul seemed satisfied with himself. "Plus they have a great steak."

"I'm all for it, as long as nobody gets shot." I gave in to the atmosphere and let him order me a Cosmopolitan.

"You have to have the Lansky salad. I mean, have whatever you like, but I will suggest, strongly suggest the Lansky salad to start." He was still trying to imitate the gangster persona, whether he realized it or not.

"What's in it?" I asked idly while perusing the menu. There was an eclectic array of appetizers and a raw bar that looked enticing.

"It's got shrimp, bacon, and string beans, if I remember correctly." Paul reached across the table then and took my hands into his own. He held my hand over the menu and then proceeded to toss me a gangstery wink.

"God, all you need is the pin-striped suit!" I accused him of role-playing to the hilt, but my mind was elsewhere. Who had he been here with before? I would have to be stupid to think that Paul Corsi had sat home every day of his life before me, waiting for me to appear on the horizon. What if he had been here with an ex-girlfriend? Did it matter? What if she was more sophisticated than I could ever be; living on the Upper East Side in a renovated apartment that screamed education and vogue? *Don't ruin this,* I began talking myself down. *It doesn't matter. Enjoy the night. He's here with you.*

I knew I had to snap out of it fast, not just for fear of ruining what was so far a great evening, but because these thoughts seemed to have a way of steamrolling in my mind. That kind of thinking is exactly what had elevated David to God-status, enabling our original relationship roll over into turmoil and leading me to a place where I never wanted to go back to again.

I'm working on it.

"Are you into the raw bar?" He inquired; unaware of the roller coaster I was riding inside of my mind.

"I am. When I was younger, my Dad and I used to eat clams on the half shell with cocktail sauce every time we went to the beach." Oh, God. Now what? Where on Earth had that memory derived from? What the hell was the matter with me? I began the night getting all choked up over the fact that he gave me a picture, then I made up a nightmare scenario in my head about the ex-girlfriend (s) that he has already taken to the very same restaurant, now…I mention my father. My father, whom I think I did the clam thing with maybe three times. Was I premenstrual? I wished I could kick myself. If it was physically possible for me to kick myself underneath the table, without grazing him in the process...then I would. I should.

I made a mental note to practice that as soon as I arrived home.

"Looks like they have oysters on the half shell. I will if you will." He suggested.

"If we get the salad, I'll split half of a half dozen with you." I said.

"Three each? All right." He kept holding my hand and released it only when he decided to take a sip of his drink.

I took a deep breath and talked myself down a little bit further. I decided on a salmon dish, and he on a filet mignon. By the time the appetizer and salads arrived, I was back to enjoying things for what they were. And he was busy telling me about his brother.

"Peter and I aren't exactly night and day, but I think it's safe to say we are dawn and dusk. There's a hazy place in between those two times where we can meet and see things the same, but for the most part...let's put it this way, he voted for Clinton."

"Bill Clinton?" I asked in amazement, surprised at the abruptness in his voice, the quick shift in conversation. Besides, I thought everybody in New York City was a die-hard Democrat.

"Yes, Big Bad Billy Boy. Or...Blowjob Bill, for those who prefer to call it like it is. I don't know how you feel about him, you probably like him; it seems like everybody does, but I despise him. Always have. But when you're kids, you don't talk about politics. You grow up, you form opinions, and then you find out you can't always relate to people–even your own relations." Paul seemed passionate suddenly, and I wanted to find out more about this guy who was unafraid to go against the grain.

"I can't say that I like Bill. I certainly don't like what he did to his wife." Truth be told, I had very little respect for any woman who stayed with a man once he humiliated her, especially as publicly as he had humiliated her. A small voice inside begged a super-direct question: Was she really so different than my mother? Did we expect more or less of those in the public eye? Mrs. Clinton had pretended to be a Super-feminist, but let's call it like it is: would Gloria Steinem have stayed with Bill Clinton? None of my business, but something most Americans had been forced to mull over at one point or another in the past few years.

"That's refreshing. I guess we're answering another big question right now." Paul pointed out.

"Which one?" I wasn't following.

"Politics." Paul smiled. "We've already attacked Religion and Politics."

"You're right. So: are you a Republican?" I assumed it was quite possible, considering how much he didn't like Bill.

"I consider myself an Independent. I voted for a Democrat in my last local election, but I voted for the Republican candidate against Bill this last time. Bob Pineapple. Though I have nothing against Bob Pineapple, I would have liked a stronger choice to go up against Billy. Although, I would have voted for Bozo the Clown against Bill." He grinned and took another bite of his meal.

"You're funny." I thought a minute. "I like the idea that you are apparently not at all interested in being politically correct. As for me, I guess I'm an Independent, too. As for Bill and Hill, I think I felt bad for their kid when they were going through their marital…situation." I mean, how else could I put it? Was there any way to put it delicately? I could certainly relate to a kid being caught in the crossfire, and that's why I think my heart was turned towards the daughter and away from the scandal.

"Yeah, I felt bad for *every* kid that had to learn about the President getting his rocks off in the Oval Office with someone other than his wife." Paul made a face.

"But if it had been his wife…?" I asked.

"I'm sure the taxpayers wouldn't have minded." Paul interjected.

I hate to admit this, but I really liked the idea that he was irked by the President's conduct. It spoke to me about faithfulness and love and perhaps even his thoughts regarding impropriety.

"What else?" I prompted.

"Now we just have to tackle: Sex, Family, and Future." And he shone that million-watt smile on me.

"No. I meant, what else do you have to tell me about Politics?" Politics wasn't a big topic for me, but it seemed like it was for him, so I wanted him to get it all out now. I didn't want any surprises popping up later on.

"Let's see. Not much else. I love Rudy Giuliani. I know that might not be a really popular view right now, but I love the things that he's done for this city. Of course, I am a white male from Long Island, so I have a particular perspective. I love the fact that he cleaned up Grand Central and the area all around Times Square. I am aware of the games politicians play, but I look at it as more of like a spectator sport, therefore I can appreciate a guy like him who doesn't take any garbage. How did we get on this topic to begin with?" He looked deeply into my eyes.

"Your brother." I reminded him, keeping his gaze. I could get lost in his eyes forever.

"Right, my brother, the Clinton-Lover. Well, let's see what else I can tell you about Pierre. He hates being called Pierre. I think I was in the third grade when I figured out that 'Pierre' is French for Peter. Well, you can imagine how I just would not let that go. I would draw it out, and say *PP—pp-iiiiii-AIR!* Really loud in front of other boys. And girls. Not that I'm proud of this, you see, but I especially liked saying the P part. Can you imagine how much fun it was at eight and nine years old to say Pee a lot in one day? Then he would tell Mom. And try and call me Tall Paul. Which wasn't nearly as much fun as Pee-air. What else? Oh, here's some trivia. Peter loves chocolate. You could say, 'who doesn't?' but my brother is by far the biggest chocoholic I have ever known. Drinks chocolate coffee in the morning; eats chocolate-flavored yogurt when he's on a diet. Not that he ever needs to diet. He and his emaciated wife can just pump tons of chocolate through their veins and still have low cholesterol at the end of the day.   Peter is also a history buff, and the best tour guide you could ever ask for in DC. When he first moved to DC, I thought he would be back within a year, but DC suits him. Besides that, Peter and I both love our parents to death. No matter what comes between us, we can usually shelve it when it comes to Mom and Dad." Paul wrapped up his seemingly endless diatribe about his sibling.

"By mutual agreement?"

"Unspoken agreement."

"That's nice."

"It can be."

I never knew what to say at moments like this, because I didn't have a similar story to tell. It was so *Cleaveresque.*

Stop it, Danielle!

"And?" Paul moved closer to the table and hunched over slightly, as if he were about to share state secrets. "Would you like to attack another of the hot topics we have left, or would you rather move on to dessert?"

I checked my watch. "Dessert sounds good. Can we share?"

"Absolutely." Paul suggested something chocolaty. "Peter would love this."

"Sounds good."

We both ordered tea and the dessert with two forks. We had fun attacking it from every angle, and once we finished, we hopped a cab to Grand Central. He let the cab go and walked me inside, insisting he could walk home from there.

"I had a great time. Thank you." I looked up into his eyes as we stood near Track 29.

"No, Thank you. You made it possible for me to get through the rest of the week." Paul showered me with another glowing smile, lighting up his eyes and his whole face in the process.

"I've got to go." I motioned towards the clock and he leaned forward to give me a good-bye kiss.

"Ummm, Bye." He unhooked his hand from my own.

"Bye." I walked away wondering if he was still looking at me. I turned around and peeked.

He was.

Chapter Thirty-Two

"We're going to Seaside." My father would announce this and my mother would scowl, as was their annual ritual.

My father loved the beach just as much as she hated it; although this same argument could have been applied to any one thing that decorated the life they chose to spend together. They were forever at odds, their wills clashing in circumstances both large and small, the perspective that one was always giving in to the other the only thing shared evenly.

"Michael, Seaside is four hours from here!" Another thing she hated was long car rides and she had no problem letting him know all about it.

"So we'll stay over night," he would say, and then he would go on to act as if this was one big adventure, drowning out her protestations with an unrecognizable tune, whistling as loud as he possibly could.

The main problem was that in the movies...adventures didn't equal tension. In our house, they always did. My father would begin by scheming and conniving a way to get her to go with him to the little ocean town that he loved, and when she repeatedly denied him, he would switch tactics, the whistling slowly turning into yelling, until he insisted loudly that we were going. At this point, there was no reasoning. That was that. Then if his wishes were not granted, he would bully her. He seemed to take special joy in calling her names, one right after the next, until a whole string of names resembled a familiar, if horrible, tune.

I would get angry inside, scared because they yelled so much, deep down knowing that he would win and we would land ourselves at the beach.

And that was that.

And she would whine.

And that was that.
And he would call her a bitch.
And that was that.
And they would fight.

I, on the other hand, I would smile secretly from my perch in the backseat and count the tolls as my father's arm would arc forward and toss in change, the lane light turning from red to green.

Each toll a milestone: one step closer to the beach.

I counted the green lights as we passed through the tolls and dreamed about my toes touching the sand. I loved the feeling of sand beneath my toes, even squishing in between them, and the spectacle of the waves crashing against the shore. My love for all things beach was so intense that I would focus on the prize; silently willing them to get along for once, just enough to deposit me at the shore. It would get so bad that I wouldn't care if they left me there, free to live among surf and sand. Eventually, I learned to drown out the sounds of their power struggle emanating from the front seat of the car. It didn't really matter as long as I could get there.

One pastime I especially loved was seeing the sandcastles as we walked up and down the beach. I would urge my father to take me past each masterpiece, and I would dream of one day creating my own special castle. I wished I could make a sandcastle like the ones I saw each year, the towering castles with a moat, or the boxy structures that looked just as formidable. Little did I know then that adults, professional sandmen and ladies worked on these charming edifices for hours a day. My little girl eyes only knew that I wanted the same.

My father understood. I think he understood me then better than he does now, understood me in a way that he never understood his wife, my mother. He would take the time to walk me past each exhibit, leaving my mother behind to guard our towels and coolers and such. Eventually we would end up at The Clam Shack, *a place that sounded very much like its name. The shack was the best option for those of us who liked the surf and the sand, for they let you walk up to their outdoor bar and order at the window, then sit on a plastic-covered stool even soaking wet and suck down as many clams as you could pay for.*

My father would always order a dozen to start, and I would wait eagerly while he splashed each clam on the half shell with a spritz of lemon, then add a heavy handful of ruby red cocktail sauce. After we demolished the first dozen, he would order another, which always led me to ask the inevitable:

"Dad, why don't you order them all at once?" I knew just like he did that we would surely eat two dozen.

"Because I like to savor them." He would reply.

I never understood his logic, if for no other reason than because I thought I was capable of savoring two dozen at a time the same way I could savor one dozen and then the next.

It took me until adulthood to realize that he was savoring his time, time spent away from my mother, time spent alone with me, time spent enjoying the foods that he loved. Time spent on a day at the beach.

Chapter Thirty-Three

"Do you think I have too many hang-ups regarding food?" I asked Constance as if the idea had just dawned on me. It was stupid, the inflection in my voice, as if I had just discovered something earth shattering and monumental.

I knew I had food hang-ups. I knew, deep down inside, that it was not normal that my most cherished memories of my childhood involved my father and various types of seafood. I knew that the way I used to fight with The Monster over him stealing food that my mother had designated just for me was sometimes over-the-top, the same way I knew that the nightly patrols of my kitchen were outdated and unnecessary, but could not delete these trips from my itinerary any less than I could help myself from mentally calculating calories burned or not burned every time I hopped aboard a treadmill.

"I think that food has played an integral role in your life. The better question would be, 'Do *you* feel that you have a large amount of hang-ups regarding food?'" Constance was Therapist Personified today, not allowing herself to get tied into answering any questions.

I knew her tactics; she wanted me to think, to answer my own questions, to reason out loud.

Today I just wanted an opinion from another woman. A woman who I liked and respected and who could be more objective, as she was on the outside peering in.

I told her that.

"I think that you have a lot of memories that are associated with food. Culturally, you were brought up around a lot of food, and food took on several meanings for you as you grew, depending on your experience." Constance offered.

And that, dear friends, was the best I was going to get out of her.

I unraveled the whole food story regarding The Monster. The Monster was not of Italian descent, he didn't understand food protocol, and since he never respected other people's property (or feelings for that matter) he would simply help himself to whatever was left in the refrigerator, with blatant disregard for all. Do you know how most people will ask an entire picnic table of party revelers if they would like the last deviled egg prior to scooping it up for themselves, and usually only do so after making several excuses for *taking the last one?* The Monster had no such predilections. He took, never gave, as that was his M.O., and he didn't think twice about polishing off the last of any one thing. I can remember having a small birthday get-together when I was fifteen years old, just my mother, a few family members and two girlfriends of mine. The Monster was on his best behavior. My mother had brought me strawberry shortcake from my favorite bakery, and I was in Heaven as I inhaled a huge piece on the day of my birthday. The next morning, I was rooting around in the fridge to try and find the leftover cake, when The Monster announced his presence loudly with a belch that would register 9.9 on the Richter scale. I looked up to find him looming over me, a nefarious look upon his face, no excuse forthcoming for his rude and odious behavior.

"Would you happen to know what happened to the rest of my cake?" I could barely keep the malice from my voice, knowing before he answered just what his answer would be.

"I ate it." *With that, he scratched himself, stepped in front of me and proceeded to lift a fresh carton of orange juice out of the fridge.*

He drank straight from the carton. I made my way upstairs and into the sanctuary of my room, steam pouring steadily from my ears, my fists clenched at my side.

"I realize that I live alone; I know this, my logical mind knows that nobody will take my food away from me any more, but it doesn't stop me from cataloguing the contents of my refrigerator every night before I go to sleep." I was admitting this out loud to Constance for perhaps the first time, unable to tie it to the memory of my father and the beach, but feeling a connection lying somewhere under the surface, deeper than perhaps I had allowed myself to go before.

"Maybe you can try to cut down the amount of times per week you do that." She suggested.

I smiled. "You mean, instead of going cold turkey? Like, don't throw out the cigarettes, just cut back?"

She shared my smile. "Sort of." She paused a moment. Was she waiting for me?

"I suppose I can do that." A thought entered my brain, a revelation I had yet to fully register. "The last time I went out with Paul, I didn't check the fridge when I got home, I actually fell right to sleep."

"That's good. That's improvement; a step in the right direction." She nodded an affirmation.

"Do you think so?" What did Paul have to do with my preoccupation with food? Maybe nothing. Maybe I was just so busy with him that I had less time to be concerned with me.

"Yes, I think so. I think that you're improving in a lot of areas. I think you don't give yourself enough credit." Her eyes bored into my own, and I found myself looking away from her then.

I blushed.

"I think I have a hard time seeing it." I still had the nightmares, the constant second-guessing going on inside, the trepidation over what could or could not be regarding Paul.

The session wound up and soon I was on my way back to work, cell phone in hand, buzzing Lanie about frozen yogurt.

Believe me, the irony was not lost on me. I grabbed two Peach Treats and then made my way back to the hole/office. Brad had yet to call Lanie and today was Thursday. As far as she knew, he was still in DC, still counting on their Saturday night date.

"Anything yet?" I asked her as I deposited her Froyo on her desk and then took a swipe at the part of mine that was starting to drip over the edge.

"No." Lanie dislodged the spoon from the center of her froyo and then shrugged. "Annemarie called looking for you though. And the fort…was being held. Just check your messages."

I checked messages and then email, finding an email from Paul. I smiled to myself. He had sent me over a Y2K joke that was actually pretty funny, so I responded with my thoughts that the world would end on New Year's Eve 1999. I didn't really think that, but the Millennium hype was in full swing, so I decided to chime in and see where he stood.

Almost the instant the email hit the wires; my phone rang and his number flashed on the screen.

"Yes…?" I answered as if I couldn't imagine why on Earth he would be calling.

"Are you stockpiling cans too?" He chided me and I indulged him with a hearty laugh. The Y2K hype had grown to a fever pitch, with people believing everything from all the world's computers coming to a grinding halt as the clock struck twelve, to Jesus Himself retuning as soon as the confetti hit the air. New York City was on alert, with every generator being checked, and every I.T. person already scheduled to work on New Year's Eve, the luckiest few being on call and not actually glued to a computer terminal. The general consensus was that the computers that ran everything the world over would not understand the rollover from 19- to the year 2000. Therefore, everything would spontaneously combust.

"I'm taking money out of the ATM on the 30th, just in case." Doomsday and Nay Sayers predicted that our money would be locked in the banks for days on end, if not forever.

"Are you really?" Paul seemed amazed by this.

"I am really." I hated to admit it to him because I didn't want him to think I was truly freaky, but when you've lived the life I've lived, you tend to have to look out for yourself and always have a contingency plan.

"Wow, you're really cool." Paul sounded awed, and I didn't know him well enough yet to be able to tell how sarcastic he was being.

"I am really." I repeated and then allowed for another laugh. "Why, don't you believe all this Y2K stuff?" We had been bombarded with so much information at work that I couldn't even harness it all, all I knew was that there were a ton of people not flying anywhere on New Year's Eve, afraid that the plane's computers would not be working. Actually, they were afraid of flying at the stroke of twelve, terrified that while up in midair, the computers would crash and therefore the plane.

"I believe there may be some glitches. Besides that, I prefer to think positive."

"THAT BASTARD!" Lanie's yell interrupted my conversation with Paul. I slapped Paul on hold quickly, only to turn and find Lanie gesturing wildly in the face of her spy phone.

"Lane? What?" I jumped up and ran over to her side to see a number with a New York exchange on her reader.

"It's Brad." She pointed at the phone as if it were a snake.

"Pick it up!" I admonished her. Wasn't this what she had been waiting for?

"I can't believe it took him until THURSDAY! What does he think he is, The Leader of the Free World?" She made an evil face as she ripped the phone from its cradle, but her voice was pure composure as she finally spoke into the handset.

Paul! Oh, was he still on hold? He was.

"Sorry, Paul." I got back on the phone hoping I wouldn't have to explain Lanie's outburst.

"Everything okay over there?" Paul chuckled nervously. "I thought maybe your Y2K virus came a little early."

"Ah, no...that's just Lanie," I responded, not offering to explain any further.

"Sounds like fun. Listen, I've got to run, but are we still on for Saturday?"

"You betcha." You betcha? The class! Maybe I should just fill my cheeks with chewing gum the minute I pick up the phone from now on.

"Alright. Have a great day. Bye." With that, he hung up the phone and I decided to eavesdrop on Lanie.

Oh, she was docile. She was actually giggling as the poor handset was returned far more gracefully to its home a minute later.

"Lane?" I inquired of the alien sitting next to me, then looked at her as if she had sprouted antennae.

"Stop looking at me like that!" She admonished. "Look, I know I'm a schmuck when it comes to him."

"You're all bark and no bite." I observed, knowing that this was part of the reason I loved her so fiercely myself, and probably the same reason—or one of many—that had led Brad to become a Lanie-lover also.

"True. True." She shook her head and then faced me head-on. "Tell anybody and you die."

I laughed so hard I almost fell off my chair. "You have a rep to protect?" I managed to push this out through the pains in my chest, my side splitting, my face cracking, all due to the similarity of our hearts.

"Of course. I really do hate him, ya know that?" Lanie asked me.

"The same way I hate Paul." I agreed. "So what did he say?"

"He said that he's been thinking about me." Lanie proceeded to blush, albeit against her own will. "He asked me if we were still on for Saturday night."

"I assume you said yes?" I asked her even though I already knew the answer.

"I said yes." She paused more than a beat. "Am I an idiot?"

I knew what she was asking, that age-old question that women the world over toil with in every relationship: how much is too much? Where do you lose yourself to the one you love? Can you be too careful?

The fact that I was trying to figure out the answers to these questions myself did not make me a prime candidate in the answer category.

"You are not an idiot. You're a human being, Lanie."

"I'm so glad we never get like this at the same time," She responded, echoing my earlier sentiment.

"So am I," I replied and then turned back to work. I had enough drama for one afternoon. "Are we still on for dinner?"

"Yes, but we have to work out first. I have a date this weekend."

And so it goes.

Chapter Thirty-Four

"I was calling to check in on you," I said to Am on Saturday, as I toyed with the various clothing options that were decorating my bed. I was up earlier than usual and figured it would be prime time to try and get into touch with her. She had called me earlier in the week to bitch about work, but I was so swamped that I really didn't have time to talk. Now I was at a loss for what to wear because I had planned on taking Paul to an outdoor eatery, and even though it was early June, the day was more than a little on the cool side and I feared that the original sundress I had in mind would now leave me with not only goose pimples, but the dreaded 'headlights.'

You get the picture.

"I'm okay. And you're helping by letting me whine about it. So what's on for tonight with Paul?" She seemed to perk up with the introduction of another topic, so I indulged her by rattling on and on about Paul and potential outfits and restaurants.

"This place we were going to go to would be much better if it were a sunny day and a warmer night, so I am thinking instead about taking him over to this little place called *Palazzo*." I mused.

"Palazzo, like the pants?" Annemarie asked.

"I guess so. Hopefully they'll have some good jeans on the menu."

"Oh, that was a bad one."

"Thank you very much. Seriously, I hope it's good. I've driven past there a handful of times, but I don't know anybody down here to ask. So I went on the web and had them fax me a menu."

"I hope that's just nervous energy in the form of a bad joke. You don't try these on him, do you?" Annemarie pressed.

"No, but I told him about my Comicsitis." I admitted.

"You revealed the dreaded disease!" Am sounded impressed.

"I did." I nodded although she couldn't see me.

"And?"

"So far he still likes me!" I exclaimed.

"I don't see any reason why he wouldn't. So when do Steven and I get to meet The Mystery Man?" Annemarie used the same title I had before I knew him as Paul.

"Lanie just asked me the same thing. When are you coming down?"

"Soon."

"Soon when?" It was always hard to get the Upstate crowd to come and visit me. It seemed as if I was still a part of the scenery up there, and therefore they just expected me to show up from time to time.

"I'll talk to Steven and let you know. When are you coming up next?"

I sighed. Soon would be too soon. I mulled it over a sec, knowing that Mikey Jr. was due for a visit, whether or not I wanted to see the man we both called Dad. My mother had recently asked the same question, and now Am made three. I glanced at the phone information on the table next to the phone. I had to call my mother next.

"I'll make you a deal; talk to Steven about coming down, and once you call me back, we'll try and arrange two dates." I thought myself fair.

"Sounds good." She agreed and we got off the phone not long after. I started running water in order to boil a pot of tea, needing the support of caffeine prior to picking up the phone to call my mother. Once the tea was steeping, I procrastinated a little more, and shuffled through my CD rack. I pulled out an old Mariah Carey and heard her powerful voice sing:

And you don't remember...How you used to hold me...How we'd melt together...

How you needed me...How we used to be...In love...

I shuddered as a feeling that was pure David rushed through my body, a feeling long forgotten, a sinking summer of depression that was better not remembered.

I skipped the track, but the next song, *Can't Let Go,* continued to stir the pot. Skipped one more and found *Make It Happen,* which was optimistic enough to make a desert flow with water.

Go Mariah.

I sipped my tea, said a little prayer, and then picked up the phone to call my mother. I had been playing phone tag with her all week (read: she'd been avoiding me) and now that I was home and could scream at the top of my lungs if needed, I was determined to talk to her about The Monster.

"Hello?" Her voice was fuller than the last time we spoke, and I felt a small twinge of hope that perhaps he had left her alone for the remainder of the week.

"Hi, Mom," I began, my words rolling out from under me. "It's me, I wanted to talk to you about the phone. I got lots of great information the other day, did you get my message?" I had left her a message detailing her options, and had to call back three times because I kept getting cut off by her answering machine.

"Danielle. Yes, I got your messages."

That was it.

I tried not to let her dissuade me.

"Well, Mom, did you get any other phone calls this week?" I decided to start easy.

"Well, his mother called."

"His mother?" Talk about incredulous: right then and there, you could have blown me over with a mere wave of the hand. I had fleeting images of The Monster's mother; from her stopping by with a casserole to her insisting in a rather shrill voice that her son's problems were my mother's entire fault. She had never done anything to me directly, unless of course you count the fact that she had spawned the devil, but I had always held something against her, however unspoken, because I fully believed the aforementioned point. She was inconsistent at best, full of blame at the least. I often wondered about her, wondered how much of his condition had to do with his upbringing. After all, how much of whom I was today had to do with the garbage I went through growing up?

My mother was detailing their phone conversation as I tried to pick up where we had left off. "Basically, she wanted me to know that when he did get out of jail, that he was not coming to stay with her. Under no uncertain terms, she said."

Oh, the mother of old would have told her to go to hell. How I longed for that empowered woman to pop up from her blighted existence, born-again in her belligerence. Even the pre-divorce Mom had more vigor, standing up to my father in ways both large and small throughout their time together. Okay, more small than large, but for God's sake, at least she *tried* then.

"So what else did she have to say?" I would have been amused, but it was simply too sad to think that this woman was afraid of her own son.

"Not much else. She asked for you."

Fine. Except that didn't really help the situation, did it?

"Well," I began and then launched into a lengthy description regarding her phone options. I told her what I suggested and filled in the spaces whenever I asked her something that she couldn't give a definitive answer on right away.

"I just really don't want to change my number," she insisted.

I took a deep breath and counted to ten.

"I know, Mom, nobody wants to change their number." I would have mentioned that I thought she should move away, too, but since I couldn't even seem to get her to change her number, I thought that would be totally fruitless. I decided to take a different tack. "What about just getting the Caller-ID option? That way if he calls, you could at least know by the area code who it is and then not even pick up the phone."

"I could do that." She was either eager to please me or just as eager to shut me up.

"Can we do that? Also, do you have a way to shut off the ringer on your phone? That way, once you see the number on the Caller-ID, you can shut the ringer off, so you don't even have to hear it ring." I proposed.

"My phone doesn't have that." It was a simple statement that she made, but my heart lurched nonetheless, because she had the best of nothing. It was difficult to have anything nice or new or updated when you lived with a man who stole from you all the time. The Monster had been away for some time now, but that hadn't made all the debt they had accumulated just get up and vacate the premises.

"Well, I happen to have an extra phone here that does. I'll ship it to you on Monday." This was a blatant lie, but my mother for all of her mistakes, still had her pride and would rarely accept any presents from me.

"How do you have an extra phone?" She asked, her voice laced with skepticism.

"When I moved in here I thought I had two jacks, so I brought two phones and then couldn't return the one." Lie, lie, lie. But if it got her to acquiesce to accepting the phone, the end would justify the means.

"Oh, all right." She sighed. "So when do I get to see you?"

"Soon." I borrowed from Annemarie. We made a little small talk and then got off the phone. I would get her a brand-new phone tomorrow, with all the bells and whistles; regardless of how many dollars it would set me back until payday. In the meantime, I had enough time for a power walk before I had to jump in the shower. I grabbed a sweatshirt and off I went.

I was lost in thought, pumping my arms and legs, my mind jumping from one topic to the next as I rounded the curve near the house with the pretty flowers. I stopped a moment to admire them and was shocked to suddenly hear a voice directly beside me.

"They're beautiful, aren't they?"

I jumped. Had I been so lost in thought that I didn't hear the sound of the woman sneaking up beside me? Where was the hyper-vigilance that I had cultivated from living on the edge so long? Could it be that I was getting better?

Or just dumber?

I turned to my right then and acknowledged the woman standing next to me.

"Oh, hello, I'm sorry. Are they yours?" I pointed towards the house they sat in front of, my heart still pounding in my chest. Since when had I allowed myself to start putting my guard down?

"They were my husband's. I'm so sorry; did I startle you?" She seemed a tad bit flustered, as if she hadn't meant to happen upon me the way she did.

"Well, yes, I was startled, I guess I didn't know you were there." I smiled what I hoped was a reassuring smile. "I'm Danielle."

"And I'm Millie Lancaster." She smiled and the deep lines in her face punctuated her grin. I took in Millie for a minute as we stood there, her gray hair protruding from the brim of her hat, her white pants perfectly creased, she was the picture of today's suburban grandma. With money.

"I didn't mean to stare. I had come across your flowers one other time when I was out walking, and I thought they were so spectacular. I wanted to paint them."

Again, I wanted to kick myself for my forwardness. What had possessed me to say that?

"Oh, do you paint?" She clapped her hands together with glee. "I used to love to paint! Maybe you can give me a refresher course." Her eyes flitted from me to the flowers.

"I...um, I don't really paint. What I meant to say is that I used to paint. I was thinking about taking up painting again, and I just thought that I might be able to paint your flowers without massacring them." My words tumbled out a mess, as I stood hopeful that she would not label me a lunatic neighbor.

"Oh, but you're welcome to paint my flowers anytime! I may just join you." She stood there still smiling as I drank in her presence in a way I didn't know I was capable of. There was something instantly likable about Millie Lancaster and I couldn't believe how comfortable I felt in her presence.

"Well, I can let you know about that," I offered and then chuckled. "I would definitely have to find and then dust off my paintbrushes."

"You let me know when you're ready. I'm right here, number thirty-five." She pointed towards her mailbox and I noticed for the first time the mail tucked underneath her arm.

"Sounds good." No matter how weird the incident may have initially seemed, it did sound good to me and I determined that I would one day darken her doorstep with paintbrushes in tow.

"It does, doesn't it? Hope to see you soon, Danielle, it was sure nice meeting you." With that, she made her way towards the front door of her well kept home.

"You too." I called after her, and then proceeded to pick up the pace and finish my power-walk. The skies had turned an ominous gray and the wind had picked up while I had stood there talking. I thought again about my original plan for the evening, which was to take Paul out to a park after dinner. It was looking like I would have to amend that and do something indoors.

My mind mulled over the options as I rounded the lake and made my way back to my house. I thought of renting a movie, then thought maybe we should go to one. I decided to let him decide.

I opened the door to my place and saw the answering machine light blinking. For a brief instant, I panicked, thinking it was Paul calling to cancel.

"Well, idiot, you won't know either way until you hit the button," I muttered to myself after staring at it for a full minute.

It was he, asking if there was anything he could bring. I smiled. Whew. Good to know there was still some lingering paranoia. After Millie Lancaster, I wasn't so sure.

I called Paul back and he answered on the third ring.

"Hello," he said this as if he were running around in circles and had just stopped to catch his breath.

"Hi, it's Danielle." I still wasn't ready to say *'Me'* yet.

"Hey–did you get my message?" He sounded like he was running.

"Yes, I was wondering if you could bring up some bagels, cream cheese, and newspapers." I said nonchalantly.

"You're as funny as those funnies you have to read. Seriously?" He still sounded as if he were panting.

"Paul, are you okay?" I felt strange asking him, but he sounded as if he were running a marathon. And coming in last.

"I'm on the treadmill." He grunted or laughed, I couldn't tell. "Sorry, I must sound like a mess."

"I thought you didn't do the gym."

"I do the home gym."

"Oh."

"So would you like me to bring up anything?" He inquired.

"No. I'm great. I would recommend a windbreaker, though. It's gotten a little bit chilly out there." I glanced outside again, only to see my landlord's hammock wrap itself up in a gust of wind.

"Gotcha. Okay, I should be arriving at 5:57. Is that okay or would you like me to rent a car?"

"Paul, there is no problem whatsoever with me picking you up." Unless he was one of those male-chauvinist-pig-men that didn't like a woman to drive. "The question is: are you okay with me driving?" Might as well know right away.

"I am fine with you driving. Don't be silly; I just don't like to impose. And sometimes I really like to drive, since I rarely drive anymore. Make you a deal, the next time it's nice out, I'll rent a convertible and drive up." He suggested amicably.

"Sounds good."

"I'll see you soon." Paul said and I heard a whirring sound in the background for the first time. He was probably kicking it up a notch. Either that or he wasn't breathing as hard. Either way, it made me see him as a little more human, and I liked that.

I stretched and gave Lanie a quick buzz.

"Have you heard from him?"

"He's on his way."

"This is good news."

"This is good news for him."

"You're a riot."

"And yours?"

"On his way."

"You have fun."

"You too."

"Mexican Monday?"

"You got it."

"Love."

"Au revior."

Lanie's favorite sign-off: Love. No 'Love you.' No 'I love ya, I'll see ya later.' Just 'Love.'

Which of course makes Lanie: Lanie.

With that thought, I hopped in the shower and scrubbed and lathered with all of my might. I found myself getting excited to see Paul, not to mention excited in general just to have someone to see.

Love.

The real reason women shave their legs.

Because, let's face it: if it weren't for the manly man thing, I'd let it hang and braid it for special occasions. Trim it like a Christmas tree one month out of the year.

These thoughts aside, I shaved my legs like a woman on a mission and doubled over the arms as well. Once out of the shower, I prepped like a model trying to win a slot as a reality show finalist, then grabbed my keys and headed for the train station.

I saw him before he saw me. I sat there for a matter of seconds, spying as it were, until he looked up and caught my eye. He looked as fabulous as he always did, in a stylish button-down and a tailored pair of khakis, brown shoes finishing the ensemble.

"Hi." I hid inside myself again, a shyness sweeping over me; so sudden even I was taken by surprise.

"Hi." He stopped right in front of me, looked at me tentatively and then swept me into an all-absorbing hug. I fell into him and after a minute, I let myself relax. There was no reason to be nervous. Would he be taking the train up to Westchester on a Saturday night if he weren't truly interested?

I answered my own question with a resounding no.

"Are you okay?" He rubbed my shoulders, easing my tension with the smallest of strokes. "Are you cold?"

I nodded reflexively. I wasn't cold; I was scared. But it's always easier to say cold.

"Let's go," I hopped into the Cavalier. "I am taking you to a restaurant called *Palazzo*. Now, I have never been there myself, so if the food is horrible, then I take no credit for that. If it's wonderful, I'll take all the credit."

"That sounds about right." He tapped his fingers on the dashboard to a tune that had just come on the radio. "You look marvelous, by the way."

"You sound like Billy Crystal." I snuck a peek at him out of the corner of my right eye as I rounded a turn. He was truly beautiful.

"You Look Maaaarvelous!" Another bad impersonation by Paul Corsi.

"Did you like that song?" Another memory of growing up, popping up when I was with him. Why did that seem to keep happening?

"I loved it, like, the first twelve hundred times I heard it." He laughed. "Do you remember that song *You Can Call Me Al?"*

"Yes!" I laughed then too. The Eighties were so eclectic. "Do you remember the video with Chevy Chase?"

"Who doesn't remember that video? I loved it! The only problem with the song being such a big hit was that I had a friend named Al in high school, and we ribbed him so hard, I'm afraid he never lived it down. Then he started using it as a line. You know, you sidle up to a girl and, trying desperately to come up with anything remotely cool, and Al would say, something incredibly geeky like: *My name's Al, but you could call me Al.* And he'd kind of sing the end; just in case the girl didn't get the joke. It was bad." Paul shook his head as he recounted the bitter end.

"So what exactly do you do when you *sidle* up to a girl?" I was feeling relaxed enough now to joke, to cajole some information out of him, and to flirt. Paul had this uncanny knack of relaxing me, and allowing me to be me to the fullest degree of the law.

"You know, you sidle." He raised his eyebrows and winked.

"Sidle actually means to go forward with a sideways motion."

"Well, then that's what we do. We go forward with a sideways motion." He cracked up then. "Sort of like when I met you on the sidewalk."

"Oh, you're hilarious." I gave in to a grin then, and turned into the parking lot of *Palazzo*.

"Is this it?" Paul asked as I parked.

"Yes. Why, is it not good?" I couldn't read the expression on his face.

"I think I've been here before." His eyes surveyed the outside.

"You're kidding? I wouldn't have thought you would have been to any place around here." I felt stupid then and I didn't know why. Could he have been here with an ex-girlfriend? Did he have an ex that lived in Westchester?

"I think…well, the name didn't ring any bells when you said it. But–and I might be wrong here–I think that Amy had her wedding here." He seemed as if he was mulling this over. "I'll know once we get inside."

"Amy?" I asked, not knowing what else to say.

"Yes, Amy White is the woman that I worked with at the job I just left. She married this guy Gary, and since it was a second wedding for both of them, they had a little shindig here and then a week in Mexico. If I remember correctly, the food was fabulous, so you made a good choice." Paul nodded as if to himself.

Then why did I feel like he had just dropped a lead balloon on my feet? I wanted to wow him a little, and I guess I wanted the credit after having researched the place several times over. Or had he just given me credit?

Stop it, Danielle. Stop trying so hard to ruin things.

Self-fulfilling prophecy: I've never known any relationship to work out well, so I intend to make sure that this one doesn't.

Was that what I was doing?

I sincerely hoped not.

I'm working on it.

"Does Amy live in the area?" I asked pointedly.

"No. She and Gary moved away, to New Mexico I believe, and last I heard they are working on having a child." He opened the door for me and I slid right under his frame and towards the hostess stand.

"One of the very few advantages to being short." I informed him.

"I would think there are a lot of advantages to being short." He opined.

"That's because you're tall." We shared a smile then and the maitre'd sat us towards a tall window that overlooked a beautiful garden in full bloom. It was too bad the day was still gray, as the grounds were immaculate and I'm sure even more inviting when the sun was shining. I said as much to him.

"Yes, I agree. Look, there's even a path along the right side of the garden." Paul turned to the waiter then and asked him about it. Our waiter informed us that the house was actually an old converted mansion that used to house a Mayor and his wife, circa 1900. The mayor was well-liked and respected by all in the community, so that when his wife took ill the entire community took it upon themselves to finish the garden path that the couple had originally begun building together. She ended up passing away once the path was completed.

"That's a beautiful story, but what a tragedy," I remarked as the waiter went off to get us a bottle of wine.

"Some of the best love stories are tragedies." Paul remarked in turn.

"Like *Titanic?*"

"Like *Titanic.*"

"What did you think of that movie?" I asked knowing that it was virtually impossible that he had not seen it.

"I liked it. I liked the history more than the love story, but I could appreciate both." He paused a second. "Do you remember the shot of that one couple, the one that just huddled up in bed together while the ship was sinking? They knew they would drown, but they didn't even try to escape. That always bothered me."

"Bothered you how?" I tried to understand what he saw in it. The defeatist in me saw two people who were resigned to their fate, knowing that the chances of them getting off the ship alive or together were slim to none, so instead they chose to remain together. The romantic in me spoke of things like not being able to live apart.

"I guess I just thought it odd. Why didn't they even try? Maybe it scared me." We both stopped speaking for a second while the waiter returned with our wine and poured us each a glass. Paul continued, "Maybe they just couldn't live without each other?"

Since he posed it as a question, I decided to try and answer it for him. "I think that they were more afraid of living without each other, more unwilling to do that than to chance only one of them—most likely the woman—getting off the boat alive. I found it romantic and poetic in a heartbreaking sort of way. But I understand how you felt about them not trying. I would have tried."

"I saw it that way too. Heartbreaking. I like the idea of loving someone so much, of identifying so deeply with someone, that your own life would be completely altered and practically unlivable without him or her in it. And although you don't know how you'd really react until you were in a situation like that, I would like to think I would try to at least get her off the boat. The chivalrous part of me would want her to go on without me, because I think that true love is like that. You give completely. But perhaps that's a little pie in the sky?" He offered.

"Perhaps. I think it's amazing to hear a man your age say this, either way." And that slipped out before I had a chance to stop it.

"Yeah," He scraped his hands across his hairline. "I think that a lot of people in general are afraid to love like that. But if I had the chance to really love someone, like my parents and the way they love each other, I would take the chance, and I'm not so sure that a lot of men can say that."

Was this guy too much or what?

"I think a lot of people treat each other badly, they get into relationships with the wrong people and then when they move on, the damage is already done. People are afraid to trust." I was shocked to be able to share this with him, and I found myself feeling as if I was standing outside myself, hearing a voice speaking, but not being able to claim it as my own.

"Are we tackling another big question?" Paul asked me then.

"Which category would this fall under? If I remember correctly, we already went over God and Politics. We had yet to discuss Sex, Family, Future." Not that I was willing to jump into any of those topics either.

"I thought one of the remaining topics was Love."

"Perhaps you confused Love and Sex." I suggested this with a wry grin.

"I...ah, wouldn't be the first time." He blushed as he said that, and I tallied a few more points for Paul the Human.

"So did we just cover Love?" I didn't want him to feel rushed.

"I guess we kind of did." We were smiling at each other over the table, the kind of conspiratory grin that people in love tend to share.

Our waiter reappeared at that moment, hands laden with a bruschetta appetizer I simply couldn't resist and a puffed pastry with shrimp something or other for Paul.

"I love bread." I mouthed this as I inhaled a triangular piece of bread dressed with tomato.

"I do too."

"I don't get the whole low-carb thing." I made a face.

"Me neither." He made a face right back, then offered to share a piece of his appetizer, and we went halfsies, all the while discussing good bread vs. bad bread.

"I don't think that you can really get good bread outside of New York," I went on to discuss how all bagels elsewhere were simply bad imposters.

"New Haven, Connecticut has a couple of great pizza places, and good bread in general."

"I've never been there."

"I'll take you there sometime."

From there, we indulged in fragrant pasta dishes with Mediterranean flair, finishing off both of our plates. We opted to share dessert again, and just as we were getting done, he asked about what was next on the agenda.

"Well, I was going to take you to this park that I like to walk around, but…" I gestured towards the rain-soaked windows. "I think not. So I thought we could either go to a movie, or rent one, unless you had anything else in mind."

"I would love to rent a movie, if you don't mind. Whenever you go to a movie with someone, you never really talk, and I want to continue our conversation." Paul looked at me steadily, his eyes saying more than anything in the aforementioned conversation.

"Which conversation?" I wondered if conversation was a metaphor for one of the five big topics as a wave of desire swept powerfully down my spine.

"Any conversation." He paid the check and we left the restaurant soon after. We scampered to the car in order to avoid the ongoing drizzle, and as soon as both of the doors were slammed shut, he leaned over and kissed me full on the mouth. It was as expected as it was unexpected, and the wave of desire pounded forcefully against the base of my spine, tunneling around to ride right into my stomach, knocking me over with the force of a thousand oceans. I let myself go completely as my lips probed his, our tongues reaching out with urgency neither of us had allowed the other to manifest until now. His kisses were deep, his breath tasted of coffee and sweet dessert, and I found myself forgetting time and place and falling deeper and deeper as the minutes ticked by.

After a few minutes, he pulled away and looked directly into my eyes.

"Danielle, you're so beautiful." He chewed his lower lip a second, but his eyes were still fastened on mine, drilling into my soul.

"No, you are." I traced his lips with my finger, unable to believe that this wonderful man was interested in me.

He shook his head but didn't take his eyes off me.

"I'm so glad I met you." Paul grabbed my hand then and gave a quick squeeze.

I took that as a sign to get moving, so I rocketed the Cav into orbit and pointed her right towards my place. I had enough movies at my place to fulfill almost any appetite, so I chose to screw the rental and go straight home. Besides, I was hoping for some more interaction as well.

Once we pulled into my parking spot, Paul made mention of the fact that I hadn't stopped by your friendly neighborhood Blockbuster.

"I thought you wanted to continue our conversation," I smiled winningly in his direction.

"I do." He returned my smile with a brilliant one of his own.

We barely made it in the door when he took me in his arms again and continued kissing me, the intensity climbing with each step closer to the couch. My mind was trying to signal my heart, my heart my mind, when I told them both to buzz off and just go with it. Soon we were on the couch, his mouth still kissing and probing my own, body heat emanating from every pore, several degrees higher than mine, legs akimbo, my own body feeling safe and warm as I snuggled up as close as I could to him, allowing various sensations to ripple through my body, conscious on some level of the very real fact that I was falling deeply in love with this man.

"You're so pretty." He had stopped kissing me for a second, and he held my face in his hands as he said this with pure conviction in his voice.

"You're too much." I whispered this as my heart beat practically out of my frame. He was, he was too much, he was too good, and he was more than I had ever hoped for, better than my dreams.

"You okay?" Again, his eyes did a quick pirouette through my soul.

"I'm okay." I shifted a little underneath him, and he took the opportunity to prop himself up on one elbow and stare intently into my eyes. I held him there for a minute or twelve.

"Did you ever think about all the stupid little things you do, so many things in one day that you can't even put them all on paper, and then one of those stupid little things opens up a door, and suddenly, when you walk through that door, everything changes."

"Like making the bet with yourself?" I was trying to follow his thoughts.

"Even better, like crossing the street where I did each morning. How many entrances are there to Grand Central?" He asked incredulously.

"You're right." I nodded my head, my fingers still playing with his hand. "What are you saying?"

"That it was Fate."

"That we met?"

"Yes, Fate." He leaned back towards me and gave me a quick kiss on the lips. "You do believe in fate, don't you?" He pulled back.

"I believe in God, so yes, and I guess I believe in Fate, but I believe in Fate more as something God uses to get us to believe in Him." It was a roundabout way of explaining it.

"Care to elaborate?" He seemed genuinely interested.

"For example: Did you ever see a painting, and although you may not know who the painter is right away, you can identify a particular brushstroke? Something speaks to you, and you see the hand of the painter in the painting, so you instinctively know then who painted it?" I wasn't sure if I was describing it any better this time out.

"Yes, I have experienced that. Not so much with a painter, but more like with music. Sometimes I will hear the strain of a particular voice, and although I may not know the name of the song, I know the singer." He was in obvious agreement, picking up the thread as I continued.

"So even if I believe in Fate, how can I not believe in God? I have to believe that He is the author of Fate. His brushstroke is in all the little instances; those stupid little things you do, day in and day out. The reason you walk a particular way to work, or the reason perhaps one day you don't. All I'm saying is that I find it hard to say 'Fate,' instead of 'God,' although I can reason a way to see them go hand in hand. There's a large part of me that believes that we walk into fate, or that our lives are fated in a way that enables us to be whoever it is that God calls us to be. The same way you can't hear a song by Mariah Carey and not know it's her, is the same way that I can't see Fate intervening in my life and not know that it's the God I serve."

"Would you be happier if I just said God?" He was trying to appease me in a lighthearted way now, that infectious smile spreading across his face for the hundredth time today.

"Do you think that God is in this?" I wanted God to be the Orchestrator of all things Paul, but I was afraid to box myself into thoughts like that ever since I suffered the devastation of David, having believed with all my heart and soul that he was the man that God had intended for me to spend my life with.

"I think He is." Paul paused a moment, looked up, then looked back at me. "I would like to think that He ushered me to walk down a particular street, at a particular time, so that out lives would intersect. What do you think?"

"I would like to think the same." Oh, but I was so very afraid.

"I even think that my getting the new job was fated. Or God's design. Whatever. Let's put it this way: if I hadn't made the bet with myself and then had Rob hounding me after I actually got the job, I'm not so sure I would have gotten up the nerve to ask you out. So maybe I got the job because I was supposed to find you." Paul waxed poetic.

"Love, Sex, Fate…what's next?" I tried being flippant, but I was revolving in a universe that was right now on a plane one notch down from sheer panic. The terror that I felt was so palpable that I was sure that he could feel the pounding of my pulse, hear my racing heart, and besides that read my demented mind, all giving me away, paranoia on display. I adjusted the way I was sitting on the couch just then, taking myself half a beat away from him, determined not to get too close. All this talk of God and Fate and Love commingling made me incredibly uneasy, afraid to reach out and grab what was directly in my grasp.

Next.

So what do I do next? I let him kiss me, I give in to the good things that are happening, I tell my swirling stomach to immediately stop taking my attention away from this blessing, and I take a chance.

Maybe this time it is for real; maybe this time love will stay.

As our lips are locked together in a fairly amorous pose, I take a plunge off the high dive and I fall completely, utterly, and hopelessly in love with him.

Because I still believe in God and Fate and Love.

Chapter Thirty-Five

I wiped the sleep out of my eyes, stretched across the bed, and did a slow head rotation from right to left. I scrunched down a little deeper into the sheets, and let a slow, lazy smile escape as I started feeling more cognizant. When did Paul leave last night? I know it was late, a little after midnight, but not too much later, because the trains took a break in between midnight and five in the morning. I flexed my toes, and then pointed, feeling the blood move throughout all of my appendages, and I stretched again, for good measure. I checked the clock and was surprised to find that it was only a little after nine. Although I couldn't rival Lanie for time slept in on the weekends, I also was not known to be an early riser. Hmmm. My lips felt puffy and my skin a little raw from all that cheek-to-cheek, the impressions of his scruff left behind as a stinging souvenir. I didn't mind one bit; I wore it like a badge. My mind started replaying the events of the night before.

I felt good about what I could remember, and I felt more desirable than I had in ages just thinking about the feeling of his lips upon my own. I relived the things that we said, and I allowed myself to feel a certain segment of peace because of the fact that the night had turned out to be nothing more than tantalizing talk and delicious kisses. What if he had wanted to sleep with me? What if he had pushed? No matter, I told myself, and it didn't. There was time.

I stretched again, this time standing, and decided to go for an impromptu walk outside. The early morning fog was burning off, the sun peeking through, and the day looked to be much better than yesterday, as least weather wise.

I donned my sneakers, wrapped a sweatshirt around my waist, and was off. There is something entirely spiritual about walking in the morning when most people are either still asleep, or this being Sunday, perhaps at church. My mind flitted to church briefly, and I mulled once again the possibility of finding a church I could call my own, but I knew that God lived inside my heart, and somehow that was easier.

I addressed God as I walked, telling Him more about Paul and asking Him to give me the strength that I needed to give this relationship a fair chance. I didn't want to fall back on my fears, and I didn't want to hurt or get hurt. I prayed as I walked, prayed for wisdom and discernment, and for faith.

I remembered anew the saying that fear and faith cannot exist in the same vessel and as I pressed forward physically, I determined to press forward mentally and spiritually as well. Three turns around the lake and I was headed home, past Millie's beautiful flowers, and then on to my humble abode.

I returned to find this message on my answering machine: *Hello, Danielle, it's Paul. I hope wherever you are that you haven't eaten breakfast yet. Call me; I'd love to have you down for brunch.*

I felt like a teenager, and the boy I had a crush on had finally called to ask me out. Like a teenager, I thrilled at the message, and hesitated no more than a second before picking up the phone to call him back.

"Paul?" I asked as soon as he picked up.

"Danielle! Did you get my message?" He inquired gaily.

"Yes, I just got it. I went out for a walk. Were you serious about brunch?" I made little circles on the table with my hand.

"Like a heart attack. I would come up again, but I thought it would be nice if I made you brunch at my place. It seems like it's going to be a better day out today too, so we can go out and do Sunday things, like go to the park, or a bookstore." Paul's words were tumbling out, a mile a minute, and I knew him well enough by now to know that it was his way of excited persuasion that made him talk faster than even the average New Yorker.

"Sounds good." I looked at the clock. "It's a little after ten now, so give me a little time to shower and get down there?"

"Sure, should we say twelve?"

"Yeah, about twelve." I calculated how long it would take to go from sweaty to super. "I'll need directions to your place."

"No you won't. I'll pick you up at Grand Central and walk you over." He offered to meet me by the clock.

"That sounds great. Okay, what should I bring?" One thing Mom had taught me that I stuck by: never go to somebody's house empty-handed.

"Nothing. Just you. I will run out and buy all of your favorite Comics, and I am making breakfast. Do you like French toast?"

"Does Gumby bend?"

"An analogy that will only work with those in our age group…I love it! Okay, I get the picture. Just call me when you figure out what train you'll be on."

We hung up then, and I snagged a muffin mix from my cupboard, determined to bring something over for brunch. I could have picked up something along the way, but I thought this would be easier, even if it could never be considered gourmet. I quickly stirred the muffin mix together, set the timer on the stove and then jumped into the shower. Two hours later, I was there.

"Hello again," I said in greeting as I approached him at the center clock.

His greeting was to sweep me up into his arms and crush me in a power hug.

"I missed you." He looked deeply into my eyes, gluing me to the spot and subsequently shutting out all those around us.

"You just saw me." I chided, but I felt the same. There was something beyond perfect about his touch.

"Lucky me." He took my hand in his and we began walking. "What's this?" He gestured towards the bag in my hands.

"I made muffins."

"You made muffins?" And his voice, if not his words, said *Awwww.*

"Don't be so impressed; it's a mix." I replied abashedly.

We walked across Lexington Avenue together, and then made our way over past Third and onto Second. His apartment building had a doorman, and Paul greeted him gaily as we passed through the lobby.

He led me up to the fifth floor and then into his apartment. Once I entered, I couldn't help but laugh out loud, as the apartment personified Paul, as I knew him. The small foyer opened up into a masculine living area, dotted with pieces from Pier One and The Pottery Barn. His treadmill took up one corner, and the balcony was just a few steps from that. His kitchen had a small nook with two stools as well as a minuscule table with two chairs. I didn't peek into the bedroom and he didn't show me, which I thought was also a very male thing to do, as women tend to 'show the house.'

He had several pieces of Yankee memorabilia placed here and there, and a pillow on his couch that said something about golf.

"Your place is great," I commented, sure he was waiting for some type of comment.

"Thanks. I wanted to see how sunny it got out before I set the table. What do you say we set up out on the patio?" He nodded towards his sliding glass doors.

"Sounds good." I walked towards the patio and waited for him to unlock the sliding glass doors. He unlocked the heavy doors and then breezed me through, and I encountered another tiny bistro-styled table and chairs as I stepped out into the fresh air. My feet led me to the railing, and as I peered down the length of the New York

City street, I took in all that the view afforded me. I swiveled around a bit, taking in his taste in outdoor furniture. The bistro chairs were made of some type of ornate wrought iron, but they were welcoming nonetheless, and I found myself picturing him sitting by himself, enjoying a full cup of Kona coffee on a sun-dappled day, legs splayed the length of the small patio, the newspaper sprawled out about him.

Something in my mind's eye whispered permanence, and home, and things that my heart longed for and soul sought, deep in the darkest night. I felt my eyes well up with tears again, and perhaps because it was not the first time I had done this in his presence, that old nervousness tried to creep back in and make me take notice. I turned my back to the chairs and peered out again over the street, taking deep breaths and trying to hold it all together. I felt a tear running down my cheek, and I heard Paul talking to me from a distance, but I was unable to speak.

I knew I was starving. My mind fought to control my emotions: would a starving person choose not to eat? Would a starving person be embarrassed by the mere thought of food moving them to tears? I thought not. I think even the person feeding them would understand. I would hope so. I prayed a silent prayer and tried to compose myself before he made his way back onto the patio.

No dice.

I felt him behind me, heard him place on the table what sounded like two mugs, perhaps a tray or dish or something. I stayed resolute, my back to him, my hands shaking, even as my mind told them to still.

"Danielle, are you all right?" Paul came up behind me then, and I nodded as I fell into his embrace, still unable to respond verbally. Oh God, Oh God, Oh God, it wasn't supposed to turn out this way. I was supposed to come down for a nice little brunch and enjoy the man's company.

I wasn't supposed to fall apart at the seams the first time he invited me into his home.

Home.

I was smart enough to know that it was the *home* part that was getting to me, more than Paul, more than whatever impatience I felt with myself.

"I'm fine," But my voice belied my turmoil as I responded to him, and I already knew that he was way too smart to not know better. "I just...I'm sorry, I have a lot on my mind."

"Do you want to talk about it?" He responded by unfolding his arms around me and gently turning me around so that I would have to look into his eyes. I looked deeply into his eyes for just a second, though I couldn't help but waver, as the lump in my throat grew large once again.

"No, I'm fine. I actually feel quite silly," and I forced a laugh, but it came out stiff, and we both knew that something was wrong. I felt bad not letting him in, but I couldn't seem to wrap words around whatever it was that I was feeling, and my embarrassment grew.

"Danielle," he hesitated a second, enough for him to make sure that I was looking into his eyes. "Your secret's safe with me."

My laugh this time was genuine, as I knew that he was trying his hardest to understand, but what he said was so cliché that I couldn't help myself.

"I'm sorry, Paul, I'm not laughing at you," I assured him as I saw his look of concern deepen. This was great, I'm sure he now thought that I was certifiable, and I was managing to do nothing except dig my hole even deeper.

I tried again.

"It's just that...things are so good...you've made me feel at home here," and I couldn't help myself this time as huge tears made their way out of my eyes and coursed down my cheeks unbidden. *Stop it, stop it, stop it!* I screamed at myself from the farthest corner of my brain, but since when did the heart ever listen to the brain?

"Danielle," Paul breathed, "I want to make you feel comfortable. I want you to feel at home here. I want you to feel free to tell me whatever it is that's on your mind…I don't care what it is or what it could be…I just don't want to scare you away. I'm so afraid that I might scare you away, that maybe I might come on too strong, that perhaps you won't feel the same." He took a deep breath and continued. "I know we haven't known each other all that long, but I know one thing and that is that on some strange level, I know that I was meant to meet you. I don't believe in coincidence. I believe in Fate, always have, and moreover, I have always believed in God. I just haven't seen Him intervene in my life in such a strong and beautiful way before, and if it makes you feel any better, I'm scared as hell too."

I smiled at him through my tears, everything he said coming at me in waves, rushing through my body, my mind, my spirit, my heart and soul. I was afraid to hope for this, but here he was, bringing me hope on a platter, and my only response was a smile fraught with emotion and the waterworks that were wiping every last trace of makeup from my face. I cleared my throat then and tried to respond.

"I never thought I'd meet you." Was all I could say, but apparently it was enough.

"Neither did I. But we did, we met, and I think it's safe to say that God has a plan for us. You and me. I thought of us this morning and I felt extremely blessed. I just want this feeling to continue, in fact, I never want it to end." Paul looked at me tenderly. He opened up his arms and I fell into them, feeling warmth and sensing a safety that I couldn't put into words. He hugged me hard, and by the time he let me go, I felt more than a little stupid.

"I think I need to go to the Ladies' Room," I said by way of excusing myself, thinking I must look a mess from the tears wreaking havoc with what was once a made-up face.

"There is no Ladies Room in this apartment, only a Men's Room," Paul teased and his signature smile lit up his face once again. He pointed towards his bathroom as I made my way there. "I'll reheat these." He gestured towards the mugs of tea he had brought out onto the patio earlier.

"Sorry." I shrugged an apology.

"Don't be; that's what they make microwaves for."

I loved him. That much was final. I made my way into the bathroom and was surprised to find a large array of plastic ducks dotted throughout. His shower curtain also boasted an inordinate amount of ducks, and after taking in the atmosphere and fixing my makeup, I exited with a line that most people would throttle me for.

"I bet when you leave that bathroom in the morning, you feel *just ducky.*" It was a groaner, but I thought adding a little levity to the already emotional day couldn't hurt any.

"No Comics for you!" He threatened, but tacked on a lighthearted grin and then a swift kiss on the cheek. "Are you hungry yet?"

"I'm starving."

At least I could admit it.

Chapter Thirty-Six

"Do you see him?" Lanie pointed and her face contorted into something resembling pure evil. "I cannot believe he's *here!*"

I could see her point. In a city of eight million plus people, what was the likelihood of her running into The Bradomeister on New Year's Eve?

"Lanie," I was going to try talking some sense into her, but at that moment the crowd erupted into thunderous shouts and downright screeches.

Ten!
Nine!
Eight!
Seven!
Six!
Five!

The noise was louder than any rock concert I had ever been to, the energy higher than any drug I could even imagine.

Four!
Three!
Two!
ONE!

Whatever decibel the noise had registered at even a minute earlier was fully eclipsed by the breaking of the sound barrier on the *The USS Intrepid.* Confetti fell from the sky, and just about anything tossable was suddenly hurled into the air, party hats, balloons, and people alike. Soon the buzz heard all around was that the computers were still working, the lights had not gone down on Broadway, and Dick Clark was still broadcasting to us LIVE from Times Square on the monolith screens that were positioned on either side of our erstwhile DJ. The Y2K foreboding was over; it was time to celebrate the year 2000.

"Happy New Year!" Paul exclaimed as he planted a sloppy kiss firmly on my lips.

"Happy New Year!" I shouted back in return. The crowd around us was jubilant at best, inebriated at worst.

We shared a relatively sober smile over the din, our eyes locked on each other despite the chaos going on around us.

"I love you," He leaned in and whispered in my right ear. His whisper would qualify as a stage whisper by anyone's standards, but I felt the softness in his voice and melted into him as we swayed to Auld Lang Syne.

"I love you too." My mind reeled as I fast-forwarded through the events that had brought us to this very moment. We were so very blessed. I still couldn't believe that I wasn't spending New Year's Eve home alone.

"Looks like we have to go back to work on the third," Lanie was referring to the fact that the anticipated Y2K Bug hadn't downed the city's systems, at least not as far as we could tell. She even looked saddened by the prospect, which was unlike Lanie, so I knew that Brad being here was really bothering her. She enveloped me in a crushing hug then, which I returned with equal force. "I love you!" She hollered in my ear.

"I love you too!" I had tears in my eyes again. Would it ever end? It seemed as if the more time that went on, the farther away I got from Upstate, the more I let my new life be my reality, the more touched I was by just about everything. My eyes had turned into fountains; my heart overflowed with gratefulness.

"Now, can you believe that he's here?" Lanie jumped back to her most pressing problem, trying to point out Brad in the crowd, in the most inconspicuous way possible. It had been a couple of months since they split, but Lanie was far from over the fact that as soon as they got past various professions of love, Brad had gone AWOL to the point of no return.

"No, Lanie, I can't." I shook my head and gestured to Paul so that he would come down closer to my height. I relayed the situation to him.

"Tell her Rob is The Bomb." He nodded towards his friend and Lanie's date for the evening, currently making his way towards us with a tray of drinks.

"Buddy, where did you get the tray?" Paul gestured towards the onyx tray in Rob's hand.

"I swiped it." Rob had a twinkle in his eyes, the same mischievous grin that he always wore, the kind that would lead a paranoid person to believe that he was making fun of them. All the time. "One for each."

I lifted a plastic glass of champagne from his tray and leaned in to Lanie. "Rob is The Bomb."

"He's really nice." Lanie nodded. "I just hate Brad."

"So? That's no different than from when you were with him." I pointed out.

"Danielle!" She admonished me and then said something I couldn't hear over the noise. After that, she took off in a flash.

"Where'd she go?" Rob shouted over to me.

"I think she saw someone she knew." I informed him in a tone that was one step away from shattering glass.

That was the understatement of the year, and even though the year was still young, my bet was that it might still win out. Unfortunately (or fortunately, depending on how you look at it) Lanie and Brad had finally called it Splits Ville the weekend of Lanie's birthday this past October. Apparently, they had had plans for the birthday weekend, and then Brad called on Friday to say that he had to stay in DC over said weekend. Lanie dumped him the Monday night after he returned, not so much because he couldn't make it, but because he had totally forgotten that it was her birthday, and nothing celebratory had been done or said. When she explained it to me the day after, she stated simply that she feared that staying with Brad would have been a long string of forgotten anniversaries and broken phones. Broken phones? I asked this believing that she had meant to refer to broken promises. No, she meant she broke her phone in a fit of rage.

I told her at the time that I thought it was a good idea to shake him loose, and that she couldn't be smashing phones for the sport of it. I surmised that Lanie did not have the right kind of personality for somebody as absentminded as Brad. I also watched her as she mourned the loss of a man she insisted she never had anyway. It wasn't pretty.

Now it was Brad's bad luck (or Lanie's, depending on how you look at it) to run into each other on New Year's Eve. I wondered whom he was with, and how he had decided to come to this place. *The USS Intrepid* was NYC's floating Air and Space Museum, an actual aircraft carrier that was docked in New York Harbor, however tonight, the ship was decked for New Year's revelers from around the world. Paul and I had decided early on to throw our party hats in this particular ring, and Paul's friend Rob had gotten a set of tickets at the same time. Rob and his now-ex girlfriend Kate split up right after Thanksgiving, so Lanie stepped in at the last minute. The tickets to get on board were expensive and had sold out from their inception, due to New York City hosting one of the biggest Millennium celebrations there was. Had Brad gotten tickets a while ago; before he and Lanie had called it quits? That didn't make a lot of sense. Perhaps he had intended to go with Lanie. Perhaps he was here in the same capacity that Lanie was: a fill-in. I didn't say a word of this to Paul. It was Paul's fervent hope that Rob and Lanie would hook up eventually, but now that she had left our side for a quick round of Brad-hunting, I thought that the likelihood of that was slim to none and Slim had suddenly shown up on the dance floor.

I decided to direct my attention to Paul and Rob rather than fret over Lanie. After about a half hour, I saw her walking through a crowd and heading right towards me.

I gave her a look as if to say, what happened?

She grabbed my hand and dragged me to the Ladies' Room. It wasn't much quieter in there, but I was able to discuss the whole scenario without tearing my vocal chords.

"So I bumped into him. Literally. I scouted him out and hit him in the shoulder. I wanted to see what he'd do. He looked surprised to see me, asked me who I was with, etc." Lanie was filling me in a mile a minute, exasperation written all over her face. And resentment. Let's not forget resentment.

"What did you say?" I crossed my fingers and hoped she told him the truth. Rob might be obnoxious, but he didn't deserve to be dissed on New Year's Eve either. I was just hoping she didn't say No One.

"I told him I was with a date. He asked after you and Paul. Then, THEN, " She was screaming now even though I could hear her perfectly well, "he asked me if I would like to get together next weekend!"

"Lanie! What did you say?" I was stupefied. I could have never have predicted this one. I couldn't read the expression on her face and that scared me. A part of me wished she had told him to go to hell. "Wasn't he with someone?" Had he come alone? He could have brought the tickets prior to them splitting up. Did that mean that he had gotten stuck for an extra ticket?

"I told him that he could give me a call sometime." Lanie paused for effect. "Then I shook my ass and wiggled my way out of there!" She had this bizarre look of triumph on her face.

"Lanie, this is not healthy."

"I am not healthy, my friend. At least…not tonight." She checked her lipstick in the mirror.

"C'mon, let's head back to the guys." I waved my head towards the general direction of Paul and Rob. This was Lanie's problem. I had my own problems to deal with, such as meeting Paul's parents tomorrow for New Year's Day Dinner.

Who in God's name held a New Year's Day Dinner at twelve noon in modern America? Paul's parents, that's who; the June and Ward Cleaver of Commack, Long Island. Needless to say, I was not looking forward to this event, but I had escaped them so many times thus far that I felt I needed to oblige the man that I loved.

Besides, I couldn't believe that it had already been six months since we met, almost seven as a matter of fact; either way, he saw it as a long time for me to not have met the family. Just the way he said it unnerved me: *the family.* As if it were an institution that was larger than life.

For me it was. I have always felt like an outsider looking in. I have never felt a part of either of my parent's attempts at family. The thought of being a part of the very American concept of family both thrills me and terrifies me, all in the same breath. I want what I have never had: the security of people who are related to you, the knowing that they will love you no matter what life throws their way, the feeling that you matter to someone.

Yet I fear it. I fear it almost as much as I have feared falling in love with Paul, except with Paul, I decided that I would rather take a chance after several false starts and see if there was anything to what was spoon-fed to us on the sitcoms.

The one thing I did notice is that nothing ever got summed up in a half of an hour, twenty-three minutes if you counted commercials. Paul and I had begun discussing the New Year's Day Dinner since Thanksgiving, and although I had trotted out every possible stall tactic I could think of, in the end I took a deep breath and acquiesced.

Because I loved him, and I would even go so far as to suggest that I trusted him, although my heart always lagged on that count. Trust was a precarious commodity. I had come to learn, in my life anyway, that not trusting someone was usually the safer route, because as soon as the scent of trust hit the air, the stench of familiarity usually wafted in to take its place, and the original trust never stood a fleeting chance.

"You ladies okay?" Paul looked after me in a way I still found endearing, and I bestowed a gracious smile upon him as I returned to our little circle. I determined to let the next day take care of itself; the New Year had just dawned and we had some dancing to do.

"I am just fine," I reassured him by dancing up close to him in as flirtatious of a way that I could. "I think we should hit the dance floor!"

My suggestion was taken well, as not a minute later the four of us were rotating our hips and everything else in tune with the music. The DJ was playing good stuff, but when he began mixing in a couple of Freestyle hits, Paul and I went completely wild.

"They play TKA and I will simply go off the charts!" Paul shouted in my ear as he jammed right beside me.

"They're gonna!" I was hopeful that the nostalgia trip would continue, and sure enough, about three songs later, we heard the telltale sounds of a group that had been dubbed 'The Puerto-Rican Beatles.'

"Ho! Ho! Hoo-ooh!" Lanie came up behind me and bumped my butt. Soon the four of us were dancing together, switching places and partners, Lanie seeming to have forgotten about Brad's presence on the ship.

We went on like that for a couple of more hours, laughing and joking and shouting over the music as we worked up a thick sheen of sweat. We stopped once for drinks, but after that quick stop to refuel, we didn't leave the dance floor until it was time to go.

Outside the museum, the boys tried unsuccessfully to hail a cab. Lanie and I sat on a nearby curb, shivering as sweat continued to pour from our bodies, unconcerned with much else besides our feet. We had been dancing in heels for hours, and now we were both feeling the effects.

"We'll have a better chance if we walk in," Rob directed as we moaned and groaned and railed against him. He was right, we both knew, but it was almost four in the morning now and the shoes were killing us.

"Carry me," Lanie suggested in a way that was coquettish yet grand.

Rob did not oblige, but took her by the arm, she leaning into him, and escorted her gently, two avenues in, to where there were more people, places, and things.

"I spy a Diner!" Paul announced and then shot across the street, almost getting clipped by a passing cab. "We need food!"

"We don't need food," I protested from across the street. Any food eaten after midnight automatically settled right on my hips. I was better off taping a bagel to my butt, rather than eating at this hour.

"We need food," Rob seconded and then unlatched himself from Lanie, crossing the street to join his pal.

Lanie and I shrugged as we hobbled across the street to join them. It wasn't as if we could get a cab.

"The diet starts tomorrow," Lanie proclaimed.

I have to admit that I had to stop myself from hitting her with the door on the way in. Lanie and Diet should not even be allowed in the same sentence.

Had I not been espousing my beliefs on this subject to my dear friend who was ignoring me anyway, I may have seen it coming. Or should I say I might have seen *her* coming? Perhaps. All I know is that the next thing I knew, there was an overly blonde and overtly bubbly woman exclaiming Paul's name and kissing him on both cheeks.

"Paul! Paul! How are ya, sweets?" Although the blonde girl with the backless dress seemed overly familiar with my boyfriend, I stayed discreetly behind, watching the interaction, keen on taking her in and discerning just how she knew Paul.

"Hi, Aimee…I, ah…Happy New Year!" Paul was gallant but blushing, and just as my head was shuffling through the possibilities of exactly who this woman could be, it dawned on me.

Aimee. Not A-m-y, but Aimee, the ex-girlfriend. Actually, *the ex.* His David.

Uh-oh. I tried to give Lanie the high sign, but she was already shuffling over to an available booth with Rob. I was stuck behind Paul, frozen in place, thinking about little more than the fact that Paul had downplayed Aimee's beauty. A lot.

"And who is this here?" She said this as if she were peering into a baby carriage, goo-ing and gaga-ing over one's latest treasure.

I gave her a smile that I hope revealed the fact that I did not find her amusing.

At all.

"This here," Paul paused a minute, looked down his nose right back at her, took my hand and squeezed, "is my girlfriend Danielle."

Okay, if I didn't already love him…

"Sooooo nice to meet you!" She trilled. Her gaze upon me would have been considered unsettling, but it was so full of saccharine that I didn't allow her to rattle me any more than her outside appearance had already rattled me. Her body and hair alone would rattle Cindy Crawford.

"Guys, we have a hunger scenario going on over here," Lanie had appeared again, pulling us away from Aimee, and the look on her face showed that she knew whom she was. Or at the very least, what she was up to. Pure contempt. Oh, Lanie was good at this.

And Rob. Let's not forget Rob.

Thank Rob. Thank God.

"Oh, I'll let you go." Aimee dripped each word and then threw Paul a look that could only be described as lascivious. She eased past us then, which is the first time I saw another girl, presumably part of her party, standing near the door waiting for her.

Lanie turned on her heel and I followed her in silence. I could feel Paul behind me, but I was at a loss for words. *Let you go?* Just who did this chick think she was? I knew who she was, and I didn't want her within a ten-mile radius of Paul. This was the girl that had broken his heart, the girl he had sworn off all women after dating, the last girl he had introduced to his family.

Worse than all that, she was the girl that had made him doubt himself.

"Now you know how I feel! In a city of eight million people...!" Lanie threw this out as soon as all four of us were settled in the booth. Comedy is all about timing. We all laughed heartily and basically forgot about Aimee.

Except me, of course, because although Aimee seemed shallow enough to drown in a kiddie pool, she was gorgeous. Truly beautiful, the kind of nightmare you picture your boyfriend's ex-girlfriend to be. I was already stressed out enough about meeting Paul's parents, now I felt I had to compare to Christie Brinkley. Scores of Super Models flashed through my brain, and suddenly none of them could compare to the likes of Aimee.

Fabulous.

I drowned myself in a juicy (turkey) burger and fries, convinced I was only following suit as the others around me ordered various heart-stopping meals, all with the type of sides that don't generally peel off of your hips.

"You okay?" Paul inquired halfway through. I must have been a little quieter than usual, perhaps allowing my nervousness to take over, maybe contemplative...either way, it was nice that he noticed.

"I'm fine." I leaned across the booth and kissed him full on the mouth. "It's going to be a great year."

Was I reassuring him or me? I hoped neither; I hoped it was a bona-fide prediction. I was smart enough to know that now is the time we would get down to the nitty-gritty; most relationships coasted on lust and excitement right up until about the six month mark and now was the time to dance or get off the floor.

Since I already had on my dancing shoes…

Chapter Thirty-Seven

I woke up in a daze, forgetting where I was and then smiling to myself as I saw Paul stretched next to me. I had planned to stay over from the outset, but Lanie and Rob ended up staying too as taxis were scarce and they were both too kicked to move, much less find their way home safely. I strained to hear Lanie and Rob chatting in the living room, and my curiosity piqued, wondering just how well they were getting along.

When we had all decided to stay at Paul's apartment last night, we stayed up as long as our eyes would stay open. Even though Lanie and Rob both lived in the city, Paul convinced them to stay, because after burgers and disco fries galore, grabbing a taxi would have been a chore, and no one could deny that we were collectively beyond exhausted. We came to find out that up all night at 21 and up all night at almost 30 were completely different scenarios, our bodies baked and done. Upon arriving at Paul's, the four of us crashed in an array of overtired bodies on the couch, our dresses and various remnants of a glitzy evening resembling something close to art as we lazed. Once our words began making less and less sense and our eyes threatened to shut mid-sentence, I took the initiative and announced that I was retiring. Paul pointed out where his extra pillows and blankets were hiding, and I stole away to the bedroom with him and left them to their own devices.

Now I could hear them laughing, the kind of laugh that you knew they were trying hard to suppress, perhaps in the hope that they wouldn't wake us. I slithered out of bed and made my way out into the living area.

"Good morning, Sunshines," I called as I shuffled into the room.

"Ah, good morning to you," Rob was grinning from ear to ear. I looked from one to the other, but wasn't able to pick up on anything other than the feeling that I had just walked in on a private joke.

"Hey girl," Lanie called out in greeting but did not move from her perch on the love seat. She was still buried in a blanket, a carefree attitude surrounding her, her face lit up as bright as Rob's.

"Did I miss something?" I wanted in on the joke. I situated myself on the stool nearest them in the breakfast nook. Swung my legs like a kid. "What time is it?"

"Almost ten. I was going to wake you up soon," Lanie volunteered this, but forgot to answer the question as to what they had been chuckling over. I was just about to tease her for being up so early when the time registered in my brain.

"Omigod!" I shot up off the stool, instant nervousness replacing the lazy calm I had just been experiencing. "We have to be at Paul's parent's house by noon!" I felt my throat constrict and my legs shake all at the same time. I didn't want to be late, I didn't want to make a bad impression, and now we would have to rush in order to get out there in time. This was not the best recipe for avoiding a panic attack.

"Calm down, Yellie. Get in the shower, I'll make coffee, and Rob can go jump on Paul." She climbed out from under the mountain of blankets and padded into the kitchen. "Just point me in the right direction."

I showed her where the coffee was and then did as Lanie had instructed, hoping that Rob didn't crush any pertinent bones when he jumped on Paul in an effort to wake him. Once ensconced in the bathroom, I took a power shower and muttered a quick prayer that the day would go off without a hitch.

Who was I kidding? The whole day was a hitch. Paul's parents represented so many problems for me; namely, mine. I knew well enough to know that it was only a matter of time now before Paul started pressuring me to meet my family. What if his parents suggested something involving both families? How could I gracefully decline? Would it be appropriate to tell them that my mother's husband was in jail, and therefore, all picnics would have to be scheduled for a visiting day? How about trying to explain that my father and his wife had yet to hear about Paul? How could I explain that to June and Ward? Should I even try? What had I done when I was with David? Nothing, I remembered now. I had convinced myself that nobody had had time to meet David before he left for college, but the truth and nothing but the truth So Help Me God was that I had never even entertained the idea. David was a separate entity in my life, and automatically deemed far too perfect to be let in to my very imperfect world.

I hadn't wanted him to run away. I was scared, but David had left me anyway, never knowing where I had come from, or what I was up against. Could I trust Paul to know everything there was to know about me and still love me in spite of it all? Would he stick around, once he was confronted with the disparity between our two families, if I ever even let that opportunity occur for us?

Did it matter? I believed that it wouldn't really matter if his parents didn't take to me anyway. I started blow-drying my hair the minute I got out of the shower, trying not to waste a minute, my heart beating wildly in spite of the deep breaths I kept taking so that I wouldn't burn out before I went over the bridge.

"Yellie, let me in," Lanie knocked on the door and I carefully unlatched it as I moved the temperature on the dryer from Hot to Warm to Cool. I was sweating.

"It's unlocked," I called out over the dryer. I tried blotting my face with my other hand, then gave up and shot the dryer on Hi/Cool directly into my face.

"That looks like my kind of blowjob," Lanie remarked, and I promptly burst out laughing. Leave it to Lanie.

"Thanks, I needed that." I shot her a grateful grin and held the dryer back towards the nape of my neck.

"Are you all right? I figured you might have tried to drown yourself by now," Lanie quipped. "Seriously. Please don't worry about this. They are people. People, that's all…just people."

"People suck." I said in return.

"That's true, a whole lot of them do. But these people helped to raise the man you love. Paul is such a great guy, Yellie, that they might not be all that bad. And he loves you, don't forget that." She reminded me gently.

"I know he loves me. That's not the problem. The problem is that I'm not so sure I'm ready for this. I feel like such a hick. I feel inept, and just not good enough. I hate this!" I sat on the closed lid of the toilet for a second. I knew I was making things worse, but I couldn't stop myself, and my legs started shaking again as I sat there, near tears.

"You'll be fine," Lanie assured me as she rubbed my back in a circular motion. "C'mon. You have to get ready and get out of here. Trust me, they won't have fangs."

"If they have fangs, I'm calling you. And you can deal with them," I threatened, wishing I was Lanie for the briefest of brief.

"Fine. I'll have my cell phone on all day. Did you forget that you would be with Paul?"

"And who will you be with?" I gestured towards the wall that Rob was sitting directly behind.

"Perhaps." Lanie was evasive. "Who knows? He invited me over for a game marathon later, and I just might go. He's funny as hell, Yellie, and we had a lot of fun last night and even this morning trading war stories." She shrugged.

"That sounds good," I said by way of encouragement.

"It is good; I can't get over how I went off the deep end when I saw the Bradomeister last night." Lanie shook her head. "I think I have some residual feelings for him."

"You think?" We both giggled and then Paul knocked on the door.

"Ladies, I smell!" He tried to coerce us out of the bathroom. Upon our exit, he told me that I looked nice, and that not to rush because he had already called his Mom and that everybody was off to a late start.

"Who's everybody?" I gulped.

"I didn't tell you that Pee-air and Co. would be there?" He sounded surprised.

"No, you didn't." Great, now I got to meet his brother too. I pondered whether it was better to get it all over with at once, or two by two? My mind registered that I didn't really have a choice.

"Well, they will be. But don't worry. Pee-air will have too much fun ranking on me to even notice you," he stated with chagrin.

He hopped into the shower then and I continued to get dressed and put on makeup in his bedroom. Soon we were ready, and Lanie and Rob bid us farewell, Lanie wishing me luck again, with Rob thanking Paul profusely for the crash pad.

Paul hailed us a cab over to Penn Station, where we were scheduled to depart for our trip out to Long Island. Somebody would be picking us up on the other end, as Paul and I had been unable to secure a rental car for the first day of the new millennium.

"If I knew a good travel agent…" Paul had quipped.

The New York City foot traffic was at a fever pitch. It was always like this during the Holidays, but this year was exceptionally busy, as New York City had thrown a New Year's Eve like no other. I had a maniacal thought of ducking into the crowd and making a quick break in lieu of meeting Paul's parents, but I soldiered steadily on towards the train, Paul holding my hand tight beside me.

Once aboard, the pounding of my heart only heightened, and as each mile drew us closer to our destination, I found myself growing uncharacteristically quiet. Paul sensed that I was nervous, and he did a good job of just being there, rather than being in my face.

"Only three more stops," He said and squeezed my hand as punctuation.

"I'm not ready for this," I blurted out to him, and then grew angry with myself for saying it. What on God's Green Earth was I afraid of? I had lived through so much worse than this; I was a survivor after all, and a little dinner at my boyfriend's family home should be a walk in the park compared to my family gatherings.

"You'll be fine. They're going to love you," Paul reassured me with his words and his eyes fixed on mine. "I love you."

"I love you, too." I pressed closer to him, determined to swallow some warmth from his arms as well as his eyes. I just hoped that love was enough.

Too soon, we pulled up against the platform and alighted from the train. We wound around the stairs to where he'd told his Dad to meet us. As soon as we came bounding down the stairs, I was accosted by an older version of Paul, leaning up against the railing, waiting there to meet us.

"The Dadster!" Paul exclaimed and then grabbed his father up into a big bear hug. A slap on the back here, a loud greeting there, and then Paul remembered I was standing directly behind them.

"Dad, this is Danielle." Paul brought me closer to him and I extended my hand to Mr. Corsi.

"Nice to meet you, Mr. Corsi." I shook his strong hand and met his eyes. His eyes looked to be kind, and I let myself relax a little bit, because I felt a good vibe coming from him.

"There is no Mister here," He tsk-tsked me in a way that was altogether affectionate. "Please call me Roy."

"Dad!" Paul exclaimed, a deep red flushing his cheeks. He turned to me. "His name isn't Roy."

I laughed then, and thanked God silently. Mr. Corsi had broken the ice and as I looked his way, I saw a hint of mischief in his eyes. There was nothing to be scared of here.

"My name is Phil." He opened the car doors with a beep and a quick wink from the headlights. I looked to Paul for confirmation and he nodded; no ruse this time. As we made our way to the house, Mr. Corsi explained that he used to do that all the time to Peter and Paul as they were growing up, and still tried to pass himself off as someone new any time he met people today. It was pure fun, he insisted, and I agreed. Paul told him about my love for the Comics, and we talked the rest of the way about the few things left in the world that could be considered pure fun.

Once we pulled into the driveway, we all agreed that we could add ice cream to the list of Pure Fun. I stipulated, however, that the working off of ice cream calories was not what I would consider pure fun.

"Marie is going to love her," Phil decided as we walked up the brick path to the front door. The house itself was typical of what I knew to be Long Island: a raised ranch laden with Christmas lights and plastic snowmen adorning either side of the front door. The front door was red; the house white with black shutters, and the whole effect was welcoming in a picturesque sort of way. I began to breathe easier. When Phil swung open the door, he called up to her from the landing.

My first impression of Marie Corsi was terribly Cleaveresque, right down to the apron tied around her waist, gaily in its joyous pronouncement: *Let It Snow!* She was shorter than her husband, but still taller than me, with a round face and an ample figure that nobody would ever call fat. She was the obvious choice to name as the person Paul had inherited his brilliant smile from, and as we made our way up the stairs, she bestowed that smile upon me.

"Danielle, so glad to finally meet you," She said this in a way that warmed my spirit, as if she really had been looking forward to meeting me. As she welcomed me, she clasped one hand under and one hand over my own, and I was surprised to note that I didn't feel uneasy around her at all. She further broke any remaining ice by asking, "What did he tell you his name was?"

Phil laughed heartily and then gave his wife a soft kiss on the forehead.

"Roy." He shrugged and then asked Paul if he wanted a drink.

"Roy?" She threw her hands up in the air as if to show us all how exasperating he was. "You could have picked a better one than Roy!"

Peter and his wife had yet to show, so I had a few minutes to get to know Paul's parents exclusively, and I found myself thanking God for at least the hundredth time that day. I always fared better with things coming at me in smaller waves, rather than one Hawaii-style wave ready to toss me about, and God obviously knew what I needed that day.

We had drinks and talked ice cream. Paul poured a drink for each of us and made sure he was right by my side every chance he got, deferring to me a little more than usual, meanwhile enabling me to feel comfortable in a way that I had not foreseen. His attention was both flattering and reassuring, and I reminded myself to thank him when we left.

Soon Peter and his wife Madeline arrived. Peter resembled Paul in certain ways, but his face was far more similar to his mother's than either Paul's or Mr. Corsi. He carried himself in a way that suggested he was far more serious than Paul or any of his familial contacts, but he seemed affable nonetheless, and obviously enamored of his wife. Madeline had reddish brown hair, a body that screamed ballet dancer, and was someone you could easily picture being called Maddy, if in fact she weren't so serious herself. After a flurry of greetings, Mrs. Corsi/Marie seated us at the table and regaled us with her appetizer wizardry.

Marie had actually created little flags, fashioned from colored toothpicks and some type of heavy paper, to adorn each of the appetizers she placed out on the table. Each flag said something like: *Curious Crab Dip* or *Quiche Me Kate,* so that the person imbibing the pre-dinner treats would not be wondering what exactly each creation was all about. She was worse than my biggest nightmare: she was June Cleaver and Martha Stewart all rolled into one, even to the point of not allowing any of us to help her serve or display anything.

"You can all help clear your plates," Was all she said, as she flitted about, determined to ply us with all things festive. Paul's Dad took care of the drinks, and before I knew it, almost two hours had passed.

"Dinner is on the way!" Marie announced with a flourish. Peter opened up a conversation about DC once she had stepped away, and I felt happy that I could contribute to the topic, having been there two or three times to see different hotels for work. I told Peter how I had been through The Holocaust Museum once, as I had scheduled a weekend trip the same as I had for Boston, with one day free to see the sights. The Holocaust Museum had touched me deeply, and the devastation that I had encountered had lingered with me for days afterward, stinging me each time my thoughts returned to that time in history.

"I have a friend whose grandmother survived a camp," Madeline interjected. "I met her once, and I have never forgotten the sight of the tattoo on the inside of her arm."

I nodded in a way that I hoped relayed that there were no words to express it, the horror that people endured, for no good reason, and in fact for no reason at all. From there, the conversation shifted to current events and was just about to ellipse into politics when Marie set down the last tray of food on the table.

"Now eat up, all of you, and no talk of politics between the boys." She said this with an air of finality, and when I looked across the table, I saw three men looking appropriately derided.

Topics shifted from the mundane to the ridiculous, and I found myself easing into my own skin as each minute passed, feeling a part of something good, albeit still waiting on some unconscious level for the ensuing eruption. I wasn't used to family events or holidays coming off with such ease; in either one of my family situations, there was always a hidden agenda behind good behavior, or people would take it as an occasion to stomp on each other in the veritable safety of numbers.

No such thing happened here, as the dinner flowed right into dessert, and Paul made a big display of teasing his mother for making Peter's, and not his, all-time favorite dessert.

"You make it sound as if nobody else would like *Death by Chocolate!*" His mother insisted.

Soon the day was over and Paul's Dad offered to drop us off at the train station the same way we came. We said our good-byes and piled into the car and were just about to pull out of the driveway when Paul's Mom came out to the front patio and began waving her hands like a wild woman.

"Marie? What, honey? Hah?!" Phil called to her from the front seat, but was unable to make out whatever she had been trying to relay to him. "Paul, go see what your mother wants."

Paul bounded from the car and came back a minute letter with a brown bag in his hands, a shameless grin reaching from one side of his face to the other.

"Leftovers?" His father questioned, one eye on the bag and one eye on the road.

"A little cake and a bag of chips. Some Heinz." He shrugged as if it was no big deal, but he gave himself away, looking like a kid who had hit the Trick-or-Treat destination that all kids long for: the house that gives away full-size candy bars.

"You still eat those sour cream and onion potato chips with ketchup?" Phil shuddered.

"I got Danielle to eat them too!" Paul decided to bring me into the fray, as if to defend his strange tastes. "She loves it."

"I don't know about love…" I trailed off in a way that suggested that Paul was absolutely bonkers.

We shared a laugh and then Phil's taxi ride came to a halt. He reiterated, as everyone else at the house had also, how happy he was to have met me. He invited me to come again anytime, with or without Paul.

Once Paul and I boarded the train, he took a deep breath, looked me directly in the eyes and said, "So?"

"So I like them. They're all really very nice." I nodded assent, and thought about the longing that had ratcheted its way up in my heart every moment as the day progressed. How could I explain to him that I had never experienced anything like that before? That not all people's holidays were like that?

"What did you think of Pee-air?"

"Pierre is really very nice." I was repeating myself.

"Madeline?"

"Was she a dancer?"

"Yeah, I think she took dance in college. Why?"

"You can tell."

"You can?"

"Women can."

"Oh, *women* can." He said this as if he had just discovered the theory of relativity. Or the Theory of Women.

"Women can tell certain things, especially about other women."

"Like what? Give me a for-instance." Paul challenged.

Don't ask me where this came from, because I really don't know.

"Like Aimee is a fake." I surprised myself even as I heard the words pop out of my very large mouth.

"Aimee is a fake." Paul paused a minute. "I really didn't know how to handle that last night, Danielle, and I hope I did well by you. Nobody was more uncomfortable than me running into her."

That's debatable, I thought, but refrained from saying this out loud.

"I know. I'm sorry. You handled yourself fine. I honestly don't know where that came from." I knew where it came from; it came from the part of me that bleeds green. The darkest part of me, where my insecurities lie, buried deep, only to arise at moments such as these.

"Well, it should have been discussed, anyway, I guess. What did you think of Mom?" His voice sounded eager to switch the topic back to family.

"Your mother is related to Martha Stewart, that I know for sure," I said in a tone that was purposely lighter.

"She is." He said this with a straight face, and then laughed his deep and throaty signature laugh. "You know she would love that, right?"

"I got the picture." I was trying to ease into our usual banter, but my heart felt heavy, and I wondered if he was able to pick up on it. I felt bad about the Aimee comment, and that bad feeling was still lingering, permeating my view of the holiday as a whole. Why hadn't he told me how pretty she was? So what if she was fake? Was it that she had been fake both inside and out, was that what was playing on my mind? Sure, she looked a little fake, but that kind of beauty wasn't just poured from a bottle; otherwise everybody would have some.

Plus, who was I to judge? David was the King of all Fakes, and I didn't hear Paul throwing that up in my face. What the hell was the matter with me? I had started the day obsessed and paranoid about meeting his family. When had my neuroses then shifted back to Aimee?

Just now. Enough. I was calling a truce with myself.

I'm working on it.

"I just wanted to make sure you had a nice time. I tried telling you that they didn't bite, but I knew you had to find out for yourself, and now I'm glad you did." Paul summed up the day as such.

"They didn't bite," I smiled and then leaned in to give him a soulful kiss. The next thing we knew, our train had pulled into Penn Station.

"Are you going home?" He asked as we walked towards the Exit.

"Yeah, I need to do some stuff tomorrow before our first day back," I said this instead of saying how I really felt, which was that I felt I needed some time alone. Luckily, New Year's Day had fallen on a Saturday, so I still had Sunday to recoup prior to returning to work on the third, which was Monday.

"Okay." He looked at me curiously. "Let's grab a cab to my place and then I'll walk you over to Grand Central."

"Fair enough." I could tell that he was more than a little disappointed.

I just couldn't express the need that I had to be alone with my thoughts, as well as my hopes and my fears. The past two days had been big ones for me, whether Paul knew it or not, and I desperately needed some space and downtime.

As I trudged in the door to my place, I saw my answering machine light blinking, but chose to ignore it a minute as I made my rounds as succinctly as always, checking around each corner and even in the fridge.

I found nothing changed or shifted or moved or stolen, but when I looked really hard, I found the same ghosts lingering in the corners of my mind, so I tried unsuccessfully to read, and fell asleep with the lights on.

I woke to find the lights blazing in the middle of the night, a soft reminder of a habit that I had almost ditched during the onset of my relationship with Paul. I felt exhausted, but unsettled, so I decided to get up and go to the bathroom, and then took another quick tour of my apartment. What was I looking for? The parents I never had? I was acting morose, and I couldn't control my feelings, nor did I necessarily want to.

I noticed the light on my answering machine still blinking, so I hit the button and heard Am, my father, and mother all wishing me a Happy New Year. I vowed to call them back in the morning, as it was presently three AM, and I wasn't so sure that they would appreciate a call right about now.

I tried reading again, contemplated a hot cup of apple cinnamon tea, but all roads led to my eventual staring at the ceiling and crying out to God. The day spent with Paul's family had left a hole in my heart; an indescribable pain that was keeping me from sleep. How could I express it? I couldn't; but I trusted God to understand me regardless, and somehow help me rise above it. Would the pain of my lost childhood ever go away, or would I always wind up maudlin and depressed after any outing with a group of people that I considered a 'real' family?

I recalled the initial shuttling back and forth between my parents, directly following their divorce, and the pain that I could not express to either one audibly. Whenever I was with my mother, I longed to see my father, and wondered when he would call and schedule our next visit. When I was visiting with him, I usually worried about her being alone and then worried on a cataclysmic level after she married The Monster, knowing that I wasn't there to protect her. When they first got divorced, I used to dream that one day they would get back together, but even my young heart knew that some dreams were better off left in just that realm, for they had never really gotten along that great when they were married anyway.

I sighed. I guess it was just a little girl's fantasy: Mom and Dad and the white picket fence. If I was going to be totally honest with myself, I would have to admit that my best times ever spent with my mother were after the divorce, for she had been a force to be reckoned with at that high point in her life, and delving deeper into the honesty pit, I would also have to cede that my best times with my father had either passed or were yet to come.

So how could I long for something I had never truly had? I didn't know the answer to that question, and as my eyes finally grew tired, I got up to shut off the light and settle into whatever sleep I had left to find. I just knew that it was there: a longing, a faceless and nameless demon that never left, no matter how much I tried to push it aside or pretend it didn't matter. Paul's family had stirred up the demons, and now I had only to face it head on.

Chapter Thirty-Eight

The next morning dawned gray, but I busied myself with taking down my tiny Christmas tree, stowing gifts in any conceivable space I could find and participating in general housekeeping that involved my apartment and my brain simultaneously. I spoke to Paul at a couple of different intervals, but I mostly ignored the phone, the television, and everything except the conversation that seemed to be going on inside my head.

I thought briefly about painting, but I felt silly putting together Christmas ornaments when the holiday had just passed, so although I shot my painting supplies a somewhat longing glance, my heart wasn't in it, so I refrained. I had finally gone out and bought a few small plaster craft pieces in the fall, but the only thing I had managed to do since was stare at them as they took up space in an already tight apartment. I had meant to do them before the holidays, I had brought seven ornaments with the intention of adorning them with paint and glitter and holiday cheer, but as of today, the pieces still sat there, bare and hoping that one day I would again pick up a brush.

My stall tactics had reached an all-time high; diversion was key in the Land of Danielle, so I sought out a new mystery and buried my head in that until the day turned dark.

Perhaps I had rested too much throughout the day, but as soon as the day fell into night, my mind was awake and running into overdrive. Although I wasn't sure if that was a viable reason, I was willing to blame my lazy day for the fact that I could not fall asleep.

The next morning came all too soon, and as I showered, I considered the approximate amount of hours I had actually slept, barring the conversation with God and self in the wee hours of the morning, minus the tossing and turning that eventually woke me before the alarm.

Why do we do this? Those restless nights when all you really need is a glass of burgundy wine or a prescription drug or two, you play the alarm clock game. You look at the clock at the ungodly hour of two AM, adding and subtracting in your mind…*if I fall asleep right now, and the alarm is set for six, I can still get four hours' sleep. I can exist on four hours, if I come home early tonight and get six…maybe eight…heck, if I hit the snooze button three or four times, I can pick up an extra thirty minutes…*

Guaranteed there's a guy in Uganda playing the Alarm Clock Game/Charade right this very minute. It's universal.

The point is that as I was doing this, I found myself making excuses for myself, and that is something I very rarely allow myself to do. The whole "if my parents had been normal parents, I wouldn't have all these problems" shtick. I caught myself at it and shook it off, the same as my shower water once my feet hit the floor, and I continued to wash away all thoughts counterproductive.

I'll be having none of that,

Thanks.

I continued getting ready for work, raced for my train, and made it to work in enough time to grab a yogurt on the way in. Like every other woman spanning the face of the Earth today, I was on a New Year's Resolution Diet.

"Welcome back and spare me," was Lanie's greeting the minute I opened the door to the hole/office. We hadn't been to work in over a week, which meant one of two things: it was either going to be an incredibly busy or a beyond dead day. Only time would tell.

"Spare you?" I inquired. "And a Happy New Year to you too." I shrugged off my coat and scarf.

"Are you kidding me with that yogurt or what? You'll be back on bagels by Thursday." Lanie huffed in a way that only truly skinny people can.

"You have nerve. I thought you were going to help me out with this," I pointed to the accused cup of yogurt.

"I will help you by making sure you don't blow off the gym. I will not help to make sure you imbibe embalming fluid in the morning," Lanie chided.

"Uck." I threw the yogurt down on my desk. "Thanks, Lane. Now I can't eat it anyway. Besides, how would you know what embalming fluid looks like?"

"I just know these things," she shrugged. Then she faced me head-on. "So how did it go?"

"With Paul's parents?" I shrugged right back. "They're unreal, Lanie." I proceeded to tell her how nice they were, how conciliatory everyone was towards me, and how genuinely in love Marie and Phil seemed to be, even after all these years.

"How was the brother?" She inquired.

"A little stiff." I explained Peter and Madeline as best I could. "They were nice as could be, but I could definitely understand how Paul and he sort of lose it with each other."

"So it was good." She summed up.

"It was. I just…" As shrugging seemed to be the order of the day, I gave in and shrugged again. "I have reservations."

"Of course you do. Why shouldn't you? Look at your background! You lived with a bunch of nut jobs, people you called family, but those same people never acted like a family should. I'm sure those martians out on Long Island probably scared the crap out of you." Lanie summed up again.

I exhaled for the first time in what seemed like days.

"I hoped, no–better yet, I knew–that you would understand." And Lanie didn't know the half of it. There was so much I never told anyone.

"Of course I get it. The question is, does Paul get it?" Lanie confronted, and I'm sure I blanched visibly.

"I don't know." I shook my head and felt again as if I were going to cry. "I haven't really told him anything."

"Anything about anything? Or just anything about your family?"

"Anything about my family. He knows about David; that's when he told me about Aimee. By the way, thanks for the quick rescue the other night." I paused and Lanie said that I was welcome, but that we could discuss that in a minute. "As for family matters, lets put it this way: he knows my parents are divorced, he knows that it was strained, I've showed him the picture I have up in my house of Mikey Jr., but that's about as far as I've ever gone. I never even told him my mother remarried. It just seemed a lot easier to leave The Monster out of things. I didn't want to have to explain the whole jail thing…the living in a trailer nightmare…it exemplifies that whole Upstate lifestyle, and I just don't want to have to deal with that anymore. He hasn't met any of them yet, and I have to admit that I kind of like things that way. I always believed that meeting his parents would mean that I'd have to reciprocate, so in part, that's why I shied away from it all this time."

"That makes sense, Yellie, but eventually you are going to have to let him in." Lanie reminded me.

"I know." I dreaded it.

"As for Aimee, what's her story?" Lanie asked, getting down to the nitty-gritty.

"Her story is that she is Paul's 'David.'" I paused a moment and let that sink in. "She was his first girlfriend after college, her family lives out on the Island too, and Paul met her at a party one night for an old high school buddy of his. She was there with a friend of a friend, having no better offers for the night, she decided to go, and Paul said that they met that night and they liked each other instantly. How could he not? Did you *see* her?" I was still wowed by her looks, unable or unwilling to concentrate on the fact that Paul was no longer with Cinderella.

"Stay on topic," Lanie directed. "She's attractive. Paul is not with her. Period, now go on."

Lanie is the type of great girlfriend that every girl needs. If I could bottle *her,* I'd make a million.

"By the way, how big of a jerk was I when I saw Brad the other night?" Lanie laughed, and I thought it good that she was at least able to laugh at herself.

"A little jerky."

"A big jerky."

"How about a beef jerky?"

"You're a beef jerky!" She exclaimed and at that precise moment, the phone started ringing off the wall.

It was a good hour before either of us was able to come up for air. We decided to finish the conversation over lunch.

"So what happened between you and Rob?" My tone indicated that I thought something had.

"Nothing happened. He is terribly nice, and very funny in an offbeat, sarcastic, loud sort of way. His humor takes a little time to acclimate to, but I definitely had a good time."

"Paul says he's a pain in the ass, but he means it in the nicest way possible. The first time I met him, he was ossified, so I thought he was sort of an idiot, but after that, he just kind of grew on me each time."

"Why was he so drunk?"

"He and his girlfriend had broken up, and Paul said he was devastated. That was why he had the extra ticket for New Year's." I explained.

"I'm glad they did. We dished a lot at Paul's house, and I admitted acting like an idiot myself over the Bradomeister, and he chimed in with some stories about his ex. Then I ended up going to his place the next day, and we had a marathon Trivial Pursuit session. He seems like the type of guy who acts all cool and funny, the life of the party so to speak, but he also seems like the type of guy who would give you his left foot if you really needed it."

Lanie paused a minute. "There's a gem lurking," Was Lanie's pronouncement.

"That's about the same way Paul describes him. He says he's the type of guy that would give you the shirt off his back," I parroted Paul's description of him.

"Foot, shirt, what's the difference?" Lanie said in her best Long Island accent.

"Not much as far as I'm concerned." I had to probe further. "Any sparks, though?"

"No."

"Just no?"

"No. I mean, I guess I could say not yet. It was a nice time, could be a good friendship. Why? Are you and Paul conspiring?" She narrowed her eyes.

"Not exactly. It goes without saying that it would be nice if you two hooked up, but I think it would be a stretch to say that we're conspiring." I hadn't really even discussed it with Paul.

"Good. I don't need you getting your hopes up," Lanie pointed a finger in my direction, stabbing home her point as she spoke. "Aren't we paying people for that express purpose?" Lanie quipped.

"Getting our hopes up?"

"No, helping us to figure it out."

"I think you're right," And I thought about the last time I had seen Constance. Boy, was she going to get an earful the next time. Just like most of the advertising agencies in the city, the majority of the businesses in New York closed for the week in between Christmas and New Years, and shrinks were no exception. In fact, they all took off the month of August too, so as most Therapy cardholders experience, the best time to have a breakdown is certainly not the last week in July.

We settled our bill and retired to the hole/office, and by the end of the day we both felt as if we had never left. I heard from Paul sometime amidst the chaos.

"Feels like you never left, huh?" He remarked as I described to him the day I had been having. "I know the feeling. I'm up to my eyeballs over here."

"I'm picturing you buried in paper, and it looks pretty funny," I thought out loud.

"I'm sure it does. Go ahead, have your fun. I'm hoping to dig out by the weekend."

We both laughed.

"So did you have a nice time yesterday?" He inquired tentatively.

"I did." I thought about what else I should say. "Your family was great." So sorry I couldn't return the favor.

"Well, rumor has it that you were a hit," Paul informed me.

"A hit?" That felt good.

"A hit. Mom already invited you for whatever the next holiday is," he chuckled. "I miss you, baby."

I felt a warm feeling move from my stomach throughout the rest of my body, and I wished I could be in his arms, if only for a moment, just enough to get me through until the next time I saw him again.

"I miss you, too. Do you want to get together tomorrow night?" I offered. I would stay down here if it made it easier to see each other.

"You have the gym tonight with Lanie?"

"Yes, and I must go, or I will hate myself profusely."

"Gotcha. Tomorrow it is. I'll talk to you more later, love you baby, bye."

I got in a quick 'love you too' before I hung up on my end.

"This is going to be a very good year," I said as I turned to Lanie. I didn't know why I felt that way, I just did, and although the announcement may have felt a little premature, it felt good and it felt right.

It was also something I had never had the courage to say before.

Chapter Thirty-Nine

"Dad!" I was surprised to hear from him again so soon after he had just left a message. "Happy New Year!"

"Did you get my message?" He inquired.

"Yes, yes, I did. I was out in the city, spending some time with friends." I said this by way of explanation in order to answer the unasked question of why I hadn't called him back yet.

"No matter. Just wondering how you were." His voice sounded low, and I pictured him hiding in a closet or crouched behind a door, as if calling me was a covert operation.

His wife had never given me even one occasion to feel that way; for all intents and purposes, she was a very nice lady. She was invested in her child, my brother, and she seemed interested in whatever was going on in my life. I thought that she genuinely loved my father, no matter how mismatched I have thought them to be through the years, and I thought that he had real emotion behind the rough exterior, for her, and for all of us.

I just didn't feel like I fit in anywhere. I felt intrusive, in my father's new life and even in my mother's chaos. I felt like I didn't matter, either way to either one of them.

This is why I am forever shocked when pursued by either one of my parents. Had their lives calmed down enough for them to consider me? Or did it just dawn on them that I had moved away?

"I'm fine," I responded after a moment's thought. I was fine. I was happy. I had a boyfriend. I met a man. I fell in love. Would he care?

"Where did you go on New Year's?" He inquired.

So I told him about The Intrepid, and my father offered out that he had once gone on a tour of the ship. I told him how impossible it had been to get a cab, and we both laughed about that truism, especially in the midst of the holiday season. He shared a funny cab story. I then told him about going to a friend's house on New Year's Day. He said he was glad I had a good time. Just as my heart thought it safe to let him in, to ease into the topic that the person was more than a friend, Michael Jr. picked up the other line and began shouting into the phone.

"Say hello to your sister," My father instructed, and I tossed it around with the little one for a little bit.

Soon it was time to go. I said good-bye to Michael Jr. and the same to Dad, giving my regards to his wife. The moment had passed and I decided there was no use in telling Dad about Paul just yet.

The truth is that I was chicken.

I delved into a new mystery and tried to convince my mind to shut off so that my body would follow. After reading the same paragraph several times, I put my book down and stared at the drop ceiling that adorned the little space that I rented. Paul's apartment was so much nicer than mine. Paul's parents were so much more normal than mine. Paul's life seemed so much better than mine. What the hell was he doing with me?

As if on cue, the phone rang again and it was Paul.

"Hi, honey, how's your night?" He opened with this and I saw the irresistible grin in my mind's eye, easily wiping away any trace of insecurity.

"Better now," I responded in truth.

"Did you kill yourself at the gym tonight?" Always interested in the most mundane aspects of my life, Paul never ceased to amaze me.

"Almost." I went on to describe in detail the kickboxing class that Lanie and I were practically married to, knowing that it would elicit at least a few laughs from him.

"So is the instructor a guy or a girl?"

"We have yet to figure that out."

He described his day to me, and somehow the whole world seemed better.

"So are you staying over tomorrow?" He asked. He had been pressuring me to try and stay over at least one night during the week, in order so that we might spend some more time together, as well as to drop my commute from the level of harassing to miniscule.

"Do you want me to?" I already knew that answer, but I needed to hear it again.

"Absolutely! You know, we need to talk about you being here even more often. How does permanently sound to you?" He said it in such a way that any woman would be flattered.

"Scary." I said the word and then realized it had popped out of my mouth. How long had we been together? About six months? It was too soon, not long enough for me to trust him, plus I didn't want to live with anybody without some bigger commitment. That was only one of the many various mistakes that my mother had made with The Monster, and I was patently unwilling to make the same mistakes.

"Okay, I can understand that," Paul said in return. "But we have to talk, Danielle. What do you say we set aside some time to talk this weekend?"

I said okay but my heart wasn't in it. We got off the phone not long after that, and my heart had sunk down to my knees. As I got up to brew a hot cup of tea, my brain shouted out: I knew it!

I knew the minute that I had stepped into his parent's home, I knew the minute that we took things up a notch…I knew that that was when he would start pressuring me into more. Sure, I thought it would come in the form of meeting my parents; sure he would begin campaigning on that platform…but now this! Alas, did it really matter? I knew that this relationship was too good to be true, I had always known it, and my biggest failure was in letting myself forget it. I wiped every positive thought from my mind in the midst of this tirade, only to scold myself a minute later on the opposite tack.

What was I doing? I had a man who loved me, who had been born into a family steeped in normalcy, and I was pushing him away (again) because I was scared.

UGH!

If I could pound my head into the wall with any positive result, I would probably give it a whirl. Instead, I picked up my book again and tried to shift all the stressful thoughts that were clouding my mind, believing for peace, striving to stay in the area where faith reigned supreme.

I filed a question for Constance way back, in the corner of my mind: would it always be this hard? Would I always struggle to maintain a sense of balance in my thought life? Would I always have to wrestle with the ghosts of days gone by, the ghouls that specialized in broken promises? When would my mind finally take the valiant step that it needed to successfully blot out the past?

When did the hurt stop? When could I trust Paul implicitly?

I tossed and turned and woke up in the middle of the night with my book collapsed upon my chest, the bookmark strewn elsewhere, and my covers all tied up in a knot. The resurgence of restless sleep was trying like hell to throw a wrench in my plans, not to mention my back, and I couldn't express how devastating I found this to be. I felt my sleeping habits giving me away: I was not looking forward to whatever talks Paul had in mind for us.

Chapter Forty

Tuesday dawned gray again, as was my mood, so I found it altogether fitting that I couldn't even rush to make my regular train, only trudge to the platform as if I were going to the guillotine.

I called Lanie from the train, but when she picked up her cell, she said that she was running late too, so whoever got there first should open and buzz the other for breakfast. I agreed and proceeded to the hole/office.

On the way there, I remembered that I had forgotten to pack a fresh pair of socks for the next day. This was just one of a myriad of reasons I didn't like staying with Paul. I wasn't in my own space, and I always forgot to pack something. Sure, he made it easy for me: like buying Equal instead of Sweet and Low, not to mention the telltale fuchsia toothbrush that I had stashed away in his medicine cabinet. But that wasn't the point. The point was that staying with him made me feel less in control of my situation, and I feared losing control more than anything.

I had seen what could happen when you allow yourself to lose control. It wasn't good.

Once I arrived at work, I got inundated with a slew of electronic annoyances that led me to completely forget to call Lanie for breakfast. She arrived cranky and then tramped out to get us something to sustain us, namely caffeine, as well as a bagel of some sort.

So much for the yogurt.

As soon as we were fed, the phones died down enough for us to reconnoiter and talk. The forecast was for snow, and we were desperately trying to connive a way out early when the phone started up again, enabling us to scramble for lunch sometime close to three in the afternoon.

It was just one of those days. Some call it the post-holiday blues; I didn't give it that much credit. Lanie didn't have to go see Clara, because Clara was still away skiing, so we dished and bitched and had a total hen fest.

Paul called in the midst of chaos.

"What time do you think you'll be paroled?" He asked succinctly.

"Unless it snows, I figure sometime around six." I still felt as if I was going to the guillotine, and I couldn't put my finger on the face of why. I just knew that I hated the mere insinuation of the word talk. Talk always meant bad things; in fact, I had grown up to equate the word *talk* with the word *pressure.*

"Good. I'll pick you up then?" He posed it as a question.

"Okay."

Before I knew it, it was six o'clock and Paul was looming in the doorway of the hole/office. I gathered up my things and locked the door behind us as Lanie and I exited.

"Let's try and get in on time tomorrow," Lanie suggested as we left the building.

"I will be, I'm staying down here." I informed her.

"Love," she said as a parting greeting and waved as she turned the corner.

Love.

Paul took my hand and escorted me across the various streets and avenues to his place, all the while throwing out endless options for dinner.

"I really don't care." I didn't; I was worried and fed up with trying to decide. I wanted him to decide tonight.

"Well, we could always order from the Chinese place around the corner, you love their spring rolls," He offered.

"That's fine." Was my reply.

"You okay?" He asked solicitously.

"I'm fine." Universal language for *not fine.*

We entered his apartment; I took off pounds of winter apparel, dropped my bag, and went and hid in the bathroom. By the time I came out, he had ordered Chinese with no help from yours truly.

"Danielle, what's going on?" He lit the lights on his tree, which was still standing in the corner, looking positively exhausted after having done its job throughout the season, wanting only to be left alone now, in the dark.

"You didn't take down your tree yet?" It came out as an accusation, and I didn't mean it to, but out it came.

"No, I thought I would do it this weekend. I wasn't ready to take it down on the second." He moved to light the three-wick candle I had brought him for Christmas. The room smelled instantly of vanilla.

"Oh." I couldn't think of anything else to say, which was more than unusual between us, so I curled my legs up underneath me on the couch and waited for him to proceed.

"The guy at the Chinese place said, *'Ten minute.'* Paul tried.

That got a small laugh out of me, because no matter when you called the place we ordered take-out from, could be the middle of the Chinese New Year, and the same guy always gave us the same approximation of time.

He sidled up to me then, and leaned in towards me, in an awkward attempt to put his arms around me. I remained where I was, not altogether stiff, but not exactly falling in to him either.

"Talk to me, Danielle," Paul said with a sigh.

"About what? You're the one who wanted to talk," I reminded him.

"I do. I do want to talk. Hey, look at me," he swiveled himself around until he was half-on and half-off the couch, and directly in front of my face. I didn't even realize that I had been looking away from him.

"I'm looking at you." I didn't want to because I knew how dangerous his eyes could be. I'd gotten lost in there before.

"Danielle, I didn't mean to scare you the other night," he began and then the doorbell rang. He got up, paid the delivery guy, and then set down the food without opening it. "I just want us to talk about where this relationship is going." He hesitated a second and gestured towards the food, but I waved him away.

"It's going good." I said this flippantly, and I knew it wasn't enough. Rather, I knew that it wouldn't be enough; for Paul could be demanding when he needed to be, which was only part of the reason he was so good at his job. Oh, why did I clam up like this? I wished I could will myself to be as open with him as I was with Lane and Am, or even as open as he was with me.

"Not *how* it's going, but *where* it's going. I know you have the gym with Lanie a couple of nights a week, and I don't want to take that away from you–"

I cut him off right there. "And you won't. What do you think, that I should just stop going to the gym in order to be with you?" I was suddenly hot all over, and there was a massive bolt of anger flaring in me that I couldn't wrap my hands around.

"I, ah...no. That's not what I was saying at all," Paul looked nothing short of flabbergasted, and if I had been in a right state of mind right then, I may have even recognized it.

"Well, what do you want then?" I was totally on the defensive and knew I couldn't stop myself. I had a roiling turmoil building in my stomach. When The Monster had entered the picture, my mother stopped dancing. She used to be on a bowling league, for God's sake, and he made her quit that too. I wasn't about to fall into any situation that even hinted at resembling that.

"I just want to see you more," He shook his head in disbelief. "Why are you getting like this?"

"Getting like what?" I knew what he was asking, but I was having a hard time defining it myself.

"Getting all defensive and stuff. I didn't ask you to quit the gym, I would never do that. Did I ever do anything to lead you to believe that I was like that?" His voice was rising and his features were falling into a pose that a generous person might call indignant.

"It doesn't matter. You'll want everything eventually. Now that I met your parents, it'll never end," And as soon as I said it, I threw my hand over my mouth, in a gesture that would hope to keep in the words that had already escaped and done their damage.

"Is this what this is all about? Meeting my parents?" He looked bewildered at best, but I was swirling around in a pit of despair, reliving scenes from my mother's unholy union as well as the few endless diatribes I had witnessed coming from my own father. I concentrated on me and not him, and I couldn't escape from the selfish vortex that was dictating this entire conversation. My mind was steadily screaming *Stop!* But my mouth appeared unable to listen, and then my stomach felt as if it was about to give, and my heartbeat escalated to the point where I thought it may just jump right out of my chest.

"It's about the gym," I spat out at him. "How much more do you want?"

"What do I want?" He was pacing now, looking at me as if I was an alien that someone had dropped into his living room, and he knew not what to do with her. "I just want to see you more. I want to know where we're headed, because I want us to be in the same place. I was going to ask you to move in with me, but apparently I already ask for too much. I don't get it, Dani; everything seemed to be going so right. Am I wrong again? Because if I am, I wish you would just tell me."

A small piece of my heart broke when he called me Dani. Nobody else called me that, and I loved it, but had never been able to tell him how precious I thought it was, only that I didn't mind it at all when he called me that, as he had asked the first time he'd shortened my name.

Pure silence.

"Paul," I began, but then choked on what would have been my very next words. "I'm sorry. I can't." I shook my head, unable to explain further.

"You can tell me anything, Danielle. What is it?" Paul waited patiently for me to speak as tears streamed down my cheeks unchecked.

"I just...I don't want to lose..." and I couldn't speak. Standing outside of myself, I couldn't believe I was doing this. I was duly embarrassed and I couldn't express myself without blubbering further.

"You won't lose me," He offered as he stood over me. He got up to get me a tissue, then handed it to me and sunk back on his knees in front of me.

"I don't want to lose me." There. I said it with clarity, and I found myself proud.

"I don't want you to lose you either," he said this with such sincerity that I promptly burst into tears all over again.

"I...I'm sorry." I shook and I cried and I knew not how to explain it all.

"Am I going too fast?" Paul asked gently. "I don't know what happened to you, Danielle, but I know that there's something...something that keeps you all wrapped up inside. My intention was never to scare you. I only want to love you. I hope you can see that."

I could see that, on the brightest of days, but then my mind got cloudy, and I couldn't see anything, except whispers on the air, and haunting cries that tried forever to drag me back to a place where everything hurt.

"It's not about David." Was all that I could think to say, and it wasn't really David, or not David per se, and I wanted him to know that. David couldn't hold a candle to Paul, and I needed him to see that, but I was struggling to tell him in any way that included a descriptive sentence.

"I believe you." He gave me a long and hard look as I tried to wipe off the tears and makeup that I'm sure had made my face look wonderful. "I need you to tell me what it is though. I need to know how you and I can make this work. Danielle, I have never met anybody like you before. You get me. *You get it.* And you can't trade that for anything."

"I know. You get me, too, more than anyone." I tried a small smile in an effort to reassure him. It was true. My so-called family didn't know me very well at all, and even Am and Lanie didn't get the nuances, or share the jokes that we did.

"Think you could tell me what's on your mind then?" He tried again.

I wonder if I wished hard enough; if it would somehow be easier or all go away.

"I can try." Where should I begin? I took a deep breath and then turned to face him head-on. "I love you, but sometimes I…get really scared. When you said you wanted to talk tonight, I panicked, and I also jumped to conclusions when you started talking about the gym. I'm sorry about that, it's just that I know a lot of people who start out great, and then as soon as they begin making demands on each other, the whole thing falls apart. I don't want that to happen."

"That doesn't have to happen. We don't have to turn out that way," Paul assured me, taking my hand in his own and staring intently at me as I wiped away another tear. "I feel as if I can't request something though, without you thinking that I'm making demands on you."

"That's my fault; I'll get over it." I tried to wave it away, wishing it could be that simple.

"It's not that easy." He stated the obvious.

"I know that. Don't you think I know that?" I was annoyed by what I felt was an attempt to dismay me. I knew I had problems in this area and I told him that I would deal with them. Why wasn't that enough? Why couldn't he simply trust me, and take me at my word?

"Well, how can I help you?" Paul offered.

"You can't."

We sat there in silence for what seemed like forever. I tried to look away from him, but I felt his eyes on me, calling me back, so I turned to face him once again. I was about to speak when he began talking in a voice that wasn't confrontational, but soothing.

"I want to see you more often. I want you to be around, I would love for you to move in here. Now, is that so bad? That's all I wanted to discuss with you tonight. I didn't want to take away your independence, and I don't want to intrude on any of your other interests or relationships. I love you, plain and simple, and I want to spend more time with you. Do you think there's a way that we can do that?" He was using logic, which would work with a logical person, but I was too far gone for that, and I think that he didn't want to acknowledge something that might make me look like I wasn't fully there.

"I think…" and I trailed off for more than a minute, playing with the golf pillow on his couch. Suddenly, I felt a wave of peace come over me, a gentle prodding that swelled within my spirit, and before I knew what I was doing, I had started to speak. "I know I haven't told you this, but I know you need to know this in order to understand me better." I took a deep breath and continued. "My mother ended up getting remarried after my parent's divorce. She married a guy that was less than nice, very controlling, and basically ruined her life." As if that summed it up.

"You never told me this." He was giving me a look that said bewildered, and the body posture of a man betrayed.

"I never thought it mattered so much. But I've been around enough to know now that this might very well be the reason that I've been reacting to you the way I have been," I took another deep breath. I mean, whom was I kidding? Of course I knew it mattered. I also knew full well that it was *the* reason I was reacting the way I was to him, no *might* about it. Anyone who had taken even so much as Psych 101 in college would have been able to see through the likes of me. That much I had figured out in therapy, right away, as soon as I heard myself talk. I thought briefly about telling him about my therapy, but I kept silent instead, easing in to telling him, and then retreating, deciding there were certain things that needed to be kept on a need-to-know basis.

"It was a very bad time for us." I began again; this time with what I thought was more gusto. "My mom and I used to be the very best of friends; we were there for each other in ways large and small when she and my father divorced, and I really admired her then. After a short time, she married The Monster, and everything changed. She changed. She began doing everything he told her to do, and it got so bad that eventually she lost herself. Then we changed. She and I have never been the same. I saw what could happen when you let somebody in like that. It's a scary world to live in when somebody else is running it for you." I shuddered at the thought.

"Does this Monster have a name?"

"No, he doesn't."

"Okay." He took this in stride, patting his leg, most possibly in an effort to not throw his hands up in the air. "Are they still together now?"

"Not really." As far as I was concerned, The Monster being in jail would stay in the need-to-know category. They weren't divorced, but they weren't together. Semantics ruled the day.

"And you think that I'm going to turn out to be like this…this Monster?" He gave me a look that said he was overwhelmed by the mere concept.

"Well, no." I was at odds about how to better explain myself to him. He made it sound so simplistic; suddenly I felt that I had made the wrong move in opening up to him. It was my own fault because I panicked. That's it: I had panicked, and now he knew too much. "I just get scared. Can you understand that?"

"I can understand that." He nodded several times. "I can appreciate that too, but I still feel like there's a whole lot you're not telling me. Am I wrong?"

I started crying again in answer, unable to conclude my part in the conversation, and second-guessing myself in every way imaginable.

"I don't know," I said through a torrent of fresh tears.

'You don't know?" He was getting agitated, I could tell by the pacing that he was now involved in, wearing a hole in his rug as he scraped his hair across his face and made sounds that were rather unintelligible.

"I don't know…" I felt like a basket case, as I had never acted this way in front of him before, and I also felt helpless, because I couldn't articulate what I was feeling. Of course there was a whole lot I wasn't telling him, but how much of that really had to do with us, and how much of what I had hidden needed to come out now? I didn't know how to tell him any more than I already had, at least not yet, and I wished with all my might that he could live with that.

For now, at least, I wished less were more.

"What don't you know, Danielle?" He stopped in his tracks and faced me again. "You don't know if there's more to the story? Either there is or there isn't."

"I don't know how much I can tell you without sitting here crying like a fool." I collected myself a moment and trudged on. I determined that I would not be a victim here, or anywhere, with anyone, ever. "I don't know how much of my life even pertains to you; I just thought that you should know that my fears are not totally unfounded. There are *reasons* that I feel the way I do, and *real reasons* that I act the way I do, and I wanted you to be aware of them."

"Well, how long are you going to use these *reasons* to put up a wall between us?" His voice was dripping with sarcasm.

"As long as you insist on making demands on my time," I replied tartly.

The silence invaded the room again, this time with a defiant air, both of us wanting the same thing, but afraid to bend, and unable to see.

My heart split fully in two as I sat there before him, knowing that I had the power of life and death in the palm of my hand, however unable I was to acquiesce to his request set aside, so I sat in a place that rendered me unable to do anything less than decide that this relationship would go the way of death.

Because who was I really kidding anyway? There was no way to tell, there was no seeing eye, and there were no guarantees. This much I knew for sure.

He took a deep breath and sat down beside me again.

"Can we try this again?" He took my hand in his and sat in such a way that I was forced to look him square in the face.

I stared at him and didn't say a word.

"I love you. I want to spend more time with you. I don't want you to have to give up anything in order to do that, I just wanted to see if we could figure out a way to make that happen. If we can't; we can't. I simply wanted to try. I would also like you to consider moving in with me. That would be an easy way for us to see more of each other without you feeling as if I was imposing on your schedule. If that makes you uncomfortable, then that's fine too, but then we do need to discuss where we both see this relationship going, if we see ourselves headed in the same direction. The other half of our conversation is about what has gone on in your past to make you so afraid of me, of us, of all that we can be together. I want to hear all about it, I want to help you through it if I can, but I need you to let me in. I never even knew your mother had gotten remarried until today! Much less that this person had such a negative impact on your life. I knew none of this, and I can't do this on my own, and I can't read minds, and I'm not even going to try. I will sit and listen to you, whenever you're ready, the same way that I did when you and I talked that night about David and Aimee and all the crap that we've been through. Do you remember that night?" His eyes searched my own; hopeful that I would count that night as a good memory for both of us.

"I remember." And I would never forget. That night was the first night I had ever stayed over at his place, and we had poured out our hearts until the wee hours of the morning, getting to know each other in all the ways that mattered.

"Good. I want you to remember. I want you to realize that I can be there for you, and that I can try to understand you, and do everything humanly possible to reassure you that I love you, but that's it. That's all I can do; the rest is up to you." He ended on that note, and got up then to cross the room to his kitchen table. "Are you hungry?"

I wasn't hungry, but I tried to eat along with him anyway, my mind focusing on our exchange, churning with every bite of spring roll, my stomach finally settling as the conversation shifted from us to the food.

We fell asleep not too long after eating, his arms wrapped around me in our usual pose, my mind unable to shut off completely, and my heart full.

I dreamed not.

Chapter Forty-One

"Has he ever given you reason to believe that he will take over, demand control, or leave you feeling powerless?" Constance asked.

"No." I answered honestly. "No, he hasn't. I just can't help feeling that way." I sighed for the hundredth time that session, each sigh getting deeper as I recounted the conversation with Paul.

"I think you're dealing with a lot of transference. All you've really known is the role of men taking over in your life, you've seen your mother give in to The Monster on unhealthy levels all of your life, and you're scared. You are convinced that no man could ever make a request that's not a demand, and you're placing Paul right into the pack. That's okay; it's just something you are going to have to work on. You're actually going to have to remind yourself, every day if it helps, that Paul is not The Monster." Constance wound up her speech by crossing her legs and readjusting her seat.

"I know you're right. The same way I know that Paul isn't about to steamroll into my life and just take over. Deep down, I know that about him; I know he's just not like that. But it doesn't make it any easier. I can tell you that I'm big enough to realize that what I have is an irrational fear, I can admit to it, but I just can't seem to stop it. And when that fear comes over me, I can't seem to put on the brakes. I try, and I fail, and the anxiety takes over without warning, sometimes getting so strong, that I feel powerless to overcome it. Then I alternate: the other irrational fear that I have is that he's going to leave me."

"Again, I see this as transference. Think about your relationship with your father. He left you and your mother. He went on and started a new life without you. It's not so far-fetched to believe that it could happen again. You have to decide to let Paul be Paul in your mind."

"Keep the ensuing cast of characters out of the limelight?" I asked.

Constance chuckled. "Sort of. Yeah, that's a good way of putting it."

I laughed too then, the laugh of an outsider, an observer that shakes her head at the craziness of it all. Why was there clarity in this chair? One that I couldn't seem to find anyplace else? I could recall clearly having felt this way in church at different times, but since I hadn't committed myself to any one church in quite some time, I knew that feeling only as a far-off memory, no longer tangible, a belief that I could feel that way only lingering in the slightest way possible. Then it was off to the real world, where emotions ruled supreme and I couldn't see straight to save my life, much less understand what I was feeling while I was feeling it.

"I really do try not to let every bad thing from my past ruin the good things in my future. I want to conquer that area of my thought life, and I want it done yesterday." I insisted.

"I believe you do try, and that you are trying. You have to actually give yourself credit, Danielle. The fact that you are even *in* a relationship means that you are hopeful." Constance nodded vigorously as she threw out her assessment.

I was hopeful.

I knew that, if I were to dig to a point where I could find my most authentic self, I would even go so far as to admit to being a sometime optimist, an often time romantic, and a person who still believed in good triumphing over evil.

I left Constance that day and trailed back to work, head still elsewhere. The January day was unseasonably warm, and I found myself looking up and drinking in whatever the sun had to offer.

"Want a coffee?" I asked Lanie, cutting off her greeting as she picked up the phone.

"Love one."

I stepped into the Caffeine Altar/Starbucks and ordered a raspberry mocha cappuccino for both of us.

Why not?

Then I proceeded back to the hole/office, determined to take control of my life in every way possible. I had done well so far: I had moved away from Upstate and all that my old life represented, I had taken control of my erstwhile relationship with my wayward mother, and I had even set boundaries with my father and his new family situation. The last frontier was my thought life; I needed to take control of it once and for all, and come away clean, with no demons to show for it.

I shared with Lanie what I had been thinking as soon as I returned to work. Her words to me were:

"Do you have a plan?"

"I have determination."

"You'll need a plan."

"Like breathing techniques? Forget it." I wasn't sold on anything New Age, and I wasn't about to be.

"I mean a plan of action. What you're telling me is that you want to rein in your thoughts, and overcome some emotional hurdles. For that you need a plan. You don't just decide and it happens. You can't just wish hard enough and see a result. Like everything else, you have to work at it."

"Like how?"

"Like the same way you picked up your stuff and moved two hours away in order to be closer to your goal. What was your goal then?" She asked me point-blank.

I thought about it a minute before I answered her. "My goal was to get as far away as I could from the Upstate mentality. Nothing ever happens up there; people resign themselves to life. I wanted to be where things were happening, I wanted to go where I could be in control of my destiny, and I wanted to get as far away from the hurt as I possibly could." I shrugged. I didn't think I had ever said that out loud before, and it felt freeing and unfamiliar all at the same time.

"Good. And you did just that. You extricated yourself from the situation. But now you have to leave your luggage at the door. You can't move into a brand-new house and bring all of your old shit with you." Lanie made a face.

I laughed at her analogy, and a minute later Lanie joined me.

"I mean it, though," Lanie elaborated. " I know it might be a crass analogy, but listen to what I'm saying here. I think you need to drop the baggage at the door, and then fill the entrance hallway with a lot of pretty pictures. You've done great so far, but now I think its time for you to take the next step."

"Which is what?" I asked in all sincerity. "I am doing all that I know how to do right now. I'm in therapy. I go to the gym pretty regularly. I pray and I still try and cultivate a relationship with God, even though I'm not going to any particular church at the present moment. I've read every self-help book on the planet. What more can I do to get some peace in my life, and trust Paul, and move on once and for all?" I was exasperated, but not with her, just tired of life expecting so very much of me.

"Tell the truth." Lanie's eyes challenged me, but her voice was soft, and the moment she said it out loud, I knew that she had touched on something valuable.

"The truth?" A scripture rose up in my spirit. *The truth shall set you free.* Like I just did? The same way I had said out loud the reason I had really moved from Upstate?

"The truth. The truth about everything that has happened to you: good, bad or indifferent. The truth about your past, and whatever events happened to make up that past. You need to tell Paul the truth. Tell him everything. What good is a serious relationship if you can't tell him everything anyway? You need to tell your mother the truth about whatever happened between the two of you. Forget

The Monster. Believe it or not, he's not the real issue there. It's your mother. It's easier to hate him, and blame him, because you have no allegiance to him. He's irrelevant to the relationship you now have with your mother. You need to speak the truth to her in a most desperate sort of way. You still rescue her too much, and you don't even realize that you're doing it. You also need to face your father. You need to tell your father the truth, about his new family, and how you felt when he left, and how you still feel inside." Lanie said.

"Lane, it's not that easy. I can't just tell everyone how I feel, despite how much that might hurt them, and say 'Okay, now I feel better.'" The mere thought of espousing the truth to these people scared me right down to the very core. What would they say? Would they hate me, would they not be able to see what it was that I needed from the telling? Who cared? Was I afraid that Annemarie would get teed off because she chose to stay, because she actually likes to live life at a slower pace, and my telling would come off like judging? Why was I so scared? It wasn't as if my father could leave me more then he already had; I was aware enough to know that neither one of my parents could hurt me anymore. Unless I let them.

"What's the alternative? Because until you do that, I can guarantee that you will always wrestle with these same type of things."

"What's the point? I mean, I lived through it already. It's over." I was all too aware that I was trying to convince not just Lanie, but myself as well.

"It's not over. You can't move on, Yellie, and you can't convince me that you can, not without getting the truth right out on the table."

I found myself unnerved by her, however conscious I was that what she was saying was right. I pondered her theory, but rejected it in spite of the verbose way that she presented it to me, because words were still words, and actions spoke louder than words.

"What about you? This is a great theory, Lanie, but what about your relationship with your father? When are you going to tell him how you feel? The truth?" I challenged her.

"I have an appointment to see him this Saturday. His secretary has me penciled in." She laughed as if she had just told the most absurd joke. "One thing I haven't had a chance to tell you yet is that that is a part of my New Year's resolutions: I need to come clean with Dad." Lanie stared at me, head-on.

"When did you decide this?" It felt delicious even to me, the thought of her dealing with her father, and facing the unspoken truth between them. Delicious, but scary, like an enticing roller coaster that you can only stare at from the ground.

"Over the holidays. I am simply too tired to keep on letting the same behaviors dictate our relationship. Look, Yellie, I know it won't be easy, but I've got to do it for me, in spite of whatever happens with him. We still walk around on eggshells, whenever we're around each other, the same way it was the week my mother died. It's too painful to pretend it doesn't exist anymore, so I decided to try and tell him the truth about how I feel. Perhaps we can begin again, though I don't know yet if I will ever be able to reach him, or if he even wants to be reached, but I do know that I'm willing to try. You should try, too…that's all I'm saying. Because trying with them has got to be better than where you are right now."

"Where am I right now?" I asked into the air, not expecting Lanie to respond.

"On the road to truth. Look, Danielle, you're getting there. Constance is right about that. I think that you need to take a few more brave steps in the right direction. Do you remember the night that you told me about David?"

"Yes," I replied, not sure as to what she was getting at.

"How long did it take you to tell me about David?" Lanie asked incredulously. "I know you don't want to hear this, but…I don't blame Paul for being frustrated after your talk the other night! How long did it take you to tell him about David?"

"The other night wasn't about David." I insisted.

"It doesn't matter! Don't you see? We love you. I think it's safe to say that Paul and I both love you very much. So what if you speak the truth to both of us, and let us know everything there is to know about you? Would it kill you? Would we go running and screaming from the room, gnashing our teeth and crying out in pain? Would we leave? Would we decide that you had too much crap to deal with, and would we cower and hide from the enormity of your stuff? No! I daresay, the answer would be N-O for both of us, but I'll just speak for me. No. Okay? Would it make it easier to speak the truth to us? Try us out for size, and then maybe turn around and try the same technique on your parents?" Lanie suggested.

"I honestly don't know how much more I could do." I felt bewildered by the turn this conversation had taken. It didn't make much sense to me now, coming from the mountaintop, only to be dragged down to yet another abyss. I thought I had a plan. On the way back from seeing Constance, the plan was to just do it. Now just talking to Lanie about it made that plan seem too simplistic, as if I were ready to sail the universe without a compass. I knew she was right; in my heart of hearts, I could nod my head to the feelings that she hit head-on. From there, I wasn't so sure.

"You need a plan," Lanie returned to her original statement. "Do you think I haven't already planned what I will be saying to my father this Saturday?"

"I'm sure you've given it some thought," I acquiesced.

"My point is this, Yellie; you don't just decide to conquer your thought life and then sit idly by and watch it happen. You decide. You break a pattern. You speak the truth, and then you get released." She said this with such authority that my heart stood up and listened once again.

The truth cannot be denied. It starts as a ringing in your chest and eventually worms it way through your veins and into your heart in a powerful way that stands up and shouts until you start listening. Perhaps I had missed the mark before, but I knew that Lanie was accurate in her assessment. It was just so painful. Did I really want to subject myself to more pain?

I toyed with the feelings that had lain there for all time: the anger towards my mother that I always tried to stifle, afraid that she would crack under the weight of one more accusation, and my willingness to overlook her weaknesses in favor of protecting her any way I knew how. Was I really doing her any good? Wasn't she far better off when she felt in control of her own destiny? The helpless shell that she represented now did nothing to disarm me in and of itself; I was motivated only by guilt to help her now, a nuisance thread of guilt for all the times when I was rendered helpless. Did we have what anybody would call a 'real' relationship?

The truth was no. No, plain and simple. Period–the end. Question was: could I tell her that? Should I? Would it really succeed in making me feel any better? Did I even need to point it out? Wasn't she aware of how much she had changed? Didn't she ever desire to change back?

Wasn't the role of victim tiring after a while? How about after a long while?

The rest of the day was slow, and Lanie and I switched to more mundane topics as the day wore on, wiling the day away with talk of books and other things. We had plans to go to the gym that night, and plans to meet Paul and Rob for sushi on Friday.

"So do you like him?" Since before New Year's, Lanie and Rob had formed their own friendship, exclusive of Paul and I, and it left me wondering if one day we could bank on them being a permanent double date.

"I like Rob a lot. He's a great guy. But I don't know if I *like* him yet, if that's what you want to know." Lanie answered.

"Too different?" I asked. Rob was quite different than Brad in many ways, and different from Lanie in others. Let's put it this way: they weren't the type of people you would try to set up with each other. But sometimes those things worked out too.

You never knew.

"You never know," Lanie echoed my sentiment. "I can tell you, though, that I think once I talk to my father, it will be much easier for me to hang a closed sign on the shop that I was tending named Brad."

"You think?" I was the one that had told her a while ago that the two were interspersed. Oh, how easy it was to see into somebody else's life!

For that I received a flying paper clip to the head.

"I know." Lanie crossed her arms in front of her chest. "I'll make you a deal. You take a leap of faith on Saturday morning and talk to Paul at the same time that I'm talking to my father."

"Talk to Paul about what?" Oh, here we go again. She was relentless.

"Anything. Pick a topic, any topic. We'll synchronize our watches and take The Nestea Plunge together. C'mon, Yellie, do it with me." Lanie was using her most coercive voice, the same one she used when she wanted me to indulge with her in ice cream. Real ice cream, not the Froyo stuff that was de rigueur.

"Like a suicide pact?" I offered, thinking myself fun.

"Something a little more optimistic than that," Lanie chided me.

"Okay, I'll try." The thought appealed to me, more than I wanted to admit.

"You'll try?" She paused a second and gave me a quick once-over. "Okay, better than nothing."
I'm working on it.

Chapter Forty-Two

"Wake up, sleepyhead," Paul nuzzled up against me in a way that had grown familiar, but was still altogether new, and I smiled to myself at the recurring realization of just how lucky I was to have found him.

"I'm up," I protested by throwing the comforter back up and over my head.

"That does not look like up to me," Paul commented.

I peeked out from the covers and smiled at him with my eyes. He was sitting next to me, sporting both tousled hair and the unstoppable grin, and I was disarmed completely by him all over again. Just who did he think he was, walking into my life, and coming into my heart, rendering me completely defenseless by the sheer force of his smile?

"You're bad." I said this for no apparent reason, at least, no reason that was remotely apparent to him.

"I am so not bad," he insisted as he leaned over, and pulled the covers away from my hidden lips and chin. He kissed me solidly and then jumped up and announced, "The tea is a-brewing. Come on, I need you to help me make French toast."

Oh, please. The man knew perfectly well how to make French toast. He just wanted me to get up because he was up.

I indulged him. We had gotten past our first fight. The weirdness was over, that uneven feeling that tries to hang on after an argument, and now I wanted only to be close to him again. I thought about Lanie and shrugged inwardly. There was a large part of me that didn't want to disturb the peace.

We made French toast together and then recounted the good time we had the night before. The four of us: Lanie, Rob, Paul and me had all taken a chance on a dive-y type of bar on the West side after several trays of sushi. We had passed the bar on the way to the sushi place, and then Rob insisted that we pop in for a drink afterwards, with the excuse that sushi made him thirsty, and besides it sounded like live music.

The bar ended up being a whole lot of fun, as there was a cover band playing all our favorite tunes of the Eighties, and Lanie and I figured we could at the very least make fun of the boys as they shouted such classics as *The Summer of '69,* along with all the other patrons. Several classic party songs later, we had made our way out onto the little strip of hardwood the place called a dance floor, and managed to join into the mishmosh/serenade. We ended up spinning around on the dance floor a time or two or twelve and the next thing we knew, the bar was closing and we were calling it a night.

"I can't help but love Bryan Adams." Paul shook his head in wonder.

"I guess I can't either," I laughed as I thought about the spectacle we had surely made of ourselves. Lanie and Rob had practically taken over the place, and we had to literally rip them from a banquette when the bartender called the last call.

"Do you think everybody feels the same way about their generation?" Paul inquired.

"How so?"

"Like, for example, I don't know about you, but I think the Eighties were simply the best generation to grow up in. The fads, the music, the ridiculous neon clothes…I mean, I wouldn't trade it for anything." Paul reminisced.

"I bet you that people only a few years older than us would argue that the Seventies reigned supreme. Think about the whole Saturday Night Fever thing, the Disco Era, even the rock bands that defined that decade." In part, it was ours too…*The Second Time Around* whispering in my ear.

"You've got a point. But I know that we're cooler." He flashed me the inescapable grin. "So what did you have in mind for today?"

Well, I was supposed to bare my soul to you. I looked at the clock on the wall behind us. Right now, as a matter of fact. Lanie is talking to her Dad; and part of the pact was to reveal something to you. I mean, I'm not sure I'm ready, but it's what I had in mind.

I said none of this out loud, of course.

"I don't know. What were you thinking?" I threw the ball back into his court.

"It's a little cold for the beach." He checked his watch. "What about the park and a Frappucino?"

I agreed. It was a little cold for a Frappucino, but it was unseasonably warm in the scope of a normal winter, so I decided that a little piece of indulgence wouldn't be all that bad. We left the apartment soon after we showered, and then wound our way over to Bryant Park, the cool and frosty drinks in one hand, my left hand enclosed in his right. We walked lazily, because the city lent itself to that sort of a pace on a Saturday.

It had been my call to go to Bryant over Central Park, as Bryant Park was smaller, and therefore cozier. We gathered up four green wire and wood park chairs and made them face each other, then spread out with our legs up on the one facing us, our faces tilted towards the sun. I slurped my caffeine cooler. In my mind, I named it: *Ode to Spring.*

"Paul, did you ever want to do something, but were too afraid to even try, because you couldn't bear to see it not work out right?" I asked this out of the blue, as the Frap made its way down my gullet and the whole world seemed sublime.

"Yeah. I mean, I guess I felt that way about lacrosse at first. All of my friends were into it way before me, but I held off for a while, because I didn't want to jump in until I felt I knew the game. I didn't want to seem like a jerk, plus

I was afraid of the ball." He looked towards me as he spoke.

"You were afraid of the ball?" It didn't fit the mental picture I had of him.

"Oh yeah! Do you know how fast that ball goes?" He made a whizzing sound. "It can hurt you if it hits you the wrong way."

"What do they call the ball in lacrosse?"

"The ball."

"Oh."

We laughed then, and he tickled me until I almost fell off the chair. I proceeded to look him dead in the eye.

"Stop!" I gave him my best scary look.

"Oh, all right. You are absolutely no fun," He declared.

"I'm fun." I protested.

"Okay, Fungirl, may I ask now why you are asking me that question?" Paul looked at me quizzically.

I looked at my watch and realized that Lanie had gone before me. I knew that already, had known that back at the apartment, but figured I would keep up my end of the deal anyway. I took my chances and plunged right in.

"Because I have fears about my painting." I shook my head and rolled my eyes, as if to illustrate how dumb I thought it was. "I used to love painting. I mean, I really got something out of it. Something like what I get out of reading, but also a sense of accomplishment, a feeling of worth that I can't even put into words. It's been so long since I actually picked up a brush and I finally figured out recently that it's because I'm afraid to." I was playing with the straw now, lifting it in and out of the domed cup, in an effort to avert my eyes.

"Why are you afraid?" He asked the most logical question, but the tenderness in his voice struck a chord inside my heart, and just as unexpectedly as I had begun the conversation, tears began to fall unbidden from my eyes.

"I don't know." I felt a little voice inside of me scream. *Tell him the TRUTH!* The voice sounded curiously like Lanie. I wiped the tears from my face, embarrassed, and unable to continue.

"There's no reason to be afraid. What? Are you afraid that somebody's going to make fun of you?" He had a look on his face that said he wished he could make it all better.

"No." I smiled through my tears. Wished it were that simple. I tried again. "Do you remember me telling you about The Monster?"

He nodded silently, his eyes glued to my face.

"Well," I began, "He was really a mean and rotten bastard." I told him how I fell in love with plaster craft, overdoing my artwork as only a zealous adolescent can, and betrothing my handmade gifts to half the universe, most often the half that resided within the walls of family. I shared with him about the toilet seat masterpiece falling off the wall, and The Monster's role in destroying it. I elaborated about how even before that incident occurred, that The Monster had always seen fit to make a snide remark whenever he saw me painting, and I told him how my mother would try and cover over it, and insist that he was just teasing me. He wasn't teasing, he was cruel, and I think everyone involved knew that truth. I went on to tell Paul about how something within me broke that day too, and although I longed to paint again, that I was too immobilized by fear to even pick up a brush.

"That's some story." He paused a beat and added, "I'm so sorry that happened to you."

"So am I." But I found myself lightened by the telling, and to my own astonishment, less angry than I had expected to be. Lanie was right. The truth was freeing; it was a new concept for me, but an altogether better one than what I had experienced thus far.

"What do you think it would take to get you to paint again?" Paul asked earnestly.

"I honestly don't know. I went out and bought several pieces of plaster craft in the fall, with the intention of making up some ornaments for Christmas, but I never quite got there. I procrastinated to the point of totally missing the holidays, and now those pieces are just sitting in my apartment, staring at me." I shrugged.

"I didn't know that you had even purchased them. You had talked to me about your painting before, but I obviously never knew this, and I think I assumed that your painting was something that you either outgrew or didn't have time for. I didn't know how much it was a part of you." His words pierced my soul, and the truth again took me by surprise. It was a part of me. Before I could respond, Paul's face lit up unexpectedly. "Will you teach me to paint?"

"I don't know about that," I hedged. It was awful nice of him to try that tactic, though.

"C'mon, it might help you to get back into it. I have no artistic talent whatsoever, it'll be like taking on a charity case."

I wiggled my butt in the seat, as it was starting to fall asleep. "You don't even come close to qualifying for charity." I looked deeply into his eyes and felt my heart jump in my chest, falling in love all over again. I was stuck.

"I will tell you one thing," he stared just as intently, right back into my eyes. "I would love to see you paint again. If you don't at least try to paint again; it's like he wins. And that would be a shame. You shouldn't let The Monster win."

I hadn't really thought of it that way. As the piece had shattered, I rationalized that if I never painted again, nobody could ever hurt me that way again. I had forgotten how much I missed it until only very recently, but I was still hiding in my shell, afraid to try once again.

"You're right." I agreed. "He's already taken too much. I shouldn't let him win again." I felt a new determination rise within me, plus the untold joy of a secret revealed, and I knew that Lanie was oh-so-very right.

You can't move into a brand-new house and bring all of your old shit with you.

Chapter Forty-Three

"What's that?" I pointed to the big blob sitting in a bowl on the counter, wondering if perhaps Leanna was making a pizza or a pie. Leanna made pies and pizzas with strange toppings and bizarre fillings, and I always looked forward to her creations, as Mom was a whole lot more unwilling to take risks with food she hadn't already tried before. The blob looked like dough, but I wasn't sure, and knowing Leanna, the blob could be just about anything.

"That," Leanna pointed to the blob in her usual theatrical way, "is a Friendship Cake, Daisy-girl."

I had never heard of a Friendship Cake before. I peered around the bowl, and back into it, waiting for her to continue. Leanna always had something exciting going on at her house, and I wanted to know all about this Friendship Cake, the same way I had insisted that Leanna tell me all about her artwork and her music, and everything else that she endeavored to do.

Leanna was my neighbor; she lived three houses down from Mom and me in the townhouse complex that we lived in right after Dad left, during Mom's 'Second time around' Time. When we had first moved in, Leanna came by with muffins and welcomed us in to the neighborhood. They were bran muffins, and they smelled funny, and I remember thinking that Leanna was weird, because I had never had bran muffins before. I was only eight years old, but I was enchanted with her even then, and she came to be a friend to me in the years to follow. Mom said Leanna was a feminist, and when Dad met her one day after dropping me off from a visit, he said she was a hippie. I didn't care what she was, I was attracted to her weirdness, and for some strange reason, she took a liking to me. I would come around after school to visit and she would talk to me about art and music and things that I didn't always understand, but I liked Leanna enough to make her a part of my after-school routine, and she liked me enough to take me under her wing.

Soon after we became friends, Leanna got pregnant, and when she had the baby, we went over to visit her and her husband Ross and the new baby they named Summer. While we were there, Leanna lifted up her shirt and let the baby suck right on her breast. She did this in front of Mom and me, and even Ross, and to say that I was shocked would have been an understatement. I had never seen anybody breast-feed before, and it was all that I could do to tear my eyes away from the scene. I looked to my mother, tugged her arm and pointed, but Leanna caught my eye, and patiently explained to me that it was natural, and that I shouldn't be concerned.

My fascination with Leanna grew, and I spent a whole lot of time at her house in the summer months, learning different things, and eating all kinds of natural foods. Leanna nicknamed me Daisy-girl, because she said I was as pretty as a daisy. I was flattered, for Leanna had long blonde hair that flowed, and a gentle smile that took up her whole face. I knew for sure that I wanted to be just like Leanna when I grew up. After Summer came, I would go over and help her with the baby, and tell her all my thoughts about Mom and Dad and the divorce. Leanna said that one day I wouldn't miss Dad so much. In so many words, I told her she was crazy.

So it happened that one day when I was over visiting, Leanna was making a Friendship Cake, and I, being the pesky little neighbor that I was, needed to know all about it.

"What's in it?" I asked, crinkling my nose as I wondered.

"A Friendship Cake can have all sorts of ingredients, but the thing that makes it special is that you give a cup of the batter to a friend, so she can start her own cake with it. That there has a cup of Jodi's batter, all I had to do was add the rest of the ingredients in order to make a *full-size cake."* She showed me the recipe with the list of ingredients on it.

"Your friend Jodi gave it to you?" This pass-it-on dessert intrigued me.

"Yes, and now I have to take out a cup of batter and give it to someone else before I bake my cake." She picked up a big spatula and played with the batter. "Would you like to take the next cup, and then make a cake for someone? The only hitch is that you also need to pass on the recipe and a cup of batter to another friend. Do you think that's something you would be interested in?"

"Of course I would! This is way better than the Holly Hobbie oven that doesn't even bake!" I exclaimed, my mind reeling with possibilities. I could make a cake for Dad and then keep a cup of batter aside for Mom, and then she could give the next cup of batter to her girlfriend Sheila.

Leanna laughed at my enthusiasm. She picked up a cup, measured out the exact amount of batter I would need to get started, and handed it to me.

"Now I just need to copy the recipe for you." She gave it a moment's thought. "Are you sure you want to do this?"

"Oh, yes!" I thought of how proud my father would be to taste my Friendship Cake. The day was Thursday, and I would be seeing him that Saturday for a visit, so I could give it to him then. Mom could bake another cake from her batter, and then pass a cup on to Sheila. I had it all figured out, and I raced home from Leanna's house that night to tell my Mom the plan. She thought it was a great idea, especially because Sheila hated to bake, but would then feel obligated to do so, and for some reason, Mom thought that was funny.

We were all set. The next day, which was a Friday, I removed Mom's cup of batter and went ahead and put together all of the ingredients to make the cake for Dad. I baked it perfectly, and even managed to remove it from the pan without any cracks or breakage. I let the cake cool and then put it in the fridge while I waited for Saturday's visit.

When Saturday came, I told Mom that I was going to keep the cake a secret right up until it was time to leave. Dad arrived, they nodded curtly towards each other, and while he was bringing my bag out to the car, I went and grabbed my beloved cake. I hopped in, and he asked what my package was, but I told him it was a surprise, and he accepted that and drove on.

Hours later, we were at Dad's house finishing dinner when I decided to present the cake. A couple of bites into it, my father asked what kind of cake it was.

"It's a Friendship Cake!" I announced, proud that my creation seemed pleasing to him.

"What's a Friendship Cake?" He asked, much in the same manner that I had asked Leanna.

I explained to him the way one goes about obtaining a Friendship Cake, and then explained further how I had started my own chain-dessert. Much to my horror, my father promptly spit out the piece of cake that was currently in his mouth.

"You what?" His fork stopped in midair. "Whom did you get this from?"

I had seen my father be demanding like this with Mom before the divorce, and I hated when he got this way, because it always made me shake inside.

"I got it from Leanna." I tried to explain it to him again, but he seemed incapable of listening to me and hearing what I had to say.

"But then who did she get it from?" His eyes were glowering, and I felt the full force of his anger permeating across the table.

"I don't know!" I was crying now, amazed at how horribly wrong the whole thing had gone. "Does it matter?"

"Of course it matters!" He thundered. "Leanna is a hippie! Her and her husband Ross; they're a bunch of no-

good hippies! Who knows whom she got this from, or where their hands have been? I can't eat this!" With that, he shoved the dish away from him as if it were a poisonous snake wrapped in sugar.

"But you know Leanna," I insisted through tears. I didn't know why he was so angry. I only knew that I had failed miserably, and that I would never attempt to bake him another thing.

Chapter Forty-Four

Sunday night loomed ahead of me. I haven't figured out why just yet, but I could never fall asleep easily on Sundays. It's as if I slept too much on the weekend, and my body just wasn't tired yet, but my head was moving still, fast-forwarding through all that needed to be done in the week ahead.

I tried tea.

Herbal tea. Sleepy-time tea.

No dice.

A nice hot bath, filled with scents to make you fall so soundly asleep that you never wake up...you simply drown in the tub.

Didn't work.

A book.

My favorite! Except...it kept me up.

Alas, a tried and true thriller addict should know: a truly great mystery will keep you up all night. Lock the doors! Check 'em again!

Not too smart to use as wind-down material.

I pounded pillows, tossed, did a turn or two, and then stared at the ceiling. I thought about Paul. I thought about my mother, The Monster, my father, and Am. I thought about calling Lanie for the fortieth time that night. I went back to my book.

I shut off the lights, and I wondered aloud if I had any red wine in the house. I wasn't partial to red, so I knew that there probably wasn't any hanging around. I stayed put and started wishing for other things I didn't have: Tylenol PM or other sleep-inducing drug, Valium, or whatever the designer sleep drug of the day might be, which was unbeknownst to me. Why is it that the ladies on the soap operas always had a plethora of sleep aids available, but in real life we were left to stare at inanimate objects for hours on end? I reminded myself that most people on soaps were born into money, and few seemed to hold any sort of real job. Enough about the soaps! I probably hadn't watched a soap since I was twelve. I pictured my favorite character on the now-defunct *Santa Barbara*. What was her name? Oooh, this was gonna drive me nuts! She had moved on to movies since then, but what was her name on the show? Now *this* was going to keep me up all night. Ugh. I could see her face, but I couldn't recall her name. I knew her name in real life. Ugh! Since I couldn't think of anything else to occupy my mind or wear me down completely, I snapped the light back on and delved back into my book, only to find myself feeling nagged by an unknown entity, as if I was supposed to be doing something more constructive.

  I closed the book and rotated around my humble abode. My eyes settled on the still naked pieces of plaster craft that were sitting on a high shelf. I felt a check in my spirit then and as if I were propelled by that inward confirmation, I slowly crawled my way out of the bed, determined to peruse my wares, and perhaps give them a pretty face. I felt the weight of each piece in my hand and checked the clock on the closest wall.

  If I was up, what did it matter? With a shrug, I lugged my brushes and paint out from another shelf, and placed my tote gingerly on my small kitchen table. Kelly! The character's name was Kelly, with a regal last name like Capwell, or Chapman, or some such thing. It didn't matter. Just being able to recall the name Kelly made me feel better. That aside, I stared hard at my project, willing myself to move, hands frozen momentarily at my side. I could do this. I knew I could. Moreover, I wanted to.

  Talking myself down: *The same way that this is your place, and nobody else has a key, and nobody else can take your food, and nobody else is in control...that's the same way you have to approach this, Danielle. You can do it. Nobody can break it, or you, anymore.*

In the still of the night, I heard Paul's strong voice whisper in my ear: *If you don't at least try to paint again, it's like he wins. And that would be a shame. You shouldn't let The Monster win.*

I spread out some old newspapers and chose carefully an ornament that would be easy to paint well, a square-shaped package that sported a wide ribbon as well as a fairly large bow. Although festive, it didn't have a lot of detail, and I felt confident that I could make the package come alive. I delved into my plastic tote, finding the base coat, and soon my hands were moving in an unforgotten rhythm. From the base coat, I added paint, and soon felt tired enough to try going to bed all over again.

An hour had passed.

I felt myself smiling within, feeling the assurance that what I had done was right, able then to fall off into a dreamless sleep filled with an uncharacteristic peace.

My body awoke with the alarm, and responded in such a way that I found myself bolting out of bed rather than opting for the snooze game. It was as if I couldn't wait to share my joy with Paul, or Lanie, or anyone who would listen. When I stepped out of the shower, I double-checked my work, and felt reaffirmed by the clean brushstrokes and very little need to touch up my work. Tonight, I would come home and seal the paint with a glittery topcoat, and perhaps share the masterpiece with Paul before the week's end.

Interestingly enough, I arrived at work before Lanie. Considering I had gotten a little less than four hours' worth of sleep, I found this to be no less than amazing, and decided to capitalize on the early morning adrenalin. I cleaned off my desk, answered several emails, called the messenger desk for all of the day's ticket deliveries, and was just about to put out The National Guard when Lanie breezed in, talking so fast that I couldn't get a word in edgewise.

"Yellie, so sorry! The train I was on was delayed due to an incapacitated train in front of us, then when I got off the subway, my subway stop was under construction, so I had to go up and over and around to the other side!" She slumped in her chair and kicked off her boots. "Plus, my cell is dead, so sorry I didn't call."

"Want a coffee?" The Italian's highest form of sentiment is always to offer food. Or beverage. Or both.

"Is the Pope Catholic?"

"Okay, let's go."

We locked the hole/office door behind us and ambled down to street level.

"The subway sucks." Lanie pontificated.

"It does." I agreed.

"Did you eat yet?"

"No, I was waiting for you."

"I say we actually *sit* in Starbucks for a minute or twelve and talk over tall coffees and some sort of breakfast."

"I second that emotion."

Once settled, I dispensed quickly of the small talk with this subtle opener:

"So did you talk to your father or not?" I hadn't heard from Lanie all weekend, and although I had picked up the phone to call her at least a dozen times, I was unsure about whether she would want to talk about it or not, so I hesitated enough to hang up those same dozen times. There was nothing I couldn't ask her; I knew that about Lanie, but I also knew that given the same situation, I would like some time to ruminate.

Now that I had her in my clutches, I was unstoppable.

"And how are you, dearie?" Lanie impersonated what sounded to me like an offended southern matron.

"Oh, please, Lane. I gave you your space this weekend, now I want details." I wasn't shy when it came to Lanie, at least, not about *her* life.

"Why did you feel the need to give me space? I was fine." She slurped her coffee as she did everything else, with tenacity.

"Because I would have wanted space." I answered.

"Fine, I'll remember that." Lanie placed her drink down on the table between us and slowly began picking at a lemon square. "I got there a little after noon. He had the housekeeper make us lunch. Crab salad and real lemonade. She had some sort of French bread on the side and it was fabulous." She waved away the details. "Anyway, we ate out on the patio. The first half of the meal was small talk, talk about his business and politics, and all the stuff you might talk about if we saw each other every week. I was getting annoyed, waiting for an opening, when I remembered that my mother had loved Crab salad, and I asked him if he remembered too." Lanie recounted.

"What'd he say?"

"He said yes, that he remembered. Then he sort of stared off into space and tried to change the subject, but I wouldn't let him. I dove in from there and pointed out that we rarely talk about her, and that I wanted to remember her more. Do you know what he said?" Lanie's face was a myriad of emotions.

"No." I shrugged apologetically.

"Well, he went on to say that he never talked about her because he didn't want to upset me. I told him that I was a big girl and I could handle it. I also told him that I wasn't so sure it was about upsetting me. I told him that I thought he was more worried about upsetting *him*. I went on to say that I was tired of the wall that he had put up, and that the gap between us just seemed to get worse year after year. I pointed out how he worked so hard that he never found time for life, and that because I was a part of his life, how I felt barely accounted for in the grand scheme of things." Lanie made another face.

I found myself envious. Lanie had balls. I had never had that honest or open of a conversation with my father. I was too afraid of the repercussions. Every time I had tried to please him, even in the tiniest of ways, I somehow fell short, and had long ago decided to stop trying. I had determined many years ago that any conversation that bordered on serious was not pleasing to my father, so I steered clear of anything that even so much as smelled like the truth.

The revelation came at me hard and fast: Lanie was right.

Lanie sighed.

"He said that he would try. To illustrate that, he told me a funny story about her, about them, which I had never heard before. It had to do with them crabbing together off the coast of Cape Cod. I think the crab salad triggered the memory, but I didn't care where it came from, because I saw him trying for the first time in a long time." Lanie polished off the lemon square and we sat in silence for what seemed like a long moment.

"Lane, I think that's fabulous. Either way, it's a lot farther than you've gotten with him in a while. I'm glad you spoke to him." And I was, whatever twinge of envy I might have felt for little old me was completely overshadowed by her victory, however small of a step that victory was.

"I'm glad too. I mean, there were a lot of other things that were said, a lot of details that I don't fully recall, but that was the gist of it, and I'm glad that I finally called him on his behavior with me. I'm not sure he was even fully aware of the lengths that he's taken to shut me out, but I do know that he is *more* aware of it. And I know that I can't expect instant miracles, but I do expect to see change, and for that I'm grateful." Lanie stood up. "We should go."

We went back to work and the day flew by. When we were about ready to pack up and go, I asked her how she felt.

"Relieved." Lanie nodded as if to herself. "That's the best way to describe it."

"Free?" I pushed, knowing she would push me just the same.

"Freer." Lanie smiled, and as if it just occurred to her, asked, "What about you? Did you take the Nestea Plunge too, or was I the only one to jump in the pool?"

"I jumped." We were walking towards the gym, and I kept myself looking purposefully ahead, unable to keep a smile from playing on my lips, yet determined to taunt Lanie, eager to make her guess.

"You jumped? You didn't say anything all day!" Her tone was accusatory.

"Well, I felt that it was your turn." I said that as if it explained everything.

"So what happened?" Lanie opened the door to the gym and then continued to hold it open for me. We checked in, made our way to the locker room, and then the interrogation began.

"I assume you talked to Paul," Lanie opened up with this.

"I talked to Paul." I nodded my head and smiled brighter. It was hard not to.

"Treadmill?"

"Yes."

Side by side on the conveyor belt for people, I finally opened up and told Lanie everything. I told her what I had discussed with Paul, and I told her how when I couldn't fall asleep last night, I finally got up and painted.

"That must have felt really good." Lanie put in.

"It did. It was totally freeing; that is, once I talked myself into it, I really enjoyed it for the first time in a long time. I was worried that I had forgotten how to paint, but once I delved into it, it came back to me, and the next thing I knew, an hour had passed. It was great. I haven't even told Paul that part yet. I figured I'd tell him tonight." Paul had been in an all-day meeting and couldn't be reached by voice or email all day. He had called me once, on one of his breaks, but it was just to say Hi and Bye and I decided that I would save the painting conversation for tonight as we would have more time on the phone.

"That sounds good. Oh, look who's here." Lanie pointed, her finger held closely to the readout on the treadmill, a strange look taking over her face.

"Who? Oh." I caught her drift as the Bradomeister logged on to the treadmill directly in front of us. He had his back to us, so I don't believe he saw Lanie or me, but you never know.

Lanie rolled her eyes.

"Wanna go?" I offered in a soft tone.

"No." She shook her head vehemently, kicking the treadmill up a bit as she did, and then gave me a look that had *Screw Him* written all over it.

"Okay." I shrugged my shoulders and upped the pace as well. I would stay as long as Lanie would, which would probably be as long as Brad would. It was all right. My only other plans were to go home, eat, and call Paul. And check my piece. I would have to touch up the edges and spray it with a topcoat tonight, then let it dry once again before I put it in a box. Unless I chose to keep it, which I mulled over as my feet pumped furiously in time with the belt under them. Perhaps I should keep it, and let it be a reminder of how far I've come. Wasn't that a tad bit melodramatic, though? No. I had fought long and hard to overcome the fear that sat stapled inside my heart, and now I would display the fruits of my labor.

Why not?

Three miles down, and I decided to call it a night. Lanie agreed, but just as we were stepping off the treadmill, the inevitable happened and the Bradomeister chose that exact moment to end his workout too.

"Oh, hi Lanie," he said as he turned, and almost bumped right into her. "Hi, Danielle."

"Hi Brad." I responded in words, but Lanie gave a half-smile that said nothing in particular. I felt uncomfortable for both of them as each of them stood there, rooted to their spot, looking each other up and down while pretending that they weren't doing just that. How tiring.

"So how have you been?" Brad nodded towards Lanie. "Did you have fun on New Year's?"

"We had a blast." She was playing the role of fake friendly, and she wasn't pulling it off very well, as her eyes were pure ice, and her demeanor rigid.

Could be because I knew her a lot better than Brad did. Plus I caught the deliberate *we*, even if he didn't.

"Good to know." Brad shot her a forlorn expression with that comment and then mumbled something sounding like, "I'll be seeing you." Then he was off to the locker room.

"You all right?" I inquired the minute he walked away. Bradomeister was a mystery.

"I'm fine." She walked erectly into the ladies locker room and I followed close behind. "Guys suck."

"That they do." Truth be told, even in the world where men like Paul existed, it was easy to relate to that phrase.

We air-kissed good-bye at the exit and I made my way on to the train, determined to finish the book that had kept me up half the night before, but as I made my way into the third car and chose a seat, I noticed an old couple sitting in a double seat that was facing me. They were perfect people-watching specimens, and they caught my attention not just because of the way they were dressed, but also because of the spirit that passed between them.

I named them Harry and Henrietta in my head, and I eavesdropped shamelessly as the train pulled from the station.

"Don't you think the place is too small?" Henrietta inquired fretfully, her eyes searching Harry's, looking for assurance.

"It's small." He nodded his head and then turned to look into her eyes. I saw his hand reach out to hers and then enclose it completely. "Remember our first place?"

"Oh, it was tiny!" The memory showed up across her face, visible in lines and wrinkles, and a smile that time had not dulled. "I just worry…"

"I worry too." He nodded, and it seemed a trademark movement for him, and even in the short space of time I had been watching, I knew that it was a familiar trait of the man I had dubbed Harry. He paused a minute and added, "They'll be fine."

I created a life for them inside my head. I pictured them having just come from their newly married granddaughter's apartment in Chelsea, having brought a bottle of wine and perhaps a quiche with them, now returning to their house on the hill in White Plains or Pleasantville. I pictured them briefly in their very first apartment, and I wondered how small it had been compared to the one in the city that they just visited, and I thought about the things that made Harry and Henrietta stay together, from apartment to house, year after year.

Before I knew it, I was at my stop. We smiled at each other as I disembarked, and I wished them well in my heart and mind. I tried to disengage from them as I pointed the Cavalier towards home, but my heart was overwhelmed at the prospect of one day being a part of something so harmonious, and I longed for the familial love that I had never encountered. I beat myself up: how could I be so pathetic? For all I knew, good ol' Harry was more than a little loose with his hands, and a nightmare to live with, and quite possibly the most cantankerous old man to ever live.

It just didn't seem that way. They seemed…happy.

Would Paul and I ever become Harry and Henrietta? Was it possible to live a dream together, and watch the days unfold from a shared prospective? More importantly, was it possible to do that without blame or shattering violence? Did the niceness always last, or was everyone inevitably harsh towards each other? I pondered marriage as I drove, thinking about how I had never seen a marriage up-close that worked well for both parties. Could I ever attain that quality, that certain unspoken *thing* that Harry and Henrietta possessed and displayed so openly on the train? Was Paul the type of person that believed in that kind of long-term commitment? I thought so. He was hinting at us moving in together. But marriage? I smiled to myself, thinking that Paul was what my Aunt Michelle would call 'a good catch.' I bet that Henrietta's aunt had once said that to her.

I took a quick shower and called Paul. He picked up on the fourth ring.

"Hello?" He sounded more than a little bit out of breath.

"Hi, are you okay?" I got a little nervous at the sound of him. He couldn't die on me, not until he was at least as old as Harry.

"I'm fine. I was on the treadmill." He made an inhuman sound.

"I'll call you back," I offered. Please. Go breathe.

"No, wait a sec." I heard some shuffling from Paul's end before he came back on. "You just gave me an excuse to get off."

"Great. Speaking of treadmills…" I filled him in on what had happened at the gym, about Lanie and I running into Brad, and then told him about Harry and Henrietta.

"Do you do this often?" He teased.

"You should've heard the name I gave you." Mystery Man.

"But did you give me a story to go along with it?"

"Of course I did." I filled him in on all the things I had thought in the beginning.

"An Amway Salesman? I would like to think I wear better ties than that!"

"You do. Anyway, I have news." I paused a second for effect. "I painted last night."

"You did?" The excitement in his voice was evident, and I swelled at the thought of someone being proud of me. "I'm so happy for you! What prompted that?"

His enthusiasm was catching. The tone of his voice was laced with genuine care, and it allowed me to open up and tell him all about it without any fear of judgment.

I proceeded to tell him all about being unable to fall asleep and how I wandered the hall (there's only one, from the futon to the bathroom) until all hours, and then finally got up the nerve to set up the paint and just go for it.

"How did it feel?" He asked, and I melted all over again. He got it.

He got me.

"It felt great." I sighed. "It's stupid, really…the amount of time I wasted, and not to mention the tons of energy I spent on being afraid. Once I got into it, it felt almost as if no time had passed, and before I knew it, an hour had passed!" I recounted my story jovially.

"So how does it look?" He inquired.

I wandered over to the table again and picked up the piece. Holding it up to the light, I could see a few brushstrokes that had overstepped their boundaries, but for the most part, I had to admit the ornament looked pretty good.

"Not bad for someone who hasn't touched a brush in about fifteen years," I conceded, hope burgeoning in my chest. I would put on all the finishing touches tonight and then show him over the weekend.

"I'm sure it looks great. I'm proud of you, Danielle. You took a chance and it paid off. Maybe you should trust your instincts a little more." Paul suggested, his voice infused with pride.

"I should. You're right." I nodded my head even though he couldn't see me. "It was so weird, Paul, it was almost like I wasn't going to fall asleep until I got up and at least tried. I know that sounds bizarre, but there was something really freeing in doing this, some little victory that I was able to glean from the exercise." I drummed my fingers on the table next to the paper I had spread out the night before, contemplating the ornament in the big scheme of things.

"Maybe God needed you to take a step of faith on this one, Dani." Paul said softly.

"Maybe." At the risk of getting overly maudlin, I changed the subject. "So when do I see you again?"

"When do you want to see me again?" Paul answered my question with a question, and I couldn't help but wonder if that was his way of backing away from making me feel pressured in any way. Familiarity had given way to a new wave of politeness since we had our little talk, but I was fine with that for now.

"Do you have free time on Wednesday?" I didn't take anything for granted, even after six months together, mostly because I wanted to set a good example.

"I do. How about you come over here, and I cook you some linguine and clam sauce? Then we could chill out and watch TV or a movie, and if you want to stay, you're more than welcome." He was being so accommodating that if I could reach across the phone lines and hug him right then, I would've.

"That sounds good." I agreed to stay, but only if he made his killer hot cocoa with real whipped cream for dessert.

"You got it." He promised.

"In the meantime, I love you." This was a sign-off that we fell into somehow, and whenever we couldn't be together, found ourselves taking turns at saying it.

"In the meantime, I love you too." Paul replied.

Chapter Forty-Five

"Tell me what happened." My voice was steady, but my heart was skipping a beat, and I felt flush.

"I can't." She was crying, and I had heard this cry before, so I knew that this was the real deal, and I steeled myself for the impending report.

"Tell me what happened," I insisted, worried for her, but needing to know what occurred, still believing I could help her.

"He came by. He's going to Florida. He wanted to torture me one last time." she gulped.

We were talking about The Monster, of course, and his recent release from prison. He finally got out, sometime around the holidays, and although he hadn't shown his ugly face right away, neither one of us thought he wouldn't show, and it occurred to me that I had been awaiting this particular call, and just as suddenly as that realization dawned, I realized that I had been holding my breath until now.

"What happened?" I insisted, my patience thinning. I wasn't there to help her, and it brought me back to the time when I was there and couldn't help her, and I felt my eyebrows knit and my back knot up by being brought there unwillingly. It was about ten o'clock at night, and I had just been getting ready to wash off my makeup and hop into bed with a book, when she called and I found that my wind-down routine would have to be put off for at least another hour.

"He stopped by with the guise of getting back together, at least that's how he started out, but then he got angry and started accusing me of all sorts of things. He actually thought I was with someone else while he was away in prison!" She was outraged by the accusation, but I was more outraged by the fact that he still felt he had the right to question her.

What nerve! As if it mattered if she had been with anyone. Hadn't that bastard taken enough from her? Did he really expect her to wait around for him, three years pining, and welcome him with open arms the minute he stepped foot on freedom's territory? What balls! I felt my body shake with anger and was fully aware of my hands balling into fists at my side. The man was incredible; he was a true believer in the sense that he was owed something from this world, namely my mother. If I didn't know him personally, I would be convinced that she was exaggerating the sheer audacity that made The Monster who he was, Earner of the Title.

"What did he accuse you of?" I asked, wanting to know, not wanting to know.

"He said…" She made a guttural sound that typified frustration. "He said that he wanted to know what I did with his old car. I told him, very calmly, that I sold it, the same way I had told him over the phone while he was still in prison. Then he said that he wanted the money from it, that he was going to Florida and could use a little traveling cash. I told him that I sold the car over two years ago, and that I had needed the money to pay the credit card bill that he ran up before going into jail."

"What credit card bill?" Any bank that would issue him credit would be beyond foolish, and deserved to get stiffed the money, in my estimation.

"Mobil." Was all she said.

"Mobil, like the gas company?" I mused about how he had gotten his hot little hands on a Mobil card.

"Yeah, well…he applied for the card in my name, but I never knew he had it. Apparently, they issued him one in my name and one in his, a joint account that he never bothered to tell me about. He used the one that was issued in his name. It only had about a three hundred dollar limit on it, but he ran that up with charges for gas and cigarettes and sodas and whatnot, and as soon as he went away, they started calling me and threatening, and once I realized what the bill was all about, I decided that I would sell his car and pay it off. It's not like he was going to be using his car while he was away anyway, and I didn't want them harassing me about the bill." A touch of defiance and my heart swelled once again over the memory of the Mom that once was.

"What *car* was this?" I asked, my voice laced with sarcasm. The Monster had owned various pieces of junk throughout the years, all souped-up and at the same time rusted, driven for the sole purpose of trying to appear bigger than the petty thief that he was, all vehicles that could only very loosely be called a car. I had memories of radar detectors and hot radio systems being the mantelpiece of a car that could really only be called a heap, and my mother continually sticking up for the work that he did on said cars, regardless of how many times the car left us stranded on the side of a long country road.

"The Nissan. Do you remember the Nissan?" She asked.

"I'm not sure," I answered as politely as I possibly could, swallowing the reminder that The Monster had switched cars more often than his underwear, and that I could barely keep up with his scams and schemes throughout the years, and still managing to feel infuriated by the fact that our lives back then had revolved entirely around him: his cars, his food, his moods, his addiction.

"Well, anyway, I sold the car so I could pay off the bill. The bill that *he ran up!*" My mother's voice belied a touch of outrage.

Finally!

"I don't blame you for doing that, Mom, that was a good move." I thought a minute about the fact that that one move had probably taken a lot of nerve, and that she had quite possibly struggled with the idea before actually doing it. I had to give her credit, and decided that an encouraging word or two could do nothing but help the situation. "So what happened then?"

"Well, then he started threatening me, and saying how he was going to sue me for the money. That the car was in his name, and therefore the money from the sale of the car was his. I basically told him to stuff it. He got a little too close to me, and I told him to back off before I called the cops. I told him I had an order of protection out against him." She was crying again, audible sobs that hurt my ears to hear.

"You got the order of protection?" I was stunned by this revelation.

"No, but he doesn't know that, does he?" Came the retort.

Go, Mom!

"Another good move. Then what'd he say? DID HE TOUCH YOU?" I was yelling now, both aware and unaware as I screamed, frustration getting the best of me. She had me hanging on the edge of my proverbial seat, and I vowed to kill him if he had so much as even laid a hand to her.

" No, he just threatened to sue me, he said that he would show me, that I hadn't heard the end of him." She huffed. "I think he's probably right."

"Do you still not want to change your number?" I asked this in the gentlest voice possible, reigning myself in, trying hard not to lose control.

"No, I don't want to change my number." Her voice was at a much calmer register. "I just want him gone. I realize now that jail was just a temporary way to get him out of my hair, and that he never appreciated when I visited him, or sent him things, he just wanted the stuff, and I thought I was doing the right thing by bringing stuff to him. I wanted to do the right thing, I thought about what the Christian thing to do was, and I wanted to forgive him. Now I just want him gone. I hope he goes off to Florida and meets another woman, and he lives the rest of his life down there with her, whoever she is, and let me just say that she can have him!" And she laughed.

It was so unexpected to hear my mother's sense of humor resurface that I laughed out loud at her proclamation, so happy was I to simply revel in it, and it took me a full minute to respond. We both laughed harder, the tension easing at the absurd thought that another poor unsuspecting suckerette might actually fancy his behind.

"Amen to that!" I could feel myself smiling. "What did he insinuate about other men?"

"Insinuate?" She took a deep breath and started again. "He didn't insinuate anything; he accused me of seeing Jake."

"Jake Next Door?" Jake Rolland had been her next-door neighbor since the day she moved into the rattrap she currently called home. He was a down-home sort of guy that would do anything to help out a neighbor, and he frequently did just that whenever my mother went knocking on his door. Jake was what everyone would call a 'nice guy,' and he seemed to have a special place in his heart for my mother.

"Yeah, can you believe that?" My mother sounded absolutely stunned by the veracity of his claim. "All because Jake didn't say hello to him when he pulled into the driveway."

"For God's sake, didn't it ever occur to him that Jake might just be sick of his crap?" Like most drug addicts, The Monster had duped everybody he knew, friends and enemies alike. Jake would have been considered a friend, except The Monster had stolen his hose once for drug money, and had always held it against him since then, because my mother had replaced the hose.

"Ever since the hose incident, he just didn't like Jake." She sucked in air and let it out slowly, obviously ruminating over that particular course of events.

As if it were Jake's fault that *he* stole the hose! Oh, I loved it! If this entire scenario hadn't played out in my own life, time and time again, I might actually consider it funny. Laughable.

Only it wasn't funny, it was sad. Tired and old and sad beyond measure, and even though he was gone for now, I had a strange feeling that my mother would be right: we hadn't seen the last of him yet.

"So he left without incident?" As if mental and verbal abuse weren't considered incidents. I knew better; I just didn't know any other way to put it.

"Yes." She seemed calmer now, and in much better spirits than when I had picked up the phone. "I hope he gets run over on I-95."

"Mom!" I extolled a little mock horror. "That isn't very Christian of you!"

"I think God will understand," she forced another laugh and I joined in with her.

"I think so too." With that, and promises to call if she needed me, we said our goodbyes and hung up the phone.

It took a few minutes to realize that the tears streaming down my face were my own, and even longer to realize that the phone wasn't fully back in its cradle. Once I fixed the phone, I waddled over to my mirror and took stock of the makeup now running down my face, and I laughed at the thought that I would now have less makeup to take off. I soaped up my face then, and as I threw a cascade of cold water over me to rinse, I caught an errant smile trying to rise through the tears. I caught myself in the mirror and forced my face into the semblance of a woman who was more of a cynic: *I'll believe it when I see it.*

I wasn't ready to believe that the old Mom was back, at least, not yet. I saw a hint of her, and felt as if God had heard the wish I had carried around buried in my heart, the dream that one day I could find her again, singing and dancing with the best of them.

As I fell into bed, I kept fighting, but as I drifted off to sleep, I was no longer sure whether I was fighting off the smile or the tears. I guess it didn't matter, because my dreams were filled with Paul and I frolicking on a beach in what seemed to be Florida.

Chapter Forty-Six

"I had a dream about you last night," I confessed as I stood to his right, chopping up what was going to be a fabulous Caesar salad.

"Taste this," Paul said as he offered a taste of his near-famous clam sauce on a wooden spoon.

I reached towards him and slurped the spoonful of sauce.

"Ummm." I nodded my head in approval. "Delicious as always."

"Hot enough?" He fretted while I chopped.

"Yep." I found myself nodding again. "Lookin' good."

"So tell me about this dream," he gestured towards me with the spoon, and then dipped it back into the pot, stirring lightly.

"The dream was you and me on a beach in what I think was Florida." I shrugged.

"That's all?" He seemed bewildered, as if he had sat poised to listen to the likes of a Hemingway tome.

"Yeah, it wasn't anything in particular…what I mean to say is that there was no plot to speak of, just a scene of us on the beach, enjoying each other and the sun, and there was this really good feeling between us, ya know, nothing I can really describe per se, but a feeling that lingered when I woke up this morning." There was a word for the feeling, and the word was *safe,* but I wasn't ready to explore that yet.

"Would you like to go away?" Paul suggested in a manner that said that he didn't know what to make of what I had told him.

"And escape this lovely New York winter? Of course I would! That's not the point. The point is…" and again, the word *safe* was the Pink Elephant in the room, "that it was a good dream."

"I'm glad you had it then." He looked over my shoulder. "How's your chopping going over there?"

"Fabulous. I just need to add the anchovies, and we're done." I arranged each and every salty fish in a way that Van Gogh would envy. If there were ever something trivial I could use to point out that Paul and I were meant to be, it would have to be the fact that we both liked anchovies. Never before had I met a man that liked the little fishies as much as me.

"Okay, great. Let's delve in to that a little bit there, then I'll throw in the linguine and we'll go to town." Paul assessed the kitchen as he said this.

"A man after my own heart." I followed him around the corner from the breakfast nook and put the two plates down in front of our respective places.

"Umm, umm, good!" Paul announced after only one or two bites in.

"Thanks." I took a bite myself and then shared a thought. "I think Caesar would roll in his grave, the way people make Caesar salads today."

"I don't think Caesar made the salad."

"Who then?"

"Some guy in Mexico."

"Surely you jest."

"I wish I were jesting."

"My point is that it has become so mainstream now, that it sucks in most places. A lot of places you can't even get anchovies on the side, and the fast food places that are touting them have desecrated them beyond belief." I pontificated.

"I agree. Nothing worse than a sucky Caesar salad."

"Bad Chinese food," I countered, thinking that I would rather have no Chinese food than bad Chinese food.

"Bad pizza wins over all," Paul put in.

"Oh yes! Bad pizza is sooooo bad," I agreed and we both laughed. I went on to extol the virtues of good bread, and how most of the people who lived Upstate had never had good bread before.

"Imagine how the Midwest…exists. Remember me telling you about my buddy, Alex? You wanna see somebody scarf down bread?" Paul shook his head in amazement.

"I thought his father owned a pizza place."

"Yeah, but Alex told me you can't get good Italian bread out there to save your life. A bagel? Fuhgettaboudit!" Paul chuckled.

"Maybe Alex's Dad owns a *bad* pizza place!" I thought aloud.

"They can't. They're too rich."

"Ah-hah." I giggled. Paul and I were falling into a pattern with circular conversations and inside jokes, and I liked the way it felt inside, to be a part of something, and to have a voice even in the mundane. "But if all you've ever had was bad pizza…"

"Then you wouldn't know the difference. I getcha."

Paul got up then and plunged the linguine into the boiling hot water on top of the stove. Until it was ready, we kept up a constant chatter over our respective days, and tried to decide what was going on for the weekend.

"I say we have a movie marathon here. I'll buy popcorn, and Sno-caps, and we'll invite Lanie and Rob over to veg out and it will be tons of fun." Paul proposed.

"Tons of fun?" I mimicked him.

"Actually, Tons *O'* Fun would probably be more accurate." Paul wiggled his eyebrows.

"Kind of like Cup O' Soup?"

"Exactly." Paul hefted the pasta dishes onto the table, then jumped up and retrieved the Romano cheese from the counter. He tossed a mound of cheese atop his plate and then returned to the topic at hand, slowly twirling his pasta onto his fork. "So what do you think?"

"I think I can agree that it will be Tons *O'* Fun," We shared a grin as we stuffed our faces. "Besides, it's supposed to snow again this weekend, at least that was the long-term forecast that I heard today, so I could think of no better plan than to be snowed in with you." I grabbed the cheese from the center of the table and threw a mound on top of my plate too. Umm, umm, umm. A man that looked like Paul and could cook too. When had I hit the jackpot?

Paul slurped a long strip of linguine from his fork and as I watched it disappear into his mouth and down his throat, I thought that he looked like a four-year-old, taken with the experience of enjoying his food, not a care in the world registering on his face, nothing at all but the simple pleasure of eating a favorite meal. We ate in silence a minute or two, and he must have noticed me watching him, or felt my gaze upon him, because he turned to me then and said, "What?"

"Nothing." I shrugged. "You look blissfully happy."

"I am. I have you, and I have pasta, and what more could I want?" He stated this with such nonchalance that I stood there in amazement, unable to speak for at least a full minute.

"I envy you." The words popped out of my mouth before I even had a chance to register them, but once they did, I found they rang true, and I knew for sure that there was something I was missing.

"Why?" He stopped eating then and looked at me as if I had just sprouted twelve heads. "What do you mean?"

"You're so simple." That came out wrong.

"I'm *simple?*" He said the word as if it were a disease.

"Yes. No. What I meant was that…" I floundered for the right words, unable to express what it was I had just been thinking. I hadn't meant to offend, only to compliment him, and to point out the fact that I had observed something in him that I found valuable, a sense of peace that I was starting to realize that I didn't have.

No matter how far I've come; I know that I've still got a way to go.

I decided to try again.

"I guess what I meant to say was that you have…a certain something that I haven't quite been able to get a handle on just yet; a knack for breathing in the simple pleasures, a peace in small things…" I swirled my fork in the air, all in a hapless effort to trail along words in the air, rambling now, trying to overcompensate for fear that I had offended him, and still I felt a little bit at a loss for words. How could I explain something so intangible? How did I even know that I was missing it, if I couldn't define it, or put my finger on it? I looked up into Paul's eyes and found my answer there. Somehow, he had taught me something about life, and deep in his eyes I knew that I had learned it from being around him, and drinking in the ambiance that being a part of his life offered to me.

"I think I know what you're trying to say." He grinned as if to himself, and I saw the wheels turning inside of his head. "You're wondering why I don't let things bother me?"

"More like I'm noticing how you don't let things bother you." I paused a thoughtful moment. "I know it may sound stupid, but even though we've been together for a few months now, I feel like I'm just beginning to notice things about you." I was a little embarrassed to admit this out loud, but since the cat was out of the bag…well, since I had lit the bag on fire and then forced the cat to jump from the fiery inferno…either way, I let the truth fall from my mouth and do away with whatever embarrassment that wanted to take over.

"You have a point there." Paul took a long swig of his drink and then focused his attention directly on me. "I don't want to start another fight with you; I don't want to go through another horrible discussion like we did last week, but can I point out one of the things that I've noticed about you?"

I nodded slowly.

"I notice that you carry a big bag of bricks around with you. I notice that you're right about one thing, if nothing else: that you don't really know how to indulge in simple pleasures. You try, I see you trying all the time, and sometimes I think you succeed–like when you're reading a book–but truth be told, that isn't a lifestyle for you. You actually have to *try* to relax, and you actually have to *try* and enjoy things without your mind going into overdrive." He looked at me intently, and stopped playing with his fork. He reached across the table to take my hand in his own. "I know I don't know everything there is to know about you yet, but I hope one day you'll trust me enough to tell me. I hope one day that you can start unloading that big sack of bricks, and one by one, let them go. You'll feel lighter. I promise." He was still talking, but I could barely hear him over the torrent of tears that were silently making their way down my face.

I couldn't speak.

"You thought I didn't know about your bag, huh?" He said softly.

I got up then, the purpose in my mind to walk away, but I found myself standing over him instead, and the next thing I knew he had pushed his chair away from the table, and I was fitting myself in his arms and sobbing uncontrollably.

I still couldn't say a word, and was thankful that he held me for a long time, not putting pressure on me to say anything, but allowing me to simply bury my head in his chest and cry. I cried for the truth that he espoused, and I cried even harder for the hopelessness that I felt in trying so hard to control it all. I thought I did a good job at hiding, good enough so that he wouldn't know or even suspect a thing until I was ready to tell him, but somehow he knew anyway, I was obviously more transparent than I thought I was, and now I couldn't stop the tears that came and I wasn't even sure if I wanted to.

"It's okay." He rubbed my back. "You're on your way."

I'm working on it.

I cried harder. He didn't know anything…barely anything…how could he know so much about me? How could he read my mind, and know my innermost thoughts? The bag of bricks…what a way of putting it…I had never envisioned it quite that way before, but I felt a heat resonating inside my heart that spoke volumes: I needed to unload.

"Our delicious food is getting cold," I blubbered after a while, pulling away from him and averting my eyes, swiping at my errant mascara. Was it just last week that a scene just like this had played itself out in this same place? Was I beginning to lose it? What was the matter with me that I couldn't hold it together anymore? Or did I just not want to?

"Yes, but that's why they have microwaves." Paul got up then and lifted both our dishes from the table to his counter, one already airborne and headed into the microwave.

"I'm sorry." I stood away from him, a little more embarrassed now that the moment was over, playing with my hands in an effort to still them, wondering just how bad I looked at this very moment.

"There's nothing to be sorry for." The microwave beeped and I saw him exchange plates.

Yes, there was. There was so much. My mind flicked to the day when he would decide that he was in too deep, and that I was a little more than a tad bit too much for him, and I sighed audibly.

The nuke machine beeped again and Paul positioned our plates back where they had been.

"Eat up," he instructed.

I did, and it was as good as it was earlier, only there was more cheese to be added and less conversation, which had a calming effect on me. I concentrated on the food and soon we were back in the rhythm of discussing all things silly and frivolous, as well as a shopping list for the weekend.

"We need all the stuff to make homemade chocolate chip cookies." Paul insisted on the Nestle Tollhouse variety and no other. "If we're going to get snowed in, we've got to do it right!"

"You really are about four years old," I informed him.

"I'm five." He corrected, then got up and enfolded me in his arms once again.

The most important ingredient that showed its face that night was peace.

Chapter Forty-Seven

"Do you remember me telling you about Dez?" Lanie asked me the minute she strode in the door.

"Dez was your old friend from high school?" I could remember Lanie mentioning her in passing, but I couldn't remember the reason that they weren't friends anymore.

"Yes. Dez Diaz. Her real name was Desiree, but she went by Dez because she always wanted to be a star, and she thought that Dez Diaz was a good 'stage name.' She's one of those people you wonder why you were ever friends with; big boobs, a fake smile, and waaaayy too much lipstick." Lanie rolled her eyes. "Anyway, I think I just saw her in the lobby downstairs."

"Do you think she got a job working for us?" That would be interesting, and not impossible, because we were the world's biggest ad agency, and always looking for fresh talent.

"I think she's shooting commercials." Lanie clucked her tongue and gave me another look that said, *Oh please.*

"Why do you think that?" I asked. "Also, why did you two stop being friends? I'm not sure you ever told me." I took a long sip of my tea and swilled the sweet hot beverage around on my tongue. There was nothing better than a hot cup of tea on a cold winter morning.

"Well, let me start with the commercial question first." Lanie reflected. " I should have said doing, not shooting, in terms of the commercials. I think she might be doing commercials because when I was home over the holidays, I ran into Jude, who we both used to hang out with, and he said that she had gotten some major acting gigs around town and that he heard that she was making her way to the big city, hoping that the Playhouse gig would translate into some minor things here, at the very least. As for question number two, the reason I no longer speak to the trollop is because she put the moves on my father."

"She *what?*" I spit out the remaining tea from my mouth and slapped the desk in front of me with an open palm. "GET OUT!"

"I will not; it's my hole/office too." Lanie shot me a wry grin and then continued. "Yeah, can you believe that? Well, I shouldn't say she actually did it, but she tried, and the innuendo alone made me want to barf. There I was, thinking she always wanted to hang out at my place because…well, I have a really nice place." She shrugged. "Jude was the one who tipped me off, actually, and I owe him to this day. *Jude* is a real friend."

"Did your Dad ever catch on?" I was outraged at the mere thought of a friend, a peer, hitting on my father. Lanie's Dad was cute, but come on now. Real life wasn't like the set of a cheesy soap opera, with characters falling in and out of lust with their girlfriend's much older, much-richer fathers.

Or was it?

"No." She waved that thought away quickly. "*My father?* Yellie, until we talked quite recently, he would barely notice if I was in the same room as he was…much less notice a gaggling teenager making eyes at him over a bowl of Mac and Cheese."

"So what happened between the two of you?" I prodded.

"I don't know anymore really. Well," she looked off into space as she recalled past events, "actually, I do remember. Jude was my pal, he had been my bud forever, and I was the one who introduced him and Dez, and then we formed a sort of unlikely trio. Anyway…Have you met Jude?"

I shook my head No.

"Jude was the guy in high school who was like, terribly asexual, but all the girls liked him. You know what I mean?"

"Every high school has a guy like that." I thought about Kyle, a guy who fit the bill from my old high school Upstate.

"Okay, so Jude and I became fast friends by sophomore year. We had three classes together, and we also had drama together after school. We probably had a mutual crush on each other at one point or another, but we never acted on it, and we managed to stay fast friends throughout our entire high school career. He had a similar family situation as I did, except both his parents were absentee to my one, but either way, we had a lot in common." She waited a beat. "I miss him."

"So call him."

"I might." She tossed me a terribly overused stress ball. "Right now, though…I need an overflowing hero."

"Done." With that, we made our way to the corner deli.

Chapter Forty-Eight

"We'll need one classic, one comedy, something scary, and something recent." Paul announced this with authority.

"Yeah, but everybody has a different idea of the meaning of the word classic," Lanie countered, and I chimed in my agreement.

"What do you ladies mean?" Rob put down his beer and peered at us over his pilsner. "A classic is a classic. Period."

We shook our heads in unison. Men know nothing.

It was Friday night, and the four of us had decided to meet up with one another for a short round of drinks in Midtown. We were discussing the impending Movie Marathon that Paul was hosting Saturday night.

Paul and me.

I guess.

"There are different types of classics," Lanie insisted as she pushed Rob in his seat. "There are classic classics, like: *Look Who's Coming to Dinner,* or *Ben-Hur.* Then there are modern-day classics, like *The Color Purple* or *When Harry Met Sally.*"

"*When Harry Met Sally* is not a classic!" Paul said emphatically, and then added an amendment to his traditional eye roll, an eye-roll-headshake sort of thing that, if it wasn't so fantastic, I would have found condescending.

"It absolutely is!" I shook my head right back at him and tried to perfect the eye roll. "Name one person that you know that has not seen that film."

"I..." I could see Paul was wracking his brain.

"Is that what deems something a classic?" Rob shook his head in utter disgust. "I can't name one person who hasn't seen *Star Wars,* but nobody considers that a classic!"

"Speak for yourself," Paul warned, and then toasted Rob specifically, the air by default.

"The point is that there are different types of classics." Lanie reiterated.

"So what makes a movie a classic in your eyes?" Rob challenged her. "Why, for instance, would you call *When Harry Met Sally* a classic?"

Lanie, ever one to rise to such a challenge, started ticking off her reasons on her fingers. "One: The plot is timeless. Boy meets girl and they hate each other. They meet again, become friends, and fall in love. Two: The actual movie had two lead actors that are themselves, considered almost timeless. Three: there's universal appeal in the theme. It spoke to the hearts and minds of our culture at that time. That's why so many people loved it."

"That's why so many *women* loved it," Rob corrected her with a gaze that was playful and flirtatious. I caught it, and when I looked over to Lanie, I knew she did too.

"You hated it?" She challenged him.

"I didn't hate it; I just wasn't passionate about it, the way most women are." Rob paused a second and then turned to Paul. "Do you think that's sexist?"

"I think that's the truth," Paul responded; with a sheepish look to both Lanie and I. "Danielle, you have to admit that's just a true statement."

"Okay. Well, what about *Sleepless in Seattle?* Would you consider that movie a modern-day classic?" I wanted to challenge their perception of women's films, or so-called chick-flicks.

"Does Meg Ryan being in it automatically make it a classic?" Rob swept a hand over our table, as if to suggest that Meg Ryan encompassed all things. "Cause then I say that *Courage Under Fire* should be in the Film Hall of Fame."

"Oh, you're a laugh riot," Lanie pantomimed riotous laughter. "I'm splitting my side here."

We all laughed at her contortionist moves, then settled back into to our discussion with a "So?" from me.

"I think *Sleepless in Seattle* is more of a classic than *When Harry Met Sally,*" Paul put in, and whether he was humoring me or just trying to be fair and answer a question, I sat by charmed by his participation in the conversation.

"More of a classic?" Rob seemed bewildered at this point.

"No, I get that. Why?" My eyes challenged Paul.

"The music." He said simply and then looked to me as if he were a game show contestant, waiting to hear if he had said the right answer. My eyes must have flashed something reminiscent of Bob Barker, because he continued. "The music was timeless, the fact that they used Jimmy Durante and songs that wouldn't date the film makes that movie more of a classic than Harry and Sally."

I nodded, and Lanie added, "Even Meg Ryan's wardrobe for the film had a timeless quality to it. When the film came out, she was totally in style, but if you were to watch it ten or more years from now, I don't think you would shout, *Omigod! Look at that skirt!*"

"Unlike *Valley Girl.*" Rob offered.

"Or any of those Eighties films…*Sixteen Candles, Ferris Beuller's Day Off, Less Than Zero…*" Paul threw in the movies we all grew up watching, again, and again, and yet again.

"I would consider *Sixteen Candles* a modern-day classic," I announced this in a voice that dared dissent.

"Fine, but let's not get that for tomorrow. I can basically quote it line for line. I want something that maybe I missed." Lanie tossed out.

"Lanie, I must say, you strike me as the type that doesn't miss a trick," Rob nudged her as he said this, and I once again caught a vibe that hinted at more than friendship.

She toasted him in answer.

Chapter Forty-Nine

"If I eat one more cookie, I will barf," Lanie announced this pleasantly, as we sat amidst the remnants of our Salt and Sugar Festival. There was still at least one half-full microwave popcorn bag decorating Paul's floor, several bowls of various chrunchies and munchies artfully arranged on his coffee table, all displaying different stages of empty, plus the overflowing tin of homemade chocolate chips that Lanie was referring to dotting the landscape of Paul's apartment. And we had been at this for hours, with two movies down and two to go.

"You cannot be done eating," Rob accused from his neon sleeping bag, which he was carefully ensconced in at the foot of the couch. Rob had insisted upon getting snowed in with style, hence the Eddie Bauer touch and the designer fleece from head to toe.

"I am. I'm done. I'm overdone," Lanie said in a voice that belied a tremendous food hangover.

"And I was just about to ask who wanted me to call and order a pizza," Paul said this without even a hint of sarcasm. I studied him for a quick second and wondered where exactly he put it all, the sugar, and the salt, the endless bags of potato chips slathered in Heinz.

I wandered over to Paul's balcony as he and Rob discussed the merits of ordering pizza now versus waiting, all thoughts dependent of course on the amount of snow God decided to dump on our fair city. I looked outside the sliding glass doors and found about seven inches had accumulated so far on the balcony, with a winter wind blowing one side into greater proportion than the other, and the snow continuing to fall at a rather steady pace. I flicked the light to the left side of the sliders and watched the snow fall steadily in the sharpness of the light. It seemed too bright, so I shut the light back off and looked farther into the distance, watching the snowfall under the streetlight at the corner. I thought briefly about how they didn't have streetlights Upstate, how most roads were dark and windy and treacherous in a steadily falling snow. I didn't miss driving in that, but I prided myself for a second, knowing that not everybody could drive in serious snow.

I could hear the ongoing banter of Paul, Lanie and Rob as I took in the wintry scene at my feet, but my mind was wandering to a time and place in my life where snowfall had meant something entirely different than a blanketing nuisance.

"Come on and try it," my father waved me on, insisting that I follow him up a hill that seemed mammoth in the eyes of a five year old, a rocky hill that wasn't made for the Sno-tube I tugged along behind me.

"I am. I'm going to try it from here," I announced, plainly deciding that he could go up farther because he was bigger than me, and that I didn't need to follow his lead.

"That's only half the ride!" He called from a space far in front, miles uphill from where I was planted.

I ignored him then, turned and pushed off with my hands, one gloved hand dug into the snow on either side of my Sno-tube. I gave a one-two-three and then shoved off, my tube hurtling me down the slope, convinced that I was brave and sure that he would see the same, as soon as he looked up and realized just how fast I was moving down the slope in front of me.

I collapsed at the end, my Sno-tube frittering to my right, my body splayed left of it in the snow, when suddenly I realized that I had forgotten to check my gloves. My mother had just purchased new gloves for me: they were the novelty winter accessory of that year, and after begging profusely from Christmas to Valentine's Day, I received them the week before from Cupid, and had prayed dutifully for snow ever since. The gloves had a hologram-type patch on the outside face, a patch that promised to turn bright blue once it was cold enough outside. The week had so far profited me nothing, but now that my hands had been hidden in actual snow…Bingo! They were blue.

"Dad! Dad!" I called to the man that was hurtling down the slope directly to my left. I grabbed my Sno-tube and lunged right, making sure I was out of his way, and once his sled came to a complete stop, ran towards him so that I could show him my gloves.

"They changed!" I was blowing smoke out of my mouth, it was so cold outside, but I stood transfixed, oblivious to anything but my bright blue gloves.

"Great." He dusted himself off as he stood. "Now come on, let's do the whole hill."

"I can't." I felt myself getting all choked up and I willed myself not to cry in front of him. I didn't want to admit how scared I was, afraid that he wouldn't want to play with me anymore, scared still that he would leave again, as he had been wont to do lately. I understood him leaving. Who would want a kid who was afraid of the bunny slope?

"What do you mean, you can't?" He huffed out big puffs of cold-air smoke. "Come on, I'll show you." He grabbed my Sno-tube in his left paw; his own sled already gripped in his right, and trudged up the hill without so much as a backward glance to me.

"Danielle, do you have a preference, or would you rather just go out and play in the snow?" Paul interrupted my memory and I was jostled back to the present. I turned to find him holding one video in each hand, my reverie having been broken, and my mind devoid of anything resembling an answer.

"Huh?" I blinked and took in the mother lode of junk food as well as the fact that there were two other people in the room also waiting on my response.

"Comedy or Horror?" Paul persisted.

"I say we end on a light note, so Horror first." Lanie said.

"Yeah, no bad dreams for me." I nodded my head towards Lanie and looked directly at Paul. "Horror first."

Paul went about setting up the movie while Rob retired to the bathroom and Lanie busied herself with rearranging her position on the love seat.

"You okay?" Paul came over to me and wrapped his arms around me from behind, as I stared back out onto the snowy landscape.

"I'm fine." Was I fine? What was the matter with me? Could I no longer do something as simple as watch a quiet snowfall and take it in for what it was? Would I always be assaulted by the memories of days gone by? "I guess I kind of got lost in the snow." I gave him a sheepish grin. I tried to remember another memory involving snow, a happier memory of days gone by, but I came up empty, so I turned in to Paul and gave him a deep hug. I inhaled his scent and smiled. Again, the word *safe* dove into my consciousness, but I swept it away completely.

"I love you," Paul whispered in my ear and I broke out in a full-fledged grin.

"I love you, too," I replied softly, and then went in for another quick hug.

"When Rob returns from the Throne, you two are done with all that," Lanie wagged a finger in our direction. I looked up at her and laughed.

At that, Rob exited the bathroom and said, "So are we ordering a pizza or what?"

"Or what." I replied before Lanie had the chance. "Unless you guys are hungry. If you're hungry, order up."

"I mean…I think we need something more than all this junk food," Paul suggested.

Lanie and I shared a look: pizza is junk food.

"Sustenance." Rob agreed.

"I'll call." Paul bounded into the kitchen and grabbed a menu from the inner reaches of his drawer. "I'm calling the place on the corner in case they aren't delivering, that way we won't have to go that far."

"And who do you think is going out there with you?" Rob asked this as if Paul had suggested burning down someone's house just for the hell of it.

"I'll go," I heard myself say. I thought about it a second and then realized that perhaps we could catch snowflakes on our tongue.

"All right." Paul called, and this being New York City, the place was still open, but no more deliveries for the night. He ordered a large pepperoni and a small veggie pizza, just in case us girls changed our minds. About twenty minutes later we left the apartment looking as if we were going to blaze a trail straight up to Alaska.

"Are you having fun?" Paul asked as soon as we got out on the street. The wind was moving faster now and the snow was blowing in our faces. I felt as if I had to yell to be heard over the wind, but at the same time there was a quiet to the city streets that was rarely heard on a Saturday night. A lone cab inched by us, its tires crunching in the snow, and I felt the need to stop and take it all in, if only for a few silent seconds.

"I'm having a great time. This was a good idea," I answered, my eyes looking for and then locating the street lamp I had been watching before.

"The pizza or the night?" Paul questioned.

"Both," I tried to estimate how much snow was on the ground as we crossed the street hand in hand. The pizza place was at the corner opposite us, so not too far of a walk, but just enough to require a double dose of hot chocolate upon return. "How much snow do you think is out here?" I asked him as we walked gingerly across the street.

"About six inches." Paul made a face. "Give or take six inches."

I chuckled then and we stamped our feet as we made our way into the pizza shop. They had our pizzas ready to go for us, and the guy behind the counter said something funny to Paul about the snow and the city, something about the bike deliveries not being able to go out as it piled up high. Paul paid for the pizza and we were on our way.

"Do you like snow?" I asked him as we made our way back to his place. It seemed strange that I had never asked him that before, but I don't think it was something we had ever had occasion to discuss. I tried to stick out my tongue and catch a snowflake, but the wind was whipping them sideways, and either way, away from my mouth, so I closed it up fast and stared at Paul as he spoke.

"I do. I think it's pretty, and it brings with it a hush to our otherwise frenetic lives. I like it more now that I live in the city. Dad used to force Peter and I to shovel not only our walk and drive, but the walk and the driveway of the old widow across the street too, every time it snowed, and as a teenager, Dads tend to really lose some rating points for things like that." Paul smiled at the memory. "Peter and I used to work side by side on each place until one day, when he decided to do hers himself. He told me to do ours. I think he thought he was getting the better end of the deal, because her driveway was shorter, but her stairs were a nightmare, so by the next snowfall, he tried to pawn her place off on me. We fought about it, and then Dad had to get involved and insist that we both work on both properties, and that was that. There was no discussion."

"Upstate snow is more like a regular part of the winter landscape," I commented. "I like it though."

"I like it best in the morning."

"When it's untouched."

"No footprints, no nothing."

"No telltale signs of dog."

"Or human."

"Yuck." Catching on, I wondered what type of human would pee in the snow. I must have had a fine expression on my face, because Paul laughed at me then, full throttle.

"I did that once in college." He admitted this as we strode through the door to his apartment, his back to me.

"You did what?" I asked in awe of the man I thought I knew.

"I got so drunk that I peed my name in the snow." He was rolling then, recalling his college antics, and Rob jumped up at that moment to hi-five Paul in the way that only guys can do.

"You're proud of this?" I was aghast.

"Not proud, exactly, but…" he and Rob seemed to be sharing a private joke. "It was so damn funny. When I looked outside the next day, I saw something that looked like a lopsided P-O-V-I staring back at me. I was just glad they couldn't identify me."

We all laughed then, and I found myself wondering about the BC grad with a penchant for acting like a five-year-old. Perhaps he could teach me a thing or twelve about being childish.

"Want some?" Paul gestured towards the pizza.

"I don't." Lanie flounced back onto the love seat. "Well, maybe later."

"Then will you barf?" Rob was riding her, and I found it pretty funny, as if perhaps I was watching two people who had met their match.

"Only on you," Lanie batted her eyes at Rob and then crossed her legs in a ladylike fashion.

"Pizza?" Paul extended his hands towards the veggie pizza.

"Maybe later." I had already eaten no less than a thousand pretzels and half a dozen cookies.

Paul and Rob piled up their plates and soon one of us hit the remote, falling back into the lazy-day routine of being snowed in and eating ourselves into oblivion. The movie itself was staggering between an A- and B-list film, so my attention wavered several times towards the door, and I found myself watching the snow pile up outside far more than the carnage playing out on the magic box.

"I can't, Daddy!" I wanted him to turn around and see the sheer terror that was playing itself out on my face, but he kept hiking to the summit, hands filled with sleds, oblivious to the pain on his only child's face. I tried stopping several times just to see if I could get his attention, but he forged ahead without me, and I knew within seconds that I had only to follow.

"You're fine." He turned around once he had reached the peak and extended a hand towards me. Finally. *"Come on up here and show me how you're not a scaredy-cat."*

"But I am," I said with all the frankness a five year old instinctively has use of, no longer caring if he spent the night at home or not. All I knew was that I did not want to go flying down the hill.

"No, you're not. Come on, Danielle! Are you a baby? Is that it? You're a big baby! Is that it?" He was frustrated. I could tell.

"I can go from here." I stepped down a bit, two or three feet, and in doing so, convinced myself that I could bargain with him. I wanted to please him, but I was scared, so scared that I was willing to go more than halfway, but no more. I didn't care what he called me, but I wished he would stop calling me a scaredy-cat, and I wished right then that I was brave, or a boy. I felt instinctively that he wanted a boy, a son who would go tunneling down the slope without even so much as the blink of an eye.

"Come on, Danielle. Just step up. It's only a few more feet!" My father made a motion with his hands, as if to say, forget about it, and shoved off himself, leaving my Sno-tube a few feet above where I was standing. I watched him fly down the hill, standing helpless all alone, wondering if I could walk up the remainder of the hill, and fly down behind him from the tippy top. I looked up, but it still loomed high above me, so I grabbed the rope on the side of my Sno-tube, and tugged it closer to where I was sitting.

My gloves were still blue. I took a breath, gave a good old heave-ho, and off I was only to finish to the far left of my Dad.

I felt a hand extended towards me.

"Let's go home," my father suggested, disappointment clearly etched in his features.

"I'll go from the top next time." I wanted so badly for him to understand.

"Sure you will." He didn't believe me, and as I fell into step behind him, I cried silent tears into my blue-gloved hands.

"Who chose that?" Lanie accused in a voice that led no one to want to confess.

"I can't recall," Rob stated, his voice dripping with sarcasm.

"There's a reason that no horror film has ever won an Oscar." Paul shrugged.

"None?" Rob was incredulous.

"None that I know of," Lanie put out.

"One comedy, coming right up. Danielle, are you checking the snow?" Paul twisted his head in my direction.

I was still staring out onto the patio, watching the snow accumulate through the dimness coming from the streetlight, and I could hear Paul calling me back to the present day, when all we really needed to ponder was Whodunit, and what we would need to imbibe next.

"Yeah, it's really coming down now," I enthused. The snowfall had picked up its pace and it reminded me once again of the type of snow we got Upstate on a regular basis. My statement warranted all of them getting up and staggering towards the patio door, gaping as it were at the amount of snow that was piling up outside.

"I got snowed in once at a friend's house in the Hamptons. You wouldn't believe how much snow they get out there compared to the rest of Long Island." Lanie shook her head. "Think we should turn on the news?"

"Why bother? We're not going anywhere." Rob pointed towards the same street lamp I had been watching throughout the night. "See how much you can see it in the light?"

We gawked at the blanket covering the city all in white. For the past two years, winters in New York City had been mild, and we hadn't dealt with the likes of this in a while.

"I had tickets for a Billy Joel concert once, and he got so snowed in out in the Hamptons that they actually had to cancel the concert." Paul shared.

"Did they reschedule it?" I had never heard of a concert being cancelled before, at least not due to snow. Overdose, maybe, but not snow.

"Yeah, I went the next night. It was great." Paul went on to tell us some details about the concert, like what song he opened with and what the encore songs were. I made a mental note about Billy Joel: Long Islanders loved him like Jersey loved Springsteen. It was almost a given.

"I have an idea. A bathroom and news break, then the comedy. Then if we're still awake, a board game." I loved conducting the slumber party, and felt a great need to join in at this point, as I had been absent for most of the slasher film.

"Sounds like a plan." Paul motored into the kitchen to reheat another slice for himself. "Anyone else?"

"I'll have one," I called out to him as I made my way into the bathroom. Why not? This night was supposed to be about fun: getting snowed in with some friends, joking around, eating food that we all knew was bad for us, and not caring one whit about anything serious. I made a mental note to speak to Constance about my memories invading my social life. I needed to understand why, after all this time; I could no longer stem the tide that threatened to overflow into every aspect of my life. Was it Paul? Was being with Paul causing me to recall every serious event that had ever occurred, to deal with those feelings, and perhaps bid all the bad ones adieu? I thought back to the time before I met him, and the truth was that most of my memories were confined then to dreams, relegated to a subconscious that only knocked on the door while I was fast asleep.

Was that true? Or did I just not notice it until now? Did it matter?

"Hurry up, lady, I've got to pee." This came from Lanie on the other side of the door.

"I'm coming." I unlocked the door from my side and let her in. "I'm ready."

Ready for what, I knew not, but at the very least knew that I was ready for the next movie and a slice.

Chapter Fifty

"I just don't understand why I'm having all these memories come rushing back now. I can't tell you the last time I thought about that day on the hill with my father." My eyes begged a question as I looked to Constance for reassurance. Had I gone completely nuts? Had it finally come to that?

"I think that you're finally ready to deal with your feelings." She paused, hung on a second, and then threw out another thought. "I think you feel safe enough to deal with it now."

I drew a sharp intake of breath as she hit the nail right on the proverbial head. There was that word again, *safe,* being intrusive in every way possible. Suddenly, the word *safe* was popping up all around me, invading my moments and forcing my thoughts to wrap itself around it. I had a concurrent thought. "Do you think that's why I'm so angry now?"

"In what sense?"

I explained to her how, whenever I spoke to either one of my parents lately, I was almost constantly trying to keep my sarcasm in check, how the anger that had always been hovering right around the surface had finally done just that–surfaced–and how I could barely hold accusations from flying out of my mouth. I confessed about how I went to great lengths to avoid them, and how the word *busy* had become a regular excuse in my life with them. I genuinely felt that I owed them nothing, but still wanted a connection with the both of them. They were the parents; I was the child. Where had they been when I needed them most? They were so far from being the keepers of the flame that I felt an intense bile rising in my throat just sitting there and talking about it. Thinking about it made me both angry and sad. My point was this: could it be that I finally felt safe enough to have and even display all of those emotions, now that I had moved on and created both a literal and figurative distance between us? Perhaps that was why all of the memories were rising up within me, calling me to address them once and for all. My mind flicked cautiously to the bag of bricks that Paul had described. Was that night with the snow all about letting another brick fall? In keeping honest with myself, I would have to admit that I had never allowed myself to feel those feelings before, perhaps because I never felt safe enough to reveal them?

"I don't know if that makes any sense." It did and it didn't and I was waiting for Constance to lay it all out for me.

"It makes perfect sense. You were living in a house filled with chaos; you didn't feel safe enough to contribute to that chaos. To break out, to show anger in a house that was so unpredictable…you weren't comfortable enough to do that, you were too busy trying to survive. Perhaps now that you've been on your own for a while, you finally feel that you're in a place where you can display your emotions, and work them out in time." Constance waited for a reply.

"I always felt like I was swallowing it. At home, I rarely spoke up to The Monster or my mother about the atrocities that were going on in that house. With my father, I never seemed to get up the nerve to tell him that I needed him more often than I saw him, or that I missed the special times we had spent together alone. I was always afraid to speak up." I cried silent tears for a long minute while Constance waited on standby.

"And now?"

"I think I'm still afraid to speak up, but the memories seem to be rallying on my behalf, forcing me to remember, and maybe to let certain things go. But on some level, I thought I had already done that. A couple of years ago, I was driving around Upstate and I went into the old development where we lived when my parents were still married. I drove past the old house, and then I decided to try and locate the hill. Well, a house had been built on the property since then, but I found the exact spot, and you know what?"

"What?"

"The hill wasn't so big after all. I couldn't believe my own eyes; I remembered it being so much bigger, and then I felt stupid all over again for having been so scared." I fought my way through the tears as I spoke, almost laughing at my own stupidity by the time I was done.

"I think that you shouldn't have felt stupid. Your father didn't know what he was doing, but he should have acknowledged your fear, instead of making you feel bad about it." Constance shook her head solidly.

"I felt like the biggest jerk, that day, and then again when I saw the hill. I felt like a jerk that day because I knew that I disappointed him, and I wanted so desperately not to do that. Of course, at that age, I took all of their marital problems and somehow found a way to blame myself." I shrugged. "Now, I felt stupid because I let my fears get the best of me."

"It's understandable to have fears."

"I know that; I just wish I had known that then. Did you ever go visit your elementary school as a grown-up?" I asked her.

"No." She had an inquisitive look on her face, possibly trying to figure out the abrupt change in topic.

"Well, I did once, I went there, and I couldn't believe how small the chairs were. The bathroom…I can remember going to the bathroom and almost falling because I didn't judge the bowl being so low," I laughed, humbled by the memory. "Everything that had seemed so big as a child seemed so small then. I had that same feeling when I looked at the hill."

"I understand." Constance nodded and then waited for me to continue.

"I want to deal with this stuff and get it over with. Now that I met Paul, I want to find a new life with him. I want to get past all the hurt and crap, and move on, and maybe that's what my mind is trying to tell me." I surmised.

The hour that was less than an hour had come to an end, and I left with no real definitive answers in tow, but the same familiar feeling that I always left with, a feeling that enabled me to see past the landscape of my past, and even the present day.

Hope?

I guess.

I stepped carefully around a patch of ice as I made my way back to the office, my mind going over my weekend plans. I was driving up to see Am, and although she had told me to bring Paul along, I decided against it for the sole reason that I was toying with the idea of stopping by to see my mother, and I still wasn't ready for her and Paul to interface.

"Tell me you brought me back a chai tea," Lanie greeted me as soon as I reentered the hole/office.

"You didn't say you wanted one," I looked at her as if she had three heads as I carefully unwound the scarf nestled around my neck.

"Leave that on!" She jumped up and wound the scarf around my neck again, a little too tight for my taste, then grabbed her purse and propelled me out the door. "You're right, I think I was talking to myself. I told myself in my head, but I thought I told you out loud."

"Lanie, are you sure you need more caffeine?"

She ushered me out the door and regaled me with stories about the various Teams that were giving her heartache while I was gone. Each account in the agency had a name like 'Team Heineken' or 'Team Kleenex' and we worked closely with the teams that traveled the most.

Team Tampax was a personal favorite.

Anyway…right before I left work, Paul called to reconfirm our date for Sunday. I had declined to make anything more than tentative plans with him for Saturday night because I knew that I would be Upstate during the day, so he was taking my lead and heading out to Long Island for the day to catch up with his Mom and Dad. I was looking forward to seeing him on Sunday, and I would be lying if I said that I was doing anything less than protecting myself by not seeing him Saturday, regardless as to what time my wheels hit Westchester pavement. I usually needed some time to digest whatever happened up there and transfer myself back into the section of my life entitled New.

"So no chance you'll want a nightcap?" Paul was persistent and sometimes greedy with the time we had to spend together.

"I don't think so. Saturday will be a long driving day," I said in return, knowing full well that if I even opened up the gates a touch that he would sashay through and be standing on my doorstep at midnight.

"I'll come to you," and because he offered this in the same manner of which he would offer a slice of pie, I was able to not run screaming from the room, the heebie-jeebies crawling the length of my entire back.

"Aren't you going to stay out on the Island that night?" I countered, knowing full well that his old room was always available if he so desired.

"No. Nah, I thought I would come in and sleep at my place, that way it would be easier to get up and make brunch in the morning. No rush." He said, and then I heard someone walk into his office and say something like *do the hand-jive.*

"What?"

"I have a meeting in five." He translated. "I'll call you a little later on."

"Oh. Okay. Bye." I hung up quickly because I didn't want to hold him up, but also because I didn't want to have to tell him no. "Are you ready?" I turned to Lanie.

"Ready to roll," Lanie affirmed as she slung her gym bag over her shoulder.

"Okay." I powered down my computer and in less than a minute, I was on my way to kickboxing heaven–or hell–depending on which way you looked at it.

Kickboxing gave me power. I can't really explain the way that I felt when I hit the bag, but it was tantamount to all the other things that make life worth living: an ice cream sundae, good Chinese food, etc. The exertion was a sensory high on a whole other level, and I always left the class feeling somehow *bigger* than when I went in. I felt pumped up and my body always got a rush along with a great workout from the class, but there was a spiritual connection that I had made early on, a feeling of control that my body craved as much as my mind. And that was precisely what always left me coming back for more.

Sometimes I would picture The Monster's ugly scowl as my arms sliced through the air, wiping that god awful grin from his inebriated face, getting him back for all the ways he had violated my mother and myself, a punch here and a kick there and a jab, jab, jab, and on the floor he would go! Beaten down, punched out, and no longer smiling, to say the least. I felt invigorated by this fantasy, and suddenly the punches weren't so hard to throw. Most nights, the class would go by in a whoosh of expelled air and stress would take its place at the door, all faces intent on the end result that kickboxing had to offer. I often wondered what the other people were picturing as I rode an angry wave and then came crashing down.

"Lane, do you think about anything in particular when you're punching?" Lanie and I were walking next to each other on treadmills following class, both bodies drenched, and my spirit renewed.

"Sometimes." Lanie shrugged. "I think I just think about stress in general, and I visualize getting it out of my body, and then it comes out."

"You visualize it how?"

"Oozing out of my pores."

"Oozing?"

"Yeah." She looked chagrined. "You asked." She added a shrug.

"So no faces then? No one in particular?" I prodded.

"Brad right after we broke up." Lanie admitted with a sarcastic grin.

"Okay, then I feel better." I winked at her. Lanie was so terrifically human; she never made me feel as if I were teetering on the edge of sanity.

Of course, I knew I was, I just didn't need friends pointing it out to me.

"So are you going to see your mother this weekend?" Lanie asked me with a sideways glance.

"I'm thinking about a drive-by." Stop-in, not shooting.

"Tell Am I said Hi." She took her speed down and was at a full stop a few seconds later. "I'm beat."

"I'm about ready to pack it in myself," I hopped off the treadmill and made my way to the locker room. I got changed and high-tailed it over to the train. There were no people worth watching, so I buried myself in a book until the conductor called out my stop, when I scrambled off the train and then hiked to my car.

On the way to my car, I said a little prayer: *God, please help me to deal with whatever it is I need to deal with in order to make my life the best life I can have.* I wanted to be victorious in all things, and although the prayer was somewhat circular, I knew that God would understand what I was trying to say. I had somehow arrived at the point of wanting more, and I thought maybe Constance was right, in saying that I was finally ready to deal with the pain rather than continue to bury it.

Chapter Fifty-One

    Saturday dawned gray and cold, but there was no real snow in the forecast, so I hopped in my buggy and proceeded Upstate as soon as I was showered and spiffed, my vanilla-scented self wrapped in fleece from head to toe. I had an avalanche of good music piled high on my front seat, and I flicked between slow and fast as I wound my way towards the place I had come from, still debating whether or not I should visit with Mom. I mulled over the plusses and minuses in my head, ultimately deciding to decide later on.
    For some reason, my mind settled on Steven as I drove. Steven was like the big brother I never had, always there for me, yet graciously respecting my relationship with Am, and maintaining some sort of distance as a result of that. Alright, maybe he was more like a cousin: someone you had great conversations with whenever you showed up together, but not exactly someone you would go out of your way to call. I often wondered how much Am really told him about me, in the still of the night, when pillow talk turned to shared confidences and deep revelations. Maybe it was egotistical of me to even think that I rated in that department.
    I tossed all my meditations out the window when I made the final turn into their driveway. The snow was piled up higher up here; last week's storm had enabled them to form a thick white wall on either side of their driveway, the end result of what I am sure was hours of shoveling. The snow was piled so high that I could barely see their front door over it, and I sighed as I remembered shoveling for hours on end, just my Mom and me and a Thermos of hot cocoa. We were the girls who could do anything, and we showed the world how we ran our own little club for a while there, snow be damned. I shook my head again and gathered up my quiche as I made my way precariously up

the drive, trying to avoid the patches of ice peeking up through the places they had shoveled.

Mom and I had been meticulous in our heyday.

The door swung open before I even had a chance to ring the bell. "Danielle!" It was Am, hugging me and pulling me in from the cold.

"Whatcha got there?" Steven eyed my quiche greedily, and I pretended for a second to not know what he was talking about.

"Oh, this?" I displayed the quiche. "You wouldn't want any of this."

"You're right." He nodded as if the quiche were poison. "I don't even think I like that stuff."

I laughed and leaned in to give him a quick hug. The quiche I had proffered was from the same place I had brought it before, this cozy little bistro in the city that made homemade quiches and pies that were absolutely to die for. The last time Steven had a piece of this yummy little masterpiece, Am accused him of making bedroom sounds at the dining room table.

We talked and ate and the next thing I knew, it was time to point my car in my mother's direction.

The tinderbox that my mother was currently ensconced in was the last place she had moved into after I decided to leave. Growing up, my seasons had been punctuated with moves from one place to another, leaving me no room to ever utter to Paul or anyone else, 'That's the house I grew up in.'

Although most Army brats could say the same, our moves had been more pie-in-the-sky than duty or anything else resembling responsibility, fragments of thought that were never carried through to the end stage, a life lived through the clouded eyes of a dreamer (my mother) and a drug addict. (The Monster) The next place would always be better…cheaper…nicer…we would get ahead at the next place, the next place would have better neighbors, and of course, the next place would solve all of their problems.

Only the next place never did, and the more my mother bought into it, it seemed the more disillusioned she became, until The Monster went to jail and she convinced herself that she didn't deserve more than what she had, which was a home in which the furnishings were done exclusively by Kmart.

As I ambled onto her gravel driveway I saw her neighbor Jake outside throwing salt on his walkway and I gave him a wave and a smile. Jake was a good friend to her as well as a great neighbor, and a secret part of my heart had always wished for them to fall madly in love and move in together. Let The Monster's accusations be true! My mother could do, and in fact had done, far worse than the likes of Jake.

"Hi Jake," I called out as I alighted from my vehicle.

"Hey there, Big City Girl! How are ya?" Jake had a smile that extended ear to ear and his greeting said *Howdy* to me even if his actual words were close, but no banana.

"I'm okay." I crunched across the snow closer to where he was standing. "Had enough snow yet?"

"Just about." He laughed and touched the top of his hat. "You should have seen your mother the day before the storm. I saw her coming into the house with about thirty bags full of groceries."

"She still remembers the days when it would take a day or two for them to plow," I laughed along with him, making small talk until the door opened up behind us.

"Danielle?" My mother called from inside her doorway. "Isn't it cold? Oh, Hi Jake."

"Well hello there! I just found a Big City Girl on your doorstep," Jake gestured towards me and we shared another grin. He was a simple man with a big heart, and I found myself glad to have made his acquaintance.

"I noticed." My mother flashed him a smile, and it warmed my heart to see it. Smiles had been few and far between in the past few years.

I made another few seconds of idle chitchat with Jake and then made my way inside my mother's humble abode. The place was etched in sameness, the quality of her goods the same as the last time I had visited, the neatness a signature of her remaining pride, and the trademark scent of good Italian cooking welcomed me inside. I turned around to take off my coat and noticed a pile of socks and candy bars piled up on the floor in front of her television set.

"Was that a lame present from Santa or what?" I pointed towards the pile.

"That is actually a present for a friend of The Monster's." She replied, her back to me as she made her way into her kitchen.

"What?" My rage was instantaneous, knowing full well where the conversation was headed, wishing I had never asked. I tried to keep the edge from my voice, but I found my face flushed, and my body temperature rising at the mere thought of my mother perpetuating any sort of relationship with any constituency of Monster-Dom.

"He had a friend in jail that was widowed while he was in there; a poor soul whose wife died of cancer. His children don't speak to him, and he has virtually no one, so I decided I would send him a few staples for the New Year." She shrugged, as if it were entirely normal to send prisoners socks and Milky Ways, as if this acquaintance of The Monster's were a fellow soldier in the army, one she felt it was her patriotic duty to serve.

"Surely you jest." I was fully aware that my voice was laced with disgust, but there was no room to hide it, and no will to swallow the truth in this instance. "Why on Earth would you do that? Do you even know him? What the hell is he in there for? Jaywalking? I mean, come on Mom, do you think that his children don't talk to him because he's some sort of great guy?" I hammered the words out at her, each syllable punctuated with venom. Would she never learn? *Why* would she never learn?

"Danielle," My mother took a deep breath and then turned to face me, her expression tired, worn out by my continuous protestations. "This…" she pointed towards the incriminating pile. "These things were purchased a long time ago, *for THE MONSTER,* and since he no longer has any use for them there, and I certainly wasn't going to offer them to him now; I thought it might be a nice, Christian thing to do, to give them to Howie."

"Howie? Howie!" I moved around her living room, uncomfortable in my own skin, glaring at the pile of socks and candy. "You shouldn't have been sending The Monster anything anyway!"

"You're probably right. Can you think of someone else that would enjoy the bag of Hanes and the chocolate? Would you like to give them to your boyfriend?" She offered this as if it were a natural train of thought.

"Are you kidding me?" I was yelling now, fast on my way to screaming, totally unable to control myself. "I don't want to give Paul socks! I am simply appalled that you would continue to support a convict…any convict…and don't you dare give me that 'What Would Jesus Do' mantra, because I don't really care! *Jesus wasn't a doormat!"* I huffed and I puffed and I almost blew her little shack down.

"Danielle, I really don't know where all your anger comes from." She shook her head as if to erase all culpability. "You should do something about that."

All vestiges of talk thrown to the ground, I wailed, "You don't know *where* my anger comes from? You can't imagine, right now, as we speak, you can't imagine why this would be a little bit upsetting to me? Can you–just once–slap yourself in my position, and see how frustrating this conversation is from my end?" I was amazed by her, simply amazed at the amount of denial one human being could steep herself in.

"I understand that you're angry about The Monster. I get it. You think I don't get it? You think I don't sit up nights and think about what he did to you...to us?" She was crying suddenly, and I found my heart splintering off into little pieces, wanting to reach out and hold her, and hug her, and tell her everything would be okay, but unable to get past the seething anger, standing implacable in my resolve to not give up, to make a point that would stick with her.

"Then why do you keep doing it?" I asked plainly. She hurt me by actions that weren't even related to me, time and again, whether she knew it or not.

"I just think that giving Howie the socks and stuff is the right thing to do. He has no one." She stated this without apology, as resolute as I, even in her weakness. "I also think that if you let go of the anger, Danielle, that you'll feel better about *you.* Forget The Monster. He'll get his. If you stop hating him, does that mean he wins? No, that means you win. Don't think I'm not aware of all that he's taken from us...I'm more aware than you know; I just choose to let it go, rather than let it consume me any more than it already has. I've spent enough time hating. Now I'm just spent. "

"Then who's holding him accountable?" I spat out the words, aware that I was railing out at God on some level, too. So what that he had served several years in prison? Did that erase or make well the fact that he destroyed a family? Did it help to take back all the awful fights; did it make my memories somehow disappear? I felt on some strange level that I had to hold on to the anger, that in some cosmic way my righteous indignation would tip the scales in such a way that he would have to pay for all the hurt he caused.

"I would like to believe that God will hold him accountable for all the evil things he has done." My mother nodded her head and then leveled her gaze at me. "But either way, I am trying to not hold on to it anymore. I've realized one thing: holding unforgiveness in your heart is like drinking poison and hoping your enemy will die from it." She stared directly at me.

"Where did you hear that?" It didn't sound like something she had made up herself.

"Joyce Meyer," she chuckled. Joyce Meyer was a motivational teacher/preacher/author/evangelist that my Mom was totally into.

I laughed at her analogy, and in spite of myself, I found the anger begin to dissipate, and I loosened up just a little.

"That's a good one."

"That's a true one."

"Well, you might be right." I reminded myself to breathe. My mind shifted to the conversation I had had with Paul about The Monster and my painting. What was it he'd said? That if I gave up painting for good that The Monster wins. He was right; she was right; I knew it; I just didn't know how to fix it.

"Want some pasta?" My mother got up then and crossed the room, heading back towards her kitchen, acting as if all was well with the world. Had we just not had a huge fight? How was she able to switch gears, so quickly, so easily, without having any garbage left sticking to her in the end? Was it maturity? A spiritual maturity that I had yet to reach, or was it a survival tactic that she had honed throughout the bad years?

"Yeah, I'll have some." I resigned myself to the fact that however she did it, it worked, and besides that the food smelled delicious.

We sat down in silence and eventually started speaking as the pasta disappeared from our plates. We talked about the weather, and the winters gone by, nothing in particular. Once we finished eating, she surprised me with a cheesecake she had made the day before.

"What did you make this for?" The cheesecake was larger than life, adorned with glistening cherries, the edge rimmed with crumbled graham. I swear I thought it was winking at me as I sat there and eyed it.

"I made it in case you decided to stop by," She said nonchalantly.

"You made this whole cake for me?" It was humungous.

"Oh, I figured Jake Next Door could help me polish it off if need be." She said 'Next Door' as if that were Jake's last name.

"So why don't you give him a call, or did you figure you'd bring it over to him?"

"Either."

"I'll call." I offered and then got up to place the call. Jake picked right up and not only accepted graciously, but proposed to add something else to the menu. He had just made a fresh jug of warm apple cider. When I told my mother, she was pleased.

"Danielle, you will love Jake's cider," She had barely gotten the words out of her mouth when the doorbell rang and our beloved neighbor appeared, cider in tow.

"Hello again," I greeted him and then led the way into the kitchen.

"Hello to you too!" Jake gave both myself and mom a quick air kiss and then settled the cider onto the table. "Now that looks good, ladies…" he waved his hand over the cheesecake.

"I deserve zero credit," I informed him, and made a gesture towards Mom.

"Oh. It's nothing," my mother insisted, already slicing into the cake, in the process of heaping huge slabs onto our plates. "I made cherry because it's Danielle's favorite."

"Mine too." Jake shot me a conspiratory look. "Although when you live alone, any home baked meal is a favorite."

"You don't cook?" Jake was always bringing over some beverage or the other, so I guess that I had just assumed that he cooked too. In the summer, he brought homemade lemonade, and in the winter, cider or hot cocoa.

"I'm not that good at it," he shook his head with remorse.

"Jake, if you haven't eaten dinner yet, I have more than enough pasta left to share," my mother was already on her feet and getting a dish out of the cabinet.

"Well..." he gave her an aw-shucks grin. "It does smell good. Maybe just a little bit."

"I can wait for cake," I announced as I got up to go to the ladies room. I figured I'd give them a minute alone while Jake caught up on the food. I made my way over to my mother's bathroom and at that precise moment I heard my cell phone chiming from deep inside my bag.

"Danielle, is that your phone?" She called from the kitchen.

"I think so." I rerouted and grabbed my bag from where I had put it down in the living room, opening the zipper as I trundled towards the back bedroom. "Hello?"

"Am I interrupting anything?" It was Paul's voice, coming alive across the miles, and making my heart skip a beat.

"No!" I found myself more than happy to hear his voice on the other end of the line. "You're not interrupting anything. To what do I owe the pleasure of this phone call?"

"To the fact that I am missing you." He paused a second and asked, "Would it be melodramatic to say that Saturday just didn't seem as good with you gone?"

"Yes, it would be melodramatic, but I love hearing you say it anyway." I sighed. "Just don't let your Mom hear you saying that, I wouldn't want her to get offended."

"Mom is in the other room, and Dad is stirring up something that resembles chili in the kitchen. Could be chili, could be battery acid soup, we're not sure yet."

"Sounds good." I laughed.

"So whatcha up to? I miss you." He was borderline whining.

"I am up to cheesecake, which will mean at least three extra hours at the gym next week." I joshed. "Seriously? I'm still up at Mom's, having cake with her and Jake, and will most likely be heading home after dessert."

"Is Jake the dog?"

"No, Jake's the neighbor."

"Jake is such a cool name for a dog."

"I'll be sure and tell him that."

"Please don't. Sounds good anyway. Okay, I miss you, and I won't ask you to come down again because I know you'll get mad at me, so let me just say that I can't wait to see you again, and I'll see you tomorrow." Paul said.

"Sounds great. In the meantime, I love you."

"In the meantime, I love you too."

I pressed End and then squeezed into the bathroom. My mother's current bathroom was so tight that it did not lend itself to being comfortable; instead it was a place you went only to get in and get out. I did so and then joined Mom and Jake back in the kitchen, where it seemed that they were getting along famously. I wondered then if perhaps they knew each other better than I had presumed. There was a familiarity between them that seemed rather obvious all of the sudden, and I wished again that Mom would either end up with Jake or someone just like him.

"Ready for cheesecake?" Jake rubbed his hands together in a greedy fashion.

"The question is: are you?" I gestured towards his empty pasta dish and smiled.

"There's always room for cake," Jake returned.

"Amen to that." My mother got out a third cake plate and distributed the three pieces evenly. Soon we were buried in the creaminess, silence all around us as we indulged.

"This is the best," I caught my mother's glance. "Thanks."

"You're welcome." She beamed.

"Ummm," was all Jake could muster.

I took a sip of Jake's cider and found it to be pleasantly warm with just the right touch of cinnamon. "You can't get this at Starbucks."

"I hope not." Jake settled into a comfortable grin. "I'm hopin' to give them a run for their money."

"Are you really?" My mother inquired.

"No, I'm jokin'." Jake did something that resembled a blush.

"Well, you should." With that, I stood and said that I had better get going. The day was getting late and I still had a way to drive. We said our goodbyes and my mother tried unsuccessfully to give me half the cheesecake to take home. I settled on a small piece about half the size of my car and then turned to go.

"Mom," I reminded her with a thoughtful glance and a finger pointed over to the offending pile by the television. "Let that be the one and only care package to Howie."

"Danielle, please," was all that she said.

Chapter Fifty-Two

I couldn't shower fast enough. I don't know why I was so eager to see Paul (with the exception of the fact that I was madly in love with him) but for some strange reason it seemed as if I couldn't get into his arms fast enough, and as I ran around my apartment shoving things into a bag, I found myself doubling back several times in order to make sure I had everything.

I ran for the train and laughed to myself as I boarded, wondering how on Earth I had gotten to a place in my life where running for the train on a weekend was perfectly acceptable, even something I could say I looked forward to, knowing who was waiting for me on the other end. I didn't mind...and for a second my heart lurched at the thought of perhaps one day not feeling this way anymore. How long had we been together? Seven months now? Was I still climbing the apex? Was there sure to be a crash? Panic settled into that familiar place in my stomach. Was I wrong to get this excited over everything I did with Paul?

Or was that my old mindset barging through the new door again? When would my heart firmly register that this man was not another David, was nothing like The Monster, was far from the father that had tossed me aside for a new model child?

My heart felt the need for conjecture, the haunting refrain of *when will it end* clouding, so I determined simply to shove my negative thoughts aside, and focus on the positive. The positive thought being that I had found a man who loved me...and for now at the very least, I was happy.

Why question it?

Why not?

My pace quickened as I made my way to Paul after getting off the train. I sought my refuge in his arms, and like a soldier who had been on a long journey; I made my way to the finish line.

"You don't have to meet me any more; you know, I know where you live now." The words tumbled out as I leaned into him for a hug. I felt my eyes flutter and I stepped into the role of a flirt with ease as I took his hand in mine. Was I still wooing him, or was he still wooing me? Did it matter?

"There's something to be said about chivalry," was his response, and as he swept me deeper into his arms, I knew that there was where I wanted to be, for all time.

"There is," I replied, holding him close, enveloped by my new life, and the precious love that I had found, walking across the street one day.

His lips leaned down to touch mine and the chaos of Grand Central Station melted into the background as we stood there, solid in our embrace, his lips searching my own as if I were getting on a train and never coming back this way again. My mind took a dangerous turn: *what if I wasn't?* What if my heart were to walk away from the questioning, and learn how to trust, never to come this way again? The path of doom and gloom behind me, what possibilities lie ahead? Could we become something far more than I had ever envisioned before? I felt I had some sort of head start: hadn't Paul already stepped out of my dreams and into my life? Would it really be so hard to cut the self-sabotage off at the knees, to decide and to then remain in a place where hope was an anchor…*to trust?*

All these thoughts swirled around inside my head as we kissed, trailing off only once we pulled apart, and his eyes caught my own in a long look that erased the various musings going on inside my head.

"You ready?" he eyed my face, and then took in my coat and bag, as if to make sure I had everything I needed.

"Yeah," I replied in a tone far quieter than the one that usually exited out of my mouth, breathless and wondering if in fact he had the ability to read my mind. Did he know just how much I had come to love the person that he was? Is? Could be in my life? I knew that I was sometimes lax on letting him in to all that was going on inside, but I believed he could tell, and on some level, I knew he knew, and I held onto a sincere need to believe that perhaps he could read my mind.

"I missed you," he looked deeply into my eyes and squeezed my hand as we made our way outside.

"I did too." I missed his touch.

"You missed you too?" He joked, and his sparkling grin accosted me the same way it had when we first met, and I couldn't help but toss him one right back.

"I did!" I allowed my grin to escalate into easy laughter over nothing at all. "So what did you make me?"

"Pancakes." He wiggled his eyebrows. "Nutty pancakes."

"Nutty pancakes? Are these a family recipe?" It was so easy to tease when there was no truth behind it.

"They are actually." Paul nodded his head with vigor. "Does everyone have one nutty relative?"

"One?" I laughed loudly now, wishing for such luck. "I unfortunately have many." I let that out without hesitation, warmed by the comfortable feeling I had found in his arms.

"Everybody has at least one," Paul informed me in such a way that I felt bolstered, normal, like one of the pack.

"Tell me about yours." I was egging him on, knowing full well that I could top just about anything he threw out at me.

"Will you tell me about yours?" He said this with a leveled gaze, his mega-watt smile laced with a tinge of seriousness, concern gracing the corners of his eyes.

"I will give you one for one," I promised, as we came upon his apartment building. Paul opened up the door, and then held it for me, and I snuck in under his arm and made a beeline for the elevator button. I loved pushing the button first.

"Okay. Well!" He shook his head, as if he couldn't believe he was telling me this. "My father has/had a brother named Rick. Rick passed away when I was about…fifteen? Yeah, I think I was fifteen. Rick was the typical black sheep of the family." Paul shrugged as we got off the elevator and opened the door to his apartment.

"Everybody has at least one," I gave a little tit for tat.

"Exactly. So, when Rick was alive, he had married someone when he was very young, I never met her…I think her name was Susan…anyway, he was married about two years and then got divorced. He married Elaine before the ink was dry on the divorce decree, and Elaine was soon after dubbed 'Strange Elaine.' My father came up with that little epithet, and whenever she wasn't around, he would draw out her name and make it sound like a rhyme: *Strange Elainge.* My father liked her in his own way, but I mean, she was nuts to the point of embarrassing. She was from some little town in Vermont, and she was always talking about the town as if she still lived there, or as if we knew all the people that lived there too."

"Kind of like Rose in *The Golden Girls*?" I offered.

"Kind of, yeah…that's actually a pretty good analogy. She was nutty and ditzy, just like Rose, and she yodeled." He laughed. "You can't imagine how embarrassing that was as a kid."

"Was she a professional yodeler or something?" I was willing to give her the benefit of the doubt.

"No, she was just weird. Rick rode a motorcycle, and she loved that, and often times they would ride up to Vermont in the fall on the back of his bike, and she would call it her 'Leaf Expedition.' Every time they went to Vermont, she would pick up jugs of real Vermont maple syrup and tie them on the back of the bike to bring back to Long Island for us."

"That must have been good."

"It was. It totally was. Anyway, she was more than a little strange, and although she was always very nice, my family merely tolerated her. After Rick died, we all thought that she would end up back in her little Vermont town, but surprisingly enough, she decided to stay out in Long Island. My mother, being the quintessentially sweet person that she is, still invites her over occasionally, and when that happens, my father generally makes himself scarce."

"Did she ever remarry?"

"No. Bizarre as she might have been and probably still is, she was unbelievably faithful to Rick and totally in love with him." Paul shook his head as if to underscore the tragedy.

"When's the last time you saw her?"

"College graduation?" Paul suggested.

"Can I ask what happened to Rick?" I was curious about his uncle dying so young.

"He died in a motorcycle accident. He was on the L.I.E one day, and he got pinned between two cars and from what I understand, died rather quickly. He was…" Paul paused a thoughtful moment. "…Probably the age I am now."

"Did you like him?"

"Uncle Rick? Yeah, he was a cool guy. I remember him being much more like a kid than an adult, which was probably why everybody in the family thought he was sort of a loser. He never grew up, not really, not like my Dad had, not like the rest of the guys he used to hang out with. They all had kids, houses, steady jobs…not motorcycles and weird wives from New England states." He shrugged again.

"I can imagine how different he must have felt. Either way, it's sad." I couldn't imagine losing my only love at such a young age, and my heart went out to Strange Elaine.

"So the whole point of this conversation is this: Strange Elaine had visited my mother recently, gave her the recipe for nutty pancakes, as well as a couple of jugs of the Vermont Maple from her hometown. Since I was out there yesterday, Mom offered to give me both so that I might impress you with my culinary skills today." Paul explained.

"Are you still trying to impress me?" I asked in a coquettish fashion.

"Of course I am!" Paul looked stupefied. "The day I'm not trying to impress you anymore; that's the day you have to worry!"

"I'll keep that in mind." I felt exhilarated by his declaration and warned at the same time. It was the same conversation I had had with myself all day long, played out in a conversation that began about someone else, but it made me feel like I wasn't the only one, and I needed that more than Paul would ever know.

"So tell me about your nutty relative," Paul prodded as he poured the batter onto the griddle, each cake a perfect circle.

I would have to take it that he meant nutty, and not certifiably insane, abusive, or downright hallucinogenic. I shuffled through the various wackjobs I knew or was related to, and in my mind went right to my Rock-star Grandma.

"Well, my father's mother is a bit much," I began, wondering how exactly one could explain the old bat. "She lives in Florida now, so I don't see her more than once or twice a year, but whenever she comes up, she manages to drive my father completely nuts with her little quirks." I sighed.

"Give me an example." Paul was egging me on.

"The pillows. A perfect example would have to be *the pillows.*" I pronounced this with fervor, figuring I might as well have a little fun with it. "You have to understand though, a little bit about the nutty Grandma before I can fully explain: The Pillows."

"I feel like I should say, 'Dun-Dun-Dun!'" Paul made a pretty good sound effect.

"You should."

"Name please?"

"Genevieve."

"Proceed."

"Okay, so Genevieve…is, well, let's put it this way…kind of like a prima Donna 80-year old rock star has-been in a polyester suit." I looked to Paul.

Paul guffawed.

I nodded and continued, "Every time she comes up to visit, she complains about my father's house as if it used to be a luxury hotel and is somehow no longer up to par. She's worse than Lanie on a six-property hotel site inspection. When she leaves my Dad's house, she runs over to Aunt Michelle's and basically puts her through the same rigmarole there, to the point where you just want to throw her in a box and ship her back to Florida early."

"Like a bad fruit."

"Like a bad nut."

"Gotcha." He flipped the pancakes.

"By the way, can I help you with anything?"

"Can you pour some juice?" He pointed towards the juice glasses he had laid out on the counter.

"I can pour the juice," I nodded affirmation and then hopped off the stool in order to pour him some OJ and me some Cran-Raspberry.

"So continue."

"Yes, well…The Pillows. Every time she goes to visit my father, she whines incessantly about the pillows at his house. One's too soft, the other too hard, too lumpy…you get the picture. The last time my stepmother knew she was coming, she went out and bought a stable of pillows, all to no avail." I chuckled at the retelling of the tale. "I don't actually know why they still try to please her."

"Because she's old." Paul put in.

"Okay, but there is also something deeper lurking underneath the skin, like an itch my father can't seem to scratch, the only salve being her approval. My real question would have to be what makes her that way? I've never met anybody who is so unhappy with everything. My father has dubbed her comings and goings *The Aggravation Tour.*" I wrapped finger quotes around the words and had the reward of Paul throwing his head back into a full-out laugh.

"Sounds like your Dad is a pretty funny guy." Paul observed as he transferred the nutty pancakes from the griddle to our plates. From there, he arranged some strawberries on top, along with a dollop of cream, arranged as if he were being judged in a contest.

Funny. I thought about it and rolled the word around on my tongue. *A funny guy.* What could I say to that comment? I guess? Occasionally? If I think of my Dad in times gone by, I sometimes think of a freewheeling spirit that loved to laugh, that enjoyed food, that was very much his own man, but was he funny? He could be funny when he wanted to be, but he could also be many more things than what one could easily describe. Occasionally, I could see the side of him that was so like his mother too, the guy who deemed my sleigh ride as not up to par, not good enough, not high enough up the hill.

But a funny guy?

"My father is…well, he can occasionally be quite funny, as he sees the world differently than most people do, and therefore sports an interesting sense of humor…but unfortunately, he is sometimes a lot like her, where nothing is ever good enough." I found out that the truth, when spoken out loud, had the power to validate the theories buried inside the heart. I had always *felt* he operated that way, but once I said it out loud to Paul, I knew that he really didn't have the capacity to be content. I thought back to the incident on the hill. His way or no way. Halfway was no good. His mother magnified that wrestling inside of his own heart, and I believe that's why he struggled with her thrice-yearly visits, and perhaps even why he called me to commiserate, because he knew that the same small piece of discontent may have been passed down to me as well.

"We are all guilty of being like our parents, whether we want to admit it or not." Paul intoned as he took a bite of pancake.

"How are you like yours?" I was deflecting *and* curious.

"Oh, I can see my father in me more often than not. Especially at work," he started talking with his hands, "always trying to be pragmatic…listen to both sides, then eventually take charge and settle on the most equitable situation for both parties. Sometimes I hear myself talking in a meeting, and I swear it's my father's voice I hear, dealing with me and Peter." Paul blushed throughout his confession.

"By the way, these are *delish!*" I exclaimed over the pancakes as I swallowed my first bite. "Sorry, I didn't mean to interrupt you." I waved for him to go on.

"Not a prob." He grinned. "They are good, aren't they?"

"Ummmm." I nodded, my mouth full of the next delectable bite.

"So I can see it, and I'm sure there are tons of other people who can't see it, but I think we all end up being like our parents in one way or another," Paul dabbed another bite into a pool of syrup.

"I don't know how much I'm like either of them." The unsaid: I barely knew my father anymore, and I feared turning into my mother. "I think I used to want to be just like my mother when I was younger. Much younger." I added this, my mind already cueing up our theme song, slowly leading me back to that time.

"Like how?" Paul seemed genuinely interested, and his eyes were riveted on me, even as his cheeks were packed with food.

"Well, first of all, she was very pretty." I laid my fork at the edge of my plate and allowed my mind to travel back to that long-ago time where nothing mattered but Girl Power. *The Second Time Around.* "My mother used to have her hair all sorts of teased, with an Aqua-net veil hanging heavily around the latest hairstyle. She wore tons of fun makeup; bright colors and big platform dancing shoes...even just to go to the supermarket. Or black. She would wear black in the middle of summer, way before it was popular to do so. None of the other Moms on the block dressed anything like her, and I vowed that I wanted to be just like her when I grew up. All the other mothers seemed gray in comparison." I sighed.

"What happened?" Paul was paying rapt attention.

"She married The Monster, and platform heels went out of style. She stopped being pretty sometime after that, not because she wasn't pretty any more, but just because she didn't want to be." I couldn't put it into better words than that.

"What else?" He studied me carefully as he sipped his coffee.

"What else about her?" When he nodded, I continued, reminiscing once again. "My mother used to be so independent. Once she and my father got divorced, she was the Queen of her World, and nothing and no one was going to stop her from living the life that she wanted to live. She had me utterly convinced that I could be anything I ever wanted to be, even at a very young age, and I think that I admired that, way before I ever knew the meaning of the word admiration." I was starting to feel that old familiar lump work its way up my throat, so I paused a minute and looked at Paul, while the long ago picture of my mother lay superimposed on my brain.

"I understand why you hate him." Paul said this so matter-of-factly that it took a minute for my mind to register, and when it did, I let out a sound, something in between a yelp and a cry.

"I'm grateful."

Chapter Fifty-Three

"So how was it?" Lanie asked as she paid for her coffee. Her cell phone chimed just then and she gave me a one-sec sign as she balanced the cup and the phone. I heard her say things like when and sure as she dove into her bag for money, paid as she nodded, then proceeded to click off immediately.

I asked her a look.

"That was my father. Apparently my mother's sister will be in town next weekend, so he wants to know if I can be out there for lunch." She explained.

"This is Aunt..." I trailed off, knowing there was an Aunt, but unable to recall her name. I grabbed my egg white and cheese on a bialy from our regular counter guy and paid for that and a hot cocoa, then joined Lanie outside the bodega.

"Aunt Cecile. She was my mother's older sister, who now lives in Florida, and still manages to pop by and visit whenever she is in New York. I should say she *is* my mother's older sister, since she's still alive. Anyway; Cecile is okay and I don't mind doing lunch with her, although I have a sneaking suspicion that the only reason she drops in on my father now and again is just to see if he is still mourning my mother, or rather if he's involved with anybody yet." Lanie blanched, and I felt sure it was not the coffee.

"Do you really think so? I mean, no offense, but it's been a long time...I don't think anyone would blame him if he were to get involved with someone now." I took a sip of the scalding cocoa as we crossed the street and then chastised myself for not waiting until it had gotten a little cooler.

"Perhaps you're right." Lanie fiddled with her computer a second before facing me again. "So how was your weekend?"

"Good. I saw Am and my mother…you know the deal. Besides that, I had a good time with Paul yesterday." I recounted the nutty pancakes and the highlights of our conversation.

"He's a really good guy, Danielle." Lanie nodded in time with her pronouncement. " I wish I could find a really good guy."

"What about Rob?" I wasn't into pushing the Rob factor, but he seemed like an obvious option.

"Here we go again: *What About Bob?*"

I laughed.

"Still no spark." Lanie grimaced. "I actually spent Sunday morning with him. We went out for brunch to a place down in the Village, a nice new bistro with a little jazz quintet, and we had omelettes and good talk. I thoroughly enjoy his company. I just don't know about there being any potential romance on the horizon."

"Well, how does he act towards you?" I took a huge bite of my egg sandwich as I waited for her to respond.

"He acts…very proprietary. He defers to me as if I were a date, but he has in no way given me any indication that he wants to be anything more than friends." Lanie seemed to dismiss it out of hand. She tapped the computer screen and then gestured towards me. "Did you see this email from Olive?"

I replied in the negative and scarfed another bite of bialy as I shuffled through my emails. About twenty in, I came across the one Lanie was referring to.

"Wanna go?" I looked to Lanie with barely concealed excitement. Our company was looking for agents to go down to Brazil and do a complete sweep of all the hotels we currently had under contract, as well as to check out two more that we were considering for our new hotel program. The offer was for us to go down on a Friday night, arrive Saturday morning, then check out the hotels Saturday and Sunday and return on Sunday night, which would have us to arrive New York on Monday morning.

The work would be simple, and the opportunity to go to Brazil immense, as I myself had never been to South America before, and the trip wouldn't cost us a dime.

"Let's!" Lanie's face broke into a monstrous grin. "I'm going to answer the email right now."

"Do you think they'll let us go together?" My mind was expanding with the possibility of Lanie and I in Brazil for the weekend, but I wasn't willing to get my hopes up just yet.

"Sure. Why not? We can even come straight to work on Monday from the airport, so why would they say no?" Lanie countered.

"I think we'll have to close early on Friday." I reminded her.

"We'll beg." Lanie was relentless in pursuit of pleasure.

I re-read the email and decided that we could get in a full day at the beach if we could manage to see all of the hotels on Saturday, one right after the other. There were a total of eight hotels, so the possibility was strong that we could schedule the site inspections back-to-back, and then be done and free by dinnertime on Saturday night. That would allow for a day at the beach on Sunday, with enough time to shower before getting back on the plane to come home. Then if we could sleep on the plane…Monday might be tough, but it would be worth it.

"Lane, have you ever been to South America?" I thought not, but wanted to make sure, convinced it would be more adventurous if we would be going there for the first time together.

"Never." Lanie breathed excitement. "And I had an idea. Do you think we could knock out all of the hotel visits on Saturday, so that maybe we can have a day at the beach on Sunday, before we return?"

"Great minds think alike." I informed her that I had just been thinking the same thing.

"If Olive doesn't call by one, I'm calling her." Lanie threw this out at me.

"Gotcha." From there on we got busy, and the morning soon disappeared into the afternoon. Just when Lanie was about to call Olive, the phone rang on our end, and I knew by the tone of Lanie's voice that she was speaking to Olive. I thought it funny that Olive had made a deadline that she knew not of.

I went to stand over by Lanie's desk so that I could eavesdrop to full advantage. After several 'Of course!' and 'We'd love to's,' Lanie turned to me.

"Can you go next weekend?"

"This weekend coming up or the weekend after?"

"This weekend. Five days from now."

My mind sorted quickly through my plans. I had no real plans except to spend some time with Paul, and although I had tried to call him earlier to tell him about the initial invitation, he had been in a meeting and unable to be reached.

"I don't think I do." I shook my head. "Nothing major."

"Good, because we're going this Friday." Lanie went back to Olive, and I let her sum up the plans as I sat at my desk basking in this new development. *This* was the entire reason I had left Upstate; stuff like this just didn't happen up there.

"So what did she say?" I bombarded Lanie the minute I heard her disconnect.

"We're on!" Lanie got up from her desk and danced a terribly unsophisticated jig, her arms flailing in the air, face crowing victory. "My day is MADE."

"Wow." I joined her in a high-five that almost twisted my wrist. "I am sooo psyched! So: what did she say?" I demanded.

"She said…" Lanie drew it out, attaching full drama to the word *said*. "That we can leave from here on Friday eve. We'll close at four, because the flight is at seven o'clockish pm, and as we well know…two hours prior. Then she said we can set up our appointments however we like, and the flight back is Sunday at six o'clockish, getting us into JFK at 6 o'clockish on Monday morning."

"Ish." I made a hand gesture to indicate *ish*.

"Exactly." Lanie paused a second. "This is so whirlwind, Yellie, are you psyched?"

"Totally." I went about getting a map out of the Rio De Janeiro area, one that a hotel had sent us long ago indicating where all the hotels were situated on the beach. "Is there a reason that there's such an urgency to this trip?"

"Of course there is! Mr. Todd and a bunch of his cronies are going down for Carnival, and since that begins in just a couple of weeks, they need us to go check out the hotels now." Lanie drummed the top of her desk. "Yellie, I think we need visas for this one."

"You find that out and I'll try and figure out the best itinerary for us to see the hotels, and maybe set up some appointments. Did Olive say where we'll be staying?" If I remembered correctly, the host hotels were always the nicest properties, and they literally tried to charm us from the beginning of our stay right up until the bitter end.

"She is going to be sending us an email with our itinerary, and all our confirmations. Apparently, they will be giving us a little dinero to spend, plus a couple of hotels are willing to treat us to breakfast and dinner, as part of our site inspections. Yellie, this is so cool!" Lanie was bursting with hyperactivity.

"It is." I nodded vigorously. "Although it doesn't really make any sense. Don't you have to book rooms for Carnival months in advance? Wouldn't you think that Mr. Todd is already booked? I wouldn't think that it really matters what we may find, it'll probably be too late for him to switch hotels at this point." I wasn't trying to kick a gift horse in the mouth, but our sudden fortune seemed strange, the timing a little bit off.

"Who cares?" Lanie waved me back over to her desk. "Oh, look at this! GIRL! I can feel the sand between my toes!" She pointed to a forecast off of the Weather Channel website. It boasted sunny days ahead in Brazil and a median temperature of about ninety degrees Fahrenheit.

"It's summer down there," I smiled at the thought of even one day away from boots and heavy clothing.

Just then the phone rang, and when I looked at the reader, I was pleased to see that it was Paul calling me back.

"Did you get my message?" I greeted him as I picked up the spy phone.

"Indeed I did. So what's up?" He sounded busy, but his interest piqued, as the message I had left him had been vague.

"I'm going to Brazil."

"What? When?"

"Friday." I said it matter-of-factly, as if catching planes to Rio was a regular occurrence in my life.

"This Friday?" His voice went up a notch.

"Yes! And I am soo excited–you have no idea. You see, Lanie and I just got this invitation from Olive, and I wasn't sure if she would let the two of us go together, but then she called us back, and Lanie talked her into it, and now we're going, but we still have to get visas, although I'm sure we can get them tomorrow, and then we're off, but we'll only be gone a few days; just the weekend…"

"Whoa! Slow down, honey, you're starting to give me a headache." I could hear Paul chuckling on his end.

"Ooops, sorry. I'm totally pumped." I didn't even realize how fast I was going.

"I can tell. Does that mean I'm on my own again this weekend?" He sounded like a child whose puppy had gotten run over in traffic.

"Unfortunately, it does. I'm sorry, honey. Can I make you dinner next weekend and make it up to you?" God, please let him say yes. No problems, no fights, just yes, and I'll miss you, and have a good time, and bring me home something nice.

"You sure can. God, I am really going to miss you. Can I see you…? Well, when do you leave?" Paul asked.

"We're leaving right from work on Friday." I took a deep breath and realized that I was going to miss him too.

"Then can I see you on Thursday night?" Paul suggested.

I wanted to, but I knew I would have to pack, and I didn't know what to say right away, because I also didn't want to disappoint him.

"Can I let you know?" It came out sounding lame even to me. I just didn't know how to juggle him, the trip, and the gym. Plus I had therapy on Thursday afternoons, which left one less lunch hour for me to run around. Could I go to the gym right after work, go home, pack, get changed, and then come down and stay with him on Thursday night? Or would it make me crazy?

"Sure. Listen, I've got to go now. I'll call you later. Are you and Lanie at the gym tonight?"

Do I have to fit into a bathing suit on Sunday?

I refrained from saying that and instead just said, "Yes. I'll talk to you later. In the meantime, I love you."

"In the meantime, I love you too." With that, he signed off and I turned around to finish scheming with Crooked Lane.

"I'm calling the hotels." I announced with fervor.

"You got it. I'm calling my father to see if we can use one of his club passes for the American Airlines lounge at JFK. It looks like we're flying Varig down, and American back. They want us to compare the flights." Lanie was preoccupied with what looked like the emailed itinerary on her computer screen.

"What are you going to tell him about Aunt Cecile?" I remembered for her.

"Oh, crap!" Apparently Lanie had already forgotten the plans she made earlier this morning. "I guess I'm going to tell him that he's on his own."

"Will he understand?"

"He'll be pleased that I'm seeing the world."

"Truly?"

"He'll be a little bent because he has to schmooze her on his own." Lanie blinked twice and shrugged it off. "I can't tell you how many times he has blown me off for lunch."

"So no guilt."

"No guilt and a pina colada." She gave me a thumbs-up.

Chapter Fifty-Four

The rest of the week went by in a blur as we packed and schemed our way to Brazil. Lanie took care of our visas and double-checked the expiration dates on both of our passports, as well as scammed her father out of two big fat tickets to the American Airlines Admirals Club Lounge. Actually, she scammed him out of four: one for each end, times the two of us. He sent them overnight, so he obviously wasn't too upset she wasn't sticking around to see her aunt, at least that's what I told Lanie. I took care of all of our appointments and scheduled them all for Saturday; so that we could visit the hotels in one fell swoop and then meet our beach destination on Sunday. Besides that, I packed, worked out like a fiend, and then packed some more. Packing was tough: we needed winter for departure, summer for arrival, work clothes, beach clothes, and then something comfortable yet workable for our return trip.

"Lane, what can we wear to sleep in on the plane, then work in all day Monday?" I was fretting over a tent-like dress that promised no wrinkles or a long sweater and knit pants, and I had called Lanie mid-fret with the mistaken idea that she would decide for me.

"Layers."

"Layers? That's all you have to offer me, layers?" I pressed and got nowhere. Obviously, Lanie was not nearly as obsessed about attire for this trip, and I was on my own with my overnight dilemma. Of course, I could pack one outfit for the plane and another to change into at Lanie's apartment or the Admirals Lounge in the morning, but either way the wrinkle plague was tightening its unsociable grip, and so I fretted once more before tossing both the 'travel dress' and the casual outfit in the rolling suitcase. I checked my watch. Thursday night and all was well. It was almost ten, and I was through packing everything that could be packed, and I felt a sense of completion as I scanned my apartment once more. Now all I had to do was throw some books in my carry-on and I was set. My hair gel, makeup, deodorant, all of that would have to make its way into the bag after one last use in the AM.

Now…books. I felt a silly little grin slide across my face as I thought about the feeling of sunshine on my shoulders and a good book in my hand. Knowing I had two plane rides ahead as well as the day at the beach, I had popped into my local NYPL branch on the way back from Constance today, and scoffed up all that looked interesting in the New and Book Express sections. I had in my hand two new mysteries and a book from the express that screamed *beach read*. I tucked the beach read in the carry-on first, since it was after all an express and needed to be back in a week (no renewals) and then hemmed and hawed over which mystery I would want to read first. After several minutes of this, I felt rescued by the ring of the telephone.

"Hello?" I figured it was Lanie, calling me back to remind me to grab something or the other.

"Good Evening," Paul trilled into the phone.

I laughed at his tone and shoved one of the mysteries in the carry-on and the other into the depths of my suitcase. It wasn't unheard of for me to finish three books in one weekend, and I didn't want to be caught without something to read on such a long plane ride. Then I took the beach read back out of the carry-on, knowing that I would start that one tonight.

"Good Evening to you too," I said. "You sound like the villain in an off-Broadway play."

"That was exactly the tone I had hoped for," he insisted.

"So what's up?"

"Nothing. Na-da. I was just thinking I could still coerce you into jumping on the train to come down here and spend your last night with me, then I thought that was crazy, but then I picked up the phone and figured I'd give it a shot anyway." Paul made no excuse.

"Well, you are crazy, but thanks for trying." I felt a little uneasy with his insistence, but shooed that feeling aside, knowing his heart and my own little paranoias far too well to give the feeling an actual voice.

"Figured I'd give it a whirl." Paul sighed. "So are you coming to my house when you get off the plane?"

"When I get off the plane?" I lost him for a sec, then caught on and shook my head in the negative, as if he could see me. "Oh no, well, worst-case scenario, we figured we could hop over to Lanie's house for a quick shower, but Lanie said they have showers at the Admirals Arrival Lounge, so I think the plan was to just go straight from the plane to there and then on to work."

"Oh." Paul hesitated and then continued in a disappointed voice, "I was hoping to catch you before you went to work, maybe grab a muffin together."

"I'm sorry, honey, but I think they expect us to report directly to the agency. Lanie and I are planning to drink caffeine all day long." I said by way of explanation, although I didn't think he needed any. Or should need any. What was the matter with him anyway? Wasn't he happy for me to be going to Brazil? Or was he jealous and needy and overwhelmed by the thought of being without me for just a few days?

"What about after?"

"After work Monday?"

"Yes. How would you like to pack an extra set of clothes and then come right over here?" He said this as if he were inviting a six-year old to Disney.

"And stay?"

"Yes, unless that doesn't suit you."

"That's not it." I felt my chest beginning to expand, and the etchings of a sudden headache coming on. "It's just that I'm probably going to crash Monday night, between the jet lag, and working all day, having slept on the plane..." I rubbed my temples, weary from trying to explain myself to him. I knew that Monday night I would just want to go home, settle in, sleep in my own bed, and crash. But I hadn't been in a relationship in a while, perhaps had never been in a real relationship ever, at least nothing at all like this one right here. Was I wrong to feel so overwhelmed by a simple suggestion? Did I owe him some more consideration than I was currently willing to give? I wasn't sure, and the uneasiness manifested itself in the form of an ear-banging headache that had arrived with no invitation from yours truly.

"You can crash here!" Paul offered with so much gusto that I felt downright embarrassed at the thoughts I was having. What was the matter with me? The man obviously just wanted to see me. When I didn't respond right away he said, "Alright, I give up. But can I have dibbs on Tuesday night?"

"Tuesday?" I thought the only thing I had on tap for Tuesday was the gym, but that could either be blown off or done early, either way factoring him into the equation without too much trouble. "Tuesday is fine."

"Good. I'll make plans for a nice dinner out." He suggested this with a tone of finality, so I didn't argue. Paul always picked a good place.

"Are you going to try and call Alex while I'm away?" He had mentioned this to me not long after I told him I was going to Brazil, as his rich friend Alex was still working on a project in NYC, as well as still living in a corporate apartment on the East side, and Paul thought that this may be an opportune time for them to hook up and reminisce.

"I tried Alex, but got a voice mail, so I left him a message in hopes that he will get back to me soon. Look, don't worry about me. I have tons of work to do, I can always hang out with Rob if I'm desperate for companionship, and my family is just a train ride away. I'll be fine. I'm just really going to miss you." Paul concluded, and I felt that old familiar tingle ease its way down my spine again.

The good one.

"I'll miss you too." I thought about the way his strong arms felt around me and knew that I would miss his touch, even if it were only for a few days more than normal, and then I willed my thoughts to settle on Brazil rather than him. "I'll call you tomorrow, probably like a hundred times."

"Sounds good." With that, we did a little kissy-face and then signed off, he to his pillow and I to a book, not yet ready to sleep.

After reading the same sentences over and over and having them form nothing coherent in my head, I put the book down on my stomach and simply lay in bed and stared at the ceiling. I went over my list of all things packed, ticking them off rhythmically in my head, reassuring myself that anything forgotten could be bought. There was something floating around at the rim of my consciousness, but I couldn't put my finger on it, and every time I came close to capturing the actual thought, it escaped me. I was reminded of the female detective in a series I often read: often times, it was the tiniest clue, dropped early in the story, that followed her around both her waking and sleeping hours, the one that she couldn't finger until the last few pages of the tome, when it would suddenly slide into place, click in her mind, and not only provide her answer, but also the peace she had been so softly pursuing.

I felt that way now, except that I wasn't solving a mystery, nor did I own a very cool gun. After several attempts to wrap my head around the reason sleep was eluding me, I gave up, got up, and boiled myself a spot of tea.

A *spot* of tea! Give me an old Agatha Christie, and I'll show you where, in each and every story, one or more characters will eventually make for themselves a spot of tea. For some reason, I loved this British way of phrasing, so I rolled it around on my tongue a few times as I set the kettle to boil. Was it Paul? Was he what was bothering me?

If so, why? I mean, so what if he was being a little bit of a nudge. What crime was he guilty of...loving me too much? Most women wouldn't complain. I let the tea steep and took a quick hop into the bathroom. What was there to complain about?

I came up empty.

Maybe the entire reason that I was unable to sleep was because I was excited for Rio, and I was trying to make it out to be more than just that.

I must have convinced myself that was the case, because the next thing I knew I was out like a light, woken suddenly by the inhuman blaring of my beloved alarm.

If every day was a race, this day was the qualifying round for the Indy 500. I sped through a shower, checked, checked, and triple-checked all things Brazil, and soon I was off to the train station, a rolling suitcase dragging behind me at no less than fifty miles per hour.

My mind flitted briefly to the fact that when I was in the third grade, we were forced to learn the Metric system. Teachers and parents alike shrilled from the rooftops that Metric was soon to be *the way,* and therefore we must adapt to Europe's way of doing things. Conversion charts and tears were the hallmark of that year: for some unknown reason, I was unable to adapt. My point was this: I would never know what fifty miles per hour equaled in kilometers!

Alas, I made it to work on time, and soon Lanie and I were cross-referencing all that was hidden in our little black bags. Set as we would ever be, we set out for a whopping breakfast of McDonald's egg and cheese biscuit, hash browns in the sleeve, and a super-size coffee for each of us, determined to indulge American-style before our legs no longer touched the soil.

"You know they'll probably have McDonald's down there," Lanie pointed this out directly after she crumbled her wax paper into a ball and pitched it into her wastebasket.

"You're right, they have McDonald's everywhere. What's your point? Because if you're worried about the calories, you're boring me to tears." I shot her an amazing glare.

"My point was that maybe we will hate the food there and have to eat Mickey Dee's for three days straight, so perhaps we should have saved this foray into fat indulgence until we touched down in Rio?" Lanie questioned.

"Perhaps." I thumbed through my email and came up with a final send-off from Olive, as well as four confirmations from hotel sales managers. "Although I happen to like Spanish food."

"It's not Spanish; it's Portuguese, remember? Have you ever had Portuguese food?" Lanie rolled her eyes. "It's very meaty."

"It's also an adventure!" I looked sideways at Lanie. "Okay, Lane, what's up? You are so not ever like this."

"I don't know. I just know that I got three hours of sleep last night and I'm PMSing, so everything seems a hassle today, and believe me when I say that I don't want it to be, but for some reason I am thoroughly annoyed by everything right now," Lanie looked at me in a way that implied she felt sorry for her companion. "You're going to have to put up with me."

"I've done it before. Look, Lane…all we have to do is polish off the day, get our butts in a town car, be deposited at the JFK lounge, and it's almost like we're on vacation. Think positive." I had dealt with Lanie before when she got like this, and it was usually a rough road only until she got some Midol or alcohol, and then the scary monster within would stop rearing its ugly head.

"I am. I will. You're right." Lanie shot me a wry grin. "Will you drink with me?"

"Of course!" I chuckled. "I can't wait to lounge, I've never been inside one of the waiting rooms for the elite yet."

"Aaah…you'll be amazed at how the other half flies." Lanie gave me a knowing glance. "My father is still unaccustomed to being rich. He gave up those tickets like a house on fire; I think he's still tres uncomfortable with money."

For the life of me, I could not imagine that feeling. I tried to envision even having money, and my mind got all scrambled in the process. Putting that aside, Lanie's mention of her Dad reminded me that I should call both of the wayward parents before setting foot on a plane out of the country, if for no other reason than to assure them that I would not end up in a ball of flame.

Would they even care?

After lunch, I began with my father.

I dialed him at work and after being on hold a bit and listening to a muzaked *Men At Work* song, he came on the line full of energy, and I was almost duped into thinking that he sounded happy to hear from me.

"Dad, I just wanted you to know that I'm going to Brazil." It came out in a rush of words, as if I wasn't sure what his reaction would be, afraid on some level that he would ridicule me.

After the when and why were transmitted, he said, "I'm happy for you, Danielle. I've never been to Brazil before, always wanted to go to Rio." He sung a bar from *The Girl from Ipanema* and then said other Dad-sounding things like "Have fun" and "Be careful" and "Call when you get back."

Painless.

Strange.

I waited a few minutes before dialing Mom, as I felt the need to steel myself for what I was sure would not be a mere five-minute conversation.

"Mom, it's Danielle." I realized after I said it how dumb it sounded, as I was her only child.

"I know who this is!" She came off as indignant, but I knew that was her way of making a joke. After awkward pleasantries were exchanged, I dropped the bomb.

"So listen: I've been asked by my company to go to Brazil."

"When?"

"Today, tonight." I forced myself to sound as casual as I possibly could, determined even in this minute interchange to underscore the point of the very important life I was now leading. So important, in fact, that a trip to Brazil became something I mentioned in passing. Even as I watched myself doing it, I knew not why. Was I trying to prove something? If so, what?

"Why didn't you tell me?" Her voice modulated from interest to alarm. " I just saw you."

"Well, I didn't know then." It was the truth and I found myself getting annoyed by the fact that she was questioning me. "Aren't you happy for me?"

"Of course I'm happy for you! It just seems so sudden, that's all. I mean, will you be safe?" She seemed outraged, whether it was the pace or the seeming lack of planning, I would never know. I had to remind myself that most of the people who lived Upstate had never seen Florida, much less Brazil.

I had to bite back the reply that wanted so badly to jump from my heart to my lips, the nasty comment about not being safe in your own house, the question about safety being relative.

"I'll be fine." Then I regaled her with our itinerary, and in a concerted whoosh of talk, took control of the conversation and stopped feeling so flustered.

Soon after getting off the phone with her, Paul called in to wish us both a good time and luck.

"Why are you calling now?" I had my ideas that the Bon Voyage Phone Call should come at the very end of the day.

"It's after three and I thought you girls would be leaving soon." Paul returned.

After three? Where had all the time went? I hadn't realized, and now I knew that if we were going to pull out by four, I really had to get my butt in gear.

"Wow. You're right; I didn't realize how late it had gotten. Well, thank you for the call. I will be sure to call you from the airport." I hustled then and turned to Lanie. "Are you ready?"

"Yeah." Her smile was back, as was her enthusiasm. "Took a Midol after lunch and now I'm ready to face the world. Let me just pee; we'll go over everything one last time and…we're off!"

"You know you shouldn't drink while you're on medication," I called after her as she made her way from the hole/office to the ladies room.

"But we're gonna!" Lanie called back, threatening any opposition that I could possibly put forth.

I convinced myself there was nothing she could do to hurt herself anyway–what was the worst thing she could do, pass out on the plane? It wasn't like she had to fly the plane or anything. A brief scene from the movie *Airplane* flashed inside my head.

Time was moving so fast. The next thing I knew, we were in the back of a town car, hurtling towards JFK airport. The driver dropped us off by the Varig counter, we checked in and then checked our rollers. We kept our carry-ons and just as we were about to inquire as to where the American Airlines lounge was, the svelte woman behind the counter informed us that our Varig sales rep had put aside two passes to their lounge. Would she like her to show us where it was?

We nodded, pleased by the surprise, and as we were following the woman from counter to lounge, Lanie leaned in to say, "Looks like Dad's getting off easy. We'll just use his tickets on the return."

"No problema." I considered this a treat and didn't care either way.

"There you go," The Varig woman said with grace as she opened the door for us and ushered us into the lounge. She spoke to somebody behind the reception desk in what I assumed was Portuguese, and soon after we were given a two-second tour and then shown to a bistro-type table right near the bar.

Left alone to our own devices, I whispered to Lanie, "This is nice."

"Yes. I feel so much more human in here," she agreed.

"Less like cattle?"

"You got it. Come on, let's go grab a drink." Lanie got up and walked three paces to the bar. The bar was unmanned but complimentary, and boasted travel-sized bottles of liquor, individual wine bottles, as well as bottles of beer in a glass-front fridge. They also had out warm nuts in little white ceramic bowls, a platter of cheese, a huge array of fruit, and bruschetta, hot off the press.

"A veritable feast!" I proclaimed, eyes wide with what lay before me. Even after working in New York City for the past few years, times like these pointed out to me how little I knew about the luxuries at my feet. *So this was how the other half lived.* I felt like a hick.

Lanie grabbed four personal wine bottles from the fridge and walked back to the table with two glasses in hand. Okay, I guess I was drinking white zinfandel. Before I could even begin to fill a dish, she was behind me again, beating me to it.

"Do you want grapes?" She inquired of me as she piled her plate high with a bunch of green grapes.

"Sure. I'll get some bruschetta," I offered as I grabbed another plate and started to fill that one up with the tiny pieces of tomato-laden bread.

"I love this," Lanie's excitement was back in full force.

"No one loves it more than I," I quipped, not sure if it was proper English, and not caring one whit.

"Try me," Lanie said in response, and then sashayed her way back to our table. I joined her there a second later, and once she unscrewed our wine bottle caps, she proposed a toast.

"A toast?" I pointed to the bruschetta, which elicited a stunning eye roll from Lanie.

"Yellie. I mean this." She cleared her throat and raised her glass. "To our friendship."

"Our friendship." It was easy to toast to that.

"And to doing this again...with men." Lanie proposed.

"What men?"

"You and Paul; me and whoever. A trip to Brazil and a lifetime of love." Lanie stared right through me for half a second, and then clinked our glasses together.

"Amen, sister!" I downed a great gulp of the Sutter Home, all the while grinning wickedly. "I feel like I'm on vacation, or like I'm doing something I'm not supposed to."

"You are doing something you're not supposed to; you're treating a business trip as if it were a vacation."

"Don't we get mad when people try to book a trip and do the exact same thing?"

"Only when they involve us and our sought-after talent."

"So it's okay for us because we didn't involve anyone."

"Exactly."

"I'll drink to that!" I felt positively decadent, drinking at five o'clock...early evening...soon to be boarding a plane to South America...at that moment, I could barely think of anything troubling. Lost in my reverie, I almost didn't hear my cell phone ring.

"Phone." Lanie pointed as I began to open it up.

"Hello?" It was Paul. "Hi, baby." I wondered if he could hear the smile in my voice.

"How you girls doing over there?" He sounded wistful, very much like he was missing out on all the fun.

"We are doing great." I filled him in on the wine and cheese and the entire lounge experience.

"Now I know why you didn't have time to call."

It didn't sound like an accusation, so I let it be.

"I'm pretty sure I can get those passes with my frequent flyer mileage. I should check it out for the next time I travel." Paul continued.

"You should. Listen, honey, I'll call you before I board?" I could have stayed on the phone with him, but I didn't want to ignore Lanie.

"Sounds good. Please do." With that, he clicked off, and I sighed as soon as I collapsed the phone.

"You love him," Lanie said matter-of-factly, "And he loves you. I hope to God you don't screw this up."

Her statement momentarily took me aback, so it took me a full minute before I could muster up a reply. "What do you mean by that?"

"I'm still waiting for the self-sabotage super hero to come flying into the picture." Lanie waved away the sentence the same instant she put it out there.

"You think I'll do that?" I asked her plainly, knowing that we both knew what I was capable of, the question not being so frightening now that it was out in the open.

"Sometimes I picture you with a cape on, and instead of *Here I come to save the Day...*" she flapped her arms like a cartoon character as she sang a bit too loudly, "You'll say...*Here I come to ruin my life...!*"

"I'm trying hard not to do that." But it was a retort with no energy, and we both felt it.

"I know you are. Sometimes, I feel like an innocent observer, and other times I feel like I'm waiting for the other shoe to drop." Lanie intoned.

"How do you think I feel?" It did me no good to know that Lanie was also waiting to see if I could conquer all the demons. It made me testy on one hand, but on the other, I felt I could use that energy to prove myself: to her, to me, to Paul.

"What if he asks you to marry him?" Lanie threw this out suddenly, and the force of her words hit me like a wave.

I didn't have time to react. The next thing I knew, the woman at the reception desk was calling out a subtle announcement that our flight was ready to board. We jumped up, grabbed our bags, and I saw Lanie sneak an extra bottle or two of liquor in the outside pocket of her carry-on case. As we made our way towards the lounge exit, I looked a question over my shoulder to Lanie.

"You will have more than enough time to find an answer to that on this trip," Lanie patted me on the arm. "Don't worry."

"I wasn't worried. Who's worried?" I asked the air.

We boarded promptly and settled in to our seats, 46 A and B. Window and next, and after a quick internal joust, I proceeded to offer Lanie the window.

"No, I have to pee a lot," and she waved me in.

I was glad because I loved the window, but would have been willing to give it to her if she wanted it, at least one way anyway. The plane was nice, and the flight attendants seemed friendlier than any I had ever had on any domestic flight–ever. How exactly does that bode for 'the friendly skies?' Once the plane took off, I was unable to sleep, for I was high as a kite, between the take off itself and the mere fact that I was in the air, headed towards a place I had never been before.

I got out my beach read and proceeded to read minus beach, while Lanie dozed in the seat next to me.

After a while, she got up to pee, and when she came back she was awake enough to chat me up for a little bit.

"How are the bathrooms?" I inquired.

"They're okay…a little tight." She lifted her right leg up on her lap and crossed it, wrenching it so that the heel of her right foot was parallel with the outside of my right thigh. "After the lounge experience, coach just doesn't cut it."

"You've got a point there." I chuckled. "They should have upgraded us too."

"We're ungrateful bastards, you know that?" Lanie chuckled.

"Of course we are. We're travel agents, for God's sake, we want it all free." This was a private joke we shared often, basically whining about our fore agents, who ruined our image long before we ever issued even one ticket.

"I'm going back to sleep. Wake me up for breakfast." Lanie pulled her other leg up under her and punched the baby pillow into something that would wedge nicely under her head.

I must have dozed off myself, because the next thing I knew, a gorgeous flight attendant was waking both of us for breakfast and the window shades were flying up all over the place. I blinked, so did Lanie, and then we both laughed at the same time as we patted our hair into place.

"I feel like I slept in a chair," I stretched and my book fell off my lap and onto the floor.

"You did." Lanie leaned over me and took a peek out of the window. "You can't really see anything yet."

"Yeah, I think we have about another hour." I checked my watch and did the math. "That's probably why they've got to serve us breakfast now."

"Do you think they have Cap'n Crunch?" Lanie mused.

"I doubt it."

"Me too." She stretched, I yawned, and then she yawned too.

"It's contagious." I struggled forward in order to retrieve my book from the depths below my chair. "Alright, Lane, a good idea would be to hop into the bathroom now, before every single person gets on line."

"Good idea." She got up and got on line, and then it occurred to me that I never did call Paul back. Didn't I tell him I would call him before I boarded? I thought so. I shrugged it off, then went to pee when Lanie returned. The flight attendant attended us then, with a warm muffin and a strange brand of yogurt.

"Lanie, look: your favorite!" I held up the yogurt in hopes that I was torturing her fully.

"Yech." She flicked the yogurt away from her on her tray. "I hope it gets better from here."

"Are you still tired?" I was curious as to how evenly matched we were in the sleep department.

She nodded. "Yeah, but we'll get through the day and then crash. Plus, we can sleep on the beach tomorrow."

"I'm with ya."

We disembarked after a fairly uneventful landing in which people still clapped and then made our way through Customs. I felt the heat as we waited in the Customs section, even through the air-conditioned atmosphere.

"Lanie, do you feel the heat?" I was already taking my sweater up over my head and smoothing out the plain shirt I had put underneath.

"Yes, I do." She looked around and pointed to the right. "That guy over there has the door opened."

I looked to where she was pointing and sure enough, a porter or someone had a side door wide open, with the hot air pouring in from the outside.

"Maybe it's too cold for him in here," I suggested.

"Maybe." Lanie shrugged and then asked me to hold onto her carry-on as she wrangled her way out of her sweater. "I'm so glad I dressed in layers."

She was too much.

Once through Customs, we reclaimed our luggage and then hailed a cab to take us to our host hotel, The Caesar Park, located on Ipanema Beach. The ride from the airport to the hotel was exciting in and of itself, as Lanie and I took in our new surroundings with pleasure.

"Look, Lane, a Coca-Cola sign!" Familiar things took on new meaning.

"I see Mastercard!" Lanie pointed to a billboard written in both English and Portuguese.

Several Ooohs and Aaahs later, we were deposited at the front of the hotel, directly across the street from a busy, crowded beach.

"That's Ipanema Beach?" I looked to Lanie, surprised to see it so full so early.

"It looks like those old pictures of Coney Island!" Lanie stood agape at the amount of people populating the sand. There seemed to be no American-style hang-ups about space or proximity, as people cavorted in various stages of undress blanket-to-blanket, chaise-to-chaise.

"Come on, let's check in." I walked towards the Guest Reception, all the while taking in and judging the hotel's décor. The lobby wasn't huge, but it was tastefully done in earth tones, with a marble hallway throughout. When we went to check in, the woman was most pleasant, and actually seemed happy to be able to do her job for us.

"This ain't the Motel Six," Lanie drawled in my ear.

I kicked her (lightly) in the shins and then palmed one keycard and gave her another. Just as I was about to turn away from the desk, I remembered to ask for an exceptionally late check out the next day. Apparently, our sales rep had already put that request in for us, and we were all set.

Our sales rep also ended up blessing us with a room that was extravagant in its appointments; a view of Ipanema beach greeted us as well as a luxurious touches throughout, all accompanied by a floor-to-ceiling marble bath. Lanie chose the bed nearest the window and I was happy with whatever they had to offer. At this point, my bed could have been on the ceiling and I would have been thrilled.

"So what's first?" She asked, lying prone on her bed, her legs kicking back and forth in the air like a small child.

"First, I think we should power-shower, and then we're off to the races; no time to dilly-dally. We have three appointments on this side, Ipanema Beach, before we head back to this hotel for a late lunch; then I scheduled all the afternoon appointments with hotels situated on Copacabana Beach, four in a row over there." I checked my watch as I said all this, doing the math quickly and then finally deciding to wind it to local time. A part of me wasn't sure if it was worth changing for two days' time; I could very easily do the math and calculate time while I was here. I mulled the plusses and minuses for the briefest of brief, then decided to just switch the clock and make my life as easy as possible.

"You are a smart cookie. Do you want to shower first?" Lanie offered, still kicking her legs.

"Sure. I'll be right out." I unpacked the outfit I had brought for our appointments and laid it out on my bed. "Do you think I need to iron this?"

"Just hang it on the door when you shower. You should be okay." Lanie jumped up then and began to rifle through her bag.

"Good idea." I did that; jumped in the shower, and reveled for the flash of moments I was in there, hot water cascading down my back. Nothing feels as good as a hot shower after a long trip on a plane.

When I got out, Lanie hopped in, and soon we were dressed, done, and headed towards our morning appointments. Our first appointment was a luxurious boutique-style hotel walking distance from the hotel we were presently at, the second a dive, the third a moderate American chain. The morning flew by as we shook hands and stuck our head into standard rooms, deluxe rooms, and suites, all the while drinking in the Brazilian hospitality and atmosphere. Once we pounded out the three, we met the sales rep for our host hotel back in our lobby, where he announced he would be treating us to a traditional Brazilian lunch that the hotel was known for. Luis was not what I had pictured over the phone. Much shorter.

"Sounds good; I'm famished." Lanie was almost embarrassing in her bluntness, her very American/New York style seeming even more ostentatious in front of Luis, who was soft-spoken in nature, and almost formal in gesture.

"Famished is good. I trust you ladies will find something you like at the *Feijoada.*" Luis showered us with a welcoming smile.

"How do you say that?" I tried to repeat after him and mangled it, but he was a good sport and repeated it several times until I said something that sounded like what he had just said. We hopped on the elevator in the lobby and were transported up to a series of rooms where they held the Feijoada. We were greeted upon arrival by a maitre'd that seemed to know Luis quite well, and shook hands with each of us jovially. He offered us a drink before entering, so being the good sports that we are, Lanie and I decided to try some. Unfortunately, it was so hot that I wanted to scream, and I could tell by Lanie's face that she felt pretty much the same.

From there, Luis ushered us in to a room that boasted a buffet-style table set up in a large square pattern. All four sides of the table boasted an array of disgusting things he called delicacies in containers that looked like gargantuan cauldrons. I caught Lanie's glance as we walked past an iron pot labeled *cow tongue,* and knew that this lunch would make the record books. *This* was a story we could tell over and over again.

From there we entered the main room, where what looked like a bunch of high-powered executives were found sitting around and eating the various animal parts from the other room. Luis sat us at a table with a view and then encouraged us to get up and please fill a plate; he would wait for us to return.

"Is there any way we can escape all this?" Lanie whispered in my ear as we made our way back to the buffet table, our feet dragging.

"I don't think so. They are putting us up for free, you know. Plus this is supposed to be a delicacy," I pointed this out with enthusiasm so contrived I thought for an instant that Lanie was just going to haul off and hit me.

"A delicacy for who? Not the cow," Lanie hissed in my ear as we went to go pick up a plate.

I laughed out loud at her, knowing she didn't give a heap about the cow. We made our rounds silently, pointing and daring each other to try different things as we eventually found enough acceptable things to at least partially fill our plates.

"This looks good," I tried to get myself psyched to eat what looked like a big heap of seaweed. It didn't matter. It was green and I was pretty sure it wasn't lamb balls, so I piled it high, and tried to steer Lanie in the same direction.

"I told you their food was very meaty," Lanie said matter-of-factly.

"Very intestine-y." I corrected.

We both made a face, got it out of our system, and then made our way back to the table. Luis seemed happy to see us return. I wondered if he was happy that we hadn't run off. I wondered if he knew that Americans in general and New Yorkers in particular simply weren't used to this much food in the middle of the day, especially this much venison.

As soon as we were settled in, he regaled us with interesting stories about his country. Luis had been born and raised in Brazil, and he seemed to know a lot about Rio in particular, even though he said he lived in another nearby town. He shared with us that he had worked for the

Caesar Park for close to nine years, and that he truly enjoyed meeting new people all the time. We told him a little about New York, and offered for him to call us for some restaurant ideas the next time he was in our town, that we would direct him away from the tourist traps and towards something that was the essence of our city.

"So how do you like the Feijoada?" He asked us in accented English. "What do you Americans say, 'so far, so good?'" He seemed like he was trying to impress us with his knowledge of the vernacular.

"I like this green vegetable very much," I spoke up since it was obvious to me that Lanie wasn't going to.

"Ah, that is what we would call cauliflower grass. At least, that's a rough translation of it." He pointed to his own dish. "I like it too."

"I think we're just not used to eating this much in the middle of the day," Lanie offered this by way of excuse, as she had barely touched anything on her plate. "I can't believe how crowded this place is!"

"This is a very popular Feijoada. The hotel is known for it," Luis paused and said, *"Feijoadado Caesar Park: Gostosa Em Todos Os Idiomas."*

Lanie and I offered him a blank stare.

"The translation is: Caesar Park's Feijoada, delightful in any language." He clapped his hands in glee. "Every day, this room is packed full of international executives, eager to take their clients to lunch here."

"Well, I don't see how any of you get any work done, with that beautiful beach directly behind you." Lanie pointed towards the backdrop of Ipanema Beach, tactfully steering the subject from animal parts that no one should eat to the famed beach right outside our windows.

"Ah, yes…" Luis told us a tale about the beach. From there on, the conversation leapt from the beach to the people, the economy of Brazil, Carnival, as well as his opinions of several other hotel properties in Rio. We got up at one point and wandered over to the dessert table, where we once again cautiously grabbed some treats.

"There's probably birds stuffed inside of these," Lanie suggested as she nodded at the pastries.

"Probably only little birds," I teased.

Our lunch was over before we knew it, and when I checked my watch, I was alarmed to see that we only had about fifteen minutes to get to our next appointment.

"Lanie, we need to hustle," I warned her as we exited the dining area.

"Okay. Two minutes. I need to freshen up and then we'll grab a cab." Lanie ducked into a ladies room and I followed in right after. Two minutes later we were outside the hotel, jumping into a cab.

"Copacabana Palace," I said to the driver, who nodded and then pulled out recklessly.

"Yellie, I cannot believe the lunch we were just subjected to!" Lanie shook her head, as if to rid her mouth of any unpleasant taste still lingering.

"When in Rome…" I shrugged my shoulders and gave her a half-smile.

"At least there's good food in Rome." Lanie could play the brat role well when she wanted to.

In less than five minutes, we were dropped off at the entrance to the Copacabana Palace. When we alighted from the cab, we both paused a minute to drink in the hotel that lay glittering before us. It was beautiful and grand, a true palace in every sense of the word. Walking inside, I felt underdressed, and until our sales rep came out to meet us, I felt somewhat like a loiterer in the opulent lobby. The smell of old money permeated every inch of the hotel, and by the time we were walking around the pool area, I was deeply in love.

"This is gorgeous," I breathed as I took in the in ground pool and the surrounding gardens.

"I couldn't agree more," Lanie looked awed.

Our sales rep was pleasant and was a regular fountain of information regarding the hotel. She showed us several different rooms and then ushered us up to the top floor.

"I have a surprise for you," she said this with a smile in her voice and a devilish grin washing over her face. "The penthouse is empty. Would you like to see it?"

Lanie and I nodded like selfish and greedy children getting a peek under the Christmas tree.

I gasped when she opened up the door, and continued to make little noises throughout. The bathroom was bigger than my apartment, than most apartments, with an amazing view of the length of Copacabana beach, all this from the claw-footed bathtub. The balcony was even more amazing, complete with its own private pool.

"We've had U2's Bono stay here, as well as your President, Mr. Clinton." Our sales rep made a sweeping gesture with her hands.

"Omigod," Lanie pointed towards the pool. "That pool is amazing. The best part is that you would never know it's up here."

"You should see how people fight over this room for Carnival." Our sales rep rolled her eyes.

"Can you tell us who's in it this year?" I pictured the likes of Tom Cruise or Harrison Ford.

"Sorry. I cannot." She ushered us out soon after, but the effect the hotel had on us lasted throughout the rest of the day. After the Copacabana Palace, we still had three other hotels to see, and not one was able to compare in any way that mattered.

"I'm afraid we're not being fair to the other hotels," I explained to Lanie as we walked back to ours. "We should have seen the Palace last."

"You're worried about a hotel's feelings now?" Lanie ribbed me as we walked along the sidewalk across the street from the beach. "I know what you mean, though. Nothing else compares once you see that place. The Caesar

Park is fabulous, deluxe and appealing in its own way, a very close second, but the Palace is so grand…and you know that Mr. Todd would love it."

"Who wouldn't." I was tired, but I kept walking, wanting to be out in the sun as much as I could in the next twenty-four hours. "This sun feels so good."

"What time is it?" Lanie inquired.

"Six o'clock." I replied. We were done with all of our appointments, and I found myself looking forward to the free time ahead. "What do you want to do about dinner?"

"I have an idea. Let's go back to the room and take a quick nap. Apparently nobody eats dinner around here until eight or nine o'clock anyway. We can nap a little, freshen up, then go out to eat and get a little happy." She raised her eyebrows at me.

"What do you Americans say, 'so far, so good?'" I did a bad imitation of Luis as we bounded into our hotel and towards the elevator. Once we got up to the room, a wave of tiredness came over me, and I insisted that Lanie set the alarm, otherwise I was sure I would sleep right through dinner.

"Gotcha," was the last thing she said. We both collapsed as soon as our heads hit the pillow, only to be woken by the sound of a ringing phone what seemed like eons later.

"What's that?" I moaned, drifting out of sleep against my will. It sounded like a phone, but it sounded so far away that I could barely place the sound.

"Wake-up call," Lanie groaned to me before picking up. "Ugh."

A minute after that, a buzzer that sounded somewhat like a nuclear reactor going off flounced us out of our beds. We showered again, woke up slowly, fixed our hair, and went to answer the call of hunger.

On the way down to the lobby, I handed Lanie a compliment. "Good call, doubling up on the alarm."

"I would have never have woken up otherwise," Lanie fluffed out her hair. "I feel like a sludge, but I know I'll feel better once we eat something." We went over to the concierge once we hit the lobby and asked him to recommend an Italian restaurant. He gave us walking directions to one nearby, and even recommended a particular dish.

"Don't you think it's a little pathetic to do Italian in Brazil?" I mulled this over as we walked to the place.

"Yellie, I only know that I cannot do Brazilian again," Lanie said in her most tortured voice.

We found the Italian place with no problem whatsoever, and were pleased to find our waiter fluent in English. He made us laugh and asked us about New York City, all the while trying to do a very bad New York City accent.

"Where do you think they learn that stuff?" I asked once he left.

"The movies, where else?" Lanie answered.

The Italian food was no Little Italy, the pasta not what I would call *al dente* and the bread…bad, just like it was anywhere except the city. We had a good time and a few drinks, and at the close of the meal, Lanie declared it a major improvement over the afternoon's smorgasbord from hell.

Sleep was catching up with us again, but as we made our way outside the restaurant, the smell and sound of the ocean as well as the stars up in the sky made us want to prolong our jaunt, so we crossed the street and decided to walk on the ocean side back to our hotel. Just as we were crossing, we stumbled upon what looked to be a flea market in the middle of the median on Copacabana Beach.

"What's this?" Lanie's eyes were filled with delight as her shopping genes kicked into full gear.

"A market?" I checked my watch, noticing that it was already after ten o'clock at night, but the stalls in front of us looked open and the people eager to sell their wares.

"What time do you close?" Lanie asked a woman at a bathing suit stall in a slower English than what I knew to be natural for her.

"Close?"

"Open until?" Lanie tried again.

"Midnight." The woman replied with a smile.

Lanie turned to me. "Time to shop!"

"Perfect," I agreed as we started to wander from one stall to the other. This would be my saving grace; that way I wouldn't get stuck trying to buy Paul some cheesy mass-produced gift at the airport seconds before boarding.

We began making our way from stall to stall as cars whizzed by on either side of us and the ocean continued to dance, in and out, away from the shore, and then back in again. We browsed and the local people greeted us heartily each time we stopped to look. Lanie got caught up in a leather stall, and although I loved the idea of sifting through purses with her, I walked away a little and tried to find something that I thought Paul would like. I was about to buy him a painting when I spied a woman standing over a display of marble chess sets, the kind that you would display in the den or library of a house. They were beautiful. I stood there for more than a minute, eyeing a particular set, wondering if Paul even knew how to play chess.

A few minutes into my perusal, Lanie came up behind me with a bag in her hand. "Look at this," she took her purchase out of the bag and waved it in front of my face. "Who doesn't need a purple leather handbag?" She seemed delighted.

"Everyone needs one of those," I agreed, sarcasm dripping from my every word.

"What are you looking at?" She peered over my shoulder and took in the various chess sets on the table in front of us. "They're gorgeous. For Paul?"

"I think so." I pictured him older, playing chess with another man who at that age could only be called a crony.

"You're gonna cart that thing back on the plane, though?" Lanie looked at me. "It's got to be super heavy."

"Yeah, I'm sure it is." I checked out the artwork by picking up a piece, what I believed to be the bishop. "I just don't want to get him a cheesy t-shirt."

"That says, 'My girlfriend went to Brazil and all she brought me was this stupid t-shirt?'" Lanie sang.

"You get the picture." I sighed, thinking about hauling what was equivalent to a slab of concrete onto the plane with me. "Let me check out what else is around, then I'll come back and make a decision."

I rotated around the various displays and picked up a small hand-sewn makeup type bag for my mother. I wasn't sure that she would use it, but I always tried to pick her up something when I traveled, perhaps because she had so little. Either way, it was something I knew she would have liked, way back in the day, so I let my nostalgia rule me once again and I bought it for just a few *real,* which was Brazil's dollar.

I thought about buying Am something, but nothing struck me as Am, so I ended up back at the chess lady's stall determined to heft a set home for Paul. She spoke hardly any English, but after three rounds of pointing and pantomiming what it was I was looking to purchase, we settled on a price and she proceeded to wrap up the chess set carefully in newspaper. I bargained so well that I even got her to throw in a set of marble checker discs, figuring if nothing else that I knew how to play checkers and could at the very least do that with Paul.

"You won't need to lift your arms for a week," Lanie observed, nodding her head and giving approval in her own strange way.

"You're right about that," I agreed as I hefted the set onto my shoulder, trying to place the bag on my shoulder in such a way that I wouldn't fall over to the side.

"He'll love it." Lanie encouraged.

"He better appreciate it." I grunted.

"Now why would you say something like that?" Lanie gave me a look.

"Men don't appreciate things. At least, not the same way women do." I said with authority borne of experience.

"I'll give you that." Lanie stopped in the middle of the sidewalk. "Uh-oh. Looks like we're going to have that talk, right now, tootsie!" She drove a line in the air with her hand, as if to cut off all other innocuous conversation.

"What talk?"

"The one we started in the lounge. Look, Yellie, I know you well enough to know that you're probably scared witless *still,* but I also know that you have a good man, and I know you know that too." Lanie took on the tone of a sister that offered advice you didn't ask for. At least, I presumed that this was what a sister would sound like.

"I know that." I agreed cautiously, not knowing exactly where she was headed.

"Well, I just don't want to see you screw this up in any way that could point directly back to you. It seems as if he's headed in the right direction, Yellie, the question is: are you?" She stared at me point-blank.

"I am." I nodded vigorously and shifted the set from one shoulder to the other. "I love him."

"I know you love him." Lanie hesitated. "I just have a very funny feeling that he's wanting to move this along a little faster than you're even aware of, and I guess I wanted to give you a heads-up on that."

"Did you talk to him?" I stiffened, not liking the idea that Lanie and Paul, however beloved, however close, would talk about me behind my back.

"No. No." She waved the thought away with the hand not holding the purple purse. "I just think he's ready to kick it up a notch, and I don't know why…it's just a feeling I get, and I guess my main concern is that you will see it coming too, and not be so afraid of it."

"Are you talking about the conversation we had about moving in together?" I shifted the bag. I had told Lanie about the fight and the pressure I had felt from Paul, because basically, I told Lane everything.

"It's not any one thing in particular. It's that, it's the fact that he's got longevity written all over his face, it's just something I feel…I don't know, but I think he's *the one.*" Lanie faced me head on, walking backwards now, two steps ahead of me, a defiant look plastered across her face.

"Do you like him, Lane?" I asked expectantly.

"Paul?" For a second, she looked confused.

"Yes, Paul…who else?"

"I…of course I do!" She turned back around and continued to walk by my side. "Do you really think I wouldn't have told you by now?"

"Well, you never say anything." I accused.

"I never say anything? Surely you jest! I never shut up!" Lanie looked positively affronted.

"You know what I mean. I guess what I'm really asking is, do you think he's good for me?"

"Again, don't you think I would have said something by now if I thought he was a schmuck?" She looked at me as if I had completely lost my mind, as we traveled down Ipanema back to the hotel, myself already regretting the chess set purchase, dying to put in down.

"I think you would have. I trust you with stuff like that." I couldn't articulate exactly what I was trying to say at first. "It's just…look, do you really think my mother knew what she was getting into when she married The Monster? I would like to believe she didn't have a clue."

"I would like to believe that also. What's your point?" Lanie asked.

"Well, how do you know? I mean, I think Paul's *'the one'* so to speak, but I also thought that David was *'the one,'* and I'm sure my mother thought both my father and The Monster were *'the one'*" I wrapped quotes around the saying with my one arm that still had feeling in it. "So my point is this: I'm counting on you to tell me if this guy's a jackass, and I'm the only one not seeing it."

"Danielle," Lanie began, and I knew she was serious, because she rarely called me Danielle, "In your heart of hearts, what do you think?"

"I think Paul's the one. Deep, deep down, I don't even question it. I just get terrified when I think of all the women out there making bad choices, and how, no matter how smart we are, we're all susceptible to it." I saw our hotel coming up on the right and I said a silent prayer because I was about to drop Paul's gift in the middle of the sidewalk and leave it there. What was I thinking? The thing had to weigh at least a hundred pounds.

"Yellie, we are all susceptible to being duped, you're right." Lanie opened up the lobby door for me as we made our way into the hotel. "But I think you know it in your knower, when you meet the man you fit with."

I allowed myself a smile, emanating from somewhere deep inside my heart. "Lane, I know one thing for sure. I feel a peace when I'm with Paul that I never felt with David, and even when I get scared, that peace always sneaks its way in to override whatever other crap I'm feeling."

"So there. You just proved my point. Just go with it, Yellie." With that, she opened up the door to our room.

"I am, I will." I rushed across the room in a final burst of energy and deposited the chess set on the table near the window. "Oh, Thank God."

Lanie laughed at me.

Within minutes of returning to our room, we changed and got ready for bed, set the alarm for the morning, and fell fast asleep the minute our heads hit the pillow. There was no more chitchat, as our bodies responded to the sleep it so desperately needed.

The next morning, the alarm buzzed in tandem with the wake-up call and the minute the two of those things occurred, I said to Lanie, "What time is it?"

"Eight." She mumbled this from somewhere deep inside her pillow.

"Eight?" Ugh. I couldn't believe she set the alarm for eight; it was so unlike her to want to get up early.

"I figured since we only have one day…" She stretched and yawned and then got up to pull the curtains. "We can sleep down there." She pointed to the beach.

I got up and joined her. "I can't believe there are already people out on the beach."

"Another reason I thought earlier was best." Lanie yawned.

"Okay, I agree. I'm up now anyway. So what's for breakfast?"

"Room service?"

"Perfect."

We ordered up while we lathered sunscreen on our bodies and quickly got changed into our suits. I had brought two suits with me, not sure how I would feel about my body until the day of, and now chose a two-piece with boy shorts, in an effort to hide a little more buttock and as much leg as possible. Lanie of course had a fabulous bikini that showed off all her assets.

"I hate you," I said as I gave her an admiring glance.

"And I love you," she returned, shaking her head all the while. "You know, you can absolutely get away with one of these; you just don't think you can."

"Whatever." I blew her off, forgiving her her genes, albeit begrudgingly.

We tramped down to the beach directly after coffee so strong it made Starbucks look like flavored water. The guy at the hotel's cabana was extremely nice, setting us up with two chaise lounges that faced the sun, fawning over us as if he had never seen a girl before. He also offered us towels and a spritz of Evian, which prompted me to say the following:

"Do we have to go back?"

"Not necessarily." Lanie sighed. "This makes all the garbage, all the 'Mr. Todd needs a circus' stuff bearable. Almost…worth it."

"Hey, I wouldn't go that far." I laughed.

"You're right." Lanie laughed too.

We lounged for a long time, basking in the sun, trading barbs about who was currently freezing their butts off back home in New York. I delved into my book, and for a moment allowed myself to inhale and exhale, and breathe in the scene. After a while, we got up and took a long walk on the beach, taking it all in, conjuring up different scenarios on how we might be able to multiply our time there, all the while knowing that we were going to be getting on the plane to return home that night.

"I feel overdressed," Lanie pointed out as we made our way back to our spot.

"I hear ya." It seemed like almost every woman on the beach was wearing some variation of a thong or at the very least a string bikini. My boy shorts seemed prudish in comparison, but the part I thought best was that none of the skimpily-clad women were what you would call super-thin, at least not what any American would call thin, and I found that I felt more and more comfortable in my own skin as the day wore on. The second time we got up for a walk, I received more than a few appraising glances, and I noticed more often than not that the men's eyes were trained on the hips.

"I do feel that hips are in down here, though," I informed Lanie later on. "I might stay forever."

"Only American men like their women eighty-seven pounds soaking wet," Lanie sounded disgusted though I couldn't understand why as she about fit that description. "Men around the world like rubenesque."

"Oh, that's it then! I've just been living in the wrong country my entire life." I acted as if I had completed a major puzzle.

"You're the one with the boyfriend, so I suggest you shut it." Lanie threatened.

"Consider it done." We walked along the beach and stopped at one point to buy a coconut. We watched the young boys stick a straw right into the coconut and hand it to us, no cup needed. We drank the coconut juice and then ordered some fresh fruit from a nearby stand. The day wore on and we found ourselves coming up with more and more outrageous schemes to get us to stay as the clock ticked. Faster than the speed of light, the clock dictated that we needed to head upstairs and shower for our return flight. We felt both lucky that we had come, and sad to leave so soon, but our job was done, and we knew that the right thing to do would be to not pretend we missed our flight.

We checked into the Admirals Lounge at the Rio airport and then wiled away the wait at the bar once again, indulging in ginger ale and vodka.

"We really shouldn't be drinking this," I pointed out to Lanie. "We are going to be so dehydrated when we get off that plane."

"Do you think I got any color?" She was ignoring me, slinging back her drink as if I hadn't even spoken.

"Yes, you're browny-red." I looked at my own arms. "I didn't get anything for anyone except Paul and my mom." I felt a small twinge of guilt.

"Well, I only got something for me." Lanie shrugged. "Do you think I should get something for my Dad?"

"Considering he had to entertain your Aunt Cecile without you, I'd say yeah." I thought about getting Michael Jr. a little something, not sure if that would mean that I would have to get something for my father, too. And his wife. What about Am?

"We have enough time. Come on," Lanie pulled me up from my chair and headed out of the lounge and back into the airport. "I saw a letter opener for my Dad on the way in, I'll grab that and then you can get something if you want to, too."

"Okay." I followed her into the gift shop and looked around quickly. They had a cool shirt that I thought a kid would like. It said *Brasil,* the way the Brazilians seem to spell it, and it had a picture of their flag on it. I grabbed that for the kid, and then proceeded to grab a few small boxes of chocolate, just in case I forgot anyone else and felt overwhelmed by guilt at not having brought them anything. By the time I checked out, Lanie was standing behind me with a bag on her arm.

"Did you get the letter opener?" I nodded towards the bag.

"Yes, and I know he'll like it." She seemed pleased with herself.

"Let's go back." We headed back to the lounge and before we knew it, our flight was called and we were boarding. I set up shop to sleep right away, even as I pondered for a second the fact that it seemed perfectly normal to be doing something as private as sleeping amidst a sea of strangers.

"Boy, am I going to sleep tomorrow night." I let out a low whistle.

"Big-time." Lanie agreed.

Our adventure almost over, we fell back asleep until the flight attendants began pulling up shades and waking people for breakfast. Once we were fully awake, Lanie checked her watch and looked over at me.

A moment later, a flight attendant put our breakfast trays down in front of us.

"What's with the freaking yogurt?" Lanie indicated the incriminating cup dotting the landscape of her tray.

"They know you love it." I shook my head and grinned. "Sure you don't want mine?"

"Stuff it." Lanie countered.

Forty-eight hours after the first time, we again got off the plane, went through Customs, retrieved our luggage, and called a town car to spirit us off to work. Sitting in the back, we both dozed until our Croatian driver slammed on the brakes so hard I thought I was playing the role of crash test dummy. Lanie and I shared a look.

"Welcome to New York," Lanie quipped.

"There's no place else I'd rather be," and when I said it, I realized that I still felt that way, no matter what great trip I had just come back from, no matter what the city had to offer: traffic congestion, subways without AC, tourists who stood in the middle of the street looking at a topographical map…it didn't matter to me, as the city still held its own magic, the same way it did the first day I began working here many moons ago.

"I'd rather be in bed," Lanie moaned.

I checked my watch. "Wait 'til four o'clock and then you can whine like that."

She did. After we were deposited at the doorstep of our workplace, we automatically adjusted to work mode and although we may have been on autopilot, we both hunkered down and managed to get our work done. After catching up on emails and voice mails, we called Olive and reiterated the entire trip to her via speakerphone, giving her a blow-by-blow description of each hotel. She asked us to write out all of our observations in an email sent to her attention, and once she asked for that, Lanie pointed to me, stating that I had stronger powers of observation. I insisted that wasn't true, but composed the email anyway, trading off and giving Lanie the job of handling all the refunds and voids from the week prior. It was a good trade: I hated doing all that paperwork, and I loved talking about hotels. Sometime around noon, Paul called, and I found myself buoyed by the sound of his voice.

"Did you get my email?" He asked hurriedly, the minute I picked up the phone. He had sent a 'Welcome Back' email that I opened first thing.

"Yeah, it was really cute. Thank you," I said. "How are you, honey?" I found myself grateful he didn't mention that I forgot to call him before we took off.

He was what I needed, on so many levels.

"I'm okay, better now that you're back and I know you're home safe. Listen; I'm in between meetings and today is shaping up to be a pretty crazy day. I just wanted to touch base with you, make sure you were okay, but I promise to call you later, as soon as I get a chance."

I found myself oddly relieved that he wasn't about to push me for dinner, to stay over, etc. "That's fine, I'm glad you called anyway. Call me later."

"I love you."

"Me too."

That was it, but it kept me going, until almost four o'clock when Lanie started whining as if on cue.

"Yellie, we neeeed a double espresso." Lanie was leaning on my desk, trying to get me to go out and get one with her.

"Lane, you're right. It's so cold here," I was whining right back at her, knowing full well that I was starting to lose it myself.

"The coffee will keep us wa-arm…" Lanie threw me my scarf. "I swear, Yellie, I need your help here. I'm beat."

There was only an hour or so left of our workday, but I decided to go along with her and indulge. She was right; we needed a little pick-me-up, something to get us both home safely. So we trudged across the street wrapped in attire that was the polar opposite of the day before, delirious from our lack of comfortable sleep.

"Remember Jolt Cola?" Lanie giggled. "I could use some of that right about now." She wobbled as we crossed the street.

Jolt Cola was a short-lived cola that came out while we were in high school. It offered about three or five times the caffeine of regular soda. I believe they discontinued it because kids were going to school practically high from it, and some parent brought a lawsuit or some such thing.

"I think a double will do the trick," I assured her, knowing full well I should be drinking more water.

"What about some choc-o-lat?" Lanie accented her speech and then tossed me a devil-may-care grin as she pointed to a sinful dessert in the display case in front of us. "It'll help wake us up."

"Tell my thighs that." I had to admit it was tempting.

"I will." Lanie moved behind me, and in her utter deliriousness, starting talking to my legs. "You can have just one."

"Get over here before I kick you," I glared at her as the barista barked our orders over at the bar. I crossed in front of Lanie and grabbed our drinks, only to turn and find her buying the two chocolaty treats.

"Yummy." She smiled at me like an angel, although I knew better, and called her satan as we left. I called her worse as I took the first bite.

"Lanie, now I have to kickbox all week!" I was still whining, but it was no longer packing a punch as I sunk my teeth into the sweetness in my hand.

"At least now I'll be able to make it home alive," Lanie said to justify her purchase.

"Hrmph." But she was right, because as we settled back in to close out our day, I had a nice little buzz rolling and I was able to keep my head from falling on top of my desk. Sooner than we knew, it was after five and we were both paroled and ready to go home and collapse.

"Give me a hug," Lanie fell sloppily into my arms before we closed the door. "I had a great time. I'll see you in the morning."

"Me too." I hugged her back. "I'm so beat." In spite of the sugar rush, I knew I was going to fall asleep on the train. My only hope was that I would wake up in time for my stop.

I did, and then I drove home and did just what I said I was going to: collapse. I was so tired I didn't check anything, not my food, not the mail, not the answering machine. I only checked the door, and even that I only checked twice before falling into a sleep so deep that there was no room for dreams.

Chapter Fifty-Five

When the unwelcome blare of my alarm woke me the next morning, I was more disoriented than usual and so bone-tired that I actually stood there for more than thirty seconds, my mind beating in time with the accusatory buzz, until my heart galloping at an unhealthy pace persuaded me to reach over and swoop the alarm straight off the table with a bang.

"Aaw," I cried out to no one in particular, tempted beyond measure to call in sick and play hooky. I still needed sleep. My body was screaming for it. I toyed with the idea for more than a minute, but ended up talking myself into getting up and forcing myself to shower if for no other reason than I knew that Lanie was somewhere out there forcing herself to do the same. It wouldn't be fair to leave Lanie to hold down the fort all on her own, not for tiredness alone. Puking, maybe. Tired was simply not enough.

As if my thought life had dictated that very bizarre thought unto my body, I began to feel nauseous as I soaped up in the shower.

I waved it off and kept showering, determined to get my butt into work.

Maybe I should give The Monster more credit than I normally did: when it came to the workplace, I had a stellar work ethic, in part due to his non-example in making calling in sick a sport, (although he always called it 'calling *out* sick') in part due to the fact that I saw what a liar and hypocrite he was, and tried desperately to distance myself from those two attributes in any way possible. There was nary a day that the man was actually sick, from anything other than a hangover–real or imagined–and therefore managed to instill in me a contempt for those who took work so lightly. Without consciously trying, he was decidedly the number one factor in my forming an opinion about those who abused the goodwill they culled within their companies, and as a result I almost became the Cal Ripken of corporate travel: three sick days in as many years.

When I got out of the shower, I weighed the idea of jumping back into bed and calling Lanie, begging off something fierce, knowing that she would easily understand. I tried to shake it off. The feeling came back again, with a force far greater than the initial greeting in the shower. I ran from where I was standing outside my closet back into the bathroom. Five minutes later, I felt better and convinced myself that I was dehydrated and perhaps the whole nausea thing was from something I had eaten in Brazil. I tied my hair back into a ponytail and promised myself I'd pick up a Gatorade on the way in. I threw a few things in a bag, determined to tell Paul that if I was going to stay over, we were going to stay in for dinner. Right now, the only dinner I could think about was a can of healthy soup.

On the way in on the train, I felt a moment of nausea slip over me again, which resulted in fervent prayers regarding not having to use the Metro-North bathrooms, not to mention crossed fingers all the way in to work. From the moment I got off the train, I was consumed with the usually simple task of not passing out on the sidewalk as I made my way in, and totally forgot about the Gatorade, as well as anything resembling breakfast.

"You look like hell," Lanie exclaimed, the minute my toe entered the space we lovingly called the hole/office.

"Thanks," I muttered, as I felt my eyes roll into the back of my head. At this point, standing up was an effort.

"Yellie, did you force yourself to come in?" She shook her head and gave me her most disappointed look. "You could have called in, you know. I can handle it."

"That's not it," I began to protest, but then realized I really didn't even feel good enough to do that.

"I know. I know; it's your deranged sense of responsibility that forces you to come in and contaminate me," she shook her head.

"You got it." I offered her a weak smile.

"Yellie, go home, you look like HELL and you'll only get me sick. I can batten down the hatch here. As a matter of fact, would you rather go to my place? You can always sack out there, if you don't want to make the trip all the way home." Lanie gave me a proprietary once-over.

"Ugh," I moaned again, looking to Lanie for some sort of permission slip. She just gave me one, but I needed more reassurance than that, and for some strange reason, suddenly wanted my mother to take care of me.

"Look, let me get you a hot cup of tea and some toast. Then you can decide what you want to do. In the meantime, you can watch the phones for me. I'll be right back," Lanie said and then she was gone.

I brooked no argument. I put my head on the desk and was happy to feel the coolness against my cheek. A thought crossed my mind as soon as Lanie left the room. I should have told her to pick me up some Gatorade, or ginger ale, or something else that was cold. It didn't matter. I knew by now that I probably wouldn't last the whole day anyway; I could just pick some up on the way home.

I must have drifted off, because the next thing I knew I was startled awake by the sound of Lanie's voice reentering the hole/office.

"You are all set, my friend." She set a bag down on my desk and started pulling things out of it. "Tea with honey, wheat toast with strawberry jelly, and a little bottle of ginger ale…my mom always got that for me when I was sick."

"So did mine." I offered her a weak smile of thanks.

"So, do you think it's something you ate? In Brazil? I was just thinking about that, but my answer came up no, because then wouldn't I be sick too?"

"I guess." I uncapped the tea and took a deep draw from the cup. It filled my mouth and I thought for a second that I actually felt it as it traveled down into my stomach. My stomach felt a mess; what I used to call *swirly* when I was young. I forced myself to get down the toast, and for a few minutes after that, convinced myself that I was better.

"In a few minutes, I'm going to throw you out. You know that rest is the only thing that will help you get rid of this thing," Lanie sounded very Mom-like in her self-imposed role as caretaker.

"I'm fine," I insisted, beginning to shift quietly through my emails. It was about nine-thirty, and I found myself trying to figure out how many more hours that left me in the day. I realized what I was doing just as a new pain shifted through my stomach, a roiling pain that prompted me to jump up and make a run for the bathroom. Once I established myself on the throne, I realized I would probably be spending the rest of the day there and that I should just go home. Lanie was right; it wasn't fair to get her sick, purely because I was so stubborn about being at work everyday. I determined to make it back to my desk, call Paul and beg off for the night, and then return home promptly and crawl right back into bed. When I got out of the stall, I washed my hands and splashed some cold water on my face. Lanie was right. I looked like death warmed over.

"You win, I lose, I'm leaving." I announced as I reentered our little sanctuary. I nodded a nod of defeat in Lanie's direction, put my hands out in the air as if to say, *'What can I tell ya?'* and then began logging out of my computer as I stood in front of my desk.

"Are you going to be alright to make the train ride home?" Lanie's concern was etched on her perfectly sculpted brows.

"I think I'll be fine." I checked my watch. "I think I'll call Paul and then I am outta here." I picked up the phone and dialed. He picked up on the third ring.

"Paul Corsi."

"Did my number not show?"

"Baby! You know, I didn't even look at the darn thing. What's going on? How'd you sleep?" He sounded very up. Busy, but up.

"I think I slept alright. I just woke up with a horrible…I don't know, stomach virus? Flu? Something's not kosher." I tried to joke it off, but as each second went by, I felt worse and worse, and my only goal now was to get home and remain horizontal the rest of the day.

"Are you okay? Do you need me?" His voice shifted from happy to hear from me to pure concern.

"I'm fine, or at least, I will be fine. I just need to go home and rest. I wanted to call you before I left." I sat down again as I was speaking to him.

"Why don't you go to my place?" Paul offered. "That way if you feel better, we can still go out for dinner tonight."

"Paul, there is no way I am going to make dinner tonight." I was flattered on one hand and annoyed on the other, thinking about that being the first thought out of his head. I reminded myself that he couldn't see how awful I looked, and that he had obviously been looking forward to seeing me, after having not seen me in days.

"So go to my house anyway. You have a key. Why travel all the way home to your place?" He was insistent in a way that unnerved me.

Instantly.

"Because I want to be in my own bed," I answered, aware that my voice was beginning to shake, as were my hands. Something in my tone must have registered with Lanie, because I saw her look up out of the corner of my eye and watch me steadily as I finished the conversation. Her concern threw me over the edge, and I was startled to find silent tears slowly begin to run down my face and splatter on my desk right in front of me.

"Danielle, I just think you don't want me to take care of you. Nobody's saying we have to go out for dinner if you don't want to. I can make you soup. Do you want me to come home right now? I'll make you soup," Paul's offer made him seem all the more oblivious, and at the same time, instilled in me a righteous anger that I had thus far not practiced around him.

"Paul," I started, my voice quavering, my heart beating faster and faster, "you obviously do not understand just how horrible I feel right now. If I'm going to puke, I would like to do so in my own home. Okay? Is that alright with you?" Righteous anger ignited, I was suddenly screaming at the top of my lungs. "I'M SORRY THAT YOU HAVEN'T SEEN ME IN *LESS THAN A WEEK*, AND I'M SORRY I RUINED YOUR DINNER PLANS! I simply wanted to call you before I went home, turned off the phone, crawled in to my bed, and...*died!* Can you understand that that's all I wanted from you right now...a phone call? I don't need you badgering me!" I couldn't stop crying, and I was amazed to find that I felt hot all over, flushed and agitated in equal measure.

"Danielle, you are a mess. Go home, okay? Get better! I'm just trying to help you out here! Call me back when you decide to be a human being!" With that, he banged down the phone.

I sat at my desk and cried, for how long, I didn't know. My mind vaguely registered Lanie standing behind me, rubbing my back, and cooing something or the other, the only words I was able to register being *fine* and *be okay*, as I sat there feeling sorry for myself. This was great; now I had a stuffy nose and a blotchy face on top of everything else. And had Paul and I just gotten in our first real fight? Over what? I had never screamed at him like that before; was that supposed to be some sort of warning signal?

"Danielle, you're going to miss the next train," Lanie's voice zoomed in and brought me back to consciousness.

"He's such a jerk!" I railed wildly, my nose so stuffed that I sounded ferocious and manly, all at the same time. I couldn't get over what had just happened with Paul, and as my hand reached for the tissue box on my desk, I felt my head swimming, my heart underwater right along with my sinuses. "Ooooooh!"

"Men can be jerks. Listen: I want you to go home, turn off your phone, get some serious rest, and then call me when you wake up. Okay? I'll call Olive and let her know that you're not in. Don't worry about anything here." Lanie waited for me to nod my head. "Then you can call me and tell me what a jerk he is. Although I think once you're feeling better, he'll be a little less of a jerk."

"I don't think so," I countered and then sniffed so loud I scared myself. I checked my watch again and found that Lanie was right. In order to make the next express, I would have to leave right now. I gathered up my things and thanked her profusely, sputtering all the while.

"Remember to call me when you wake up."

"Okay."

I marched over to Grand Central and made the train by the hair on my chinny-chin-chin. The minute my butt hit the seat, I practically passed out, to be woken only by the sound of the over-zealous conductor announcing the stop before mine. Normally, a guy like him would drive me insane, screaming into the microphone as he was, but today I was grateful, as he jolted me out of my slumber just in time for my stop.

Walking to the car was not fun. My mind registered my bones beginning to ache and I knew for sure that I was in for a doozy. I willed myself to stop at the Stop-and-Shop on the way home, and basically ransacked their shelves for all the diet ginger ale and fruit punch Gatorade my little hands could hold. I also grabbed a new bear of honey and pastina-style pasta, not sure I had any in the house, and knowing that I was not about to venture out again. The pastina was another Mommy remedy: I could easily call up the smell of her Italian medicine, the best thing in the whole world for a swirly stomach when you're little. I paid the portly cashier and then scowled at the bagger with all my might, my excuse being that I didn't feel well enough to be nice. The truth was that I never liked that particular bagger named Claude.

Surly and brokenhearted, I aimed my vehicle towards home, amazed at how light traffic was in the middle of a Tuesday morning. My mind flitted briefly to the bevy of housewives that made up the general population of Westchester on any given day. Or should I say, doctor's wives? Was there a PTA meeting today? A lunch date at Nordstrom's? Where were all the minivans?

I didn't really care, I was being nasty and cranky and felt the need to offer all that goodwill out to someone. The next thing I knew, I was on my way into my driveway, and found myself letting out a big sigh of relief as soon as I settled the car into park. Home. My own home, where nobody would drink my diet ginger ale or Gatorade. I stepped out of the car and dragged the plastic bottles in their bags behind me. Once I reached the door, I hoisted them on my hip, victory coming after only three attempts with the key. I wiped some sweat from my brow and then lifted my newly bought beverages into my place, carefully taking inventory as I started putting things away. Everything was the same as before I left for Brazil, save for the pile of mail and the still-full suitcase on the floor near my bed. After taking in the suitcase, I had an overwhelming desire to empty it before I laid down, but my common sense won out. I made what I hoped was a final trip to the bathroom and then took a huge swig of ginger ale. I thought about what Lanie said and turned the phone off. In less than a minute, I was out like a light.

Chapter Fifty-Six

I woke to a grayness outside that belied impending rain or worse, and found myself wondering if there was any snow in the forecast for the upcoming week. My mind registered that I hadn't been around, and then I began to wonder what exactly I was doing in bed in the middle of the day. Ah, the flu thing. I looked down and tried to figure out what was going on inside my stomach. Nothing you could see from the outside. I turned towards my alarm clock and was surprised to see that it was almost four o'clock. What time had I gotten back? I think after eleven, maybe even closer to twelve. So that meant I had slept for about four hours.

Good.

I stretched and then got up and walked gingerly to the bathroom. Once I was up, my stomach rumbled, and I realized I was starving. Oh God, I hated this. I was hungry but afraid to eat, scared that once again, my food would go right through me. I debated my choices and then opted for food, hunger coming out on top of any other concerns. I decided on pastina, and as the water began to boil, I checked in with Lanie.

"Travel." Lanie sounded the same as she always did. Normally, I would love to try and disguise my voice, trick her into thinking I was a real pain in the neck customer, and ask her to jump through hoops for me, but today I simply did not feel well enough to try.

"Lane, it's me." I watched the pot.

"Hey, Yellie, feeling better?" She seemed genuinely glad to hear from me.

"I am. I think." I explained to her about how I slept and now about how I was going to try to get down some food.

"Keep chugging that ginger ale. It might be mind over matter, but to this day, it always makes me feel better when I drink it." Lanie advised. "So what happened between you and Paul?"

"I..." I shrugged, then remembered she couldn't see me. "I really don't know. I'm sure he was disappointed about dinner tonight, but he was just really driving me nuts today. He kept wanting me to go to his house, but you know when you feel sick, you just want to be left alone? I don't think he gets it, and I was just...extremely frustrated with him." Pissed off was probably even more accurate. Easier said now that my head was a bit clearer. Still didn't mean that I knew how to fix it.

"I think he just doesn't know." Lanie asked if she could put me on hold a sec. I said yes and then she came right back. "As I was saying, I think he just has no clue. Remember what you told me, way back in the day, about Brad? I don't think Paul realizes how much he puts pressure on you. I just think he tries to help out, over-tries sometimes, and then he gets frustrated when he feels he can't do anything for you."

"Which would be fine, but I have been taking care of myself for a very long time, Lanie. I don't need him jumping in and trying to play hero with me, then getting all nasty when I don't let him do what *he* wants to do for *me!* I mean, don't you think that's a tad bit selfish?" I was angry again, and I could feel my body heating up as I conveyed this to her. I stirred the pastina and then took it off the stove. I cracked an egg in it, whisked that around, added the I Can't Believe it's Not Butter spray and a tablespoon of Parmesan cheese.

"I just think he's oblivious," Lanie said, echoing my earlier sentiment.

"You're probably right." I shook my head and continued, "I just didn't need anybody's garbage today." I stirred my creation and then tasted it. It was great. Comfort food deluxe.

"Listen, kid, I'm going to be getting out of here soon to go home and catch a little more shut-eye myself.

But I'm leaving the phone on. So if you wanna call, just call, I will pick up for you." Lanie said, while computer keys clacked in the background all the while. "What are you thinking about tomorrow?"

"Tomorrow I intend on being in," I replied heartily.

"Of course you do," Lanie chuckled. "Just see how you feel and call me."

"That's fair," I answered and then hung up the phone. I hit my answering machine and discovered only one message from Am, telling me to give a call when I got back. Paul had yet to call, and as I sat there eating my bowl of pastina, I began to wonder if he going to call me at all. Maybe it was over. Maybe I would never hear from him again. What had he said? He had told me to call him back when I decided to be a human being. Since I was still a grouch, I decided to wait a while longer.

It's a good thing too. As savory as the pastina was going down…well, you can imagine how much fun it was to get rid of it not fifteen minutes later.

I was really starting to hate this day.

Then I decided that I was really starting to hate Paul. Granted, I yelled, I blew up at him…but I was the one who wasn't feeling good. Did he care? No. He cared more about dinner than about me. Was he really that concerned with his schedule getting screwed up? I mean, if he wanted to see me, shouldn't he care how I felt while he was spending his coveted time with me? I grappled with that in between trips to the bathroom and finally fell back asleep sometime around six.

When I woke the second time, it was pitch black outside. I checked the clock. Eight twenty-three. My stomach seemed more settled than it was earlier, but I was afraid to eat again and then spend the balance of the night in the bathroom. I was still so tired. I got up and put my teakettle up to boil. I felt miserable. I tiptoed over to my answering machine, only to find the message light unblinking, aloof in its electronic capacity. I felt even more miserable.

I poured my tea and fluffed my pillows as it steeped, then went over and checked the phone for a dial tone.

It was working. Okay, so who was the victim here? I was sick; he was screamed at. He obviously didn't care about me, otherwise wouldn't he have understood a little better that I was acting like an idiot just because I was in pain? That he couldn't fix everything, or control me? What would it take for him to understand how I felt today? And, was it my mission to make him understand? Did I really need this?

I took my tea by the handle and brought it over beside my bed, but after just a few sips I couldn't hold my head up any more. I fell back asleep but was woken in the early morning hours by a lurching in my stomach that would give The Exorcist a run for his money. Somewhere about three o'clock in the morning, my body issued my brain a quick order: Thou Shalt Not Even Try To Go To Work Today.

I got the message, but I started crying anyway, tears that couldn't be explained, but popped up simultaneously along with the feeling that my body was betraying me. I hated being sick; I was not a good sick person. I tended to not get sick very often, but when I did, it was usually something like this one here: a tide of virus that would hang on with all of its might.

I was frustrated. I didn't like missing work for any reason except travel. I didn't like leaving Lanie in the lurch. It made me feel irresponsible, and although I knew there was little to no rationale to that thought process, it sure didn't make it easier to just sit home and let nature take its course. On top of that, I also didn't like the idea that Paul had never picked up the phone to see how I was doing. I convinced myself that if the tables were turned, that I would have at least checked in to see if he was still alive.

He didn't care. I had picked the wrong guy after all. All this swirling around with my stomach, and soon after praying to the porcelain god, I was out again, the covers thrown off me because of the heat.

I woke shivering. The day was as dark as the last, but still no snow. I checked the clock and was surprised to see it read five in the morning. What time had I been up hugging the bowl? I think that had been about three. It seemed as if I had slept more than two hours. I piled my blankets back on top of me and didn't wake again until my regular alarm went off. I called Lanie at some point and admitted defeat.

"Stay home, you big dork, and stop worrying," she mumbled with as much force as one could mumble.

"I feel bad." I meant that in many, many ways.

"I know. Did Paul call?" She inquired lightly.

"No." I sighed, and then almost started crying again. "I can't believe him."

"You were pretty fierce, Yellie, give him some time."

"Yeah." Whose side was she on anyway?

I fell back asleep, but when I woke back up around ten, I felt for some reason that I had turned the corner. I couldn't put my finger on it, but I felt less rumbly in my stomach, and when I got up to go to the bathroom, I didn't feel nearly as weak or woozy. I decided to try and eat again, and miracle of all miracles, it stayed down.

I spent a quiet day reading or watching shows on television that I normally am never home to watch. I wondered about the plight of the suburban housewife: what the heck did they watch all day? Most of the stuff on TV was positively mind numbing. I convinced myself that they had no time to watch, what with taking care of the kids and all.

I decided to give Am a buzz. She had called the other day and left a message, so I left her one back at work, stating that I was home and to give a call back when she had a chance.

Today would be the perfect day to catch up and chitchat. At least on my end, I had an unlimited amount of time to talk.

So I guess it was no surprise that when the phone finally did ring that I thought it was Annemarie calling me back, and not Paul, the man currently masquerading as my boyfriend.

"Hello?" I knew I must have sounded like sheer hell.

"Hi." Paul's voice and nothing else.

"Oh, hello." I wasn't going to give him any more than he was giving me.

"How are you feeling?"

"Why?"

"Why?"

"Yeah, why do you care?" At that moment, I knew I must have sounded like a petulant four-year-old, but I didn't care.

"Because I care." He took a deep breath and I could see him in my mind's eye, scraping his hair back from his face.

"Well, why?" Oh, he was not about to get off easy.

"Danielle, please. Stop acting as if you think I don't care about you. You know I do. I would have called you yesterday, but I wanted you to get some rest. Now cut it out."

"If you think that what you just said qualifies as some sort of an apology, you're out of your mind." With a resounding bang, I hung up the phone. Huh! My turn! My lip started quavering then and I willed myself not to start crying all over again, as I was just starting to feel better and I didn't need to get myself all sorts of upset, and trigger the fever, not to mention the whole retching experience. I wasn't even sure if your body could do that simply by being upset, but I wasn't willing to find out. I hunkered down into a mode that I had perfected during adolescence, the glacial heart and the numbness running through my veins. I didn't care; it wasn't worth caring about.

I buried my head in a book. I looked at the clock. What would Lanie be doing right about now? I gave her a call.

"Lane. You busy?" I must have inquired with some urgency, because she told me to hold but came right back.

"What's the matter?"

The numbness broke and I started telling her about the conversation I had with Paul. By the time I was done, I was crying again.

"He's such a jerk!" Apparently, this was as much as I could articulate over the past two days.

"I think you're both being stubborn."

This is a true friend here. The response that you least want to hear, delivered to you with a dash of disgust; this and only this is the hallmark of a true blue friend.

"How am I being stubborn?" I acted absolutely galled by what was being said, but I knew in my heart of hearts that the burning sensation in my chest was nothing close to heartburn.

"You *both* are." Lanie paused a second. "Listen to yourself here, Danielle. You're mad because he was badgering you about going to his place yesterday. You're mad because his mind seemed to be more on the dinner and less on you, and you're mad because you felt crowded. You expected him to understand just how you felt, without having to explain yourself to him, and you're doubly pissed off because he can't read minds. He, on the other hand, is ripping pissed because you won't let him take care of you. Did you read Mars/Venus, girlfriend? Okay, the man always wants to fix things. That's their thing; that's what men do best. He could not help you yesterday, you and I both know that, but he believes you would not *let* him help you; there's a big difference in perception here. Then he calls today, but that's not good enough–he should have called yesterday. Fine. So then you move right ahead into accusing him of not caring about you. He tells you to cut the crap, you get your back up, and now the score is one hang-up for him, one for you, and nobody wins."

Silence etched its way through the phone line.

"Thanks for the brief recap, Dr. Lanie. But what I need help with is: NOW WHAT? What the hell do I do now?" I was consumed with frustration. I didn't know how to fix it. At the risk of sounding like a serial guest on Oprah: I had no role models for stuff like this. What did people in my family do when there was a lack of communication such as this? They fought. Sometimes they threw things. They accused, they pointed fingers, and most of all they walked away.

"Call him." Lanie suggested.

"Screw him." He could call me.

He *should* call me.

"Fine, but then you can expect this to go on a few more days at the very least." Lanie asked me to hold a sec and then came right back again.

"Is it busy?" I asked her when she returned.

"No, it's fine."

"Okay."

"Yellie, look…you have to determine what's more important to you here. Being right? Or sorting this out? If I told you that you were right, would it make you feel better?" Lanie offered.

"Do you think I'm right?"

"Does it matter?"

"It kind of does." I convinced myself that if I was right, then maybe I could be the bigger person and forgive him.

"Then I'll tell you that you're right. You were right for wanting to be alone yesterday. You were right for doing what you needed to do for you; you should never give in to someone else's pressure just to make them happy. Especially when it has to do with your body. But you were also wrong for playing games today. For hanging up on him, and for expecting him to read your mind in the first place. You're wrong now because you're acting like a brat and you could very well be straightening this out with him, instead of calling me up and complaining to me about him." Lanie cleared her throat. "So how do ya like them apples?"

"You suck," I told her, but there was no venom in my assessment of her, if for no other reason than I knew that she was right. Just like any human being the world over, I hated being wrong, and didn't very much like having it pointed out to me when I was. But. But I knew Lanie was right; I just wasn't used to fixing things, and I really didn't know where to begin.

"Fine, I suck, what the hell." Lanie chuckled then. "I'll take that as a compliment. Yellie, remember what I said in Brazil? I'll amend it a little. You and he *both* have fabulous opportunities to just go right ahead and screw this thing up for all it's worth. And you know what I have to say to that? Don't do it, Yellie. Life's too short."

"You're right; I know you're right." I felt that I knew what I had to do. "Thanks, Lanie."

"Don't thank me. I'm only good with this stuff when it comes to other people's lives."

"Me too." I thanked her again and briefed her on my medical condition before hanging up the phone, assuring her that I would be in to work tomorrow.

"Don't rush it," she advised, but we both knew that I would.

I hung up with Lanie and made yet another trip to the bathroom. Once I crawled back into bed, I resolved to call Paul, but before I did, I said a little prayer.

Lord, please help me to navigate the waters of this relationship. I don't know how to proceed and I'm terrified of drowning.

I took a deep breath and picked up the phone. He should still be at work, and as I dialed, I hoped he was at his desk and not at one of his perpetual meetings.

"Paul Corsi."

"Hi, it's me." Much softer than my earlier hello.

"Hi 'Me,' how are you feeling?" He sounded better too, and I had to wonder if he just had the same talk with Rob that I had had with Lanie.

"I'm okay." I paused a second, and the silence almost ate me up inside. "I'm really sorry about before."

"So am I." He waited a beat. "It really bothers me that you think I don't care about you, or about you being sick. I care a lot. I just don't always know how to show it, except to offer to make you soup and stuff like that."

"I know. I mean, I know that now." I drew a deep breath and then forced myself to go on. "I think I expected you to know that I really needed some alone time. I'm not saying that's right or fair, I'm just saying that I think that's where my head was at."

"For all the talking we do, we really don't say much, now do we?" Paul observed.

"I guess not." I took the covers and rearranged them so that the bottom was wrapped around my feet. "I just want you to know that I still love you."

"Still? After all this?" His voice was dripping with sarcasm, and I couldn't help but laugh when I thought about just how stupid this whole thing had become. Lanie was right; life is way too short for the likes of this.

"Yes, in my own crazy way, I can't help myself."

"The operative word in that sentence being…"

"Crazy?"

"You got it."

2001

Chapter Fifty-Seven

"You know what will be really cool? When we have kids, we can say that we met in the 1900's!" Paul thought himself funny.

"And that will be cool because it will make us seem older than we are?" I inquired.

"No, it'll just be cool." Paul offered me his most charming smile.

"I still can't get over writing '2000' on things, much less '2001.'" It was true. I would occasionally still write checks out with a 19--, and then have to either write over it and make the check sloppy or void it and start a new one.

"You have to admit that New Year's was better this year." Paul was convinced that spending New Year's Eve at home with friends was the way to go from here on in.

"It was definitely less tiring," I agreed. Plus I didn't have to run into any of Paul's cloying ex-girlfriends. Yes, New Year's Eve was a good time had by all, I just didn't want to agree so quickly that he may think that I was willing to stay home to party year in and year out.

Since I fully intended to spend many years with this man, I was more than aware that a little something such as that, which always seemed like a non-issue in the beginning, could very well sprout and grow wings and turn into a full-out Issue. So I agreed, but I left the back door open. The same way I approached the kid issue: I let comments like that last one there just sort of float over the top of my head, acknowledging it but not, almost as if I couldn't approach the subject one more time. We had discussed the kid issue at length: Paul definitely wanted some eventually, but I didn't want our lives to change just yet, and although I was confident I would feel a stirring sometime before I was forty, there was very little to persuade me at this point in time.

Am and Steven had had their little precious, my honorary godchild, the one, the only Jocelyn Joy, (aptly named because she was everyone's pride and joy) late last year, and although I loved her sweet baby face, I especially loved the fact that I only saw her for a short amount of time, and then could transport her right back to her parents. For me, this was an obvious indicator that I was simply *not ready,* and no amount of cootchy-cootchy-coo could persuade me just yet.

Besides, Paul and I had yet to get engaged. Much less married. Needless to say, there would be absolutely no transmogrification of this body until my last name rhymed with Horsey. But I had hope, hope in the form of Lanie, via Rob, telling me that the question would be popped sometime before GM put out its year-end report. I was okay with that. In fact, I was more than okay, because although I loved Paul with every breath in my being, I still had to let him meet my parents, the trick there being that I was sure I would suffer a sudden stroke in the process.

Procrastination is a beautiful thing.

"So what do we do for the Big Day?" Paul threw it back in my lap. He had veered off course a little with New Year's, but at the beginning of the conversation, we had actually been discussing Valentine's Day, which was a little over a week away.

"I was thinking about The Supper Club?" The Supper Club was a swing joint located on West 47th that all dancing New Yorkers visited at one point or another. It boasted a huge dance floor with a 25-foot ceiling art deco backdrop, and it was fun and sexy all at the same time. "It might be packed, but it'll definitely be fun." I also figured he couldn't deny me, considering that I had sat home for New Year's.

"I haven't been there in forever. That does sound good. I bet they have some sort of package available or something. I'll check it out." Paul got up to make a note in his Palm Pilot.

"See what you can do. In the meantime, we better get ready." I gestured towards the clock. We had just been lazing around drinking Paul's homemade cocoa, but if we were expected to be at his parent's house in two hours, that meant we had to get going and get on the train.

"You're right." He made his way into the bathroom and I tried putting some finishing touches on in the mirror outside the bathroom in the hall.

As I put a dab of under eye concealer under each eye, I wondered just how my eyes had gotten the rings underneath, and how on Earth the puffiness had taken up permanent residence there. Five years ago, I don't think I had even owned under eye gunk, and now I carried it around in my purse. Yuck. I slathered on some cherry Chapstick and reminded myself that I still wore less makeup than half the urban population.

We were going to Paul's parent's anniversary party. They didn't know it yet; they just thought that we were meeting them for dinner out on the Island, but Paul and Peter had planned a little shindig at a local family restaurant and invited some of their friends, that part being the surprise. They anticipated the dinner and they knew Peter was driving up from DC, and of course; Mr. Corsi would be picking us up from the train station. The people popping out from behind potted plants that were six feet tall…that part would be sure to put one if not both of them into full cardiac arrest. Paul's parents were married on an actual Valentine's Day forty years ago, but since this was the only time the boys could coordinate their plans, plus bring everybody else together, we were having the party today. I told Paul that the week or so early might help to throw them off a little, plus I had a sneaking suspicion that Mrs. Corsi would promptly burst into tears once she got to the restaurant, surprised or not. She was just that kind of gal. I had grown to like her more and more over the past almost two years, and although I knew I could never possibly be able to live up to her happy homemaking standards, she didn't seem the type to try and make me feel bad about it.

Paul's Dad Phil, who whooped and hollered when we stepped off the train, almost as if he hadn't seen us in years, ceremoniously met us the same way he always did: arms outstretched and the trademark Corsi grin swallowing his entire face.

"I've got my whole family together for dinner and I'm still in love with my wife! What more could a man ask for?" he asked rhetorically while he slapped Paul on the back and then tried to capture him in an immense bear hug. Phil then turned to me and did the same, and I found myself responding gladly, as Phil was one of the most non-threatening men I had ever encountered in my life.

"Hi, Mr. Corsi," I said with a smile and a big squeeze.

"Danielle! You look stunning! You know, if I wasn't married thirty-nine years to someone else..." His eyes crinkled when he smiled and I wondered briefly if Paul would look the same at the same age.

"Forty, Dad. Let's not forget why I'm here. I don't come out to the Island for a measly thirty-nine years." Paul grinned.

"Well, I never! Hey, hold up a second," He stopped to buy a paper from the man at the stand nearby. As he walked away, we heard the guy yell, "Bye Les!"

"Les?" Paul rolled his eyes.

"Oh, you know me, I answer to anything," Phil waved his hand away as if it made no matter.

Paul and I shared a look. "Dad, I really think you should have gone into acting."

"I do that all the time. I *act* as if I like your Aunt Helen," he quipped.

"I sure hope he can pull that off again today," Paul said in an under voice as he ushered me into the car.

"Don't worry." I assured him with a quick squeeze of the hand. Both he and Peter had been fretting all week about minor details, things I had heretofore believed only women had the corner on worrying about, like streamers and favors and the like. I helped Paul out by thinking up a gift, which ended up being a pair of tickets to a Broadway show, and a dinner gift certificate for Angelo and Maxie's. He said his parents would love it and I agreed. Peter's wife Madeline had insisted on buying them a very expensive, very heavy bowl from Lenox that Peter seemed to be proud of (evidenced by him actually emailing Paul a jpeg of it) but that Paul confided seemed like an overgrown ashtray.

    We arrived on time to find Peter and Madeline already there, and as soon as everyone hugged all around, Peter began ushering us into his car so that we could get to the restaurant on schedule. Peter, I had come to find out, was big on everything happening *on schedule.* He must have emailed Paul no less than a dozen 'schedules' regarding the event. But how much can you schedule a bunch of people in a restaurant? I had this absurd picture of Peter in my mind, orchestrating when the bread would be served at each table, and if the Anniversary cake comes out five minutes off schedule…God Help Us all.

    Don't get me wrong; even though I had little contact with Peter, I had grown to really like him in the time we had spent in one another's company. He was just a man with a plan, and I knew that, so it didn't really bother me.

    It bothered Paul.

    "How you doing there, Anal-Man? Did you pop a vein yet?" Paul rubbed Peter's shoulders from the backseat as Peter took the right turn out of the development.

    "I'm doing fine. I just hope the Petersons show up. And how are you, Danielle?" Peter moved the conversation over to me with a quick look in the rearview mirror.

    "Did they not RSVP?" Paul cut in before I could say a word.

    "They didn't either way, although I can't see them missing it. You know how they are; they're tremendously flighty, so I included them in the head count." I saw Peter's eyes flick towards me again in the rearview.

"I'm fine, Peter. Don't worry, you guys did a great job, and you know your parents will love it either way." I stepped into the role of cheerleader with ease, wishing at the same time that Madeline might jump in and help me. My eyes moved to the back of her head as I pondered the woman that Peter married. She was never anything but nice to me, but we had yet to form any real sort of friendship, and I would wonder occasionally what exactly that was all about. Paul said she was just shy, but I had another word for her, and to put it simply, it was cold.

"I just hope that blowhard Stapleton doesn't start ranting and raving over the election again. The last time we saw him, I wanted to shake him until his teeth fell out." Peter shook his head in pure disdain. Jerry Stapleton was a long-time friend of the Corsi family, as well as head of the local Republican party. The Corsis invited he and his wife over to share their traditional New Year's Day Dinner, and Peter and Jerry had almost come to blows over who actually won Election 2000. Peter was a die-hard fan of Al Gore, and needless to say, Jerry was quite happy with the current man in the Oval Office. It wasn't a pretty sight, and although I didn't say anything either way, I knew how Peter felt. I was hoping no one would say anything today either, as the whole debate had went from polarizing to tiring, and I just wanted to see everybody have a really good time.

"No politics today," was all Madeline said.

"I second that emotion," Paul agreed from the seat next to me. I squeezed his hand again and gave him a look that I hoped belied my pride in him; the same way Peter had felt about Jerry Stapleton, Paul almost had to be restrained from tossing Peter's face directly into a banana cream pie on New Year's. I was just the lucky girl who got to hear the endless diatribe on the way home: *How the hell could he have voted for that bumbling idiot? Clinton I could even understand; at least he had some charm! I just don't understand my brother…what the hell is the matter with him?*

And on and on and on and on.

We pulled into the restaurant's parking lot right in front of their parents, so both Peter and Paul took off quickly and ran in to make sure that everything was running on or close to schedule.

"I wonder if I should take our gift in now, or just wait and run back out for it." Madeline seemed perplexed. "I don't want to give anything away by running in with a big box under my arm."

The purveyor of Broadway tickets had no such problem.

"I can run back out with you," I offered and then graced her with my biggest smile. "Let's try to stall them."

"Ah, my three favorite girls," Phil smiled wide and then took in a deep breath as he approached us in the lot.

"You ladies look so fashionable!" Marie moved her hands down across her skirt, picking off some imaginary lint.

"Thank you," We both said at the same instant, then looked at each other and smiled. Madeline was so pretty when she smiled.

"After you, after you, and after you," Phil held open the door for us, and I caught Paul's glance in our direction. They were ready. Just as Phil was about to start chatting up the maitre'd, Paul came over and announced that he and Peter had already snagged a table in the back.

"Come on, Padre, you're gonna love this one," Paul's megawatt smile was settled firmly in place as he guided his unsuspecting father towards the back of the restaurant. Three steps from the door to the private room, Paul grabbed Marie's arm too. He made like he was going to sit at a nearby table and then faked left while Peter swung open the door to the twenty or so friends that had gathered inside.

"SURPRISE!" There was yelling and screaming and people running up to crowd them. Paul and I stood off to one side with Peter and Madeline. We took it all in, sharing a secret smile and shaking hands with a lot of people I didn't know. When I looked over at Marie, she was crying as predicted, and after a few minutes, extracted herself in order to come over and thank her boys.

"You guys are too much!" She exclaimed as she wiped tears of joy from her eyes. " I didn't know a thing! What did you do?" She chastised them in a way only a loving mother can, her way of saying they shouldn't have. Phil came over to us too and thanked us all profusely, Madeline and myself included. For some reason, when he hugged me hard, I felt tears well up inside my own eyes too. There was something so tender about these people, a niceness that emanated from their core, a something indefinable that made you want to be a part of whatever they were involved in. They always made me feel included, and the moment that thought jumped into my consciousness, I started to get all choked up and had to take a minute to excuse myself.

I bolted out of the room and asked the first waiter I saw where the restroom was, then made my way there expeditiously. I needed to fix my makeup, I told myself, but the truth was that I just needed to cry for a minute, alone, and process the feelings that were coursing through my brain. What was the matter with me? It had been a long time since I had experienced anything like this; was I crying because of my unexpected reaction to their kindness, or was I crying because this whole scenario jumped out at me and spoke to my brain all the things that my heart longed for still? How many years would my parents have been married, had they stayed together all this time? I ticked their wedding date off inside of my head and counted the years forward. Thirty-three years. If. If only…ah, I wiped my face and blew my nose, knowing that I needed to compose myself and then trot right back in there and join the fun. Ah, good thing I had that under eye concealer: now I had red rings to add to the lovely black that currently made me look twelve years older than I was.

Joy.

I fixed my face quick and then returned to the party. When I walked in, I found Paul right away, chatting up someone I recognized to be an old friend from their church: a Mr. Antonelli? Something like that.

I approached Paul and stood silently by his side since I didn't want to interrupt. He acknowledged me by wrapping his arm around my waist and then reintroducing me the minute there was a break in the conversation.

"Mr. Antonelli, this is my girlfriend, Danielle." Paul looked from him to me.

I offered out my hand. "I believe we've met before. Nice to see you again."

"Danielle, I have been telling this boy here to call me Anthony, ever since he left the youth group, ten, fifteen years ago. It's a no-win situation." He chuckled. "But I say to you my dear friend Paul, that everything happens for a reason."

I believed that. I looked at Paul and my eyes asked a question.

"Don't tell Madeline, but we were *discussing politics*." He said it like *hunting wabbit.* "I was just saying to Mr. A here…Anthony…that I'm still upset that Giuliani didn't end up running for Senate. Now we're stuck with another Clinton." Paul could no longer hide his disgust, and he rolled his eyes almost straight into the back of his head.

I was an Independent, so I really didn't get into party politics. My problem was this: I still couldn't get over the fact that the woman had not left her wayward husband, and yet had the nerve to call herself a champion for women's rights. When you get married, does that automatically mean you check your rights at the door?

I said nothing.

"You never know; God has a plan for all of us," Anthony was saying. "Right now is just not Giuliani's time." He splayed his hands.

"You think it was God's plan for that atrocity to be in office?" Paul looked about ready to spit.

"If you believe in God, you have to believe He's still on the throne." Anthony chuckled in a way that endeared you to him instantly. "He's aware of all that's going on down here. He's more than aware."

"Ugh." Paul shuddered. "I just can't get over it."

"Think of it this way, Paul..." Anthony paused. "People on both sides of this argument *just can't get over it*."

In the man's point, I saw instantly why he had been such a good youth group leader: he had an uncanny knack for getting you to see both sides, without coming across as preachy, or even revealing his side of the argument. Maybe more people like Mr. A should run for politics.

Soon we rotated around the room, and I was able to stop feeling sorry for myself simply by losing myself in the people and the myriad of conversations going on throughout. There was talk of the Election, but nobody came to blows, and most people were just having fun, loudly reliving their memories with the Corsi's. I had prompted Paul to put a guest sign-in type of book over by the bar, and I moseyed over there at one point to take a peek, happy to find people actually signing it and writing their own little antidotes all over the pages.

"Do you want to dance?" Paul whispered in my ear as I read one person's scrawled handwriting: *Remember the Cruise!*

"I would love to, Sir, but there seems to be no music," I pointed out as I turned towards him and fell into his arms.

"Ah, but there will be!" Paul looked around, as if he was about to share top-secret scientific data with me. "I just paid the waiter to pop in a Frank Sinatra CD for the 'rents."

"How did you know they had a stereo?"

Paul pointed to the speakers in the corner of the room.

"Oh, you're good," I complimented. "And the CD?"

"Stolen from Mom and Dad's little buggy," he admitted with a sly smile. "I've got it all under control."

"I think I should be worried about you," I intoned. Just then, *Fly Me To The Moon* came blaring through the speakers. The crowd seemed surprised but happy.

"Dance, my lady?" Paul offered his hand.

"But of course." We began to dance in the middle of the room and soon several other couples had joined in with us.

"Good call, little brother," Peter gave Paul a thumbs-up as he moved past us, Madeline pressed firmly against him, her posture still labeling her the ballerina she once was.

"Amen," Paul called back to him and then looked down and winked at me. "I'm so glad we pulled this off. It's really nice seeing everyone."

"I'm proud of you." And I realized that I was, as I said it, but not just for the party. There was so much about Paul that made me proud to have him on my arm.

"I love you," He leaned down and punctuated that with a kiss.

"I love you too," but I turned away slightly then, afraid that I would be overcome again, and not willing to spill my tears on the middle of the makeshift dance floor.

The party flew by. Paul's parent's friends were a really nice bunch of people. They showered them with gifts and good will, and they kept thanking us profusely, as well as Peter and Madeline. At the very end, I was collecting the disposable cameras from each table and handing them back to Madeline, who had brought them and then offered to get them developed too.

"It was nice, wasn't it?" Madeline asked worriedly, as she took the four cameras out of my hands and packed them in her shoulder bag.

"It was great," I assured her.

"I'm thinking about making them a photo album, you know, a mini-one though, so they can have it always, and still take it to show their friends." Madeline said.

As if they would be unable to heft a regular-sized photo album all the way to a friend's house.

"I think that's a great idea," I reassured her. Madeline was a weird one. What my father would call a tough nut to crack.

We left then and went back to Paul's parent's house to relive the entire thing over another cup of coffee while we waited for the train. Phil in particular was sad to see us go.

"We had such a good time!" He looked all choked up for an instant, but then composed himself through the guise of one of his signature smiles. "Aw, when will I have you kids all together again like this?"

"No pressure, of course," Marie put in over his shoulder.

"Soon, Dad. Easter." Peter looked at his watch and then turned to Paul. "Paul, do you want me to drop you guys off at the train station?"

"If you can, it'll save Dad the trip." Paul looked towards his father. I got the impression that his father didn't mind driving us, but he waved him on to go ahead with Peter.

"You kids go. Your mother and I have lots to talk about," Phil insisted.

So we piled into Peter's car a few minutes later, said a warm goodbye to him and the usual to Madeline, and the next thing you knew we were on our way back into the city.

"Whatcha thinkin'?" Paul sidled up next to me on the train, interrupting my reverie as I watched the scope of Long Island pass through the window.

"I'm thinking about how lucky you are to have parents who are still married," I decided to come clean with him even as the words popped out of my mouth. "I had such a nice time today, and I was so happy for you and your family, but I couldn't help be a little sad for me, because I know I'll never have that." I turned and faced him head-on.

"Do you still want that?"

Oh, only a child of divorce could understand how badly we all want that. I've grown up now; I've come a long way. I know better. I know that my parents would have killed each other eventually, whether physically or in spirit, or both…as an adult, I can see that they had probably never been good together, should have never have gotten married in the first place. But the child inside me still wanted them back. A whole family, the fantasy land that I had never lived in. Did I still want that? How could I explain to someone who has always had that…that I would always want that? That desire to be loved, to have a home to go home to…it never fades. It never goes away. It permeates my very being; for better or worse, it has made me the person I am today.

"Do you realize how lucky you are?" I was fine with answering a question with a question.

"I do." Paul spoke past the obvious lump in his throat. "I do, I realize it all the time. So many of my friend's parents are divorced. Or, if their parents are still married, they don't get along at all." He shook his head. "Mine are still in love. I'm very lucky."

"Do you think we'll be in love like that someday?" I wanted to be, so badly I could taste it, but there was still that pessimistic hanger-on inside my head, a little guy that only popped up when hope lay silent.

"I hope so." Paul kissed my forehead. "I want to be."

"So do I." And I thought, inside myself: *So do I.*

Chapter Fifty-Eight

"Waiting for the ring positively sucks," I announced this to Lanie late one night, after the gym and midway through a platter of sushi.

"Waiting for the phone to ring sucks even more," Lanie countered, and as a result, I laughed out loud and almost started choking.

"Don't you just wait for email now?"

"Zip it."

"No really, Lane, why are you doing this again?" I was still rather surprised at Lanie's new choice of dating aids, namely the computer. Lanie had recently signed up for an online dating thing, and since had been out with two duds and one guy that she liked, but he was moving to South Africa.

"Because I'm desperate! Why else do people do these things?" She reveled in the sardonic. "Seriously? I thought I'd give it a whirl. Why not? Nothing else seemed to be happening, and do you know that girl Alana on Team Cheer? She met her fiancé on line, at the same site I registered at."

"Alana from Team Cheer? What does that tell you?" I made a face and threw my hands up in the air, cheering. "Where's he from? Disney?"

"Oh, you're a regular laugh riot," Lanie couldn't help but laugh though, in spite of her obvious desire to bang me in the head.

"I am pretty funny. The point that I was trying to make was that you've never been that interested in pursuing anything before; I have heard you refer to your status in the past as preferring to be the hunted, not the huntee. So what gives?" I titled my head and waited for an answer.

"What gives?" Lanie stalled or paused, I wasn't quite sure. "I guess I am finally getting to the point where the idea of permanence appeals to me, more than it has so far, and since I hadn't been meeting anyone of, let's put it this way...*Lanie caliber*...I figured what the hell." Lanie seemed nonplussed by the whole thing, which in and of itself means that she deserves a whole lot of credit. There were a ton of other women our age that were veritably obsessed with bagging a man; Lanie was just checking out her options.

"What about Rob?" It seemed that I always came back to this very same question.

"Here we go again...*What About Bob?*" Lanie broke into peals of laughter. "Don't you think if anything was going to happen, it would have happened by now?"

"I do." I nodded agreement. "But I guess we're still holding out some hope."

"Ah, the proud Momma and Poppa bear...holding out hope for the younguns!" Lanie illustrated her point by clasping her hands together in overacted glee.

"Lane, you know it's not like that." I hated the idea of making her feel that way.

"Yellie, I know it's not like that, because I know you. And I know that you're not condescending, or selfish, and that you probably do sincerely think that Rob might be the man that God dropped from the center of Heaven right down to the Earth just for little old me. Just keep in mind that I would have positively killed basically anyone else by now, simply for asking." Lanie warned me with her scary face.

"I know that. I get it. I just want you to be happy. The South Africa guy seemed really great; I would have loved it if he would have stuck around and then you would have seen where that whole thing went..." I read Lanie's face. "I guess it is irrelevant."

"Kind of." She sighed. "He was very cute."

"Why did he have his stuff out there, though, if he knew he was going to leave?" This is the type of stuff that made me wary for her and the whole online dating scene.

"He didn't know when he posted. He works for Pepsi, and apparently they offered him a 'once-in-a-lifetime' chance to work in South Africa, so I can't say as I blame him." Lanie shrugged and sang a line: *"Someday, my Prince will come…!"*

"He will." Though I have to admit that I wondered briefly if having the Prince and not knowing when he would become The Official Prince was on some level harder than the initial waiting for the Prince to pop his head onto the screen.

"Okay, so whine to me, because you know you're gonna." Lanie poked a maki and then swished it around in some soy.

"Have I really started whining about this?" I didn't want to become one of *'those girls'*–one of those women that I had never understood until I was in their position. I just didn't understand what was taking so long; I knew that we were going to get engaged soon, I just didn't know when, and I found myself crawling all walls lately trying to anticipate the when and the how and even the where.

"A little." Lanie confirmed. "You're getting nervous."

"I am?"

"You are. You're dwelling on it, whether you realize it or not."

"I am."

"I just don't see any real problem here, Yellie. You know the man is crazy about you. You know he has actual plans to marry you. You know it's just a matter of time before he slips a rock on your finger. So why are you projecting?"

"I don't know." I concentrated on my food. "I can't explain it, Lanie. It's like, every time he says, even the most casual thing…*Danielle, can I ask you something…*I get totally wound up inside. I feel like I can't wait another minute. Then I almost balk, I get so scared, I wonder if marriage is something I really should even try my hand at, given my family history…and then an hour later, I'm back to Square One again, wondering when the heck he's going to make his move."

"Did you speak to Constance about this?"

"I did. I have. She wants me to try living in the moment. I try. I'm just not good at it. She said that since I grew up the way I did–always trying to protect myself, plan ahead for the next altercation, etc.–that I need to develop these skills now. And I really do try. I just can't help the fact that I am always projecting." I took a deep breath and toyed with my chopsticks. "I'm going to be in therapy forever."

"You're not going to be in therapy forever. I am." Lanie joked and I gave her a wry grin as a result.

"You're doing better than I am."

"Did I tell you I ran into Jude last weekend?" Lanie changed the subject, while separating the last two pieces of sushi on the platter, one to my side, one for her.

"No, how is he?"

"Still the same." Lanie shook her head in wonder. "Still partner-less, in either persuasion. But I ran into him at a coffee house out on the Island, and I ended up having about three coffees just so we could sit there and catch up with each other. He's still a magnificent friend. Very uplifting."

"You should invite him out with us sometime," I suggested, having wanted to meet Jude for the longest time.

"I should. I will." Lanie demolished her last piece of sushi and then said, "Do you want tea?"

"Does Gumby bend?"

"Okay. Back to you, anyway. Tell me why this is pressing on you again, all of the sudden. You haven't been this strung out over this particular topic in quite some time."

"I think it bothered me because of Paul's parent's party." I tried to figure out how to explain it to her. "It's bizarre, I know, but it just seems as if Madeline has a lot more clout than I do."

"Do they treat you like that?" Lanie inquired.

I took it that she meant Paul's parents. "No, not at all. Marie and Phil are really great people. It's just that she's the *wife,* and I am still the *girlfriend.*" I wrung my hands and then threw them out as if to say, *I dunno.*

"Yeah, but from what you've said, Madeline's no prize." Lanie wasn't exactly following.

"Madeline is almost irrelevant. My point is that when Paul introduced me to his old youth counselor, he introduced me as his girlfriend. It sounded so juvenile, and I felt like a jerk. When does the girlfriend ever get respect? The wife seems to come with at least a small amount of respect built-in." I surmised.

"You're assuming a lot."

"You're right. But can you understand what I'm saying?"

"I do. So what's your mission? Is your plan to hound him until he drops to his knees?"

"I have no plan. I just need to tell you these things."

"Let's put it this way: Do you think you can hold on tight until the man actually decides to do it?"

"I think I can." I nodded as if I were taking orders from a superior officer.

"I hate to go all Nike on you, but then Just Do It. He really is worth the wait, Danielle." Lanie the Mom.

"I know that." It was the one thing I knew for sure. "I know."

Chapter Fifty-Nine

It was Valentine's Day and I was just finishing up, putting final touches on my hair and makeup one last time before I exited Paul's bedroom and walked out to meet him in the living room. I played with my hair and checked my watch for the umpteenth time. Something would just not allow me to propel my feet towards the door.

What if tonight was The Big Night? What if Paul was about to use the backdrop of Valentine's Day to usher in a new life, a new beginning for both of us? Would he do that? I wasn't sure. I remembered telling him once that I didn't think I would like to be proposed to on a holiday; I wanted the day he proposed to me to stand alone on the calendar, not something to be remembered each year only by the onset of something Hallmark raked in the money for. Did that make any sense? Would he even remember me saying that? I wasn't sure if it mattered anymore…I didn't care…I just wanted him to do it and get it over with already…I felt…UGH! I felt just like one of those girls I hated.

Why oh WHY was I doing this to myself? And how had I gotten to this very ugly, insecure little place? I didn't want it to go down like this. I knew what the real problem was here: I had no control over this situation, and I didn't like it. I wasn't used to it. I was used to controlling my own environment. I had become an expert at it. Now that I found myself waiting on someone else, being held in an artificial limbo so to speak, I found that I did not like it, not one bit. And why was I held in limbo to begin with? All because I didn't have the nerve to just go ahead and get the ball rolling all by myself. And why not? I considered myself a feminist. Why then was I not so eager to simply move ahead and begin to facilitate my own happiness?

Because I was old-fashioned? Because some small part of me still believed in chivalry, and couldn't help but like the manly-man things that Paul did for me?

The truth, the little voice inside of me commanded. Tell yourself the truth.

Because I needed to know, beyond a shadow of a doubt, that this man loved me for all it was worth, and that he walked into a lifetime with me under absolutely no duress, and that nothing would ever shake the abiding love that we had found.

"Danielle, are you ready yet, honey? We have reservations." Paul called from outside the bedroom door.

I checked my watch again, the hair, and the face. I looked okay. Good enough. It was time to go. I concentrated on wiping every hysterical thought from my head as I opened up the door and sashayed into his arms.

"You look stunning." There was an awe in his voice that was inherently real.

"Thank you, baby. You don't look too shabby yourself." I gave him a slow once-over. He was dressed in a dark suit that was tailored to fit him perfectly. He had on a pinstriped shirt and a dark maroon-colored solid tie, looking every bit of the dashing GQ man, a portrait he wore so well. It reminded me of the first time I saw him in a suit on the street. It seemed like ages ago.

"Where in the world did you find this masterpiece?" He spun me around and I giggled, confident once again, in us, and in the way I looked tonight. The dress I was wearing I had found in a little boutique downtown on a Saturday before Christmas, when I was out shopping with Lanie, supposedly looking for gifts for others. I bought it on a whim, figuring I could wear it to Paul's coworker's wedding that we had in March, also knowing that I could very well wear it if we were to go out on Valentine's Day. The dress itself was all black, with a fitted top and a full skirt, and a tiny red flower that was smattered across the right side of my waist. It was simple but chic, and the main reason I bought it was because every time I stepped into it, I felt about ten pounds lighter.

"Downtown, with Lanie." I twirled again, confirming that this skirt was going to be totally perfect to dance in. "I'm glad you like it, because I'm wearing it to John and Sara's wedding in March."

"You can wear that every day for the rest of our lives and I will be happy," Paul professed with a big grin.

The rest of our lives…I snapped myself back to reality and looked him square in the eye. "I love you." I said it with such seriousness that I almost scared myself.

"I love you too." He smiled. "You okay?"

"I am one hundred percent more than fine." I liked the idea that I was taller in heels and didn't have so far to go to lean up and kiss him, so I did, once or twice or perhaps seventeen times.

"We should go," He pulled away after a little while and checked his watch. "We're going to be late."

"You got it." I went to grab my coat and was thrilled to see him try and help me into it, the way a chivalrous man does.

He grabbed his keys and we left the building, hailed a cab, and were soon deposited at the doorstep of The Supper Club. We got there only ten minutes late, and were pleased to see the party just beginning. Everybody was in a festive mood; people were already dancing and crowding the bar, and the kitsch level was totally over the top. There was a woman at the door sporting a fake diamond about the size of a cantaloupe, and some people even went so far as to dress in zoot suits and flapper-style dresses. As we walked deeper into the room I spied an older couple that I found instantly endearing, he in a tux and she in a ball gown, and I pointed them out to Paul. Although most of the women wore dresses similar to my own, some people really outdid themselves, what with clothes that could be considered costumes. One couple in particular looked like protégés of Fred and Ginger, and I couldn't keep my eyes off of them.

"They are amazing," I whispered to Paul as we stood nearby and watched them bringing energy to the place that you could feel in the air, as well as supreme reverence from the onlookers. They had a circle of people standing around them, cheering them on, and getting all caught up in the music.

"They make me feel like a klutz," Paul smiled abashedly.

"You are a klutz," I teased.

"Thanks." Paul poked me in the rib. "Let's go, klutzy." He took me by the hand and spun me out on to the dance floor. The floor was crowded. We danced a few sets and then got off for a little while, had a drink, a little bit of food, and that's when Paul thought he saw something going on in the balcony. He grabbed my hand and pulled me upstairs, where we were pleased to find an employee about to start breaking down a couple of swing moves. We learned three moves and with that (and our newfound confidence) we plowed right back out there, twirling and spinning the night away. We proved rather quickly that neither one of us deserved the title of klutz. Towards the end of the evening, the band took a break, so we did too.

"This joint is jumping!" The MC ended his announcement with this, which the crowd responded to by a collective whoop and a clapping of hands.

Then Paul proceeded to say something that almost made me have a heart attack.

We were standing by a table, each swallowing the last bit of our cocktails, when he put down my drink, spun me out, then folded me back into his arms, swing-style. That's when he whispered into my ear, "How would you feel if I told you something truly unbelievable?"

This is the part where my heart officially stopped beating. I paused too long and lost the beat, then stared at him, utterly unable to speak as my feet kept dancing. Was that the way he wanted to open up to *the question?* Was what he just said a precursor to the great big pop? I reminded myself that he said tell, not ask, and either way...he was grinning at me now, blinding me with the radiance of his smile, and I found myself wondering how I would feel if he decided to do it right now. A tingle ran down my spine, and I reminded myself that he was still waiting for a response.

"I don't know how I'd feel, so why don't you just tell me?" I had almost said ask me, but I caught myself again, and now I tried to wait patiently for a response as my heart practically jumped right out of my chest. I tried to be coy, but I felt like a dolt, superimposing a fake smile right on top of my real one. Coy was not a strong suit for me, so whom exactly was I trying to kid?

"I feel like I never want to do this with anyone else, ever again." He shrugged; his eyes gleamed. That was it. Whew. Another false alarm. On the right track to proposal, but not an actual one. I slowly let out a breath and decided that it was perfectly okay to keep breathing.

"I'm glad. For a minute I thought you were going to leave me for Ginger over there." I pointed my chin in the direction of the couple that was still tearing up the dance floor. A small circle had formed around them and people were openly gawking and cheering them on.

He smiled in acknowledgement of my comment, but barreled on ahead with his latest revelation. "Sometimes, I just can't believe that I feel this way about someone; I can't begin to tell you how many times I heard about stuff like this before I met you, and I would always wonder if it would happen to me. I felt like falling in love like this was something that other people did. Now that's it's happened to us, it still has some sort of unreality to it, a quality that isn't always believable...and I find myself sometimes, in my darkest moments, waiting for it to fade. But it doesn't. It hasn't, and I know now it won't. I guess I just wanted to share that with you."

And give me a heart attack in the process. Gee, thanks.

Instead of giving my thoughts a voice, I moved closer to him and allowed him to swallow me up in his embrace, not sure if I was still moving in time with the music, and not caring either way. "I don't ever want to do this with anyone else, ever again, either," I gave him a reassuring smile, but I felt the same way he did, standing in awe of the situation. I could remember after David and I split up, thinking: Hey, maybe that was as good as it gets. Maybe you'll never fall in love completely again. Maybe you will, but after a while, your feelings will fade, and you'll be stuck with a man who is only a shell of his former self, the man you thought you fell in love with originally, but who was really just a great big faker on his best behavior. I had always harbored the fear that if I did give my heart to someone again, that I would either be consumed with looking over my shoulder, or obsessed with looking ahead, and not able to settle in to a comforting thought, like *this feels right,* or even the wish that I would never have or want to do a particular something with a particular someone else.

"I love you, Danielle. I love everything about you." He whispered lovingly in my ear and I felt his hot breath on my cheek. "Promise me you'll always be my dance partner."

You still don't know everything about me.

"I promise. I love you." And then, almost as an afterthought, "Happy Valentine's Day."

Chapter Sixty

LOVE IS RISK.

Somebody was sending around an email entitled Love Is Risk, in all caps, as some sort of deranged forward that was supposed to make you think and realize Love was *worth* the Risk.

I thought it was a virus. I was just about to call up Am and tell her to stop forwarding viruses, when I decided to risk my life and open it. What's the worst thing that could happen; that I wouldn't forward it to at least seven people in the next hour, and my eyeballs and hair would fall out simultaneously? What did I care about minute details such as those?

I opened up the email and read the little ditty. It was a story about a woman who never truly risked anything. She was in a relationship her whole life, with a man that she completely adored, but she was unable to risk anything more than a casual closeness. She tried to open up to him, but every time he told her he loved her, she would answer by saying 'Me too,' and never would the actual word *love* be uttered from her lips. They never married. She loved him with all the love in her heart, but she remained his girlfriend always, because she was too afraid to take the risk and marry. One day the man died suddenly and she never even got a chance to say good-bye. She realized when she lost him that she would have risked anything just to see him one last time. The forward went a little something like this: *Love Is Risk. Take a risk and forward this on to all the people you love today, whether they know you love them or not. Whether they love you or not; because love is always a risk worth taking.*

Sappy. Sap-sap-sap-sap-sappier than sappy. What the heck was going on Upstate? Annemarie popped out a little one and all of the sudden she was the unparalleled Queen of Sappy Emails, not to mention the Duchess of

Digital Pictures, her baby's face (and heinie) flying across the Web at regular intervals.

My, how things have changed. Three years ago Annemarie was adverse to email; you could only get her to send or receive any at work, and then only if it was completely necessary. I would send her countless jokes and forwards, and never once did I receive a reply. Now she was sending me Sap at a regular rate. That's okay. I knew that this email was more about me and less about her, but I wasn't able to see the whole picture. I mean, I was waiting for Paul to propose, wasn't I? And I told him I loved him every single day. So how was I not risking? Was she talking about my parents? Or was I simply reading way too much into this?

I forwarded it to Lanie separately from everyone else in my address book: *Tell me what you think of this one.* Then on to Paul and Rob and every other unsuspecting inhabitant of my virtual address book.

About two seconds after I forwarded it to Lanie, she turned around and said, "I think it's supposed to make you think."

"Well, isn't that obvious?" I looked at Lanie as if she had marbles running around inside of her head.

"Sure, but then I don't understand what you're asking me."

"It's sappy."

"Sure it is, but almost every email you get is either sappy or raunchy. Why, did this particular email bother you or something?"

"I guess it did its job: it made me think. But to tell you the truth, I'm thinking my question should have been, do you see me in that scenario? Do you think that's why Am sent it to me?" I was trying to be introspective, but now Lanie was looking at me as if I had marbles running around inside of my head.

"I think Am sent it to you because she is now the Queen of Sap, and because that's what Sap-Queens do, they forward amazingly sappy emails to the ends of cyberspace, in hopes that somebody will forward them something sappy too. As for your first question, I can see you a little bit in that scenario. You're still afraid of letting your two worlds collide. You haven't taken a real risk regarding Paul and your family yet." Lanie stared down her nose at me.

"Why does Paul even have to meet them?" I was whining again, and I knew it, I could hear myself doing it, and I wanted to yell, 'CUT!' like an angry director in a low-budget film, but I was rolling…rolling…ACTION! I think I was still scared that somehow my old life could contaminate my new one; keeping them apart seemed the only viable option, and had been for years now. Plus I was afraid about getting my father's approval. If that one incident on the hill had proved nothing else: halfway wasn't good enough. And I wasn't sure that my father would be totally enamored of Paul, although I wasn't sure that he wouldn't be either…so I guess that, all summed up, I *was* still afraid of risk.

If love was risk, then I was on the right track with Paul–singularly–in fact, I was doing quite well in the Opening Up Department. The other night, I had actually taken it upon myself to–

"Because they are a part of you." Lanie interrupted my thoughts. "Whether you like it or not, they are a part of you, who you are, your life…" Lanie made a weird motion involving her hands, neck, and head. "Nobody's saying they have to be buddy-buddy. They just need to meet, shake hands, you know, the whole shebang. Just get it over with. I guarantee it will not be as scary as you think it is."

"I was waiting until we get engaged." It was a lame protest and I knew it.

"Why? What difference will that make?"

"I don't know. I just think it'll be better."

"So you can prove something? Yellie, what the hell are you still trying to prove to these people? That you're better than they are? Here's a shocker: they already know that! Even at their self-involved worst, I would venture a guess at the fact that your parents know they were not the best parents! So you go up there with a ring on your finger, to prove what? That you didn't marry the guy with the gun rack on the back of his truck? That somehow you picked yourself up by your bootstraps, and managed to marry someone who wouldn't ensconce you in a singlewide trailer in lieu of a first apartment? Hello! If they had half a brain in either one of their heads, they should know that you never would have done that anyway. So you wear yourself out, trying to prove something to people who don't really matter in the big scheme of things. This, my dear friend, is not smart. And I know you're smarter than that. What on Earth are you thinking?" Lanie shook her head as if she normally thought better of me.

"I'm thinking that," and I paused a second as Alex walked into the hole/office and dropped our mail on my desk–Hi's all around–then resumed, "I'm thinking that, if Paul and I go up there and they reject him or me or we, that I will have a ring on my finger, something to represent that I am part of a family of my own, and that somehow that by being there…like that…they can't hurt me anymore. Not too much anyway." It was wayward logic at best, but it made sense to me.

"They can only hurt you as much as you allow them to hurt you," Lanie reminded me. "You can't use Paul as a shield."

"The question is, is it worth the risk?" It was a rhetorical question, because I knew not what I would gain from allowing Paul to enter my already fragile relationship with them, except that it would be intellectually honest and perhaps enable me to surmount my fear. Would that alone make it all worthwhile? Or would my relationship with Paul somehow become ensnared in the cobwebs of my past and former life? Couldn't we just go away and get married on a beach somewhere, far and away from all the people in our lives? I thought about it a minute. Paul's parents would flip. It wouldn't be fair to them, and whatever goodwill I had managed to cull from that relationship would automatically go down the drain. Did I want that? Simply because I was unable or unwilling to take the risks that I needed to take with my own family?

No. I did not need another awkward family situation. That I knew for sure.

Love is Risk.

No kidding. I felt as if I risked my heart exploding out of my chest every single time I picked up the phone and called my father: what if he was too busy, with the new wife, the new kid, the new house? I put myself on the line, both literally and figuratively, and no one knew the extent of risk I undertook except for me. Was Lanie telling me to go on and risk just a little bit more? Why? So their rejection of me could be complete?

That would be fun. Then I could call up my mother and *risk* another argument with her, just to air it all out, and watch her travel on the precarious edge of sanity, thanks to yours truly. How could I possibly want to pass that one up?

The real truth was, the equation just didn't work out for me. Love=Risk=Love? That's what the email was insinuating, and the point that I kept clinging to was clear and simple–thus far, I could not agree with that theory. Or was the email trying to say that if you love someone you should take the risk and let that love be known, regardless of the consequences? That one day it might be too late to show your love, and with no way to convey it, you would live in a world colored with regret? Was that the message? Then perhaps I should forward it to my parents!

Besides the fact that my mother couldn't afford a computer and my father could barely operate one, neither one of them struck me as the type to heed this sort of circular message. I mean, by God, my mother had to reside with The Monster for years on end before she felt the lightning bolt of truth, zapping her into believing the fact that the man was an abusive bastard, with no hope for reform. I wasn't too confident that she would get the message right away, at least as it pertained to me. I admit I was too scared to send it: in her warped mind, she might very well turn the whole thing around and decide that she needed to take another risk and love The Monster again. And that I simply could not have.

As if she had just formed the ability to zone in on my brain waves, the phone rang and it was her. She was just calling to say hello, to tell me something inane about the new laundry soap she got on sale this week at the supermarket, when I heard a voice that sounded strangely like my own say:

"Mom, why don't you come down this weekend for a visit?"

"Oh, it's so far to get to you. No. I don't know." I could see her wringing her hands on the other end.

"Mom, you have seen my apartment exactly once. Why don't you make the trip down for a change? I'll make you a deal. I'll invite Paul over so you can finally meet him," and even as the words popped out of my mouth, I couldn't believe I was saying it. But I was, and I had to believe that my mouth was betraying the desires of my heart. Maybe I was willing to take a risk, more willing than I originally thought I was.

"It's such a long ride, Danielle. Why don't you come up here?" She offered instead, but for some reason, this inflamed me to the point that I could not even describe, her obvious blocking of all things that pertained to my new life. I started to get hot.

"Because I always come up!" I had to remind myself to breathe. Was it too much to ask for her to simply get into the car and drive down to see me for a change? Did I really ask so much from her? If it were The Monster asking, OH, then she would run to the gas station and be fueling up her tank right now, as we speak! "Where exactly do you have to go?" I spat the words out, still trying to control my volume and not allow this conversation to escalate into a full-fledged fight.

"I don't have to go anywhere."

"That's my point exactly. You have no plans," I knew this before I called her, although I hated to point it out to her. Since The Monster went and took over every aspect of her life, she lost whatever friends she had, and since her self-esteem had been ransacked, she didn't try to make any new friends, so she never had what I would call a full social calendar to contend with. You would think that she would be interested in spending the afternoon with her only child.

"Can I let you know?" She asked in her meekest voice, and it was all I could do to not bang down the phone and forget it all. All of it. Whose brilliant idea was this anyway?

Control.

"Sure." I conceded, admitting defeat to the many neuroses that floated around inside of her head. "Let me know tomorrow."

"Okay then," and she prattled on about the new dryer sheets that went along with the laundry soap that she was lucky enough to get on sale.

A few minutes of allowing her to babble was about all my heart could permit. I agreed with her that it couldn't be all bad, considering that the same people who made Cheer made the new laundry products, and she had loved Cheer for too many years to count. I made a mental note to ask Lane to ask Alana to see if we had any samples lying around the agency from Team Cheer.

"You are not going to believe this," Lanie announced, her disgust undisguised and dripping from each syllable. "Look at this utter crap." She was pointing to The New York Post's Page Six column, a New York tradition/staple for all the goings-on of Who's Who in New York society. Celebrities, Wall Street power brokers, and all the old money inheritors shared space on a page that millions of New Yorkers turned to every day for their dose of gossip a la New York.

"Who's that?" I sucked in a breath. "Oh…" It was a picture of Dez Diaz, Lanie's old friend, posing for the camera with a fresh look of innocence, a man draped on her arm that looked to be at the very least fifty-five or so years old. Pushing sixty, maybe.

Lanie threw the paper over her shoulder with dramatic flair.

"Okay. Focus! We have bigger fish to fry here." I pointed over to the stack of new hotel and resort information packets that we had blown off the day before. Olive wanted us to shuffle through them and see if there were any that we would recommend just by looking at them, then narrow it down to a couple that we could go visit in order to see if they were appropriate for an upcoming meeting we had to plan. Lanie had insisted that we tell Olive we couldn't judge a book by its cover, and that we needed to go see the properties for ourselves. Although I was always up for free travel, I insisted that we wade through the overflowing box of brochures, and then concentrate on scamming free travel to the ones we really liked. A method to the madness.

"Fine." Lanie started separating out the packets, one for me, one for her. Once we got into a rhythm, Lanie went back to our earlier conversation, which had originated from the email. "Take the way I am now putting myself out there, plastering my face on the Web, in hopes of meeting–if not Mr. Right–a very nice guy to whittle away my time with. That's a risk," Lanie pointed out.

I threw aside a brochure for a resort in Scottsdale, Arizona. Nice, but not enough nonstop flights in and out of Phoenix to accommodate this group. "Fine. You are risking…what? Humiliation? Not finding someone? All I'm saying is that once you are in a relationship with someone, the risks are far greater. You have more to lose. The initial risk isn't really the crux of the problem here."

"The crux of the problem is in your head," Lanie pointed to me several times in repetition, gangster-style. "It's all a matter of perspective."

"Give me an example from *your life*." I felt the need to underscore, as I was generally exhausted mulling over mine.

"Perfect example: there is a guy right now that I have a modicum of interest in. I have yet to contact him, all because of one very strange thing he wrote on his online profile. Okay? Get this: He's a nice Jewish boy from Long Island, works in the city. Lives in the city, is a professional, has all the right buzzwords. Except do you know what he wrote on his freaking profile? 'Likes Hello Kitty.' Now tell me, Yellie, would you not be more than a tad bit cautious about responding to something/someone like that?" Lanie laughed in such a way that I couldn't help but laugh myself.

"He really wrote that, Lane? Meaning that he likes the character, 'Hello Kitty'? From when we were kids?" I was stunned.

"I take it that's what he means. Although what do I know? Could be some really cool computer game that I'm just not in on. Okay. So, what do I do now? Everything else lines up…he seems like the type of guy I might have more than a passing interest in. Perhaps the 'Hello Kitty' reference is his idea of a bad joke…and all he wants is to test it out, see if he could meet someone as off-the-wall as he is. Right? Then that would appeal to me; I obviously have a thing for strange people." Lanie indicated me with a dramatic roll of the eye. "My point is this: I will never know unless I take the risk."

"So you're contacting the Kitty guy?" What if that was just code for him trying to say, but not say, that he was a pedophile? I worried for Lanie.

"I might." She shrugged, then handed me a pile of brochures. "These are all Disney. Chuck 'em." The one place the agency did not want the event held was Disney. Nothing against Mickey Mouse, but the employees tended to all want to extend if we held a meeting at Disney, and after the last time that happened, the agency had alerted Olive to scrap Disney as a resort destination. If I remember correctly, the last time that happened, Lanie and I had gotten overwhelmed with requests for personal reservations, car seats in rental cars, cribs in rooms, rollaways, etc. I chucked the brochures into my garbage can with a resounding bang. I was not at all interested in who needed a Park Hopper Pass and who did not.

The phone was dead, so we capitalized on that and made our way through the pile faster than we had expected. Soon we had narrowed it down to four different places: two in Florida, one in California, and one on Hilton Head, South Carolina, although we knew that one would probably be harder to get to, due to less flight options per day.

"I don't know, Lane. I agree with you, but I don't. I just tried to talk to my mother, you know, take the emotional risk, and ask her to come down on Saturday afternoon and meet Paul. And she was like…" I searched for the right words. "Very noncommittal, not impressed, and she just balked at the idea of driving down to see me. Sometimes I feel very invalidated by the Upstate bunch, be it my father, or my mother, or even Am. They never offer to come down and see me; it's as if because their life revolves around Upstate, mine still should too. And I guess you could argue that I'm not taking a huge risk by inviting her down, but I'm just not sure I need Paul to see the "mobile home" that she currently resides in. I would be willing to take a risk in small doses. Does that make any sense?" I wanted Lanie to agree with me.

"It makes perfect sense. Look, you're obsessing about the email. Just get the general message, forward, delete, and move on."

"The general message being…?" I also wanted to see if I was on the right track.

"The general message being that if you don't at least try to love, you risk losing out on something really special."

"You think that's it?"

"I do." Lanie shrugged. "Not everybody takes everything to heart the same way you do, kid."

"It's a gift and a curse." I had learned that over time. If you felt things deeply, you sometimes got more out of life than the average Joe, but if you felt things deeply, you also ran the risk of getting hurt a little more deeply too. I guess if I had learned nothing else from life, I had learned that that was why I was still so scared. I'd been burned before and I didn't want to travel down that road again; so I closed myself off in bits and pieces, trusting few and trusting slow.

I was probably my own worst enemy. Maybe I could start praying to become a little shallower, revolving in a demeanor that automatically enabled me to feel things less, and be involved with the superficial more.

It wouldn't work. I knew it, but I still held on to these vague beliefs that somehow women who were totally caught up in fashion magazines and getting their toes done always ended up being a little less brokenhearted than I did.

Think about it, right now, wherever you are: everybody has that one song that just tears you to shreds every time you hear it. I can think about a song that became popular when David and I broke up, and to this very day, so many years removed from all things David, I could still feel the bitter shame and the utter hopelessness I felt on that ride home from New Orleans. Give yourself a minute, and if you're not the type to block it all out, you'll find you can recall every single word and nuance of searing melody, your heart constricts, and the next thing you know, you're right back in the place that defined pain.

I don't want to go back there.

I never, ever want to go back there again.

Chapter Sixty-One

"So what's on tap for this weekend?" Paul asked nonchalantly over a bowl of Ramen noodles. We were at his place, he indulging in his bachelor's specialty, and I taking the high road, and slurping the latest concoction from Healthy Choice: low fat soup that actually tasted pretty decent.

"We have no major plans. I..." My mother still hadn't gotten back to me, but I knew that the likelihood of her driving down to see me was slim to none, unless I badgered her with all my might, and the bottom line was that I was just not sure if I had the energy. "I thought maybe we could hang out at my place on Saturday." Just in case.

"Rent some movies?" Paul suggested. "There are about three new releases I really wanted to see."

"Sounds good." The weather report had said cold and gray, a chance of snow, though nothing definite as of yet. The winter was the best time to bury yourself under the blankets and have a movie marathon with the one you love.

"Can we pick them up by you?" Paul asked.

"Sure, I can grab a few movies either when I get home on Friday, or I can grab them on the way to pick you up at the train station on Saturday morning." Either way would be fine.

"You're staying home on Friday night?" He gave me a look that said he didn't comprehend.

"Well..." I still had this ridiculous notion that my mother would call at the last minute and want to come down, and then I would want to clean and tidy things up a bit more than when it was just Paul and me. I didn't know how to tell Paul this, because I still hadn't told him about the earlier conversation or that I had even invited her. Instead, I opted for, "I was thinking about making a quiche."

"From scratch?" He sounded impressed.

"Yeah." I gave him a look. "I know how to make one from scratch, you know. It may not be as good as your Mom's, but I manage." Mrs. Corsi was a force to be reckoned with in the kitchen.

"I didn't mean anything by that." His mouth turned up in a slow smile. "You ladies sure are competitive when it comes to kitchen stuff."

"I'm not competitive." I was slightly taken aback by the way he obviously saw me. Did I come off that way?

"Sure you are. All women are." He nodded, as if he were the authority on all things woman.

"You so don't know that." I reached over and smacked him in the arm. "You're assuming."

"So?" He got up to put his bowl in the sink.

"So? You're making generalizations and assuming an awful lot." I rolled my eyes at him, and then followed him to the sink with my bowl. I ran some water in it and then turned to face him head-on. "You're a jerk." I slapped him again. Same arm, same place, but harder, and with a little more meaning.

"I'm a jerk?" He seemed as if this put him off. "I am *not* a jerk."

"You are. You can be." I walked around him then, unable to decipher just why I was feeling so irritated by his earlier comment. What reference did he have to call upon, that all women were competitive when it came to cooking and baking and the like? His mother's 4H Club? Or better yet, the various church bake sales that he attended regularly throughout his childhood? Give me a break.

"Take that back." He stood over me now, glaring down at me in a way I had not experienced from him as yet. "You're the one being a jerk."

"I am not!" I went to hit him again, at same place on his arm, but this time he grabbed my arm in time and twisted it in the opposite direction.

"Stop that!" He looked at me as if I were a bratty little child that he had no control over. "Stop hitting me!"

"What?" I looked at him as if he were the crazy one. "What do you mean, stop hitting you? Let go of me!" I tried to wrench my arm away from him in a way that showed that I meant business. I had no recollection of hitting him.

"I'll let you go if you promise not to hit me again," He said this in a level voice, but his eyes looked scary, and for the first time ever, I found myself getting outwardly defensive around Paul, and feeling old feelings that were better left buried.

"I only hit you because you were being a jerk." I spat the words out one by one, then pulled my arm closer and into me, but he still had his hand on me and wouldn't let me go. "Let me go, Paul, I mean it!" I was starting to breathe faster and I knew that in less than a minute, I would start hyperventilating.

Here it was: the big boom I was waiting for. *All men are alike. They think that they run the show. They grab and they hit and they cannot be trusted.*

He wouldn't let go of me. He stood there, still as a statue, looking at me as if I were some foreign creature, afraid to let me out of his grasp.

My mind went to a far-away time and place, the sounds of a struggle, and The Rolling Stones blaring in the background.

"Danielle, what the hell's the matter with you?" His eyes were almost popping out of his head.

I tried to focus, but I felt myself reacting with venom.

"There's nothing wrong with me. NOW LET ME GO!" I screamed at the top of lungs, which enabled me to get out of his grasp, as he was completely stunned for almost a full minute. The next thing I knew, I was crying. *All alike. They're all alike.* Hysterically crying. With blinding tears cascading down my face, I turned from him and started shoving my things into my bag. Like an erstwhile soundtrack, I started hearing The Rolling Stones playing in my ear…*If you start me up, I'll never stop…never stop…never stop…never stop…*

"Danielle, where are you going?" He was incredulous, standing beside me wringing his hands, afraid to reach out and try touching me again.

"I'm going home. Now." I could barely speak through my tears, but I knew one thing for sure: if I didn't get out of there at that very moment, that I would never forgive myself and that things would turn ugly. Or should I say uglier?

"You're not going home like this." He shook his head as if to demonstrate that as his final word.

"The hell I'm not." I looked up through my tears and showed him what I hoped was a look of utter defiance. My bag was packed and I was ready to go, but he was standing in front of me now, blocking my path to the door. "Step aside." I would barrel through him if I had to.

"Step aside?" He looked around the room crazily, searching everywhere for something, someone to help him with this alien side of me. "Danielle, there is no way in hell that you're leaving like this."

"Wanna make a bet?" I challenged him with my eyes, crazed over with the intent to get away from his presence as fast as humanly possible.

"Why are you doing this?" He threw his hands up in the air. "I'm not touching you. I had no intention of hurting you. Can't you just stay; talk this out? I don't even understand what the hell just happened here."

"Get out of my way," I had found my most threatening tone. It was recalled from the depths of my being, from a time and place that he wouldn't understand. I stared him down then, determined to flee, regardless of whatever opposition he posed.

"I want you to stay," He had taken his voice down a few notches, but I could barely hear him, and all I could see were blurred images, my mother running, pleading, my heart pounding…juxtaposed against what I thought was his unfair treatment of me.

"I don't care what you want." And right then, I didn't. I just wanted out, and away, and free. I wanted control over my situation. I wanted to be alone.

"Obviously. Danielle," He reached for me again but thought better of it. "I'm sorry. I'm sorry for being a jerk, but you just can't hit me like that. I won't…"

I pushed past him then, past his upcoming diatribe about what he would or would not stand for, past my future, into my past, being swallowed up whole by fear and things assumed on either side.

I ran to the elevator, and once I was outside, I began gasping huge chunks of fresh air, trying to regulate my breathing, and above all else, stop crying. I felt disoriented for a minute. Where was I headed, and what had just happened in there? I answered the first half of the question as I pointed my feet in the direction of Grand Central. About halfway there I realized how cold it was outside, and wrapped my scarf tighter around me. I didn't care. He was a jerk. As my feet pounded the pavement on my short walk to the station, I started a rhythm in my head: *I don't care. He's a jerk. I don't care. He's a jerk.*

I jumped onto the first available train, and the first thing I did once I grabbed a seat was to take out my small cosmetic mirror and check my face. Sure enough, I found black smudges all over the top half of my face, my eyes already showing the stress of my crying by a puffiness that I couldn't do anything about. I swiped away at the mascara and the tears, and then shut the compact quick, not wanting to get a look into my eyes and see what was festering there.

My breathing started getting better with each mile of track, and by the time I was deposited at my station, I felt an overwhelming sense of calm take hold of me and lead me to my car. I began crying once more on my way home in the car, but I stilled myself, telling myself that I had to drive and to stop the histrionics. Once I arrived at my house, I checked the mail and the refrigerator, mentally checking the contents, and assuring myself that my refrigerator was the same way I had left it when I left that morning. I closed the door to the fridge and went into the bathroom to wash off the final residue of makeup, fully aware of the fact that I didn't want to look too closely at myself in the mirror if I didn't have to.

When I exited the bathroom, I noticed the light on my answering machine was blinking, and I paused a minute before I decided whether I wanted to hit the button or not. What if it was him? What could he possibly have to say? Better yet, what would I have to say to him? I checked the lock on the door, then opened up the fridge again and started counting the eggs. Ten. Had there been ten in there when I left for work this morning? Would ten be enough to make a regular-sized quiche? I couldn't remember.

I scowled at the light on the answering machine, wanting to be alone with my thoughts, but also wanting to know what the light had in store for me. After a second check of the door lock, I decided to press the button and get my answer.

Hi Danielle, it's Mom. I don't know if you're still interested, but I thought about it and I would like to come down on Saturday and meet your boyfriend. Let me know what I can bring. Love you, Bye!

Oh, the timing could not have been more perfect!

I grabbed my book and settled in for a read, but could barely concentrate on anything, and ended up staring at the ceiling for what seemed like hours on end.

I know I must have fallen asleep at some point, because I woke in the morning, unsure of whether what had transpired between Paul and I was a dream or had actually occurred. I found the evidence in my puffy eyes, and the dampness on my pillow, and a brokenness in my heart that I hadn't felt in years.

Chapter Sixty-Two

I thanked God the next day was Thursday as I made my way to Constance's office. I feared that I could not wait another minute, much less another day, to unload the whole thing to someone that was, in fact, a professional.

Lanie came close, but let's face it; she was only a professional in her own mind. And I had unloaded on her all morning, as the phone remained mercifully silent, while she sat and listened and said nothing in all the appropriate places, and something whenever something needed to be said. But what could she tell me, really? Because I couldn't define it myself.

So I trudged south towards Constance, thinking that if this was the end of Paul and I, that I could handle it so long as I could up my sessions to…let's say, six times a week. That and a bottle of wine after each session. Scratch that, a gallon. Or two.

Either way, when I entered Constance's office, I was barely able to pull off a sheepish sort of grin before I collapsed into tears that wouldn't stop coming. I cried for a full two minutes, my only interruption being her soft questions, "Danielle, why are you crying?"

"I think I just broke up with Paul." I flailed my arms as if to demonstrate that I was grasping for the needed words, "Or he me. I don't know."

"Well, why don't you start by telling me what happened?" She asked plainly, in a soothing voice, and then she waited for me to collect myself and speak.

I told her everything. I told her how I had smacked him on the arm, and how even as I did it, I convinced myself I didn't do it. I told her how I was both ashamed and terrified, not knowing which emotion I felt more either last night or today. I relayed to her how explosive I had been, suddenly angered by the slightest offense, and determined to deem him a typical man, typical at least to all I had known before. I was scared that Paul was just like all the other men in my life, but I was even more scared that I had lost him by my erratic behavior.

After a long minute of silence, Constance asked, "Danielle, did he raise his hand to you in any way?"

"No."

"Are you sure?"

"I'm sure." I hung my head. "He only touched me that one time, to keep my hand away; to stop me from hitting him all over again."

"But you thought he might hit you." It was a statement, not a question.

"I panicked." I gave a self-defensive little shrug. "I thought he might be like The Monster. He looked at me in a very mean way."

"So what started all the hitting?"

"I don't know. Like I said, I didn't even realize that I did it at first. I just did. I did it and then I couldn't stop." I felt the need to defend myself even further. "It wasn't really hard. I just…tapped him?"

"If you had tapped him, would he have gotten so upset?" She directed the question towards me, deferring if you will, to the one that knew him better.

"Probably not." I took a deep breath in and exhaled, "So what do I do now?"

"First of all, you have to stop the hitting. Under no circumstances should either of you be hitting the other. And the name calling. The name calling has to stop." Her face was resolute.

I thought that was obvious. I knew what I should be doing; I just didn't know how to do it. I didn't say anything as my mind wandered, and I began to wonder how we had even gotten to that place.

"You're right." I replayed the scene in my mind again. It was ugly.

"Can you think of where you got that from?"

"Got what?"

"Your behavior. You had to learn it from somewhere. Can you think back to where you may have picked up that sort of behavior?"

"Of course I can, that's easy. The Monster. I owe it all to him." I made a sweeping gesture with my hands, as if to say that explained everything.

She waited.

I thought harder, deeper, and forced myself to go to a place I wasn't so sure I wanted to go to.

"My father." I started crying again, softly this time, heartened by the revelation at hand. "My father is always calling people names." He called my mother names all the time when they were married.

"And do you want to carry that into your relationship with Paul?" She asked gently.

I shook my head, *No,* tears flowing freely.

"Then you need to be more aware in the future. Danielle, I may have never met Paul, but from everything you've told me, he seems as if he has some genuine love for you. I don't think he is abusive; I don't think he wants to be abusive to you. He may be a little narrow in his thinking, but you can't consider that a crime of the highest order. I think he's probably bewildered by now, wondering what really transpired between the two of you. Can you talk to him?" Constance suggested this in a voice that hinted that talking to Paul should be an easy thing.

"I guess I could," but I got scared again, immobilized by the thought of approaching him and admitting to my erratic behavior and begging forgiveness. "I don't want to have to go and beg forgiveness."

"I don't think you should have to do that. I think if you approach this in a civil tone, that the two of you can work past this and perhaps get somewhere. It's not about begging forgiveness. Maybe this situation will even open up a new line of conversation for the two of you. Do you think you can tell him why you did what you did that night?"

I was barely on the edge of understanding it myself. I wasn't sure. I shook my head. Too scared. Not ready. I didn't know.

"I'm not sure."

"Well, I think you can give it some time, and maybe gain some perspective from it, and then pick up the phone and call him when you're ready to talk. I believe he will listen to you." She reassured.

"I don't know." I may have been sitting still, but I was drowning in despair, the feeling of failure washing over me in monstrous waves. After all that I had done to get away from it…to distance myself…to prove how unlike them I really was at all…when the rubber hit the road, when all the chips were down, I was no better than the people who raised me, with all their faults and casualties. I shared this thought with Constance.

"But you are better, Danielle, because you are aware of it. You are sitting opposite me right now, trying to make some sense out of it all, and wanting to effect change in your own life. Can you say that about either one of your parents?" When Constance pointed this out, it sounded logical, and I wanted so badly to believe that I was one step ahead of the game.

"I can say that they are definitely not aware." I knew for sure that neither one of them knew of the burdens they had dropped at my doorstep.

"Then you're one step ahead of the game," Constance offered her most reassuring smile and urged me to call Paul and unburden myself to him.

I reluctantly agreed. My session over, I thanked, paid, and exited out onto Lexington Avenue. I meandered back to work whichever way the lights were going, and found myself feeling pretty low by the time I reentered the hole/office.

"Any better?" Lanie looked up at me hopefully.

"No." I shook my head, and tears started spilling at the same time. I flounced down onto my desk and let them spill.

"You're human, Yellie." Lanie stood beside me.

"I am one messed-up human," I hiccupped.

"Look, I'm not saying that what you did was right, or even that it should be dismissed in any way. You're going to have to deal with it. I just think that it is forgivable. If Paul really loves you, he will forgive you." Lanie put in.

"I just…I want…" my words trailed off and I tried to explain with my hands. I found a tissue, blew, and then tried all over again. "I know all that. What I don't know is how to explain myself to him."

"One step at a time." Lanie suggested.

"I'm not sure where to begin." I was so disappointed in myself.

"Start at the beginning?" Lanie looked up at the sound of her phone and then ignored it, deciding to let the call go to voicemail. "Look, Yellie, I know that you don't see this in yourself yet, but there are times when I can't get over how normal you actually are. You've had a tough life, and yet you still managed to draw up these very impossible standards for yourself; you moved, you made it on your own; you created a new life for yourself. That's not to say that you didn't take more than a couple of backward glances over your shoulder, but that is to say *look how far you've come.* So you had a little misstep. What are you going to do now, jump off the Brooklyn Bridge?" Lanie painted a rather funny picture without being intentional.

"I was wondering if you would drive me to it?" I pointed a wry grin in her direction and smiled through tears. I knew deep down that all she was saying was true.

I just didn't know how to get to the other side.

"No dice." Came Lanie's succinct reply.

"I'm embarrassed." I let the word out in a whisper and struggled to continue. "I guess I thought that if I could hide myself completely from Paul, that the old behaviors, the things that skulk around and permeate the halls of my memory would be buried, and that I wouldn't have to deal with them at all. That I would only have to deal with them on my own, not involving someone else, as if somehow I was convinced that I had fully separated myself from all that I took in. Now I feel as if I've been found out."

"I think it was naive of you to think that you would never have to share the tough part of your life with him. Correct me if I'm wrong, but don't you want to know everything there is to know about him?" Lanie asked.

"Of course I do."

"And would you love him any less if he told you he had been raised by wolves, and that perhaps he had picked up some of their wolf-y habits?"

"No." I shook my head in response. "I would deal with it."

"Then give yourself some more credit." Lanie smiled. "You really are worth all the trouble."

Chapter Sixty-Three

Paul didn't seem to think so. Days passed and my phone remained eerily silent. I ended up fudging with my mother and telling her that although I would love to have her down sometime soon, that Paul had an emergency meeting that he had to attend at work that Saturday, and I myself was suddenly coming down with something that she did not want to catch.

She bought it, as there was no reason not to, and I found myself completely alone on Saturday, huddled under a lapful of covers, trying to escape with a recent blockbuster from a writer whose work was currently off the charts.

It didn't help.

I was ashamed, I was steeped in embarrassment, and no matter how many pages fell to the left side of my bookmark, I found myself totally unaware of anything that was going on in the world outside my own. I couldn't concentrate. I kept playing and replaying the scene from the other night in my head, and no matter how I sliced it or diced it, I still couldn't believe that I had let loose with my hands and hit Paul. No matter how gently, no matter how much it may have meant next to nothing in the big scheme of things…as the excuses rolled around inside of my head, I knew that I was wrong, and my actions caused me to burn. I tried calling him several times. I would pick up the phone and dial his number, only to hang up before the connection went through, still unsure about how to approach it.

All I knew was that he wasn't calling me. I wondered where he was and I wondered what he was doing. I wondered if he told Rob about what had happened between us, or if he had just alluded to a fight that didn't include anything physical. I wondered further if Lanie had told Rob. Lanie had called earlier in the day, but she had a date with the Hello Kitty guy tonight, and although she was appropriately concerned about the fate of my relationship, she was also caught up in some elaborate pre-date prepping.

It was understandable. I mulled over the idea of sharing my dilemma with Am. Am had been with me on more than one occasion when a fight had broken out at the old homestead, or on the receiving end of me on her doorstep by the time the wrap-up occurred. I told myself that Am would understand; she had all the back-story and wouldn't need much by way of explanation.

I hesitated there too. What if the baby was crying and I couldn't get a word in edgewise? Was it right to assume that Jocelyn always needed her more than I did? Shouldn't I at the very least give her the opportunity to be a friend?

I was incapable of picking up the phone, however, and by midafternoon, my thoughts had once again given away to tears. What was I doing with my life? Had I just lost the only man I ever loved because I did something stupid and now couldn't or wouldn't own up to the fact that this reconciliation would have to come from me?

Did I really expect him to pick up the phone?

I wandered around the apartment aimlessly and tried to pray. My words came out muddled and in collusion with a bucket full of tears, and only once I had cried myself out, did I have any sense of peace or direction regarding whatever it is I had to do to get myself on the right path.

Chapter Sixty-Four

A week passed and although I started every time my work, home, or cell phone rang, I knew from the depths of my soul that the person on the other end would not be Paul.

Would never be Paul again.

I convinced myself that I was okay with that, but every so often I would start to cry, and for no apparent reason, I was eating more than three Sumo wrestlers should attempt to eat in the course of any given year. I was overly involved with the inhaling of a muffin at my desk that next Wednesday when I heard Lanie close the door to the hole/office and then come up behind me. She lifted the muffin top deftly out of my hand (mid-bite!) and then pulled her chair up close beside me.

"This is the last time we will have this conversation." She began with a sigh. "If for no other reason than I have just about given up on you."

"What conversation?" I narrowed my eyes, daring her to come into my space. It wasn't a pretty place to live lately.

"The conversation that is your life!" Lanie's voice got louder with each syllable. She glared at me and then, "Danielle, how long has it been since you spoke to Paul?"

"I left there last Wednesday night. After…the incident." I hung my head in shame and looked longingly at the muffin top that she had brazenly taken from me.

"The incident. I love it! As if what you did cited an International Incident! You act as if you plunged a knife into his mother's chest. Or better yet, that he had happened in on you in various stages of undress with a whole army of men. Yellie, you did something no one should be proud of. You reached out and took a swipe at a man that you love. You acted out of violence instead of love; you tried to communicate with your hands rather than your words. But…ENOUGH!" Lanie slammed her hand down on the desk as if to illustrate just how fed up with me she was. "I have had enough of you castigating yourself. It's over. Get over it and pick up the phone. Not that I think it's his turn to call you, but either way, you know what a stubborn bastard he can be and you know that he's not going to. That should be clear by now; each of you just let a week roll by without even the slightest hint of reconciliation. And I think it's ridiculous. You have too much going for you. You can't let something small like this trip you up and annihilate any chance that either one of you has to pursue a healthy relationship. Aren't you willing to fight for this? For him?" Lanie looked me square in the eye.

"I am so tired of fighting." I looked right back at her, my appetite gone, and my day shattered. "My whole life has been fighting. Fighting is what got me into this problem in the first place."

"Then call him and don't fight." Lanie prodded.

"And I'm even more scared of that. Look, don't you think I've given this a hell of a lot of thought this past week, Lanie?" I threw my hands up in the air. "Give me a break! I've done little else but think and rethink our relationship every minute since *the incident* in his apartment."

"So what are you going to do now? Are you just going to walk way, and let the whole thing fade? A love like that doesn't just fade." Lanie shook her head at my utter lack of perception.

"I don't know what else to do, Lanie! I mean, last Saturday, I thought about calling him all day. I thought about it, I cried about it, I prayed about it…and the only peace I found was when I decided that the best thing to do would be to just let the whole thing go. He deserves better than me. I am…a broken pot. Damaged goods. I thought I was so far removed from all the images that shuffle through my brain. I thought I was…*not violent.* I thought I could handle anything…that I was enlightened. Just like an alcoholic whose Daddy was an alcoholic, I told myself that

I would never go down that road. But I did it! And I'm smart enough to know that I just might do it again. Don't you realize, Lanie, that while I was hitting him, that I wasn't even aware that I was doing it? It snuck up on me in such a way that I now have reason to believe that it's part of who I am. No matter how much I try to shed the skin of someone who grew up on the wrong side of the tracks…it's still there, Lane, and I don't trust myself to ever fully get rid of it." I summed up with that thought, knowing full well that although it was the first time I had spoken that thought out loud, that it was the truth as I knew it.

"So you're just going to walk away without giving him a chance to know the motivation behind your actions? Without ever getting a chance to know the real you?" Lanie looked at me as if she had never seen me before. "You know, Yellie, I know everything there is to know about you and I still happen to love you anyway."

"You are not my lover." It was different. Couldn't she see the difference?

"But I am your very best friend. And if Paul is the one you want to spend the rest of your life with, then shouldn't he have that chance too?"

"A chance for what?"

"To be your friend, Yellie. A real friend doesn't run when the going gets rough. A real friend hangs around for every season."

"Do you think that we're not friends?" I believed that I had worked hard to cultivate the friendship side of my relationship with Paul.

"I think that you and Paul are friends, but I also believe that you have the potential to be much better friends. I think if you tried trusting him a little more that you would be surprised at just how much he could take."

"If you're wrong, I'll never forgive you." I wanted so badly to believe that, but fear kept me paralyzed and shame had its own way of keeping me in check.

"Tell me: what exactly do you have to lose right now anyway?" Lanie gave me a knowing glance.

"Not very much." I acquiesced.

"Plus, and I hate to mention this right now because I feel as if you're just becoming somewhat rational…" She paused a beat and then forged on anyway, "I think you owe him an apology, regardless of whether you feel as if you owe him an explanation or not."

"You're right. I definitely owe him an apology." I thought about exactly what words I could say.

Chapter Sixty-Five

After bandying about thirty-seven levels of anguish, I finally decided to do what Lanie said and reach out to Paul. She was right; he was never going to call me. He was too stubborn, and let's be honest…I was the one who needed to do the fixing here.

So Thursday came and went rather uneventfully. I worked all day, went to see Constance, and then attended my kickboxing class at the gym. I drove home from the train, checked the mail, food, and locks several times.

Then I decided that I needed a nice hot shower before I confronted the situation with Paul. I hopped into the shower and allowed vague thoughts of drowning to enter my mind. I thought about what I would say to him and failed to come up with anything that made an iota of sense.

After my shower, I wrapped my wet hair up in a towel and proceeded to make myself a hot cup of tea. While letting the tea steep, I gave myself a mini-pedicure, just touching up here and there, still unsure as to just what my approach should be. How could I tell the man that I loved that I was afraid he wouldn't love me if he really knew me? That my background would send him running for the hills? That I was afraid to lose him, so I hid in the shadows, and had done so for so long now that I didn't know how to step out into the harsh and glaring light? How could I explain away my behavior to someone else when I didn't quite understand it myself?

If I had buried all the ugly, how did it have the ability to reach through the grave and assault me?

I sighed and checked the clock on my kitchen wall. It was 9:43. I knew if I was going to call him tonight, that the time to call was now.

I took a deep breath and dialed.

One ring, two.

Good. Maybe he was out with Rob.

Perhaps he was out with another woman?

No, I told myself. Too fast. I drummed my fingertips on the table that held the phone, and practiced breathing as if I was a Lamaze enthusiast.

He picked up on the cusp of the fourth ring, breathing heavy into the phone.

"Hello?" His voice called to me, but it took me a second to respond. "Hello?"

"Hi, it's...Danielle." We had long since gotten to the point of saying *me,* but I felt the need to qualify, as if the past week had erased all recollection of my voice.

"I know who this is," and his voice sounded distant, not chastising or anything else, simply far, far away.

"Were you on the treadmill or moving heavy furniture?" I tried to score a point with humor, perhaps loosen him up a little.

"The treadmill." It was Paul, but Paul was usually not abrupt, so it didn't sound like him.

"Oh." He was not going to make it easy on me. "Well, I'm sure you're wondering why I called..." I cleared my throat. "I was wondering if we could talk."

There. I said it.

"What would you like to talk about, Danielle?" He sounded wearier than outright mean, but either way, his demeanor was fully disconcerting.

"I...well..." How exactly could I sum that one up? We both knew full well what I was calling to talk about. If this was any indicator of how the conversation would go, well maybe then I should just cut my losses and say goodbye right away. "I wanted to talk about the incident last week, and I was hoping to have the chance to apologize."

"Go ahead." His clipped answers were wearing on me already, and throwing me off to the point where I couldn't establish any sort of rhythm in my thoughts or speech.

"Well, I'm really sorry about the way I acted last week. I…" I fumbled for the right words, took a deep breath, and began again. "I got a little crazy and I just wanted to say that I was sorry."

"Apology accepted."

Wow, he was really being a hard-ass. I guess I hadn't known what to expect, although I wasn't so sure that I had expected this. Maybe it was over, well past over, and I had no right to expect anything more than this kind of treatment from him now. If that were the case, then I would determine to extricate myself and walk away quick. An image from that time long ago flashed promptly across my brain: I could remember walking in on David and then walking right back out again. There was no need to linger. It was over; it was plain.

Was Paul looking to cut his losses and walk away clean? Should I give him that on a platter, and not worry about picking up my own pieces until this conversation was finished? There was a silence between us but I could still hear him breathing on the other end of the phone.

My next reaction was completely out of fear.

"Well, I was wondering if I could stop by sometime this week and give you back your key, you know…pick up all my stuff." I was calling his bluff, so to speak, although the pounding in my heart would have told you otherwise.

"That'll be fine. Just let me know when is good for you and I'll be here." His reply was flippant at best; nasty at worst.

"Is tomorrow night good for you?" I threw it right back at him, determined to keep my voice level until we got off the phone.

"That's fine. I'll be here after six," and he said it as if he was making an appointment with the carpet cleaner.

"I'll see you then." I hung up the phone unwilling to believe what had just transpired between us. Was that it? You spend almost two years of your life with someone, only to find that one stiff breeze can blow down your entire house of cards?

    Was every relationship like that, or was it just the ones that I got involved in?

    Was there never a happy ending?

Chapter Sixty-Six

"You look like hell." This was Lanie's greeting the minute she walked in the door the next morning.

"That's great. I was hoping to win back my boyfriend tonight. Now you go ahead and tell me that I haven't got a shot in hell." My reply to her was biting, but if she knew me at all, she would know that even though I had my armor on, that I was just about two steps away from total collapse.

"I said you *look like hell.* So what happened?" Lanie came close and peered directly into my eyes.

I told her.

"So that's it. It's over. I just wasted almost two years of my life being with someone who I thought was 'The One,' *again, I might add*–for nothing. To have my past come back and slap me in the face." I laughed a maniacal laugh. "How's that for an analogy?"

"I just can't believe that. Ugh!" Lanie pantomimed pulling out her hair. "You two are impossible!"

"Uh-uh." I shook my head vigorously. "You cannot blame me this time, Lanie. I was playing off of him. I took his cues and ran with it."

"You're both stubborn. You and your stupid pride, this I-won't-let-him-hurt-me-or-see-how-much-I-hurt bullshit, and him covering up his real emotions just because he does not get it." Lanie laughed bitterly. "You know, this just proves you two are perfect for each other."

"Well, I really feel that it's too late now. I screwed up. He's unwilling to budge. It seems apparent to me that he doesn't want to hear my excuses, and the truth of the matter is that I don't think he even considered my apology." I pushed my emotions down and chose to abide in anger, feeling that was a safe, if not familiar, place to reside.

"I find that sad." Lanie stated in a voice so low I almost didn't hear her. "You both have baggage. *Everyone has baggage.* There's no real reason you can't work through it."

"I would tend to agree with you, and I would even promise you that I would try one last at-bat with this man, but he gave me no indication last night of wanting anything less than good-bye." I massaged my neck and tried to roll my shoulders back. I wanted to will the tension from my body, but I knew right now that no amount of willpower would get me through this feeling. I would just have to stay strong until I saw him tonight.

As if reading my mind, Lanie asked, "When do you see him?"

"He said to stop by after six," I looked at my watch and saw that it read ten o'clock. "Only eight more hours to the guillotine."

"Do you want me to stick around?" Lanie offered.

"No, I'll be okay. Besides, I think I've really got to do this on my own." I pushed together whatever resolve I had left in me and decided to try and concentrate on my day. The same way I had gotten through countless incidents at home on my own, I would get through this with my nerves of steel, and I promised myself I would not cry in front of him.

5:56 pm.

I took a deep breath and tried to fix my face as best I could. Lanie was right, though…I really did look like hell. I had bags under my eyes enough to open up my own luggage store, and even as I tried to affix those eyes with a fresh coat of mascara, I found my hand trembling so much that I got black on the bridge of my nose.

I gave up then. I mean, the whole thought of putting on mascara was just a hair shy of ridiculous anyway, because even if I could manage to walk out of his door with my dignity intact, I knew full well that my tears would begin to flow the minute my feet hit the pavement. Hence the prepping slowed down to a halt and the hand wringing began.

"Will you call me right after?" Lanie pressed as she glanced over her shoulder at what I'm sure was a sight to behold.

"Yes," I nodded my head and bit down hard on my lower lip as tears threatened to flow once again. I don't know why, but I was much worse now, knowing that I was about to see him…worse than I had been the entire week, jumping every time the phone rang.

Lanie came over to me and enveloped me in a warm hug. "You'll be okay."

"I know." I nodded again, unsure on the inside, but sure in another way that could not be defined. I had gone through so much worse; surely a break-up of this magnitude would be tough, but I vowed it wouldn't break me.

"Call me," she ordered again as she made her way out the door.

"I will." I promised. I stood there for a moment, alone in the hole/office, and uttered a convoluted prayer. *Please, God, let it all work out right; whatever form right takes. I need you now. Please help me out here.*

I checked my watch and saw the time was 6:24. He should be home by now.

It was Do or Die time.

I made my way over to his apartment slowly, stopping at each light and taking a deep breath each time. No jaywalking tonight. I could do this; I knew I could. I just needed to put one foot in front of the other and know that it would all work out in the end.

I'm working on it.

Sooner than I was ready for, I was at the foot of his doorstep, and I knocked on the door tentatively in lieu of using my key.

The door opened and for the first time in a long time, he seemed larger than life.

"Hi." He seemed tentative too, as he swung the door open and motioned for me to come in.

"Hi." I bit back another round of tears that threatened to push its way to the top, and looked him over from head to toe. He was so beautiful, and even in this rather uncomfortable circumstance, I felt attracted to him the same way I had the first day I saw him crossing Lexington Avenue.

"I…ah, I just got in." He gave me a sheepish grin and I saw color rise in his cheeks. It seemed as if he didn't know what to do with his hands.

"I know. I don't want to waste your time, so…" I held out the hand that cradled his key, my eyes willing him to reach out and take it, as my heart splintered into a million or more tiny little pieces. However had we gotten to this god-awful place?

"Okay. That's it, I guess?" He made no move to take the key from me as a thousand emotions flashed across his face in an instant, but then he settled on angry and I knew that there had to be something more.

"I guess so." My eyes studied his intently, unwilling to let go completely and walk out the door, my heart believing that I had no right to try and ask for more.

"Fine." He took the key out of my hand then and slapped it on top of his breakfast counter. He stared me down.

I stood completely still, turned on my heel, and proceeded to walk out his door for the very last time.

"Danielle, don't you want to know why I didn't call you all week?" His voice sliced through the silence just as my hand came to rest on his front doorknob.

"I know why." At least, I thought I did. I turned around again and faced him.

"No, you only *think* you know why." His voice came across as condescending and the look on his face offered little else.

"Well, why don't you tell me then, Paul?" I gave it right back to him, as much as I could anyway, curiosity winning out over the soap-opera exit.

"I didn't call you not because of what transpired between us per se, but I did not call you simply because you didn't give us a chance to work it out together. I am so tired of banging down your door, only to find nobody home–all the time. Whatever prompted the fight, your behavior…I'll never know, because you don't trust me enough to let me in." He took a deep breath and held my eyes in his intent gaze. "I will always love you, Danielle, but I cannot and *I will not* stand idly beside you, unable to reach *inside you* and get to the you I know is in there. I can't make you believe in a kind of love that can move mountains. This past week has enabled me to do a lot of thinking, and I know now that you will never trust me enough to tell me all the bad things that happened to make you act the way you do. I can't force it out of you and I just got done trying."

"So your not calling had nothing to do with my slapping you?" I needed to clarify, but I sounded like a sarcastic wench, even to my own ears.

"The way I see it: your hitting me was just a symptom of a bigger problem. And you're not about to tell me what that problem is." He wrung his hands out and then waved them in the air in sheer frustration. "I can forgive you hitting me. I can't forgive your hiding."

There is a moment in every person's life: you are standing on the precipice of something, and you need desperately to jump off and make that one decision that will change things forever.

This was my moment.

I chose to jump.

"You're right." I slumped against his couch and the tears came unbidden, taking over in a fashion that I was at a loss to conceal. I couldn't believe the way I was crying and carrying on, which was exactly what I told myself I would not do. "I'm sorry. I need you to forgive me." I took a deep breath and swiped at my tears. "I'm...done hiding."

He came towards me then and wrapped me in his arms, holding me closer than he had ever held me before. After a minute or so of getting mascara all over his sweater, I felt his arms around me begin to shake and when I looked up into his eyes, I saw that he was crying too. Fat silent tears rolled down his cheeks and he took pains to swallow as our eyes locked.

"I'm not going to make this easy on you," he warned me with a voice that belied so many different emotions that he couldn't manage to sound either mean of threatening.

"You shouldn't." I was still crying while holding his gaze. I took a deep breath and admitted, "I haven't made it easy on you."

"Why don't we go sit down?" He motioned towards the couch and I dropped my bag right where I stood and followed close behind. Once we both settled on to the couch, I picked a place on the wall behind him, focused in, and told him the story of my life.

I told him everything. No matter how big or ugly something was, regardless of how incidental something might have seemed, I let it all spill out in a rush of words that had been contained for far too long. Occasionally, I would look right at him, but eventually I would settle back to looking past him, recalling the memories and digging back to a place of pain. I told him about the father I still felt disconnected from, ever since the day he divorced us...the mother I mourned for...The Monster...the mother I had left to deal with today...the angst...the nightmares...the trust issues...the scathing memories of abuse...the longing to be a part of a whole...the inability to hide myself completely...the desire to stop hiding and move forward, into another kind of life with him. Time was of no consequence as I unloaded everything that came to mind.

Paul proved to be a sympathetic listener. Every so often, he would interrupt to ask a question or share a thought, but he mostly provided a rapt audience with whom I could feel safe sharing. There was that word again: *safe*. I let it roll over me and cushion me, instead of intimidating me the way it usually did.

He got up at one point to get a box of tissues.

"Is this the reason I've never met either one of your parents?" He asked without malice.

I nodded yes. "I hate to admit that I've been ashamed, but...the truth? I've quite possibly been ashamed. Have you ever been Upstate?"

"I've been as far upstate as Westchester County." Paul replied.

"Westchester County...isn't reality." I tried to be fair as I explained the landscape of the little town I came from, but the only way I could see it now was through the eyes of one who had gotten burned and ran away. "I hate it up there."

"I could see why." Paul reached out for my hand then and gave it a little squeeze. "I just don't understand why you hesitated...why you were unable to share this with me for such a long time." He shook his head, searching for clarity that I wasn't sure I could provide.

"Because I am...damaged goods." It hurt to say it, but I believed it to be true on some level, and it was even harder to try and extrapolate that feeling.

"Why do you think that?" Paul's look was incredulous, his sadness palpable.

"I don't know." I started crying again, a torrent of ragged tears that could not be controlled. "I can't remember the last time I didn't walk around with that feeling inside my heart." I choked out the sentence, but once again in the telling, I felt a spark of freedom rise up inside my chest and take hold of my insides. A swell of emotions rose up in my heart. Oh, for how long had these words longed to be uttered? To what end?

"You are so…not…" Paul paused a minute and swallowed hard. "Danielle, I have something to confess. I think–no–I *know* that a large part of the reason that I fell in love with you was because you were so refreshingly unaware of how special you are; I had been through Aimee and people like her, and they were always so busy telling me how fabulous they were that it grew absolutely tiring. You are special. You are not broken, or damaged, and even if you are a little bit bruised…it doesn't really matter to me. I just want you to be honest and be faithful and the rest doesn't matter at all. Do you hear me?"

"I hear you, but I can assure you of the one thing I know for sure: my heart doesn't readily accept words spoken in the moment, or speeches and declarations of love brought on by a tidal wave of emotion. My whole life has been a string of broken promises up until I met you, and now…" I was at a momentary loss for words. "Now I'm scared."

"Does it help at all to know that I'm scared too?" Paul tried.

"It does and it doesn't. And believe me, it's not as if I am just dismissing all of the words you said. I'm not." I sniffled hard and then grabbed another tissue. "I've been in therapy for almost three years now; trying like hell to sort it all out on my own. I'm so sorry."

"I know you are." He looked down to the couch and then back up to meet my eyes again.

"I can't seem to say I'm sorry enough. I know you may not believe this, but when I reached out and slapped you that night, I didn't even realize I was doing it at first. It was only when I realized what I did that I knew I had to get away from here." I felt shamed all over again, rehashing it in all its vivid Technicolor here on the couch, but I knew now that it had to be dealt with.

"I believe you, Danielle, and I don't see it in you to act that way all by yourself. I believe you have a gentle spirit and I know that you're sincere in what it is you're telling me now. But the solution is not to simply run and hide. You can't do that. You can't expect me to not run away when the going gets rough, but then deem it perfectly acceptable for you to do that very thing. We can work through this, but I need you to work with me. I can't do it alone." Paul raked his hands through his already tousled hair.

"I would never ask you to." I waited a moment and breathed in the silence that had turned from being fraught with emotion to a state I could almost call comfortable.

"I need to know…is there…anything else?" Paul steadied his gaze and his eyes searched my own.

"No. I've told you everything. And although I still feel a little stupid in the telling, well…I still feel the need to ask you not to judge me. I need you to be patient." I felt it was a lot to ask, even in the asking, but I knew that whatever relationship problems I had hadn't surfaced overnight and wouldn't be done away with that easily either.

"What if I told you," and now he bent towards me and lifted one hand up to play with a lock of hair that had fallen in my face, "that I want to work things out? That I have no intention of leaving, or judging, and that my only desire is to love you for all time? What if I told you that there is nothing you can do to make me change my mind? Nothing–short of running away and blocking me out again–nothing on this Earth that could conspire to tear us apart?" His eyes searched my own, willing me to believe.

"I would tell you," and I could barely finish, what from the tears that were once again flowing freely down my face, "that I love you. That I am amazed by your capacity to love me. That whenever I am around you, I sometimes get scared of being found out, and knowing that, if you knew the real me…" I waved away the rest of the sentence.

"Danielle, will you marry me?"

I stared at him, wide-eyed, unsure as to whether I had heard him correctly or simply dreamed those words into existence.

For a long moment, neither one of us said a word.

"I...are you sure?" I found a voice, but it sounded rather unlike my own. Everything seemed surreal; the fight, this conversation, the words that I had longed to hear...being uttered now, with little to no pretense...unexpectedly, the same way we had met, suddenly...just like the way we had fallen in love.

"Of course I'm sure." He shared a small portion of his usual grin. "It's the only way I can think of to make you understand that I love you unconditionally. That I am never going to leave."

The words *never going to leave* permeated my heart and closed a wound that had been open too long now, a tear in my soul that seemed as if it had always been there.

"I love you, Paul." I was engulfed by yet another round of tears, unable to get a grasp on the sudden turn of events, but knowing in my heart that nothing could be more right than the way things stood right now. He took me in his arms and I stayed there awhile, crying softly and clutching on to the man who loved me more than I had ever been loved before.

"Can I take that as a yes?" He was crying again too, and soon enough, our tears turned to laughter, and eventually we fell away from our embrace.

"Yes." I confirmed for him once we broke apart. As if there ever could have been another answer for me. Never in a million years could I have predicted the way the night had gone.

"Then let me do this right." He jumped up from the couch and was gone in an instant, only to return a minute later with a tiny velvet box in his hand. He got down on one knee in front of me and proceeded to formally propose.

I didn't think I had any tears left, but when he took my hand in his and asked me to be his wife, I couldn't answer for what seemed like forever, as a fresh round of tears rose up inside of me and took control over my tongue.

"Yes," I eked it out and we embraced again, this time sealing our fate with a promise to last forever.

"I love you, Danielle, and I always will," Paul declared his love for me as I gaped at the diamond glittering on my left hand. I had never owned anything so nice in my entire life.

"I love you more," I protested. The truth was that I fully believed it. I would always love him more; because he came along and found me, and decided that I was worth the love I had been missing all this time.

"I don't know if that's possible." He countered my statement with a tender kiss on my forehead, and another quick squeeze.

I stared again at my ring and then looked up and directly into his eyes.

"I guess this means that you'll have to meet my parents."

His response to me was an airborne golf pillow chucked in my direction and a fantastic eye roll.

Chapter Sixty-Seven

"Let me see!" Lanie barged into the hole/office, almost tearing the pathetic little door right off its hinge. She trotted three steps in my direction and made a sound that was something akin to, Ooh-Ooh-ooh...OH!

"Lane, are you alright?" I was swimming in happiness, stunned by the outcome; standing on legs that I prayed wouldn't give out before the day was through. After our talk and his proposal, I had only managed to get about three hours of sleep total.

"You really look like hell today," Lanie observed as she swept me into her arms and hugged me so hard I thought my insides might fall out.

"Thanks, Lane." I pretended to kick her in the shins and then stood apart from her, extending my hand so we could both have a better look.

"It's beautiful," Lanie surveyed the ring and then filled me in a little bit about it, knowing full well that I wouldn't know a real diamond from a cubic zirconium.

"Is it big?" I thought it was enormous, especially for my petite hand size, but I really didn't care about the dynamics of the ring, and I was just asking for the sport of it.

"It's a little over two carats." Lanie held it up to the light. "It is truly brilliant, Yellie, he did a great job."

"I know." I whispered this almost to myself as my chest puffed out with pride. I had never had it this good: the ring, Paul, my life...I stood in awe of all that was going on around me, and when the fear came and insisted that one day...*all good things must come to an end*...I tucked it away and shushed the voice that made me stop and question whatever good fortune came my way.

Not this time.

Come hell or high water, this time would be different. I suddenly felt my life expanding rather than contracting, and it was a good feeling.

"So what have you two decided to do about…the other issue?" Lanie tried for tactful.

"Believe it or not, I am taking him with me on Thursday to see Constance. He's taking a half-day and coming up here; we'll go together and then I will come back to work as usual. He said that he can catch up on paperwork at home, and then I intend to meet him after." I was proud of the plan we had come up with and wanted somebody else to be proud of me too.

"Very nice." Lanie acknowledged. "Look, I know you know this, but I'm going to say it anyway: all this would mean nothing," she gestured towards the ring, "and I mean, *Na-da,* if you don't take care of all your other crap."

"I know, Lane." I laughed out loud and looked her way. "Lanie, I have no intention of moving into a new house and taking all of my old shit with me–if that's your concern."

"Good! At least you learned *something* throughout all this!" She joined me in easy laughter and I knew for sure right then that it was going to be a fabulous day.

Chapter Sixty-Eight

"Well, we have to go out there by next weekend, or I am afraid that they will spontaneously combust," Paul warned in a jovial tone. "They already saw the ring...I don't know what all the commotion is about." He shook his head.

"Perhaps all the commotion is about me?" I suggested plainly. Paul just didn't understand; his family, and his mother in particular, would now feel an intense need to fawn over the likes of me, due entirely to the recent turn of events.

"Aaah...!" Paul threw his hands up in the air, Italian-style.

"Are you regretting this?" I waved my finger in his face, but there was no energy behind my words, unless you counted the sheer delight that I felt at seeing him flummoxed.

"Never." His one word had a ton of energy behind it, and when he swept me up into his arms, I knew for sure that he meant it, and that I was finally in the very place that I had always–so desperately–wanted to be.

"Paul," I drew away from him after a minute or two, "How are you feeling about what Constance said?"

I was referring to the meeting we had with her the day before, the one in which it took me a full fifteen minutes plus a watershed of tears to settle in and perhaps begin making sense at all. At first, it seemed incredibly strange to find Paul in the same room with me during my Thursday afternoon pow-wow with Constance, but eventually I adapted, and by the end of our session, I felt as if we had made some headway. I felt validated by the fact that she admonished Paul to be patient; she went on to reiterate that he could not, and would not, ever be able to fully understand the exact nature of the things I had gone through in my formative years and beyond. He asked her some very insightful questions, and although I let him have the floor for the majority of the time, I never felt overlooked, or somehow as if I were eavesdropping on someone else's conversation. By the time we left, she congratulated us on our engagement, and made an appointment at a different time to see us the following week.

"I feel good. I liked her," He was nodding as he settled onto the couch with a pillow under his arm.

"Is that all?" I was hoping for something more, a shining moment or feeling of clarity that he received from the experience. I rearranged my pillow so that I was facing him directly and sat down next to the arm.

"Should there be more?" He looked perplexed for an instant, as if I were quizzing him on the fly. "Look, I think it's great that we're doing this for us, for our relationship. I'm glad you feel safe talking around her. I'll be honest—I wish it could have come about without either one of us having to take that road. There's a part of me that wishes we could just deal with all of our issues on our own, but…I know that's not realistic. So it's fine."

Fine? I thought that to be a strange way of describing things. I was expecting something more, even as the thought occurred to me that maybe I was expecting too much. But what did he mean by 'that road?'

"Paul, what did you mean by 'that road?'" I had to ask.

"You know, the whole family therapy route, or…what should we call it? It's not marital counseling, at least not yet." He looked to me for an answer.

"Couples counseling." I offered.

"Exactly. So…let me put it to you this way: no guy likes to go to couple's counseling." He had a sheepish grin on his face, blushing as soon as his admission hit the air.

"So what do you suggest we do?" I could feel myself getting defensive, and I warned myself not to go there. At least not yet.

"I suggest we keep going. Why should my opinion change? I'm sure we're both whacked out in certain areas. My only point was that I would liken it to going to the dentist."

The dentist?

"Go ahead, " I urged, and then shifted on the couch. I could barely wait to hear this.

"Danielle, nobody likes going to the dentist. Okay? All right. I can see you're with me so far. But you've got to go to the dentist in order to have nice teeth. Same principle applies here. Can you think of one guy that you know that would thrill at the idea of going and sitting in a therapist's office with his girlfriend or wife or whoever and talking about how they got to be the way they are? No! Any guy I know would rather have a tooth extracted." As Paul wound up with this thought, I could see a self-satisfied grin slowly replacing the rose in his cheeks.

"You've got to be kidding me! You are such an old-fashioned Italian!" I jumped off the couch we were sharing and flounced onto the adjacent love seat.

"Ah-hah, but now I am *your* old-fashioned Italian!" He followed me to where I was sitting and boxed me in on the smaller couch. "Where are you going, my pretty?"

"Away from the old-fashioned, self-righteous Italian." I looked to the wall.

He touched my chin with his finger and gently swiveled me around.

"Didn't we just talk about honesty?" He proposed this by way of excuse for his narrow-minded ideology.

"We did. But do you think you can be a little more sensitive and perhaps a little less brutal right now? That was just our first session. So much has happened in the past couple of weeks, I guess I was hoping you would be a little more excited about us and a little less critical of your…dentist appointments." I gave him a look that was intended to make him feel guilt, but instead he leaned over and began kissing me, unabashedly, content to ignore his remarks, my reaction, and whatever else was going on at the same time. I melted in to him and stayed there, until he eventually climbed up onto the couch, where I found a way to make room for two.

Chapter Sixty-Nine

"So what are you going to do?" Lanie gave me a sideways glance as she kicked her treadmill up a notch.

"About what?" I had just run out of the kickboxing class with her, and was busy adjusting the controls on my treadmill.

"About the whole meet the parents thing," Lanie rolled her eyes and then gestured towards me, expecting what for an answer I did not know.

"I guess I will have to take him Upstate in the very near future," I'm sure I sounded as if I were pronouncing a death sentence, but however fixated Lanie was on this particular topic, I had it all over her. I kept putting it off and making excuses, yet I knew the day was not too far off in the distance, where I would have to ante up and just go.

"I can't believe you didn't even tell them yet." Lanie shook her head as she escalated from a fast walk to a slow jog.

"I can't believe it either." I confessed. It had been almost two weeks since Paul proposed and I accepted, but I had not had any inclination thus far to call either Mom or Dad and share the news. What was I afraid of…judgment? Rejection? Both? Why did I even care?

"What are you afraid of?" As always, Lanie dove right into the farthest recesses of my brain.

"I don't know." I hesitated. "I'm not scared. At least, I don't think I'm scared. Maybe I'm holding it close to me because I'm afraid that they might step in somehow and ruin it. I just know that I can't tell my mother over the phone, and since my father found out about the existence of Paul rather recently…well, I guess I was hoping to tell him in person also."

"But you told Am over the phone." Lanie pointed out.

"That's different. I couldn't wait to tell Am. Hell, Am's already got Jocelyn all but dressed up as a flower girl, and the child can't even walk yet. Plus, she keeps making noises about me finding a dress." I gave Lanie a look that said *You know Am.*

"Do you even know what you want to do yet?" Lanie was referring to my last brilliant idea: running away to a Caribbean island and telling everybody about it after the fact.

"No." I fixed my ponytail and made the elastic band tighter as I walked. "I really have no clue. What about you? Enough about me…what do you think of me?"

Lanie and I shared a smile. It was a favorite line of ours from *Beaches,* and we made a sport out of working it into conversation whenever we could.

"I think you still need a lot of work." Lanie laughed out loud and then took the treadmill back down. "I've got to be a crazy person to try and run after that class. Murder! Look, what can I tell you? Adam is a freak…he likes Hello Kitty…he's got a weird predilection for unsalted pretzels and show tunes, but besides that, I am positively smitten. If that's what you're asking. "

Hmmm.

"Lanie, did it ever occur to you that perhaps…"

"Adam is gay?" She finished for me. "I think about that every minute of every day."

"And?"

"I called Jude."

Lanie gestured and was just about to contiunue when her cell phone rang. She picked it up from the display area of her treadmill, and a second later; I saw her hop off, a foot to each side, the belt still running beneath her.

Tears popped out of her eyes and began instantly streaming down her face.

"Lanie, what the hell's the matter?" I stopped my treadmill abruptly, hopped off instantly, and practically jumped on to hers.

"Alright. Yes. I'll be there. I'm leaving the gym right now. I'll be out there as soon as I can…thanks, Marissa. Yes. Yes. Tell him I said to hang on, dammit. I don't care if he can hear or not…I'll be right there." She disconnected and looked at me.

"What, Lanie? Tell me what happened." I insisted.

"My father just had a heart attack."

Chapter Seventy

We ran into the locker room from there, Lanie calculating the fastest way to get out to Long Island amidst a bevy of tears and I trying Paul on my cell as we ripped off our gym clothes and shrugged on our street clothes. There was no time to stretch or shower, and by the time we made it from the locker room out to the lobby of the gym, I had Paul running over to Avis to rent a car and Lanie and I were on our way to meet him.

"You're sure he doesn't mind…?" Lanie hiccupped, fear etched in her features, her face awash in tears, her voice much higher than its usual tone.

"Of course not! What the hell else are you going to do, Lanie, wait for the next Long Island Railroad train to get you to…where? And then grab a taxi? Uh-uh. Friendship doesn't work that way." I shook my head as we crossed Lexington Avenue and made our way over to Third. There was an Avis not far from Paul's place, and I had told him to rent whatever they had available and that we would meet him there.

"I could have gotten a limo." Lanie replied, but her words trailed off at the end, and if the moment wasn't so tragic, I might have laughed, because the disparity in our respective backgrounds came alive at times like this. I would have never even have thought to hire a limo.

"You need friends right now," I assured her, and then motioned towards the sign. "We can go." I ushered her across Third.

We ran up to the neon red and white sign indicating Avis and found Paul already strapped in to the driver's seat, ready to pull out of the small parking garage attached to the building. He had the windows rolled down and yelled as soon as he saw us approach.

"Ladies! Over here!" He gestured from the front seat of a Chevy Lumina.

"Thanks, baby." We shared a concerned look and then I held open the front door for Lanie, indicating that she should sit in the front seat.

"No, I think I'm better off in the back." She climbed in back and after I hustled into the front seat, we were off and pointed towards the land they both hailed from.

Lanie and Paul exchanged notes about the fastest way to get out to the hospital that Lanie's Dad was in, and once that was settled, Lanie started crying again. I took off my seat belt and rearranged myself so that I could reach through the seats and hold her hand.

"What else did Marissa say?" I asked gently, trying to get as much information out of her as I could, because what I had received so far was muddy and unclear.

"She said…" Lanie sniffed hard and then dropped my hand in order to shuffle through her bag and look for a tissue, coming up with a pocket pack a few seconds later. "That she was wrapping up her day and she buzzed him to see if there was anything else he needed. He didn't reply to her buzz, and after a few minutes, she decided to pop her head in and just see what he was up to–wrap up the end of their day–and when she went in to see him, she found him face-down on his desk, and then she said that when she felt for a pulse, he still had one, thready, I think she said…so she called 9-1-1, and then me…he's unconscious now, but they think he's got a good chance…I don't know…" and once again the tears came, so I reached for her hand again and squeezed it, not knowing what else to do.

I looked at Paul, driving silently, seemingly paying attention to the road in front of him.

"And Marissa is his assistant?" Paul asked and then looked to me for an answer.

"Yes." I nodded, looking to Lanie for clarification.

"He's at the hospital with his assistant." Lanie laughed at the absurdity that picture presented. "I wonder if he's still taking calls?" She laughed again, bitterly, but then the laugh collapsed into tears and I stood there feeling as helpless as anyone could possibly feel.

"How much longer?" I turned to Paul and asked in my helplessness, believing that if I had more information that somehow I would be in better control.

"Maybe twenty minutes." He tuned the radio to an all-news station. "Depends on this traffic."

"Lanie, don't...try not to worry. Men his age, with his responsibilities...heart attacks are almost common at this point..." I was babbling, knowing inside what I really wanted to say, but unable to articulate it.

"I'm not ready to lose him yet. I can't...there would be far too much left unsaid. We just started trying to be father and daughter again." Lanie's voice came from a faraway place, but her words reached out and grabbed me, and my heart ached for the little girl lost inside that very simple plea.

She was right; it was too soon by anyone's standards. It was bad enough that she didn't have her mother anymore. She needed him, and whether he was aware of it or not, he needed her. I began to pray silently as Paul honked his horn and the man on the radio garbled on.

Once we arrived at the hospital, things started moving really fast. Lanie ran in ahead of us and we almost lost sight of her, only to find her huddled with whom I assumed was Marissa and her father's doctor a minute after. We stood back from the circle, wanting to give her space, waiting to hear the prognosis from Lanie.

"I'll be right back," she said to us and then trailed off with Marissa and the doctor.

Paul and I exchanged a look and then turned to find a place to sit in the waiting room behind us. I hadn't been in a hospital in quite some time, and I was surprised to see the muted décor and the small television sets, also muted, tuned to CNN. There was a homey feel to the space, and even though it was still unmistakably a hospital waiting room, I felt myself begin to calm as I settled onto a nearby couch.

"You okay?" Paul looked over from the chair beside me and offered a sweet smile.

I nodded. "I'm just worried about Lanie." I tried to put myself in her shoes and I couldn't even fathom it. I could empathize with her plight; I wasn't ready to lose my father either, regardless of whatever distance stood between us. I had readily convinced myself that there would always be time to sort out whatever miscommunication had brought us to the place our relationship now sat in.

I found myself suddenly convinced of just how foolish that was. I saw life as a precarious thing; and as I weighed in my hands both the push and pull of time, I fell silent in thought and reverted once again to prayer. I prayed that Lanie and her Dad would have another chance; I prayed also that I would take the entire situation as a lesson learned in my own life, and not ignore the budding regret in my heart.

Soon Lanie came back to join us. The woman I assumed to be Marissa followed.

"I saw him." She smiled at me through tears. "He looks...well, he's out like a light, but the doctor seems to think there's no real reason that he won't wake up soon."

"You father will be fine," Marissa agreed and then nodded as punctuation.

"I assume you're Marissa?" I offered my hand out to her and shook. I was just about to introduce Paul, when Lanie broke in and apologized for not doing so herself.

"Stop it Lanie," I admonished. "You're not supposed to have manners at a time like this."

She managed to squeak out a smile.

"What on Earth would I do without you?" She was just about to fling herself into my arms, full-speed ahead, when she stopped and glared gratefully in Paul's direction. "You too. Come here, both of you." Then she threw herself at both of us, and we enclosed her in a hug that was tighter than Super-Glue.

I squeezed Lanie hard and then motioned over my shoulder for Marissa to join the pack. She came in cautiously, but her hands felt warm, and her smile was so tentative but nice that I decided right then that I very much liked her.

Finally, we broke apart, and Lanie addressed Marissa.

"Marissa," Lanie took a deep breath before continuing, "Thanks so much for calling me like you did. Please feel free to leave; my friends are going to stay with me. You don't have to stay all night." Lanie gestured towards the two of us and we nodded our heads silently.

"Lanie, if you don't mind…" Marissa's voice trailed off and she proceeded to get all choked up right in front of us. "I'd like to stay."

"No, of course I don't mind. Not at all! I just didn't want you to feel as if you were obligated to stay." Lanie smiled again and then reached out and touched her hand.

"Should I call someone?" I offered in a tone that was meant to interrupt their moment, as I was picking up on a vibe that, if called correctly, I wasn't so sure Lanie would be able to handle just then.

"Oh, would you call Jude for me?" Lanie looked gratefully in my direction. "He's not that far from here and he would want to know."

"Gladly." I grabbed her cell phone and scrolled through her programmed numbers searching for Jude. Once I found him, I told Lanie I was going to pop outside real quick and give him a buzz. I motioned for Paul to join me.

Paul followed me into the corridor and then outside the automatic doors. We stood under a bright purple awning with the hospital's name on it as I waited for Jude to pick up. Paul pointed to an ashtray filled with sand.

"Somehow that seems utterly ridiculous outside the entrance to the Emergency Room." Paul observed.

"Do you know how many doctors smoke?" I countered, although incredulous that anyone even smoked at all anymore, I knew full well that the medical community was guilty for puffing away in spite of their knowledge.

"I thought only the cancer doctors still smoked; you know, the guys who specialize with the lungs." This was Paul's attempt at nervous humor.

I gave him a thumbs-down sign as someone picked up the phone.

"Tough crowd," Paul mumbled.

"Hello, may I please speak to Jude?" I felt a tinge of nervousness, realizing in that instant that I was about to be the bearer of bad news.

"This is Jude." Jude replied. He had a smoky voice that was inherently asexual in tone, and I almost choked back a laugh, because Lanie's impersonations had apparently been spot-on.

"Hi, Jude, this is Danielle, Lanie's friend from wor–"

"Oh please, honey, I *know* who you are." He tsk-tsked me for a nanosecond and then shifted to instant panic. "Danielle! Is Lanie alright?"

"She's okay. She's fine. I…I'm calling you because Lanie's father had a heart attack tonight, and well, he's fine too–at least, we believe he'll be fine, Lanie just wanted me to call you and let you know that we're out here at the hospital. She thought you'd want to know." I let my words tumble out at break-neck speed, not wanting to panic Jude any more than he already was.

"Oh Dear God!" Jude seemed to let out a big breath and then he continued. "Okay, I will be there in no more than eight minutes. Please tell her I'm on my way."

"You go it." I hung up then and shook my head. "I guess I will be meeting Jude sooner rather than later."

"What about Rob?" Paul offered.

I stifled a laugh, as that joke was strictly between Lanie and me. "I think you should buzz him too."

Paul took a minute to call Rob as I continued to contemplate the ashtray outside the Emergency room doors. What were people thinking?

I heard Paul click off, and just as he suggested we head back in, I gave him a sign that indicated I wanted him to come closer.

"Do you think there's anything going on between Lanie's Dad and Marissa?" I whispered this as if there were spies in the lobby.

"Whatever gave you that impression?" Paul looked at me as if I had antennae growing out of my head.

I shrugged. "Just something I picked up on…a girlie thing."

"Like a sixth sense?"

"Yeah." I nodded. "Something I think Lanie would also have picked up on, were she not entirely distraught."

"Does it matter?" Paul was as perplexed as any man would be.

"It might." I waved my hand in front of me, as if to wave away any such incrimations. "We should really go back in. Is Rob coming out?"

"What do you think?" Paul looked at me as if I should know better.

"I think he is." I gestured towards the door. "After you."

"Oh, no, here: let me get that." Paul waved his hands in front of us and the automatic door slid right open.

"You are a Prince." I smirked.

"You're catching on." He threw a ridiculous grin my way and grabbed my hand as we made our way back to where Lanie was seated. Marissa was still sitting on Lanie's left, trying to fix whatever makeup was left on her face with a crumpled tissue and a mirror that had seen better days.

"Did you get Jude?" Lanie asked as soon as she spotted us.

"Yes. He said he'd be here in no more than eight minutes." I relayed.

"Other people say five, or ten even…but Jude; well, he's Jude. You'll see what I mean." Lanie allowed a fraction of a smile to inch across her face.

"In less than eight minutes," Paul quipped, and fortunately, that sad attempt at nervous humor broke through the proverbial ice. We all laughed, and although it might have crossed all of our minds to feel guilty about laughing, we didn't.

The next thing we knew, Jude entered the waiting area with a flourish. I knew who he was even before Lanie introduced us.

"La-la-la-Lanie!" He trilled and then proceeded to dance around her in a sloppy circle. "Come here, give me some sugar."

Lanie rose to greet her dear old friend, who, contrary to the image I had conjured was surprisingly handsome in a Robert Downey Jr. (minus the drugs) sort of way. In addition to all I already had filed away about Jude, I found myself deciding that I liked him immensely, just by the way he held Lanie close. Gay–not gay–it didn't matter. He was protective of her and he obviously cared a great deal about her; his desire to protect her rather obvious, his hug deep and prolonged.

Paul and I sat silently nearby while Marissa kept wringing the same tissue she was using earlier to try and fix her face.

Eventually, Jude gave up his grasp on Lanie, and Lanie turned around and introduced him to each of us in turn. When I extended my hand towards him in greeting, he passed it up and simply pressed me into a smaller version of the same hug he had just given Lanie.

"You're just what I pictured!" Jude appraised me openly, while I stood by and offered out my friendliest smile.

"And you're not." I blushed a little, but he seemed to love my candor, and somehow we all became fast friends in the midst of chaos.

Lanie introduced Jude and Marissa next, and then Paul offered to go get us all a round of coffee.

"Hope it's not sludge; I bought Bailey's." Jude indicated a bag that was shoved deep into the inside of his jacket. I could see the bottle's seal peeking out through the top of the paper bag, and I found myself surprised that I hadn't picked up on it while we hugged.

"Emergency serum?" I pointed to the contraband.

"No better night than tonight." He told Paul to hold up a minute and then took the bottle from his side, placing it between my legs. "You hold on to that. I'll help Paul with the coffees."

"Gotcha." I looked up, hoping to share a smile with Lanie, but she was staring off into space just then, and I didn't want to interrupt any moment she might be having. I looked towards Marissa and noticed that she was doing pretty much the same. I wondered what each of them was thinking.

Was Marissa just a concerned employee, rocked by the thought of the man she worked so closely with being in some sort of lethal danger? Or was she a woman who loved that same man, almost as much as the girl to her right? I shook my head and told myself it didn't matter. Not right now. I would refuse to think about it and I would especially refrain from pointing it out to Lanie. After all, what did I have but a hunch?

So what that my hunches were almost always right?

In allowing both Lanie and Marissa their space, I got up and started to paw through a rack of dog-eared magazines in the far corner of the room. There was tons of material to pick through, but there was basically nothing I was interested in. *Highlights* was not my speed; *US News and World Report* too serious for the moment, and the latest Martha Stewart almost seemed a mockery in a place as precarious as this.

Who gave a flying leap if your placemat matched your napkins when someone you loved was inside fighting for their life?

The boys returned with coffee in tow the minute I gave up my perusal, and I was silently grateful once again for their efforts on Lanie's behalf. They broke her reverie and helped the time to pass that much quicker.

"And when you finish that," Jude indicated the coffee he had spiked for Lanie, "I found an ice machine. From there on forward, it's Bailey's straight up."

He wiggled his eyebrows and Lanie started crying all over again. I was about to get off the couch and go to her when Jude wrapped his arms around her once more and said in jest, "That's okay honey, I won't force you to drink."

I looked away, biting back my own tears, trying to bury the tidal wave of thoughts that were tempting to take over my brain. What if it were my father? Would I be better or worse? Would I be even remotely sane right now?

What if he didn't wake up?

"I want to go check on him," Lanie stood up then and made her way over to the nurse's station. I was torn between wanting to follow her and give her space, and since I wasn't sure what to do, I remained put and tried hard to make inane conversation with Jude and Paul. I kept my eyes on Lanie's back as she retreated and then stood up a minute later and stretched. When I turned back around my eyes connected with Rob's, who was just then striding purposefully through the entrance.

"Where is she?" Not known for formalities at the best of times, Rob was an obvious ball of nerves as he approached where we were sitting, and barely broke his stride as I pointed down the hall. "I'll be right back."

"Wait up; I'll go with you." I joined him. I decided that if Lanie wanted to be alone with her father that she would just tell us. Either way, I could barely sit anymore. I warned myself that it might be a very long night, so I scurried to meet Rob, hoping that Lanie would somehow be insulated by our love and support.

"How is she?" Rob's eyes flashed possessiveness, not unlike Jude.

"I think she's going to be all right," I pointed again as we neared the door indicating where Lanie's father was resting. I motioned for Rob to walk in before me.

As we walked into the room, we found Lanie sitting silently beside her father, her hands enclosing his own, the tracks her tears left still staining her cheeks. She looked up as we approached but didn't say a word.

"Hey there Lane," Rob smiled crookedly and then moved a bit closer to her, reaching out his hand. "You okay?"

Lanie nodded silently and then looked away. She focused on her father while I found myself getting all choked up and having to look away again. Oh, I was practically useless at a time like this! I took in the machines surrounding her father and I wondered exactly what his prognosis was. I knew next to nothing about medicine, only that the machine that was beeping had better keep doing that same rhythmic beeping, otherwise Lanie's Dad was in a world of trouble.

I barely heard her at first, but after a minute passed, I heard Lanie mumble something that I couldn't quite make out.

"Lane? Do you need something?" I reached towards her as Rob had, alas–to no avail.

"I need more time with him," She was still mumbling, but this time the words made sense and my heart broke all over again for her.

God, please let her have that wish.

I slithered out into the hall, determined to give her whatever alone time she needed. I traced my steps back to the waiting room only to find the mismatched trio still sipping their Bailey's-laced coffee; Marissa on one couch, Paul on another, and Jude silently pacing directly in back of them.

"You okay?" Paul asked sweetly as I approached the open seat next to him.

"I am. I'm fine. I'm worried about her," I scrunched up my nose and made what I'm sure was an awkward face.

"We all are. Come here, you," He offered me his arms then and I fell into them gratefully, safe in the crook of his shoulder, in between his arm and his heart, and stayed there for what seemed like forever. Paul was gently brushing the hair off my face and alternately kissing my forehead when Lanie resurfaced with Rob.

"You all right?" Jude and I said this at the same time, which caused Lanie to force a quick grin.

"I'm fine." She plopped down on the couch next to me and I reached out to hug her close, in chain fashion, with Paul hugging me and then me hugging her. I could see Rob out of the corner of my eye on Paul's right. He was pacing. "I'm hungry, but I don't want to leave."

I made eyes at Jude, who promptly offered to order a pizza. Rob said he could go pick one up and while we made further introductions and decided on sustenance, I noticed Marissa slowly edging her way off the couch.

"Marissa, will you want some pizza?" I wanted to catch her before she made her way back in to see Lanie's Dad, in an effort to make her feel as included as I possibly could.

"That would be nice." She nodded plainly.

"Any preferences?" I asked.

"Anything." She walked away then, and I made eye contact with Paul. He shrugged his shoulders almost imperceptibly, as if stating that he didn't know just what to make of the situation. If Lanie's Dad was more than just her boss, then why did she have to go through all this alone? Did she have friends? If so, where were they?

Maybe I was wrong. Perhaps I was jumping to conclusions because we were all in turmoil: therefore I was focusing on the most inconsequential part of the drama. What would Constance say about that? I was lost in my thoughts, still hugging Lanie, when I thought I heard Jude and Rob bickering over the pizza.

"Lanie likes olives," Jude insisted, and when I turned, I saw Rob roll his eyes and begin to try and edge away from where Jude was standing.

"I know what Lanie likes." Rob grumbled as he turned around to address Paul. "Do you wanna take a ride?"

"To get pizza?" Paul nodded as he disconnected himself from me, gingerly, and rose off the couch.

"Yeah, I know a place not far from here that Lanie would like. I figure I'll go pick up a couple of pies." Rob made a motion towards the door with his head.

"She hates DeMario's." Jude intoned.

"Did I say I was going to go to DeMario's?" Rob challenged Jude with his eyes, and at the same time, Lanie popped her head up.

"Lanie's right here, you know…" she admonished both of them with a glance. "And right now just about anything would be fine."

"Let's go," Rob said gruffly to Paul. Paul reminded us to call his cell if we thought of anything else and the two of them took off.

"Children." Lanie whispered.

"Ah, boys will be boys." I said, and then patted my chest in an effort to get her to lean on me again.

"Yellie, you're being a good Mommy to me right now," she exhaled deeply and then settled in closer.

"I'm trying." I sighed. We were too young to lose our parents. Surely God knew that, didn't He? Grandparents…okay, nobody wants to lose a grandparent either, but it was the circle of life and all that…somehow it was easier to reconcile. Lanie's Dad was so young, so vibrant...he had to pull through this. He simply had to.

We sat in silence for what seemed like a long time; Lanie on my lap and Jude on the couch adjacent us, slowly sipping a Bailey's. Eventually, Marissa reappeared and some time after that I noticed another family enter the waiting room. Several of the family members were speaking in Spanish as one woman in particular sat off to herself in a corner and cried softly. I wondered what they were here for; whose life was hanging in the balance while they waited along with complete strangers to hear the news?

"Chow time!" I heard Rob's voice behind me and turned slowly in my seat. It felt as if Lanie had dozed off in my lap and I wanted her to wake up on her own, so I made a motion with my hand as if to indicate that he should tone it down a little.

Rob's eyes begged a question.

"I think she's just wiped out," I looked at my watch then and was surprised to find it was almost eleven. Wow. Time sure flies when you're having fun.

"Let her rest," Jude suggested as he rose off the couch and stretched.

"I'll feed you," Paul offered. He shrugged off his jacket and then opened up a box of pizza. "By the way, I called Mom and Dad just to let them know we're out here. They said if any of us need to stay, that we're more than welcome. They're not too far from here."

Besides me, everybody else had ties to Long Island, so it was unlikely that any of us would have to take them up on that. But it was nice of them to offer. My in-laws...my heart skipped a beat at that thought becoming a reality.

In-laws!

For the first time in hours, my gaze shifted my most recent accessory. There were times that I still couldn't believe it. I wasn't used to dreams becoming reality. I felt almost as if I were finally part of a very exclusive club…The Engagement Club…and I felt different still, even though I was determined to be the same me regardless of my marital status.

Paul started to feed me a piece of veggie pie, but I must have shifted somehow, because moments after my first bite, Lanie woke up and decided to join us. She wolfed down three pieces of pizza in succession and then started chugging Pepsi at a frightening pace. It was nervous eating and I didn't blame her for it–I just didn't want her to get sick. Once we were all sated, we offered the remaining pieces to the Spanish family on the other side of the room. They accepted gratefully with nods of the head, while the youngest of the group said *Thank You* in heavily accented English.

We settled in again, only to be interrupted a few seconds later by a nurse that was calling Lanie's name from the edge of the room.

"I'm Lanie!" Lanie bolted up and almost spilled an entire bottle of Pepsi all over herself. She accosted the nurse that was waiting patiently for her. "What? What do you need? How is he?"

"He's awake." The nurse said the magic words, and Lanie almost attacked her in her exuberance.

"Can I see him?" Lanie changed that fast. "I need to see him."

"This way," The nurse ushered her out the door and I felt the rest of us breathe a collective sigh of relief. I couldn't sit still, so I followed them out into the hall and then stood outside the door to her Dad's room.

Jude, Paul, Rob and Marissa followed me a moment after, and we were all there to greet Lanie as she walked out of the room to find us.

"They think he's going to be okay. He's awake, but he's tired, and they want him to sleep. I'm going to stay, but please go–all of you. You've been so great, but you all need to go. It's late, and I've taken enough of your time."

Lanie was smiling now, a genuine smile that projected relief in spite of the tears that were still flowing down her face.

"I'm staying." Jude shrugged, and then in an effort to explain, "I live practically around the corner from here."

"I'm staying too," Rob insisted, with a roll of the eyes to Jude.

"You can stay if you want to, but I really insist you go," Lanie said to me. "Obviously, I'm going to be out here for a few days, so you will need to go to work and open up shop for us. So go get some sleep, and do me one more favor: call Olive for me in the morning, explain the situation, and tell her I will call her as soon as I get a chance. I just…I really need to be here right now."

"That's totally understandable." I nodded my head. "Are you sure you're going to be alright?" I was reluctant to leave her, even though I knew what she was saying was true.

"Of course." She nodded graciously. "I have Jude and Rob with me and I have just given Marissa permission to call in sick tomorrow."

"You're too much. Promise me you will call me if you need anything. I mean it–anything–and I will be right out here." I knew that Lanie knew that, but I felt the need to say it anyway.

"You got it." Lanie wrapped me up in a big bear hug. "I love you, Yellie."

"I love you too." I shed yet another tear as we parted, then hugged every other person in turn.

Chapter Seventy-One

After barely a minute of debate, we decided against staying at Paul's parent's house and drove back into the city that night. The thought process was that we would hit a lot less traffic at one in the morning than during the morning rush. As we made our way back, I was busy watching exit after exit go by in the side mirror, when I felt Paul's hand on my knee, palm-up, waiting for me to drop my hand in his.

"You okay, babe?" Paul took his eyes off the road for a split second and glanced sideways at me.

"I'm fine. I'm just worried for her. I know that Jude and Rob and even Marissa are still there, but I just wish I could help her out more." I sighed.

"I know this is going to sound inconsequential, but you're helping her out just by being at work, allowing her to feel free to spend as much time as she needs to there." Paul squeezed my hand as punctuation.

"Would you mind coming out here again tomorrow night?" I glanced sideways at him.

"Not at all. In fact, I rented the car for two days, because I wasn't sure how long we'd need it." He made a turn to get on the bridge. "Rob really does not like that Jude character."

"You think?" I couldn't help the sarcasm. "Jude *is* a character. What do you think it is…a little like sibling rivalry?"

"I think the old meeting the new…sometimes they just don't fit." Paul shrugged. "Look, there's my building." Paul pointed out of his window, where the New York City skyline rose up to meet us as we passed over the Brooklyn Bridge.

"God, it's so beautiful." I smiled and thrilled the same way I did the very first time I saw the skyline at night.

"The city that never sleeps," Paul intoned as he tried to sneak looks and drive at the same time.

"It really is my favorite. I mean, am I prejudiced or what?" I stayed with my eyes glued towards the window until we were off the bridge and on the city streets.

"Yeah, but you're prejudiced in the very best of ways." Paul smiled in my direction.

"Thanks."

We got to his place and then fell right into bed. The next thing I knew, the alarm was blaring and I was digging a hole, burrowing under the covers, unwilling to give in to the very early light of day.

"Wake up, Danielle. You've got to go hold down the fort."

"I have no clothes." I mumbled, still tangled in the comforter, debating whether or not I should tickle Paul's feet.

"What do you mean, you have no clothes?" He moved the comforter so that he could see the top of my head. Defeated, I looked up at him and then inched my way towards him for a kiss.

"I mean that I had no intention of staying here last night. I have my gym bag, the clothes I wore to work yesterday shoved in a corner of said gym bag, plus the clothes I wore last night to the hospital, which are basically after-gym clothes and therefore not suitable for work."

"After-gym clothes?" Paul tried to stifle his grin. "Okay–whatever–why don't you just take my credit card and run out and buy an outfit on the way to work?"

"No place will be open." I shook my head.

"Well, take it anyway and buy yourself something for tomorrow. You're going to need something if you're staying here tonight." He propped his head up on his elbow and stretched his legs. "You showering first?"

"Yeah." I delved into the gym bag and tried to see if I could rearrange what I wore yesterday into something that might work out okay for today. "I don't need your credit card, though."

"Okay." A beat. Then, "Why not?"

"Because it's yours." I felt uncomfortable taking money from him; letting him buy me things…I didn't want him to one day feel as if I owed him or something.

"Don't be ridiculous. It's ours."

"How is your credit card mine?"

"Because we're engaged, silly, and now what's mine is yours."

"I'm getting in the shower." I padded into the bathroom, all the while tossing that thought around in my head. What's mine is yours? I wasn't so sure about that, at least not yet. My eyes automatically went to my hand and the everlasting reminder that sparkled there.

Ugh.

Once I was in the shower, I remembered the jeans I had left here. A while back, Paul had cleaned out the proverbial you're-not-living-here-but-you-stay-here-enough-to-warrant-a-drawer drawer for me in his dresser. I kept nothing but a few incidentals: Tampax, an extra pair of pantyhose, the toothbrush holder for the toothbrush that was now jammed into a slim bathroom drawer, and an extra (black) sweater for when it got cold. I mulled my options as I rinsed myself off. The good thing was that I could wear the jeans to work. Even the CEO of the Ad Agency wore jeans to work, so if I could piece that together with the black sweater, I was sure I could deal with that for today. Then when the stores opened, I would go pick out something else to wear tomorrow.

I toweled off and then wrapped the towel around me toga-style. I tiptoed from the bathroom back into the bedroom and passed Paul on the way. While he was in the shower, I shrugged on the reserve jeans and sweater.

Good enough.

I emptied my gym bag and put all the clothes that needed to be laundered in the same pile where Paul kept his. Was this what married life would be like?

What's mine is yours…

My thoughts flicked briefly to The Monster and how when he came into my mother's life he just took over. What was hers became his–even my things were fair game. There were no boundaries; no respect for other people's possessions. Although Paul was by definition lending a hand rather than taking from me…I could barely reconcile myself to the understanding of *ours*.

I pushed my thoughts down, focusing instead on my workday and Lanie's situation. I decided to wait a little while before calling her this morning. I hoped that she had been able to get some sleep.

I also prayed that her father was out of the woods.

By the time Paul got out of the shower I was almost ready to roll. I finished dabbing on a little bit of makeup and then went to give him a hug and kiss goodbye.

"You're still wet," I pointed this out as he was trying to press me close and therefore dry his chest on my sweater.

"I am." He shook his hair and sprayed me in the process, a mischievous grin taking up residence the full length of his face.

"Is it your goal to get me wet?" I admonished him, although I couldn't help but smile, as his smile was contagious. I think I had a little something for a man in a towel.

"It is my goal to get you to trust me." He smiled more evenly, this time looking deep into my eyes and then punctuating his sentence with a kiss.

"I love you." Something inside insisted that he would never know how much.

Chapter Seventy-Two

My day started out busy. First, I called Olive and let her know about Lanie's situation. She assured me that however long Lanie needed to be out would be fine by her, and also offered me help if I needed it. I declined graciously, but told her that if I felt overwhelmed that I wouldn't hesitate to give her a call.

Then I was inundated with calls for a meeting that was going to happen a little over a month from now. I started telling people that they would have to be patient, and if they wanted their reservations done ASAP to please understand that I was one woman down and still trying to juggle the day-to-day stuff amidst the bevy of meeting requests. All this fell on deaf ears. In the city that never sleeps, people get accustomed to doing things fast, and having things done like…yesterday. Eventually I had to let all calls go to voice mail, which I made sure sported a very nice, very new message that stated that all reservation requests for the upcoming meeting would have to be sent in via email. I advised the impatient crowd that I would respond to them as soon as feasibly possible.

Mid-morning, I tried Lanie's cell. I wasn't sure if she was sleeping or just unable to get cell service in the hospital, so I left her a message and then tried Rob. I also got his cell. I left a message there too and tried Paul.

Vive le voice mail! I left another message.

I was all too soon buried in work again, so I called out for lunch to be delivered and continued to plow through my emails as I waited for some word from Lanie.

She checked in about two o'clock, sounding much calmer and at the same time extremely tired.

"Hey Yellie, how's it going over there?" I thought I heard her stifle a yawn.

"Forget me. How's it going over there?" I didn't even notice that I had been holding my breath until I felt myself exhale.

"He's stable." She sighed, a deep sigh that was edged with concern, but signified relief nonetheless.

"Lanie, that's great. Now what?" I shoved away my computer keyboard so I could give her my full attention.

"Now he gets to stay here a little while longer. I had them put him in a private room so that he can rest. Apparently, he's going to be fine, but this happened because he's a stress bomb; that and because he had some sort of clotting problem. They're giving him a drug called Plavix, as well as a prescription for rest and stress therapy."

"What's stress therapy?"

"I think it's like regular therapy. They just focus on what's stressing you out all the time." Lanie offered.

"You think?" I wasn't sure.

"Who knows? All I know is that I'll make sure he takes his medicine. The rest is his responsibility." She took another deep breath. "I'm going to go home now, though–his house, well, you know what I mean. I need a nap. I slept all night in a chair, and the doctor recommended that I go home and come back in a little while, since it seems like he'll be fine."

"Is Jude still there with you?"

"No, but Rob is and he's going to drive me. Then I'm going to come back here tonight."

"Paul and I want to drive out also."

"You don't have to. But if you'd like to…well, you know I always want you here."

"I know I don't have to, but I *want* to."

"So come. By the way, is it busy?"

"No," I lied, "I'm doing just fine."

"You're a bad liar," Lanie came back with this and I couldn't help but laugh.

"And that's a *good* thing," I reassured her, and then proceeded to remind her no less than a thousand times to call if she needed me, that I would get out there sooner rather than later if need be.

"You got it." Lanie told me to hold on a sec and seemed as if she was talking to a nurse or someone else. "Alright, Yellie, I'm off. I'll see you later."

"You got it." I replied in turn.

After work, I ran across the street and purchased yet another pair of black pants and two different tops that I could work with. I let myself into Paul's apartment and made hot tea in travel mugs while I waited for him to get home from work, all the while *contemplating* calling my own father. I would be a bald-faced liar if I didn't admit that Lanie's tear-sodden words kept ringing through my head: *I need more time with him.*

I checked my watch and decided I probably still had a few minutes before Paul got home and we needed to get on the road. I approached Paul's phone tentatively and then dialed the numbers, hesitantly, each finger lingering more than the usual millisecond as I depressed the familiar digits.

His voice rushed through me when he picked up the phone and I found myself feeling calmed by the assurance it gave: he was alive and well, albeit AWOL.

"Dad?" I heard my own voice squeak a little and I chastised myself inwardly.

"Danielle? You alright?" He must have sensed something or heard the catch in my voice.

"Yes, Dad, I'm fine." I exhaled, tapping my fingers on the counter in rhythmic fashion. "My question is, how are you doing?"

"I'm good. Good! Spring is coming and car sales should be picking up soon. So what's up?"

"I got engaged." The moment the words flew out of my mouth I wanted to kill myself for telling him this way. I took a deep breath and closed my eyes as I waited for his reaction.

"You got engaged? Well–Wow, I mean, isn't this a little fast?" Came his reply.

"Fast?" I was lost for a second, and then realized that I had only recently told him about Paul. Of course he would think it was fast...I hadn't been truthful about how long we'd been dating.

Oh, what a tangled web we weave!

"I mean, I haven't even met the guy!" He forced a chuckle, and even though his tone was jovial, I could tell that he was a little put off by that.

I hesitated briefly, and then plowed ahead. My initial reaction was to tell him to go to hell. Did he really think we had the kind of relationship that would warrant my seeking his permission before I made a major life decision? His stamp of approval was something I had given up on...long ago...halfway up a snow-filled hill.

"Dad, I was going to ask you if you would like to do just that, this weekend, or sometime soon." I waited for a reply that didn't come. "Would you like that?"

"Well, sure, I would like that." He seemed taken aback by the entire subject matter. "Is that all?"

All? What did he mean by all? Did he still know me, better than I thought he did? Did he hear the catch in my voice? Was he able to pick up on something, some subtle nuance that allowed him to zone in on my brain waves?

"Well, I have some other...not-so-good news." I stopped drumming my fingers as I dropped the second bomb. "Lanie's dad had a heart attack."

And I started to cry.

"Is he alright? What happened, Danielle?" His voice registered alarm and yet his tone became softer, more reminiscent of the bearer of oft-smuggled shrimp.

"He's going to be okay. He...Lanie's dad owns his own company, so he's a bit of a stress bomb...we were out at the hospital last night, and Lanie says he's coming along nicely. We–Paul and I–are going to go back out to the hospital to sit with her tonight. I guess I was just worried about you." I swiped at an errant tear.

"Why are you worried about me? I'm fine." His voice changed again, from caring to flippant, as if to dismiss any and all concern I might have held on his behalf.

"You're fine. Well, I guess that's all then." I pushed some more air out of my lungs and was just about to hang up when I decided against it. "No. Wait a minute, that's not all. That's not all at all."

Normally, I would laugh at my little play-on-words, at the very least take notice of it, but for now, the words sat secondary to the point I was trying to make.

"What happened?" He seemed put out by my vacillating.

"Nothing...*happened.* Lanie's dad having a heart attack, that's something that happened. But between you and me? Nothing has happened in a very long time. I want things to happen, though...I think it's time that we had the type of relationship where things happened on a regular basis. Like; for instance–and call me crazy here if this is just too much for you–how about my best friend's father has a heart attack and I am allowed...I am in fact encouraged...to call you up and discuss this with you, not because *something happened,* but because of the way it hit too close to home and the way it made me worry about you. Can you imagine that?" Somewhere in the background I heard a key turn in a lock and then I felt, rather than saw, Paul come in through his door. I turned my head towards the wall and tried to quell my shaking hands as I waited for my father to respond.

"I can imagine that." His voice was small now, and I felt my heart lurch as I waited for more.

Nobody said anything for what seemed like eons, and then I felt Paul as he came up beside me. I'm sure I was a sight, but I turned to him anyway and gave him a sign as if to say, *One minute.* He stood silently nearby, his mere presence an encouragement.

"I need to know that I'm not going to find you one day, the way Lanie just found her father, and be afraid that you won't wake up…because there's still so much left to say." I was speaking softly myself now, as the hammering in my heart had started to subside just a little, but I pressed on past the fear and even the pain, because I felt that since I had started this entire line of conversation that I had better well finish it.

"You won't. I'm fine. There's no need to worry about me, Danielle." He came across as tired, dismissive, as if this subject was just too uncomfortable and he wished he could talk about anything else.

"What about us? What if I told you that I worry about us, about this relationship that is nothing but a shell of its former self?" I waved my hands as I spoke, Paul-style, my frustration mounting once again as his responses flowed inadequately. Hot tears ran the length of my face, and I allowed them to keep going, silently falling onto the floor.

"What is there to worry about?" He was back in the game again, frustration evident in the rising volume on the other end of the line. "I am fine. Physically fine. I don't intend on having a heart attack any time soon. I can't promise you that, but I can tell you that I take good care of myself. As for us…Danielle, I have always been there for you, even if I haven't physically been there for you." He sighed deeply. "Just because you didn't live in the same house as me doesn't mean that I loved you any less than the one that did."

"This isn't about Michael." I warned.

"Then what's it about? Danielle, if you're worried about me, then maybe you need to worry about you too."

"You're not making sense. I just…can't…*reach you.*" I collapsed into tears then, the truth hitting the air like a sucker-punch directly in the heart, knowing full well that I was talking to my mother as well as to him, and the shared frustration had no place else to go but out.

"You can. Don't you think that there are times I feel the same way?" He got a little choked up as he continued. "Look at you…you're all grown up, you're getting married for God's sake, and there are times I feel as if I barely know you."

"Whose fault is that?" I spit this out, venom lacing each word, secure in my belief that he was to blame.

"Oh, sure, I'll take the blame for the majority of the rift that stands between us, but what I won't do, my dear child, is take the blame for all of it. I just won't." He huffed. "I could have done a better job, sure…I could have called a little more…but I didn't want to be a pest to you, to crowd you in the new life you have. I worry about you; do you really believe that I don't worry about you?"

" I don't know. I really don't know." I shook my head.

"Well, now you know. I do. Plain and simple. I just don't know how to make you know that." He said this forcefully, his frustration coming across loudly, regardless of tone.

"Why don't you start by telling me?" I suggested this plainly.

"I guess I just did."

"Okay, maybe you did."

There was a ream of silence again and then we both began to laugh. The impossibility of our relationship…the fact that we were probably a lot more alike than either of us wanted to admit.

"I am fine." He began again like this, in a controlled tone, as if he were ticking off the bullet points on a memo. "I feel fine and I intend to continue feeling that way. I am sorry about your friend's father. I'm also sorry that it made you have a panic attack over you, and me and my health in general. But–and I don't mean any disrespect here–maybe it's a good thing. You obviously had some things you wanted to get off your chest."

"You think?" I sighed, chuckled, and tried to remember the point I was originally trying to make. "I wish I was a kid again."

Words unbidden again running from the annals of my brain, but like so many things we hide and control and try so hard to bury…they're just sentences waiting to be pushed from the tips of our tongues out to touch the waiting air.

"Oh yeah? Why?"

"Because I do." I wanted him to remember and understand without having to ask. Perhaps I was asking for too much too soon.

"We all do," my father said wistfully, and then changed the subject to Paul. "So when do I get to meet this guy?"

"Is this weekend good for you?" I offered with a quick look in Paul's direction, reading his eyes, nodding as he gave the go-ahead.

"It can be. I'll make you a deal: I will talk to my wife and we will make some plans to have a nice dinner, and then I'll call you back to reconfirm." He said this with a touch of salesman-swagger, but I chose not to be offended, as this was just his way of closing the deal.

"Sounds good." I nodded involuntarily. "Dad, I've got to go out to see Lanie now. Just leave me a message and I'll talk to you soon."

"You got it." He signed off with that, and as I turned to face Paul, I finally wiped the remaining tears from my face.

"Your father?" Paul said it like a question, and I knew that what he meant to ask was more than just who had been on the other end of the phone.

"Yeah." I smiled dimly, then looked and locked eyes with the man I loved. "I'll tell you on the way out there. Come on, it's…" I checked my watch. "We gotta go."

Chapter Seventy-Three

We piled into the rental and as Paul shot the car East, I began filling him in on the entire conversation.

"Did you intend to tell him tonight?" I had to give Paul credit for being delicate. Last he had heard, I was ducking and hiding and insisting I would tell my parents in my own time.

"No." I waited a beat as I collected the words I would need to elaborate. "I had absolutely no intention of telling him on the phone…it just poured out along with everything else…and now it's done."

"How do you feel?" He looked sideways as if to catch a glimpse of my face.

"I feel relieved, in a weird sort of way. It also feels totally surreal; the conversation from beginning to end was one that I had tried out in my mind too many times to count." I looked out onto the rush of traffic, squinting my eyes, forcing the headlights to blur.

"I'm glad you told him. Even if it was not the way you planned it. I mean, he is still your Dad." Paul looked at me again. "Dads want to know these things."

"He never seemed as if he was that type of Dad." I shrugged, then turned sideways in my seat to face him. "Do you find me unreachable?"

"Sometimes." Curiously, Paul now had his eyes glued to the road ahead of him.

"You do?" I was stunned. "You find me unreachable."

"Not so much since we got back together…but there were times, yeah…when I felt like you held me at arm's length and I didn't know what to do to make things better."

"Were you frustrated?"

"Sometimes."

"How 'bout now?"

"Not yet." He graced me with an open smile and then gestured towards my cell phone, currently resting on the console between us. "Do you want to give Lanie a call and see if she wants us to pick something up?"

"Good idea." I dialed Lanie and got her voicemail. I left her a message and then pressed *End.* "No dice. Would you be willing to run back out once we get there?"

"No problema," Paul responded, and then reached across in order to put his hand on my knee. "I love you, Dani."

I smiled widely in his direction. "I love you too."

Chapter Seventy-Four

We retraced our steps through the hospital only to find Lanie's Dad had been moved to another room. Once we were instructed on which way to go, I recalled Lanie having said something about having her father moved to a private room.

"I'm sorry, I should have remembered," I said plaintively as the elevator doors closed, mad at myself because I wasn't in charge of the incidentals.

"I *like* touring hospitals," Paul insisted, with a quick wave of the hand. "Stop being so hard on yourself."

"Do you think I'm hard on myself?" I was intent on looking in, even as the elevator moved us up.

"What is this tonight, twenty questions?" Paul looked bemused as he extended his hand to hold open the elevator doors.

We exited and I didn't answer.

I didn't really know what to say.

After several arrows and turns, we came up to Lanie's Dad's room only to find Lanie and Rob fiercely ripping apart deli sandwiches over his feet.

"Hey!" Lanie exclaimed loudly as she spotted us and then hopped up to greet us with a warm hug. "Dad, you remember Danielle and this is her *fiancé,* Paul." She put the emphasis on fiancé and then winked at me over her shoulder as she led me to her father's bed.

"Hi there." I shook his hand and smiled widely. "You sure had us scared. How are you doing?"

"I'm fine." He returned my smile with some effort, although there was a light in his eyes that had not been extinguished throughout his ordeal.

We each grabbed a plastic chair and then settled in to eat and hang out. Lanie had sent Rob out for various deli delights knowing that we were coming and once unloaded, we had the bottom half of the bed covered with a picnic feast that could feed several kings.

Nurses popped in and out, and eventually Marissa darkened the doorway. I tossed Paul another look and Lanie caught me. Her eyes said she would talk to me later.

After a couple of hours, Lanie told her father that she thought it was time for him to get some sleep. The role reversal was evident, but it was something she had seemed to step into with ease, so I tipped my hat to her as she walked us out to the elevator.

"You're doing a great job, Lanie." I assured her as I linked my arm in hers.

She touched her head to my shoulder and then stepped in front of me, turning her face to mine. "He's usually in charge of everything; it's really kind of weird being in charge for a change."

"I guess it would be." My mind flicked as I tried to measure about how long I had tried taking charge of my mother's mess and how many times I had run things in lieu of her absence.

"So what do you think of The Marissa Situation?" Lanie's eyes challenged mine, warning me not to act as if I hadn't noticed.

"I think it's…interesting." I was about to follow up, but Paul guffawed loudly in my brief pause and therefore directed attention to him.

"Delicacy is not your strong suit," Paul admonished me.

"It isn't. Although nobody's saying it can't be," I reminded.

"All I want is an opinion," Lanie trilled as we reached the exit doors.

"Here's my opinion: if you're fine with it, I'm fine with it." I gave it to her the same way that I knew that she would give it to me.

"I don't know how I feel yet," Lanie said candidly as she looked between Paul and I. "It's not that he's not entitled. It's just…weird. I feel as if I was the last to know."

"Maybe you were. Maybe he was worried about your reaction and therefore decided not to say anything right away. What did he say to you about it?" I asked.

"He knew I figured it out, and he basically broached the subject by saying that the only reason he didn't tell me sooner is because he wasn't sure how long it would last." She shrugged. "I'm fine with her just as long as she doesn't get in my way."

"And if she does you can kill her," I offered this as if it were the next logical step.

"Of course." Lanie waved us away with two big hugs and a load of thanks.

"I'll see you…?" I didn't want to pressure her. I just wanted an idea.

"Definitely by Monday."

"Gotcha." I paused to wrap her up into another hug. "By the way…have you heard from Hello Kitty Guy?" For the life of me, his name had escaped me, as he seemed peripheral now, while Rob and even Jude marked time with her at the hospital.

"Adam?" Lanie sighed. "He's left me several messages, but we're more or less playing phone tag right now and the truth of the matter is that I really don't care."

"I hear ya." I secretly still held out hope that one day she and Rob would decide to confess their undying love for one another.

"Get going." She patted me on the arm and then turned to give Paul a goodbye hug. "I'll talk to you tomorrow."

Paul and I pushed our way through the doors and left her then, myself walking slightly backwards until I saw her disappear from view.

"He looks good," Paul observed as we walked over to the rental car. "Are you glad you came?"

"Yeah, I am. Even though I know Lanie will be just fine, I still wanted to be there for her," I settled into the car and then turned sideways in my seat. "I guess the verdict is in on that guy Adam."

"What's with the Hello Kitty thing?"

"God, who knows? He's just a weird guy, I guess…but I think he really sunk his ship by not at least trying to come out here and see her." I shook my head.

"I wish she'd get together with Rob." We both laughed, as we had spoken the same thought at the same exact moment.

I looked at him then, my love, my whole heart, and as I settled into my seat I had that feeling of knowing someone and being known in a way that I always hoped I would be. I think that's what we're all trying to find anyway…a heart like ours…someone who knows it, *who gets it,* who is willing to put it all out there and not be afraid to melt right into you. How long had I run from him? I contemplated this as we drove towards my city, and as I inhaled and then exhaled deeply, I chose for myself again the path that would lead me directly to Paul.

"Are you ready for this weekend?" I asked precariously, although I knew deep down that I would be more nervous than he.

"I've been ready." Paul glanced at me as he drove. "This is the stuff of life."

"Who said that?"

"I did."

"No, I mean…" I caught his grimace and then added my own. "You better buckle your seat belt."

"It's already on."

Chapter Seventy-Five

I stayed at Paul's that night and then dragged myself into work the next day, immeasurably tired for no apparent reason.

I yawned several hundred times, waved hello to Alana from Team Cheer, and picked up the phone absentmindedly.

The third call of the day was my mother.

"Hello there," I trilled into the phone, trying to remain even in tone, although my heart always skipped a beat at the mere existence of her digits on my screen.

"Hi Danielle, it's Mom. What's new?" She sounded more even than me for a change.

"I got engaged."

Omigod! Rather...OH MY GOD! What the hell did I just do?

I did it again.

No plan, no foresight, na-da, just the opening of the drawbridge and then the plunging into the moat...

"You what?!" Her amazement shattered my endless inner diatribe and shuttered me straight back to reality. For a brief second I couldn't tell if she was angry or just steeped in full-out shock.

"I got engaged." I said it this time with more conviction, as if I had actually prepared to tell her just then.

"When did this happen?" She must have realized that she sounded more than a bit harsh, as she tempered her tone and then started again. "I mean, Wow...I guess I'm just a little shocked. When did he propose?"

Since I wasn't about to tell her the whole ugly scenario about how a near-fatal break-up had suddenly shifted into a promise of forever love, I decided instead to focus on the events of the past few days and relay that to her all in one fell swoop. "Well, he proposed the other night, but I didn't have a chance to call you right away because Lanie's Dad had a heart attack, and then we were out on Long Island…" I finished wrapping up a few minutes later, and even as I waited for her response, a still small voice whispered that I would have told the old Mom instantly.

Was it a sign of growth? Of not needing my parents so much, of distancing myself from them? Or was it a sign of my wanting to assert a grand old screw-you in the most silent of ways? You weren't there for me; therefore you get the very least of my attention now. You contributed to my pain; therefore your share in my joy is lessened, for you shouldn't get to partake in it all. Did that make any sense? Or was I still lugging that big old bag of bricks around, even when it came to the incidentals?

Food for thought.

"Well, I am really and truly very happy for you. I wish…well, I wish I had met him a few weeks ago when we had those plans…although I'm sure you picked yourself out a good one." She signed, perhaps resigned to our fate. Her voice broke through all that she was unwilling to say: when had the day arrived that we could no longer proclaim to be the very best of girlfriends? Had it shuffled by in the years when she had been too engulfed in her own pain to notice that she had a daughter slowly growing into a woman right under her very nose? Was it some strange form of poetic justice to now see her vying for attention on the sidelines of my life?

"Thanks, Mom." What else was there to say? My voice held a tinge of sarcasm, but I forced myself to curb whatever animosity I might still be holding onto and choose to enjoy this mother and whatever relationship we had today.

"So when do we celebrate?" She asked me with what seemed to be forced enthusiasm. The shifting of gears was intentional, so I went with it, removing from my mind the whys and the whynots.

"Well, I have plans this weekend, so how about the weekend after?" I suggested this as the other line started to ring. I hesitated, as always, to inform her that the plans I held were with my father. I glanced over to the reader on Lanie's phone and determined that Danny from Team Mazda could leave a voice mail.

"Do you want to come up? I could have Jake Next Door over for cake; I'm sure he'd love that." My mother suggested.

"I'm sure he would." I laughed. Jake Next Door would take a piece of cake any way he could get his hands on it. I crossed fingers inside my heart for them again. What would be better than her hooking up with Jake, now that The Monster was gone and she finally seemed as if she was actually getting her life together? "Can I let you know? I mean, is there any possibility that you can come down? You can bring Jake with you." The other line was ringing again, and I saw that it was somebody else from Team Mazda. That could only mean one thing: Drama on the eleventh floor. I would have to get off the phone with her soon.

"I will ask Jake if he wants to take a ride with me. Why don't you talk to your…*fiancé*…and then let me know when is good for the two of you." Each minute, she sounded more like the Mom of days gone by. Or more like Lanie. I couldn't tell.

"I will. I've got to go. I'll talk to you soon, bye." I hung up on her and then grabbed the third incoming call from Team Mazda. I was greeted by a shrieking banshee in the form of Tia Modena, the only girl on the Team.

"Danielle! Danielle! Dan said he called and left you a voice mail, and then Guy tried you and didn't get you and then they gave it to me because we just got invited to the car show and now Mazda wants the new print ads done by then, so they're in a meeting, but they left this with me, so here I am and I need to get all of us out to their headquarters tomorrow because they need to decide and the car show is right around the corner." Tia said this in a whoosh of air that was downright frightening to have to be subject to. If she weren't the ripe young age of twenty-four years old, I would demand a blood pressure test be administered immediately.

"Tia: Breathe! I command you to b-r-e-a-t-h-e. Okay, where do you guys need to go again?" I had temporarily forgotten where Mazda was located, as her frenzy was oozing through the phone and I felt my own blood pressure rise in turn.

She filled me in and I got busy soon after arranging travel for the entire Team. From there, I had three calls from Adrienne and then it just escalated. By the end of the day, I was lighting my hair on fire and sacrificing it to the God of Travel and Tourism.

"Travel, it's Danielle." I said this by rote, not even having the two seconds it took to look at the reader.

"Hello, Gorgeous," Paul infused life into my end of the phone, and I couldn't help but break out in a nice big grin in spite of my heavy workload.

"Gorgeous? I don't know about gorgeous. Frenzied, harried, overloaded, and a little more than pissed…but gorgeous, I don't know."

"How about hungry?"

"Could be." I checked my watch and was surprised to see that the day was almost through. "What did you have in mind?"

"Dinner. Dancing. A night on the town." Paul chuckled softly. "Actually, just dinner, although I could probably be talked into everything else."

"I can't be. I have…" I looked around me and tried to figure out about how long it would take me to get unburied. "How about I meet you over at our favorite little Mexican Diner for a whole load of comfort food?"

"That sounds like just what the doctor ordered." Paul hummed. "I think I can get outta here before the clock strikes twelve. How 'bout you?"

"I think I can get outta here before the clock strikes seven," I crossed my fingers and my toes, hoping that my prediction was in the ballpark of reality.

"I'll meet you there." He paused a beat. "By the way, are you staying over tonight?"

"Well…" I needed clothes desperately, but was too tired to want to haul my buttocks home. "If I can fudge another outfit out of what it is I have with you, then I'll stay. I need sleep."

"Sounds like a plan. I'll pick you up at seven."

"Ciao for now." I put the phone down, ran out to the cubby-kitchen, made myself a jolt of caffeinated tea and then resumed my frenetic pace.

I had a date.

Chapter Seventy-Six

"So I told my mother today." I said this matter-of-factly, as I rested my fork on the side of my plate and then looked Paul straight in the eye. I took a swill of my frosty peach margarita as I waited for him to respond.

"Whatever prompted you to do that?" He had a curious expression on his face, one step down from amazement; one step up from knowing me too well.

"The same thing that prompted me to suddenly tell my father: my big, fat mouth." I sighed, took another sip of my drink and then snuck a peek at the glittering diamond on my left hand. I looked back at him, sinking myself deep into those baby browns. "Paul, I should warn you now...you can still probably get your money back on this thing."

"And miss all this?" He indicated our little corner in the back end of the diner. "Never."

"Well...the truth of the matter is that I have no real idea why I told her, after promising myself that I was going to tell her–each of them, really–in person. I just couldn't hold back. It's like this: I want to protect myself from them, so they can't hurt me anymore. I want to prove that I am fine in my new life without them, almost to the point of throwing it up to their face and/or excluding them from whatever events now make up my life. But then as soon as I think I don't need them, something deep inside me calls out to them, and I end up revealing myself and including them far more than I ever thought I would originally. Am I making even one bit of sense?" It was the first time I had ever let those words hit the air; held inside my heart for so long, they felt funny, and I wasn't sure at that moment if I made sense to anybody but myself.

"Sure you are. It's just that you have to make a decision. You should probably decide whether they're in or they're out, whether you let them in on that decision or not." He shrugged, put down his napkin, and then grabbed for a tortilla chip. As he leaned back in his chair crunching all the way, his eyes swept over my face.

"It's not that easy." I couldn't just decide whether they were in or out: wasn't that obvious?

"I can imagine. But either way, you need to stop torturing yourself. Have you talked to Constance about this?" Chip, dip, face, chip, dip, face.

I had to bite back the sarcasm before I replied. *Just what did he think I was paying her for?* This roller-coaster ride was almost our sole topic of conversation, presented in a different format week to week, the characters on the stage providing the only variation. The story was almost always the same.

"Of course I talk to Constance about this. It isn't as if there's an instant answer available, though. I mean, I want to connect with them. I want them in my life. I just want to know in advance that if I let them back in, that they're not going to cop out on me all over again. I want…" I laughed a second at the ridiculous thought that had just flashed through my mind. "I wish I could just have them sign a contract or something…a statement saying that they wouldn't hurt me anymore…that they would act like responsible parents for a change, and be there if I needed them, and step out a little when their presence got to be a bit too much."

"You're looking for perfection. I hate to be the one to give you this newsflash, honey, but it doesn't exist." Another chip, dip…oops, almost lost the salsa…quick save into the mouth.

"I think I figured that out already." I broke the chip I was holding into tinier pieces.

"You think?"

"Perhaps."

"So what are we going to do with your father this weekend?"

"I don't know yet. I haven't heard from him. He said he would speak to his wife and then get back to me…but I haven't heard from him yet…although if he called my house, I haven't been home." I shrugged as the possibilities walked through my mind.

"Didn't you tell him to call your cell?"

"I don't remember."

"Okay. Well, so here's the deal: how about we deal with your Dad this weekend and your Mom the weekend after?" He proposed.

"Can I have a week off in between?" I didn't want to have to beg, but if I had to I would. He would soon see first-hand why I might need some time off in between the two.

"I think that can be arranged." Paul hailed a waiter and ordered another Corona. He gestured towards me, did I want another drink? I shook my head no.

"I just don't think…" I trailed off as I finished the chip I had been playing with and then dove back into my meal. "I don't think you know what you're in for."

"They'll be fine. Look, Danielle, people are people. And most people want to be liked, loved…at least liked. They will be on their best behavior in front of me and I won't let them hurt you. Ever. Again." Paul gave me a serious look and I held his eyes for a minute as my heart held onto his promise.

"The truth of the matter is that I am more worried about how I may act around them. *I* may not be on my best behavior around *them.*" I sighed. "I can't even explain it to you. It's like I always start out trying to do well by them, to maintain my patience, forget the past, bury the anger…but then my mother goes and says something seemingly inconsequential…and I blow up inside–or outside–and, so…I think that's why I've been so scared about the fact that one day you would have to interface."

"Do you think you can lower your expectations of them…just a little," He made a sign with his fingers to indicate a pinch, "And raise your trust in me…just a schoche?"

"I think I can." I nodded. "By the way, I have lowered my expectations of them. I had to. I got tired of being disappointed all the time."

"No, you haven't. You just think you have. You're still hopeful. Always hopeful that one day they will give you the credit you so rightly deserve."

"For what?"

"For turning out good in spite of them."

"You think?"

"I do." He raked his hands through his hair in a familiar gesture. "But don't ask me. I'm totally prejudiced."

"Thank God for that."

We laughed and then finished up our Mexican feasts: all burritos ordered on the premises were as big as at least a leg. A human leg. Actually, an NBA-player's leg. Soon we walked back to Paul's place and eventually we went to bed. I made a promise to myself to make sure to go back to my place tomorrow.

As I drifted off to sleep, I smiled to myself. Soon the day would come where I wouldn't have to worry about having enough clothes at one place or another, or a toothbrush here or my book collection there.

I couldn't wait.

Chapter Seventy-Seven

"What are you doing here?" I almost fell off my chair as I saw Lanie breeze into the hole/office behind me, making a steady beeline for her own workstation.

"Oh please! I was about to kill Superman, so I had to just get away!" Lanie rolled her eyes and looked at me as she took off her jacket and began settling in. "Besides, Lovergirl can take care of him."

"I take it Superman is Dad and Lovergirl is Marissa?" I couldn't help but smile and feel happy that Lanie was back in, like a breath of fresh air, providing color in the grayness of the hole/office.

"Of course my father is Superman! He can have a heart attack, fall into a coma, check into the hospital and out, then rush back to run his company all in the space of just a few short days! In fact, he can do all that with a cape on!" Lanie's sarcasm couldn't be missed.

"What about Lovergirl?"

"Oh, didn't you know? She can take care of him *and* his office all in one leap and a half of a bound!"

"Perhaps they're made for each other?"

"I guess." Lanie sat down and began to peruse the various mail and Post-its that littered the top of her desk. "Would you walk with me and go get a coffee, before I plunge into all this?"

"Of course!" I put all our calls over to voicemail and then crossed the room in order to give her a big hug. She returned it with a sigh.

"I just hope he doesn't overdo it, Yellie."

"I hope so too."

"He checked himself out! I mean, he says he's going home to rest, but you and I both know that it'll be a matter of hours before he has some folder in his hands and a phone on his hip." She shook her head. "He's stubborn."

"It's what made him a good businessman," I pointed this out to her, trying hard to find the silver lining.

"Yeah. You're right." Lanie grabbed her purse and gestured towards the door. "I just wish he'd get stubborn about his health."

We took the elevator down to street level and then crossed the street to the Caffeine Altar. Lanie ordered a double espresso and I joined her. After a few sips on a comfy couch, we decided to finish them back upstairs and catch up while we worked.

"You going back out there tonight?" I asked her as we re-boarded the elevator.

"I am." She nodded. "The good thing is, he asked me to hire him a personal trainer for when he's feeling better. So I get to audition a lot of buff men for Daddy Dearest."

"By audition, you mean…?" I wagged my eyebrows up and down.

"I wish." She unlocked the door and then sat down at her desk. "You know I blew off Adam?"

"I kind of figured as much. I found it odd that after we left the hospital that first night that not one of us remembered to call him. Not even you." I said this to her in the way of expecting an answer.

"Yeah…it was just so weird. There I was in a moment of crisis, and all I could think about was calling Jude. I thought about where Rob was, and suddenly he was there. This new guy didn't even cross my mind." Lanie shrugged. "The whole Hello Kitty thing was a little bit creepy anyway."

"I agree." Just then, the phone started to buzz, so I gave her a one sec signal and picked it up. The next thing I knew, it was almost afternoon and I still hadn't had a chance to pick up the phone and call Paul, even just to tell him Lanie was in.

I checked my watch and told Lanie I would be ready to go to lunch in five minutes, right after I called

Paul and ran to the bathroom. As I dialed his number, I was reading an email, and needless to say, completely caught off guard when I heard a raspy female voice pick up the other end.

"Paul Corsi's line," the voice said.

I sat stunned a second as I registered that there was another woman picking up his phone. Okay, so it was his office phone, but still...

"Is Paul available?" I tried to remain calm and sound as if I were not talking through gritted teeth. Just who the hell was this and why was she picking up his phone?

"No, I'm sorry, he just stepped out. Can I take a message?" I heard a giggle then, but it sounded more like it was in the background than coming directly from the person on the phone.

Were there two girls in his office? Several women? If so, why were they picking up his phone? Hadn't they ever heard of letting a call roll over to voice mail? And why did it sound more like a party than a planning meeting in there? What gave them the right to–

"Can you please tell him Danielle called? Thanks." I cut myself off and hung up the phone before I allowed my voice to betray me any farther. As I hung up, I swiveled around to look at Lanie and stated, "That was weird."

"What's up?" Lanie inquired as she shrugged her jacket on and switched her phone to Off.

"I don't know. I just find it entirely strange. I just called Paul's office and some woman picked up his phone and asked if she could take a message. I just...I've never heard that happen before." I was a little bit unnerved but trying hard not to let it bother me.

"Don't worry about it. Come on, grab your bag and let's go eat. I would worry only if you called his *house* and heard some other chick picking up the phone."

"You're right; it's nothing." I had a glittering reminder on my hand, a telltale beacon that insisted I not worry. I shrugged it off and began to follow Lanie downstairs. We ate salads and drank Snapples, then headed back up in order to finish out our day. In a matter of minutes, we got busy all over again and almost missed a call coming in from Olive, checking in to make sure we were not over our heads in ten feet of water. She asked after Lanie's Dad, and once we gave her the stats on the day, we assured her that we were fine and continued to bang out reservations until well after five.

"God, I missed this," Lanie laughed out loud then as the phone buzzed and the display read Adrienne.

"It's all you." I picked up the second call that had buzzed in right after Adrienne, thinking once again that I had yet to hear from Paul all day long. It was unusual, not to mention unsettling. I wondered if he had even gotten my message.

Lanie was fluffing her hair and 'doing' Adrienne to a T by the time I finished up my final call and then moved the phone back over to the Off position. Tomorrow was another day, and anything that I hadn't gotten done could be done then.

"You done?" I asked her as I heard her hang up.

"Yeah, that was an *urgent* phone call for a trip he needs to take next week." Lanie rolled her eyes. "I see it's still the same old."

I smiled. "Yes, except I missed you. So how are you getting out there tonight?"

"I'm going to take the LIRR train and Jude is going to meet me to pick me up. Then I will probably come in from there in the morning." Lanie brightened. "At least coming in from Long Island, I'll have a real excuse to come in late for a change."

"Lane, you know if you need to stay out there that you don't have to come in at all. I was surprised to even see you today." I grabbed my overnight bag, which was wedged under the far right side of my cube. "I will be home if you need me, doing a load of laundry, checking to make sure my apartment is still there, and generally fretting over the weekend. Call me if you need me."

"Likewise, my friend."

We gave each other cheek kisses and were on our way. On my way out I checked my cell phone to see if it was on. It was on, there were no messages, and my battery had a full charge.

Chapter Seventy-Eight

"Hello?" I ran for the phone but tried to answer it in a voice that sounded as if I hadn't run for it.

"Is there a Dan-yell Darrucco there?" Came the synthesized voice from the telemarketing abyss.

"There's nobody here by that name." I replaced the phone feeling as if I had stated a complete truth. I swore to myself that if any one of them ever got my name right, that I would listen to their spiel as a reward. Until then...sorry, no takers.

After replacing the phone, I placed my bag on the couch and then backtracked to the floor behind me in order to pick up my mail. I collected all of it, but before I sat down, I pressed the button on my answering machine, hoping to hear Paul's voice.

The first message was from my father: *Hey Danielle, it's Dad. I talked to the wife and the kid and it looks like we're all free on Saturday. How about we go to Carmine's and eat fried calamari by the handful? Let me know what you think.*

Carmine's. Okay–touristy, but good. I remembered what Paul said about lowering my expectations. Carmine's would be fine. I would call him back in a little bit. I looked around, making sure everything was in the same place as when I had left it. I felt as if I hadn't been home forever. My place looked smaller than usual, and as I perused my main room, the refrigerator, and then the mail, I decided that I wouldn't mind the move from my place to Paul's. In fact, I was looking forward to it.

Paul.

I checked my watch and found it to read almost eight o'clock. I still hadn't heard from him all day, and even though I knew deep down that everything was fine between us, I still felt a small sense of alarm building in the back of my brain.

I decided to call my father first. Get it over with, and get my mind off of Paul. Surely he would give me a call sometime soon…so far in our relationship he hadn't let a day go by without at least a quick call or two to say hello. I felt my mind begin to conjure up some fantastic scenarios about the woman who had picked up his phone earlier today.

I shoved those thoughts aside and dialed my father. After three rings, little Mikey picked up, and after a play-by-play reiteration of his soccer practice earlier today, my father cut in and we firmed up our plans.

"So what do you think of Carmine's? I thought that would be a good idea for everyone." My father seemed proud of his suggestion, so in an effort not to disappoint him, I agreed.

"That will be fine. Great. What time were you thinking of?" I was hoping we could still get reservations.

"Early work for you?" He suggested, probably factoring in his long ride back Upstate when he left the city that night.

"Early like around four?" Carmine's was always jammed, but I felt we might have a better chance to get in if we went a little earlier. Plus, that might leave Paul and I some time alone after the Summit.

"Works for us." He called something unintelligible out to my brother. "Do you want to meet there?"

"Are you going to the one near Times Square?"

"There's two?"

"Yes. There's one in the Nineties also. But we can meet you at the one in the Forties."

"Then it's a go. If anything changes, I'll give you a call."

"You have my cell phone number?" I wasn't sure if I had ever given it to him; either way, he had never once called me on it.

"I've got it here." He gave me another recap and then we both hung up.

8:35 pm.

Still no Paul.

I convinced myself I was just getting anxious for no good reason. I mean, what on Earth was the matter with me? When Paul was smothering, I ran to the hills, and then when he had a busy day, I acted as if he had abandoned me for good.

I needed to shake it off.

I looked at my watch again and tried to determine if it was too late to go out for a walk. I needed to burn some nervous energy and had a trusty little flashlight that I used for just such occasions. Besides, where I lived, safety was an assumption. I knew that bad things could very well happen anywhere, but the worst thing I had ever heard of happening in my neck of the woods was a maid claiming the neighbor's antique gravy boat for her very own…using…the five-finger discount. You get my drift.

The scandal!

I don't even own a gravy boat.

I wondered briefly if we would get one for the wedding.

So I suited up, donned my brightest workout gear, and then slapped on a pair of kicks, determined to not worry and wait by the phone like a desperate woman on patrol. What was that saying? *A watched phone never rings.*

(Even if you are engaged to the guy.)

As fate would have it, the minute I stepped outside and began to slide my sliding-glass door shut behind me, I heard the phone ring through the glass, so I reached inside to pick it up.

"Hello?" I had one foot outside and one foot in, straddling the track.

"Hey sweetie, how have you been all day?" It was Paul, sounding as happy as ever to hear from me.

"Fine."

(Not fine.)

"Good! Well, listen to this! You are not gonna believe what happened to me today!" and he proceeded to rattle on a full ten minutes before realizing that I hadn't said one word in return.

"Danielle?" He came up for breath. It must have suddenly occurred to him that I had said barely more than one umm-hmm in the spaces between his speech.

"Yes?" I had steeled my heart against him, and I knew not why.

"Are you there? Honey, what's the matter? I thought you would find this interesting." He sounded perplexed.

"I do. I also find the girl who picked up your phone today pretty interesting." Score one for me, soap-opera style.

"Who? What are you talking about?" Still perplexed.

"Why don't you tell me, Paul? I mean, were you really that busy all day, that you didn't have thirty seconds to pick up the phone and just give me a quick call? Is that the way things are going to be now…we're engaged…screw me…I can wait…I'm on the back burner…nobody even needs to give you a message regarding me because *everything* is more important than me now!" I realized I was crying only once I felt the tears on my face. My mind flashed quickly to Lanie and the way she had felt about the Bradomeister.

"Danielle, I don't know what the hell you're talking about. I had a very busy day today–with some major developments–all of which I was just calling to share with you. I don't know why you take my not calling you so personally!" Paul replied angrily, his voice edging up with each word.

I took a deep breath before I responded.

"How am I supposed to take *you* not calling *me* NOT PERSONALLY?" The grammar sucked, but I felt sure that he would get the point.

He sighed.

I tried again.

"I called your office today and somebody picked up your phone. She didn't seem to know who I was, and she didn't seem to care. I had never heard her voice before and was a little taken aback by the fact that you obviously gave this person permission to pick up your private line. She told me she was going to give you the message that I called. Obviously, she didn't. I just wonder if that was a true oversight, that's all. Plus I wonder how long we'll be married before you really start taking advantage of me." My voice had edged up also, and my heart was straining against my chest.

"Is that what you believe about me?" Paul seemed farther away than when I had first picked up the phone, farther away than he had seemed all day long.

"I don't know." I sat there dazed for a second. "No, I don't think I believe that about you. It's just…"

"It's your past. That's the problem, Danielle. There's got to come a day when you no longer let your past dictate how you feel about me; what you believe about me." Paul hesitated a beat. "As for the woman who picked up the phone, it was probably Victoria. She was in on the entire deal with me today, and was in and out of my office all day long."

"I'm sorry." I didn't really know what else to say and I found myself feeling a little more than foolish for jumping to conclusions and lambasting him the way I just had.

"So am I." He made a noise that belied his frustration. "You just took the wind out of my sails."

"I'm really sorry, Paul. I just…" I had no words to describe the way that I felt about it. "Believe me when I say that I didn't set out for things to end up this way."

"I believe you, but I'm tired and now I think it's best that I just get off the phone." Paul said. "We can talk about this with Constance tomorrow."

"Do you want to tell me about the rest of your day?" I offered anyway.

"No, not now. I'm not mad, I just want to go. I love you." He hung up the phone before I could get out my reply.

I loved him too. I was just afraid to.

Chapter Seventy-Nine

"So how did you feel when you heard that person pick up the phone?" Constance looked at me and waited, as did Paul.

"My heart stopped. I can't explain it. I knew, even as I stood there, that I was overreacting…I just couldn't help it. And now that I think about it…if Paul had called me earlier in the day, it probably wouldn't have been such a big deal. It's just that it…escalated." I knew I wasn't acquitting myself well, but I felt unable to reach and do any more than that thus far.

"I'm pretty diligent about calling you during the day," Paul returned defensively.

"You're right. You are. Usually." I sat there on the other side of the couch, tears streaming down my face, as they were wont to do, every time I sat in this office.

"What did you want Paul to do for you, Danielle? Can you articulate it?" Constance gave me a look that said: *Continue.*

"I wanted him to call me."

I saw Paul's hands shoot up in the air out of the corner of my eye.

"I guess I wanted him to reassure me." I continued, realizing that it sounded dumb when I said it out loud. "I think I'm really nervous about him meeting my father this weekend. And I think I have it in my mind that once we get married…that he'll take advantage of me. And it scares me."

"Your father and your impending marriage are two separate issues. Let's go through them one at a time." Constance made a gesture as if to give Paul the floor.

"I have never given her the impression that once we are married, that I will automatically take her for granted and summarily take advantage of her." Paul huffed.

"Danielle?" This from Constance, our erstwhile conductor.

"I'm not saying that *he* gave me that impression. I was saying that I felt that way." I struggled to make him understand.

"Because of your past! Danielle," Paul took a deep breath and rolled his eyes. "You have to trust me. Me. Paul Corsi. You need to learn how to trust our love, and not look to what anybody else has or doesn't have, or the way they treat each other. I can't help the way other people treat each other. I can only show you what I can give."

"I know that." I said this in an almost whisper, fighting against the feelings inside that tended to clash with all that he was saying. I looked to Constance, my eyes begging her to translate.

"I think that you have to keep Danielle's past in the forefront of your mind, Paul, at least for right now." Constance began, "With the onset of your engagement…meeting her parents…the impending wedding…there's bound to be a lot of things that get stirred up. Right now is the time to be patient."

"I feel like that Billy Joel song, *Innocent Man.*" Paul scoffed and turned in my direction. "Now, don't go saying that it figures–you know–a Long Island boy, relating everything to a Billy Joel song."

"I won't say it." I smiled a peace offering.

"Do you know that song?" Paul referred the question to Constance.

"I do." She nodded. "In a way, there is some truth to it. It's unfortunate that you have to, sort of quell the nervousness, and reassure Danielle about things that you didn't precipitate. I think you'll fare far better if you keep this all in the forefront, though. It seems as if you stuff all the knowledge you have about Danielle's past–all the things that she has confided to you–in the back of your head."

We waited a moment for Paul to respond to that.

"You're right about that. I probably do. I..." he trailed off a second, then tried again. "I just don't think it should affect us."

"If only we lived on a desert island, we would have no problems." I intoned.

"I'm not looking for a desert island situation," Paul insisted with vive.

"I know you're not." I sighed. "Believe me when I say that I really do try."

I caught his eyes for the first time in the session, and I looked deeply into them, hoping to drive home the earnestness with which I had just spoken.

"It's unfair to you to have to deal with all this..." Constance validated Paul with both her words and a heartfelt glance. "But...you have to remember how unfair life has been for Danielle. She's just now getting together the tools that she needs to succeed. If you can keep that in the forefront of your mind, and be patient, I truly believe that you two can make a success of your life together." She sat back and waited to see which one of us would reply first.

"Do you think I'm getting better?" I dared to ask.

"I think you're making great progress. What do you think?" She threw it back to me in typical therapist style.

"I think..." and my voice got shaky as I tried to respond. "I think that there are days that feel as if I am a world away from all that occurred to me in my prior life, Upstate...and then there are days where I feel as if I am climbing a mountain and I will never, ever reach the top." Ugh. There were times that the hour in her office was as tedious as trying to swim through a vat of pea soup: muddled and murky, my arms getting tired with each push.

"You're doing rather well." Constance addressed Paul again. "Danielle is very invested in her recovery and progress."

"No, I know. I get that. I just...I could kill her parents for all that she's had to lug around for so long." He explained his theory about the bag of bricks. "And now that I'm about to meet them…I guess I don't know what to expect either."

"I think you'll be fine." Constance reassured us both with her heavy smile, her *constant* companion, part of the reason I liked her so much.

Chapter Eighty

"Do I look alright?" I was growing tired of preening and desperately wanted to make my way out of the bathroom, but kept fidgeting and fixing in spite of myself.

"You look fine." Paul enveloped me in a great big hug, and I stayed there for a full minute, taking strength from him. When he pulled away, he said, "You'll be fine. I'm the one who should be worried about things here. How do I look?" He made a little circle on the bathroom rug, showing off his new khakis and a Polo shirt.

"You look fine." I returned, and then turned back to the mirror for one last dash of makeup. "My father will be less concerned with how you look and more concerned with how you shake."

"My behind?" Paul shook his tush.

"Your hand." I eyed him mischievously. "Although you could shake that thing for me any old time."

"Wow. How long for dinner?" He shook his butt again and made a face. I laughed.

I took my thousandth deep breath of the day, turned to him and said, "Ready?"

"Yup." He gave me a satisfying once-over. "Ready as I'm ever going to be."

We made our way downstairs and Paul hailed a cab. As we piled in, he grabbed my hand and held it safe in his. We looked at each other and shared a smile as we hurtled our way across town in the yellow cab, our ears accosted by a seat belt reminder from the likes of Joan Rivers.

Soon we were deposited in front of Carmine's. We looked at each other one more time, and I gave Paul a nervous smile as he opened up the door for me. I scooted in underneath the canopy of his extended arm, and then grabbed his hand again as soon as he released the door. We squeezed each other's hand at the same moment, and I wondered briefly exactly who was reassuring who.

As we walked into the crowded waiting area, I spied them standing over in a corner to our left. They had their jackets slung over their respective arms, and they looked preoccupied as they were taking in their surroundings, waiting patiently for us.

"That's them." I gestured with my chin, squeezed his hand again, and then made my way towards them.

"Hi Dad, Michael, Beth." I nodded at each of them in turn and then tried to scoop Michael up into a hug. "You're getting so big!"

"I told you!" My father beamed at his son.

His son.

His son who lived with him, who he never left, who probably slept soundly under his roof, secure in the belief that the father he knew was right next door, that he cared enough to protect him from the things that went bump in the night. I couldn't remember that feeling. I got lost for a fraction of a second, those thoughts flashing through my mind at lightning speed, and then I reached back for Paul, and pushed the past behind.

"Everyone, this is Paul." Now it was my turn to beam, as he leaned forward to shake my father's hand, and from where I was standing, seemed to hold his own. "Paul, this is my father Michael, Michael Jr., and his mom Beth." I smiled at Beth, whom I held some genuine affection for, but who just didn't seem to fit the Dad I once knew.

Greetings were exchanged, my brother Michael openly perusing Paul from bottom to top, while Beth did the same, except she did it in a manner that would have gone unnoticed by anyone but me. I smirked and caught her eye as the host turned towards the group of people waiting and called out Paul's name. Looked like Beth thought Paul was just as cute as I did. Sometimes, it *is* just a girl thing.

"That's us." Paul did one of his famous hand gestures and we followed the host single-file over to a table towards the back of the room.

Something funny: When my father and Paul went to sit down, I noticed that they both gravitated towards the two chairs, whose backs were to the wall, Godfather-style. Call it an Old Italian tradition/superstition; call it whatever you want, but you would have had to be me at that precise moment in order to see the pure humor that one action evoked from the depths of my soul. I almost couldn't help myself, but I managed (with a load of self-restraint) to stifle the chuckle that was fighting to surface as they scraped out their chairs and positioned themselves, back to the wall, oblivious to their habits.

I situated myself across from Paul, my father was on his left, Beth was next to me on my right, and Michael Jr. claimed the seat at the head of the table. Soon enough a waiter dumped a heaping basket of bread on our table, sloshed our glasses full of water, and then dropped a bundle of menus before promising to come right back.

"This is sooo goood!" Little Michael inhaled the bread and I shot an appreciative grin in his direction.

"You like that? I knew you'd like the bread here." I winked.

"Ummm-ummm!" Michael took a second piece before he was even finished with his first one.

"So I hear congratulations are in order," my father singsonged in a voice that suddenly seemed very unlike him.

I looked up then and allowed for a thought that hadn't entered my mind until that minute: could he be nervous too?

"Oh, yes! Let me see!" Beth lunged towards my left hand, and then placed her bread on a napkin in order to take my hand in hers. "Ooooh, Danielle, that's gorgeous."

"Thank you." I must have blushed. I let her hold my hand, and although I pretended to gaze upon my ring right along with her, I was really concentrating on my father.

"You did good." He said this looking at Paul, his eyes flicking only slightly over the ring. For a second, I wasn't really sure whom he was saying this to.

"Thanks." I answered for us, waiting for his attention to turn to me. After the tiniest pause, our waiter picked that moment to make his way back over to the table, and take our drink order. He told us the specials, his voice resting somewhere between rehearsed and spoken with flourish. At Carmine's, most of the dishes are served family-style, with mounds of food piled high atop an unadorned platter, tempting from its mass alone. After a quick debate, we settled on a platter of fried calamari, a platter of Caesar salad, a platter of ziti, as well as a special chicken dish that the waiter had recommended.

"That should be enough to feed an army," Paul remarked.

"At least this army," Beth giggled and then reached over to ruffle little Michael's hair. He tried to duck her oncoming hand, but still managed to get a piece of her, and as I caught Beth's wry grin on the retreat, I thought about the woman inside.

I had never really gotten to know Beth. Don't get me wrong; it's not as if I saw her as the enemy, or that she turned me off in any way that mattered. I just kept my distance, and so had she. It was the unspoken contract between us, and as the smell of garlic permeated the already heavy air, I wondered briefly if that contract needed to be renegotiated.

"So I don't suppose you own a car, living down here," My father turned again to Paul, directing the conversation, asking a question outside of the usual question format.

Okay, so he was nervous. Cars were always his failsafe position: it was something he knew well, a topic that wouldn't cause anything controversial to come in to the conversation. I took it under advisement that perhaps this day wasn't any easier for Dad than it was for me.

Paul began discussing cars with my father then, and Beth began inquiring after the wedding, in typical gender typing fashion. Michael Jr. seemed entranced with the whole Carmine's scene, and slowly but surely, as the conversation began to flow and ideas were bandied about, I began to settle in to a sense of family, whatever that was in my life, whatever it would be.

"I kind of almost want to elope," I confessed as Beth prodded me for details.

"Oh, you couldn't do that! Your father would be so upset if he didn't get to walk you down the aisle." She said it matter-of-factly, as she gazed across the table at her husband, and then back to me.

"He would?" It seemed so long ago since I had had that picture in my mind: the one of the loving father, advocate, and friend.

"Oh, Danielle, you don't know." She shook her head. "You just don't know."

I found that familiar ring of defensiveness building around me once again. How could I know if he never told me? Was I supposed to read his mind?

"Well, I can't imagine Paul's parents being happy with that decision either. So it looks like we are going to plan a pretty traditional wedding." I tried to shrug off my earlier, divisive thoughts. "Sometimes I can't even believe it's real. I mean, I haven't made one actual plan yet…for anything…I guess just because I can't believe I have to plan a wedding. That it's happening to *me*." I found myself suddenly tempted to tell Beth more; to confide in her as I never had before, to begin to share with her the very tangible emotion that there were many times I simply could not believe that *my life* had been happening to me.

My new life.

"Have you decided where you're going to live?" My father cut in at this point, before I had a chance to try it on for size.

Paul and I looked at each other. We hadn't really discussed it, perhaps because it seemed obvious to us, but I felt sure that his apartment was the only answer for now.

"We'll live down here." I answered for us again, as I reached for Paul's hand underneath the table.

"Then what are you going to do with your car?" My father inquired.

Having a car in the city was a humungous expense; the end result being that most non-millionaires opted out completely. I hadn't even thought that far ahead yet. I had only been engaged a couple of weeks, and I certainly wasn't prepared for his handful of probing (albeit practical) questions.

"I..." I shook my head and looked at Paul.

"You know, we haven't really discussed it yet, but..." he turned to me, "My parents have offered for you to store your car at their house if you still want to keep it."

"Oh. Okay. So I guess we'll do that." I shrugged. I wanted more. I wanted less discussion of the logistics, and more about this very large change that was coming up in my life. Was this what both Paul and Constance meant when they warned me about not expecting so much? Was my father or his wife capable of connecting on a deeper level, or should I just stick to talking about the inconsequential, concentrating on the myriad of details that would, in fact, need to be negotiated before The Big Day? I found myself worrying more about the reality of having a wedding with both parents sharing the same space than the aesthetics. Was that wrong? Was this time supposed to be filled with joyous and carefree thoughts, my mind free of tension, my only worries pertaining to choice of florist and the inevitable debate of band vs. DJ? If it was, I was failing miserably, as my mind was focusing more on how I would navigate the murky waters of marriage, rather than the details of joining two lives together in one adrenalin-injected evening.

"You know what I want to know?" Michael spoke up and interrupted the conversation that seemed to be going on around me. "I want to know how you two met." He said this with the candor of a child, however I caught an adult voice peeking through, and my heart smiled just listening to him.

"You mean you don't know?" Paul acted surprised. Well, perhaps he was. "Your sister knocked me over!"

"No!" Michael found this rather funny. "She didn't!"

"She did!" Paul insisted, holding court for all of them. "Seriously? We met crossing Lexington Avenue."

"And she just picked you up?" Michael asked unabashedly.

"*He* picked *me* up, I'll have you know." I insisted swiftly.

"Ah, but did you orchestrate the bump?" My father wiggled his eyebrows in a way that was not unlike Paul.

"The bump?" I shot a disdainful look towards the man who dared to question my intentions.

"Yeah, *the bump…*" My father turned to confront Paul. "How spontaneous was the bump? Was it…a natural bump, or was it a bump contrived?"

"Do you think I would contrive a bump?" I acted as if I was appalled by the insinuation, but inside I was enjoying his attention, and the playfulness that I knew was lurking right underneath his burly, uptight surface.

"Would you have contrived the initial bump?" Paul had a look of mock surprise on his face, his hands gesturing in a way that said he was just as appalled as I.

"How do I know that you didn't contrive the initial bump?" I threw this back at him, then sat back and took a long pull on my water, my smile hugging the brim of the glass.

"If I remember correctly, I was the one that got the briefcase knocked right out of my hands!" Paul huffed.

"Not to mention your heart…stolen right out of your chest!" I clutched my hands in front of me and mooned a little for all of them, pretending to be Paul.

"Aw, mush…" My father shook his head, not interested in anything too potentially sappy. He was rescued a moment later by the waiter with a tray full of entrees.

We dug in, and the night carried on with more of the same. Good food, great barbs, and after fully settling in to the idea that family could be a good thing…even I had to admit that I had good company.

After dinner, they wanted to walk around Times Square for a little bit, so we indulged them, all the while narrating as we walked.

"Dad, do you see that place in the middle over there?" I pointed to the TKTS booth and turned around so I could see him.

"Yeah." He nodded.

"That's the place where you can get discounted tickets to Broadway shows," I pointed again and traced the line snaking out from the windows. "It's always like that."

"Can you get Off-Broadway there too?" He inquired as his head swiveled to take in the length of the line. "This guy at work–his kid is in something going on downtown."

"I think so." Paul answered as we crossed the street. "I think you can only get tickets for the day of an event though."

I nodded. "Do you know the name of the show downtown?"

"Nah." He dismissed the thought with his paw and a quick shake of the head.

"Maybe we should do that sometime, Michael," Beth suggested as we walked past the booth. "We can come down here and visit Danielle and Paul and go see a play."

"Sure. Sure. By the way, when are you kids coming Upstate to visit us?" My father threw this out as if the thought had just occurred to him.

Okay–and I determined to give him the benefit of the doubt here–maybe it had.

"Soon." I could barely choke it out. *One thing at a time here, Dad.*

"Sounds good. Michael wants to take you to a game." He acknowledged my brother with a head gesture.

"A Yankee game?" I pretended to be excited about a chance to see the Yankees. "Are you treating, Michael?"

"No." He laughed and shook his head. "My soccer game."

"Gotcha." I purposely dropped Paul's hand then and moved over to ruffle Michael's hair. "I'll come up soon."

"Okay." He looked up at me and smiled. He didn't seem bothered by my touching him.

"Where did you guys park?" Paul asked nonchalantly as we kept moving North, all the while taking in the sights and the smells of a Saturday night in Times Square. The area was beginning to get crowded now, the pretzel guy on the corner still hawking his wares from the height of the afternoon crush, while people from around the world circled him, the steam rising from his cart, enticing, wafting over the heads of tourists and natives alike. I nodded my head as the vendor caught my eye and then observed his handwritten pretzel sign: easily a dollar more than the price of the guy who was set up outside of Paul's place.

Capitalism at its best.

"Over by…" My father made a faraway motion with his hands. "Beth, did you write it down?"

"Of course." Beth replied, as she leapt to attention and began tearing apart her purse with a ferociousness of a bear ripping through a campsite. I shuddered as I took her in: *"It's in here somewhere. Oh, where is that little piece of paper?"* Fretfully, she worked her fingers through every pocket and zippered pouch while my father loomed over her somewhere in the background, his demeanor growing more apprehensive second by second, my eyes not focused on him, my heart alone able to detect him.

I remembered what is was like to want to try to please him, and as that memory shot through my brain, I felt a buried sense of shame rise and color my cheeks in this present day.

"Did you find it?" He was demanding in a tone that was meant to sound light, but I knew better, and so did she.

"I have the ticket right here..." she produced the ticket and then waved it at him. "I just...I wrote down the street on a separate piece of paper." She ferreted around inside her bag.

We were stopped now, on a street corner at the North end of Times Square, people jostling us as we took up valuable sidewalk space.

"Maybe we should move in," I suggested and then pointed to the nearby side of a building. "We're probably in the way here."

Us four adults moved in to stand on the side of the building while Michael trailed along, his eyes still wide as he took in the sights. He seemed oblivious to my father's demeanor as well as the slowly disintegrating Beth, caught up as he was in the blinking lights and nonstop neon. I tried to catch Paul's eye, but the entire scenario registered as no big deal to him, and he had begun making an effort to talk to Michael as I looked on towards Dad and Beth.

"Why didn't you just write it on the back of the ticket?" He demanded of her, his voice laced with an accusatory tone. "I mean, wasn't that more than a little dumb to write it on a separate piece of paper?"

"Michael," She was referring to my father, "I thought...I wrote it down as soon as we pulled in and we didn't *have* the ticket yet!" I saw a blush creep up her cheeks and for the second time that night I felt my heart lurch towards her. I found myself wanting to protect her, to try to tell her that, in the big scheme of things, it really didn't matter.

"Do you remember the name of the place?" Paul moved closer to the huddle, cutting his conversation with Michael short, as he stepped in and offered to help.

"I think it was Kinney. Yes, Kinney!" Beth pronounced as she came up out of her purse for a second. "Does that help?"

Paul and I exchanged a glance. There was a Kinney parking garage on every other street in New York, plus they sat in triplicate in the more touristy areas like Times Square. No, it didn't help much.

My father now had her purse and was double-checking her work as Beth stood a few steps away from him.

"What we can do is this," Paul proposed and then waited to speak until everybody was looking at him, "We can take the ticket you do have to the nearest Kinney and see if they can trace the numbers on it or something and maybe point us in the right direction. Or," and this was Paul's attempt to lighten things, "it's a beautiful night…we could just walk around from one garage to another until we find the car."

I shot him a wry grin, my father hrmphed, and Beth looked grateful at the diversion that his suggestion provided.

"Let's start here," I suggested and then pointed left.

Beth shrugged her shoulders and then trailed behind us as we hung a left and proceeded to make our way down the street to the nearest Kinney. I strode next to Beth, and tentatively put my arm around her. "Don't worry; we'll find it."

"I just can't believe how stupid…!" She trailed off then, blaming herself for not being able to please him, whether she knew that was what she was blaming herself for or not. She shoved her hands deep into her jacket pockets, and as if doing so reminded her of something else, she mumbled, *"Wait a second..."* and then reached into her jacket. She fuddled around an inside pocket for a second or two and then emerged triumphant with a yellow slip of paper in her hand.

"I got it!" She screeched and waved the paper towards my father. Then again, "I got it."

"Well, what does it say?" He didn't share her joy in finding the elusive slip of paper. His manner indicated that he would have known where it was all the while, and that Beth was somehow his cross to bear.

"It says 45th Street between 5th and 6th," she informed him.

"Okay, so we'll walk you down." I walked to the front of the pack and lead the way without another word. I grabbed Paul's hand and held on tight. I found myself suddenly wishing for them to leave: a quick exit before the old Danielle buried herself in the disappointments of her former life, mired in the behaviors that repeated themselves over and over again in this tenuous relationship.

As we walked down to the garage where their car was parked, I focused on chitchatting with Michael about school and friends and of course, soccer. The kid loved soccer like a European, much to my father's chagrin. I think my father still held on to the illusion that one day Little Michael would evolve from a kid who loved running the length of a soccer field to a kid who would one day become the star quarterback on his high school football team. He would wait a long time, this I knew. I may not have or make the time to see Michael often, but I knew the kid instinctively, and there was a link between us that was more than a sharing of the same chromosome.

"This is it," Beth crowed as we approached the front of the Kinney that was supposedly garaging their car. My father went up to the attendant and handed him the ticket as we all continued some idle chitchat on the sidewalk.

"You sure you guys don't want to do or see something else?" I offered this half-heartedly, knowing they would leave, but feeling as if I should offer nonetheless.

"No, we're fine," Beth reassured me. She took my hands in hers then and played with my ring for another second. "It's beautiful, Danielle."

"Thanks." I'm sure I blushed. "I…you know what, Beth? I've never seen yours!" I had probably seen it no less than a hundred times, but I had never really looked at it, and now my curiosity was piqued. I flipped her hand over then and gazed upon a nice-sized stone set in a flower-type design. It looked older, almost vintage, and I wondered briefly if she wanted it that way.

"They're so different now," she sighed, then held her hand out against my own. "Mine was so trendy at the time. Yours is truly timeless."

"I think yours looks vintage. Very cool," I reassured her, my head nodding and my eyes latching on to hers.

"You know it's not about the ring?" Beth held her gaze steady on my own for what seemed like eternity.

"I know." I looked over to where Paul was shooting the breeze with my father and Michael. "I know that I love him."

"He seems really great, Danielle. I'm happy for you," and with that, Beth leaned towards me and enveloped me in a hug. I hugged her tentatively at first, my mind trying desperately to recall if I had ever once hugged her in the past, my heart feeling lighter just by the slim connection that we made.

"Thanks. I'm happy for me too." I said this with a chuckle, and we broke apart just as the car was produced. My father waved us over and then proceeded to wish us goodbye with a chaste hug for me and another firm handshake for Paul. I got another chance to ruffle Michael's hair and soon they were off, disappearing quickly into the throng of New York City traffic. I stayed where I was, looking after them until they were only a speck of blue light, until I could barely see their car in the mishmash of cars heading towards the major highways.

"Are you okay?" Paul came up beside me and casually fit himself into me, pressing close against my left side.

"I'm fine. It's just so weird still…nothing's easy with them, and I don't know why. I feel drained. I feel like I needed them to leave when they did, but for some strange reason, I'm always left behind wanting more." I sighed. "I don't get it myself, so I really don't see how I can explain it to you."

"You did fine," Paul reassured me, and I smiled then, because the conversation should be being held in reverse; me reassuring him that he was well liked and well received.

"I need a hug." I leaned into him face-on and received a gracious hug. As I moved away from him, I locked eyes with him and shared a smile. "You were great."

"Should I hail a cab or do you want to walk?" He paused for my direction and then grabbed my hand in the process.

"I would love to walk if you would. It's turning out to be a pretty nice night." I was indicating the weather, but I realized as we began walking home that no major catastrophes had ensued, and that all in all, it could have been worse.

"Your father seems like an okay guy. He just…doesn't express himself well." Paul looked sideways at me in order to catch my expression. "I think it's safe to say that he likes cars?"

"Oh yeah, I should have warned you in advance about the obsession with cars," I rolled my eyes and smiled.

"I think he really cares about you." Paul put it out there and it took me almost the length of one city block to respond.

"You think?" I mulled it over a minute. "I think he might, but even with me keeping my expectation level at below zero, it's hard to tell."

"They're your family, Danielle. They might not be perfect, they may even be a little bit wacky, but the point is they're yours. And there's not much you can do about that."

"Oh, you are so right, my friend. Too right."

Somewhere between the West side and the East side I reconciled myself to the fact that not only was Paul right, that they were my family, and that was that, but that he was displaying once again that uncanny knack for remaining unruffled. Family wasn't like friends or lovers: you couldn't choose them. You did the best you could with what you had–with whatever God gave you to work with–and then you choose the rest of the people in your life to make up for the blighted holes that the family left behind.

Late that night, while Paul was sleeping, I got up to grab a drink of water. I wandered out onto the terrace and wondered again about the people we chose: did we really choose them, or did they choose us? My mind recalled my father's effort at a joke: *was it an orchestrated bump?* Perhaps it was orchestrated…by God himself…knowing what I would need and when. Knowing far better than I that Paul was the remedy for all the people I couldn't choose.

When I slipped back into bed, I kissed him on the cheek and then played softly with his hair until I fell back asleep. I was so grateful.

Chapter Eighty-One

"Victory!" Lanie shouted from the seat next to me.

I indulged her with a wicked grin and then laughed at my own reticence. "They came, they saw, they left promptly. And that's what I'm grateful for." I took a small bow.

"Ah, but you came to an agreement and that's the most important thing." Lanie gave me a knowing smile as she kicked her legs in a childish fashion and then whirled around in her chair.

"An agreement? With whom?" I was only a tad bit puzzled.

"With yourself." Lanie swiveled once again and then threw her hands up in exasperation. "You're slow today. Read my lips: you made an agreement with yourself, conscious or no, that you were not going to let them rattle your cage the other night. It sounds like–and stop me if I'm wrong here–that you didn't fall into any of the same old pitfalls with them. You didn't leave in tears, you didn't allow them to run the conversation, you weren't drowning in disappointment, and you even had a fuzzy warm feeling at some point during the night."

"You're right." I acquiesced. "I felt grateful, and although some of that was directed towards them, it was mostly a deeper thing, a God-centered gratefulness, and a feeling towards Paul that I can't even…put into words." I found myself getting all choked up as I spoke, recalling the way I felt when I woke up in the middle of the night, that surge in my heart that I couldn't define.

"It's your turn." Lanie said this so softly that I thought at first that it was an utterance of my own heart, a thought that transpired only in my own brain. However when I looked up at her, she had a dopey grin on her face, and I realized that she said it after all.

"I guess it is." I looked around me as if searching. "I know I've said this at least a million times: it just doesn't seem real."

"Then let's make it real!" Lanie insisted and then jumped out of her chair. "We need to go shopping for wedding dresses!"

"Already? Oh, God, Lanie, I can't…"

"Why not?!" C'mon, Yellie, you're killing me here! You need to get in the mood. You're a *bride, for God's sake;* start acting like one!" Lanie looked over her shoulder at her phone display. "Did the phone just ring?"

"I didn't hear anything." I checked mine.

"Okay," She waved it away, as if work was inconsequential compared to The Wedding. "Here's the deal. What are you doing tonight?"

"Tonight? I thought we were going to the gym."

"Ixnay on the gym. Let's go to Saks and Lord and Taylor and try on every fancy dress they have!" Lanie was bursting with enthusiasm. "This is the kind of stuff we dreamed about as little girls! Do you have any idea how long I have wanted to try on a wedding dress?"

"Lanie, I hate to remind you, but this is not an episode of *Friends*. We can't just go in to some store somewhere and start ransacking their entire line of formalwear."

"Why not?" Lanie was indignant. "You have to lighten up, my friend. This is the fun part! In fact…" she looked behind her as if she had forgotten something, "I picked this up on the way to work this morning!" From the southeast corner of her desk she hefted what at first appeared to be a hotel catalog. Only once it landed on my desk with a *whomp* did I realize that it was the latest tome of *Bride's* magazine.

"You are really just…too much." But her enthusiasm was catching, and I found myself thumbing through the pages in spite of myself. The next thing I knew,

Lanie was beside me, her head right next to mine, her chin practically digging into my shoulder.

"Ooooh, look at that one!" Lanie pointed to a dress that was more chandelier than couture.

"I think I want something a little more plain." I made a face.

"You mean classic."

"Right. Classic."

"Well, look at that one." Lanie pointed to the layout on the opposite page.

"I think that's a little…revealing." I wanted to look like a bride, not a hooker.

"That's why you have to try them on! Yellie, you can't possibly tell what you're going to look like in one of these until you try them on…and *whirl* in them." Lanie made a small pirouette in the middle of the hole/office. Just then Alex walked by and tipped his cap to both of us.

We collapsed in giggles and Lanie called out after him, "Wanna dance?"

Alex called back a smothered greeting something along the lines of "I'll be back."

"Don't you think it's just a little too early?" I wrinkled my nose at Lanie, hoping she would see my point. Although I wasn't sure just what my point was. I think I was afraid to jinx things.

"No. Absolutely not! It's never too early to look! Plus, I need to start trying on some bridesmaid dresses. You are not going to put me in one of those drippy little pastel numbers, are you? I think I like beige." Lanie mused, her hands back on top of the magazine, flipping the pages animatedly.

"Beige?" Although I would have never entertained the color beige (is beige even a color?) I found myself picturing Lanie in it and I knew full well that she could pull it off with panache.

"Or something neutral." Lanie lifted the magazine off my desk then and moved it over to hers as her phone rang. She answered her phone then, began making reservations for someone, and continued to comb through the book in between various computer inputs.

I shook my head and marveled at the woman I shared so many hours with. How Lanie could be so cavalier with something as momentous as my wedding dress left me feeling more than a little bit uneasy. I had always thought of the search for The Dress as something akin to a bright light shining down from heaven; a chorus of *Alleluia* trumpeting from the rafters as I scuttled around, the light gathering power and then settling on the perfect dress in just the nick of time. Shouldn't a shopping day that had so much significance attached to it be planned weeks, even months, in advance? Didn't I have to enter a bridal shoppe with a bevy of women in tow? Would they even let me in without my mother by my side? My mind flicked briefly towards thoughts of my mother. Did I want her to be involved in this on any level? Was I ready to trust her with my dreams again?

I tried to throw out all of my preconceived notions and focus on what I wanted. What did Danielle want to do? I mean, what did I desire? This was my one and only chance to run the whole shebang any which way I wanted to: was I going to acquiesce to anyone's view of what my wedding day should be? What about everyone's view? Did anyone or everyone have any say…except Paul? I shook my head, and the phone rang almost instantaneously. It was Paul.

"I was just thinking of you." I smiled on my end, unable to hide the excitement that bubbled up inside me every time his digits hit the frame.

"I am guilty of the same." He said this in a voice that said, *you caught me.* "Whatcha upta?"

"Not much. Did you try to rhyme that?"

"You like that, huh?"

"Oh, you are without a doubt too cool for me." I smiled again at my good fortune. The ring on my finger punctuated my feelings for him, and as I gazed upon it, I made a decision and put it into words. "I'm going shopping with Lanie tonight. For wedding dresses."

"Good for you! I was wondering when you girls were going to get around to doing that. Can I meet you for dinner afterwards?" Paul voice was genuine; his happiness extending through the phone.

"Of course. Call Rob and see if he wants to join us." I made a motion towards Lanie and she nodded as she continued to talk into her headset. "Lanie says yes."

"Cool. I'll catch up with you later." Paul said *wait one sec,* and then I heard some background noise, questions pertaining to papers he had or didn't have. "Baby, I gotta go. But call me later and remember one thing–"

"You love me?" I interrupted, believing I knew the closing.

"That too, but what I was going to say is have fun."

"Gotcha."

Chapter Eighty-Two

"Are you ready?" Lanie smacked her newly glossed lips together, shut her makeup mirror with a severe click and then began shoving on her jacket. "Get your shopping shoes on, honey, because here we go!"

"Lanie–seriously–I don't have the right shoes for this," I looked down, suddenly alarmed at the backless espadrilles that were adorning my feet. They were worn brown leather and they looked fabulous with my denim capris and brown top, but probably wouldn't work well when trying on formalwear.

"You're not getting a dress hemmed tonight," she countered and then gave me an evil glare. "No more excuses out of you, Yellie! You are trying on dresses and you are having fun doing so even if it kills you." She clicked her computer off and turned to face me, hands on hips, ready to roll.

"I don't even have on the right bra," I was beginning to whine. I hated myself for it, but I couldn't seem to stop and I didn't know why.

"Let me rephrase: You are trying on dresses and you are having fun doing so even if *I* kill you." Lanie smiled complacently.

"Okay, okay, you win, I lose…I'm going." I shrugged on my jacket and grabbed my purse. "Maybe I'll buy a new bra while we're there."

"That's the ticket!" Lanie graced me with an approving glance. "You are the *worst* bride so far! Yellie: don't ruin this for me."

I had to laugh at the outrageousness of it all.

She was right, after all, and I guess that's what was bugging me the most. I had this strange feeling coursing through my chest, hammering in my ears and trying to talk me out of going with her all day long. It was as if trying on a dress would bring it all to life, and I was afraid to step into it—literally and figuratively.

But what was I going to do, hide from a dress? If I couldn't get over this first hurdle, I would never be able to plan the rest of the wedding. Besides, Lanie was right; what was I waiting for? Paul and I had discussed a wedding in the spring. If we were aiming for next spring, then I had to get a move on, because a year was not a lot of time to plan a wedding anywhere, and New York City moved faster than any place else in the world. There was a fair chance that a lot of things were already booked, and the things that we'd find available would be through the roof price-wise. Ah well, I would just have to see what happens when the time comes.

One hurdle at a time.

"All right, you ready?" I acted as if I had been waiting on her all day long.

"I thought you'd never ask."

We made our way down to the lobby and out the doors before we decided on any sort of game plan.

"Want to hail a cab?" Lanie asked with the energy of someone who was dreading the very thought.

"At rush hour?" I looked at her as if she had three heads. "We'll get there faster walking."

"You're right." Lanie hung a left at the corner and began sprinting to the west side. She left a space for me and gestured forward. "March!"

"Now, is that any way to talk to the bride?" I was beginning to get into the spirit of things. "Lanie, do you really want to wear beige?"

"I really want to wear whatever it is that you want me to wear," Lanie batted her eyelashes at me coquettishly, "Isn't that what a good bridesmaid is supposed to say?"

"Yes." I nodded my head vigorously. "Even if I put you in fuchsia tulle."

"You will no longer have a friend, much less a bridesmaid, if you put me in fuchsia tulle." Lanie huffed as we walked up from Lexington Avenue to Park. "Seriously, Yellie, what're you looking for?"

"For me or for you?"

"Both."

"Okay. Well, like I said to you before; for me I want something a little on the plain side." I put my hand up to stop her before she corrected me, "Classic. Whatever–just no beads, no pearls, no yards and yards of lace, nothing that looks like I am *dripping* anything."

"Except class."

"Exactly."

"Do you want a full gown?"

"I guess so…I don't want anything too form-fitting." I indicated my hips.

"I think girls like you should wear stuff that shows off your curves." Lanie made an hourglass figure with her hands and then put one arm behind her head as if she were posing for the camera. "I have it on good authority that you don't know what the hell you want."

"You're probably right. Go ahead: what do you want?" I knew that she was champing at the bit to tell me all about her coming-out party: i.e., my wedding.

"I want sexy, not frumpy. I want something classic, too…but not dowdy. I want to be able to wear Manolo Blahniks with the dress, not those awful dyeables that all the girls from Long Island force their bridesmaids to wear." Lanie crinkled her nose.

"Do I look like the dyeable type to you?" I feigned offense.

"No, but I betcha the girls Upstate are guilty of the same." Lanie tried to stare me down over her shoulder as we crossed the street right in front of Sak's.

"I was only in one wedding: Annemarie's." I made a face to her back.

"And…?" She turned as soon as we were safely crossed, her eyes pinning me to the sidewalk as it were.

"She had dyeables." I gave in, rolling my eyes and chuckling at the same time. "What are you, the human nature guru? How do you know these things off the top of your head, and still manage to not look snide in the delivery?"

"You need to learn to give me more credit." Lanie swept her arms out in front of me as she indicated the revolving door. "After you, madam."

"Hrmph," I acted exasperated, but I knew better and so did she. One quick turn of the door and I was enveloped in a melee of scent: Cosmetics, First Floor, Vultures. I turned to look at Lanie and gave her a warning glance.

"You know you're going to need a new scent for the Big Day?" Lanie propelled me towards the next counter where, as luck would have it, sat a perfectly adorned cardboard bride atop a fluorescent spill of various ointments on display. "See?"

Within minutes, she cried out: "I got it!" Lanie exclaimed as she barreled towards me, arms outstretched in sheer delight. "Sniff!" She commanded this in a voice that fell somewhere between drill instructor and sensory coach.

I did as instructed and then gave her what I thought was my most ingratiating smile.

"It's called *sampling,*" Lanie reminded me as she ushered me away from Cosmetics and over towards the escalators. "Just remember that scent." She pressed a cardboard swatch into my palm.

"Gotcha."

We rode the escalator up what seemed like a hundred floors to the area that was dubbed *Formal, Eveningwear, And Bridal Salon.* When we stepped off the escalator, we each looked one way and then the other, shrugged, and then proceeded towards a landscape of blinding sequins.

"Now this is what I *don't* want," Lanie pointed to something that looked like it belonged in The Ice Capades, circa 1979.

"I think that's more for a mother of the bride," I turned the dress over in my hand. The dress was so sparkly that I saw spots.

"Whose mother?" Lanie quipped as she barreled through a bunch of gaudy selections. "I expected better of Saks."

"Lanie, look!" I spied a blur of white, cream, and ivory silk from where I was standing. "That must be the bridal salon." I found myself getting excited for the first time all day. True excitement, the type of stirring in your soul that can't be defined, the whirring of your internal organs, the instant flexing of a smile across your face.

"Let's go!" Lanie hung the sequined horror in her hand back up on a nearby rack, the hanger facing backwards, the dress askew. She proceeded forward without a further glance in its direction.

The dresses were all hung up in a U-shaped fashion; the entire area roped off with a discreet velvet rope at the entrance; almost as if to indicate that these dresses deserved a particular reverence. I padded in on the heels of Lanie, my eyes taking in each sheaf of silk and satin, from right to left, all the way around the U.

We didn't speak for a full minute, and I allowed myself to get swallowed up in the moment: I was a bride. I was The Bride. I was going to make my dreams come true, and now all I had to do was pick out a dress.

The surreal factor was shooting through the roof.

Added to that: "Hi, can I help you with something?"

I whirled around to find a woman who was probably just a little bit older than me, but so perfectly pulled together that she looked as if she had been emulating fashion magazines from the time Cosmo originated. She was thin, too thin, and she seemed angular even in the smile she presented. She reeked of an old pro that had been doing this forever: sizing up brides and whipping them into shape in no time whatsoever. She had an air about her that commandeered instant respect, and although I wasn't sure right away if I liked her, I tried to smile and decided to give her a shot.

"Hi. Um, thanks. I'm just looking…" The stand-by 'just looking' response seemed inadequate now, amidst yards of fabric that were held aside for only a small amount of the population. I smiled weakly again. I remembered that I was wearing espadrilles and not the right bra. Maybe she knew that I just wasn't ready.

"Are you a bride?" She trilled this in such a way that I found myself leaning quickly towards not liking her, as I took in the way she held her fake smile firmly in place, long after the question had hit the air.

There was an evil speck in her eye that hinted that she was questioning me, and by that I mean that she was questioning my right to be there.

"Oh, yes." I extended my hand promptly, blushing in spite of myself, as I practically shoved my diamond in her face. What was the matter with me? I was acting like Lanie! Who, by the way, was presently across the U from me, buried in yards of silk. "I just don't know what I want yet."

"Well, I'm sure you can let me know when you know." She offered me a catty little smile, one that assured me that I was wasting her time, and then she turned on her heel and strode swiftly away.

I was officially and utterly dismissed. There were no overtures towards help: no prying questions that looked for the buzzwords in my speech, no mild flattery thrown about in a guise to cinch the sale, no inquiries pertaining to my upcoming nuptials.

Nada.

Oh-ho-ho-ho-ho-ho! She was messing with the wrong girl if she thought that I was just going to roll over and play dead to her superior attitude. I had fought hard to get to this place in my life; I wasn't just some dippy society girl who was trying on dresses because I had a free afternoon. I was Danielle–and it was my turn.

"Find anything you like?" Lanie appeared next to me suddenly, a big white puff of dress slung over one arm.

"I...not yet. I can tell you I just found something I don't like." I pointed low, concealed somewhat by the dress Lanie was holding, looking directly at the saleswoman who had just strode away. I must have made a face, because Lanie's response was, "That bad, huh?"

I nodded.

"Then I say we try on some dresses!" Lanie gave me the evil grin that she generally reserved for when she ran into a new boyfriend's ex-girlfriend. "What do you think of this one here?" She unwound the dress from her arm, and then straightened it out for display. It was all white, with a classic, timeless cut: off the shoulder, fitted to the waist, a nice flare in order to hide the hips.

"I like it!" I nodded vigorously. "But didn't you say that we should try on *a lot* of dresses? That I wouldn't know what I would like until I tried them on?" I read her eyes and said no more. She gave the signal: we were in cahoots.

"Of course I did!" Lanie acted as if she had just lost her head, and then proceeded to do what she did best: she put on her Adrienne voice and whistled for the saleswoman.

She whistled like she was hailing a cab in the middle of a busy Manhattan street, she whistled as if she was in the last round of the North American Champion Whistle-Off Contest, and as a result, she startled the poor Salesmonster half to death.

" Muffy" turned around so abruptly that I thought her head was about to snap off her neck. Whoever would be so rude to summon her in such a way?

"Hiya, over there, do you tink you can help us ovah heer?" Lanie was Adrienne Plus: and I was about to lose it, trying to play good cop to her bad.

"Did you need some help with something?" Muffy steadied her gaze right on Lanie-cum-Adrienne and tried not to hide the fact that she looked as if she was sniffing shit.

"Oh shurr, here: You hold this." Lanie shoved the dress that she had been holding into her arms, bunched it up a little for good measure, and then indicated the dressing room to the right. "The *Bride* and I are going in there. You–find us some other stuff that looks sorta, you know, kinda like this one here, and bring them in. In fact, just bring in a whole loada dresses and keep 'em coming 'til I tell ya we're done. We'll wait for ya." Lanie tromped right into the dressing room then, while I averted my eyes from the salesgirl and tiptoed in right after.

"Lanie!" I was hissing through tears, she was making me laugh so hard, and I wasn't going to be able to hold it in much longer. *"You're crazy!"*

"Are you having fun?" Lanie peeked out the door and tried tracking Muffy.

"Yes!" I giggled like a schoolgirl who had just received her first issue of *Tiger Beat* in the mail; Scott Baio's face plastered on the front cover, unable to control myself...because he was a *fox*.

"Good. She...isn't." Lanie pointed with her chin to the woman we were currently harassing. She was haphazardly pulling a dress out of one of the racks, her face showing not an ounce of love for my dear friend. If you looked really hard, you could see the steam pouring out of her ears.

"We are sooo bad!" I laughed heartily, and then danced a jig in front of the floor-length mirror. "I like it though."

"Good. My goal here is to make you feel good." Lanie was fluctuating between spying on Muffy and keeping an eye on me. "I did like that one dress though."

"So did I." I stepped up onto what seemed like a small platform, placed strategically in front of the mirror. "Lanie, aren't you supposed to have a fistful of M&M's in your hand right about now, and preen, and cry over me as I rotate?"

"A la Harry Met Sally?" Lanie guffawed. "That's for when you find *the* dress. Don't rush things. You're not buying anything today. Not yet anyway. Don't rush me."

"Rush you? Who's rushing you? And what if I do find *the* dress here, tonight?" I stepped into the Fret Zone for about a half second.

"You shall not buy it here on principle." She jerked her head towards Muffy. "Our goal is to look, and now of course, to drive Muffy crazy. If you do find *the dress* here, we copy down the SKU number, make, model, whatever, and we order it from somewhere else. Oh, here she comes." Lanie moved away from the entrance and made room for Muff.

Muffy entered the room with her fake smile fixed firmly in place, her left hand still holding the dress Lanie had thrown at her, her right hand clutching three similar dresses, each one with their trains trailing on the ground behind her. She said not a word, but kept flashing us a saccharine smile, while she violently situated each dress on the bar closest to the rounded display step.

"Whatcha got there, toots?" Lanie came up behind her and began manhandling the dresses one by one.

"I believe…" Muffy smiled again, but you could tell she really wanted to roll her eyes, "…that any of these would be appropriate."

"Gotcha." Lanie gave her the cheesiest grin I have ever seen in real life and then Muffy quickly made her exit.

We rolled.

"Okay, so now what?" I deferred to Lanie, as my self-appointed expert.

"Now you try them on. Lose the shoes and pants, Yellie, but keep on your top. I think you have to step into these," Lanie had the first dress in her hand and was looking for the zipper.

"Oh." This is something I hadn't thought of, something I wondered if my mother would know.

Lanie unzipped the dress fully, and then positioned it on the floor so that it looked like I had to step into a big, fluffy, synthetic donut hole. "Try this. Step in…gingerly. Now take off your shirt."

I heaved off my shirt and began adjusting the bra straps so that they fell right off the shoulder.

"Forget about the bra. Remember: this is preliminary." Lanie clucked.

I stopped fiddling with the bra and gently pulled the dress up around me. It was probably a couple of sizes larger than the one I would actually wear, but I got the general idea as Lanie proceeded to zip me up the back, and the whole thing began to take some sort of shape.

I have to admit that my heart fluttered just a little bit as I took a long look at myself in the mirror.

"You like?" Lanie was circling me, and then stopped in front of me in an effort to read my face. "What do you think, Yellie?"

"I like it!" I giggled and grinned and felt truly beautiful for the first time ever. "Oh, Lanie, what do you think?"

"I think you still need to try on those other dresses." She gave me a warning glance. "Don't go falling in love with the first one here that catches your fancy."

"As if." I preened a little, but eventually removed the dress, and tried on the other three in rapid succession. I found out quickly that I had a slight problem: I liked all of them.

"You still need to try on more," Lanie insisted after I asked her if she thought we should at least take all the information off of the first dress. "But write it down, because you're right, you never know."

I rummaged through my purse and found a pen and a stray piece of paper. I jotted down the designer's name, the model number and all of the other information on the tag, whether I understood it or not. I hung the dress back up on the rail and gathered my things.

"Next?" I was on a roll and wanted to keep going.

"Next we go to Lord and Taylor. Maybe there we can get someone to help us who doesn't have ice in her veins." She shook her head and we exited the dressing room together.

Just when I thought it was over, I heard Lanie call out, "Bye-bye, Muffy!"

It was louder than her whistle.

Chapter Eighty-Three

"So how'd you guys do?" Paul met us by the bar with a beer in his hand and Rob at his side.

"Miss Danielle *finally* came into her own," Lanie pronounced this with a beaming smile and a quick pat on my back. "I'll let her tell you." She gave Paul a hug hello and greeted Rob with a quick kiss on the cheek. She then hopped up on the bar stool right next to him, and gave me the floor.

"Well, first we had to deal with Muffy…" I cued in the drama and rolled my eyes for full effect.

"Who's Muffy?" Paul questioned.

"The Ice Queen." I went on to establish the presence of Muffy in the life of the wayward bride. Lanie and I told the story in tandem, embellishing all of her worst characteristics, exaggerating to the hilt.

"Girls, I am quite sure she did not have fangs," Rob said this in his trademark deadpan voice, then rolled his eyes and took a drink.

"Ah, but she did, my dear friend, and if it wasn't for Lanie, she would have eaten us alive!" I bowed to Lanie. "But then, *then…*" I let the suspense build as my last word hung in the air.

"Then?" Paul held out his hands in a gesture that said, *Come on.*

"I think I found it." I gave a satisfied smirk and then took a long pull on the beer Rob had ordered for me.

"You think you found your wedding dress?" Paul was a little slow on the uptake, but I thought I would keep him anyway.

"I think so. Lane?" I deferred to Lanie for the final say.

"I think so too." Lanie gave me the thumbs-up sign and then started a separate conversation with Rob.

Paul turned to me.

"You really think you found it?" His eyes belied genuine happiness for me.

"I think so." I grabbed him then and crushed his lips against my own. Crowds be damned, I was having my way with him right in the middle of a crowded bar. "I think I found it." I whispered this as we pulled apart, he gasping for air, somewhat taken aback by my forwardness, but liking it too, I could tell by the way his lip curled up on one side of his mouth. "I think I found it…in more ways than one."

Chapter Eighty-Four

"So when are we meeting your mother?" Paul inquired this lazily over breakfast one Sunday morning a couple of weeks later.

I sighed. "I've already met my mother."

The expression on his face: *not funny*.

"Okay. I guess…" I trailed off, with no words left to say. There was no use waiting any longer. I was smart enough to know that the bigger I made this…the bigger it would be. "I guess I could call her now."

He nodded, probably afraid to pursue the topic, definitely hungry, as he shoveled a mound of Western omelette in his face and kept my gaze, chewing thoughtfully.

"What are you thinking?" I ventured, still toying with my own breakfast.

"I'm thinking that it's not going to be as bad as you think. I'm thinking that you tend to get yourself all worked up over nothing–"

"Nothing?"

"Not nothing, just that you need to trust me."

"It's them I don't trust." By *them* I meant my parents, and although I knew that needed no further elaboration, I wanted to clarify.

"Okay, then trust *us*." He grabbed his coffee mug and took a long swill. "At the risk of sounding like a total geek, look at us Danielle: everything's coming up roses. Our meeting with your father went just fine; my parents practically drooled over your ring, and then basically did everything short of giving you a key to their city in terms of welcoming you into the family. Hell, even Madeline cracked a genuine smile when she acknowledged our engagement. Things with Constance are flowing nicely…you may have even found your wedding dress already! I need you to trust that this initial meeting with your mother is not going to do even one tiny little thing to set us off in the wrong direction, because you're hitting your stride, whether you realize it or not."

"You think I am?" I was touched by the way those words just rolled off of his lips, as if he didn't need to give them a second thought.

"I do." He nodded his head vigorously. "Everybody has tough times in life–we all know that you've had your fair share–but I think that time for you is drawing to a close. In some ways, I can feel your healing, and it warms my heart to think that maybe your life is getting better."

"Do you want to take all the credit for that, or just part of it?" I gave him a quizzical look, waiting patiently to hear how he understood his role in my life. I took a deep sip of my tea and sat back, wondering just how many of our thoughts were alike.

"You know what I mean." He made a hand gesture that looked as if he was trying to pull something out of his throat. "I mean, I would like to think that I am a part of your…turning the corner, would you say? But the truth is that maybe God is just using me in your life, kind of like a…"

"Soft place to land?" I whispered, my heart speaking words that had been known inside the very depths of my soul, for some time now, but hadn't been spoken out loud.

"Yeah." He reached across the table then, and enveloped my hand in his own, closing securely, needing no further instruction. "See, I can't take all the credit."

"So I guess I'll call my mother." I picked my napkin up, dabbed the corners of my mouth, and lifted my plate off the table. I gathered his empty plate to me and then exited the terrace, making my way towards the phone.

"Mom?" She answered so abruptly that it almost didn't seem like her.

"Yeah, hold on, I…" I heard a huge crash in the background, like a pot and pan convention where everyone was drunk and rowdy. Three clanks later, she picked back up.

"You okay?" I smiled to myself, picturing her fighting with a Bundt pan.

"I'm fine. I'm just trying to rearrange this cabinet." She was huffing, whether she realized it or not.

"Do you want me to call you back?" I offered.

"No, I'm fine. It's just tricky, that's all. So what's up?" It seemed as if her breathing was slowing down and she was getting herself together.

"Well," Insert deep breath on my end. "I was wondering if we could come up next weekend."

"You and Paul?" She brightened.

"Paul and me." Yessirree.

"I thought you wanted me to come down." No emotion, just fact.

"Well, I did. I do." But you know what, Mom? I decided it's time for Paul to see Upstate New York in its entire glorious splendor.

"Which one?"

"Well, I'm thinking if it would be easier for you…we could come Upstate. We just want to see you, I mean…I want you to meet him…" I was faltering a little, but I remembered what Paul said about me hitting my stride, so I kept right on going. "Why don't we come up next Saturday?"

"I think next Saturday would be fine! Well! I really thought you were going to expect me to come down. Now I can cook all your favorites…what does Paul like, by the way? Does he have any special 'eating things' I should know about?" I could hear her drawing up a menu in her head.

"Eating things?" I chuckled, knowing full well what she meant, but I couldn't resist. "Ah, no, there are no dietary restrictions for Paul. He'll eat just about anything."

"Okay! That's good then, I think I'll make tortellini salad, and some kind of fish. Would you mind if I invited over Jake Next Door?" She asked this as if she was the child and I was the Mom.

"No, of course not! Paul will love Jake Next Door. Can I ask...is there something going on between the two of you...?" I didn't know how else to ask that question, so it just came out, and then I figured that that was probably the best way anyway.

"Are you kidding me? I've sworn off men forever!" She said this with such belligerence that it scared me, but it also made me sad, to think that it was true, and that she had been ruined by such a lowly character–i.e. The Monster.

"That's too bad, Mom. Jake Next Door seems like the right kind of guy." I stated this as a well-known truth, no malice, just fact.

"Maybe." She sighed. "I just can't get past the fact that he's 'Jake Next Door.' I wouldn't even know his last name, except that it's printed on the side of his mailbox." She chuckled, and then sighed deeply once again. "Plus he knows all of my business."

I would never get her. Wasn't that all the better reason to be with someone; someone who was safe, who didn't care where you came from or what got you to where you are today, someone who loved you in spite of yourself?

Look who was talking? Don't think I didn't miss the irony there–the fact that I had just gotten a hold of that premise in my own life did not escape me–but it was like a good restaurant: once you found out about it, you wanted to tell everyone else, and have them all go out and try it too.

"Okay." I decided not to comment on her concerns surrounding Jake. "Well, what I'll do is this: I'll call you sometime towards the end of the week, and reconfirm. But expect us up there around noon?"

"Noon is great! Oh, Danielle, I'm so happy for you!" She gushed.

"Thanks, Mom. I am too." I replaced the receiver then and when I turned around I saw Paul standing behind me with an empty mug of coffee in his hands. "Were you eavesdropping?"

"Not really. I was looking to get another cup of coffee." He indicated that I should move, as I was standing directly in front of the coffee machine.

"Gotcha. Well, it's all set. We are going to be going up there next Saturday, sometime around noon. I guess–and tell me if this sounds good to you–that we can stay at my apartment the Friday night before and then I can drive up from there."

"Sounds good to me." He went through the motions of sugar and cream, seemingly not bothered by anything at all.

"It's not much, you know..." I hesitated a moment and then felt the need to add, "Her place is small, and the whole–well, whatever you've pictured about Upstate, it's probably..." I wrung my hands in an effort to try and express myself.

"It'll be fine, Danielle. Stop pre-worrying." He leaned back against the cabinet and fixed me with a steady gaze.

"I'm not." I mulled a sec. "Okay, I am. I just feel the need to preface the entire event..." I trailed off.

"Danielle, it's where you came from."

"In that case, you're right."

Chapter Eighty-Five

The week flew by. Lanie had begun her quest to hire her father a personal trainer/physical therapist/wunderkind, and I was trying hard to keep the pre-worrying to a manageable limit.

We exited the elevator and walked out into bright sunshine. I sighed. "I'm walking over to Paul's. What are you up to?"

"I am going downtown to my place, waiting for Rob, then we're heading out east to my padre's place. We figured we'd visit with him and then hang out on the island tonight. I told him he could stay at my father's."

"Nothing yet?" She knew what I was asking.

"No, we're just the very best of friends." Lanie shrugged. "Are you two heading Upstate tomorrow?"

"Yes. All prayers accepted, gratefully." I nodded my head a hundred times consecutively; then swished it back and forth.

"You'll be fine. Your mother will love Paul. And I guarantee that this will even bring you closer." Lanie nodded once, like the old wise woman that she was.

"I hope so. You know what I love?"

"Paul. Besides that?"

"The fact that it doesn't get dark out so early anymore." I smiled, then looked up, indicating the simple pleasure of longer days.

"I know. Me too. Summer's coming," Lanie lifted her eyebrows and then reached out to give me a quick hug good-bye. "You'll be fine. Call me when the weekend's over."

"Love you."

"Love you too."

I hustled to the corner to cross and then walked the rest of the way over to Paul's at a slower place, taking in the fresh air and enjoying the sunshine as it continued to warm my face and arms. I loved the sun. I thought about the summer that was just around the bend and the fun times we were sure to have: at the parks in the city, at the beach on Long Island. There was so much to do in my little corner of the world…Movie Mondays at Bryant Park…food festivals, concerts galore…my mind turned then to all of the summers Paul and I would share…and I smiled inside, feeling the warm glow of the sun radiating straight out of my center.

One sneaky little thought interrupted my reverie: I really needed to start making wedding plans soon. If we wanted to get married in the merry, merry, month of the very next May…I had this nagging, recurring reminder going off inside my head several times a day that I would need to get my butt into fifth gear very, very soon. I dismissed the thought and decided not to worry, choosing instead to pour myself a tall glass of water and then wait out on the terrace for Paul. I took in the sun, trying hard to focus on today. I convinced myself that we had a long drive Upstate tomorrow and we could venture into the minefield of our wedding at some point during the drive.

The next thing I knew, I heard the door open, and I felt my heart flutter like it always did. I watched him from the terrace, plunking down his briefcase, shifting through the mail at top speed, calling out then, "Danielle? I'm home."

I got a little choked up and found myself surprised by my emotions all over again. Would this feeling ever end? Did I really want it to?

"I'm out here." I called to him from the terrace, then placed my glass on the tabletop and walked into the room to join him. A few seconds later: "Hi."

"Hi."

We stood still for a second, our eyes focused on each other, until we slowly leaned closer, our bodies gravitating towards one another as if there were a magnet planted in each of our chests. He kissed me, and then continued to kiss me, tender little kisses that trailed all the way down from my lips to my chin and then my neck. I got caught up in the moment, and I returned his kisses, one by one, until I felt the need to tilt his chin back up to me and then began devouring his mouth like a starving, desperate woman. It was a while before we broke apart, and forever before either one of us uttered a single word.

"I can't help but love you," I inhaled deeply and then looked him dead in the eye, "I love you so much." I felt tears well up inside me, my mind registering once again the incredible gift I had been given.

"I love you more." He said this with such certainty, it was as if it were the most true statement in the world, a known fact, and he stood there in front of me, just daring me to defy him, as if any question of his sincerity would be met with a blast of reproach, and that he would take that as license to show me exactly how much he cared.

"I'll take your word for it." I smiled a shy smile, gently grasping his hands, keeping eye contact until the smile grew bigger, my smile extending to him, growing contagious, and soon both of us were indulging the other, and making silly faces to see who would crack first.

He won; he always won, and I laughed out loud and turned away when it became clear the victory was once again his.

"You're too easy." He shook his head as if to say, *what am I going to do with her?* It seemed particularly funny because he was playing to an audience of none.

"Your face is going to freeze like that." I assured him, as I sat on the couch and waited for him to remove his jacket.

He settled next to me. "So tell me about your day."

"Okay, so what are you thinking? Do you want to go to my place now, or eat here first?"

"It's so nice out. Aren't there any places up by you that offer outdoor dining, even if it's a shack?" He suggested as he poured himself a drink.

"Shack-dining…shack-dining…hmmm…" I pondered the question with a grave look in place. "Perhaps. But I have a better idea. I know you love *Friendly's,* and since there are no *Friendly's* in the city…"

"Yes!" He looked like a little kid whose coach had okayed ice cream after the winning game. "I am so desperately in need of a *Reese's Pieces Sundae…* I can't even articulate it!"

And so it went. I helped him pack, we jumped on the train, and the next thing you know, we're ordering a seven thousand calorie desert.

"Do you want me to drive up tomorrow?" He offered as he licked the area surrounding his mouth free of dripping hot fudge.

"No, I know the way, so I thought it would be easier if I drove and you got to play passenger for a change." I dug for a huge wallop of peanut butter sauce and came up full.

Yum.

"Do I get to yell Moo out the window to cows along the way?" He actually asked me this with a straight face, his cheeks packed full of ice cream.

"You will see no cows along the way. If you would like, I can arrange for us to visit a farm before we leave there tomorrow." I took a few pieces of the candy off the top and munched on those.

"That's all right. Seriously, is there anything I should know in advance?"

"No." I said it with all the conviction my little heart could muster.

"No?" He paused a second, spoon hovering over what was left of his dessert.

"No, I've decided not to pre-worry, and I've been doing a pretty good job of it–so let's not ruin that, okay?" If I was going to do this whole family thing, I was determined to do it right. I didn't want him to go into it with any more preconceived notions than he probably already had; and I found something very freeing in deciding to take that tack and just run with it.

"Well, far be it from me to…" he hesitated a second and graced me with his ever-famous smile. "You're something else, kid."

"I'm working on it."

Chapter Eighty-Six

"What time is it?" Paul growled as the alarm clock buzzed, sonic-boom style.

"Eight." I muttered, reaching out to swipe the clock and offer myself the Snooze Package: an additional nine minutes.

"Eight?" His growling became fiercer. "Please, do tell: why on Earth did we set the alarm for *eight?*" He had rolled closer to me now and was determinedly pulling my covers off, in an effort to make me pay.

"Stop!" I wrestled him for my comforter. "I set the alarm early because I want to go for a walk or a run." I sat up now, pulling the comforter around me, and growled back. "You don't have to come with me, so stop complaining. It's just that I can't very well indulge in *Friendly's* on Friday and tortellini on a Saturday and still expect to fit in my jeans on Sunday."

"Oh, sassafras," he mumbled that or something like it into his pillow. He made another unintelligible comment before he turned back around to face me. "Is your Mom making tortellini?"

"Yes. At least, that's what she said." I yawned and ran my fingers through my hair, still trying to get my eyes into some sort of focus. "Why? Does that sway you?"

"Into taking a walk? No. But maybe you can sway me..." he tried prying the covers off me again.

"Forget it, buster. I need *serious* exercise." I gave him a look.

The wailing of an air raid siren, otherwise known as the snooze alarm, blocked his next comment.

"Enough!" He got up and started hitting every button in order to stop the nonsense. "Oh MY GOD, how do you live with this thing?!"

"Ah, now you see why I go through so many alarm clocks each year." I smiled knowingly.

"Did you ever once consider waking up to music?" He looked at me as if I was a creature from another planet.

"Sure. Then I hear a song I like and I assume it's the background music to a good dream I'm having, so I just sleep on and on, and on…" I made a hand gesture that I hoped conveyed the full extent of my dilemma.

"I gotcha. All right. Well, I'm up now. Might as well go for that walk with you." He bolted out of bed then and headed straight for the bathroom.

Okay, so it looked like I was about to have a walking partner. I felt unsure as to whether or not I really wanted him to come; there was a small part of me that was looking at the walk as a time of contemplation, and prayer, and well…just a little bit of prep time before the big day I had looming ahead of me. I pondered telling him thanks, but no thanks, but then he bounded out of the bathroom door with a sincere smile and said, "Actually, I think it's a good call, since we're going to be sitting so long in the car anyway."

So much for that.

"You're right." I padded past him, into the bathroom, and began vigorously brushing my teeth.

"Do you want to do breakfast before or after?" He called through the door.

"After," I called back, hoping he could understand me as the toothpaste continued to foam and take over the insides of my mouth.

"I'm ready!" He announced the minute I stepped out of the bathroom.

"Okay, can you give me second? By the way, where did the grouchy guy from the bed go? I think I liked him a lot better than this…*morning person*…that is currently standing in my way." I sidestepped him and made my way to the closet, in an effort to find my sneakers.

"Yikes!" He made a face. "Come on, Danielle, whatsa matter, do your workouts have to be miserable for you to feel as if you accomplished something?" He gave me a pouty face, which I assumed was supposed to on some level represent me.

"Of course they do!" I graced him with The Evil Eye, but to no avail. I picked through my clothes and found something suitable, then grumbled to him that I was ready. "Let's go."

"Don't wait up on account of me," he said sarcastically, as I started walking briskly from my driveway, up and around the bend.

"You'll be fine." I assured him. "Stop whining."

The general bickering went on for at least a quarter of a mile, until I realized we were approaching Millie Lancaster's house; the one with the beautiful flowers.

"Paul," I grabbed his arm and directed him to walk all the way to the left side of the road. "Take a look at these flowers. Aren't they gorgeous?" I was just about to tell him about the woman who lived there and the conversation we had when, almost as if I had summoned her, Millie Lancaster herself popped up from behind a row of hedges.

"Good morning!" She greeted us gaily, her gloved hands full, a garden hoe in the left, and what looked like pulled weeds in her right. "I see you have found yourself a walking partner."

"Hi there, good to see you!" I felt tempted to greet her with a big hug, but I refrained, if only because I wasn't sure how she would respond. Millie Lancaster radiated warmth, in ways that couldn't be defined, and I found myself liking her all over again, and wishing that I would have a chance to get to know this friendly old woman better. "Yes, I do have a walking partner today. Paul, this is Ms. Lancaster; and this is Paul." I said this by way of introduction.

"Please call me Millie." She threw down her garden tool, along with the weeds, and then removed her gloves and offered her hand out to Paul.

"Nice to meet you, Ma'am." Paul nodded as he shook her hand delicately. "You sure do have a beautiful arrangement of flowers here."

"Yes. Oh well, you know, they were my husband Hank's...he was so invested in his garden, meticulous about those flowers, right up until the day he died." She smiled, and it was born of reminiscence, but there was still a small amount of pain that betrayed itself in the openness of her face, and I couldn't miss it.

"I'm sorry." It took me a second to realize that Paul and I had said that at the same time. We shared a look, and then turned our attention back to Millie.

"Oh, it's been a long time now. And it seems so silly..." she trailed off a second, looking far into the distance, or perhaps the past, and when she turned her head back to us, it seemed for a minute that she was focusing her eyes directly on me. "I can remember being jealous of the time he spent out here gardening. I can still recall the silly things, the stupid tiffs that we would have...it all seemed so important then, but now..." she moved her hands in a fashion as if to say she couldn't explain. "Now I take care of his flowers for him, and I think about the time I wasted, and I would give anything to have him back here, tooling around in his flowers, calling out to me to bring him a glass of iced tea with lemon. He always liked fresh lemon."

"I think he would be proud; you've kept them so nice." I didn't really know what else to say. She had revealed so much of herself in so little time that I found myself caught off guard, trying to process all that she had shared, all while still trying to keep up the conversation as it were.

"Oh!" She changed the subject abruptly, and her demeanor shifted too, back to the loving Grandma around the corner. "Did you ever decide you wanted to paint those flowers?"

I blushed. "I actually started painting again. I made a few little things for the Holidays...but no paintings yet. I guess now that summer's coming I should give it a whirl." I shrugged.

"Oh, anytime, Danielle, you just let me know! And Paul…you're welcome too…anytime you want to come over, you two can just pull up a brush and we can all take turns trying to paint something that looks like flowers!" She laughed, her whole persona filled with glee, and I knew that no matter what, it would be hard to try not to get caught up in her enthusiasm.

"That sounds good. I'll definitely let you know," I smiled at her and we caught each other's eye.

"He's a good-looking gentleman," she jerked a finger in Paul's direction, "Or what do they say nowadays, 'a hottie?'"

Paul and I both burst out laughing, and I saw my future husband's face turn as red as a fire engine. "I think that's the word." I said, and then tickled him on his side.

"Well, you look good together. Now go! Get going, don't let me interrupt your walk any more, just let me know if you want to paint, and I'll be here." She chuckled, almost as if to herself. "I'm still up on the lingo."

"That you are," I assured her. We shared another smile and I thanked her for her offer, then we waved good-bye as we took off around the corner. Once we were a few lengths away from the house, Paul turned to me and said:

"That woman has good taste."

"Oh, puh-leese!" I rolled my eyes and kept on walking.

Chapter Eighty-Seven

"I have to warn you; it's really not very much." I was about five miles from my mother's house at this point, and although I prided myself in having done a good job by keeping my pre-worrying and my over-explaining to a bare minimum, I now felt as if I had to try and at least prepare him for whatever it was that we were about to encounter.

"Oh, like I grew up in a mansion?" He gave me look as if to say, *Don't worry.*

"That's not it–it's just–it didn't have to be this way." I felt my stomach bubbling because only I knew how starkly true that statement was…had the old Mom resurrected herself from the dead…earlier, sooner, had she tried a little harder…had she been able to stand up for herself and me and the life we had planned together…*The Second Time Around*…I felt the words reverberating from my heart, pounding now at the base of my skull, and I knew that a deep breath was about the only thing keeping me from having a full-out panic attack.

I took a deep breath and smiled uneasily over at Paul.

"It's okay." He reached across the center console and wrapped his left hand around my right.

"We're almost there." I knew he knew that, I had been saying stuff like that repeatedly for the past fifteen minutes, and now I had to stop a second and wonder if I was saying it for him or for me.

It didn't matter.

I made a right down a road that was actually called JOE'S MOTHER'S ROAD.

"Did you catch that?" I pointed to the sign.

"Yeah, I wasn't about to say anything." He shook his head in wonder. "It's like another world up here; it doesn't even feel like the same state."

"Yeah, I find it funny...did you ever meet someone from Europe who has only been to or heard of New York City? They tend to think the entire state is like that." I smirked. "Now do you understand why I left?"

"I understand why you left." That's all he said, but it seemed like, even in that one statement, that he was saying so much more.

The third road on the left was MY mother's road, aptly named Elm Street. Living here with The Monster, I had often quoted the movie, *Nightmare on Elm Street*. It just seemed to fit...too well.

We swung the left and then followed the road from asphalt to gravel, my eyes trying to take in the scenery as I drove, trying to imagine seeing all this for the first time, trying to see this place through Paul's eyes. About a half mile of gravel under our feet, I braked and pulled into a makeshift spot.

"That's my mother's house," I pointed left, "And that's Jake Next Door's house."

"Well, that's about where I would picture Jake Next Door's house to be: next door." Paul smiled at me and made googly eyes, but I graced him with only a wry grin in exchange.

"Come on." I lifted my buttocks out of the seat, stood up straight, and stretched. It had been a particularly long ride today, or at least, it had seemed that way to me. Paul came around to my side and arms outstretched, offered me a hug. I indulged myself and then reached into my backseat to grab the bag of bread that I had brought up from the city. "Let's go."

I grabbed his hand and he followed me up the rickety stairs to my mother's front door. I went to ring the doorbell, but the moment my hand was extended, the door flew open and my mother greeted us with an enthusiastic hello.

"Hi!" She was grinning from ear to ear and I couldn't help but think that she looked like a giddy teenager. She was wearing light colored blue jeans and a bright green top, and my mind registered quickly that it was nothing that I recognized from her closet. Had she gone out and bought something just for this occasion? I hoped not, as I knew her money situation, and I hoped even more that she hadn't felt the need to try and impress Paul.

"Hi Mom," I said as I tried to edge my way into her place, "This is Paul..." I said it in a sing-songy kind of voice, not exactly meaning for it to come out that way, but not exactly knowing how else to introduce them.

"Well, it's so nice to finally meet you!" She reached forward and gave him a hug, and if it caught Paul off-guard at all, he didn't show it, instead he leaned in and hugged her right back.

"You too." He looked back and forth between us. "You ladies definitely have the same smile."

"You think?" I appraised my mother quickly and she did the same. I shrugged. "You might be right." I headed off into the kitchen then, to put the bread on the counter, and to simply move around for a second. The kitchen smelled good. "Mom, I'm leaving the bread in here."

"Okay, that's fine. Oh, you didn't have to bring any, but thanks...is that the bread you brought up from New York, like the last time?"

"You got it."

"Oh, that's good." She turned to offer Paul a seat. "Oh, please make yourself comfortable. Danielle, I...Wait! Didn't you even show me your ring?"

"You didn't ask." I held the ring out to her then, and gave her a chance to fawn over it, as only a mother can. After a two-minute rendition of the Oooh and Aaah song, I asked her where Jake was.

"Let me guess: next door?" Paul piped this in from the ottoman that he had found to sit on, looking sheepish only once I looked over and gave him the thumbs-down sign.

"Good guess." My mother chuckled. "He should be on his way over, any minute. Come see what I made," she said to me, and I followed her dutifully into the kitchen. She showed me the covered dish full of all different color tortellini and sliced peppers. Then she let me peek into the fridge, where I spied a pineapple cheesecake taking over the entire center shelf.

"Wow." I licked my lips. "Looks good."

"Danielle," she hissed my name from across her small kitchen, then continued whispering conspiratorially as she moved closer, "He's very cute." She nodded vigorously. "And tall. Cute and tall."

"He's a great guy." I smiled in spite of myself. "And you're right; he's awfully cute, isn't he?" My stomach, which had been gurgling for at least the past hour, subsided briefly, as I had a minute flashback to the Mom that had once been my pal. Maybe we could be friends again. Maybe…I steeled myself against getting too hopeful, reminding myself of the strategy that Constance had said to deploy: *Lower your expectations.* Maybe one day soon.

I offered to slice the bread, and just as I was about to call Paul inside with us, I heard another male voice enter the premises, and as my mother rushed out to greet Jake, I heard the boys making introductions amongst themselves, and the fanfare moving towards me.

"Hey there Danielle, you big city girl!" Jake walked into the kitchen carrying a tray of steaming salmon steaks. "I hope you like salmon, because these puppies here are hot off the grill, and ready to be inhaled!" Jake put the tray down on the counter and then walked over to give me a hug. "I heard you have a rock there on your finger, too…a real cause for celebration! Well, well, will you look at that! I bet your Mom really likes him already!" Jake winked and my mom acted insulted.

From there, the day moved on as steadily as could be expected. We inhaled (as Jake so aptly put it) the lunch that he and my mother had put together for us, we bantered back and forth, and once again, I found myself almost losing my place, and forgetting where I was in the midst of that warm fuzzy feeling. Things weren't perfect: I found myself fielding all sorts of wedding questions that I wasn't ready to answer, and I had to admit that there was more than a couple of times I clammed up and refused to join into their seemingly innocuous conversation, but for the most part, a good time was had by all, and the hours flew by, swiftly, as often does when you find yourself having a pretty decent time.

Once dessert was about to be served, Jake jumped up and ran to get some fabulous beverage he had concocted from over at his place, and I took that as a good chance to get up and use the bathroom. I hesitated a second, a little nervous about leaving my mother alone with Paul, but I dismissed my worries, partially because my bladder was about to burst, and partially because things had been going well thus far.

Upon returning from the stifling closet my mother called a bathroom, I overheard them talking and decided to eavesdrop a second before I re-entered the kitchen.

"Well, I don't know how much Danielle has told you, Paul…about our life together…I guess I just want you to know that I'm happy for you both. I hope life brings you good things. It's obviously brought you each other." She sounded a little hoarse, as if it were hard for her to talk about this, her failings as a mother, or her hope for our future.

"Well, I'm grateful, I know that for sure." Paul was trying to be polite, and I could tell that he didn't know how to respond to her. I was about to do a little rescuing when I heard her voice again and what she said brought me up short.

"I just wish Danielle could understand how sorry I am…" she trailed off a second, and sounded as if she was trying to clear her throat. "I know what I did–and didn't do–and I wonder sometimes if she knows how aware I've become."

    I took a deep breath and decided that the time had come for me to rescue Paul; there was no need for him to have to respond to her newfound guilt or introspection. I backed up a few steps (silently) then made an absurd amount of noise as I clamored back into the kitchen.

    "So where's Jake?"

Chapter Eighty-Eight

"Do you want to go back tonight, or do you want to stay here again?" I wanted to offer Paul the choice, as I felt that he had already gone out of his way for me all weekend long.

"To my place?" He looked at me as we came up upon my exit. "No, that's all right. We'll stay at your place tonight, and then maybe you could come back with me tomorrow?"

"That sounds more than fair." I looked over at him in the darkness. There was a small light edging his features, and I took him in for a second and then transferred my eyes back to the road. "Thanks again for coming with me today."

"You're welcome. They're—or should I say she—is really not that bad. And Jake is a heck of a guy. You sure there's nothing going on between them?" He asked.

"I'm sure, and yes, it's a shame. He really is a great guy. She just doesn't see it. Either that or she's afraid to. I don't know." I turned onto my road and then slowed as the car came closer to the driveway. Paul hadn't said a word about what my mother had said to him while I was in the bathroom and I wasn't about to ask. That was the main problem with eavesdropping: you couldn't very well admit to hearing what you weren't supposed to hear without giving away your position. I must have sighed out loud, because a second later we were standing out on my patio, and just as I was fitting the key into the lock, Paul came up behind me and said, "She loves you, you know."

"I don't *know* anything when it comes to my parents."

"It seems that I'm going to be forced to say the same thing to you that I said the night we saw your father's side in the city: they're yours. You can hope for them to change, you can beg them, you can even wish for a whole new family…but the truth of the matter is that this is the family God saw fit to give you. Period, The End."

"You're right. I know you're right, it's just…" I turned to him and shook my head, unable to express the myriad of feelings that were coursing through my brain. "I may be getting a little ahead of myself here, but I worry about the wedding, and the fact that I am just beginning to have relationships with these two people called my parents. I don't want that to ruin things. And I worry…believe it or not, I actually feel bad for you…you get the short stick of the in-law deal, and I think I am somehow convinced that one day that's all going to come back to bite me."

"You can't worry about the future, Danielle…you can only try and do your best, and let the chips fall where they may. Just think: you can plan and execute a big, splashy, expensive wedding, with everyone on their best behavior, a whole fabulous support system in place, and…and the roof can cave in, and it could end up raining cats and dogs, and the next thing you know, the caterer could pull out a gun and murder the lead singer of the band, who he's been having an affair with for exactly four hundred weddings. The blood would get all over your dress, and…" Paul was tossing his hands around, furiously accentuating the drama.

"Okay! Okay, I get it–I get it. Four hundred weddings and a funeral, huh? Not your best joke." I graced him with a big grin, my eyes scolding.

"Hey! I wasn't even trying for that…although that's not bad…but that's not the point. The point is…do you get my point?" He had been standing behind me, telling me his story, but now he swiveled me around and his eyes were probing, causing me to question myself and eventually agree: I had more than most people ever would. I found a safe harbor in his eyes, and nothing could sway us now.

"I always get your point." I kissed him deeply, breathing in his fading scent, and the nighttime air that surrounded us. "I can't wait for summer to truly begin."

"Why?"

"I don't know; I guess I'm anticipating a great summer. Summer always holds such promise; for me, you can't beat the longer days, and endless nights, the beach, the whole gentle laziness of it all…I'm really looking forward to spending this summer with you."

"I'm really looking forward to spending a lifetime with you."

"Think you can handle it?"

"Definitely."

Chapter Eighty-Nine

It was one of those mornings that I just didn't want to go to work. It was a beautiful September morning, but it still felt like summer, and I daydreamed as I crossed Lexington Avenue that Paul and I had decided to play hooky and high tail it out to the beach.

I sighed and settled in, but my heart was contemplating one last day to tuck my toes in the sand.

"Lanie! Danielle! Come to Reception!" Alex ran into our hole/office with an urgency which I have never seen before, his hustle all the more hustled than the norm, his face barely readable as he turned his back towards us and bounded right back into the hall, in the same direction he had just come from.

"Another star?" Lanie drawled in a way that spelled out boredom.

"HOLY SHIT!" This was shouted from an unidentifiable voice down the hall. And then a chorus of voices, raised in a way that shouted this was surely more than a sighting of a random star in the ad agency's hallowed halls.

"Oh My God!" This now, and then a collective gasp, as if half the agency were finding out some sort of terrible news.

"Lanie, I think it's got to be something else," I had this overwhelming sense of something bigger than the usual drama, my stomach instantly feeling rumbly. "Let's go see."

Lanie and I scuttled out into the hallway, made a right towards reception and were surprised to find a gaggle of coworkers crowding around the various television sets that usually were there for the sole purpose of playing our ads on a continual loop and allowing us to look and feel the part of a New York City ad agency, or at the very least, what our clients *thought* an agency should look like.

"What happened?" Lanie questioned as she pushed ahead of me, while I hung back just a bit, used to being the short one in the crowd, and never able to see from the back. I would get the goods from her, and I was confident anyway that the crowd would disperse after the initial rubbernecking.

"A plane hit the World Trade Center." Another voice, from which face, I did not know.

My mind raced towards Paul, and before I even knew what I was doing, I had pushed my way to the front of the crowd, and touched my hand to the horrible images on the screen in front of me.

"LANIE!" I screamed, and the crowd parted a little, everyone moving just enough to make sure that she got to me quickly. I gasped and gaped at the horror portrayed in full vivid Technicolor. I pointed to the buildings. "Lanie, which one is Paul's?" I knew that Paul was in Tower One, but I was disoriented, and couldn't tell them apart, or perhaps my mind simply wasn't able to.

"Tower One, sweetie. Okay. Okay. I'm sure he's okay. What time does he usually go in?" She was holding my hands now, grasping my fingers hard, and although I was aware of her, I couldn't process a word that she was saying, and I couldn't tear my eyes away from the surreal images currently unfolding on the TV screen.

"Paul?" I was looking at Lanie, but I could see right through her, or rather, I could not see her at all.

"Yellie, come with me." She moved away from the screen and pushed me through the crowd and back to our hole/office. "You need to call Paul. What's his number, Yellie?"

"Paul's number?" I repeated after her, and gave her a look which I'm sure betrayed my bewilderment. "Lanie, I...what's going on?" I had the beginnings of a headache, and I found myself floundering, trying to piece together what appeared to be an amazing Hollywood special effect, and the reality that it was not in fact just that.

"Yellie, we don't know yet, but you have got to snap out of it. NOW!" Lanie roared at me and then jumped right into her take-charge mode, putting her hands on my shoulders and almost shaking me into action.

"I am. Okay, I can do this," For fear of Lanie's wrath or otherwise, I will never know, but I collected myself instantly, talking to myself as I picked up my phone handset and dialed Paul's business number. It rang four times and then I heard his voice mail pick up, the same message as always: *You have reached the desk of Paul Corsi. I'm not available to get to the phone right now, please leave a message and I'll* ...blah, blah, blah. I hung up the phone, thought quickly, then called back and left him a message anyway.

"Paul, it's me, Danielle. Baby, if you get this message, please call me back right away. I'm watching all this on TV, and I want to know that you're okay. Please call, sweetie. I love you." I hung up the phone and tried collecting myself further, my mind back in action and running a mile a minute. Hadn't he said something about an eight o'clock meeting? Maybe he overslept. Or perhaps he hadn't even gone into work today. For all I knew, he was lying around in bed, waiting to call me while I got settled in at my desk. Playing hooky. That's it: he was playing hooky. It was an absolutely beautiful day outside; why not? Why shouldn't he be right around the corner, trying desperately to catch one more summer-like day before fall settled in? Should I try the apartment? I had a key; I could run over there and wake him–

"Call his cell," Lanie directed over her shoulder as she tried to get online. "Shit! Every friggin' news website is…being updated, I guess. I can't get on Fox News, CNN, nothing." She shook her head in frustration. "Then try his place."

I picked up the phone and dialed Paul's cell, but as soon as I started dialing his number, I saw the phone blinking with an incoming call, so I hung up and grabbed the call, praying it was him.

"Danielle?" He sounded far away, and his voice was shaking.

"PAUL!" I gulped some air and tried to calm myself down as tears popped out of my eyes and came pouring down my face. "Are you okay?"

"I can't find Rob. I don't know. I'm up…we went up the stairs as soon as we felt the impact. I was on 105, in a meeting, but I was standing by the stairs and I…I think I'm on 107, I don't know, I just ran up, it's so damn hot. We're trying to get to the roof. Do you know what happened?" His voice was filled with urgency, and a raw emotion that belied how terrified he must be. "I see smoke."

"Baby, can you get down?" I felt my knees fall to the floor, a wave of nausea emanating from the pit of my stomach. For some reason, I knew that Up was not the answer, but I didn't think he could get down either.

"The plane is below us. This can't be an accident. OH MY GOD!" Paul screamed and then I heard what sounded like him dropping the phone, and a muffled boom a second later. "Another plane just flew into the other tower! Danielle, I love you. I think…the world is ending…baby, I've got to go up!" He was getting scratchy as he said this, fading out just a little. I prayed with all my might that he would be able to hang on the line with me.

At the same instant, Lanie and I heard screaming coming from the reception area outside of our office. I heard someone yell something about a second plane.

"Paul, I love you. Go! Run! I'm sure they'll have helicopters to come and get you, get to the roof! Baby, I love you," I was crying now, harsh jerking sobs that came from a scared and ugly place somewhere deep inside, unsure if he could even understand me through tears, but determined to talk him through it if I could.

"Baby, I'll call you. In the meantime, I love you." Paul sounded all choked up and I could tell he was breathing heavy.

"In the meantime, I love you too!" I called out to him, but the call was lost, and I knew now that all I could do was pray and intercede on his behalf. Since my knees had already buckled under me, I stayed there and sobbed for I don't know how long, and when I finally looked up, I saw Lanie standing above me, her eyes rimmed with red.

"Yellie," She kneeled down next to me and hugged me, held me close, and we sobbed together openly for what seemed like eternity.

"I just had him…" I gestured toward the phone and then looked around the room. I was torn between sitting by the phone and going back out by the television screens to see about the second plane.

The phone rang.

Lanie jumped up to get it.

"Travel, Lanie."

I looked up to her, and as I heard her talking, something in the back of my head registered for the first time that these were commercial airliners that had dove into the building and that we could in fact have passengers on either one of those flights.

"Yeah, I will check that out. Sure. I promise." Lanie hung up the phone and shook her head as tears continued to stream down her face. She wiped her nose with the back of her hand and then gestured wildly as she reached for a tissue. "That was Adrienne. She wants me to double-check and make sure that we don't have anybody on those flights. Oh, God, I hadn't even thought of that yet."

No impersonation this time.

"I'll call Olive," I offered in an effort to keep myself busy, but as soon as I said it, I realized how futile that would be. Olive also worked at the World Trade Center, also in Tower One, although she was on the fifty-ninth floor.

Lanie and I shared a look.

"I don't even know…" Lanie looked at me as if she did not know what to do. Where to begin, how to proceed. "I'm going to go out to check the TV screens again. You man the phones. I'll be right back; I need to see what's going on out there. Try to get online."

I did as Lanie instructed, like a zombie I moved, going through the motions, trying to see if any of the news websites had been updated. Nothing. I couldn't even get on. I was operating in a sphere outside myself, trying desperately to do the most mundane thing, yet screaming inside and praying to God that he would keep Paul alive for me. I didn't care about anyone else. I just wanted Paul.

The phone rang again and I lunged for it.

"Hello?" I forgot the whole 'Travel' spiel as I picked up.

"Danielle? Are you okay? I didn't know where you worked and I…" My mother was hysterically crying on the other end of the phone.

"Mom, I'm fine, calm down. It's a couple of miles from where I am." I tried to steady my quavering voice.

"OH, THANK GOD!" She blew out a large whoosh of air. "I had no idea…I was so worried…" She kept weeping, but I could pretty much make out what she was saying, and either way got the general gist.

"Mom, I need to go now, though. I have to figure out if we had any people on those planes. I…" And then my voice cracked, and I could barely speak any more. "I need to find Paul."

"Oh, Dear Lord, okay. Please keep in touch with me. I'll be praying for you," She sniffed loudly and then hung up reluctantly, only after three more quick reassurances from my end, and my promise that I loved her.

That's right Mom, keep praying, I can barely think straight right about now.

Lanie entered the room again, and I could tell that she was more than shaken, her eyes having taken on a frenetic look, her hands wringing mercilessly. "Yellie, it looks bad. Did anybody call?"

"Just my mother." I shook my head and got caught up in another round of wracking sobs.

"I better call my Dad." Lanie walked past me to her desk and dialed her father's number as I stared blankly at the computer screen that was failing to show me any information. I tried to will the phone to ring. I turned on my cell phone and made sure the battery was full.

"Yellie, I can't get through. There's something wrong with the phones." Lanie looked perplexed, as I had just told her about my mother calling.

"Don't say that, Lane." Right now, my only lifeline to Paul was the phone. I picked up the handset and dialed his cell phone number again. No answer. It just rang; I didn't get voice mail or anything. Then I tried his business number. The voice mail picked up there, and I left another stupid message through tears, knowing full well that he was no longer at his desk.

"I'm sorry, Yel, but I can't get anyone." Lanie banged the desk in frustration. "I tried my father's work, cell, and home, but I can't seem to get connected. But there's a dial tone here. I just don't get it."

"Do you think that the planes could have knocked out the power lines?"

"On Long Island?"

"I don't know." I felt as helpless as I'm sure I sounded.

"I don't know either." Lanie rubbed her eyes. "I'm going to run back out, see if there's any news about that."

She ran out of our hole then, leaving me alone to face my greatest fear: what if Paul wasn't able to make it out alive? What if they were able to get helicopters to the roof, but just like *The Titanic*, it was women and children first and there was no room for him? There shouldn't be any children, I prided myself with that wee bit of fact, then banished all Titanic-type thoughts with a quick shake of my head. I wasn't going to think about anything like that, I was going to stay positive until I got another phone call.

"They just hit the Pentagon."

"Who are 'they'?" I was feeling panicky.

"Apparently, it's a bunch of terrorists from the Middle East."

"Are you sure?" Whatever had we done to them?

"I'm as sure as the guy on the news." Lanie leaned into me and sobbed. "Stay here, I'll go check again."

The Pentagon?

Lanie was gone more than a few minutes the next round, no doubt viewing the carnage at the Pentagon on the tube. I thought about what Paul said, about the world ending, and I started to shake and cry some more. The world might as well end if he wasn't going to be in it. I made myself stop thinking like that again and again willed myself to think positively, knowing that if there was a will, there was a way. A million little proverbs wormed their way across the marquee of my brain, and time was something I simply could not measure.

"The FAA just shut down all flights nationwide." Lanie checked our computers again, but you couldn't get much off of the Web. "It's definitely terrorists."

Terrorists. I rolled the word around on my tongue, but it was foreign to me, and I couldn't wrap my head around the image of what I believed to be a terrorist, and what was going on in America today. Didn't terrorists use bombs, like the idiot that blew up the building in Oklahoma, or the guys that tried to bomb The World Trade Center the first time a few years ago? Or hijacking planes…I could even understand that, but hijacking a plane and then using it as a bomb?

I didn't get it.

"What do we do now?" I looked at Lanie and saw the confusion that was in my heart reflected in her eyes. I had lived through a lot of garbage: neglect and abuse and all things domestic, but this one was completely out of my realm. I didn't know what to do.

"I can keep getting information from the TV, as long as you keep watching the phones...if they ring..." Lanie threw her hands up in utter frustration. " I don't know, Yellie. What did Paul say about Rob?"

"He wasn't with him." His actual words were that he couldn't find him, but I felt no need to tell Lanie that until we knew a little more. "Did you try his cell?"

"I did, and I got voice mail, but there was no answer." Lanie checked her watch. "That was before. It's ten o'clock. Do you think I should try again?"

"Why not?" At this point, there was nothing left for us to do, nothing except wait. "I want to go check on the TV. Promise me you'll run for me if Paul calls in again." I hadn't been out to see the television since my initial look, and now I wanted to see what had happened at The Pentagon. I grabbed my cell phone and held it tight in my hand, just in case it decided to work and ring again.

"Of course. I'm not going anywhere." Lanie settled in to her desk. "I'm actually going to pull a manifest off of Sabre to see if we had anybody on any of those flights. I think I remember how to do it...I think it's called running a spectra..."

I left her there, talking half to me and half to herself, and I made my way back out to the reception area. What I found there was utterly unreal: people that I knew mostly only from seeing their faces in the halls, all crowded around various television sets, their eyes glued to what was going on just a few miles down the road. Some of the people were sitting on the floor, slumped over, and crying buckets of tears, with tissues clutched in their one hand and a useless cell phone in the other.

"Do you know someone?" Alana from Team Cheer came up behind me, her cheerleader persona thrown three sheets to the wind, as black gobs of eye makeup decorated her face in ways it was never meant to.

"My fiancé." I clutched at my heart and heard a little gasp escape from what seemed like my mouth. My tears flowed openly. "You?" It was all I could mutter as I looked at Alana from only the corner of one eye, unable as I was to peel my eyes away from the split image on the screen: one side, the Towers billowing smoke, and the Pentagon opposite, with a huge hole on one side, spewing fire and smoke.

"My father works in the Towers." She hung her head and started to cry. "I haven't heard from him."

I patted her on the shoulder, unsure of what else I should do to comfort her, if anything. I knew how she felt, but I had talked to Paul, so I was still hanging on to some irrational hope that perhaps I was in a better state than she was, having at least gotten one phone call so far. I turned around to see people getting on the elevators behind where we were standing.

"Where are you going?" I called out to Alex as he hopped on the elevator going down.

"I'm going home." Although as soon as he said it, Alex waved for the people already in the elevator to go without him, then turned to me with concern etched on his face. "Are you okay, Danielle?"

"I'm…yeah. But how are you getting home?" Lanie had told me that Mayor Giuliani had shut down all the trains and bridges, and I didn't think there were buses running either.

"I live nearby here, I can walk. Danielle, do you need a place to stay? You and Lanie can come stay with me." Alex waited patiently for an answer as I promptly burst into tears, overwhelmed by his kindness, and unable to speak. The next thing I knew, Alex put his arms around me and was holding me in a firm embrace.

"I…I'm sorry, Alex," I sniffled hard and then pulled away, sure that I was ruining his shirt with tears and makeup. "It's just that Paul…" and at that moment, I wasn't sure if I had ever told Alex about Paul, if he knew that I thought my fiancé was currently climbing to the roof, waiting for a rescue...

"I...Oh, God, Danielle, please don't be sorry," Alex's voice got fuzzy as he continued to hold me close. "There's no reason to be sorry."

"I am. No, go. You were leaving." I pointed towards the elevator. "There's nothing we can do except wait. Please go home." I didn't want to hold him up from whatever friend or family member was waiting for him at home.

"Okay, now wait a second. Come in here so I can give you something," he pulled a piece of paper off my desk and began to address both of us as he wrote. "Just in case the phones are not working, and you girls need me. This is my address. If you can't get home and you need to...just be with someone, you come to me. You call. You come to me, you hear me?" He was looking directly at me and trying to get me to acknowledge what he was saying. I heard him, and I believe I nodded, but my head was jamming and my heart overflowing. There was little I could manage to do besides nod my head.

"I live in the city, too, and if we can get downtown, Danielle's going to stay with me." Lanie stated. I thought I heard them exchange numbers.

"That's good." Alex looked from one to the other. "You be strong." He gave us each a hug then and he left. The minute he left, I started another crying jag, and after a few minutes, I was unsure if I would ever be able to stop.

"Yellie, you don't know. You don't know what's going on down there yet. Please, Yellie, please try to calm down just a little bit, honey; you're going to make yourself sick. You know they're trying to rescue him. Do you hear all the sirens?" Lanie gestured towards the window, where the sounds of endless sirens were emanating from the street.

I nodded, but I couldn't say a word. All I wanted was for Paul to call me back again, to hear his voice...I wanted to be with him, incase he needed me...I wanted to pray for him and with him on the phone. I made a sound then, something that sounded inhuman to anyone who could hear, but it was about all I could articulate, this keening for Paul that had no end, this longing for the man I loved, who I knew to be in danger, but that I could do nothing for or about. Why? Oh, God. Why was this happening to me? To us? To the United States? I felt a hundred different emotions at once. I looked down at my ring and tried to find some solace in the brilliance on my finger, but it was nothing but a cold hard stone, nothing without the warm man that gave it to me.

"I want to go check the TV's again," Lanie looked at me, giving me a long once-over. "Are you going to be okay?"

"I'm fine," I lied, because what could I say right now besides a lie? *Okay* wasn't a word that I could relate to right now. I needed Paul, and something inside me knew that without him, I would never be okay again. Fine seemed appropriate; it was chilly and the truth of the matter is, everyone knew that fine had come to mean not fine anyway. So I stuck with fine.

"I'll be right back." Lanie tiptoed out of the room again and into the corridor towards the bank of televisions.

I tried unsuccessfully to log on to a news site again, and vaguely registered another soaring of expletives from the crowd outside.

Lanie came running back in.

"Yellie!" She was pacing around the room, literally pulling her hair out, her sobs so loud that I thought they would break the sound barrier. "Yellie, the south tower fell. It just..."

"Fell?" I didn't understand.

"It isn't there anymore." Lanie hiccupped.

"Lanie, what do you mean?" I realized I was yelling about a half a second after I spoke. "Lanie, what–?"

We both stopped still for a second as the phone rang in our office. Without a word between us, we collectively lunged for the phone, Lanie picking up before I did.

"Hello?" She dumped the travel spiel also, her voice steeped in urgency. "What?"

And then from her: "Excuse me?"

I decided it wasn't Paul, as I knew she would have handed the phone right to me.

She banged down the phone.

"I need to go look at the TV, Yellie. Maybe you should too. I don't know." Lanie slumped down in her chair. Then: "OH!" She jumped up and crossed the room. "The radio!"

We had been so involved with running out to check things on the tube that we totally forgot that we had a radio in our office. It was an older-style boom box that Lanie had brought in a long time ago, and even though we had it on more often than not, neither one of us had given it even so much as a second thought this morning. Now Lanie was up and tuning it into our favorite station, the one we usually listened to at work.

"We are just receiving a report here that another commercial jetliner, we don't have the...we think it's United...has crashed in a field in a small town in Pennsylvania. We are receiving reports that this hijacked jet was headed for another destination...perhaps the White House..."

Lanie and I stared at each other above the voice of our favorite DJ.

"Paul said the world is ending..." My voice was barely above a whisper, but I knew that Lanie heard me, as she acknowledged me with a slight nodding of her head.

"It might be," Lanie concurred in a soft voice, as if that option just occurred to her. "I want to try my father again."

That thought touched off another, and I decided to try my father also, but I found out quickly that I could no longer get into the Upstate exchange. I tried my mother again, just to make sure, and I even tried Am. No dice. It was as if all the lines were jammed, and there was no Operator or even recording to inform us regarding what exactly was going on. I looked to Lanie after a minute and realized that she couldn't get through either.

"What do you think we should do?" I was unsure of whether we should stay or go, as people were leaving the agency in droves, and this seemed to be the closest thing I could ever recall qualifying as a national emergency/disaster. Did they expect us to stay? Should we, as the Travel Department, stay nearby the phones until we knew for sure that Olive was accounted for, and that there was no other information that could be given out from our end? Or did everybody know by now that the flights were shut down, and that we were basically powerless to do anything anyway?

"I think we should call the travel agency's call center out in Kansas and let them know we're leaving." Lanie took the reins and I nodded silently. I wanted to go to Paul's apartment and wait to see if he could get to me there.

"I agree." I nodded again.

We should leave.

"It sounds like it connected!" Lanie seemed excited by the fact that our phone service might be restored. A minute later I heard her talking to the regular operator there, whose name was Casey, and after Lanie reassured her several times that we were no where near the Towers, they figured out a way for the phones to be forwarded so that we could leave.

"Wait!" I waved my hands in Lanie's face before she hung up with them. "See if they can call your Dad." If we were still unable to get through from where we were, I didn't think it would be too much to ask to see if Casey could do her that small favor.

"Good idea," Lanie agreed, then placed Casey on hold as she tried all of her father's numbers again at warped speed. She shook her head to signify no service, then went back and asked Casey if she wouldn't mind trying her father, just so he knew that she was fine. Casey agreed, and as Lanie rattled off one of her father's numbers, it occurred to me that I should try Paul's parents. Surely they knew what was going on by now.

True, but if Lanie couldn't get through to her Dad in the 631-area code, what would make me think that I would be able to get through to Paul's parents? I thought a split second about having Casey call them too, but what would I say? That I hadn't heard from him in…how long? I wasn't exactly sure. Time was a deceiver on a day like today.

I dismissed the idea as futile, and pictured Paul's face in my mind's eye. As I conjured up his image, my heart began to fold all over again. *Dear God, please let him come home safe to me. You know. You know how much I love him; you can't give him to me and then allow him to be taken away so soon. We have plans, Lord, a lifetime of plans together.*

By the time Lanie got done with her call, I was crying all over again. A fresh torrent of tears cascaded down my face, and it was all I could do to look up and acknowledge Lanie now standing beside me, whispering something unintelligible and cooing in my ear.

"We should go home, Yellie." Lanie said as she cleared her throat and then reached for a new clump of tissues.

"I can't get home." I shook my head. There were no trains up to Westchester.

"Would you like to come home with me?" Lanie offered. "It'll be a hell of a walk, but I don't think you should be alone right now."

"I want to go to Paul's." I knew that one thing, if I knew nothing else. I wanted to be where Paul could find me. I wanted to be around his things. Plus, it seemed the easiest thing to do at this point, as Paul's place was only a few blocks away from where we were right now.

Lanie nodded sagely. "Okay, I'll go with you."

"I'm sorry, Lanie. I just…I need to be there. You can go home if you want to, I'll understand." But we both knew that we didn't want to be alone right now.

"No. That's not even an option. Come on, Yellie, let's pack up our stuff and get going. It's almost ten thirty. I think we've done all we can do here." Lanie looked around the room as if it was her first day in the office and she didn't know where to begin. She crossed the room then and shut off the boom box, our fave DJ sounding more serious than we had ever heard him before.

"Lanie, what if he calls back here?" I was suddenly panicky, wondering if leaving really was the right thing to do. What if Paul tried to call me back again here? What if he tried my cell and it wasn't working; would he even think to try his own phone? Or would he try me at my place, where I would probably not be for days?

"He won't." The finality with which she said it really bothered me and I told her so.

"Lanie, how can you be so sure?" I gave the phone a longing look, willing it to ring one more time and release me. "How come some phone numbers are working and some you can't dial out to?" I was afraid to leave. I knew well enough to know that I might find Paul injured, if I was lucky enough for him to survive this thing. What if he had amnesia, and could only remember the last succession of numbers to run through his head, which would be my work number? Would he be able to find me, to find his way home to me again? Did it matter? I would find him. I knew I would.

"Yellie, listen to me. You are in shock. We all are. The best thing to do would be to go to Paul's place right now and sit by his phone there, where we can at the very least have full disposal to a television set, his phone line, as well as both of our cell phones on standby. We can cry comfortably, on a couch with a blanket, and we can make hot tea when we want to. Plus…this is a corporate building.

Not a landmark, but a…I think we'll be safer at his apartment. We need to leave." Lanie had her authoritative voice in full effect, and I knew better than to argue with her when she got like this.

"You're right. I know you're right." Through tears, I grabbed my bag and slung it over my shoulder, reassessing the room one last time. There was nothing else we could do here. I knew that. I knew it, I just couldn't think about being parted from the phone, which was the last time I heard his voice. What if it was the last time I ever…? I shoved that thought aside, determined anew to trudge over to his place and wait for his phone to ring or for him to walk through that door.

Lanie pushed me out of the hole/office and then carefully locked the door behind us. As we went out into the hallway, we saw several people still littering the floor, crying in the arms of their coworkers or friends. I tried not to look, but some morbid curiosity got the best of me, and I found myself fixated, staring at Alana, who was currently clutching on to a guy I knew from the Media department, whose name I believed to be James.

As Lanie boarded the elevator, I waved to her to hold onto it a sec and reached into my bag for a stray piece of paper and pen, and then before I even knew what I was doing, offered my cell and Paul's address out to James and Alana.

"In case you can't get home."

I scurried onto the elevator after that, afraid that my voice would crack further and that I would make an even greater spectacle out of myself than I was sure I already had. It didn't matter. I was overcome with emotion regardless of my attempts to tell myself that I was overreacting, and my heart was no longer able to listen to my mind's instruction to calm down. I started crying again the minute the doors closed.

When we stepped off into the lobby, the lobby appeared different at first, as if I had not breezed through the same lobby earlier that same morning, without a second thought to the security guards that were a staple at the door. Every person milling about looked bruised, and unlike the regular New York rush, eyes met eyes and individuals were acknowledged.

"Lanie?" I looked to my right and caught her wiping a tear from her already tear-stained face.

"Yeah, toots?" She smiled through her tears at me.

"I love you." It seemed more than appropriate to say it then.

"I love you too." Her smile grew deeper, and she went through the revolving door in front of me as we exited out onto the street.

We were at the street corner, taking in the surreal quality the day held: the picture-perfect blue, blue sky…the slight breeze in an air that held not a trace of humidity…the groups of people gathering on corners, talking and crying and holding each other…some just staring into space, wondering why…and there we were, just waiting for the sign to change from *Don't Walk* to *Walk* when we heard somebody shout to us from a small group on the opposite corner, and I felt my whole world come crashing down.

Literally.

"THE SECOND TOWER FELL!" Screams and screeches were the backdrop to this announcement, when all I could do was stare, trying to decide who I could walk over to and possibly kill, which one of the crowd had uttered such a preposterous and utterly thoughtless thing. I felt Lanie grab me from behind just then, and I knew that even though I must have thought that I kept that thought inside, I was able to register that she was restraining me, and so I made her job easy and proceeded to collapse into her arms.

The streets are dirty and I shouldn't be sitting on them.

If I sit on the street, I should not touch it, and if I touch the street, I should not wipe my eyes…you could get pink eye. Oh, where had I learned that? I told Lanie, but she didn't seem too concerned. I would have been. If I were she, I would have been concerned with pink eye, because she could catch it too. Pink eye was not fun.

    Not fun for anyone.
    NO FUN FOR NO ONE.
    I giggled. That was funny. What was that called?
    An unintentional rhyme! I remembered.
    Now, why was Lanie insisting that I stand up? Didn't she realize that I was perfectly fine right where I was right now? I knew she didn't know. She couldn't know what I knew, for I knew that Paul was dead and that there was no way I would ever see him again.

    I knew it, knew it like I knew my name, but I could not utter another syllable, and I couldn't seem to put one foot in front of the other, and I couldn't see anything, except Lanie trying to talk to me, but I couldn't make out her words, because all I could hear was the pounding of my own heart and a sorry little voice that told me Paul was no more.

    "NNNnnnnooooooOOOOOO!" I shouted as loud as I could shout anything. "It can't be true!" I felt limp as a rag doll as Lanie tried once again to pull me up to my full height and demand that I put one foot in front of the other. "It can't be true!" I told her again, I told anyone who would listen, but I knew in my heart of hearts that I lost him.

    "...Can't take care of you here. Please, Yellie..." some of what I heard Lanie say was starting to get through to me.

    "I love you, Lane." I said this for the second time in less than ten minutes. I was blubbering now, but I made myself try and stand up, for her sake if not for mine.

    "I love you too, Yellie. Come on now, we've got to get you to Paul's." She yanked me closer to her until she had a firm grip on my arm.

    "Hey, that's a death grip," I pointed out to her, all the while trying hard not to find myself funny. I felt that right now might not be the appropriate time to whine about a death grip, but the absurdity reached out and choked me, and I found myself mixing tears and laughter all over again, like a college kid, reckless with too many beers and then liquor. What was it they said? Stick to one, one or the other, don't mix…some little sing-songy saying came to mind, but then took off just as quickly.

"Yeah, well, I've got to get your ass home and off this street." Lanie steered me away from the corner and held on tight as we began walking. I noticed Lanie was cursing a lot today. Lanie hardly ever cursed. I also noticed people were crying all around us. They all seemed to have the same problem I did.

I trudged along and let Lanie take the lead, more than willing to give up control and allow her to lead me, fully aware that I could not do this alone.

I cried. I cried and I cried and soon the laughter was nothing but a fleeting memory, a space in time used to remind me of how off-balance I was in the first place. I could feel my sandals scraping the pavement as Lanie dragged me along, my toes scrabbling, and although I thought vaguely about the shoes on my feet, I was aware that they were Paul's favorite sandals.

Sandals.
Why?
Because it was a beautiful day.
A beautiful day in the neighborhood…!

I pictured Mr. Rogers, with his valium-laced smile, peering into the homes of so many little kiddies. The song changed tune abruptly: Eddie Murphy ripping him to shreds on an old episode of *Saturday Night Live.*

All of the sudden we were there, standing outside of Paul's apartment building, the city frozen around us, the air replete with fear.

I let Lanie press the button for the elevator, and once inside, I straightened up, consumed with the task of waiting for Paul to arrive.

"Do you think he'll come right here?" I asked Lanie with a hopeful lilt in my voice, trying to convince at least one of us that Paul would eventually show up.

"I think if he can, he will," Lanie said carefully as she unlocked the door to Paul's apartment.

I entered the hallway wondering why it looked the same as it always had, for some reason expecting the interior of his place to be altered in some chaotic way, depicting all that was going on in the world outside.

"It looks the same." I said this to Lanie directly before I collapsed again, this time in the center of his hallway parquet floor. "Lanie…Lanie…" Huge sobs heaved in my chest, and I found myself unable to articulate anything I was feeling at that precise moment. "I know he's not coming home."

"You still don't know yet." Lanie's words fell flat; she knew it and so did I.

"I need to see it." I jumped up then and ran towards the TV, trying to snap it on, in the process managing to forget all about the remote control.

Lanie stood behind me and handed it to me silently.

"I need to see it." I repeated myself. As if seeing it would make it all better. I think I was so far gone at that point that I just didn't know what else to do.

I pressed the appropriate buttons and ended up on the Fox News channel, which I knew to be Paul's favorite. I deferred to him in lieu of his presence. The screen showed a news reporter standing outside of The Pentagon, gesturing rapidly and firing various facts loudly into a microphone. I stood as still as a rock, waiting for the screen to change. I could feel Lanie to the left of me, slightly behind, doing the same.

Back to the World Trade Towers.

Or…what were the Towers.

The picture in front of me was a smoking mass of pure rubble, concrete and wood reduced to panels and sticks, and around it the buildings that were still standing dusted with smoke, never having been even half the size of the ones that were now a burning pile in the center.

My heart stood still.

It looked like a war zone, or at the very least, what I had pictured a war zone to look like. Firemen were milling around in a white dust, with gray clouds of smoke getting in the way of the cameras, their faces etched in utter shock, their usual larger-than-life demeanor rattled, oblivious to another screaming news man in front of the camera, trying to get it all in.

The screen switched and we were able to see an instant replay of Tower One collapsing into a grotesque demolition, the mere sight burning my eyes as if the smoke had permeated the room straight from the screen. My heart lurched. How could that have happened? How could buildings that tall, that big, a structure so sound…my mind flitted briefly to Paul and I watching a Discovery Channel special on the ins and outs of the Twin Towers…how could they just fall down?

The image repeated itself, shoving another knife deeper inside my already battered soul, making me wonder if I would ever be able to wrap my head around what had transpired downtown.

Paul was gone.

Buried somewhere in all that carnage, my only solace being that perhaps he didn't suffer; for who could have known that those buildings would come down? I thought of his flesh burning and I willed myself to focus on the fact that I hadn't heard from him in a while and although not likely, it was possible that he had escaped somehow, and was either injured or simply unable to call me.

And even as my heart made this fantastical wish, I chided myself.

I knew better.

As much as I wanted to believe it, my heart meted out the truth in irregular beats, my tear ducts dry for the moment, as reality fitted itself inside of my hopelessness.

I knew in my heart of hearts that he was gone. That I would never see him again; never hold that hand that swallowed my own. Never would I feel his touch, or see that brilliant smile that lit a thousand nights for me, and I knew with a knowing far beyond my years that I would not even find a grave to bury him in.

His grave would now be a pile of rubble, a towering inferno, the likes of which no man should have to endure.

His life defined now by his death, my heart but a useless organ, the damage irreparable…my life altered…evermore.

Sept 11, 2002

I woke with the dawn and felt gratified to, at the very least, see the sunlight peeking through my blinds, a day not unlike the one I had experienced only one year before.

Was it a year already? I realized the date that the calendar was hawking, but times like these dared the calendar to be false, since time had become a precarious thing for me.

I went through the same mind-numbing routine that I did every day upon waking. I shuffled past a vision of Paul, saw his Tower collapse again in my head, and acknowledged the dull ache in my chest, the one that never went away.

I sighed.

I checked my watch, but it was still a little early to call Lanie and see whether she was going to come up or not. Besides, I hesitated calling because I knew she would once again try to reconfirm whether or not I was definite about not wanting to be down there today. I had told her more than once and although I knew that she was just looking out for me, I was frustrated by having to reassure countless other people that Ground Zero was not where I wanted to be today.

Ground Zero was the name they had given it, the reference to mark the massive grave where the Towers had once stood, so tall, gleaming in the sun or moonlight, their glittering façade lighting up our skyline, back dropping tons of movie scenes, standing for New York in so many different ways.

I didn't mind the name; it seemed fitting.

What I minded was the fact that The Twin Towers no longer stood proud at the tip of Manhattan Isle. I minded the fact that although Paul's family had bought a plot out in some cemetery out on Long Island, that I really had no one place to go and feel close to Paul this day. I minded the fact that my life had changed, in the blink of an eye, and no amount of prayer or petition could change it back.

Not ever.

There's so much I still can't explain. I find myself looking for answers when there are none. There's no real reason that what occurred on that fateful day happened to us at all; sure, the TV hosts and the desk jockeys have hammered out all the facts by now, but did any of it make any real sense to anyone who lost someone that day? A bunch of sick bastards, terrorists, so-called religious people, took some planes and destroyed three thousand American lives because of their interpretation of…God? Was their mission to get us to believe? Did they really think it would win us over? What about all that's happened since then? Do they really think they can win this war?

So none of it makes sense to me still. I think back now to the swirl of events that happened in the days following the disaster: how we made up flyers with Paul's name and picture on it, and how Lanie and I scoured the downtown area looking for both him and Rob, finding nothing more than anyone else did, just a lot of 'I'm sorrys' and not nearly enough John Does in the hospitals. We wandered around fruitlessly, and once the city opened back up, Phil and Marie and even Peter Corsi sat with me, in an apartment that Paul wouldn't come home to, watching a phone that was completely unwilling to ring.

Time passed and the days began to get shorter. I walked around in daze, unwilling to believe that I no longer had a wedding to plan. Eventually Paul's family decided to have a memorial service out on Long Island, at their old church where all of their friends and family could attend. There were so many people there for Paul, friends I had only heard about in passing, as well as friends I had come to call my own in the years since we first met. He would have been proud to find out that every single one of his Boston College roommates had showed, each year there represented well by the suitemates and friends that stood still in their shock and disbelief, clutching on to one another with a volume of tears that almost drowned them alive. There were colleagues from his current job, but they weren't recognizable to me, as so many of his inner circle from work had also perished that day. There were family members I had aspirations of meeting at our wedding…and there were even some politicians that stopped by, people I had never anticipated meeting. When Mayor Giuliani showed up, there was a hush in the room and I felt validated in a way that I could not explain. He shook hands and said nice things, and he was gone in an instant, but I heard later on that he had seventeen funerals that he attended just on Long Island that day, and so I was thankful that he had even popped his head in to acknowledge Paul's life. I remember thinking that Paul would have been pleased, as he had always liked Giuliani. The funny thing was that everybody liked him now, people being what they were, desperately seeking leadership during a time of utter crisis.

Paul also would have been thrilled to know that Hillary Clinton did not show. No other politicians showed their face, with the exception of his hometown Mayor, and I truthfully cannot recall whether I met him or not. I knew he was there only because Paul's old youth group leader, Mr. A, pointed him out to me at the reception afterwards.

We 'buried' him in October, but it was as surreal as anything else I could have ever even imagined going through. I was a widow before being a bride.

And time was not my friend. Some days it moved slower, some so fast I thought I could no longer see his face, and it terrified me like nothing else to think that one day perhaps I wouldn't be able to visualize Paul the same way I could before.

I missed everything about him. I missed his face, and that mega-watt smile that he would turn on just for me. I missed his touch and the way his body heat would keep me warm when I curled up next to him, warm in a way that a blanket could never come close to. I missed his jokes, our repartee, even the fact that I trusted him, had slowly begun to trust him in a way that I trusted no one else, and I missed that closeness. I thought back sometimes to the times I wasted; being afraid to disclose and afraid to move closer. Oh, how I would give anything for those minutes back, those hours…those days when I felt unsure and then shied away from him. Time played tricks on me; there were times when I thought that my wounds had begun to heal, but then I realized that not enough time had passed. Every day was an anniversary of something else.

I received a deluge of sympathy cards, letters written from people I had met once or twice, to missives from those who had exited my life long ago. One thing I can say about coming from a small town in Upstate New York: everyone knew my story. People like Julie, my old friend from high school, and even her old boyfriend Brick…they sent cards with sayings meant to comfort. I was still receiving them now; people who had just found out or wanted to let me know that they were thinking of me on the anniversary of the day my whole life fell apart. Alex, Paul's old college roommate, called me every two months like clockwork, letting me know that he was still praying for me. Most offers to keep me in prayer came off as nothing if not sincere, however, each drop of kindness caused my bucket of tears to overflow, and I was transported back to that horrible instant in a flash, drowning as it were.

Then time would escalate and I would be back here again, trying not to imagine Paul the last time I spoke to him on the phone.

Time. It ambled on, never seeking my permission as the seasons changed and somehow I ended up here, laying in bed, and deciding not to go to Ground Zero. I agonized over that decision, but in the end I didn't think I could handle all the publicity surrounding the one-year anniversary. I wanted to be alone, to steep in my misery, to cry unabashedly if need be. Alone. Without Paul to pepper my life with love, I had a great desire to give in to the tears, to let them cleanse me if they were able. I told the Corsis how I felt and they said they understood. They were going anyway. They felt they needed to be at Ground Zero, and I understood that too. Peter and Madeline would be coming up from DC for the ceremony.

I would be watching it from my television, a box of tissues ready on standby. I had convinced myself that I needed to mourn one last time, as if the day would come and go and somehow I would be better in the morning. I think I hoped for that, but then I felt guilty hoping. I talked to Lanie about everything, and she was more than any one could ever ask for in the Friend Department. She was tried and true, and as my thoughts turned to her, I found myself already biting back a tear or twelve, wondering if she knew how much she meant to me now.

If I was up, I was going to wake her now too. Tough nuggies.

"Hello?" She sounded sleepy, but not sleeping, so I felt very little guilt.

"Are you up?" My voice sounded a little too loud to my own ears.

"I am." Lanie let loose a low humph. "I can't sleep. I would like to sleep today, sleep right through the reading of all those names, but of course, I can't. Not today."

"Are you all right?" It was a stupid question to ask on a day like today, but I asked it anyway, knowing that she was also grieving, having an exceptionally hard time letting go of Rob.

"I am as okay as I am going to be. Do you need me? I can bring up some Bailey's." She was referring to her earlier invitation to come up and accompany me through tears.

"No, I think I'll be all right." My mind flicked to her own hour of need, and I thought about Jude smuggling

Bailey's into the hospital. I got up then and flicked on the TV, then muted the sound. "They're setting up down there."

The cameras were all adjusted to the scene at Ground Zero. People were setting up podiums and there was a long line of mourners waiting to be released into the pit, as they were so aptly calling the now empty foundations where the buildings once stood.

"Yeah, I see." Lanie breathed deeply into the phone. "You know what pisses me off?"

"What?" I was watching the mourners congregate at the top of the ramp leading down.

"I feel like the rest of the country is…I don't know, like…over it already. I'm feeling very isolated today, like nobody except us New Yorkers are still mourning."

"Lanie, you know that's not true. We're completely attached to the situation. I mean, look what happened to us, here…you can't really blame the people out in California for not feeling the staggering losses the same way we did, or not wanting to rehash the whole thing again." I found myself sticking up for hypothetical people in a far-way state, assuming we even knew how Californians felt about anything.

"Yeah, I guess I didn't get this riled up about Oklahoma City." Lanie replied.

"I remember feeling horrible for them, but not really understanding it, not the way I do now." I couldn't help but notice the irony. "And that was nothing compared to this."

"Isn't that the sad, sad truth."

Something occurred to me. "Do you remember seeing that movie, *The Siege*?"

"With Annette Benning and Denzel?"

"Yeah, remember we saw it together?" The four of us had seen it one night avec pizza. I could vividly recall feeling shocked and overwhelmed by the movie the first time I saw it, as it was about something we knew very little about back then…terrorists. I had caught it again on cable, just a few months ago, and I forced myself to sit down and take it in again, hoping on some level for a greater understanding, or perhaps a catharsis. I was left only with shock by my change in perception; the two hundred some-out loss of life seemed minor compared to what we had suffered.

"I remember some of the stuff the FBI was saying in that movie, I can remember some of it going over my head." Lanie recalled. "Who knew then?"

"Do you think we'll see Paul's family?" I changed the subject then, knowing we could go on and on forever about fiction, when real life was clanging like a gong, forcing me to stand up and pay attention. I knew that Marie and Phil had made up a cardboard picture of Paul to hold up for the cameras. They weren't looking for face time for themselves. So many survivors only wanted the faces to punctuate the meaning, to establish silently what they felt the day should be about.

Never Forget.

A crop of bumper stickers and house signs graced every open corner of space, from Westchester to the tip of Montauk, from sea to shining sea.

We Will Never Forget.

9/11 Heroes: FDNY and NYPD. Thank You.

Firefighters and police officers that had lost their lives in the line of duty were unanimously deemed heroes, from that day forward, Mariah Carey's popular song *Hero* was recycled, and the word was bandied about with an almost religious fervor.

I agreed with the assessment, however, I was touched by the sadness that the mere word evoked in my heart. I had known two heroes at different points in my life: my father and then my mother.

Now Paul.

Freedom Isn't Free!

I Love New York…Now More Than Ever.

The American Flag saw a quick resurgence and a newfound respect. It was suddenly cool again to wave the flag.

Paul would be miffed about that: he had always had a healthy respect for the Red, White, and Blue. I'm sure, if he had been alive today, that he would have loved to witness the budding patriotism cross-country, but I knew Paul well enough to know that it would have irked him too, simply because it took a tragedy of this magnitude to make the flag regain its place in the lives of the everyday citizen.

Paul also would have wanted them to rebuild the Twin Towers exactly the same way they were, maybe even a story or two higher, if for no other reason than to give the terrorists a big old screw-you in the form of another landmark. Paul loved those buildings. He loved working there. He loved the view. He loved the way they exemplified New York City, and I knew beyond a shadow of a doubt that he would want them rebuilt at the foot of his grave. What was it he had said about my not painting ever again, solely because of The Monster? That I couldn't and that I *shouldn't* let him win; that giving up meant on some level that he had won.

Paul would not want the terrorists to win.

He would not want them to take any more than they already had.

He would cry out from his final resting place if he could, a strong and steady voice, insisting to the masses that it was okay by him, even if it was now considered hallowed ground.

I understood and even had a respect for the other mourners and their concerns about the Towers being rebuilt. I got it. I just know full well how Paul would have felt.

Lanie answered me after a minute or so of silence, in which we both watched the events unfurl on the television screen. "I think...there are so many people...I didn't picture so many..." her voice trailed off and her sentence ended in a heartrending sob that could be felt across the miles.

"There are." It was all I could do to not break down completely. The sheer volume of people at the site was a staggering reminder to all that we had lost. Loved ones that would never come home again.

"Did Alana call you last night?" Lanie collected herself as she referred to the coworker that had become a close friend to each of us.

"Yes. She said she'd be there." Alana, as suspected on that horrible day, had lost her Dad. We now had a bond that no one could sever.

"I feel so bad…for everyone." Lanie's voice was muffled again as she continued to cry on her end. Not a minute later I joined her, my tears coming unbidden, even before the first moment of silence was announced.

"I know. I do too." I felt the worst for me, but I felt bad for everyone who lost Paul, and Rob, and even Olive. Olive was another person we knew who had never made it home that day.

"Things will never be the same." Lanie stated plainly, and I posed no rebuke.

She was right.

I kicked up the volume on the television, my eyes scanning the crowd for Paul's family even as my ears focused on the somber tone of the television journalist as he went about reading the order of events. There would be music and several politicians would speak at different points of the day. Moments of silence would illustrate the times designated that the planes hit the buildings, and there would be a complete reading of all the names, of every single person that perished that day.

I found it to be an appropriate tribute. Whoever thought of this type of memorial, whoever arranged it, deserved credit for picking something that would infuse the remembrance with the memories of the victims, and validate their deaths by acknowledging their lives.

They were here, they worked here, and they were innocent civilians that exemplified the old adage: they were in the wrong place at the wrong time. They loved, they were missed, and our lives would never be the same without them in it.

There were days where I still didn't get it.

Sometimes I got mad at God, and I railed out at Him as pure venom spewed from my heart to my lips, unable to understand why Paul had to perish on that fateful day. Couldn't He have at least saved Paul? There were so many stories of people oversleeping, or showing up late to work, even one of a man who had an overwhelming craving for a particular coffee and was saved by having to go get the coffee across the street from the Towers…other people's miracles had grown to exhaust me. Yet even as I questioned my God, I fell into Him in a way that I never had before, knowing that I would only get through this under the safety of His wings.

"Lane, I'm gonna go." I offered no further explanation, and I knew she knew without my saying that I needed to get through this one on my own.

"Promise to call if you need me." Lanie pressed.

"I promise." And I would.

"I'll call you later." She warned, the mother hen, constantly checking up on me.

"I know you will." I let a semi-smile escape from my prison of pain. I remembered what I had said to her the day her father had the heart attack, when she said that Paul and I didn't have to drive her out to Long Island. I insisted, and told her: *Friendship doesn't work that way.* You don't leave your friend high and dry in their time of need; I led by example and she picked up the mantle and carried me through all this. I would be forever in her debt.

I had also found the most unexpected friend in the lovely lady down the street: Millie Lancaster. Millie heard about what happened to Paul, and she showed up one day not long after, with a zucchini bread in her hand, and her arms outstretched in comfort. She had been a widow a long time, she said, and she knew that although nothing would ever take away my pain, that she was there whenever I needed a shoulder to cry on. I took her up on it occasionally, but more often than not, we got together to paint.

I settled into my bed then, armed with the remote and a box of tissues, burrowed deeper under the covers, and then shivered in spite of the near-perfect weather.

I wanted to hear them read Paul's name.

I needed to.

The cameras flicked to the crowd, and I saw so many faces I had come to recognize. The same faces that had graced the walls of the Armory, the hospitals, Grand Central, subway stations, even lampposts...those same faces now clutched in the hands of loved ones, vying for the camera, populating the scene at the end of the world as we knew it. The faces of the victims felt familiar to me, as did several of the faces of the loved ones now gathered at the pit. Perhaps I had met them, or shared a tear or a hug on any one of those days after the tragedy. I felt like I knew them. Either way, they felt like a family to me now, a family borne of circumstance, an unspoken bond between us that no man could shatter.

I wondered for all of us how we would get through this day.

Name after name, I felt as if someone was wielding a hammer, and as each name was read, the guy with the hammer aimed right at the center of my heart, only to exact another blow to a heart that had almost stopped beating. Oh, when would the pain ever end? I told myself to get up, get off the couch, to shut off the television, to turn away from the drone of pain, but I was unable to do that, and I knew that I needed to do this, even if I couldn't express why. Tears streamed down my face as each name was uttered, some mangled by those who couldn't get the pronunciation quite right, others said in spite of the obvious lump in the speaker's throat. I began to shake as they got into the C's.

Kevin Francis Conroy...
Helen D. Cook...
James Corrigan...

I held my breath for what seemed like an eternity.

Paul Corsi...

Forget the hammer. Even a knife would feel better than this. When they said his name, I felt as if somebody knocked the wind right out of me, and be it a gunshot or another type of wound, I was convinced in the moments that passed right after they said his name that anything at all would be better than this pain.

My tears engulfed me. I thought back to the day we first met and I remembered not thinking about anything except getting to work on time as I knocked his briefcase out of his hand. I was simply rushing by a stranger, not even giving him a second glance at that point. Who knew?

The World Trade. I couldn't escape the irony here. He made a bet with himself: if he got the job, he'd ask me out. If he hadn't gotten the job, would he have ever gotten up the courage to ask me out? Perhaps no. Then we wouldn't have ever been together, but by that argument, Paul would also be alive today.

I grabbed for tissues and before I knew it, I had gone through more than half the box. For some strange reason, this made me laugh, laugh in a way that made the heartache seem alien to me, as if I could laugh enough to simply will it all away.

I missed him.

I missed having someone around to cheer me on, I missed my soft place to land…I missed believing that I had somehow hit my stride.

I missed his hands.

I twisted the ring on my finger and then gazed down upon the diamond again, breathing in all that we had meant to each other, then breathing out in a way that was meant to forestall additional tears.

It didn't work. Caught up in my reverie, I was unable to register at first the sound that seemed to be coming from somewhere out by my door.

Was that a knock?

I turned around, expecting to find Lanie, knowing that it would be just like her to ignore my protestations and come up anyway, but was surprised instead to find my mother standing there with a plastic container in her hand.

"Mom?" I slid open the sliding glass so-called front door and stood there a full minute, unsure as to whether what I was seeing was real or just a figment of my imagination. She looked pretty and despite the obvious anguish that was written all over her face, she looked as if she was taking care of herself again.

"I thought you shouldn't be alone today." She choked back tears and then gave me a solemn look. "I brought cheesecake."

And I started to cry. Her kindness and her presence, the fact that she drove all the way down here to offer support and a piece of cheesecake…overwhelmed me to the point where there were no words. I cried a river of tears in her arms, and as I inhaled her scent, I realized that she smelled today so much like the old mother, the mother of my dreams and long-ago memories.

"Mom…" I clutched on to her and I cried desperate chunks of tears, the kind of tears that jump out of your system, buried so long that they hurt as they exit

"Danielle, I am so, so…sorry." She cradled me in her arms and kissed my forehead like she used to. I could feel her tears mingling with my hair, and I embraced the dampness, knowing that I needed her now, and feeling grateful that she had taken it upon herself to come down.

"I love him." I stated plainly through a flood of tears. "He loved me."

"I know. Oh, honey, I know." And she hung on for dear life, comforting the only child God saw fit to give her.

Eventually we heard the names still being said in the background. We broke apart and I looked at her, tears in my eyes, and a lump in my throat. "I think I missed Olive's name being read."

"That's okay." She nodded. "There's so many."

"Too many."

"Yes." Again, she nodded. "I'll put the cheesecake away."

"Okay." I climbed back up onto my bed and wrapped the blankets tightly around my torso. I sniffed loudly, focusing again on the litany of names. Somewhere towards the end, I looked over to find my mother sitting on the bed right next to me, weeping silently into a handful of tissues. Even in my grief, I felt comforted by her presence. I had my mom there to take care of me.

I had lost Paul. Had I gained my mother?

She stayed all day and well into the night. When the time finally came for dinner, I had her order Chinese food to be delivered.

I couldn't help but order the shrimp fried rice.

The End

Acknowledgements

"In all thy ways acknowledge Him, and He shall direct thy paths." (Proverbs 3:6)

With gratitude to the people who encouraged me to take action, those who cheered me on, and the reader…for letting me tell you a story.

Elizabeth Browning was instrumental in planting this very valuable seed: *"Anything is Possible, and Everything is Okay."*

I can't thank Lindsay Miserandino enough; she is not only a stellar friend, but an amazing editor. Thank you from the bottom of my heart for handling me and my work with the utmost care. My instincts were right. You're the goods.

To THE CLASS: You all rock. You are tremendous artists and I am humbled to be in your presence. My mother helped me get my ass to class by pitching in tandem week after week, so many thanks to her as well.

To my Brother John…I hope you dance. Always.

To every New Yorker that was in The City on that fateful day: I hold you in my prayers. I will never forget the way I felt that day or the losses that we all suffered.
May God richly bless you.

Made in the USA
Middletown, DE
12 August 2017